Shelley
and the
Chaos of History

Literature and Philosophy

A. J. Cascardi, General Editor

This series publishes books in a wide range of subjects in philosophy and literature, including studies of the social and historical issues that relate these two fields. Drawing on the resources of the Anglo-American and Continental traditions, the series is open to philosophically informed scholarship covering the entire range of contemporary critical thought.

Already published:

J. M. Bernstein, *The Fate of Art: Aesthetic Alienation from Kant to Derrida and Adorno*

Peter Bürger, *The Decline of Modernism*

Mary E. Finn, *Writing the Incommensurable: Kierkegaard, Rossetti, and Hopkins*

Reed Way Dasenbrock, ed., *Literary Theory After Davidson*

David Haney, *William Wordsworth and the Hermeneutics of Incarnation*

David Jacobson, *Emerson's Pragmatic Vision: The Dance of the Eye*

Gray Kochhar-Lindgren, *Narcissus Transformed: The Textual Subject in Psychoanalysis and Literature*

Robert Steiner, *Toward a Grammar of Abstraction: Modernity, Wittgenstein, and the Paintings of Jackson Pollock*

Sylvia Walsh, *Living Poetically: Kierkegaard's Existential Aesthetics*

Michel Meyer, *Rhetoric, Language, and Reason*

Christie McDonald and Gary Wihl, eds., *Transformation in Personhood and Culture After Theory*

Charles Altieri, *Painterly Abstraction in Modernist American Poetry: The Contemporaneity of Modernism*

John C. O'Neal, *The Authority of Experience: Sensationist Theory in the French Enlightenment*

John O'Neill, ed., *Freud and the Passions*

Sheridan Hough, *Nietzsche's Noontide Friend*

E. M. Dadlez, *What's Hecuba to Him?*

Shelley
and the
Chaos of History

A New Politics of Poetry

Hugh Roberts

The Pennsylvania State University Press
University Park, Pennsylvania

Library of Congress Cataloging-in-Publication Data

Roberts, Hugh, 1962–
    Shelley and the chaos of history : a new politics of poetry / Hugh
Roberts.
        p.   cm. — (Literature and philosophy)
    Includes bibliographical references and index.
    ISBN 0-271-01640-X (cloth : alk. paper)
    ISBN 0-271-01641-8 (paper : alk. paper)
    1. Shelley, Percy Bysshe, 1792–1822—Political and social views.
2. Politics and literature—Great Britain—History—19th century.
3. Political poetry, English—History and criticism.   I. Title.
II. Series.
PR5442.P64R63   1997
821'.7—dc20   96-20029
                                                                          CIP

It is the policy of The Pennsylvania State University Press to use acid-free paper for
the first printing of all clothbound books. Publications on uncoated stock satisfy
the minimum requirements of American National Standard for Information
Sciences—Permanence of Paper for Printed Library Materials, ANSI Z39.48-1992.

Contents

Acknowledgments

This book began life at McGill University as a doctoral thesis, which would never have been completed without the generous financial support provided by a Canadian Commonwealth Scholarship from 1986 to 1991.

I first developed an interest in Shelley's writing under the guidance of my tutor, Harry Ricketts, in an undergraduate course on the Romantic poets. Without Harry's deep love of literature and rare ability to share and communicate his interest in it, I doubt I would ever have pursued a degree in English literature.

At McGill I had the good fortune to work with Chris Heppner. Professor Heppner's detailed and thoroughly considered response to all my work would be a model for any teacher. Chris's support and encouragement as a close friend has also been invaluable to me.

Some of the ideas in this book were developed in a project written under the supervision of Gary Wihl, who also read and provided useful comments on an early draft of Part One and who was encouraging and instrumental in the transformation of thesis into book. Stuart Curran provided some gracious words of encouragement at a crucial stage, which were more important to me than he could know. Tony Cascardi's enthusiastic and incisive comments as reader and editor were a pleasure to receive. Without his support for the project, I doubt this book would have ever emerged. The thoughtful criticisms of Penn State Press's second (anonymous) reader were intelligent and helpful. Keith Monley's astute and intelligent copyediting helped save a rookie writer from many embarrassing slips.

Most of this book has been read, in one form or another, by Maggie Kilgour, and those familiar with her work on the Gothic will recognize its influence on my ideas. My debts to Maggie as friend, mentor, hostess, and chef are all immeasurable, but these debts are to me a comfort, as a token of enduring friendship, and not a burden. Peta Bowden, who proved to me (twice!) that a thesis really *could* be completed, and Dick

Ounsworth provided rigorous intellectual challenge and warm and loving support according to need. Caroline Greenwood collects *another*
prize for being Caroline Greenwood, thereby establishing a world record unlikely to be broken in our lifetimes. Katharine Cukier's humor
and wisdom made all the difference, particularly in the last trying
months of completing the dissertation. Without the love of John, Kay,
Mary, Kate, and Tim Roberts, strong enough to reach me halfway across
the world, none of this would have been possible.

Last, my deepest debt is to Rachel Gamby, whose love and patience
are inexhaustible. I cannot express the extent of my love and my grati-
tude: "And for that riches where is my deserving?"

Parts of Chapter 1 have appeared in different forms in "Usage and
Abusage: The New Historicism and History," *EIDOS* 9 (1990): 175–93,
and "Critique historiciste et politiques de l'histoire," *L'Âne: Le Maga-
zine Freudien* 56 (Winter 1993): 33–35. Parts of Chapters 6 and 7 have
appeared in "Chaos and Evolution: A Quantum Leap in Shelley's Process," *Keats-Shelley Journal* 45 (1996): 156–94. Parts of Chapter 3 have
appeared in "Shelley Among the Post-Kantians," *Studies in Romanticism* 35 (1996): 295–330.

A Note on Shelley Texts

The complex, confusing, and unsatisfactory history of editions of Shelley's writings is all too familiar to the Shelley scholar. The Longman edition of the poems, currently emerging under the editorship of Kelvin Everest and Geoffrey Matthews, and the Oxford edition of the prose, being produced by E. B. Murray, seem likely to solve these problems for future generations. Unfortunately, most of this book was written before even the first volumes of these editions became available. As a result, I have had to refer to a number of different editions of Shelley's work, checking textual cruxes in as many sources as possible.

For citations from Shelley's prose, I give the source in the references (I have drawn first on the Donald H. Reiman and Sharon B. Powers Norton edition and, for works not included in that edition, on the Roger Ingpen and Walter E. Peck "Julian" edition). For citations from the poetry, all references, where possible, are to the Reiman and Powers edition; for poems not included in that edition, I have used, for lyric poems, Judith Chernaik's *Lyrics of Shelley* and, for all other poems, Thomas Hutchinson's Oxford *Poetical Works*, in the edition corrected by G. M. Matthews.

For my parents, Kay and John Roberts

> *Thus let thy power, which like the truth*
> *Of nature on my passive youth*
> *Descended, to my onward life supply*
> *Its calm—to one who worships thee.*

Introduction

Few authors have made claims as bold as Shelley's for the direct political efficacy of poetry. The ringing declaration that ends his *Defence of Poetry*—"Poets are the unacknowledged legislators of the World"—is something of a litmus test for our belief in the political significance of poetry; the extent to which we can avoid an ironic response to the claim is the extent of our willingness to dispute Auden's despairing conclusion that "poetry makes nothing happen."

The major impediment to our taking this claim seriously lies in the philosophical underpinnings of our habitual ways of conceiving the political nature of the text. Our reflex assumption that a "political" reading of the text must be broadly historicist in fact drastically reduces the possible political effect of literature. The contemporary dominance of this assumption can be traced to the post-Kantian response to the disintegrative threat of Enlightenment analytics, which has its political expression in the "fury of destruction" of the French Revolution. The attempt to conceive of a politics in which all (phenomenal) revolutionary negation is preemptively recuperated by a (noumenal) absolute moral and political order—be it the state, history, or culture—ultimately renders any politically effective action (which is to say, an action that results in a *change* in the existing social and political order) unthinkable.

Shelley's divided intellectual inheritance from, on the one hand, the skeptical revolutionary Enlightenment and, on the other, the emergent Romantic response to that Enlightenment makes him acutely aware of the attractions and dangers of both camps. The skeptical revolutionary (who is, increasingly, the "standard" Shelley of contemporary critics) enjoys the possibility of radical negation of the status quo, the openness to transforming "process" that the idealist Romantic cannot allow. On the other hand, he is only too conscious of the dramatic failure of the promise of that process, as represented by the French Revolution and the power of Burke's conservative critique, according to which the skeptical Enlightenment's openness to radical discontinuity is an invitation to disintegration of the organic body politic, from which only annihilation can ensue.

Shelley may have no sympathy with Burke's political vision, but he is aware that Burke's political critique of Enlightenment revolutionism exactly matches the Romantic critique of the disintegrative, analytic Enlightenment that he finds in the work of such admired "precursor poets" as Wordsworth, Coleridge, and Goethe. He knows that the two approaches share an organicist drive toward an inclusive totality that will reveal the divisions and disjunctions of our ironic world to be the merely phenomenal by-product of our fallen vision, and that real political change—change that implies some unrecuperated negation—is therefore no less unthinkable for the true Romantic than for Burke.

It may seem the oldest of old hats to describe Shelley as torn between his "skepticism" and his "Romantic idealism"; ever since C. E. Pulos's *Deep Truth* this has been the keynote of descriptions of Shelley's intellectual career. Most systematically drawn by E. R. Wasserman, who makes Shelley a progressively more "idealist" skeptic, the idea is fundamental even in the work of more recent critics who insist more strongly upon the predominance of skepticism in Shelley's thought.[1] I propose a new solution to this old problem, however. The answer to this paradoxical division in Shelley's thought does not lie in deciding that Shelley was "really" an idealist or "really" a skeptic. I show that with the aid of Lucretius, Shelley develops an alternative approach to the issues of history, change, time, and process on which his double intellectual legacy divides. This alternative approach incorporates the most compelling features of both the skeptical and the idealist positions, without attempting either a schizophrenic "skeptical idealist" view or a "synthesis" of the two antithetical tendencies.

The implications of Shelley's reconciliation of being and becoming

---

1. Wasserman, *Shelley;* and see, e.g., Abbey (*Destroyer and Preserver*), who refers throughout to Shelley's "Platonic skepticism," and Hogle (*Shelley's Process*), who speaks of Shelley's "skeptical idealism" and "idealistic skepticism" (294). Some recent restatements of this old dilemma, which prove its currency in Shelley criticism, include Fuller, 212, and Duff, 196–97. Hamilton's "Old Anatomies" provides a good short critique of this tendency.

are far-reaching. They can be seen as part of an ongoing revolution in Western thought, a revolution based upon a reconsideration of the scientific and ethical significance of living in time. The latest and most far-reaching manifestation of this revolution is the new science of complex dynamics popularly known as "chaos science." I use some of the key concepts of chaos science to illuminate both the wider implications of Shelley's new approach and, conversely, the implications of chaos theory for literary studies—a subject that is still controversial.

When we read Shelley's poetry with this new theory of time and process in mind, much that has previously seemed baffling falls into place. Above all, a thoroughly new understanding of political process emerges, one that allows us to comprehend and accept, without excuses for "poetic license," Shelley's claim that "poets are the unacknowledged legislators of the World." Shelley gives us an understanding of the political role of the text that greatly broadens our definition of what is "political" in literature, and gives literature an effective political role without straining our credulity. Perhaps most welcome of all is the fact that Shelley gives us a way of going beyond the all too familiar disputes between historicist and deconstructionist critics—our contemporary version of the skeptical and idealist division that ruled Shelley's intellectual climate.

My argument falls into three more or less independent parts. In the first part I begin by discussing some of the general philosophical and critical issues that underlie any attempt to conceive of the literary text as a political entity. I argue that our "zero-degree" critical assumptions about the literary text are almost exclusively historicist and contextualist. I go on to explore some of the philosophical history underlying this fact, and find that the crucial period for the development of the philosophical frameworks of the "historical turn" is that which sees the emergence of mainstream Romanticism. I then explore Shelley's relationship to that Romanticism, arguing that the bulk of Shelley criticism can be divided into two streams, those who believe that Shelley always was or eventually became a proponent of the same "idealist" approach as, say, Wordsworth and Coleridge, and those who believe that, drawing on the tradition of the skeptical and revolutionary Enlightenment, Shelley maintained a sustained attack on conventional Romanticism. I explore both these options and suggest that, aside from their inherent inadequacies in accounting for the political nature of the text, they each have characteristic weaknesses—as well as undeniable strengths—when we turn to Shelley's own poetry. Moreover, I argue that the complexity of Shelley's engagement with the major philosophical issues of his time has been underestimated. I contend that we find in his work a very conscious exploration of the relative strengths and weaknesses of Romanticism and the revolutionary Enlightenment to which it is a response.

Although the persistent attempts to read Shelley's philosophy as a "mix" of skepticism and idealism have serious problems, I accept their central point, which is that elements of both approaches can be found in his thought. I argue, however, that these elements are parts of a heretofore unrecognized "third way" that allows Shelley to accept aspects of both the Romantic-idealist and Enlightenment-skeptical approaches while correcting the political incoherences that plague them both. In extended readings of Shelley's *Revolt of Islam* and "The Triumph of Life" we see him struggling with these two approaches, eventually moving through and beyond them.

This "third way" I explore in Part Two, which is the most "theoretical" part of the book. There I argue that Shelley draws on the work of Lucretius, and on the Lucretian influence in the Enlightenment, profoundly to rethink the nature of process, identity, and our relationship to time. Drawing on Michel Serres's reading of Lucretius, I use recent developments in what is popularly known as chaos theory to explore some of the more radical poetic and political implications of Shelley's Lucretianism. Using Martha Nussbaum's *Fragility of Goodness,* I argue that Shelley's acceptance of radical contingency in hermeneutical and political processes has profound ethical and political implications. In particular, it forces us to rethink entirely the nature of the poetic text, and the meaning of its political "engagement" with a society in constant evolution.

Last, in Part Three, I engage in a number of extended readings of selected poems and prose works from throughout Shelley's career to demonstrate the wide-ranging implications of this approach for our understanding of Shelley's entire oeuvre.

PART ONE

DEATH IS BUSY EVERYWHERE

1

The Political Nature of the Literary Text

POLITICS IN CONTEXT

In literary criticism, political criticism usually takes the form of an attempt to engage the text with a sociohistorical "context." Be it a Marxist like Frederic Jameson, exhorting us "always [to] historicize" (*Political Unconscious,* 9), or a New Historicist like Louis Adrian Montrose, telling us that historical/contextual "facts help us imaginatively to return a now-lifeless Elizabethan text to its living context in the material relations of Elizabethan people" (59), we are assured that "real power" (Howard, 15) is granted to the text by elaborating its connections with political institutions and events more or less contemporary with its production. In this chapter, I explore some of the problems with this claim and some of the philosophical underpinnings of its commonsense appeal.

There are two basic versions of this appeal to the "living context," and one can roughly align them with the two principal critical models of political interpretation: the recent ill-defined but influential critical movement known as New Historicism, and Marxist criticism. Proponents of the first see the context as a receptive metatext. I use the term "metatext" as a version of Gregory Bateson's "metacommunication": "those signals which should tell the individual what sort of a message a message is, i.e., . . . signals of the same logical type as 'This is play'" (167). The historical context is read as a set of continually present metatextual markers indicating the way in which we are to "take" the text "itself." This model, however, suffers from the problem that Hans-Georg Gadamer identifies in criticizing the concept of the "contemporary audience": "This idea of the contemporary addressee can claim only a restricted critical validity. For what is contemporaneity? Listeners of the day before yesterday as well as of the day after tomorrow are always among those to whom one speaks as a contemporary. Where are we to draw the line that excludes a reader from being addressed? What are contemporaries and what is a text's claim to truth in the face of this multifarious mixture of past and future? The idea of the original reader is full of unexamined idealisation" (356). New Historicist critics are usually careful to murmur the occasional warnings about the inherent contradictions of the text's "historical context," but they cannot but hypostatize the metatext, which they use to guarantee the "real power" of the text and as a key to its "meaning."[1] The very contradictions themselves come to be regarded as characteristic, and are found mirrored in the texts themselves.

Such idealization represses the very real contradictions within which all textual production and consumption is caught. To produce an "age" from the tangled threads of history requires, as the quotation from Gadamer suggests, a considerable amount of not always justifiable cutting. Once we propose one historical context as metatext, how can we stop, without recourse to the implicit violence of this "unexamined idealisation," the infinite regress of all the other possible metatexts that could in turn bracket the text "itself" and the context in which we are reading it? Not only must New Historicist critics exclude all the competing "contemporary" contexts one might propose as the "real ground" of the text in question (few texts, after all, are strictly occasional; an Elizabethan or Jacobean playwright, for example, could envisage a number of different potential audiences for any one work he might produce), they reveal the full extent of their arbitrary idealization of the "contemporary context" by also excluding from consideration as clues to the text's "real meaning" all the wide variety of contexts in which it has been found significant since, approximately, the death of its author. We must suppose an original moment of creation in which text and meta-

---

1. This tendency to repeat the hypostatization they elsewhere decry is particularly noticeable in more recent attempts to provide New Historicist criticism with a more complex theoretical underpinning. Marjorie Levinson's contributions to Levinson et al. (*Rethinking Historicism*) are a case in point. She provides some excellent criticisms of any historicism's inevitable idealizations of "the past" (see, e.g., 8–10) and yet cannot avoid, ultimately, talking of the "necessity of [Wordsworth's] solutions" (50) to the problems posed by his age, and attempting to place our "present" into a productive hermeneutic dialectic with this self-contained "past" (33–35, 50–51).

textual context are perfectly fused—the text crystallizes its productive context and becomes a total cultural fact—every subsequent evocation of the text errs from that originary plenitude of significance. Shelley notes in his *Defence* that *Paradise Lost* becomes, "by a strange and natural antithesis," a "chief popular support" of the same Anglican Church-and-state system Milton abhorred. For a New Historicist critic, however, the subsequent career of the poem is virtually irrelevant; only the relationship of the text to "the context" in which it was produced is allowed to tell us something about the nature of the text.[2]

If every text may begin to mean something new when placed in a different context, then it is only at the cost of violently repressing the possibility of a multiplicity of contexts within which the text may be "at home" that New Historicist interpretation can get off the ground at all. On the other hand, within the indefinite chronological boundary of con-temporaneity, New Historicist critics are quite happy to determine the "contemporary significance" of the same text with reference to widely differing contemporary discourses. The virtual absence in New Histori-cist criticism of controversy over *which* contemporary discourse is the appropriate "home" for a given text indicates the limitations of the New Historicist approach for understanding the political role of texts in his-torical change. What "real power" can a text be considered to possess if it must be capable of representing, and expressing, any and all aspects of its "contemporary" culture? Political effectiveness would seem to re-quire some partiality, a conceptual and material ability to negate aspects of the status quo. Individual studies seem to strive to find such specific political "homes" for given texts, but the overall impression we are left with is of a collective effort to reduce, but not eliminate, the text's "promiscuity": it is a question of keeping it in the (chronological) family.

Proponents of the second model of relating the text to its historical context regard the historical context as the *locus of textual production* (these approaches are not mutually exclusive). This seems on the face of it to be a more promising way of directly articulating the text with political/historical action. The model's commonsense core is an appeal to the idea that, to understand something, one must return to its origins and seek to understand the conditions to which it was a response. Texts are thus to be explained with reference to the sociopolitical conjunc-ture that conditioned their emergence.

2. There are exceptions to this rule: Michael Bristol's *Shakespeare's America, America's Shakespeare* is one of the best examples. The British "cultural materialists" (particularly Alan Sinfield) also show an interest in the politics of "reception" (or consumption) as well as those of production.

The focus on "production" moves us into the realm of Marxist theory. Karl Marx argued that although production and consumption must be seen "as moments of one process," nonetheless "production is the real point of departure and hence also the predominant moment" (*Grundrisse*, 94). In Marxist theory, the author is redefined as a literary "worker," whose textual production can be understood as a socioculturally determined product of a given set of relations of production. The text is viewed, not as a response to its context, but as an active part of a social dynamic: "Rather than ask, 'What is the *attitude* of a work to the relations of production of its time?' I should like to ask, 'What is its *position* in them?' This question directly concerns the function the work has within the literary relations of production of its time" (Benjamin, "Author as Producer," 222).

The corollary of this emphasis on literary production is hostility to those critics who focus on the moment of consumption. The writer as "ouvrier de son texte" produces that text in determinate historical conditions, and literary theorists are guilty of a pernicious fetishism of the literary work in abstracting it from historical process: "La critique prétend traiter l'oeuvre comme un produit de consommation: ainsi elle tombe aussitôt dans l'illusion empirique (qui est la première en droit), puisqu'elle se demande seulement comment *recevoir* un objet donné. Cependent cette illusion ne vient pas seule: elle se double aussitôt d'une illusion normative. La critique se propose alors de *modifier* l'oeuvre pour mieux l'absorber. Elle ne la traite plus alors exactement comme une donnée dans la mésure où elle là refuse dans sa réalité de fait, pour n'y voir que la manifestation provisoire d'une intention encore à effectuer" (Macherey, *Pour une théorie*, 30).[3] The writer as laborer produces the text in a determinate time and space, but the reader as consumer is apt to engage with the text with no regard for the labor the writer invested or the exigencies to which the writer was responding. Just as the laborer works in a determinate self-present context to produce goods that are subsequently rendered alienated commodities by their uncontrollable availability to the indifference of the consumer's cash, the nonhistoricizing critical reader retroactively alienates the writer's product by enacting the pernicious divorce of text and productive context. Raymond Williams sees this erasure of the moment of production

3. "Criticism claims to treat the work as an object of consumption, thus falling into the empiricist fallacy (first in authority) because it asks only how to *receive* a given object. But this first fallacy is closely followed by a second, the normative fallacy, in which criticism proposes to modify the work in order to assimilate it more thoroughly, denying its factual reality as being merely the provisional version of an unfulfilled intention" (*Theory*, 19).

as one of the principal elements in the construction of the notion of "literature" in the early nineteenth century. Literature becomes "a category of use [consumption] and condition rather than of production" (Williams, *Marxism and Literature*, 47).

But the problem with this model of the text's relationship to its historical context is that its proponents, by suppressing the moment of consumption, render a crucial moment of the text's political activity unavailable for analysis. A text that was produced but never consumed could have no political effect.

Ironically, and surprisingly, both of these supposedly "political" models of the text's relationship to society are characteristically weak when it comes to providing us with any way of understanding how a given text might act politically. In both of them there is a considerable distrust—even fear—of the most distinctive "power" of texts. The problem with reading texts out of their context of production is not that they become mute and lose significance but that they become all too voluble. The text's basic promiscuity, the ease with which we appropriate texts from the past to uses their authors could not have foreseen, is what calls for limitation by the "authentic" historical context. One could speak of a "historical-context function" analogous to Michel Foucault's "author function," which similarly

> allows a limitation of the cancerous and dangerous proliferation of significations within a world where one is thrifty not only with one's resources and riches, but also with one's discourses and their significations. . . .
>
> [T]he author is not an indefinite source of significations which fill a work; the author does not precede the works, he is a certain functional principle by which, in our culture, one limits, excludes, and chooses; in short, by which one impedes the free circulation, the free manipulation, the free composition, decomposition, and recomposition of fiction. . . . The author is therefore the ideological figure by which one marks the manner in which we fear the proliferation of meaning. (Foucault, "What Is an Author?" 159)

It does not seem self-evident that a radical politics of the text must take the form of a contextual historicism. The insistence upon the primacy of the contemporary response seems an arbitrary limitation, a purely ideological attempt to restrict the text's basic promiscuity, its ability to be read and reread long after its "moment" of production.

Since at least Horace's *Exegi monumentum aere perennius,* a part of
the writer's "conditions of production" has always been a realization of
the text's future promiscuity, its ability to outlive the historical conditions of the day.[4] A historicist approach seems singularly unsuited to
theorizing what must be the key moment of a radical politics: social
change. To read texts as extremely rich historical "evidence," to elaborate in detail the myriad ways in which they belong to and rise out of
particular sociopolitical conditions, can tell us much about why a given
text might be produced at a given moment, but it involves two key
blind spots with regard to the political nature of the text.

First, it cannot account for the *political* nature of the text; if the text
works as an agent of social change, it must operate as a negative moment in the process of social reproduction. If it is to change society, it
must force a discontinuity between the society that produced it and the
society that consumes it. Detailed contextualization, by focusing on the
text as a product of given historical conditions, cannot convincingly
theorize this negative moment.

Second, it cannot account for the political nature of the *text.* By insisting on tying the text to the context of production, these approaches
suppress the text's most distinctive attribute as a politically effective
expression—that despite being produced in a specific historical context, the text only ever *acts* politically as it is consumed in quite other,
subsequent, historical moments. Political literary criticism has, by and
large, ignored the *literary* nature of its material and assimilated it to a
model far more appropriate to the speech act in a total speech situation,
in which production and consumption are (ideally) simultaneous. Historicist critics cannot allow themselves to accept the possibility that the
consumption of texts may be a politically "creative" (or destructive) moment. The text in historicist criticism has an audience, but it is always
one so chronologically homologous with the author that author and audience form a corporate productive nexus. Take, for example (one of
many such), this comment of Stephen Greenblatt's: "[H]istory is not
simply discovered in the precincts surrounding the literary text or the
performance or the image; it is found in the artworks themselves, as
enabling condition, shaping force, forger of meaning, censor, commu-

---

4. Which is why Steven Jones's historicist criticism of Shelley's *Swellfoot the Tyrant,* that it
is too highbrow and too eclectic for its audience (134–35), is misplaced. Why must the
poem's "audience" be its "contemporary" audience? Shelley would argue that one of the
things a poem can legitimately do is hope to create the audience that is capable of understanding it. In "The Third World of Criticism" (105) Jerome McGann seems to be working toward a
similar understanding of the text-in-history.

nity of patronage and reception. And the work of art is not the passive surface on which this historical experience leaves its stamp but one of the creative agents in the fashioning and re-fashioning of this experience. Hence Montrose's assertion that the play creates the culture by which it is created" (*Representing the English Renaissance,* viii). The "locus of production" has become an idealized factory in which society works collectively on its symbolic order. This vision of largely harmonious "negotiation" ignores what must be the crucial political moment of negation. Or in other words, the blindness to the textuality of the literary work is precisely what conditions the inability to grant it real negative power. As long as the text seems dedicated to a particular receptive/productive context, it cannot act against that context without destroying its own conditions of being.

Both Marxist and New Historicist critics would argue that they do give the text an active role in society, and even (sometimes) an active role in social change. This is true; but in both cases it is notable how ill equipped either theoretical approach is to account for the text's political activity. There are two basic models of the text's political action available in this historical contextualization. Either it is a crucial moment in supporting and constructing the sociopolitical order that produces it, or it is "subversive" of that order. Each argument has its problems.

The first is well exemplified in Jean Howard's attempt to give a theoretical account of New Historicism, in which she makes the suggestion that this approach gives the text "real power." Although she is at pains to argue that "'history' is not objective, transparent, unified, or easily knowable and consequently is extremely problematic as a concept for grounding the meaning of a literary text," she cannot avoid the "unexamined idealism" that makes the "context of production" precisely such a "ground": "Rather than passively reflecting an external reality, literature is an agent in constructing a culture's sense of reality. It is part of a much larger symbolic order through which the world at a particular historical moment is conceptualized and through which a culture imagines its relationship to the actual conditions of its existence" (Howard, 15). Her apparent willingness to regard "*both* social and literary texts . . . [as] opaque, self-divided, and porous" (15) rapidly collapses into a thoroughly hypostatized, synchronic pseudo-dialectic. "A culture" engages as a singular, selfsame agent in the act of "imagin[ing] *its* relationship to the actual conditions of *its* existence." The claim that this restores the text's "real power" seems at best ironic. Can the text choose not to reproduce this "much larger symbolic order"? If all texts act in this manner, how can we possibly know that they are politically effective? There seems to be no theoretical ground on which we can distinguish between the text as cause of this symbolic order (even as a dialectical moment of its self-reproduction) and as mere symptom or evidence of it.

Much the same criticism might be made of Marxist claims for the text's role as an effective weapon in the struggle for ideological hegemony.[5] The claim can be made, but there seems to be no way of proving that the text plays any positive role in maintaining the social structure. In any case one might cite as evidence, we already know that the political structure persisted; the problem is to prove a given text's role in this persistence. It is rather like the old English music-hall joke about the man in the railway carriage throwing sheets of his newspaper out the window "to keep the elephants away." To the inevitable comment "But there aren't any elephants in England!" he retorts triumphantly, "See!" It may be that Montrose is right, for example, to suggest that the Elizabethan "pastoral of power" played a crucial role in perpetuating the Tudor sociopolitical order: "Pastorals that celebrate the ideal of content function to articulate—and thereby, perhaps, to assuage—*dis*content" (36). "Perhaps," indeed. *Perhaps* without the Elizabethan pastoral there would have been a bloody revolution, but Montrose cannot demonstrate the mechanism that connects these defusings of political discontent with actual political processes.

The idea of "subversiveness" is equally problematic. Subversion is a model of political action that relies upon the more or less extended existence of the very thing it fights against. Stephen Mullaney's attempt to ground English Renaissance drama in the physical "context" of the theaters in which it was originally performed—located in the politically and symbolically ambiguous "Liberties" on the margins of medieval and Renaissance London—is a good example of this problem. He wants to suggest that the drama gains a subversive potential by being thus marginalized, but we are free to wonder what radical political threat can come from a marginality created and controlled by the power structures that are supposedly being subverted: "The purpose of this study is to delineate the traditions of moral and cultural license that had for centuries been maintained in the Liberties, and to examine the ways in which popular drama appropriated such license to achieve, for a relatively

---

5. See Ernesto Laclau and Chantal Mouffe's *Hegemony and Socialist Strategy.* Williams has a useful chapter on the subject as it relates to literary criticism (*Marxism and Literature*, 108–14). See also Jorge Larrain, *Marxism and Ideology.*

brief period of time, an ideological liberty of its own" (Mullaney, 9). The emphasis on tradition and continuity here ("maintained for centuries") is seeking to impress us with the plenitude of metatextual significance the Liberties bring to the drama, and with their active role in the "production" of these texts. But can a site of "cultural license" really be a source of disruptive "ideological liberty"? Or is it not "licensed" in the other sense, permitted a certain controlled freedom to become society's "all-licensed" fool?

Texts in this kind of "political criticism" wear their "subversiveness" like a badge. They exercise "real power" only in the sense of a "powerful" affectivity; it is a powerful experience to marginalize temporarily what one habitually regards as central. But there is an unavoidable moment in historicist criticism when the critic must opt for this ineffective affective "subversiveness" or allow the possibility of genuine negation. Typically, they find, like Greenblatt, that "[t]here is subversion, no end of subversion, only not for us" (*Shakespearean Negotiations,* 39). Barbara Reibling puts it more bluntly: "[T]here is nothing in the subversion/containment model that can account for genuine conflict or change" (179).

Marxist criticism, if it gives the text a role in social change, is less likely to define that change in terms of subversion, but its models are problematic in the same way as when it sees the text as a tool of the hegemonic order. Marxist criticisms tend to align the text with particular social forces. The text becomes evidence of the class struggles in which its author/producer is engaged, as it does for Georg Lukàcs in *History and Class Consciousness* (2–3, 175–77), where he reads the text as a vital element in bringing about the self-consciousness of the emergent dominant class, the proletariat as subject-object of history. Or as it does in Williams's concept of "dominant, residual, and emergent" forces in cultural production (*Marxism and Literature,* 121–27). But this merely repeats, at a lower level, the problems of the historicist infusion of the text within its "contemporary context." The "context" is no longer the whole society, merely an "emergent" or "dominant" *part* of the society, but the text plays the same role in that part as it does with regard to the whole in the New Historicist view. It is still impossible to understand how we can conceive the text as politically effective. A class that failed to coalesce, because of inadequate literary representation, simply would not present itself as such for historical analysis. At best, it seems a way of deciding which writers are on the side of the angels—as, for example, when Walter Benjamin gives us this set of criteria for recognizing the politically sound author: "Does he succeed in promoting the socialization of the intellectual means of production? Does he see how he himself can organize the intellectual workers in the production process? Does he have proposals for the *Umfunktionierung* of the novel, the drama, the poem? The more completely he can orient his activity toward this task, the more correct will be the political tendency, and necessarily also the higher the technical quality, of his work" ("Author as Producer," 238). Even if we can see value in this politics of *engagement,* it seems to have nothing to say to us about the political role of the text beyond its context of production.

One way to begin to understand what motivates this seemingly paradoxical resistance to history on the part of avowedly historicist critical practices is by examining what is at stake in the resistance to the text's promiscuity. This might seem to be complicated by the fact that New Historicists, at least, are notoriously uncomfortable with stating the theoretical grounds of their critical practice (Howard, 21). "Theory" involves the (at least temporary) bracketing of the very contextual determinatives that, for the historicist, are essential. This is why literary theory, particularly in its deconstructivist versions, which problematize any appeal to grounding contexts, meets with such deep political suspicion from historicist critics. This suspicion of "theory" makes Greenblatt, for example, claim he can only accept "an embedded theory, theory glimpsed lurking in the thickets of narrative pragmatics" ("Capitalist Culture and the Circulatory System," 257). This very suspicion is, however, an important clue to understanding the appeal of historicist criticism.

We can relate this historicist resistance to theory to the pragmatic argument "against theory" mounted by Steven Knapp and Walter Benn Michaels in their paper of that name:

> [T]he only relevant truth about belief is that you can't go outside it, and, far from being unlivable, this is a truth you can't help but live. It has no practical consequences not because it can never be *united* with practice but because it can never be *separated* from practice.
>
> The theoretical impulse, as we have described it, always involves the attempt to separate things that should not be separated: on the ontological side, meaning from intention, language from speech acts; on the epistemological side, knowledge from true belief. Our point has been that the separated terms are in fact inseparable. (741)

The historicist argument is that separating the text from its specific historical context somehow renders it inauthentic and abstract, strips it of its illocutionary force; it is to "separate things that should not be separated."

One source, at least in New Historicist criticism, of this sense of the text's embeddedness in social action is an anthropological model of socially constructed meaning. References to the work of Clifford Geertz and, though to a lesser extent, Victor Turner and other anthropologists are far more frequent in New Historical criticism than references to the work of any historian or historiographer (Howard, 24, 29).[6] Greenblatt repeatedly acknowledges his indebtedness to Geertz and describes his own work as an attempt to "practice a more cultural or anthropological criticism" (*Renaissance Self-Fashioning,* 4). Mullaney claims to be "[e]mploying a kind of 'thick description' in Clifford Geertz's sense of the phrase," and Montrose's work has been described as "show[ing] the strong influence . . . of cultural anthropologists such as Victor Turner and Clifford Geertz" (Howard, 24).

The concept that recurs constantly in New Historical studies associated with Geertz's name is that of "thick description." For Geertz, this practice, outlined in his paper "Thick Description: Toward an Interpretive Theory of Culture," relates action within "a culture" as densely as possible to the culturally relevant structures of understanding that call for and make comprehensible that action. The relevance to New Historical practice is obvious: "As interworked systems of construable signs . . . culture is not a power, something to which social events, behaviours, institutions, or processes can be casually attributed; it is a context, something within which they can be intelligibly—that is, thickly—described" (Geertz, *Interpretation of Cultures,* 14).

To describe an anthropology that has long since engaged in profound internal debates over synchronic versus diachronic modes of analysis as inherently opposed to history-as-change may appear to be a stale caricature, and yet in a recent article, "History and Anthropology" (for a colloquium on the New Historicism in the humanities), Geertz has shown just how stubborn the difference of orientation can be. As he puts it, no doubt ironically but by and large accurately: "Anthropology gets the tableau, History gets the drama; Anthropology the forms, History the

---

6. It is interesting to note that this is particularly true of recent book-length studies of Shelley in the New Historicist vein. See, e.g., Steven Jones, *Shelley's Satire,* 7, and Timothy Morton, *Shelley and the Revolution in Taste,* 2–4.

causes" (326). Anthropology's inveterate attachment to synchronic models of cultural analysis, and the inevitable corollary of a persistent idealization of the notion of "a culture," provide exact analogies of all the historicist traits identified above. Geertz, in *The Interpretation of Cultures,* variously describes "culture" as a "pattern of life," a "context," an "imaginative universe," "structures of signification," "webs of significance," and ubiquitously refers to it as "a culture," as if it were a simple unitary reference point, a *Weltanschauung.* The complex disjunctions of actual life patterns must be constantly transformed—despite many unconvincing proclamations to the contrary—into a unitary totality so as to validate a methodology based upon "cultural analysis."

Geertz, like most anthropologists, seeks *Verstehen:* "A good interpretation of anything—a poem, a person, a history, a ritual, an institution, a society—takes us into the heart of that of which it is the interpretation." And he resists "theory": "When it does not do that, but leads us instead somewhere else—into an admiration of its own elegance, of its author's cleverness, or of the beauties of Euclidean order—it may have its intrinsic charms; but it is something else than what the task at hand . . . calls for" (*Interpretation of Cultures,* 18). When Greenblatt tells us that he "began with the desire to speak with the dead" (*Shakespearean Negotiations,* 1), we can recognize the same impulse that generates anthropology—the belief (or hope against hope) that one can indeed be "taken into the heart" of the radically other.

One cannot, however, simply argue that historicist criticism is a disguised anthropology, and that this accounts for its difficulties in conceptualizing "history" per se. Geertz's essay is in fact seeking models of cultural understanding from outside the available anthropological methods. It is an essay written in some ways against anthropology. He sends us to two further models for understanding the significance of culturally embedded action, each of which suggests a wider context for the distinctive features of historicist literary criticism than simply an "anthropological" methodology.

The first of these figures prominently in his title, and is, simply, "interpretation." By "interpretation" Geertz understands specifically literary interpretation, comparing cultural "analysis" to the work of "the literary critic" (*Interpretation of Cultures,* 9). This suggests that to some extent New Historicism, in seeking to go beyond the hermetic theoretical world of literary criticism, has reached out to itself in the guise of an other. This possibility would not be without consequences for our understanding of New Historicist practice. The model of literary criticism Geertz has in mind is not fully explicated, but we can recognize in it many features of the New Critical approach. The transformation of "cultures" into the New Critical version of literary texts (self-contained literary "artifacts") would be a reasonable description of the idealization of "the contemporary historical context" that characterizes so much historicist criticism. The "subversiveness" that never subverts would be analogous to the "irony" that is always found to be at play but that never undoes the ultimate dynamic unity of the literary work of art. One might speculate that the popularity of Geertzian anthropology in New Historical criticism stems from the ease with which critics trained in the close reading of literary texts can adapt those techniques to considering the text-in-society as a hermeneutical unit like the motif-in-the-text. That such an approach has difficulty conceptualizing historical *process* comes as no surprise.

The second model Geertz reaches out to steers us in a more specific direction, but with interesting implications for the historicist critic's sense of the "political." Geertz borrows the term "thick description" from two papers of Gilbert Ryle's that put forward one of the central arguments of ordinary-language philosophy: that language is essentially *public* (Geertz, *Interpretation of Cultures,* 6). As Geertz puts it: "Culture is public because meaning is" (12). Geertz draws equally on the work of such ordinary-language philosophers as the later Ludwig Wittgenstein and Stanley Cavell to construct his sense of meaning-in-social-action, of the embeddedness of all symbolic languages within shared systems of meaning (or "language games"), inscribing his own work within the "generalized attack on privacy theories of meaning . . . since early Husserl and late Wittgenstein" (12).

In the ordinary-language perspective, language—meaning—can only be approached in terms of instantiations of shared conventions for "meaning this." The test for whether a given speech act is to be regarded as successful (felicitous) is whether it fulfills publicly available criteria for being that kind of speech act, not whether it reflects the "internal" intentions of the speaker or establishes some transcendental bond between words and things.

This connection to ordinary-language philosophy, with its emphasis on the public and the shared, provides us with a new way of understanding historicist criticism's version of the text's relationship to its context, which has important consequences for our understanding of what it means for that text to be "political." If we read the historicist project as an attempt to restore to literature its original illocutionary force, to recapture the performative power of the text, then this entails a subtle but crucial change in the way we conceive of "historical con-

text." Rather than define "historical context" as a preexisting and separate locus of conjunctural demands to which the text must formulate a
response (and which troubled us because of the New Historicism's lack
of elaborated mechanisms by which the text could make that response),
we should, as J. L. Austin argues, regard the "total speech act in the total
speech situation [as] the *only actual* phenomenon which, in the last
resort, we are engaged in elucidating" (148). If we propose even a
purely analytical separation between the two moments—context and
text—this is a sign of our corruption by epistemology: the foolish "separating" desire to go "outside" our lived form of life in order to "know"
something absolutely. Wittgenstein makes the same point in arguing that
there is no such thing as a meaningful act considered separately from a
"language game": "Our mistake is to look for an explanation where we
ought to look at what happens as a 'proto-phenomenon.' That is, where
we ought to have said: *this language-game is played*" (167).

The text in historicist criticism, according to this model, should be
regarded not on the model of text/context but as the concrete manifestation of a "form of life" (Wittgenstein, 226). The context does not
exist, even virtually, beside the practices that instantiate it, any more
than the rules of a (language) game can be separated from the playing of
that game:

> It is not possible that there should have been only one occasion
> on which someone obeyed a rule. It is not possible that there
> should have been only one occasion on which a report was
> made, an order given or understood; and so on.—To obey a rule,
> to make a report, to give an order, to play a game of chess, are
> *customs* (uses, institutions).
>
> To understand a sentence means to understand a language. To
> understand a language means to be master of a technique. (81)

This in turn gives us a very different understanding of the political.
The title of Cavell's contribution to the symposium "The Politics of Interpretation" gives us a sense of what this might mean: "Politics as Opposed to What?" Even to begin to demand an explicit demonstration of
the mechanism by which a text "enters" the political realm and "responds" to its "context" is to betray a conception of language that is
essentially mimetic (that "separates what should not be separated"): first
the context, then the "image" of that context in the textual mirror. This
is the epistemological model Richard Rorty criticizes in his *Philosophy*

and the Mirror of Nature from the perspective of his philosophical pragmatism—a position closely allied with ordinary-language philosophy.

The question, "politics as opposed to what?" suggests that by seeing "the politics of interpretation" as merely one aspect of interpretation— one area to which we can either address the text or not—the real political nature of the text has already been denied. This is a less heroic conception of the political: the political conceived not as a violent, negative, and external impact upon history but as the constant negotiation of our commonness, of our sense of responsibility toward each other, and of the respective claims upon each other of, on the one hand, the community that gives us being and, on the other, ourselves as representatives of that community. For Cavell, *Coriolanus* is a political play, not because it wreaks change upon society, but because it "celebrates . . . the condition of community," so that we realize a "performance is nothing without our participation in an audience; and this participation is up to each of us" ("Who Does the Wolf Love?" 214).

This emphasis on what is "up to us" is the key to ordinary-language philosophy's ethical stance. Jacques Derrida argues that "speech act theory is fundamentally and in its most fecund, most rigorous, and most interesting aspects . . . a theory of right or law, of convention, of political ethics or of politics as ethics. It describes . . . the pure conditions of an ethical-political discourse insofar as this discourse involves the relation of intentionality to conventionality or to rules" ("Limited Inc," 240). This explains the perennial interest of the ordinary-language philosopher in promises and contracts, in all those speech acts that force us to ask, Who is speaking? and Can they be held responsible for what they say? Ordinary-language philosophy is above all an ethics of responsibility. The resistance of ordinary-language philosophy to skeptical/theoretical language (which occasions the controversy between Derrida and John Searle from which the above quotation is drawn) is a resistance to language that does not take its responsibilities seriously. It is a resistance to language that never fulfills Wittgenstein's criterion that it be "actually used in this way in the language-game which is its original home" (48). Hence the importance for Cavell of establishing that skepticism occurs in a "nonclaim context," that it is language that makes no serious claims upon the world and responds to no claims the world makes upon us (*Claim of Reason*, 219–21).

This is analogous to the historicist resistance to the promiscuity of the text; it is not a denial of the fact that texts can operate in diverse contexts but a belief that, divorced from the context in which and for which they are primarily responsible, texts lose their "thickness"—their communally invested richness and authenticity.

The key terms in Cavell's terminology for the appropriate moral stance toward the world are "acceptance" and "acknowledgment": "To let yourself matter is to acknowledge not merely how it is with you, and hence to acknowledge that you want the other to care, at least to care to know. It is equally to acknowledge that your expressions in fact express you, that they are yours, that you are in them. This means allowing yourself to be comprehended, something you can always deny. Not to deny it is, I would like to say, to acknowledge your body, and the body of your expressions, to be yours, you on earth, all there will ever *be* of you" (*Claim of Reason,* 383). This is an acceptance of our givenness to the world, an acceptance of our finality, which means a continual affirmation (acknowledgment) of the responsibilities we owe to the world and the world's responsibility for us. Above all, it means that, as Wittgenstein puts it, "[w]hat has to be accepted, the given, is—so one could say—*forms of life*" (226). We must realize that "the chain of reasons has an end" (106), and that we cannot make a complete rational account of our being in the world. This does not mean that our way of knowing is inadequate for this world, but that it is grounded in an acceptance of always already given conventions, not in pure reason.

Everything comes down to an acceptance of the "therapeutic" power of Wittgenstein's desire "to bring words back from their metaphysical to their everyday use" (48): "[I]t is evident that the reign of repressive philosophical systematizing—sometimes called metaphysics, sometimes called logical analysis—has depended upon the suppression of the human voice. It is as the recovery of this voice (as from an illness) that ordinary language philosophy is, as I have understood and written about it, before all to be understood" (Cavell, "Politics as Opposed to What?" 197). This militant phonocentrism is an attempt to restore to the individual a political power that "repressive philosophical systematizing" takes from us. This is a positive power exactly analogous to the "real power" of the text in historicist criticism, the power of acknowledging one's engagement with the community: *communitas.*

We now have a new understanding of what motivates the New Historical model of the text's relationship to the historical context. In this view, the question of a confrontation of text with context, a negation of the one by the other, is unthinkable (or should be). What looked like a suspicion of the dangerous promiscuity of the text at the moment of its consumption should perhaps now be understood as an attempt to restore to the text its power as "human voice," to restore to it its responsibility—a responsibility both to and for the "total speech situation" it does not so much find itself *in* as acknowledge as the condition of its being. For the text to "challenge" its history would be a moral failure rather than a political success. The text is given to history and must, to be meaningful, to avoid the disaster of a skeptical withholding of itself from history, accept and acknowledge its history as what is given to it, a given that the text is morally obliged to acknowledge. The text's "real power" is this positive power to voice its belonging to history, its finality, when the alternative is not freedom *from* history but being lost *to* (our) history.

The model of political action (mis)applied above to historicist criticism was one of change and discontinuity, cause and (negative) effect. But as Austin argues, from an ordinary-language perspective: "[T]he sense in which saying something produces effects on other persons, or *causes* things, is a fundamentally different sense of cause from that used in physical causation by pressure, &c. It has to operate through the conventions of language and is a matter of influence exerted by one person on another: this is probably the original sense of 'cause'" (113 n. 1). Political power, in this view, is not exercised in the brute negation of one force by another, but in the mutual acknowledgment by two forces of a defining situation. Only by fully inscribing the text in the total speech situation can we understand its historical causality, a causality now to be defined as the instantiation of a shared cultural code.

NARRATIVE AND CHANGE

I wrote, above, of two "models" to which Geertz had turned in an attempt to define his anthropological practice. These were loosely defined as "interpretation" and "ordinary-language philosophy." The distinction, however, is more apparent than real. Ordinary-language philosophy is a part of the general nineteenth- and twentieth-century philosophical turn to language we associate with pragmatics, ordinary-language philosophy, and hermeneutics (to add a "school" to each of the names—Dewey, Wittgenstein, and Heidegger—that Rorty sets up as his triumvirate of philosophers who define this new direction of philosophy [5ff.]). Heidegger's claim that *"Logos* is *phonē" (Basic Writings,* 80) is perhaps the most succinct statement of this retraction of epistemology within the linguistic horizon, which posits, in Cavell's words, that the "wish and search for community are the wish and search for reason" (*Claim of Reason,* 20). The common ground of all these approaches is their resistance to the theoretical "separation" between text and context, speech act and language game, which opens the possibility of a skeptical assault upon the relationship between language and world. From the perspective of these "hermeneutic" approaches the world is constituted in and through language, and we can only lose sight of this fact if we attempt to analyze the "parts" (speech acts, individual "facts" about the world) without regard to the "whole" (the "total speech situation," or "form of life") that gives them meaning. As David Couzens Hoy puts it: "Since Kant epistemology has been conceived as a foundationalist enterprise—one that attempts to separate knowledge from other forms of belief, with the intention of ascertaining what is objectively certain. Hermeneutics, in contrast, rejects the idea that the primary task of philosophy is to supply foundations and guarantee certainty. It sees knowledge as pragmatically relative to contexts of understanding. The paradigm of the phenomenon of understanding is the interpretation of texts" (92).

Hoy makes it clear how natural it is that literary criticism, in seeking to conceive of the literary text as a politically active force, should do so in historicist terms. In trying to shrug off the straitjacket of textual hermeticism and to open itself out to wider concerns, literary criticism seems to have an uncanny knack for discovering what are simply larger objects for the familiar practices of textual hermeneutics.

In theory, at least, applying this model to Marxist criticism is problematic. Marxist theory proposes a utopian moment of revolution that negates the social context; such a moment cannot be theorized by philosophical pragmatism. But while Marxist critics are willing to grant that a socioeconomic class has the power to transform its historical conditions of existence, they are less willing to admit that works of literature can do so. In practice most Marxist critics read literary texts as symptomatic of an underlying socioeconomic reality, and would agree with Williams's strictures against "separating the social from individual meaningful activity" (*Marxism and Literature,* 36). Williams's arguments against this theoretical "separating" hinge upon his pragmatic definition of language as "practical consciousness": "[T]he fusion of formal element and meaning . . . is the result of the real process of social development, in the actual activities of speech and in the continuing development of a language. Indeed signs can exist only when this active social relationship is posited. The usable sign . . . is a product of this continuing speech-activity between real individuals who are in some continuing social relationship. . . . What we have . . . is a grasping of . . . reality through language, which as practical consciousness is saturated by and saturates all social activity, including productive activity" (36–37). This is not merely the natural prejudice of the literary critic. Antonio Gramsci refers to Marxism as the "philosophy of praxis" in his prison notebooks; his argument that "man cannot be conceived of except as historically determined man—i.e. man who has developed, and who lives, in certain conditions, in a particular social complex or totality of social relations" (244)—is a neat summary of the basis of philosophical pragmatism.

This quotation from Gramsci returns us to the idea of "history." It is interesting to note that Rorty, one of the most prominent contemporary pragmatist philosophers, specifically pits his philosophical pragmatism against "traditional philosophy as an escape from history" and argues that the "moral" of his *Philosophy and the Mirror of Nature* is "historicist" (9, 10). Williams's arguments for a Marxist conception of language as "practical consciousness" is equally an argument for language as historical consciousness (*Marxism and Literature*, 44). For the anti-"epistemological" pragmatist, the tie to history is the tie to meaning—or the ability to mean—and the hermeneutical capacity to understand. To share meanings, to communicate, is always to invoke, or rather to instantiate, some coexistent historical "whole" within which one can "mean this." We could describe this position with a word taken from hermeneutical theory: all communication requires "charity." This is the demand, as Hoy defines it, that "[t]here must be *some* shared belief if there is to be any understanding at all" (97).

This brief exposition of the philosophical roots of historicist criticism may have seemed to be getting further and further from "history," but in fact the pragmatic insistence that "history" is the hermeneutical "whole" to which we must refer our statements and actions in order to understand them suggests rather that we are dealing with radically opposed understandings of the meaning of history. Moreover, the concept of history underlying historicist criticism is the dominant one in modern thought, and one that underwrites the "turn to language" of the hermeneutical philosophies discussed above.

I have opposed diachronic "history" to synchronic "language" and "culture," but that distinction is foreign to the fundamental impulse of modern historiography; the opposition to history-as-change is as basic to "history" as it is to anthropology or ordinary-language philosophy. When it comes to *Verstehen,* a philosopher of history quite literally wrote the book. Wilhelm Dilthey founded modern hermeneutical theory in the nineteenth century in an attempt to construct a "Critique of Historical Reason" as an extension of the three Kantian *Critiques* (Dilthey, 95).

For Dilthey, whose influence upon modern historiography is immeasurable, history is a hermeneutical totality that gives meaning to the parts of which it is composed and with reference to which all future actions (speech acts, texts) are conceived: "[T]he historical world . . . [is] a system of interactions centred on itself; each individual system of interactions contained in it has . . . its centre within itself; but all are structurally linked into a whole in which, from the significance of the individual parts, the meaning of the whole context of the social-historical world arises; thus, every value judgement and every purpose projected into the future, must be based exclusively on this structural context" (82). Hayden White helps us understand the political consequences of adopting this version of history as the hallmark of history as an academic "discipline": "What it marks out for repression in general is utopian thinking—the kind of thinking without which revolutionary politics, whether of the Left or the Right, becomes unthinkable. . . . And it does so, moreover, by so disciplining historical consciousness as to make realism effectively identical with anti-utopianism" ("Politics of Historical Interpretation," 125, 126). Utopias are, by definition, negative. A politics of the text that accepted the text's promiscuous ability to belong nowhere and everywhere, always to bring us, in a sense, "news from nowhere," would be a utopian politics. The literary historicist emphasis on the text's definite location in a concrete historical topos is profoundly anti-utopian.

Change is, in fact, a major dilemma for the philosophy of history—as much as it is for anthropology or historicist criticism. R. G. Collingwood, for example, in his *Idea of History,* tries to distinguish between valuable, positive "progress" and amoral, ungrounded "change." He does not renounce the hope of progress, but it is only possible if change is grounded in a complete historical self-consciousness that subsumes both the before and after of historical time within the continuity of the historical whole: "This understanding of the system we set out to supersede is a thing which we must retain throughout the work of superseding it, as a knowledge of the past conditioning our creation of the future. . . . It may be impossible to do this. . . . But if that is so, there will once more, as so often in the past, be change but no progress" (334). The historical consciousness of the superseded past fully recuperates the negation threatened by change, because "all history, is the re-enactment of past thought in the historian's own mind" (215). But this negation of the negation in historical consciousness problematizes the very concept of "progress." If the historian's consciousness of history is essentially the self-consciousness of reason ("historical knowledge is the only knowledge that the human mind can have of itself" [220]), then what presents itself to historical knowledge will not really admit of genuine improvement; we can at best hope for a certain clarification of a truth that is ultimately universal. The very demand for an accession to a complete historical self-consciousness capable of comprehending the individual's relationship to both past and present (or present and future) as essentially one relationship rules out the possibility of a genuine dehiscence in the seamless absolutism of historical knowing. In fact, to comprehend (in both senses) history is to condemn ourselves to an endless repetition of its singular truth: "Historical knowledge is the knowledge of what mind has done in the past, and at the same time it is the redoing of this, the perpetuation of past acts in the present" (218).

Nancy Partner, a historian whose work is closely related to the New Historicism, helps us see why this version of "history" is so appealing to literary critics. She too tries to construct a theory of change in history, drawing principally on the work of the hermeneuticist Hans-Georg Gadamer: "All past events, persons, and phenomena, however abstractly defined, emerge into identity only as part of a formal pattern which controls time. 'Tick' = origins, causes, predisposing factors, fundamental premises. 'Tock' = results, effects, achievements, recovered meanings. In the 'middle,' our plot enables us to identify manifestations, symptoms, developments, characteristics. The most rigorously eventless, characterless, 'non-narrative' history has to tell something, has to begin somewhere and proceed and conclude" (93). One can have change, it appears, as long as it is recuperated within the unifying framework of a narrative structure. "Tick" always calls forth "tock." History always takes the form of story, with the kind of narrative closure that allows us to turn a sequence of events into a hermeneutically accessible whole. Or as Dilthey put it (74-75): "Where the meaning of the life of an individual, of myself, of another, or of a nation, lies, is not clearly determined by the fact that there is such a meaning. That it is there is always certain to the person remembering it as a series of related experiences. Only in the last moment of a life can the balance of its meaning be struck so it can be done only for a moment, or by another who retraces that life."

The role of the hermeneutical historian is to recuperate change, to assiduously negate the negation of historical change by turning it into narrative, turning a sequence of events into a plot, finding the appropriate "whole" for each historical/phenomenological "part." Far from being a turn away from history, then, one could argue that historicist criticism, and the entire twentieth-century philosophical linguistic turn, with its antifoundationalist assault on theoretical "separation" and insistence upon the hermeneutical elucidation of action and meaning with reference to the pragmatic context of sociocultural convention, should, by rights, bear the name of history, while noting the attendant irony that in this historical age we seem to be almost unable to conceptualize change.

We have come a long way toward understanding the "inevitability" of the historicist turn of contemporary political literary criticism. Wherever literary critics turn to connect with issues "beyond" the text—to anthropological models of society, philosophies of effective speech acts, or even to history itself—they find a familiar hermeneutics that is based on textual interpretation. What could be more reassuring for the literary critic than to have risked the integrity of the text as aesthetic object, as organic/hermeneutical whole, only to find that text figuring as a dynamic instance of the wider, cultural whole of its metatextual "social context"?

To turn from one of the greatest nineteenth-century theorists of history to one of its greatest practitioners is to complete this sequence of historicist criticism's discoveries of the self in the guise of the other. Jacob Burckhardt's *Civilization of the Renaissance in Italy* captures the essence of an idea of history that remains a dominant theme of Western discourse to the present day. It is not only a great achievement of historiography but equally a pioneering work of anthropology; it does not seek to account for the coming-to-be of the Italian Renaissance, but to allow us to understand it as a "form of life." But surely what made Burckhardt's picture of the Italian Renaissance so influential, what makes it still such an exciting study, and what made it one of the principle factors in constructing the "Renaissance" as the historical "period" par excellence, was his conception of the Renaissance state as a "work of art" of which the citizens were consciously the authors.[7]

To make the state available to us, hermeneutically, as an organic, aesthetic object, of which the parts consciously embody the whole, is the anti-utopian utopia secretly or openly promised by all the historicisms of the last century. It is the reason that Stephen Greenblatt, 120 years after its first publication, says that "one of the best introductions to Renaissance self-fashioning remains Burckhardt's *Civilization of the Renaissance in Italy*" (*Renaissance Self-Fashioning*, 161).

---

7. Robert Darnton, a historian whose quasi-"anthropological" work has close affinities with New Historicist practice, remarked in a seminar at McGill University that he regarded Burckhardt as perhaps the greatest of historians, and as great an anthropologist as he was a historian.

2

The Politics of Skepticism and
the Politics of Idealism

What the last chapter has shown us is that in order to rethink the political role of the text, we must rethink this hermeneutical concept of history. This is where Shelley is useful. The drive to reconcile disjunctive change with coherent narrative totality—or, more generally, the hermeneutical drive from the fragmentary "part" to absolute "whole"— is the most abiding legacy of Romanticism in Western thought. Dilthey's hermeneutical historicism is an attempt to systematize this insertion of the newly discovered "Man" into the pragmatic contexts of "life, labour, and language"—as Foucault describes the new "anthropological" cast of the Western *epistēmē* that overthrows the classical order of the Enlightenment at the end of the eighteenth century (*Les mots it les choses*, 340). The Romantic conception of history is ruled by what Charles Taylor calls Romantic "expressivism" (*Sources of the Self*, 368ff.), the belief that individual lives and actions must be understood as the "expression" of a contextualizing "framework" (17)—those "horizons within which we live our lives and which make sense of them" (27). From such a perspective, the resistance to theoretical "separation" is utterly predictable: "stepping outside these limits [the "horizons" above] would be tantamount to stepping outside what we would recognize as integral, that is, undamaged human personhood" (27).

Shelley was fully aware of the attractions—and fully versed in the theory—of this anti-utopian attempt to render the relationship of the individual and individual action to a defining sociohistorical framework self-consciously transparent. However, Shelley, to an extent not true of any of the other English Romantic poets, also drew on utopian, revolutionary models of historical change that he derived from various sources in the radical Enlightenment. Shelley's attempts to reconcile these "idealist" and "skeptical" aspects of his intellectual heritage ultimately led him to develop a theory of historical process critical of them both, a theory that will enable us to reexamine our understanding of the political role of the literary text. In this chapter, however, I explore the philosophical roots and the political implications of Shelley's divided legacy. I show how compelling—and how flawed—each approach could be for Shelley. Moreover, I show that they each remain defining influences in our contemporary debates over the political role of the text.

Before returning to idealist "expressivism" and its relationship to the "therapeutic" urge of the "turn to language," I shall discuss the radical alternative vision of the political engagement with history available to Shelley from the skeptical Enlightenment.

THE POLITICS OF SKEPTICISM

I

The French Revolution was the central political fact of Shelley's time— what he called "the master theme of the epoch in which we live" (*Letters,* 2:504). In an important sense, this is still true. The Revolution— or, more precisely, the revolutionary Enlightenment—still haunts our thoughts; it is the bad dream from which the "therapeutic" imperative of the "turn to history" seeks to awaken us. It is not hard to understand why. The Revolution proposed itself, at least in one light, as a complete negation of all the historical "frameworks" within which the French had defined (and "expressed") their "culture."[1] Alexis de Tocqueville puts this particularly well: "Tandis que l'esprit humain hésite encore et, retenu dans les routes anciennes, s'efforce déjà d'en sortir, le peuple français, brisant tout à coup le lien des souvenirs, foulant aux pieds ses vieux usages, répudiant ses antiques moeurs, échappant violemment aux tradi-

1. Marx points out that the Revolution "draped itself alternately as the Roman republic and the Roman empire" in his "The Eighteenth Brumaire of Louis Bonaparte" (*Surveys from Exile,* 147). In some respects the Revolution was a moment of absolute negative change, but its protagonists could be as appalled and frightened by that fact as its detractors, and did much to disguise its novelty.

tions de famille, aux opinions des classes, à l'esprit de province, aux préjugés de nation, à l'empire des croyances, proclame que la vérité est une, qu'elle ne se modifie ni par le temps ni par les lieux, qu'elle n'est point relative mais absolue, qu'il faut la chercher au fond des choses, négligeant la forme, que chacun peut la découvrir et doit s'y conformer" (44).[2]

When Gadamer constructs, in our century, a historical textual hermeneutics, it is still this idea of revolutionary change against which he feels he has to work. For Gadamer, the Enlightenment's "global demand" for the "overcoming of all prejudices" from the standpoint of "absolute reason" (244) is "abstract and revolutionary" (249) and "impossible for historical humanity" (244). Our "historical consciousness" demands a dedication to the continuity of the state and its "traditions" as guarantee of the continuity of our subjective identity and its moral significance: "In fact history does not belong to us, but we belong to it. Long before we understand ourselves through the process of self-examination, we understand ourselves in a self-evident way in the family, society and state in which we live. The focus of subjectivity is a distorting mirror. The self-awareness of the individual is only a flickering in the closed circuits of historical life. That is why the prejudices of the individual, far more than his judgements, constitute the historical reality of his being" (245). In this view, even what is false and oppressive in the tradition is valuable because it lies within the "horizons" of what we understand as the realm of the ethical—more valuable than any attempt to move beyond those horizons. Such an "abstraction" (or separation) from the moral concreteness of our "form of life" would be a loss of "thickness" that would leave us unsituated, unsure what ethical language game we were playing.

Gadamer is rehearsing here the essential arguments of the first great response to the French Revolution: Edmund Burke's *Reflections on the Revolution in France*. Burke's is one of the most complete attempts to create a politics based upon the fragility of ethical meaningfulness. In his view, revolution is execrable, not so much because of the specific physical and mental hardships it brings in its train, but because it under-

2. "While the human mind still hesitates and, confined to its accustomed paths, already forces itself to leave them, the French people, suddenly breaking the thread of memory, trampling its old usages, repudiating its ancient customs, escaping violently from family traditions, from class opinions, from provincialism, from national prejudice, from the empire of beliefs, proclaims that truth is single, that it is not modified by time or place, that it is not relative but absolute, that it is necessary to seek it in the essence of things, and not in their form, that each one of us can discover it and must conform to it" (my translation).

mines our recognition or acknowledgment of the order of the state, which alone guarantees the stability of meanings: "Good order is the foundation of all good things. . . . The magistrate must have his reverence, the laws their authority. The body of the people must not find the principles of natural subordination by art rooted out of their minds" (372). This "by art" recalls Gadamer's "abstract and revolutionary" Enlightenment; "art" here stands for the theoretical "separation" that extracts itself from tradition in a moment of ungrounded negativity. Burke's ideal attitude toward the given conditions of our existence is one of "wise prejudice":

> To avoid therefore the evils of inconstancy and versatility, ten thousand times worse than those of obstinacy and the blindest prejudice, we have consecrated the state, that no man should approach to look into its defects or corruptions but with due caution; that he should never dream of beginning its reformation by its subversion; that he should approach to the faults of the state as to the wounds of a father, with pious awe and trembling solicitude. By this wise prejudice we are taught to look with horror on those children of their country who are prompt rashly to hack that aged parent in pieces, and put him into the kettle of magicians, in hopes that by their poisonous weeds, and wild incantations, they may regenerate the paternal constitution and renovate their father's life. (194)

The state is "consecrated"[3] because a moment of negative "inconstancy" is sufficient to break the continuity of the genealogical chain of tradition upon which our understanding of the world and our place in it depends. Once one disrupts a continuity based solely on the contiguous links of succession, it is impossible to mend the chain. This is the abyssal gap between "tick" and "tock" that must be short-circuited by reducing the two moments, the "before" and "after" of historical action, to the repetition of the same: "I would not exclude alteration neither; but even when I changed, it should be to preserve. . . . In what I did, I should follow the example of our ancestors. I would make the reparation as nearly as possible in the style of the building" (375).

3. This declension from historicist criticism to anthropology, to twentieth-century philosophies of language, to historical hermeneutics, and back to Edmund Burke supports Terry Eagleton's attack on "the varieties of American neo-pragmatism, [which] complacently consecrate . . . the given culture, protecting it under the guise of a 'radical' or faintly scandalous anti-foundationalism from fundamental critique" (*Ideology*, 383).

Burke's and Gadamer's horrified response to Enlightenment "separation" is, however, prefigured in the Enlightenment itself. They are both correct to identify the core of the Enlightenment project as the theoretical or analytical "separation," against which modern historicism still maintains its desperate struggle. Taylor suggests that the origin of this "separation" lies with Descartes's "disengaged subject"; this is "one of the most important developments of the modern era" (*Sources of the Self,* 159) because it initiates the divorce between mind and world, individual and "tradition," subject and object, that underwrites the Enlightenment project and its ability to decree that "chacun peut . . . découvrir [la vérité] et doit s'y conformer," regardless of his or her past and current "history." And yet the Enlightenment philosophes are always conscious of a political dilemma in this "disengagement." How does one restore the link between the disengaged elements? What "kettle of magicians" will "regenerate the paternal constitution"? As Charles Taylor and Terry Eagleton point out, moral sense theory—the favorite ethical solution of the Enlightenment—is one such attempted restoration (Taylor, *Sources of the Self,* 248–84; Eagleton, *Aesthetic,* 31–69). Before the Enlightenment abstraction of the individual from "tradition," the problem of *why* we have moral sentiments did not require this kind of answer.

Similarly, the problem of the individual's allegiance to the polis suddenly becomes a nagging anxiety. Social contract theory, from Hobbes and Locke onward, is the typical Enlightenment response to this problem. C. B. Macpherson reads this persuasively as a response to the "possessive individualism" of emergent capitalism, but it is equally a response to the Enlightenment's atomistic "disengaged subject," whose "political obligation" to the state is no longer self-evident (70ff.).

Denis Diderot makes the tensions within the Enlightenment approach to society particularly clear in his *La rêve de d'Alembert.* In this work, Diderot, trying, as A. M. Wilson puts it, to answer the "Lucretian" problem of "how simple elementary forms could combine and differentiate into complex ones" (559, 561), turns to the traditional image of the swarm of bees as an example of the *e pluribus unum.*[4] D'Alembert poses the question, "A travers toutes les vicissitudes que je subis dans le cours de ma durée, n'ayant peut-être pas à présent une des molécules que j'apportai en naissant, comment suis-je resté moi pour les autres et pour moi?" (Diderot, *Rêve,* 216).[5] In other words, how, within the En-

---

4. For an interesting discussion of this model in terms of information flow, see de la Carrera, 131–33.

5. "Taking into account all the changes I have undergone in the course of my life, and in view of the fact that at present I probably haven't a single one of the molecules I brought with

lightenment's "disengaged" atomistic materialism, can one conceive of organic unity? Dr. Bordeu's answer is telling: "[C'est] par la mémoire qu'il é[st] lui pour les autres et pour lui; et j'ajouterais par la lenteur des vicissitudes. Si vous eussiez passé en un clin d'oeil de la jeunesse à la décripitude, vous auriez été jeté dans ce monde, comme au premier moment de votre naissance. . . . Tous les rapports auraient été anéantis. Toute l'histoire de votre vie pour moi, toute l'histoire de la mienne pour vous, brouillée" (216).[6] Already, in 1769, the description Tocqueville will make of the French Revolution has been adumbrated here in this account of the individual liberated (or violently estranged) from *la mémoire* and *l'histoire,* along with the revolutionary topos of the rebirth of society. But it is when Mlle de l'Espinasse rephrases this argument in terms of the *grappe d'abeilles*—in which, without memory, "il n'y en aurait pas une qui eût le temps de prendre l'esprit du corps" (217)[7]— that, like Mandeville, Diderot opens the image out to the question of social continuity and social cohesion. Mlle de l'Espinasse explains her image: "Je dis que l'esprit monastique se conserve, parce que le monastère se refait peu à peu, et quand il entre un moine nouveau, il en trouve une centaine de vieux qui l'entraînent à penser et à sentir comme eux. Une abeille s'en va; il en succède dans la grappe une autre qui se met bientôt au courant" (217).[8] The anticlerical Diderot's choice of a monastery as the image of the mechanism of tradition is hardly innocent, and it might seem that we are already in the midst of the revolutionary Enlightenment here, with its attacks on the dead hand of the church and tradition, on all the Gothicisms of *l'ancien régime.*

But Diderot wants some principle of individual and social unity. He locates that unity in an "origine du faisceau," which, by the power of memory, organizes the random bundle into an active organism. Tellingly,

---

me when I was born, how have I [remained 'me'] for myself as well as for others?" (*D'Alembert's Dream,* 201; with my modification).

6. "That it [the organic being] remain[s] itself both for others and for itself thanks to memory. And I would add because of the gradualness of change. If you had passed from childhood to decrepitude in the twinkling of an eye you would have found yourself thrown into the present world as you were at the first moment of birth. . . . All relationships would have been nullified and the whole story of your life as I know it, and of mine as you do, would have been a jumble" (*D'Alembert's Dream,* 201).

7. ". . . it would be like the swarm of bees in which no bee had had time to learn about its membership of the swarm" (*D'Alembert's Dream,* 202).

8. "I am saying that the corporate spirit of a monastery keeps its character because the monastery replaces its membership only gradually, and when a new monk arrives he finds a hundred old ones who influence him to feel and think like them. One bee goes away, but another replaces it in the swarm, and he soon knows what's what" (*D'Alembert's Dream,* 202).

the terms he uses to describe either successful centralized control by this "origine" or its overthrow by the atomistic elements of the *faisceau* make the social analogies quite explicit and are equally pejorative: *despotisme* and *anarchie:*

BORDEU: Dérangez l'origine du faisceau, vous changez l'animal. Il semble qu'il soit là tout entier, tantôt dominant les ramifications, tantôt dominé par elles.
MLLE DE L'ESPINASSE:—Et l'animal est sous le despotisme ou sous l'anarchie. (220)[9]

That "anarchie" is pejorative here is made clear in Bordeu's further description of the state: "C'est l'image d'une administration faible, où chacun tire à soi l'autorité du maître. Je ne connais qu'un moyen de guérir" (220).[10] If Diderot seems uncomfortable with the despotism of memory, he is no less so with an anarchy—Taylor's "damaged personhood"—whose "cure" Dr. Bordeu sees as his (therapeutic) duty.

If Diderot is unsure what to make of the political significance of Enlightenment particularism, he has nonetheless identified the point of entry for the revolutionary Enlightenment's distinctive political program. This is the "politics of skepticism," one of the principal influences on the young Shelley. Shelley's debt to the skeptical tradition has been more than adequately covered by Pulos, Wasserman, Lloyd Abbey, and, most recently and thoroughly, Terence Hoagwood; my aim here is not to add historical detail to this debt, but to reexamine its political implications. Of the authors mentioned above, only Hoagwood is specifically interested in this question; his argument that skepticism, by attacking dogma, simultaneously subverts the ideological underpinnings of monarchy (*Skepticism and Ideology,* 30ff.)—while true as far as it goes—allows him to skip over some of Shelley's deeply felt problems in maintaining a skeptical revolutionism in the postrevolutionary era.

Significantly, the skeptical politics that most directly influenced the young Shelley derived from attempts to answer Burke's response to the

9. BORDEU: Upset the centre of the web and you change the nature of the whole creature whose entire being seems to be concentrated there, sometimes dominating outlying threads, sometimes being dominated by them.
MADEMOISELLE DE L'ESPINASSE: So that the animal is either ruled by a despotism or in a state of anarchy? (*D'Alembert's Dream*, 204-5)

10. "It is the epitome of a weak political administration in which each one usurps the authority of the ruler. There is only one way of curing this that I know of" (*D'Alembert's Dream*, 205).

French Revolution. The political tracts of the English '90s radicals—
including William Godwin's *Political Justice,* Thomas Paine's *Rights of
Man,* and Mary Wollstonecraft's *Vindication of the Rights of Man*—
were all attempts to counter Burke's decisively influential reading of the
Revolution as an unmitigated disaster. All three of them employ a skeptical form of argument principally derived from David Hume. Indeed, as
Frank B. Evans argued a long time ago, Godwin's "necessitarianism" is
little more or less than applied Hume.

Hume's associationism and "necessitarianism" are two names for the
same theory. Hume's skeptical reduction of cause and effect to a perception of a "constant conjunction," which takes place solely in the
mind of an observer, might appear to be an attack on Enlightenment
materialism; and so, in a sense, it is. But the radical conclusion Hume
draws from his argument is that the "same course of reasoning will
make us conclude, that there is but one kind of *necessity,* as there is but
one kind of cause, and that the common distinction betwixt *moral* and
physical necessity is without any foundation in nature" (*Treatise,* 171;
see also *Inquiry,* 97). The strict necessity of physical causality is also the
rule in the intellectual, ethical, and (therefore) political worlds. The sequence of ideas follows the rule of association according to the same
principle of "constant conjunction" that obtains for things. Tradition (or,
a more Shelleyan word, custom) is demystified here to become a sequence of associated ideas—as mechanical a process as physical causality.

The ineluctable tendency of any politics drawn from this theory is
toward a skeptical revolutionism that conceives of political change as
absolute negativity. It holds out the promise of a decisive intervention in
the order of association that will bring about what Diderot could not
decide if he feared or desired. It will overthrow the despotism of *la
memoire* by, in the words Tocqueville uses to describe the effect of the
French Revolution, "brisant tout à coup le lien des souvenirs." In a necessitarian moral order, to *dérange* the sequence of associations is to
ensure that "tous les rapports sont anéantis" with the same absolute
necessity[11] as would occur if one interrupted a sequence of causes in

---

11. Paradoxically, for the skeptical Hume this means only relative necessity. Hume's argument is a pragmatic one: if there is no *practical* difference between our experiences of moral
and mechanical "necessity," why artificially separate them? The relationship between Hume
and the pragmatist ordinary-language philosophers who tend to demonize him is much closer
than they realize. See his argument against excessive, or Pyrrhonian, skepticism in the *Inquiry*
(168). However, this pragmatist bent was no more influential on the nineties radicals than it is
on Hume's contemporary reputation.

the physical world (as, for instance, if one were to turn one domino out of a standing sequence). In such a case, there is simply no connection at all between the old system and the new: "jeté dans ce monde, comme au premier moment de votre naissance."[12]

It is no wonder that Coleridge, in *The Statesman's Manual* (a work read by Shelley in 1816 [White, *Shelley*, 1:542]), identified Hume as one of the principal purveyors of corrupting gallic influence in English thought: the "Scotch philosopher, who devoted his life to the undermining of the Christian religion . . . [was] the same heartless sophist who, in this island, was the main pioneer of that atheistic philosophy, which in France transvenomed the natural thirst of truth into the hydrophobia of a wild and homeless scepticism" (*Lay Sermons*, 22).

Hume occasions Coleridge's ire here—of which the above is merely a representative sample—for the seemingly venial offense of attributing "motives" to historical individuals in his *History*. But Coleridge is quite correct, within his perspective, to see this as politically disastrous: if the politico-ethical world is one of necessary motivation, we will not approach the state with Burke's "trembling awe and pious solicitude," but rather like so many mechanics setting about to fix a machine that does not function properly. The necessitarian politician will no more expect the functional society to bear traces of (to remember) its dysfunctional past than a mechanic would leave a worn spark plug in the engine for old times' sake.

Like Diderot, Hume radically calls into question the necessary organic unity of individual identity. Personal identity, in Hume's opinion, is produced purely by the reconstitutive effect of memory. As in Diderot's example of the "esprit monastique," he compares this to a society reproducing itself in its constituent parts: "I cannot compare the soul more properly to anything than to a republic or commonwealth, in which the several members are united by the reciprocal ties of government and subordination, and give rise to other persons, who propagate the same republic in the incessant changes of its parts. And as the same individual republic may not only change its members, but also its laws and constitutions; in like manner the same person may vary his ideas, without losing his identity. Whatever changes he endures, his several parts are still connected by the relation of causation" (*Treatise*, 261). This passage, like Diderot's, cuts several ways. Clearly its implications are as much political as they are personal. If memory can be adequately

---

12. "thrown into the present world as you were at the first moment of birth" (Diderot, *D'Alembert's Dream*, 201).

guaranteed for all time, then individual and political identity is as safe as Coleridge would wish. But by reducing the basis of that identity to sheer causal continuity, Hume opens up the possibility of truly radical disjunctions in social and cultural "development." If the "lien des souvenirs" is broken, revolution will create a literally "new" society.

This is what makes Godwin's *Political Justice* still such a challenging book to read if we take it seriously. Godwinian "perfectibility"—the claim that all human qualities, moral as much as intellectual, are capable of "perpetual improvement" (1:109–19)—is a simple deduction from Hume's necessitarianism. Godwin establishes (following Hume's appeal to "motive" in his *History*) that "the voluntary actions of men originate in their opinions" and that, therefore, there is no "original bias in the mind that is inaccessible to human skill" (1:52); correct the opinion, and, "man" being "by the very constitution of his nature, the subject of opinion" (1:55), you "perfect" the action. The task of the political reformer is simply to order society according to "the immutable voice of reason and justice" (1:162; Gadamer's "absolute reason") irrespective of "prejudice" and "tradition" (1:55).

Despite Godwin's personal belief in gradualism, and a political program in his *Political Justice* that largely involves people's chatting about the principles of government in their drawing rooms, the irresistible conclusion of his necessitarian views is a sweeping negation of the entire social order Burke so anxiously seeks to maintain. All precedent, all tradition, all origins, are, at least implicitly, irrelevant. Nothing, in a necessitarian view, can be taken for granted, because everything is open to question and reformation (revolution) if found wanting according to strict principles of reason.

Godwin sets about casting out all the social bonds founded on "dark tradition," hoping to arrive at a slimmed-down vision of a society in which all action and all thought can be consciously justified at all times. This exhausting ideal of a life lived in pure self-consciousness, in which everything is open to challenge and reformation, is a direct assault on the "framework" morality and epistemology proposed by Taylor. Here, all frameworks, all horizons, other than "reason," are open to transgression; individuals constantly reconstruct themselves in a kind of ethico-political free fall. (The exception of "reason" itself from attack is significant, however. A rather hypostatized notion of "reason" as guide and substrate of political change—fatally abstract and empty, from an ordinary-language perspective—is Godwin's own safety net that ensures that revolutionary change will always be part of the process of "perfection.")

More immediately, this ideal is a direct attack on Burke's *Reflections.*
Godwin writes:

> [I]f reason be frequently inadequate to its task, if there be an
> opposite principle in man, resting upon its own ground, and
> maintaining a separate jurisdiction, the most rational principles
> of society may be rendered abortive, it may be necessary to call
> in mere sensible causes to encounter causes of the same nature,
> folly may be the fittest instrument to effect the purposes of wis-
> dom, and vice to disseminate and establish the public benefit. In
> that case the salutary prejudices and useful delusions (as they
> have been called) of aristocracy, the glittering diadem, the mag-
> nificent canopy, the ribbands, stars and titles of an illustrious
> rank, may at last be found the fittest instruments for guiding and
> alluring to his proper ends the savage, man. (1:55)

Godwin intends this to be a *reductio ad absurdum* of Burke's champi-
oning of the "decent drapery" of social usages, but we see here how the
nineties radicals allowed Burke effectively to define the terms of political debate by phrasing their major political statements as responses to
his *Reflections.* Toward the end of *Political Justice* Godwin becomes
increasingly nervous about the problem of generating social cohesion
out of the intense individualism that is the necessary corollary of his
assault upon sociocultural "frameworks"—the same Lucretian problem,
of generating a whole from discrete parts, that troubled Diderot. Godwin firmly believes that "individuality is the very essence of intellectual
excellence," and that "every thing that is usually understood by the
term cooperation, is, in some degree, an evil" (2:501); he goes so far as
to speculate whether, in the truly rational society, there will not be a
withering away of "concerts of music" and "theatrical exhibitions,"
which "include an absurd and vicious cooperation": "Will it not be prac-
ticable hereafter for one man to perform the whole?" he asks (2:504).
Yet he acknowledges that "human beings are formed for society"
(2:499) and that social cohesion must be preserved, particularly in ethical conventions: "Moral independence . . . is always injurious" to the
"wholesome [*sic*] temperament of society" (2:496). "Reason" alone cannot achieve this unity, and Godwin will not allow the state to play such
a positive role. He relies upon neighborly surveillance, or what he calls
"public opinion" (2:473), to achieve this esprit de corps; he proposes "a
censure to be exercised by every individual over the actions of another,
[and] a promptness to enquire into and to judge them" (2:496), al-

though he acknowledges that some will find this "unpalatable," and even his boundless self-confidence seems slightly shaken when he asks defensively: "Why should we shrink from this?" (2:496).

It is telling that these appeals to communal censure occur only, but repeatedly, in the concluding series of chapters dealing with "objections" to the institution of the future communist, anarchic society (e.g., 2:473f., 486f., 492, 497). It seems that in trying to overcome the (Burkean) opposition to the revolutionary society, Godwin is forced to concede his main point: folly may indeed be the fittest instrument to effect the purposes of wisdom—the "rational" society may be no better equipped than "savages" to dispense with community "prejudice."

This need not be fatal for a radical politics. It was possible to use Burke's own logic against him. Many radicals did nothing to dislodge it; they merely tailored their argument to fit its terms. E. P. Thompson describes a widespread tendency in British radicalism to fight for a restoration of ancient (and largely mythical) "Saxon" laws and privileges— "'that magnanimous government which we derived from our Saxon fathers, and from the prodigious mind of the immortal Alfred'" (95)— which had been disrupted by the "Norman Yoke"; one person's "tradition" is another's lengthy interregnum.

More interesting is to see the appeal of Burke's traditionalism to a thinker like Paine. Paine's answer to Burke, *The Rights of Man*—easily the most influential of them all—mounts a skeptical attack on Burke's notion of the generational continuities that underlie and legitimate contemporary government: "What can a monarchical talker say? What has he to exult in? Alas! he has nothing. A certain something forbids him to look back to a beginning, lest some robber, or some Robin Hood, should rise from the long obscurity of time, and say, *I am the origin!*" (319).

But despite this effective skeptical undermining of the appeal to tradition as a "ground" for our ethical lives, Paine's argument leads in directions clearly parallel to Burke's preoccupations, as we see in Paine's own vision of the future of American and French government: "A thousand years hence, those who shall live in America, or in France, will look back with contemplative pride on the origin of their governments, and say, *this was the work of our glorious ancestors!*" (319).

It would seem that Paine is really aiming not to undermine Burke's goals but rather to see them more adequately achieved. If we reconsider his skeptical attack on the "origin" of Burke's traditions, we can see that in arguing that a government founded fraudulently remains fraudulent forever, Paine lends support to the appeal to a legitimating origin; he merely disputes that England's monarchy can provide one. This is borne out by his curious reverence for written constitutions, which cannot be reconciled with his famous scorn for Burke's willingness to "consign over the rights of posterity for ever, on the authority of a moldy parchment" (257). It says a great deal about the extent to which Burke's defense of the "despotism of memory" was central to the thought of the period, that the man who symbolized revolution and Jacobinism to the English should have incorporated this into his vision of the postrevolutionary society.

It says as much for the intellectual daring of those willing to pursue the skeptical implications of an attack on Burke's position to their logical conclusions. As Wollstonecraft found in her answer to Burke, *A Vindication of the Rights of Men,* attacking Burke's "wise prejudice" could lead one not just into political controversy but to skeptical inquiries undermining all certainties. "A simple question," she says, "will silence [Burke's] impertinent declamation"; but that question is not as simple as she claims: "What is truth?" The sweeping implications of this question, as she outlines them—in strikingly proto-Shelleyan language—demonstrate the close connection between radical skepticism and radical political negation: "[W]ho can discriminate the vagaries of the imagination, or scrupulosity of weakness, from the verdict of reason? Let all these points be demonstrated, and not determined by arbitrary authority and dark traditions. . . . Perhaps the most improving exercise of mind, confining the argument to the enlargement of the understanding, is the restless enquiries that hover on the boundary or stretch over the dark abyss of uncertainty" (37–38).

Unlike Godwin or Paine, Wollstonecraft is willing to abandon any hope of a definite ground of ethical and political action—even the ground of "reason." She even posits the transgression of the "horizons," or "framework," of our ethical life as itself potentially enriching: "We should be aware of confining all moral excellence to one channel, however capacious" (38).

There are direct echoes of this work of Wollstonecraft's in Shelley's work (the "dark abyss of—how little we know" in "On Life," for example [Reiman and Powers, 478]), some of which I explore in more depth later, but the most important source, for Shelley, of this kind of radical skepticism was William Drummond's *Academical Questions.*[13] Although,

13. Drummond's influence on Shelley has long been realized, but Hoagwood's is, surprisingly, the first detailed examination of the relationship between the two. C. E. Pulos's classic, but now outdated, study of Shelley's skepticism, *The Deep Truth,* gives a plainly inadequate account, dubiously attributing to Drummond a project of reconciling skeptical empiricism with a vaguely defined, Berkeleyan "idealism" (24–41; see also 105–12). Wasserman has al-

or perhaps because, he is not expressly writing political theory, Drummond makes the key skeptical attack both on Burkean traditionalism and the Enlightenment faith in reason that undermines both traditionalist and rationalist guarantees for change-as-progress. Drummond disallows all certainties in the cognitive world. Unlike Godwin, who relies on a universal and self-evident "reason" and "justice" to provide a baseline of continuity to contain and control the potential infinitude of necessitarian change, Drummond views the human mind as a highly dubious instrument about which we cannot make any adequate judgment: "The modern disciple of the academy [i.e., skeptic] will argue . . . that there neither is, nor can be, positive certainty in any conclusion made by the understanding of man. . . . He may smile, but he will not be convinced, when he sees Dogmatism, mounted upon the stilts of criticism, pronouncing her decrees infallible" (362–63). Drummond provides Shelley with a profound critique not just of our faith in sense-data (the classical target of the skeptic) but of the very structures of thought that organize our perception of the world—what Kant would call the categories (Drummond engages in a lengthy critique of Kant in the *Academical Questions*). In his view, mathematics, logic, reason are all quite possibly flawed systems that appear certain to us only because of the type of beings that we are—or, more radically, that we are *at this moment:* "I have always thought, since I was capable of reasoning, that many of the truths which appeared most certain to me, had not other foundation, than that my own mind was so constituted, as to admit them without hesitation" (378). Not only does he provide powerful arguments for this kind of intellectual relativism, but he refuses Hume's pragmatic escape clause—that despite the intellectual power of these arguments we should continue to *act* as if reason and logic were immutable laws (see *Inquiry,* 168): "Tell the savage, that the sun is bigger than the earth . . . [and he will call you a liar]. I will instruct the savage, say you, and he will have the same opinions with me. But to instruct him, is to give him new perceptions, and with them a new belief. It is to change the state of his intellectual being; to render him perceptive of many things which he did not before see. . . . Is it absolutely impossible, then, that you yourself should be capable of a similar change?" (153).

---

most nothing to say about Drummond. Hoagwood's reading gives an excellent account of Drummond's skepticism (although he ignores, and implicitly denies, Drummond's fideist theism) and its relationship to the tradition of skeptical philosophy. The only other book-length study of Shelley's skepticism, Abbey's *Destroyer and Preserver,* relies on Pulos's account (see Abbey, 1–2).

On one level this is a justification of sorts for Burke's advocacy of wise prejudice, because the startling implication of Drummond's argument is that to change one's mind is quite literally to *change* one's mind. This is why I suggested above that he adds an "at the moment" to Kant's a priori grounds for the possibility of experience. The potential incontinence or infinitude of change that Burke fears is made a central fact of human existence by this argument that any mental change is an effacement of former identity (a new birth "brisant tout à coup le lien des souvenirs") and an absolute discontinuity. Moreover, Drummond's question radically undermines our own sense of continuous identity, challenging us to reconceive what we perceive as growth, or change-within-identity, as a sequence of possibly unconnected, contiguous but not continuous, states of intellectual being.

The one certain moral wrong in Drummond's largely relativistic morality is dogma—the hubris of proclaiming our feeble and dubious conclusions to be immutable and unassailable truths. In this sense, his work, seemingly nonpolitical (although Hoagwood points out that, though no political firebrand, he was regarded with some hostility and suspicion by the government of the day [*Skepticism and Ideology*, 35f.]), can be seen as a late (1805) addition to the skeptical reply to Burke's *Reflections*. For Drummond, as for Shelley, "wise prejudice" would be an obscene phrase, suggesting a mixture of pride and sloth: "In proportion as men are rude, uncultivated and uncivilised, they are determined in their opinions, bold in their presumptions, and obstinate in their prejudices. When they begin to doubt, it may be concluded, they begin to be refined. The savage is seldom a sceptic" (39). The effect of this radical skepticism on Shelley's politics is marked. The most striking and conceptually disturbing aspect of Shelley's politics—insofar as they derive from this brand of skepticism—is his acceptance of Drummond's idea that change is by definition a leap into the unknown. In Drummond's theory, change on the model of Collingwood's "progress"—change whose "tick" anticipates its "tock"—is not really change at all. This is the source of one of the most distinctive aspects of Shelley's radicalism: the lack of a definite goal, or telos, of revolutionary change. For Shelley, the struggle is usually against the existing order rather than toward a utopia. Or, if he does posit utopias, they are literally utopian: no-places, blank spaces whose meaning will only be filled in on arrival.

In recent years this argument has become more or less the mainstream of Shelley criticism, but the conventional idea of Shelley's politics is still significantly different. Shelley is often described as a philosophical anarchist or mystical idealist painting portraits of ideal societies but short on practical proposals for bringing them into being. In fact, Shelley very rarely gives any positive detail of the good future society, unlike Godwin, who elaborates visions of the anarchic society ordered by the strict a priori laws of reason and—when these fail—neighborly surveillance. Typical of Shelley's attitude is the conclusion to his note on marriage and prostitution in *Queen Mab*. After tentatively beginning to debate what new system may develop after the abolition of marriage, he stops and writes:

> But this is a subject which it is perhaps premature to discuss. That which will result from the abolition of marriage will be natural and right; because choice and change will be exempted from restraint.
>
> In fact, religion and morality, as they now stand, compose a practical code of misery and servitude. (Hutchinson, 808)

His concern is with eliminating the known present rather than achieving a posited future.

We can see how well Shelley and Burke understood the bases of their respective positions if we compare this with Burke's sneer at Dr. Price: "Let the noble teachers but dissent, it is no matter from whom or from what. This great point once secured, it is taken for granted their religion will be rational and manly" (*Reflections*, 95). This is not an unfair description of skeptical revolutionism. Both Burke and Shelley are in agreement with Drummond that change is a moment of complete discontinuity with the past. Let there be "but dissent," and the system has been changed, "brisant tout à coup le lien des souvenirs." What the new system will be we cannot know, or it would be a phenomenon of the present one. This is why Burke argues, fearfully, that we must admit no change at all, while Shelley follows Drummond in praising the virtue of change over the stagnation of dogma: "Constancy has nothing virtuous in itself" (Hutchinson, 807).

Shelley's greatest political work in prose, *A Philosophical View of Reform*, is often read as a statement of cautious, gradualist reformism (e.g., Cameron, *Golden Years*, 148–49; Dawson, 6–7, 187–88), but this is to misread badly the implications of his argument. It is because of his open-ended, atelic concept of social change that he can present the most radical and revolutionary propositions within what appears to be a gradualist program. Unlike the person with a clear vision of the millennial society, who cannot bear to linger and dawdle on the way to its realization, Shelley, like Burke, argues that *any* amount of change is sufficient, because any change is already revolutionary: "If Reform shall be begun by the existing government, let us be contented with a limited *beginning,* with any whatsoever opening . . . it is no matter how slow, gradual and cautious be the change; we shall demand more and more with firmness and moderation, never anticipating but never deferring the moment of successful opposition" (Ingpen and Peck, 7:46). Shelley establishes intermediate goals in the essay merely to provide a point of leverage against the present system, but the essay as a whole is consistent in its refusal to suggest a point at which reform and revolution could ever be completed: "A government that is founded on any other basis [than the total acceptance and happiness of all its members] is a government of fraud or force and ought on the first convenient occasion to be overthrown" (42). Shelley, contrary to his reputation as someone who conjures up visions of the ideal future but is uninterested in how to achieve it, devotes the last third of his essay to a complex theory of graduated resistance—from constitutional forms of protest through civil disobedience to open revolution, through all of which runs the necessity, as in Drummond, of change almost for change's sake, or at least for the sake of avoiding the deathlike stultification of dogma and the authority of "dark tradition": "The strongest argument, perhaps, for the necessity of Reform is the inoperative and unconscious abjectness to which the purposes of a considerable mass of the people are reduced. They neither know nor care. . . . Unless the cause which renders them passive subjects instead of active citizens be removed, they will sink . . . into that barbaric and unnatural civilization which destroys all the differences among men" (49–50).

Even the process of philosophical reasoning about these issues must eschew goals, as Shelley writes in his essay "On Life": "[Philosophy] leaves, what is too often the duty of the reformer in political and ethical questions to leave, a vacancy. It reduces the mind to that freedom in which it would have acted but for the misuse of words and signs, the instruments of its own creation" (Reiman and Powers, 477). As so often in Shelley's landscape of the mind, the point of expected origin or of revelation of telos is revealed instead to be a vacancy or abyss. In stark contrast to Paine's attempt to ground change in a new once-and-for-all constitution, in the *Philosophical View of Reform* Shelley praises the American form of government erroneously, but tellingly, for "a law by which the constitution is reserved for revision every ten years" (Ingpen and Peck, 7:11). The writers of the constitution, says Shelley, saw the history of humankind as "a history of his mistakes and his sufferings arising from his mistakes," and realized that any constitution would come to seem yet another such mistake. This view of history as a sequence of mistakes under the form of corrections is the closest possible political analogy to Drummond's intellectual disjunctions.

Perhaps most indicative of all is Shelley's *Prometheus Unbound*. Despite delivering us to "this far goal of Time" (III, iii, 174), which seems to pronounce some kind of achieved telos, Shelley is once again concerned with "change from," not "change to." The much-remarked "negative forms" in this poem make this clear (see Dawson, 120–33; Scrivener, 197f.; Hogle, *Shelley's Process*, 195). Consider the description by the Spirit of the Hour of the new "paradise gained" of the postrevolutionary society (III, iv, 190–97) that closes the third act and was originally the end of the drama. Structurally—if this poem really were an example of the utopian "poetry of idealism" that Wasserman reads it as (*Shelley*, 253, 255ff.)—this would be the place for a rousing evocation of the Ideal City. It is interesting, in contrast, to compare how much is positively asserted as achieved and how much negatively described as overcome: "Man" is now "Sceptreless . . . uncircumscribed . . . unclassed, tribeless and nationless, / Exempt from awe, worship, degree." Shelley's vision of change, even at the moment of triumph, remains profoundly negative.

In a similar vein, there is Prometheus's comment in his speech on his and Asia's activities in their cave of retirement. They will be visited by the progeny of "arts, though unimagined, yet to be" (III, iii, 56). This seems a weak, indeed empty, statement—in the way Lear's "I will do such things—what they are yet I know not; but they shall be the terrors of the earth" is so pitifully weak—typical of that strain of Shelley's verse so despised by the New Criticism. Yet it should be read as a powerful and radical statement of a willingness to embark upon change without controls, a refusal to accept dogma or prejudice, which is finally borne out by the remarkable fourth act of *Prometheus*, in which the total disappearance of the hitherto principal characters of the drama is an eloquent statement of Drummond's view that change of "mind" is change of "being." Act IV ends not by announcing the arrival of the new era but by proclaiming the continual threat of the possibility of return to the Jupiterean world of the reader's present (IV, 565–80).

As with Shelley's necessitarianism, readers unable to face this disturbingly unstable world of goalless change have tended to read Demogorgon as some kind of hypostatized "Necessity" or "Power" that underwrites and provides continuity for the process of change.[14] But to do so

14. Wasserman reads Demogorgon as "Power" (*Shelley*, 329f.). Cameron reads him as "ne-

is to ignore everything that is said, or rather not said, about Demogorgon, that shadowy relativistic figure who speaks but as we speak, and calls himself, for convenience, "Eternity," warning, "demand no direr name" (III, i, 52). By his own account, unless he is "eternal love," he is subject, as all things are in Shelley's radical necessitarianism, to "Fate, Time, Occasion, Chance and Change" (II, iv, 119). To suggest what Demogorgon "stands for" (be it "people-monster" or "necessity" or whatever) is always to seek to do what the poem as a whole warns us not to do, to seek for certainties in a world without them (Neufeldt, 67). Demogorgon is a cipher that Shelley challenges us to leave blank—the vacancy left by the Burkean "good order," or Taylorian "framework," that Shelley wishes to leap beyond.

II

This atelic change is not without problems, however, and Shelley is very sensible to them. The most obvious problem is that of political engagement. How can the "disengaged" skeptic who is willing to transgress all and any "frameworks" of individual and cultural identity reap the positive rewards of "therapeutic" *communitas?* What kind of politics could be built upon the ever-shifting sands of atelic negation, and how effective could any politics be that renders the political "solidarity" of fighting for a common cause impracticable? Hoagwood addresses some of these problems. He attempts to read Shelley as a pure and uncompromising skeptic, and yet at the same time wants to see him as an engaged and (at least potentially) influential political radical. He expects that his readers will see this as, *prima facie,* paradoxical, and the bulk of his book is devoted to trying to convince us that Shelley has found a way of squaring this particular circle. His solution is to suggest that Shelley makes a distinction between statements about the world that involve some truth-claim ("is" statements), which are by nature undecidable, and "moral statements" ("ought" statements) that are injunctions to (political) action (*Skepticism and Ideology,* 200–201). The one category is severely constrained by the "epistemological circle," but the other operates in the freer confines of the "experiential circle"—the domain of "political right" (150). Events within the experiential circle are those which have unavoidable consequences for us but which we cannot claim to "know" absolutely. In other words, the thoroughgoing skeptic is quite right to jump out of the way of an onrushing truck, even if incapable of "proving" the truck's existence, because the truck is en-

cessity" ("Political Symbolism," 743), and Matthews as the "people-monster," the volcanic energy of the revolutionary masses ("Volcano's Voice," 222).

dowed with "facticity"; it is an event in our "experiential circle" that we cannot simply wish away. The political agent is right to respond to perceived infringements of political liberty even if unable to "prove" their factual status.

In Hoagwood's view this distinction gives Shelley's skepticism all the political bite it needs without ever having to compromise itself by suggesting dogmatically that it knows some truth about the world. Shelley makes moral claims about the way the world should be that do "not pretend to truth but rather to utility" (113). The "moral statement" involves no claim to "pre-statemental truth" (200) and therefore cannot be invalidated by events in the "experiential circle." Nonetheless, for Hoagwood, the explicit relativism of this position guarantees the radical nature of the political argument it produces: "[T]o revitalize criteria of truth and forms of thought—in abstract metaphysical discourse or in politicized ideological analysis—is to challenge the reigning order" (140). If I am advocating action according to my perspective on the "experiential circle," the argument goes, then I cannot be doing so in accordance with the dogmatic perspective of the ruling class.

There are many problems with this, but I will identify three principal ones. First, the distinction itself is more ingenious than plausible. It is difficult to imagine making a "moral statement" about how the world ought to be that does not presuppose a series of truth-claims about how the world is presently. Even if it were possible, any such statement would be so hopelessly vague ("if anything exists, it ought to continue to exist" perhaps?) that no one could recognize it as a *political* statement. The examples Hoagwood does give, such as the advocacy of universal suffrage and annual parliaments (208), are meaningless without a nearly infinite host of ancillary "truth statements" such as "parliament exists," "changing the way parliament operates will make a change in the lives of many people," "many people exist whose lives are affected by the current state of parliament," "the change effected by a reform of parliament will be beneficial for the majority of people it affects," and so forth. The distinction between "truth" and "utility" is meaningless as soon as we inquire, as any effective politics must, how we are to assess the "utility" of our actions.

The second problem with Hoagwood's approach is that relativism need not always be politically radical. Burke's political theory is a form of historicist relativism, although ultimately underpinned by divine revelation. Hoagwood does not address the fact that in Shelley's time it was the *dogmatism* of the revolutionary Enlightenment that made it seem so frighteningly radical—the fact that it was willing to ignore all precedent, all the "forms of life" to which a given view of the world is relative, in the pursuit of an uncompromising theory of social perfectibility.

It is true that Shelley consistently criticizes the dogmatism of the conservative forces in society, but Hoagwood's skeptical relativism is a poor ground from which to launch such an attack; how are we supposed to distinguish committed relativism (good) from obstinate dogmatism (bad)? Dogmatists are merely propounding the truth as they perceive it relative to their "form of life." Beyond the dubious distinction between the truth-claim content of "is" statements and "ought" statements, it is impossible to see what difference it makes in the "experiential circle" whether we are relativist skeptics or not. If Shelley advocates the reform of parliament while maintaining an undetectable mental reservation to the effect that parliament may not exist, he does not differ "experientially" from the credulous dogmatist who advocates the same thing with no such mental reservation. In the experiential circle, dogmatists and nondogmatists alike still have to jump out of the way of onrushing trucks, unfavorable ballots, and revolutionary mobs. If we are to find a radical (and radically new) theory of political/textual action in Shelley's writing, we have to go beyond the simple opposition between the daring skeptic, willing to call in question any and all forms of social being, and the dogmatic idealist, stubbornly clinging to the actual because too timid to let it go.

We could, of course, disagree with Hoagwood's admiration for the distinction between the "epistemological" and "experiential" circles but accept that Shelley did make it and maintain it. But this brings me to my third point, which I explore at length in the next section: is it really possible to argue that Shelley was a hard-line, uncompromising skeptic, or can Hoagwood only achieve this by focusing upon a selectively created "Shelley"? Hoagwood ignores all of the poems and the *Defence of Poetry* in his analysis, wanting to consider Shelley strictly as a philosopher. Poetry, however, was not marginal to the political and philosophical battle against Enlightenment "disengagement"; it was one of the principal "therapeutic" tools by which the Romantic reengagement with the world was to be achieved.

THERAPY: THE POLITICS OF IDEALISM

I

One response to the Enlightenment "disengagement" was to see it as a critical opening within the systems of meaning that define our lives—an opening that enables us, from that separated, abstracted position, to rewrite those systems from the "outside." But there was another response, the response I am calling "therapeutic," which presented by far the greater challenge to Shelley's political thought and whose most powerful formulations (nearly all contemporary with Shelley's life) underlie the "turn to history" I discussed in the first chapter. To place Shelley in relationship to the philosophical and political itinerary that takes us from the revolutionary Enlightenment to present-day historicist criticism allows us to understand both the constant struggle within Shelley's own work, as he tries to reconcile and, eventually, go beyond this divided inheritance, and the radical implications of his work for our own critical practice.

The "therapeutic" drive is an attempt to "heal" the division between mind and world, subject and object, citizen and state, that the radical Enlightenment had forced open. I take the term from Wittgenstein's *Philosophical Investigations* (sec. 133):[15]

> It is not our aim to refine or complete the system of rules for the use of our words in unheard-of ways.
>
> For the clarity we are aiming at is indeed *complete* clarity. But this simply means that the philosophical problems should *completely* disappear.
>
> The real discovery is the one that makes me capable of stopping doing philosophy when I want to.—The one that gives philosophy peace, so that it is no longer tormented by questions which bring *itself* in question.—Instead, we now demonstrate a method, by examples; and the series of examples can be broken off.—Problems are solved (difficulties eliminated), not a *single* problem.
>
> There is not *a* philosophical method, though there are indeed methods, like different therapies. (51)

This typically rich and dense web of aphorisms recapitulates most of the central tenets of ordinary-language philosophy and the linguistic/historicist turn of twentieth-century philosophy that I have already described. Words must not be used in "unheard-of ways"; their first allegiance is to the defining linguistic context. Abstract theorizing is rejected in favor of a pragmatic concern for the particular and the near: "problems . . . not a *single* problem," "the philosophical problems

---

15. Cavell's use of the term in his "Politics as Opposed to What?" also influenced my decision to use it.

should *completely* disappear [leaving only a *practice*]." It is the inescapable tendency of philosophy to fall into skepticism ("questions which bring *itself* in question"), from which we must "recover." Any doubt, any question that might divorce us from the language games we live through, is a potential threat: "The philosopher's treatment of a question is like the treatment of an illness" (91).

One of the first things we might note about this, and a remarkably consistent factor in all therapeutic arguments, is the tone. Philosophy is in crisis ("torment"), and we have to mobilize both philosophical and political resources to "heal" the damage this is doing. It is the same tone we heard in Taylor's claim that "stepping outside" our defining "framework" would be stepping outside "what we would recognize as integral, that is, undamaged human personhood" (*Sources of the Self,* 27). The claim is not, quite, that such a skeptical move is impossible, but that to make it is, as Cavell argues, a "tragic" error, cutting us off from all that is valuable and meaningful in human life (this is the central argument of Cavell's *Claim of Reason,* that "skepticism concerning other minds is not skepticism but is tragedy" [xix]).

It may seem strange that a philosophical approach to life that is, as I have tried to show, so dominant in our time should still phrase itself in terms of an anxious response to impending disaster. This anxiety, however, which we might call the reverse of an anxiety of influence, is inherent in the revolutionary Enlightenment against which therapeutic philosophy pits itself. From the very beginning, the discourse of "disengagement" is also a discourse of therapy. We saw this in Diderot's indecisiveness faced with revolutionary disengagement, and one can hear it also in Hume's withdrawal from "excessive" skepticism:

> [H]ere is the chief and most confounding objection to *excessive* skepticism, that no durable good can ever result from it while it remains in its full force and vigour. We need only ask such a skeptic, *what his meaning is? And what he proposes by all these curious researches?* He is immediately at a loss and knows not what to answer. A *Copernican* or *Ptolemaic* who supports each his different system of astronomy may hope to produce a conviction which will remain constant and durable with his audience. A *stoic* or *Epicurean* displays principles which may not only be durable, but which have an effect on conduct and behaviour. But a *Pyrrhonian* cannot expect that his philosophy will have any constant influence on the mind or, if it had, that its influence would be beneficial to society. (*Inquiry,* 168)

The similarity to Wittgenstein's attack on skepticism is intriguing. Like the ordinary-language philosopher, Hume proposes to try the extreme skeptic's statements by the litmus test of ordinary use: we ask the skeptic "what his meaning is," and he suddenly realizes he has been using words in "unheard-of ways," "he knows not what to answer."

The subtle interweaving of the two approaches in Enlightenment thought is perhaps best exemplified by Burke's use of the image of the social contract in the *Reflections*. We have seen Godwin's attempt to dismiss the Burkean subject as a "savage" amused by the baubles and trinkets of monarchy rather than persuaded to adhere to the polis by reason. Part of the reason that Godwin, despite this fairly acute polemical gibe, was not able to escape making his own appeal to extrarational forces of social cohesion lies in Burke's powerful rereading of the social contract.

John Locke's classic version of the argument, *The Second Treatise of Government,* is an attempt, like Diderot's, to think the unity of a society composed of atomistic individuals. In that sense, it is witness to the therapeutic anxiety of the early Enlightenment. But it is equally a document of revolutionary disengagement. It attempts to show that social cohesion is a reasoned response to the situation of men living in a state of nature. We are back in Hume's historical world of "motives": "The reason why men enter into society is the preservation of their property; and the end why they choose and authorize a legislative is that there may be laws made and rules set as guards and fences to the properties of all the members of the society to limit the power and moderate the dominion of every part and member of the society" (*Second Treatise,* 123–24). This argument opens the social order up to the revolutionary negativity of disengaged, reasoned evaluation. If a social contract is found wanting according to reason, it must be scrapped. Locke provides for "the establishment of a new legislative, such as they ["the people"] shall think fit," whenever the legislative oversteps its rights (124). This, if we pursue the "such as they shall think fit" to its radical extreme, is a blueprint for the amnesiac society of Diderot's speculations; it was this revolutionary implication that underlay, if not Rousseau's own idea of the "contrat social," at least the invocation of the concept by the French revolutionaries under his name.[16]

16. Lynn Hunt, in *Politics, Culture, and Class in the French Revolution* (12–13), traces the origin of the problematic modern relationship of "politics and society," and the loss of the "givenness" of tradition, to the French Revolution as a product of "Rousseau's conviction that the relationship between the social and the political (the social contract) could be rearranged." Although Rousseau, following Locke's argument, does make this point in his *Social*

Burke, with his typical skill for exploiting the anxieties and contradictions of his audience's thought, seizes on the idea of the social contract, but rewrites it so that it can speak of nothing but our desire for community, purged of "rational" interest and "motive":

> Society is indeed a contract. Subordinate contracts for objects of mere occasional interest may be dissolved at pleasure—but the state ought not to be considered as nothing better than a partnership agreement in a trade of pepper and coffee, callico or tobacco, or some other such low concern, to be taken up for a little temporary interest, and to be dissolved by the fancy of the parties. It is to be looked on with other reverence; because it is not a partnership in things subservient only to the gross animal existence of a temporary and perishable nature. It is a partnership in all science; a partnership in all art; a partnership in every virtue and in all perfection. As the ends of such a partnership cannot be obtained in many generations, it becomes a partnership not only between those who are living, but between those who are living, those who are dead, and those who are to be born. Each contract of each particular state is but a clause in the great primeval contract of eternal society, linking the lower with the higher natures, connecting the visible and invisible world, according to a fixed compact sanctioned by the inviolable oath which holds all physical and moral natures, each in their appointed place. . . . The municipal corporations of that universal kingdom are not morally at liberty at their pleasure . . . wholly to separate and tear asunder the bands of their subordinate community, and to dissolve it into an unsocial, uncivil, unconnected chaos of elementary principles. (*Reflections*, 194–95)

Undoubtedly it is the response to the political crisis of revolution that lends this an urgency and anxiety still to be heard today in the therapeutic resistance to an "abstract and revolutionary" Enlightenment. But it is also to be observed how exactly Burke has picked up Diderot's Lucretian dilemma of constructing an "eternal society" out of the "chaos of elementary principles." He takes the two halves of the dilemma, part

---

Contract (174), one could equally cite this version of the argument as an example of Enlightenment therapeutics; the "general will" is a mysterious unity prior to the establishment of any actual government. It is not entirely certain whether it can ever be "revoked" (184–86, 250). The French Revolution may have confirmed the revolutionary potential of Enlightenment disengagement, but it did not create it.

and whole, and uses all his immense rhetorical powers to place them in a decided hierarchy: the "low concern," "fancy," and destructive "separat[ing]" of the "unsocial, uncivil, unconnected" part, which seeks to "tear asunder" a whole that almost disappears under the weight of laudatory adjectives. Burke places us within a "framework" so vast, so thoroughly rooted in both past and future, heaven and earth, mind and body, that it becomes quite unthinkable to act upon it; one can only act within it.

It is not surprising to see social contract theory reappear in the work of an ordinary-language theorist such as Cavell as a viable model of our commitment to the given polity (*Claim of Reason,* 20ff.). As in Burke's case, Cavell's social contract is one to which we have always already given our consent; to be human is to be always already subject to the claims of the past and the future; it is to act against "a background of pervasive and systematic agreements among us, which we had not realized, or had not known we realized" (30). To step outside this framework of "pervasive" agreements is not a political act for Burke or Cavell, it is tantamount to madness: "The alternative to speaking for myself representatively (for *someone else's* consent) is not: speaking for myself privately. The alternative is having nothing to say, being voiceless, not even mute" (29). It is a revealing and disturbing moment when Cavell declares that the end point of any encounter with those who will not lend their voices to the community is to declare them insane (115–18). We cannot "reasonably" criticize the state, because there can be no reason outside the state: "The wish and search for community are the wish and search for reason" (20).

Romantic philosophers saw it as the special role of literature to effect this "community": a community not merely in the social sense, but an absolute community of Being in which all phenomena, natural and social, could find their true meaning. If Descartes "disengages" the observing subject from the world, Romanticism preaches "a reintegration which will restore his unity with himself, his community with his fellow men, and his companionability with an alien and hostile outer world" (Abrams, *Natural Supernaturalism,* 145); if the radical Enlightenment has rendered the relationships between citizen and state, and citizen and citizen, "abstract and revolutionary," then "the aesthetic intervenes here . . . as a dream of reconciliation—of individuals woven into intimate unity with no detriment to their specificity" (Eagleton, *Aesthetic,* 25). Poetry, as Taylor demonstrates convincingly in his *Sources of the Self,* becomes the chief vehicle of the new "expressivism" that underwrites the "turn to history" discussed in the first chapter; it is the field in which we recognize our "frameworks" of understanding to be communal.

Shelley's relationship to this therapeutic drive from the "diasparactive" fragment (to use McFarland's term) to the defining Absolute is the question I pursue in the remainder of this section. At the same time, I must explore some of the ways in which that drive underlies the historicist viewpoints explored in the first chapter. This second point has been thoroughly examined in the works cited above—among others—and I shall not attempt to give a complete historical account; it is necessary to point out one or two key connections, however, because it is these that make Shelley's relationship to Romantic therapeutics crucial for my argument. We need to see that Shelley saw "conventional" Romanticism as a live issue, a worthy challenge to skeptical revolutionism that required a real response. Although this might seem self-evident, in the contemporary climate of Shelley criticism it is anything but. Ultimately, I hope to show that by critiquing his revolutionary skepticism from the standpoint of his Romanticism, and vice versa, he develops an alternative approach that avoids their respective weaknesses and unites their strengths. By showing the tight connection between the contemporary historicist account of the role of the literary text in history and therapeutic Romanticism's privileging of the literary text, I will establish the urgency, for us, of Shelley's alternative approach.

II

The pivotal figure in this revaluation of the text is Kant. This seems at first a surprising claim. Kant, in the first *Critique,* might appear the ultimate prophet of the Enlightenment "disengagement." Setting out to complete and correct the work of David Hume, that "intelligent and estimable man," "the most ingenious of all sceptics," who "at the outset of his enquiries was certainly on the right track of truth" (*Pure Reason,* 491, 492), Kant intends in the *Critique of Pure Reason* to define rigorously the boundaries of what the subject is permitted to know. For Kant, in a favorite image, every man is an island, and the transcendental critic is both customs officer and coast guard: "This domain [of "pure understanding"] . . . is an island and enclosed by nature within limits that can never be changed. It is the country of truth (a very attractive name), but surrounded by a wide and stormy ocean, the true home of illusion, where many a fog bank and ice that soon melts away tempt us to believe in new lands, while constantly deceiving the adventurous mariner with vain hopes" (187; see also 276).

Kant seems not only to have hopelessly isolated the subject from the world (the *Ding an sich*), but to have taken the Lucretian particularism that haunted Diderot to new extremes; each individual is a bundle of tenuously related "faculties" whose unity as person or "personality" is a matter for speculation: "From the point of view of a stranger . . . perceiving in the soul no permanent phenomena, except the representation of the I, which accompanies and connects them all, we cannot determine whether that I (being a mere thought) be not in the same state of flux as the other thoughts which are chained together by the I" (260). In his geography of the human mind there is a fundamental and seemingly unbridgeable chasm between an understanding, which perceives and responds to the phenomenal world, and a practical reason, which acts according to the transcendental "ought": "two distinct jurisdictions over one and the same territory of experience" (*Critique of Judgement*, 13).

But Kant is aware of this separation as a crisis in contemporary thought. He hopes that through this juridical process of demarcation he will "prevent violence" (a violence inherent in the Enlightenment dilemma) by encouraging us to abandon certain debates as "transcendental illusions." In this sense he is, surprisingly, rather like Wittgenstein; he wants a philosophy that is willing to call a halt to its own project and concede that certain fundamental problems are not approachable. As a cartographer of the subject-in-the-world, he wants to be able to write "here be dragons" on certain regions and then forget about them.

Kant is not entirely at ease with this solution, however. Throughout the first *Critique* he keeps returning to the (therapeutic) problem of building wholes out of the discrete elements into which he has broken the world. Two examples will prove particularly fruitful: the "productive imagination" and the "organicism of pure speculative reason."

The imagination plays a crucial role in bridging the gap between the understanding and sensuous intuition. It is not, yet, a Coleridgean leap beyond the subject, but it does take the "intellectual" to the threshold of the physical. The "productive imagination," by bringing into a synthetic unity the chaotic manifold of the sensual intuition of phenomena, allows that intuition to be referred to the higher unity of understanding—the synthetic unity of apperception: "We have therefore a pure imagination as one of the fundamental faculties of the human soul, on which all knowledge *a priori* depends. Through it we bring the manifold of intuition on one side in connection with the condition of the necessary unity of pure apperception on the other. These two extreme ends, sense and understanding, must be brought into contact with each other by means of the transcendental function of imagination, because, without it, the senses might give us phenomena, but no objects of empirical knowledge, therefore no experience" (*Pure Reason,* 114). Imagination is a productive principle that creates a unity out of the Lucretian chaos of the phenomenal manifold. Its highest empirical function (the "recognition of phenomena" [114]) is a form of associative memory that prevents the radical Enlightenment threat of an absolute disjunction between "tick" and "tock": "Without our being conscious that what we are thinking now is the same as what we thought a moment before, all reproduction in the series of representations would be vain. Each representation would, in its present state, be a new one, and in no wise belonging to the act by which it was to be produced by degrees, and the manifold in it would never form a whole, because deprived of that unity which consciousness alone can impart to it" (103).[17] Kant's most compelling image for this therapeutic unity is one that will become the central metaphor of post-Kantian idealism and its drive to the Absolute: organicism. The complete interdependence of part and whole, which reassures us in the face of the disturbing divisions and incommensurable languages that rive the Kantian subject, will reappear in Dilthey's hermeneutics, which underwrite so much of contemporary historicism: "[P]ure speculative reason is so constituted that it forms a true organism, in which everything is *organic,* the whole being there for the sake of every part, and every part for the sake of the whole, so that the smallest imperfection, whether a fault or a deficiency, must inevitably betray itself in use" (xliii).

It is in the third *Critique* that the therapeutic drive finds its fullest, and most influential, expression. If the first *Critique* is the culmination of the Enlightenment disengagement, the third *Critique* is the first work of the "post-Kantian" therapeutic "reengagement." Kant's avowed aim in the work is to allow the understanding to "feel itself at home in nature" (*Judgement,* 35), and Kant promotes the aesthetic response to the world to the all-important role of extending a unity and totality to the subject-in-the-world, which previously could only be thought of the subject over against the world.

In the third *Critique* Kant sets out to knit together all the "separa-

---

17. The highest principle of unity in the Kantian subject of the first *Critique* is the synthetic unity of apperception, the "I think" that accompanies every representation of the mind. Without it, "I should have as manifold and various a self as I have representations of which I am conscious" (79), which is the fear or desire that haunts Diderot. But this Kantian *cogito* has nothing like the influence in post-Kantian thought of his concept of the imagination, which, following his use of it in the third *Critique* takes on the role he originally assigned to the synthetic unity of apperception.

tions" that inhabit the first *Critique*. The principal one, which is the "great gulf fixed" between the first and second *Critique*s, is the opposition "between the realm of the natural concept, as the sensible, and the realm of the concept of freedom, as the supersensible." The aesthetic response will knit these two realms ("so many separate worlds") together into a "unity": "it renders possible the transition from the mode of thought according to the principles of the one to that according to the principles of the other" (14). It does this by suggesting a new relationship between mind and world, subject and object: the free conformity to law of the aesthetic object (see 86).

The beautiful object is one that, without any actual finality for the subject (i.e., being "good for" this or that purpose) is nonetheless final "in itself," and thus pleasing to our minds, which desire order and unity. The object is no longer, in the third *Critique,* a dangerous iceberg in the noumenal sea surrounding the subject-island; we now find ourselves in a world that seems made for us; the aesthetic object's finality is a gratuitous revelation of the intellectual in the sensible. The "finality without end" of the aesthetic object is an extension to the sensible object of the organic auto-finality of pure reason that pertained only to the subject in the first *Critique.*

The aesthetic judgment gives us a sensible intuition of the prime mystery of the second *Critique:* how we can be ruled by a moral order despite being subject to a deterministic physical causality: "[I]f it were possible for us to have so deep an insight into a man's character . . . that every . . . incentive to these actions and all external occasions which affect them were so known to us that his future conduct could be predicted with as great a certainty as the occurrence of a solar . . . eclipse, we could nevertheless still assert that the man is free" (*Practical Reason,* 102–3). The aesthetic object is merely physical, but partakes in an intellectual order. As such, it allows us to conceive the unity of the sensible and supersensible directly: "Taste makes . . . the transition from the charm of sense to habitual moral interest possible without too violent a leap, for it represents the imagination, even in its freedom, as amenable to a final determination for understanding, and teaches us to find, even in sensuous objects, a free delight apart from any charm of sense" (*Judgement,* 225).

In the third *Critique*, then, Kant makes two crucial extensions of the therapeutic gestures of the first. The organicism of the intellectual subject has become an organicism of the object in the world (the work of art or the beautiful product of nature), and the internal unification of the subject via the productive imagination has become a unification of mind and world in which the imagination still plays a central role. There remains one crucial extension of these therapeutic gestures that is, in effect, their unification: the organic totality of the mind-in-the-world.

Although this concept is not explicitly spelled out by Kant, it is the most important legacy of the third *Critique* for post-Kantian criticism. The free conformity to law of the aesthetic object, or, rather, of the imagination in its encounter with the aesthetic object, is the key extension of the role of the imagination. It is here that it meets with and becomes a therapeutic organicism. In its conformity to law, the imagination relates the particular phenomenon to a universal condition. The aesthetic response in its universality as "thinking from the standpoint of everyone else" (152) forces us to think our humanity as a species-being. This, at least, is the most radical conclusion to be drawn from the description of aesthetic taste as a *"sensus communis"* that makes an appeal (difficult to imagine in the first *Critique*) to "the collective reason of mankind" (151).

That we are not far from either Cavell's "wish and search for community as the wish and search for reason" or Burke's social contract as defining totality is underlined in a footnote to the "Critique of Teleological Judgement": "[I]n the case of a complete transformation, recently undertaken [Kant is writing in 1790], of a great people into a state, the word *organization* has frequently, and with much propriety, been used for the constitution of the legal authorities and even of the entire body politic. For in a whole of this kind certainly no member should be a mere means, but should also be an end, and, seeing that he contributes to the possibility of the entire body, should have his position and function in turn defined by the idea of the whole" (*Judgement,* 23).

The ability to think the (sensuous) particular being as freely instantiating the (intellectual) law of the whole is the most influential therapeutic legacy of the Kantian aesthetic sensibility. It is the leitmotif of all post-Kantian idealism. From Fichte via Schelling to Hegel, we have a line of thought that picks up the desire for the unity of the subject and object and makes that unity an absolute fact, rather than a tenuous synthetic achievement. Meyer Abrams's description of Hegel's *Phenomenology* as "a work which manages the feat of epitomizing the cultural history of the maturing spirit entirely in terms of the diverse separations, conflicts, and incremental reconciliations of subject and object" (*Natural Supernaturalism,* 92) can stand for the entire post-Kantian project.

POST-KANTIANISM

For all the post-Kantians, life and history begin with a fall (often explicitly compared to the biblical one) from an original absolute unity into the fundamental division of subject and object. The goal of history is to reunite what was once divided, to raise the consciousness of the subject to the point where it intuits the object as an aspect of its *self-consciousness*—the point that Hegel will call Absolute Knowing.

We saw that the historicist approach makes history a narrative totality in which every part is determined by the unity of the whole. Schelling's *System of Transcendental Idealism* (1800) helps us understand the post-Kantian roots of this approach. Schelling, like Kant and Burke before him, recognizes the possibility of a historical order in which change would always be infinitely negative, but he dismisses this threat with a new confidence: "The question arises . . . as to whether a series of circumstances without plan or purpose can deserve the name of history at all, and whether in the mere *concept* of history there is not already contained also the concept of a necessity which choice itself is compelled to serve" (199). The answer to the question is, of course, yes; but Schelling's proof is interesting. He rereads the infinite skeptical disengagement from history as a *felix culpa*, a "fall" from the original unity of being, which is, however, necessary to get history going at all. Because all of history writes itself in the space between the fall from unity and the gradual recovery of that unity, it always (already) has a plot, a unitary meaning that it displays through time:

> Man has a history only because what he will do is incapable of being calculated in advance according to any theory. Choice is to that extent the goddess of history. Mythology has history begin with the first step out of the domain of instinct into the realm of freedom, with the loss of the Golden Age, or with the Fall, that is, with the first expression of choice. In the schemes of the philosophers, history ends with the reign of reason, that is, with the Golden Age of law, when all choice shall have vanished from the earth, and man shall have returned through freedom to the same point at which nature originally placed him, and which he forsook when history began; . . . neither absolute lawlessness, nor a series of events without aim or purpose, deserve the name of history, and . . . its true nature is constituted only by freedom and lawfulness in conjunction, or by the gradual realization, on

the part of a whole species of beings, of an ideal that they have never wholly lost. (200)

"Freedom and lawfulness in conjunction": the Kantian aesthetic "free conformity to law" becomes a means for reconciling atomistic individual wills with a coherent historical "plot."

History is unified, and the subject of history is always unified. Choice may be the goddess of history, but individual choice only attains meaningfulness in the context of necessary law; there is a "lawfulness which runs, like the weaving of an unknown hand, through the free play of choice in history" (208–9). This "system of providence," "the common ground of the harmony between freedom and intelligence," is *religion in the only true sense of the word*" (209). In this providential order of history, we can no longer be tormented by the threat of the negativity of change. All our actions, if understood aright, can be seen as "a progressive, gradually self-disclosing revelation of the absolute" (211).

The key to attaining this therapeutic self-consciousness is the literary work of art, which, because it exists in the world as a determined object while being recognized by the creating mind as an intellectual product of its free subjective activity, promotes the final coming-to-self-consciousness of the absolute unity of subjective and objective. Through the work of art this unity of subject and object, free and conditioned, becomes not just a fact of speculative philosophy, but absolute self-conscious knowledge. The mystery of art realizes "the aim of *our whole science*," it explains "how the ultimate ground of the harmony between subjective and objective becomes an object to the *self itself*" (217). In this sense art and philosophy are one: "[A]rt is at once the only true and eternal organ and document of philosophy, which ever and again continues to speak to us of what philosophy cannot depict in external form, namely the unconscious element in acting and producing, and its original identity with the conscious. Art is paramount to the philosopher, precisely because it opens to him, as it were, the holy of holies, where burns in eternal and original unity, as if in a single flame, that which in nature and history is rent asunder, and in life and action, no less than in thought, must forever fly apart" (231).

Art allows us to grasp the totality of being as a simple absolute unity. History is revealed to have a providential "plot"; the random "series of events" can only justify itself as "history" when it becomes a narrative totality with the "organic" unity of plot—a concept of plot as old as Aristotle's definition in the *Poetics,* where he compares the plot as a "whole made up of parts" to a "beautiful living creature" and argues that this whole must be "a complete whole, with its several incidents so closely connected that the transposal or withdrawal of any one of them will disjoin and dislocate the whole" (*De Poetica*, 1462, 1463). Similarly, Coleridge, under Schelling's influence, defines the "end of all *narrative*" as being "to convert *a series* into a Whole" (McFarland, 51).

Schelling argues that in fact "there is properly speaking but one absolute work of art . . . even though it should not yet exist in its most ultimate form." When it achieves that ultimate form, it will bring about the conclusion of history: the Absolute will become reality, bringing God into the world, or, rather, making the world the being of God. At this point, when unity has passed through the fallen state of division and been returned to unity, Schelling's philosophical project is complete: "A system is completed when it is led back to its starting point" (232).

Hegel's is the more famous and the more influential version of this impulse toward the Absolute, and he allows us to complete our own circle by linking the post-Kantian response to Enlightenment disengagement directly to the late-nineteenth- and early-twentieth-century historicisms we began with.

As Eagleton has pointed out, the Hegelian reconciliation of the individual and the universal is, like Schelling's, aesthetic; Kant's "free conformity to law" is reborn as "a law which is now entirely at one with [the individual's] spontaneous being" (*Aesthetic*, 22). Hegel develops this into a far more fully realized political and ethical conception than Schelling does, however. Hegel's concept of *Sittlichkeit*—the ordinary German word for "ethics," which Hegel enriches into an untranslatable term signifying the individual's ability to live, as Cavell puts it, "representatively"—underlies all the therapeutic philosophies of the last two centuries.

Hegel's concept of *Sittlichkeit* grew, significantly, out of his response to the destruction wrought by the French Revolution. Like Burke, Hegel feared the revolutionaries' abstraction from the frameworks of custom and history, which enabled them to unleash pure negative change upon the status quo. Driven by an abstract notion of utility, the revolutionaries act with "absolute freedom" (*Phenomenology*, 356); their disregard for existing social forms reduces society to a tabula rasa on which they will draw the purely rational outlines of the new order: "[A]ll social groups or classes which are the spiritual spheres into which the whole is articulated are abolished; the individual consciousness that belonged to any such sphere and willed and fulfilled itself in it has put aside its limitation; its purpose is the general purpose, its language universal law." This Rousseauist *volonté générale* destroys Hegel's aesthetically unified state. It presents us with the universal, but the individual cannot be located expressively—or "representatively"—within this universal: "[E]ach individual consciousness raises itself out of its allotted sphere, no longer finds its essence and its work in this particular sphere, but grasps itself as the *Notion* of will, grasps all spheres as the essence of this will, and therefore can only realize itself in a work which is a work of the whole [i.e., at the level of the total system]" (357).

This oppressive Godwinian attempt continually to rethink the system, to create, obey, and police laws that are entirely "self-given" and therefore open to complete change from moment to moment, fails because Spirit as Absolute Freedom, unable to divide and delegate the necessary functions of society in accordance with a system greater than itself *in* which it can realize itself, "can produce neither a positive work nor a deed; there is left for it only *negative* action; it is merely the *fury* of destruction" (357).

We have encountered this fear of change as absolute "negativity" before. It inhabited Diderot's unease with the *anarchie* of discontinuous systemic change. It was the basis of Burke's politics of tradition and social contract. Schelling's refusal of the title "history" to a mere sequence of events is its immediate precursor. But it is Hegel above all who transmits the therapeutic solution to this Enlightenment anxiety to the historicist philosophy and criticism of our century.

The key is *Sittlichkeit*, which Taylor has suggested is the defining ethical and political vision of the post-Romantic era. In Hegel's vision of "ethical life" the citizen's relationship to the historically given state is equivalent to the self-conscious subject's relationship to the Absolute; the individual member of society sublimates personal desires within the norms and goals of the total society (a word related to *Sittlichkeit, Sitten,* means "custom") and finds individual fulfillment in the realization of general goals. Not that, in theory at least, individual citizens are mere tokens in the larger game of the state; individuals play a creative role in constituting the norms and ends of the society in which they are situated, but, as Taylor puts it, these are "sustained by our action, and yet as already there, so that the member of society 'brings them about through his activity, but as something which rather simply is'" (*Hegel and Modern Society,* 89).

There is a dialectic of individual and society in which the individuals create (or re-create) the social norms through practice but act, "as it were, out of instinct" (Hegel, *Die Vernunft in der Geschichte,* qtd. in

Taylor, 89) with reference to the norms as established. It is this that
gives rise to the idea which Taylor champions and in which we recognize the fundamental ethical thrust of the historicist "turn to language":
the concept of a "situated freedom." Taylor accepts Hegel's argument
that the concept of freedom as liberation, as an escape from the bondage of dogma into free self-definition, leads inevitably to vacancy and
vacuity (158). We cannot help thinking of Shelley's negative character-
izations of the postrevolutionary society in *Prometheus Unbound* when
Taylor writes that liberationist politics, "whether Marxist, anarchist, situ-
ationist or whatever, offers no idea at all of what the society of freedom
should look like beyond the empty formulae: that it should be endlessly
creative; have no divisions, whether between men or within them, or
between levels of existence . . . involve no coercion, no representation
etc. All that is done in these negative characterisations is to think away
the entire human situation. Small wonder then that this freedom has no
content" (155). What we need to do then, he argues, is to discover a
content for freedom, to make it other than the irresponsible "let[ting]
go the rein" (*Reflections,* 354) that Burke deplores: "This means recov-
ering a conception of free activity which sees it as a response called for
by a situation which is ours in virtue of our condition as natural social
beings, or in virtue of some inescapable location or purpose. What is
common to all the varied notions of situated freedom is that they see
free activity as grounded in the *acceptance* of our defining situation"
(Taylor, *Hegel and Modern Society,* 159–60).

This emphasis on a wise "acceptance" of the given situation stems
from Burke's "wise prejudice"; but Burke's admonitions are largely negative, designed to frighten us with the consequences of revolutionary
change. Hegel promises us, on the other hand, a freedom with real content, a freedom in which every part knows its place in an absolute
order. This positive content of freedom is the same proffered by Cavell
when he talks of the need to "acknowledge" the community that defines us, and to live "representatively" of that community; it is the same
that underlies Gadamer's defense of "prejudice" as the necessary basis
of our ethical life; it is the basis of the anthropological derivation of
significance from the cultural "framework."

Politically, the condition of existence of Hegel's concrete ethical life
means an absolute willing of the state (as Universal) by the citizen (as
particular): "[I]t is the moral Whole, the *State,* which is that form of
reality in which the individual has and enjoys his freedom; but on the
condition of his recognizing, believing in, and willing that which is
common to the Whole. . . . Law, Morality, Government, and they alone,

[are] the positive reality and completion of Freedom. . . . The Individual living in this unity has a moral life [*Sittlichkeit*]; possesses a value that consists in this substantiality alone" (Hegel, *History*, 38). "Recognition" here is the same moral demand as Cavell's "acknowledgment." The historicist belief that every text instantiates—or "represents"—a defining "context," every speech act a language game, is the latest development of the Kantian aesthetic's "free conformity to law" become, through Hegel, the citizen's free conformity to the ideal of the state: "For Truth is the Unity of the universal and subjective Will; and the Universal is to be found in the State, in its laws, its universal and rational arrangements. . . . When the State or our country constitutes a community of existence; when the subjective will of man submits to laws—the contradiction between Liberty and Necessity vanishes" (39).

We saw that Schelling, by reading both state and history as a unitary, absolute truth, resisted the Lucretian problem of the disaggregation of the elements of the state and of historical process. Events could only become historical through their relationship to the one "ideal" that governs the order of history. Hegel's history is, similarly, the temporal manifestation of an eternally selfsame Spirit: "It is only an inference from the history of the World, that its development has been a rational process; that the history in question has constituted the rational necessary course of the World-Spirit—that Spirit whose nature is always one and the same, but which unfolds this its one nature in the phenomena of the World's existence" (10).

Change may appear to occur, but it is mortgaged to the Absolute: our only true "freedom" is the freedom to accept the necessity of history's unitary truth. Absolute Knowing is the absolute (self-)consciousness of the positive necessity of the world-as-it-is.

This conception of history underlies that aspect of historicist criticism which most troubled us: a "history" that cannot accept "change." If we consider the Hegelian roots of Dilthey's and Collingwood's approaches to history, this history without "event" is no longer a surprise. Sheer "events" are inadmissible in a Hegelian model of process; any happening is only truly part of history if it is already contained in the absolute Notion of history. Each part presupposes the whole. This is history as communal memory, and makes Hegel the supreme instance of the affirmation of the *lien de souvenirs* against the Enlightenment threat of discontinuity. Hegel's *Phenomenology* culminates with the uniting of history and Absolute Knowing as "comprehended History . . . [which forms] the inwardizing [*Er-innerung*, a pun on "internalizing" and "remembering" (Abrams, *Natural Supernaturalism*, 235)] and the Calvary of absolute Spirit, the actuality, truth, and certainty of his throne, without which he would be lifeless and alone" (*Phenomenology*, 493). This "inwardizing" of an absolute recollection of the progress of Spirit is the means of (hermeneutically) turning the process of history into a narrative unity within which (or as which) Spirit knows itself; and that knowing is an Absolute Knowing. The promise Hegel holds out to us here is one to which "we moderns" are particularly susceptible, as Taylor's *Sources of the Self* makes particularly clear. We live with the perception that we suffer from a certain rootlessness, that "our public traditions of family, ecology, even polis are undermined and swept away" (513). To know the self as a moment of the absolute self-consciousness of Spirit is a promise of the "infinite harmony" Schelling found in the work of art. It is to see ourselves as "rooted," defined by a whole that accounts for all our particularities. If history has a single meaning and purpose, we can stop shoring fragments against our ruins, and confidently articulate the part with the whole.

Particularly powerful is the implicit religious promise within this. Like Schelling, Hegel translates the history of the subject into theological terms. For him, "the history of the world . . . [is] the true *theodicaea*, the justification of God in History" (qtd. in Abrams, *Natural Supernaturalism*, 189). Reading Spirit's journey to Absolute Knowing as Christ's Passion is simply an extrapolation of the underlying providential order elaborated by Schelling. Yet it is remarkably potent. Schelling's "God" is rather abstract and nonspecific (it is merely the absolute unity of the subject reflected back into the subject's temporary division). The role of Christ in Christian thought is as a bridge between the sacred and the profane. It is Christ who allows us to think our own (at least potential) divinity not only because God has become a man but also because Christ's dying for our sins implies a communal unity in Christ: it is only if, at some level, all humanity is united in Christ that Christ's death can be representative for all humanity.

The reintroduction of Christian myth into the *Phenomenology* gives Hegel a figure that allows us to think our particularity and universality simultaneously without being shocked by the apparent paradox. It does not resolve the paradox, unless one makes the same leap of faith necessary to resolve the Christian one, but it makes it *thinkable* for anyone familiar with Christian mythology. Schelling's providentialism is repeated by Hegel: the "cunning of reason" figures as the providential guidance of the Absolute; the artistic "man of destiny" returns as the "world historical individual"; and the tripartite historical progress of Hegel's *Philosophy of Right*—from Abstract Right via Morality to Ethical

Life—is a reflection of Schelling's own tripartite millennial eschatology, in which the third period is the being of God (Schelling, 211–12). Schelling's providence threatened to be rather abstract and mechanical, however; our role vis-à-vis the hidden hand of the absolute is rather passive and alienated. The absolute inevitability of arriving at the millennial reconciliation of subject and object seems to undermine the dramatic value of the original separation; the unity of particular and absolute seems in danger of becoming simply the undifferentiated absolute. Hegel's specifically Christian version introduces a dynamism that allows us simultaneously to bear in mind the duality of particular and universal and to conceptualize the progress from the one to the other without collapsing that original duality into a merely transient "stage."

Hegel's "Calvary" better represents the sense of struggle to overcome our fall into "disengagement," which we have seen is a hallmark not only of post-Kantian idealism but also of the very aspects of the Enlightenment against which it struggles. The Christian myth, with its implicit admission of doubt and struggle, brings us much closer to Shelley's own interest in the therapeutic. This conception of human life as riven by the paradoxical demands of a fallen and divided reality and intimations of an absolute, unified origin to which we might return is the particular preserve of those post-Kantian philosophers whose writings we associate with the concept of Romantic Irony. It is these writers, many of whom directly address the difference between the classical and Romantic aesthetics, whose understanding of the therapeutic as a lived process defines the Romanticism to which much of Shelley's thought is a response.

ROMANTIC IRONY

It is necessary briefly to reconsider the nature of the Romantic Ironic condition, because both Ann Mellor's influential *English Romantic Irony* and David Simpson's *Irony and Authority in Romantic Poetry* have firmly established a picture of Romantic Irony, insofar as it is a specific literary program, as a kind of proto-deconstructionism, apparently greatly at odds with the therapeutic effort to bring God into the world.[18] There is some truth in this view, but it should not be over-

18. Mellor in fact says "the romantic ironist must be sharply distinguished from modern deconstructors. . . . [M]odern deconstructionists choose to perform only one half of the ro-

stated. Romantic Irony's "postmodernism" stems largely from its compli-cated self-referentiality—for example, Schlegel's delight with the second half of *Don Quixote,* in which everybody has read the first half, so that it becomes "an opus which, as it were, contemplates itself" (*Dialogue,* 70). But this self-conscious self-referentiality, while it may be enjoyed, is also a symptom of our fallen condition. We enjoy our ironic awareness of the "artistry" of the work of art because that awareness is the first step in our constant struggle to overcome such artistry.

Schiller, in his *On the Aesthetic Education of Man in a Series of Letters,* situates our modern (Romantic) mentality as little more than halfway through this painful struggle. Schiller's *Letters,* written five years before Schelling's *System of Transcendental Idealism,* anticipates most of the central tenets of the major post-Kantian philosophers. Like Schelling, he holds that the chief promise of the work of art is to recon-cile subject and object, intellect and senses, and return them to the unity they enjoyed in the prelapsarian classical world. Like Hegel, he argues that the first cure for the "wound" that "all dividing intellect" (39) has inflicted upon "modern humanity" is to be found in reconciling the individual with the state: this should be a process of "the individual *becoming* State" (32), a uniting of the individual's expressive power with the Absolute as condition and product of that expressivity. In this ideal state, "only because the whole subserves the parts may the parts submit to the whole" (33).

But despite these strong similarities there is an important difference of emphasis. Schiller may propose an *Aufhebung* (88) as the "path to divinity," but he immediately wonders whether "we may call a path what never reaches its goal." This is the crucial difference between the two approaches. The first is a systematic idealism that culminates in the Absolute. Its emphasis is always on the final destination of Spirit. The second posits that Absolute as a goal, but its emphasis is on our present fallen condition. Its idealism is unsystematic, rooted in a divided world that retains hope for the future, but not the certainty of Absolute Know-ing.

---

mantic-ironic operation" (5). However, her portrait of romantic irony in *practice* identifies it with a series of "postmodern" gestures (the refusal of closure, the interrogation of the unity of the subject), while the "reconstructive" second half of its program is simply the rather vague humanist affirmation that we infer from the "first half": "Human knowledge increases; the mind expands; life merrily multiplies, not without pain and loss, but always with energy" (70). L. Furst's *Fictions of Romantic Irony* and D. J. Enright's *Alluring Problem* both bring a useful corrective to this view, but err in reducing Romantic Irony to a simple literary technique, leaving one to wonder what makes it specifically "Romantic."

One can see this best in Schiller's *Naive and Sentimental Poetry.*
Here, he picks up the schema of the *Letters*—a classical "naive" world
of original unity-with-nature, and a modern "sentimental" world of division—but relegates the third stage (the return to harmony at a higher
level, which Schelling and Hegel will make the culmination of their systems), to a never-to-be-realized future. Schiller argues that the ancient
Greeks lived in perfect unity with the natural world. This gives their
writing its "naive" quality, by which he means a kind of innate Words-
worthianism. The "naive" writer achieves (without being aware of it as
an "achievement") a perfect simplicity and quiet strength in which "nature [is] victorious over art" (*Naive and Sentimental*, 89): "Unac-
quainted with the rules, those crutches for weakness and taskmasters of
awkwardness, led only by nature or by instinct, its guardian angel, it
goes calmly and surely through all the snares of false taste" (96). We, on
the other hand, having been through the fall of division from the natural
world, still reach out to nature, but now "[o]ur feeling for nature is like
the feeling of an invalid for health" (105). We can no longer seek the
natural unselfconsciously, and this self-conscious yearning for a simple
bond with nature is the "sentimental." It is the desire of the civilized
sophisticate to unlock the repressed expressive potential of the "heart,"
to find the child within: "[T]he feeling by which we are attached to
nature is . . . closely related to the feeling with which we mourn the lost
age of childhood and childlike innocence. Our childhood is the only
undisfigured nature that we still encounter in civilized mankind, hence
it is no wonder if every trace of the nature outside us leads us back to
our childhood" (103–4).

The modern, sentimental writer is caught in a Catch-22. Desiring nature, our very consciousness of that desire debars us from "naive" access to the natural. If the essence of the "naive" is to "*be* nature," that of
the "sentimental" is to "*seek* lost nature" (106); they "felt naturally," we
"feel the natural" (105).

But surprisingly, perhaps—and crucially for the theory of Romantic
Irony—Schiller reads this fall from original harmony as a *felix culpa*.
The "naive" poet is a "perfect" being, the sentimental indubitably imperfect, and yet this very "perfection" is the "naive" poet's problem: "[T]he
goal to which man in civilization *strives* is infinitely preferable to that
which he *attains* in nature. For the one obtains its value by the absolute
achievement of a finite, the other by approximation to an infinite greatness. But only the latter possesses *degrees* and displays a *progress*"
(112–13). The sentimental poet inhabits an anxious void between the
"actual" and the "ideal" (116–17), drawn toward a unity we know to be

unrealizable because of our very consciousness of needing to attain it. But this spurs "us moderns" to flights of expressive power inconceivable for the "naive" poet, who is limited to—though able, as the sentimental cannot, perfectly to express—the actual.

Schiller's unsystematic idealism places us in a world in which we are constantly aware of our fallen, divided nature, and constantly strive (as invalids do for health) to re-create the original therapeutic unity. This unleashes our creative potential, but, in contrast to Schelling's artistic millennium, Schiller finds what glory he can in the striving, not the attaining: "What [the sentimental idealist] demands of himself is boundless; but everything that he achieves is limited" (183–84).

Schlegel's Romantic Irony is, like Schiller's sentimentality, the product of a fall from classical unity into a dynamic world of incomplete becoming: "In the ancients, one sees the accomplished letter of entire poetry: in the moderns, one has the presentiment of the spirit in becoming" (Aphorism 93 from the *Lyceum; Dialogue,* 130). In our fallen state, we have the same Schillerian yearning for the Absolute. In the same millennial language as used by Schelling or Hegel, Schlegel projects the desire for the Absolute as the "third stage" toward which history is tending:

> The revolutionary desire to realize God's kingdom on earth is the elastic point of the progressive development and the beginning of modern history. Whatever is without relationship to God's kingdom, is for it only incidental. (Aphorism 222 from the *Athenaeum; Dialogue,* 144)

> Every good man progressively becomes God. To become God, to be man, and to educate oneself, are expressions that are synonymous. (Aphorism 262 from the *Athenaeum,* 146)

This can hardly be regarded as an attack upon the "metaphysics of presence," and, indeed, makes Schlegel's later conversion to Catholicism less surprising than it might seem. Despite the apparent confidence of these claims, however, Schlegel, like Schiller, is more concerned with exploring our fallen condition than describing the glories of self-consciousness become epiphany. Even more than for Schiller, this fall is a *felix culpa.* Schlegel can delight in the "chaos" of the paradoxical ironic predicament of striving for the Absolute with inherently limited means. This is Schlegel at his most "postmodern," and it comes out most clearly in his descriptions of and prescriptions for the truly "Romantic" text. Poetry for Schlegel, as for Schiller, is a form of "play"

("Man shall *only play* with Beauty and he shall play *only with Beauty*," [Schiller, *Letters,* 80]), but for Schlegel this has a radically ludic edge absent from Schiller. The "arabesque," the poetic "chaos" and "confusion," "permanent *parekbasis* [digression]"[19] are all cases in point, and ripe for a poststructuralist celebration of the refusal of closure. This is the nub of the celebrated Aphorism 116 from the *Athenaeum:*

> Romantic poetry is a progressive universal poetry. Its mission is not merely to reunite all separate genres of poetry and to put poetry in touch with philosophy and rhetorics. It will, and should, now mingle and now amalgamate poetry and prose, genius and criticism, the poetry of art and the poetry of nature, render poetry living and social, and life and society poetic. . . . [I]t too can soar, free from all the real and ideal interests, on the wings of poetic reflection, midway between the work and the artist. It can even exponentiate this reflection and multiply it as in an endless series of mirrors. . . . Other types of poetry are completed and can now be entirely analyzed. The Romantic type of poetry is still becoming; indeed, its peculiar essence is that it is always becoming and that it can never be completed. It cannot be exhausted by any theory, and only a divinatory criticism might dare to characterize its ideal. It alone is infinite, as it alone is free; and as its first law it recognizes that the arbitrariness of the poet endures no law above him. (Schlegel, *Dialogue,* 140–41)

This appears to speak for itself, but another picture emerges if we look at what has been left out in the ellipses and relate it to the therapeutic imperative we are exploring. This "progressive universal poetry" is as "universal" as it is "progressive." Not only does Romantic poetry perfectly express the poet's "originality" (*Dialogue,* 87), it aspires to the perfect expression of the entire universe—a purely therapeutic aspiration of linking the "within" and the "without":

> Romantic poetry alone can, like the epic, become a mirror of the entire surrounding world, a picture of its age. . . . It is capable of the highest and the most universal education; not only by creating from within, but also from without, since it organizes in similar fashion all parts of what is destined to become a whole; thus, a view is opened to an endlessly developing classicism.

19. For an excellent discussion of these terms, see Eichner, 62ff.

"Destined to become a whole": closure may never in fact be invoked in the individual Romantic poem, but this "permanent *parekbasis*" operates in a field charged by an eternal promise of closure. Romanticism aims to return to the unity of "classicism" at a higher level. This may be a thrilling freedom from the law—the liberation from a stultifying logocentrism that both Mellor and Simpson describe—or it may be a licensed freedom in which we are free to play at denying closure, because we know that our most radical "arabesque" is actually part, when seen at a sufficient distance, of the Grand Design.

There was a second version of the ironic predicament, which we might call "tragic irony" in contradistinction to the Schlegelian "comic irony." Schlegelian irony is a frenetic celebration of our self-conscious disengagement from the world even as we strive to overcome it. Tragic irony, which is nowhere better exemplified than in the poetic work of Coleridge (his theoretical and political writings have a quite different emphasis), places the poet in the same ontological and epistemological position as Schlegelian irony, but the poet is no longer able to transmute the anxiety of our fallen state into creative exhilaration. The consciousness of separation from the world and from God-in-the-world haunts the poet, and this gives rise to a Romantic irony remarkably similar to Schlegel's in form but everywhere quite opposed in feeling.

Coleridge's awareness of separation from the world liberates him, or condemns him—as it does the Schlegelian Romantic poet—to a self-conscious, self-reflective artistry. The dramatic contrast between the "naive" Wordsworthian "actual language of men" and Coleridge's medievalizing in the *Lyrical Ballads* is the obvious illustration of this. The medieval Romance is the origin of "Romantic" literature for Schlegel—hence the Romantic fascination with the medieval past—and Coleridge's additions to the text of *The Rime of the Ancient Mariner* (the gloss in seventeenth-century prose style and so forth) are textbook examples (as Simpson notes [98–101]) of Schlegel's ironic desire to mix poetry and prose, to confuse and confound styles in a "chaotic" and self-reflexive harmony.

But, for Coleridge, this self-conscious artistry leads only to a feeling of being more and more cut off from the Absolute; that "impossibility and necessity of total communication" that Schlegel celebrates as at once the spur and the dilemma of the ironic condition (Aphorism 106 from the *Lyceum; Dialogue,* 131) is Coleridge's lived nightmare, all the more harrowing in that he is constantly confronted by the therapeutic Wordsworthian ideal of the poet who "considers man and nature as essentially adapted to each other" and "binds together by passion and knowledge the vast empire of human society, as it is spread over the whole earth, and over all time" (Wordsworth, "Preface to the Lyrical Ballads [1802]," 604).

Occasionally Coleridge will approach this ideal, as in "This Lime-Tree Bower My Prison," where, in imagination, he exhorts Charles Lamb, whom he has not been able to accompany on a nature walk, to

> gaze till all doth seem
> Less gross than bodily; and of such hues
> As veil the Almighty Spirit, when yet he makes
> Spirits perceive his presence.
>
> (40-43)

This is recognizably Schellingian, but it is to be noted that this therapeutic dissolving into nature-as-God is performed by proxy. Coleridge does suggest he has shared the experience ("stand, as I have stood" [38]), but typically it is not here, not now; he writes while trapped in a bower/ prison. Even there he can assure himself "That Nature ne'er deserts the wise and pure," but this only begs the question: is he among that number? For both Schiller and Schlegel our fallen condition is the trigger for a turn inward to discover our expressive depths and "originality." Coleridge follows the same path, but only to be paralyzed by the fear that perhaps there is no such expressive richness within him. His clearest, and most distressing, statement of this is in "Dejection: An Ode."

Despite what I have argued above, there are some significant parallels between contemporary poststructuralist criticism and the post-Kantian philosophical endeavor. It is possible to trace a line of thought back from the contemporary enthusiasm for "theory"—particularly in its most compelling and influential form in the various branches of French poststructuralist thought—to some central aspects of Kant's project, and important to do so because it highlights the two-sidedness of Kant's thought, its debt to the paradoxes of the Enlightenment "separation." Moreover, poststructuralist theory is the major alternative to historicist therapeutics in contemporary critical discourse, and a brief examination of its debts to the Enlightenment helps us to consider some of its strengths and weaknesses.

In Derrida's controversy with John Searle over Austin and ordinary-language philosophy, the therapeutic and antitherapeutic approaches confront each other directly.[20] Derrida breaks completely with the ethi-

20. Derrida's original paper on Austin ("Signature Event Context") and his reply ("Limited Inc: a b c . . .") to Searle's response, "Reiterating the Differences: A Reply to Derrida," are

cal imperative of ordinary-language philosophy to find a context within which and for which all utterances can be "responsible." In his view the enabling condition of communication is that messages are capable of breaking from their productive contexts. Meaningfulness depends upon "iterability" (what I have been calling "promiscuity"), a refusal of the dedicated metatext on the grounds of language's conventionality, the very foundation stone of ordinary-language philosophy. If language can be said to belong to "the community," that could just be another way of saying it "belongs" to nobody and to no context: "[E]ven in the extreme case of my writing something in order to be able to read (reread) it *in a moment,* this moment is constituted—i.e. divided—by the very iterability of what produces itself *momentarily.* The sender and the receiver, even if they were the self-same *subject,* each relate to a mark they experience as made to do without them, from the instant of its production or of its reception on; and they experience this not as the mark's negative limit but rather as the positive condition of its possibility" ("Limited Inc," 186).

Derrida is not arguing that messages come to us in some pure world beyond the context. He does, however, question the therapeutic conviction that all messages can be "happily" (to use one of Austin's key words) located within "the presence of a fulfilled and actualized intentionality, adequate to itself and to its contents" ("Limited Inc," 203). Derrida insists that "[e]very sign, linguistic or nonlinguistic, spoken or written, . . . as a small or large unity, can be *cited,* put between quotation marks; thereby it can break with every given context, and engender infinitely new contexts in an absolutely nonsaturable fashion" ("Signature Event Context," 320). For Derrida this implies a liberatory politics of the text. The urge to confine statements/texts to defining contexts is, for him, an authoritarian attempt to maintain a given order of signification ("Limited Inc," 250).

Foucault helps us to understand the significance of this antitherapeutic and antihistoricist argument for the historicist politics of the text explored in the first chapter, and helps us to tie it back to Kant. Foucault argues that the hermeneutical approach to history, which aims at "the slow exposure of the meaning hidden in an origin" ("Nietzsche," 151), is a mystification of the true nature of historical interpretation. His description of a history purged of metaphysical illusion resumes all the

---

most easily accessible now in *Limited Inc* (Searle's text, unfortunately, is not reprinted in that work). I have used a different translation of "Signature Event Context," from *Margins of Philosophy* (307–30), and have referred to the "original" "Limited Inc" from *Glyph 2.*

points of anxiety of the Enlightenment problematic that gave rise to the
therapeutic discourse, but he embraces and promotes the fragmentation
that therapeutic discourse seeks to "heal": "[T]he historical sense can
evade metaphysics and become a privileged instrument of genealogy if
it refuses the certainty of absolutes. Given this, it corresponds to the
acuity of a glance that distinguishes, separates, and disperses, that is
capable of liberating divergence and marginal elements—the kind of
dissociating view that is capable of decomposing itself, capable of shat-
tering the unity of man's being through which it was thought that he
could extend his sovereignty to the events of his past" (152–53).
Foucault is engaged in explicating Nietzsche's second *Untimely Meditation*, and Derrida's *Spurs: Nietzsche's Styles* contains a neat exemplification of the problem of text and context, making its connection to a
Nietzschean problematic explicit.[21] For both authors, texts and speech
acts exist in a "'non-place,' the endlessly repeated play of dominations"
(Foucault, "Nietzsche," 150)—Nietzsche's realm of the irrational will to
power.

Gilles Deleuze helps us link this back to Kant. In his *Foucault*, he
suggests that Foucault's concept of "power" is a transformation of the
Kantian "imagination" that unites the understanding with the faculty of
sensuous intuition; the homology stems from their role as a third position from which two discrete "languages" ("distinct jurisdictions," to
use Kant's formulation) can be brought into contact. "Pouvoir" bridges
the gap between "le déterminable et la détermination, le visible et
l'énonçable, la réceptivité de la lumière et la spontanéité du langage"[22]
(75; see 76ff. for the link to "pouvoir")—a gap that Deleuze identifies as
Foucault's Nietzschean "non-place" from "Nietzsche, Genealogy, History": "un 'non-lieu' qui témoigne de ce que les adversaires n'appartien-
nent pas au même espace" (75).[23]

This irreducible division that calls forth a "higher" order—even if
only an "order" of the irrational "play of dominations"—is central to the
poststructuralist "fragmentation" of discourse and subjectivity. If we
pick up on Kant's juridical language, we can trace this, in particular, in
the work of Jean-François Lyotard. Judgment, for Lyotard, is precisely

---

21. See the discussion of the "unreadable" Nietzschean fragment—"I have forgotten my
umbrella"; it is all too easy to make this text "mean" despite the impossibility of referring it to
a context, which makes us aware of how ephemeral the bond between our own speech acts
and their "performative context" is (Derrida, *Spurs*, 123–45).

22. "the determinable and determination, the visible and the articulable, the receptivity of
light and the spontaneity of language" (*Foucault*, 68).

23. "a 'non-place' which bears witness to the fact that the opponents do not belong to the
same space" (*Foucault*, 68).

the problem; the archetypal political situation occurs when conflicting discourses come into conflict, with only an uncertain access to a third position within which the conflict might be "judged." This absolute and irreducible conflict he calls "le différend," and he notes that it inhabits or produces a "néant" rather like Foucault's "non-lieu": "[L]a politique n'est pas du tout un genre, elle témoigne du néant qui s'ouvre à chaque phrase occurante et à l'occasion duquel le différend naît entre les genres de discours" (*Le différend*, 204).[24]

One model for this situation is the Kantian "antithetic" of pure reason. Here, two fundamentally different ways of approaching the world, the transcendent and the phenomenological, come into conflict: "Le *Streit*, le conflit qui divise la raison avec elle-même dans son usage dialectique, ne peut pas être tranché (*nicht abzuurteilenden*) devant le tribunal qui en est saisi. On se dispute pour rien (*um nichts*)" (Lyotard, "Judicieux dans le différend," 209).[25]

All the elements of the *différend* are here, except that this is resolvable. Kant dismisses the conflict(s) as a *question mal posée:* each approach is correct in its own terms. The true *différend* presents itself as an ironic conflict where both the "impossibility and necessity" of a solution are fully felt. But unlike the therapeutic irony we have so far examined, the poststructuralist irony refuses any appeal to a resolving Absolute. The subject is riven by the political struggle of the different discourses that seek to incorporate it (218).

Kant helps the poststructuralists conceptualize this division and disengagement as not just a fact of the subject's being in the world, but a fact of the subject's relationship to itself. In the first *Critique*, Kant writes that the "intuition of self . . . is not, as if it could represent itself immediately and as spontaneously and independently active, but according to the manner in which it is internally affected, consequently as it appears to itself, not as it is" (40). This is roughly the same "break" that Derrida identifies in the subject's communication with itself.

The antitherapeutic and therapeutic derivations from Kant are "half-full"/"half-empty" ways of approaching the same Kantian dilemma. Both accept the (ironic/fallen) fragmentation of the subject and world as a starting point. For both of them, a third, higher position is called forth

24. "[P]olitics is not at all a genre, it bears witness to the nothingness which opens up with each occurring phrase and on the occasion of which the differend between genres of discourse is born" (*The Differend*, 141).

25. "The conflict (*Streit*) of reason with itself in its dialectical usage cannot be resolved (*nicht abzuurteilenden*) before the tribunal of reason. We would be arguing about nothing (*um nichts*)" ("Judiciousness in Dispute," 37).

by this fragmentation. But for one this higher position is a sheer imposition, always liable to be repeated in a *horizontal* realm (a "non-lieu") of "endlessly repeated dominations"; for the other this third position is the aesthetic absolute in which all the fragments find their expressive location. Kant is radically undecided on the point (even in the "therapeutic" third *Critique* he talks of the "distinct jurisdictions" of reason and understanding). When Taylor writes that "Foucault disconcerts" because "certain of Foucault's most interesting historical analyses, while they are highly original, seem to lie along already familiar lines of critical thought" ("Foucault on Freedom and Truth," 69), this uncanny familiarity stems from the "critical" origins of Foucault's thought.

Eagleton is wrong, however, to suggest that Lyotard's "judging without concepts is clearly a derivative of Kant's aesthetic taste" (*Aesthetic*, 398). The therapeutic model of a free conformity to law is radically called into question by the poststructuralists, who reread such a conformity as the product of political imposition. Where the Kantian aesthetic does enter the antitherapeutic approach is, above all, through Schopenhauer and his influence on Nietzsche and Freud.

Kant defines the work of art as that which pleases us *"apart from any interest"* and *"apart from concepts"* (*Judgement*, 50). The therapeutic import of this is that we discover in the sensuous world a purely intellectual interest, thereby reconciling the two halves of our divided being. Schopenhauer rather turns this around; for him, the separation of the aesthetic object from "interest" and the "concept" becomes a radical disengagement from the fallen world of the implacable will: "[A]esthetic pleasure in the beautiful consists . . . in the fact that, when we enter the state of pure contemplation, we are raised for the moment above all willing, above all desires and cares; we are, so to speak, rid of ourselves" (2:390) It is the work of art's disengagement from this world that allows us to see the world for what it is. The Nietzschean/Foucauldian view of the world as a "'non-place,' the endlessly repeated play of dominations," makes sense only from a perspective in which we can envision an art product or speech act beyond the will—or outside history. This is the Derridean "break" that allows us to imagine the message falling promiscuously under the regime of a will different from that which initiated it.

When literary criticism tries to develop an antitherapeutic approach to the text, it is not surprising that this Schopenhauerian aesthetic looms large. But the consequences for an antitherapeutic politics of the text are problematic. This is perhaps best exemplified in the work of Paul de Man.

De Man's entire critical endeavor could be seen as an attempt to prob-

lematize the relationship between the literary work of art and the world
of the will. Although de Man is now a favorite target of those seeking to
prove deconstructionism's dubious political import, or, rather, its dangerous refusal of political "engagement" (Eagleton, *Aesthetic,* 358), de
Man's approach to the text is relevant to my argument because it is
expressly a political one (*Resistance to Theory,* 10–11). The Schopenhauerian perception that a text divorced from the world exposes the
"play of dominations" that seek to control it gives a direct political significance to de Man's problematization of the rhetorical force of the
text:

> Literature is fiction not because it somehow refuses to acknowl-
> edge "reality," but because it is not *a priori* certain that language
> functions according to principles which are those, or which are
> *like* those, of the phenomenal world. It is therefore not *a priori*
> certain that literature is a reliable source of information about
> anything but its own language. . . . What we call ideology is
> precisely the confusion of linguistic with natural reality. . . .
> Those who reproach literary theory for being oblivious to social
> and historical (that is to say ideological) reality are merely stating
> their fear at having their own ideological mystifications exposed
> by the tool they are trying to discredit. They are, in short, very
> poor readers of Marx's *German Ideology.* (11)

This acontextual perspective enables de Man to "unmask" the resistance to theory as "in the last analysis . . . always based on some form of
religious faith" ("Return to Philology," 26), but it remains politically
problematic. At some point, if the text is to act in the world, and if we
are to act politically, we need to be able to theorize our engagement
with the world as something other than a mere genre confusion. While
de Man stresses that the "notion of a language entirely freed of referen-
tial constraints is properly inconceivable" (*Allegories,* 49), he gives us
no way out of Schopenhauer's Olympian distaste for the world. His entire critical movement is to problematize a connection that he assumes
we take for granted.

Moreover, while it is useful to "expose" the sublimated theological
underpinnings of the therapeutic "acceptance" and "acknowledgment"
of the world, we also need a critical position that can understand and
accept (even as it tries to move beyond) the very real rewards of the
therapeutic imperative. "Exposing" the roots of the therapeutic tendency is not a very devastating blow for it. The whole point of our

fallen nature is that it requires a leap of faith to carry us back to the Absolute. That the Absolute is not "actually" present is not a revelation. The essence of faith is that, by acting "as if" the divine order is immediately present to us, we shall make it so. This is why Cavell, in his struggle against skepticism, insists that "skepticism is a *natural* possibility of [our] condition; it reveals most perfectly the standing threat to thought and communication, that they are only human, nothing more than natural to us. One misses the drive of Wittgenstein if one is not . . . sufficiently open to the threat of skepticism (i.e., to the skeptic in oneself) or if one takes Wittgenstein . . . to deny the truth of skepticism" (*Claim of Reason,* 47).

3

Shelley's Idealism

SHELLEY AMONG THE POST-KANTIANS

To understand Shelley's position in this problematic, we must examine the nature of his interest in Romantic idealism, asking what access he had to the principal formulations of the therapeutic imperative and whether a specifically therapeutic idealism can be discerned in Shelley's writing. Although Shelley's idealism is hardly a new topic in Shelley studies, there have been surprisingly few convincing attempts to identify and describe that idealism. It is no longer necessary to make the argument against reading Shelley as a committed Platonist,[1] but we should beware of falling into the error of assuming that if he was not a Platonist, this means either that he was completely uninterested in idealism or that his idealism was completely idiosyncratic. Most Shelley critics who invoke Shelley's "idealism" do so with little or no explicit attempt to define the term.[2] It is true that Shelley is a powerfully origi-

---

1. Curran sums up what remains the contemporary near consensus on Shelley's attitude to Plato in his excellent bibliography ("Shelley," 620–21). William Scott observed a long time ago ("Shelley's Admiration for Bacon") that Shelley almost always collocates praise for Plato with praise for Bacon, which demonstrates that Shelley's admiration for Plato did not necessarily imply agreement with him. Shelley's remark that he would take Plato as his "model" in writing a "systematical" account of "the genuine elements of human society" (preface to *Prometheus Unbound*, in Reiman and Powers, 135) is actually an echo of the arch-skeptic Drummond, who with utter indifference to their opposed philosophies proposes Plato as the ideal model for all philosophical writing (318).

2. This claim is difficult to document; one cannot quote examples of Shelley's idealism not being specified. One telling case may serve to suggest the general state of play. In William

nal and syncretic thinker, but if we understand the ways in which his thought can be related to the mainstreams of philosophy and critical/poetic practice in his time, we are better able to understand the originality of his contribution.

The best available discussion of Shelley's idealism remains Wasserman's influential account in *Shelley: A Critical Reading.* Although he notes in passing that Shelley "followed in his own peculiar way the direction of eighteenth-century empiricism toward idealism, and then . . . advanced to something like the philosophy of the post-Kantian idealists" (140), the main thrust of his account is the portrayal of a specifically Shelleyan idealism: the theory of the poetic "One Mind."

Wasserman's erudite account is very useful; the idealism he describes is recognizable as a Schellingian therapeutic idealism with the role of the poet vis-à-vis the One Mind substituted for the poet's self-discovery in the Absolute. There are two problems, however. First, he rather overstates Shelley's commitment to this idealism; and second, he manages to draw this portrait with not a single reference to Schiller and two passing nods to Fichte and Schelling that go no further than to evoke the fusion of subject and object in Schelling's "objective idealism" (142; see 140, 143 n. 36). Although Wasserman's "One Mind" has found few champions in subsequent Shelley criticism, it should be held accountable, in large part, for the curious critical isolation of Shelley's idealism from contemporary idealist philosophy. Those critics who reject his portrait of Shelley as a thoroughgoing idealist still retain the notion that insofar as Shelley did dally with idealism, it was some peculiar Shelleyan version.

Meyer Abrams's two classic studies of Romantic theory, *The Mirror and the Lamp* and *Natural Supernaturalism,* do, in a sense, place Shelley in relation to the grand lines of Romantic and post-Romantic thought. Although these works remain essential analyses of Romanticism, there are good reasons to be dissatisfied with his account of Shelley's position. His perspective is so dominated by the Platonized, or Neoplatonized, Christian redemption he sees as underlying all Romantic thought, that he either misreads Shelley as more enthusiastically Neoplatonic

---

Ulmer's conscious attempt to reopen the question of Shelley's idealism and to swim against the skeptical current of Shelley criticism it is remarkable that his definition and description of Shelley's idealism hardly ever go beyond the generic and that he implies that Shelley's idealism is *sui generis,* evidently feeling no need to place it in relationship to any other philosophical or literary school (*Shelleyan Eros;* see, e.g., 11ff. and 24, where he makes the case for Shelley's "metaphorical idealism"). It is equally revealing that in Curran's Shelley bibliography, after having disposed of the Shelley-as-Platonist question in the "Shelley's Thought" section, he does not even address the question of other possible frameworks for Shelley's idealism.

than he was or marginalizes him as a troubling anomaly. The marginalization is particularly troubling. When Abrams suggests that Shelley had "imperfectly assimilated" his skepticism and his idealism, or that he "knew little or nothing" of post-Kantian idealism (*Mirror and the Lamp*, 126; *Natural Supernaturalism*, 256), it is possible to discern a strategy of exclusion that rereads Shelley's complex use and criticism of the idealist position as simple "confusion," rendering the threateningly disruptive merely muddled.

One of the more suggestive accounts of Shelley's idealism remains Harold Bloom's *Shelley's Mythmaking*—generally regarded as hopelessly outdated. Particularly useful is his suggestion that Shelley's poetry can be read, with "less violence than the Platonized readings," as a "prayer for the continuance of co-operating grace" (42). Although Bloom overreads the theological ramifications of Shelley's search for epiphanic relationships with various Thous, it is true that a search for grace, with all that implies of the agony of doubt, the brief and unsustainable moments of epiphany, and the aching sense of the profanity of the self and the purity of the other, captures well the uncertain, unsystematic, and punctual nature of Shelley's moments of aspiration toward the supersensible.

I

Shelley was not as ignorant of post-Kantian criticism as critics have suggested. His access to their thought was largely secondhand, which makes it implausible to suggest particular debts or borrowings, but he was well aware of its major outlines and understood its significance as a response to the perceived limitations of Enlightenment thought.

It is part of our historicist prejudice against inquiring into the promiscuous career in consumption of the literary text that makes this kind of "influence" seem inaccessible to, or insignificant in, critical analysis; only immediate contact with the moment of production "counts" as an authentic experience of the text. For my purposes, however, it hardly matters that Shelley may never have read any of the principal works of post-Kantian idealism, if I can show that he had access to its most important arguments (and, even more important for the poet, its patterns of imagery) as well as the impulse of the Enlightenment dilemma to drive him to explore these arguments and this imagery to their depths. He did not need to be able to relate them completely to their context of production in order to be able to use them for his own poetic, political, and philosophical purposes.

We can divide the question of Shelley's access to therapeutic idealism into two different but related areas: first, his access to the sources that the post-Kantians themselves drew upon, and second, his access to their thought. Much of the first area has been more than adequately covered by existing Shelley criticism. Abrams, for example, reads Shelley as a product of the same Neoplatonized Christianity that produces post-Kantian idealism, and we know that Shelley, even if we do not wish to see him as a "Platonist," was well versed in Platonic and Neoplatonic theory.[3] More important, he was an excellent biblical scholar, and particularly fascinated by the figure of Christ.[4] While he explicitly repudiates the Neoplatonic influence on Christianity as a corruption of its original message,[5] there is no doubt that Shelley is interested in a complex of Christian motifs that are central to the more or less sublimated theology of the therapeutic imperative. One such motif is the search for grace identified by Bloom, which implies both the desire for a sustained contact with a divinity, or Absolute, and our fallen condition, which renders that contact frustratingly inconstant; another is the apocalyptic accession to a new order that will heal our fallen and divided state, which many critics have detected in Shelley's liberal borrowings from Revelations.

Two important sources of therapeutic idealism whose impact on Shelley awaits a definitive treatment are Spinoza and Winckelmann.

Spinoza's influence on post-Kantian thought is pervasive.[6] From 1817 to 1821, a period that covers the production of most of his major poetry, Shelley returned again and again to the task of translating Spinoza's *Tractatus Theologico-Politicus* (*Letters*, 2:486). In it, he would have found adumbrated several of the central ideas of the therapeutic imperative. Spinoza's fundamental goal is the intuiting of the individual within the Absolute. His *deus sive natura* suggests that to see ourselves as

---

3. The classic study remains Notopoulos. Rogers is also helpful for details of Shelley's reading of Plato and others.

4. Webb's *Shelley: A Voice Not Understood* and *The Violet in the Crucible* are particularly useful in understanding the biblical influence on Shelley, and his interest in Christ. See also David Fuller's useful "Shelley and Jesus."

5. In one of his notes to *Queen Mab* Shelley writes on the corruption of the original reformist, revolutionary potential of Christ's message by its "rolling through the lapse of ages, [meeting] with the reveries of Plato and the reasonings of Aristotle, and acquir[ing] force and extent until the divinity of Jesus became a dogma" (Hutchinson, 820).

6. This is particularly true of Coleridge, who earns a special section under the entry "Spinozism" in the *Encyclopedia of Philosophy*. Shelley's and Coleridge's shared interest in Spinoza must have done much to help Shelley understand Coleridge's often rather disjointed philosophical arguments.

completely given to the coherent, unified, and unbreakable laws of nature is also to see ourselves as united in the one, absolute substance that
is God. In this sense, he anticipates the Kantian aesthetic free conformity to law. The final goal of Spinoza's ethics is for individuals freely to
acknowledge the conformity of their wills to the absolute, necessitarian
order of nature. This is a "law without a law" in that there is no punishment for transgressors beyond the sense of one's disengagement from
the higher order: "[W]e see that the highest reward of the Divine law is
the law itself, namely, to know God and to love Him of our free choice,
and with an undivided and fruitful spirit; while its penalty is the absence of these things, and being in bondage to the flesh—that is, having
an inconstant and wavering spirit" (62). That this opposition to "division" is specifically an opposition to the "disengagement" of Cartesian
dualism would only add to the urgency of Spinoza's argument for someone as steeped in the Enlightenment dilemma as Shelley.

Spinoza's ardent defense of freedom of thought and speech, and promotion of (for his time) a radically open democracy, might appear standard elements of the Enlightenment attack on superstition and tradition;
in fact, they stem from a vision of the citizen's relationship to the state
that contains key elements of the therapeutic relationship. Spinoza's argument for freedom of opinion (the premise on which he allows himself to submit the Bible to a rational exegesis) does not stem from a
belief that all opinions are ultimately equal and that we must therefore
support, in Lyotard's phrase, "the multiplication of small narratives"
(qtd. in Eagleton, *Aesthetic,* 399), but rather from the certainty that the
open discussion of ideas will eliminate significant error, hastening the
ultimate conformity of our will and belief with the absolute order of
reason and nature. Spinoza's democratic state is the ideal context for
this free conformity to reason because it anticipates the Hegelian *Sittlichkeit* in which we give freedom content by freely willing our subjection to the law. Subjection to arbitrary power, Spinoza argues, has given
us a "slave's" conception of freedom—in which we recognize Burke's
and Hegel's "abstract, revolutionary freedom"—that "slaves obey commands and free men live as they like; but this idea is based on a miscon-
ception, for the true slave is he who is led away by his pleasures and
can neither see what is good for him nor act accordingly: he alone is
free who lives with free consent under the entire guidance of reason"
(206).

Spinoza suggests that a democracy is the best ordered and most obedient of all societies because its subjects, like those of Hegel's ideal
State, recognize the will of the law as ultimately their own: "[A] subject

[opposed here to a "slave"] obeys the orders of the sovereign power, given for the common interest, wherein he is included. . . . [N]o one transfers his natural right so absolutely that he has no further voice in affairs, he only hands it over to the majority of a society, whereof he is a unit" (207). The freedom of opinion and speech central to democratic society ensures that the majority's commands will always be in conformity with reason; the individual instantiates the state, and through the state, the absolute order of nature, which is revealed to us in reason. Spinoza shows us just how far one can go toward post-Kantian idealism in a Judeo-Christian tradition without drawing on a Neoplatonized Christianity.

Like Schelling, Spinoza attempts to intuit history as an Absolute, if not diachronically, at least synchronically. If God is nature, and nature is an absolutely necessary unity, then everything must "fit together" in any given time. Significantly—in Shelley's day, notoriously—this leads Spinoza to an argument for the historicist interpretation of the Bible as a revelation adapted to the minds of its contemporary readers: "[T]he books of both Testaments were not written by express command at one place for all ages, but are a fortuitous collection of the works of men, writing each as his period and disposition dictated" (170). This gives Shelley a preview of the movement from the therapeutic location of the citizen-in-the-state and the individual-in-the-world to the historicist placement of the text-in-(social)-context. It is interesting to note that the immediate effect of such a placement, in this case at least, is to *strip* the text of much of its "real power." To tie the Bible to its historic conditions of production has always been resisted by believers because it threatens to make its consumption in the present seem inauthentic and irrelevant.

Winckelmann also addresses the question of the relationship of the text to its productive social context. The study of Shelley's indebtedness to Winckelmann (whose *Geschichte der Kunst des Altherthums* he read—in a French translation—in late 1818, early 1819 [White, *Shelley*, 2:66, 75]) has been restricted rather unreasonably to his influence on Shelley's artistic (in the narrow sense) sensibilities. It was in large part Winckelmann, however, on whom both Schiller and Schlegel drew in the construction of their naive/classical–versus–sentimental/Romantic dichotomies. Winckelmann argues that the greatness of classical art lies in the ancients' untrammeled connection with the natural world. Their art is the triumph of an absolute simplicity and unity to which we cannot aspire: "Much that might seem ideal to us was natural among them" (114; see also 118-19). The union with nature, which they took for granted, was natural to them *because* they took it for granted. It is now our "ideal" and for that very reason unattainable because we self-consciously strive to achieve it.

If Winckelmann does not quite make the argument in this Schillerian/ Schlegelian form, he gives us all the elements. For him, the decline of Greek art comes with the "Style of the Imitators" (133): artistic self-consciousness (the ironic gap between intention and action) is the origin of our fall from grace. Through Winckelmann, Shelley had access to a rough sketch of the therapeutic imperative: the subject was once in a state of absolute union with the object, but by becoming aware of itself as subject over against the object, it has fallen into a state where it yearns for its original unity as an ideal whole. The only route Winckelmann leaves partially open for attaining that ideal is the expressive unity of the work of art. Winckelmann is not very optimistic about our chances. Classical art stands, for him, as a high-water mark of artistic endeavor that we shall never pass again.

There remains one other important "source" of therapeutic idealism that Shelley was familiar with, though it is, in part, a negative route to the therapeutic. This is the Enlightenment dilemma to which post-Kantian idealism is in large part a response. I have been at pains to emphasize the fact that the attempt to think the Many as One can be derived as much from atomistic materialism as from Neoplatonic emanations, because Shelley's profound debt to the philosophers of the Enlightenment is amply documented. The relationship between Shelley's Enlightenment skepticism and his idealism usually figures in Shelley criticism as either a paradox or as alternate stages: problem and solution. This duality, as I have shown, was always central to the Enlightenment project. If Kant appears to us as a pivotal figure, with his divided imagery of organic synthesis, on the one hand, and cartographic analysis, on the other, we should realize that Shelley had access to the same divided imagery in the very heartland of the Enlightenment: Diderot's *Encyclopédie*.

Diderot's *Prospectus* to this work (which Shelley probably read,[7]

---

7. Shelley ordered the *Encyclopédie* in late 1812 from his publisher, Hookham (*Letters,* 1:342) and urgently and repeatedly renewed the request shortly afterward (1:354). He also ordered Diderot's *Oeuvres* at the same time (1:342), which, if he was referring to the Paris edition of 1798, included Diderot's *Prospectus* to the *Encyclopédie*, on which I shall be drawing. If he received (or came across elsewhere) either set of volumes, it would be reasonable to assume the *Prospectus* (in either work) would have been among the first things to which he would turn. The Abbé Barruel had already suggested to Shelley that the *Encyclopédistes* were part of the great conspiracy that led to the French Revolution (Darnton, 183; I am indebted to Darnton's discussion of the *Encyclopédie* in what follows), and the *Prospectus* was one of the principal texts outlining the aims and methods of the editors. Shelley's *Proposals for an Asso-*

though we cannot be sure) suggests, on the one hand, that philosophers are, like Kant's subject, stuck on a tiny island of certitude with a "mer d'objets qui nous environnent" (7-8).[8] This sea is, like Kant's, a hostile one; the few definite objects appear "comme des pointes de rochers qui semblent percer la surface et dominer les autres" (8),[9] because (Diderot is reverting to his Lucretian atomistic dilemma) "[l]a nature ne nous offre que des choses particulières, infinies en nombre, et sans aucune division fixe et déterminée" (7).[10] On the other hand, however, the project of the *Encyclopédie* is to impose order on this hostile sea of irreducible data. D'Alembert's image for this, which Kant will revive, of a "mappemonde" (Darnton, 194-95), places this attempt squarely in the classical *epistēmē* of "grands déroulements horizontaux de la *taxinomia*"[11] described by Foucault (*Les mots et les choses*, 263). This taxinomia, however, suggests to Diderot an *organic* image: the "arbre de la connaissance humaine" (*Prospectus*, 7),[12] which he draws up for us as the unifying, organizing principle of the mass of "chose particulières" dealt with in the *Encyclopédie*'s individual entries. The "tree" captures the double movement of Enlightenment thought, down toward the "horizontal" world of facts, to be sure, but equally upward in a vertical aspiration to the Absolute, which Foucault only recognizes in the Romantic rejection of the classical *epistēmē* (*Order of Things*, 251): "[L]e premier pas que nous avions à faire vers l'exécution raisonnée et bien entendue d'une Encyclopédie, c'était de former un arbre généalogique de toutes les sciences et de tous les arts, qui marquât l'origine de chaque branche de nos connaissance, les liasons qu'elles ont entre elles et avec la tige commune, et qui nous servît à rappeler les différents articles à leurs chefs" (*Prospectus*, 7).[13]

---

ciation of Philanthropists frankly (and with a measure of anticipatory glee) avows that "the Revolution of France was occasioned by the literary labors of the Encyclopaedists" (Ingpen and Peck, 5:264), whom he then proceeds to praise as bringers of wisdom and encouragers of enlightenment, much like the members of his proposed association.

    8. "sea of objects that surrounds us" (my translation).

    9. "like the tips of rocks that seem to break the surface and dominate the others" (my translation).

    10. "nature only offers us particular things, infinite in number, and without any fixed or determinate division" (my translation).

    11. "great horizontal deployments of the *taxinomia*" (*Order of Things*, 251).

    12. "tree of human knowledge" (my translation).

    13. "The first step that we had to make toward the reasoned and properly understood execution of an Encyclopedia was to form a genealogical tree of all the sciences and of all the arts that marked the origin of each branch of our knowledge, the connections that they have between themselves and with the common trunk, and that allowed us to place the different articles under their proper headings" (my translation).

The tree unfolds all human knowledge from the three faculties of memory, reason, and imagination, which in turn are the principal divisions of the original trunk: the understanding (28, fig.). Diderot insists on the unity this brings to the work; the *Encyclopédie* is a "system" of human knowledge, not a mere aggregation of "what we know now," just as a swarm is something more than a mere aggregation of individual bees. The very word "encyclopedia" carries this promise of organic unity: Diderot returns again and again to the image of an "*enchaînement* des sciences*" (his translation of the Greek [1]), which guarantees the absolute organic necessity of every entry in the work: "[I]l n'en est pas ici des omissions comme dans un autre ouvrage. L'Encyclopédie, à la rigeur, n'en permet aucune. Un article omis dans un dictionnaire commun, le rend seulement imparfait. Dans une Encyclopédie, il rompt l'enchaînement et nuit à la forme et au fond" (6).[14]

We are far, now, from the apparent paralysis before the chaotic infinity of "choses particulières," and the gap to, say, Schelling's attempt to intuit the Absolute seems very narrow—briefly crossed, perhaps, in d'Alembert's suggestion that "the universe, to someone who could embrace it from a single point of view, would be so to speak only a single fact and one great truth" (qtd. in Darnton, 204).[15]

Turning now to Shelley's direct access to the products of post-Kantian idealism, the first question that confronts us is whether or not he read Kant. Unfortunately, we cannot say with any certainty.[16] His direct references to "the criticism of pure reason" are inconclusive.[17] There are

14. "Omissions here are a different matter from those in another type of work. The Encyclopedia, rigorously speaking, does not allow a single one. An article omitted from a common dictionary simply renders it imperfect. In an Encyclopedia, it is a break in the chain that damages both form and substance" (my translation).

15. This is from the *Discours préliminaire* to the *Encyclopédie,* which Shelley could only have read (but, again, undoubtedly would have) if he had access to that work.

16. The question is discussed in both Stokoe, 156–57, and Klapper, 51ff.

17. That phrase occurs in a letter to Claire quoted by Stokoe (156–57), with some general comments about German versus French philosophy. Not mentioned by Stokoe or Klapper are three references to "pure anticipated cognition," by which Shelley evidently intends the synthetic a priori. The first of these is in the note to line 534 of "Peter Bell the Third," where Shelley, punning on Wordsworth's name, suggests that the progenitor who selected it must have had "*a pure anticipated cognition* of the nature and modesty of this ornament of his posterity" (Reiman and Powers, 341). The second is in a letter to Mary Shelley where he refers to a freak apparition of "the *perfect figure* . . . of a Capuchin friar" in the marble of a church in Ravenna as "a pure anticipated cognition of a Capuchin" (*Letters,* 2:321). The last is in a letter to Leigh Hunt in which he refers to his portrait of the Lady in the *Sensitive Plant* as "*pure anticipate cognition*" of Jane Williams (2:438). While these suggest at least some acquaintance with the details of Kant's philosophy, the only direct references that offer any judgment upon Kant's work, with the exception of his apt reference to Kant in the "Triumph of Life," seem to

several remarkably "Kantian" moments in Shelley's writing, but none that conclusively proves direct influence. M. R. Klapper emphasizes how ardently Shelley pursued copies of Kant's works at different times (51–52), and F. W. Stokoe rightly suggests that Hogg's opinion that Shelley never read Kant, supported by his well-known quip about the uncut Latin edition on Shelley's shelves, is dubious evidence (156–57). Hogg may have thought he was doing Shelley a good turn by dissociating him from German philosophy. The chief threat to Shelley's early reputation was the attempt by a conservative criticism to marginalize Shelley's poetry as "Babylonish jargon" and "insufferable buffoonery" (White, *Shelley,* 2:132). To call someone a Kantian at this time in England was as good as calling that person an incomprehensible and rather ludicrous mystic (as Coleridge knew to his cost). This also makes Peacock's comic portrait of Shelley as Scythrop dubious evidence. On the one hand, Peacock identifies him as a Kantian, which might be some indication that Shelley had tried to interest Peacock in Kant's work, but on the other hand, "Kantian" here seems to mean nothing more specific than an adept of "mystical jargon and necromantic imagery" (Peacock, *Nightmare Abbey,* 191). No doubt Peacock would smile wryly at the notion of trying to use his books to "prove" anything at all.

Perhaps the most intriguing piece of evidence, though hardly conclusive, is Mary Shelley's claim, from her 1840 preface to Shelley's *Essays, Letters from Abroad, Etc.,* that the "theory of mind" Shelley was gradually constructing was one "to which Berkeley, Coleridge, and Kant would have contributed" (Ingpen and Peck, 5:xi). It is hard to imagine what would have suggested these three names to Mary Shelley other than some concrete recollection; Shelley's predilection for Scythropian metaphysics rather pained Mary, and one would assume she would have preferred not to draw more attention to it than honesty compelled. Mary Shelley partook of and witnessed a more representative sample of Shelley's intellectual life than anyone else—including that most revealing and most ephemeral area of intellectual labor, private conversation. Her descriptions of Shelley's philosophy should not be discounted, as they too often are.

In Drummond, as I have mentioned, Shelley found a long and detailed critique of Kant's philosophy. Drummond, however, misreads Kant, in a

---

be under the influence of Drummond's (and Peacock's) view of Kant as a flighty mystic. The "pure anticipated cognition" seems to figure in Shelley's mind as an occult prescience rather than an axiom of the understanding, although in all these cases (and in the most sustained evocation of the first *Critique,* lines 518–32 of "Peter Bell the Third") Shelley is joking; the whole point of the joke may be the incongruity of the Kantian term and the subject matter.

way typical of Englishmen of his time, as dogmatically proposing that we have some mysterious direct intuition of the categories. It appears that the mere conjunction of "mind" and "a priori" was a red rag to a bull for Englishmen in the Lockean tradition.

Shelley was, however, profoundly influenced by the work of two authors both characteristic of post-Kantian philosophy: August Wilhelm Schlegel and Coleridge.

The impression made upon Shelley by Schlegel's *Lectures on Dramatic Art and Literature* (in John Black's lively 1815 translation, which he read in 1818) has been noted (Klapper, 53–54; Curran, *Annus Mirabilis*, 33), but the significance of this text as a direct link to post-Kantian idealism, not only for Shelley but for early-nineteenth-century English literary culture in general, has not been fully appreciated.[18] Our lack of interest in this text stems from our prejudice for the moment of production. We know that A. W. Schlegel was not a philosophical "originator" but a popularizer of the work of others; therefore his work becomes inauthentic and unimportant. Yet Schlegel's extraordinary contemporary reputation, both as one of the first to apply post-Kantian philosophy directly to literary theory and as an interpreter of that theory for Europe's educated classes,[19] in fact makes him ideally suited to convey to Shelley a virtual digest of the characteristic forms of therapeutic idealism; as Foucault says in a related context: "Qu'importe qui parle?" ("Qu'est-ce qu'un auteur," 95).

I shall focus on two fundamental elements of the therapeutic imperative that Shelley would have found fully articulated by Schlegel. The *Lectures on Dramatic Art and Literature* are written completely within the framework of the theory of Romantic Irony expounded by Wilhelm's brother Friedrich, giving Shelley access to the backbone of German Romantic theory. Simpson distracts us from this fact, in his discussion of the links between German and English Romantic Irony, by focusing too narrowly on Schlegel's use of the term "irony" itself (Simpson, 189). To be sure, Schlegel's allusions to "irony" are narrow and technical in emphasis (see, e.g., 140f.). But even here, Schlegel is less dryly technical than Simpson suggests. He refers to Shakespeare's irony

---

18. Wasserman makes no mention of it in his account of Shelley's idealism in *Shelley: A Critical Reading,* nor does it figure in Abrams's *Natural Supernaturalism;* Simpson, too, hastily dismisses Schlegel's account of irony as merely "technical," and on that basis discounts him as a serious influence upon English Romantic Irony (*Irony and Authority,* 189).

19. His prominent role in Madame de Staël's *De l'allemagne* (see, e.g., 2:67–76, 141ff.), a work whose role in expanding the influence of German thought beyond German-speaking countries cannot be overestimated, bears eloquent testimony to his proselytizing role.

as an irony that extends to "the whole of the action," meaning an authorial detachment that Keats, in an important statement of English Romantic irony, will call his "negative capability." But only an inappropriate emphasis on the productive origins of Romantic Irony should lead us to quibble about precise terminology. When A. W. Schlegel writes that "the poetry of the ancients was the poetry of enjoyment, and ours is that of desire: the former has its foundation in the scene which is present, while the latter hovers betwixt recollection and hope" (16), he is summarizing Schiller's and Friedrich Schlegel's schemas: a past of pure connection and unity with nature, and an ironic present of self-conscious "disengagement" and equally self-conscious struggle to recover the lost Absolute.

Even if the word "irony" is not used (Schlegel preferring the obviously related "melancholic"), the pattern of a fall into division and a consequent desire for redemption is unmistakable. The Greek's "natural harmony" (16) was perfect, but also stagnant: "they were conscious of no wants, and aspired at no higher perfection than that which they could actually attain by the exercise of their own faculties." Schlegel makes the post-Kantians' implicit image of the *felix culpa* explicit: "We, however, are taught by superior wisdom that man, through a high offence, forfeited the place for which he was originally destined; and that the whole object of his earthly existence is to strive to regain that situation, which, if left to his own strength, he could never accomplish" (15). Like his brother, he argues that this makes modern "Romantic poetry" (8), although "artificial" (14), a poetry of infinite and progressive striving, haunted always by the ironic/melancholic knowledge that "the happiness after which we strive we can never here attain" (15)—"the modern [art and poetry] can only do justice to its endeavours after what is infinite by approximation; and, from a certain appearance of imperfection, is in greater danger of not being duly appreciated" (17).

Second, like the other post-Kantians, Schlegel understands the role of art in this ironic/melancholic situation as a therapeutic bridge between the divided realms of subject and object, mind and nature: "The moderns . . . have arrived at the consciousness of the internal discord . . . and hence the endeavour of their poetry is to reconcile these two worlds between which we find ourselves divided, and to melt them indissolubly into one another. The impressions of the senses are consecrated, as it were, from their mysterious connexion with higher feelings; and the soul, on the other hand, embodies its forebodings, or nameless visions of infinity, in the phenomena of the senses" (16–17). It would be possible, on the strength of this alone, to argue that Shelley here had tapped directly into the therapeutic line of thought that under-writes the present historicist understanding of the political role of the text. But Schlegel makes the political implications of this aesthetic al-most explicit—quite clear enough, certainly, for a reader like Shelley, whose natural inclinations lead him that way.

It is only too predictable that Schlegel will seize upon organic unity as an image for the complex unity of the Romantic work of art, and he does so in a way that underscores its role as a therapeutic response to the Enlightenment dilemma of aggregation versus integration, to "sep-arating what should not be separated": "It was, generally speaking, the prevailing tendency of the time which preceded our own; a tendency displayed also in physical science, to consider what is possessed of life as a mere accumulation of dead parts, to separate what exists only in connexion and cannot otherwise be conceived, instead of penetrating to the central point and viewing all the parts as so many irradiations from it" (126). The paradigmatic Romantic text—Schlegel's example is Shakespeare—is an intimation of the Absolute in which every part dis-plays its "inward necessity . . . with reference to the whole." Like Burke's or Hegel's counterrevolutionary society, it is an organic totality from which "nothing could be taken away, nothing added, nothing oth-erwise arranged, without mutilating and disfiguring the perfect work" (127). Schlegel makes the connection between the hermeneutical or-ganicism of the text and the organic totality of society quite explicit. The cephalic "central point" about which the therapeutic text is orga-nized is derived from an earlier definition of the "true critic" as the person of sufficient "universality of mind" to "transport himself into the peculiarities of other ages and nations, to feel them as it were from their proper central point" (3).

Schlegel puts these two organicisms together to advocate a histori-cally relativist criticism in which texts are to be read as the "realization" of their productive social context: "[T]he spirit of poetry, which, though imperishable, wanders as it were through different bodies, so often as it is newly born in the human race, must, from the nutrimental substance of an altered age, be fashioned into a body of a different con-formation. . . . No one should be tried before a tribunal to which he does not belong" (95). Schlegel has given Shelley a crash course in the therapeutic-idealist politics of the text.

The relationship between Coleridge and Shelley has not received the attention it merits in Shelley criticism, although John Hodgson's book-length study may indicate that this is changing (*Coleridge, Shelley, and*

Transcendental Inquiry).[20] In 1816, Shelley wrote to Peacock from Geneva, inquiring after "the political state of England—its literature, of which when I speak Coleridge is in my thoughts" (*Letters,* 1:490). While it is true that Byron was with Shelley at this time, and therefore tacitly excluded from Shelley's request, it is nonetheless revealing that Shelley singles Coleridge out in this way as the only contemporary English writer of whom one might expect exciting work. Mary Shelley's comment about Berkeley, Coleridge, and Kant is as interesting in this context as the other.

While Wordsworth's influence on Shelley has been the subject of a great deal of study and speculation,[21] Coleridge's has been comparatively ignored, and yet it is remarkable that while Wordsworth always figures in Shelley's writing as equal parts poet and apostate ("What a beastly and pitiful wretch that Wordsworth! That such a man should be such a poet!" [*Letters,* 2:26]), Shelley's references to Coleridge are unfailingly respectful. Twice, in his poetry, they are directly compared: in the poems "To Wordsworth" and "To _____" from the *Alastor* volume, and in "Peter Bell the Third." In both cases the portrait of Coleridge is markedly more sympathetic than that of Wordsworth. In the later work, particularly, Coleridge is portrayed as a "mighty poet" and "subtle-souled psychologist" (378, 379) whose only failing is an inability to understand his own immensely complex mind; moreover, he directly inspires Peter's/Wordsworth's greatest poetry—a shrewd observation, and an indication of Shelley's estimation of their relative intellectual stature. To this, one might add his repeated urgings to the Gisbornes to press Coleridge to undertake the translation of Goethe's *Faust* (a poem Shelley recognized as one of the greatest of European literature): "No one but Coleridge is capable of this work" (*Letters,* 2:407; see 376).

In the verse letter to Maria Gisborne, Coleridge appears as

> he who sits obscure
> In the exceeding lustre and the pure
> Intense irradiation of a mind
> Which, with its own internal lighting blind,

20. Hodgson, however, is largely interested in drawing a familiar contrast between the two authors, Coleridge the idealist and Shelley the protodeconstructionist. His account is interesting, but not directly relevant to my argument here.

21. Among others, one could mention Blank, *Wordsworth's Influence on Shelley;* Bloom, *The Visionary Company* and *Poetry and Repression;* Wasserman's reading of *Alastor* (*Shelley,* 15–46); and Curran's reading of "Peter Bell the Third" (*Annus Mirabilis*).

Flags wearily through darkness and despair—
A cloud-encircled meteor of the air,
A hooded eagle among blinking owls.

(202–8)

Although there is an element of (apt) criticism in this, it also expresses
an admiration for Coleridge as *philosopher,* which poses a problem for
the more rigorously anti-idealist readings of Shelley. While Wordsworth
always appears in Shelley's writing as a great poet *despite* his odious
political beliefs, Shelley suggests here, in 1820, that Coleridge, whose
political attitudes were equally incompatible with Shelley's, has drawn
erroneous conclusions from a philosophy that at least deserves our serious attention. Shelley marks his critical distance from Coleridge, but
we should attempt to understand what value he saw in a set of ideas
that had led Coleridge to a conservatism not dissimilar to Burke's.

The question of Coleridge's relationship to post-Kantian philosophy is
complicated by the problem of Coleridge's plagiarism (see McFarland;
Fruman). Both his attackers and defenders on this issue share a commitment to the production-oriented author function that obscures one of
Coleridge's major roles for his contemporary readers. To his detractors,
his plagiarisms invalidate his text, rendering it inauthentic (or even "un-
authored") and therefore irrelevant. His defenders can choose either to
bracket them off and salvage what is genuinely "Coleridgean" in his
thought or to argue that the transmuting power of his imagination transformed all he borrowed and "wove it into a larger context of his own,
where 'the organic Whole' is greater than the sum of its parts" (Bate
and Engall, cxviii). Both these approaches fall into a curious paradox
whereby the more detailed and extensive Coleridge's borrowings from
German authors, the less significant their impact on his argument is
supposed to be. When Coleridge outlines the basis of his system in the
Biographia Literaria by translating and paraphrasing the first five pages
of Schelling's *System of Transcendental Idealism,* it is hard to read such
a large and important part of Schelling's "organic" system as an equally
integrated part of some significantly different Coleridgean argument. In
such cases, Coleridge's defenders will fall back on an appeal to our better natures: "In connection with the 'plagiarisms' the reader should bear
in mind the chronology of the work, the circumstances, the pressures
to get it done rapidly, the self-doubts, the exhaustion" (Bate and Engall,
viii). It is remarkable that this "explanation" (as opposed to an "excuse")
for the plagiarisms should be made by the same authors who suggest
Coleridge transforms his borrowings into a new "organic Whole."

While this attempt to cast Coleridge's plagiarisms as an unfortunate lapse (which it would be impolite and cruel to insist upon) is well meant, it obscures for us one of the chief interests of the *Biographia* as a text in consumption—an interest, moreover, upon which Coleridge himself particularly insisted; writing of the "Dynamic System" begun by Bruno, "reintroduced" by Kant, and perfected by Schelling building on Fichte, he says: "[T]o me it will be happiness and honour enough, should I succeed in rendering the system itself intelligible to my countrymen" (1:163). If we insist upon extracting an original Coleridgean genius from the textual patchwork of the *Biographia,* we are unable fully to appreciate the philosophical interest of his, admittedly awkward and disingenuous, attempts in the text to excuse his plagiarisms. Against the tendency of his own Romantic philosophy, Coleridge consciously offers his text up for a promiscuous consumption, quite independent of its context of production: "I regard truth as a divine ventriloquist: I care not from whose mouth the sounds are supposed to proceed, if only the words are audible and intelligible" (1:164). Although they would differ over the "divine" unity of the "truth," there is an interesting homology between this "ventriloquism" and Foucault's "qu'importe qui parle?"

What is important about Coleridge's texts, from the point of view of their influence in English literature and philosophy, is not what went into their production but what people, including Shelley, could derive from their consumption. To begin with, consider the *Biographia,* which Shelley read in late 1817 (Mary Shelley, *Journals,* 1:86) shortly after it was first published. No one could extract any systematic or detailed knowledge of any philosophical position from this dauntingly tangled and disjointed work, but Coleridge does provide a brief sketch of the history of his "dynamic system" in chapter IX, moving through Plato and the Neoplatonists via Giordano Bruno, Jacob Boehme, and Spinoza to Kant, Fichte, and Schelling. Although he gives only a brief sketch of the thought of each, this would have given Shelley at least a rough picture of the development of post-Kantian philosophy, and some knowledge of the different approaches of its principal figures, which is more than most references to his isolation from post-Kantian thought would allow. One could speculate on the relationship between Coleridge's attack on Fichtean egoism (1:158–59) and Shelley's denunciation, in the essay "On Life," of the "monstrous presumption, that I . . . am that one mind" of which we are all but a portion (Reiman and Powers, 478).

More important, the *Biographia* is a poet's cornucopia of brilliant fragments and arresting images drawn almost indiscriminately from all corners of this "library cormorant's" measureless philosophical diet, insistently incorporated (with more or less success) into an unsystematic therapeutic idealism, which rehearses in no particular order almost all the key patterns of images (although more rarely the accompanying arguments) of the post-Kantian idealists. As the voluminous notes to Bate and Engall's edition of the *Biographia* make clear, to read this work is to read, albeit unwittingly for most of Coleridge's contemporaries, a representative selection of key moments from the principal works of Kant and the post-Kantians.

In reproducing the opening pages of Schelling's *System,* Coleridge gives us a précis of the entire work that clearly expresses the therapeutic drive to allay the political and conceptual threat of skepticism by founding epistemology on the original ontological unity of the subject and object. As Coleridge puts it, in his own words, although still drawing heavily on Schelling: "[I]f we elevate our conception to the absolute self, the great eternal I AM, then the principle of being, and of knowledge, of idea, and of reality; the ground of existence, and the ground of the knowledge of existence, are absolutely identical, Sum quia sum; I am because I affirm myself to be; I affirm myself to be, because I am" (1:275).

Coleridge translates a passage of the *System* addressing the problem of how the subject and object, if they are originally one, could generate a dynamic universe: "Des Cartes, speaking as a naturalist, and in imitation of Archimedes, said, give me matter and motion and I will construct you the universe. We must of course understand him to have meant; I will render the construction of the universe intelligible. In the same sense the transcendental philosopher says; grant me a nature having two contrary forces, the one of which tends to expand infinitely, while the other strives to apprehend or *find* itself in this infinity, and I will cause the world of intelligences with the whole system of their representations to rise up before you" (1:296–97; see *System,* 72–73). This division of the original Absolute into a dynamic opposition that tends toward the reestablishment of the Absolute (when the particular is able to "apprehend" itself, by a self-conscious free conformity to the law, in the infinite) is the essence of Schelling's system (qua system) and lies at the heart of the entire therapeutic-idealist project. It is the same enabling opposition that in Fichte's system is characterized as the dynamic interaction of the "centrifugal" and "centripetal" impulses of the absolute ego in its divided state of I and not-I. Significantly, Coleridge also gives his reader this Fichtean account of the Absolute in its dynamic phase: "Bearing then this in mind, that intelligence is a self-development, not a quality supervening to a substance, we may abstract from all *degree,* and for the purpose of philosophic construction reduce it to *kind,* under the idea of an indestructible power with two opposite and counteracting forces, which, by a metaphor borrowed from astronomy, we may call the centrifugal and centripetal forces. The intelligence in the one tends to *objectize* itself, and in the other to *know* itself in the object" (1:286).

If the therapeutic imperative is a response to the radical Enlightenment "separation," or "disengagement," then it is via this movement that that separation is narrativized as a necessary interval between moments of absolute integration. We can recognize here all the branches of the therapeutic imperative that we have explored thus far: the passage from an original Absolute as thesis (naive/classical/static) via the *felix culpa* into the divided, disengaged antithesis (sentimental-ironic/Romantic/dynamic), into divine synthesis, the return to the Absolute at a higher level—the work of art, or Absolute Knowing, where the divided parts become conscious of themselves as moments of the Absolute.

For Coleridge, as for Fichte, knowing commences with the unconditioned act of the absolute ego: "[T]he spirit (originally the identity of object and subject) must in some sense dissolve this identity, in order to be conscious of it: fit alter et idem. But this implies an act, and it follows therefore that intelligence or self-consciousness is impossible, except by and in a will. The self-conscious spirit therefore is a will; and freedom must be assumed as a *ground* of philosophy, and can never be deduced from it" (1:279–80). The self-awareness that is the fruit of this fundamental act, initiating the history of consciousness, is the same "knowledge of good and evil" for which Adam and Eve brought sin and disharmony into the world, and Coleridge's "act" would be easily identified by Shelley, a year later, with Wilhelm Schlegel's "high offense," which precludes we Christian Romantic moderns from attaining the original classical unity-with-nature. In the *Biographia,* as in the *Lectures,* this fall is to be read as a *felix culpa;* we fall into division only to overcome it by developing our self-consciousness into a consciousness of the self as Absolute: "We begin with the I KNOW MYSELF, in order to end with the absolute I AM. We proceed from the SELF, in order to lose and find all self in GOD" (1:283). Coleridge, like Fichte and Schelling, insists upon the importance of self-consciousness as our route to the Absolute. Only in self-consciousness, he argues, can we conceive "an absolute something that is in and of itself at once cause and effect (*causa sui*), subject and object, or rather the absolute identity of both. . . . [I]n a self-consciousness . . . the principium essendi does not stand to the principium cognoscendi in the relation of cause to effect, but both the one and the other are co-inherent and identical" (1:285). If self-consciousness can be led by philosophy to this point, which is also Hegel's Absolute Knowing, then it would deserve the name of a "total and undivided philosophy" (1:282)—that ultimate therapeutic goal which Coleridge can only relegate to his never-to-be-completed *Logosophia.* At such a point, Coleridge, somewhat wistfully, notes: "[P]hilosophy would pass into religion, and religion become inclusive of philosophy" (1:283).

The *Biographia* gave Shelley a more-than-useful crash course in therapeutic idealism. If, after reading it, he could not have described with any accuracy the details of Fichte and Schelling's methodologies, he would nevertheless have had a firm grasp on their goal: to restore the original unity of subject and object, but at a higher level, by developing the self-consciousness of the individual subject to the point where it can intuit itself as an instantiation of the Absolute. Moreover, he would have understood, particularly in the context of his reading in Enlightenment philosophy and of Spinoza, the therapeutic import of these goals. He would have realized how directly they aimed to solve the problems of division and disengagement that haunted Diderot and Hume. Finally, Coleridge would have made clear to him how much the therapeutic promise of this philosophy is both a supersession and confirmation of the redemptive promise of Christianity.

It would be reasonable to object that this leaves Shelley a considerable amount of work to do in order to apply this theological therapeutic to the question of the individual's relationship to the state, and the problems of conceptualizing the political role of poetry. A year before reading the *Biographia,* however, Shelley had read the first of Coleridge's "Lay Sermons," *The Statesman's Manual* (Mary Shelley, *Journals,* 1:153), in which the specifically textual and political versions of the therapeutic imperative are powerfully and clearly stated. Reading the *Biographia* back into *The Statesman's Manual,* Shelley could not have failed to see how Coleridge's metaphysics underpinned the earlier work's political and literary arguments.

We have already seen that in this work Coleridge sets himself to overcome the evil effect of the Enlightenment's rationalist approach to the state: specifically Hume's pernicious obsession with "motives." Coleridge, like Burke, suggests that the "antidote" for this rootless, modern "restless craving for the wonders of the day" will be found in "the collation of the present with the past, in the habit of thoughtfully assimilating the events of our own age to those of the time before us" (*Lay Sermons,* 8, 9). By placing history firmly under the aegis of Mnemosyne in this way, Coleridge—like Burke, Schelling, and Hegel—is able to conceive of the state in time as an organic Absolute. Coleridge applies the same organic image to the state that Diderot and Kant applied to knowledge: the tree (21–22).

This image, a cliché of conservative attempts to win respect for the antiquity and organic unity of the English constitution, allows Coleridge to neutralize the negative potential of all historical change and revolution. The tree of state has a history; it has been "rocked in tempests—the goat, the ass, and the stag gnawed it—the wild boar has whetted his tusks on its bark"; and "even after its full growth . . . the whirlwind has more than once forced its stately top to touch the ground." But Coleridge follows his imagery through to emphasize the mnemonic trace that all these events leave behind on an organic body that incorporates, preserves, and unifies them: "The deep scars are still extant on its trunk, and the path of the lightning may be traced among its higher branches" (22). What to the radical skeptic is unbridgeable discontinuity is to Coleridge narrative peripeteia—in Aristotle's sense of dramatic incident that ultimately serves the unity of the plot—and organic growth.

Imagery like this makes it hard for us to imagine how Shelley could have responded favorably to Coleridge. Had not Shelley, in his *Proposals for an Association* (1812), expressly disavowed the relevance of such arguments? "I hear much of its [the British constitution's] being a tree so long growing which to cut down is as bad as cutting down an oak where there are no more. But the best way, on topics similar to these, is to tell the plain truth, without the confusion and ornament of metaphor" (Ingpen and Peck, 5:261).[22] But as early as 1811, Shelley was avowing to Hogg that "I may not be able to adduce proofs, but I think that the leaf of a tree, the meanest insect on wh. we trample are in themselves arguments more conclusive than any which can be adduced that some vast intellect animates Infinity. . . . I confess that I think Pope's 'all are but parts of one tremendous [*sic*] whole' something more than Poetry, it has ever been my favourite theory" (*Letters,* 1:35). To see himself as a part defining and defined by a wider whole, if philosophically problematic, had undeniable political and emotional appeal to Shelley. Its most pressing form was the desire of the political reformer to feel that he is able, in Hume's words, to "have an effect on conduct and behaviour," to know that he is not so "disengaged" from society that his actions are quite without influence. Shelley's first letter to Godwin, after his remarkable letter of introduction, commences a long and

---

22. Readers of Shelley's prose can judge for themselves how closely Shelley himself adheres to these strictures against metaphor.

never-resolved controversy over the most desirable means of promoting political reform.[23] In opposition to that uncompromising anarchist's hostile suspicion of all associations, which threatened to blur the individual's disengaged integrity, Shelley, in his most active years as a political reformer, insistently sought a point of contact with some broader social movement. He pointedly criticized Godwin's atomistic, piecemeal program for reform: "I am not forgetful or unheeding of what you said of Associations.—But Political Justice was first published in 1793; nearly twenty years have elapsed since the general diffusion of its doctrines. What has followed? have men ceased to fight, has vice and misery vanished from the earth.—have the fireside communications which it recommends taken place?" (*Letters,* 1:267).

The sore point in their dispute was Shelley's second pamphlet, the *Proposals for an Association of Philanthropists,* in which Shelley tried to establish a discussion-and-agitation society whose principal goal would be to bring the pressure of moral suasion to bear on the government. In it, Shelley makes the political basis of his desire for a transindividual solidarity clear: "I think that individuals acting singly, with whatever energy can never effect so much as a society" (Ingpen and Peck, 5:256).

In the same work, Shelley scoffs, evidently with Burke in mind, at those who "make the favour of Government the sunshine of their moral day" and "think things that are rusty and decayed venerable, and are uninquiringly satisfied with evils as these are, because they find them established and unquestioned as they do sunlight and air" (258–59), and we might imagine that the Coleridge of *The Statesman's Manual* would fall easily into this category. In this work, however, Coleridge subtly moves away from Burke's attempt to awe us into submission by displaying the wounds and grey hairs of our stately father, and instead emphasizes the therapeutic rewards for the individual in being organically bound to the state. What is more, he does it in terms that make its derivation from, or relationship to, a therapeutic aesthetic quite explicit. The individual's (temporal) organic integration with the (quasieternal) state reappears in the *Manual* as the role of the symbol with regard to the universal truth it symbolizes: "[A] Symbol . . . is characterized by a translucence of the Special in the Individual or of the General in the Especial or of the Universal in the General. Above all by the

23. See the series of letters from Shelley to Godwin discussing his trip to Ireland: *Letters,* vol. 1, nos. 160, 163, 170, 173, 176, and 181. Duff (*Romance and Revolution,* 103–4) offers a very useful analysis of this controversy that is generally similar to mine; but see Clemit 1993 for a rather different approach.

translucence of the Eternal through and in the Temporal. It always partakes of the Reality which it renders intelligible; and while it enunciates the whole, abides itself as a living part in that Unity, of which it is the representative" (*Lay Sermons,* 30). Coleridge's great example, the Bible, is both religious and literary, but he makes its political significance quite explicit. The key to the Bible's literary and moral excellence is the hermeneutical integration of all its disparate elements: "In the Bible every agent appears and acts as a self-subsisting individual: each has a life of its own, and yet all are one life. The elements of necessity and free will are reconciled in the higher power of an omnipresent Providence, that predestinates the whole in the moral freedom of the integral parts" (31). We can recognize in this providential reconciliation of necessity and free will yet another version of Kant's aesthetic free conformity to law. Coleridge draws the same therapeutic political conclusion from this as Hegel, and applies it to the same social disorder: the French Revolution. He turns almost directly from the passage quoted above to this outstanding example of the wages of living in contempt of the Bible's theologico-political message. He attributes the French Revolution to "the rising importance of the commercial and manufacturing class," "the spirit of sensuality," and "irreligious philosophy," but, most important, "the extreme over-rating of the knowledge and power given by the improvements of the arts and sciences . . . and the general conceit that states and governments might be and ought to be constructed as machines, every movement of which might be foreseen and taken into previous calculation" (33–34)—in short, the terrible regime of motives.

Yet it is not so much the Bible's *message* that the revolutionaries have failed to follow, at least not the message contained *in* the Bible. Although Coleridge cites a passage from Isaiah about not following "astrologers and stargazers" as evidence that the Bible contained explicit warnings sufficient to deter us from being misled by the *Encyclopédistes* (34–35), the rather dubious application of the passage signals that this is not the real force of his argument. Rather, the Bible itself stands as a model for the state, in its perfect hermeneutical unity: politically, the individual citizen should be the "symbol" of what, in the second "Lay Sermon" (which Shelley will read in 1817), Coleridge will call "the Spirit of the State" (*Lay Sermons,* 223). Coleridge's literary, political, and religious ideal, like the Hegelian *Sittlichkeit,* is to read the individual hermeneutically—as the historicist critic reads the literary text—as "an actual and essential part of that, the whole of which it represents" (79). The revolutionists offended against the therapeutic imperative because they refused to live their lives as narrative—according to Coleridge's

Aristotelian definition of the "end of *narrative*" as being "to convert *a series* into a *Whole*" (qtd. in McFarland, *Ruin*, 51)—breaking them down into the atomistic aggregations of a chemical or mechanical experiment, or, in Schelling's terms, into a "series of events without aim or purpose." This refusal to live *symbolically*, the refusal to "enunciate the whole" in one's individual being, is recognizably the same refusal to "reaffirm the polis," to "acknowledge" that one speaks "representatively" of a language and a community, which Cavell describes as the "tragic" result of skepticism (Cavell, *Claim of Reason*, 27, 29).

There is one link yet to be provided before I can claim that Coleridge allowed Shelley a full understanding of the therapeutic appeal of this organic and hermeneutical approach to the text and to the state. Although God has never been far from the examples and images I have discussed, Coleridge's appeals to the Bible are, as we have seen, appeals to literary qualities that are not dependent on its divine authority. Although Coleridge has spoken of providence, he has done so with reference only to the characters in the Bible story itself, and the unity they "enunciate"; the gap between the political and textual therapy of the *Manual* and the theological therapy of the *Biographia*, although small, remains.

Fortunately, Coleridge bridges this gap quite definitely. "Religion," he argues, "in all ages and countries of civilization . . . has been the parent and fosterer of the Fine Arts, as of Poetry, Music, Painting, &c. the common essence of which consists in a similar union of the Universal and the Individual. In this union, moreover, is contained the true sense of the IDEAL." (*Lay Sermons*, 62).

Coleridge gives two images in particular that convey the total therapeutic promise of this idealism, which evidently impressed Shelley. The first is an attempt to elucidate the mystery (or perhaps to impress us with the mystery) of the Kantian antinomy: "That hidden mystery in every, the minutest, form of existence, which contemplated under the relations of time presents itself to the understanding retrospectively, as an infinite ascent of Causes, and prospectively as an interminable progression of Effects . . . in Space . . . as a law of action and re-action . . . this same mystery freed from the phenomena of Time and Space . . . reveals itself to the pure Reason as the actual immanence of ALL in EACH." Having thus outlined the argument as baldly as he can, Coleridge reaches for a potent traditional symbol (see, e.g., Marvell's "On a Drop of Dew") to sum it up: "Are we struck with admiration at beholding the Cope of Heaven imaged in a Dew-drop? The least of the animalcula to which that drop would be an Ocean contains in itself an infinite problem of which God Omni-present is the only solution" (50). Beyond the delusive, fallen world of time and space, we are all one in God. The part is able to reflect the whole, the character the work, the citizen the state, the dewdrop the cope of heaven, because the Absolute can only be "enunciated" in the postlapsarian world by fragments. This allows us to read each fragment, symbolically, as a gage of future absolution.

The second image picks up on the centrifugal/centripetal imagery that both Fichte and Schelling develop at length, but translates it into a static spatial metaphor rather than a dynamic one. In the first appendix to the *Manual* Coleridge tells us that he is assuming on the part of his reader "a humble and docile state of mind, and above all the practice of prayer." His ideal reader, charitable in the Christian, everyday, and hermeneutical-theory senses, will be a Christian, able to understand his argument because already, at the deepest level, in agreement with it. True Christians can recognize themselves by their returning to a number of key questions, most important of which is the following: "Am I *at one* with God, and is my will concentric with that holy power, which is at once the constitutive will and the supreme reason of the universe?— If not, must I not be mad if I do not seek, and miserable if I do not discover and embrace, the means of *at-one-ment?*" (55). This image, like the image of the dewdrop that reflects and "enunciates" the heavens, knits together the textual and political concerns of the *Manual* with the theological ones of the *Biographia* and places them both within the framework of a Spinozist dynamic monism. It is an image of contextualization that neatly conveys the metaphysical and ethico-political program of therapeutic idealism.

Before leaving the *Manual,* we should also note that it contains one of the best short definitions of the Romantic Ironic urge toward the Absolute, a definition that would have made clear to Shelley the difference between the Wordsworthian and Coleridgean poetics. The passage, although long, deserves to be quoted in full because it so completely covers the major points of the therapeutic imperative: the original, naive bond with the Absolute; our present, fallen condition of "dividuous" separation; and our redeeming desire for a return to the Absolute, which, through its "preventive and assisting grace" is known to us as an ideal even in our fallen condition:

> I have at this moment before me, in the flowery meadow, on which my eye is now reposing, one of its [the book of nature's] most soothing chapters, in which there is no lamenting word, no one character of guilt or anguish. For never can I look and medi-

tate on the vegetable creation without a feeling similar to that
with which we gaze at a beautiful infant that has fed itself asleep
at its mother's bosom, and smiles in its strange dream of obscure
yet happy sensations. The same tender and genial pleasure takes
possession of me, and this pleasure is checked and drawn inward
by the like aching melancholy, by the same whispered remon-
strance, and made restless by a similar impulse of aspiration. It
seems as if the soul said to herself: from this state hast *thou*
fallen! Such shouldst thou still become, thy Self all permeable to
a holier power! thy Self at once hidden and glorified by its own
transparency, as the accidental and dividuous in this quiet and
harmonious object is subjected to the life and light of nature
which shines in it, even as the transmitted power, love and wisdom, of God over all fills and shines through, nature! But what
the plant *is,* by an act not its own and unconsciously—*that* must
thou *make* thyself to *become!* must by prayer and by a watchful
and unresisting spirit, *join* at least with the preventive and assisting grace to *make* thyself, in that light of conscience which in-
flameth not, and that knowledge which puffeth not up. (71)

II

Stokoe's comment that Shelley "manifest[s] a much more intelligent appreciation of German literature than did either Coleridge or Scott" (174)
deserves reflection. Shelley did not, so far as we know, read widely in
German literature, but he did read well. The German post-Kantians, like
their English emulators, had close ties to the literary world, and Shelley
was acquainted with some of the key products of those ties.

The effect of Goethe's *Sorrows of Young Werther* on the young Shelley's imagination, as on the entire theory and practice of Romanticism,
is incalculable. Most characteristic is Werther's infinite desire as an artist
for an absolute union with nature; his desire is for such a complete
union that it destroys his ability to create; art becomes an embarrassing
barrier between the artist and nature:

> I am so happy . . . so absorbed in this feeling of peaceful exis-
> tence, that my art is suffering. I could not draw now, not a single
> line, and yet I have never been a greater painter than in these
> moments. . . . I am alerted to the thousand various little grasses;
> when I sense the teeming of the little world among the stalks,
> the countless indescribable forms of the grubs and flies . . . and
> feel the presence of the Almighty . . . then I am often filled with
> longing, and think: ah, if only you could express this, if only you

could breathe onto the paper in all its fullness and warmth what is so alive in you, so that it would mirror your soul as your soul is the mirror of God in His infinity!—My friend—But it will be the end of me. The glory of these visions . . . will be my undoing. (26–27)

We can recognize here one source of Coleridge's and Shelley's shared longing for a therapeutic vision that unites the fragmentary and multiple world of "the meanest insect on wh. we trample," "the least of the animalcula," in a "tremendous whole" or God. Like Coleridge, Goethe solves the problem with a reflective metaphor: the soul as the mirror of God, like the dewdrop and the cope of heaven.

Schiller describes *Werther* as a naive poet's description of the sentimental condition (*Naive and Sentimental,* 137–38). Werther's dilemma defines the ironic condition and its need for a therapeutic philosophy. He yearns for nature, as, in Schiller's words, "an invalid for health"; he is painfully aware that the ancients, with their "quality of childishness" (86), achieved an unthinking union with nature that no longer seems possible in the present age. Indeed, his very consciousness of his desire for what Coleridge calls "at-one-ment" prevents the consummation of that desire. In an age in which poetry has become self-conscious it only seems a barrier between the artist and nature: "[W]hy trouble with poetry and scenes and idylls? Must we go tinkering about with Nature before we can enjoy it?" (35).

Nevertheless, as his "if only I could express this" shows, Werther cannot be content with the naive and mute appreciation of nature's wonders. He wants to express his unity in an artistic act that would be as unconscious as "breathing," but at the same time he is, cripplingly, conscious of this desire for authenticity—always already artificial as soon as consciously willed. Caught in the ironic dilemma, his desire for "absolution" becomes a *Todessehnsucht,* or longing for death, that recurs throughout the Romantic imaginary as the flip side of the exhilaration of the ironic infinitude. His disgust with this fallen and delusive world of the will prefigures Schopenhauer's recourse to the Indian concept of "Mâyâ," in which death is a release from the world of willing: "That the life of Man is but a dream has been sensed by many a one, and I too am never free of the feeling. When I consider the restrictions that are placed on the active, inquiring energies of Man; when I see that all our efforts have no other result than to satisfy needs which in turn serve no purpose but to prolong our wretched existence, and then see that all our reassurance concerning the particular questions we probe is no more than a dreamy resignation, since all we are doing is to paint our

prison walls with colourful figures and bright views—all of this . . .
leaves me silent" (30-31; see, e.g., Schopenhauer, 1:8). Werther's
brands of *Weltschmerz* and *Todessehnsucht* are more directly traceable
in the work of Byron, Schopenhauer's favorite author, but one can find
direct influences in Shelley. Shelley's "veil which those who live call
Life" ("Sonnet: Lift not . . . ," 1; *Prometheus,* III, iii, 113), which has
prompted so much Platonic speculation, has a more immediate ancestor
in Werther's agonized contemplations of suicide: "To lift the curtain and
step behind it!—That is all!" (113).

Shelley translated some of the first part of Goethe's *Faust,* and his
admiration for the work was boundless. Faust's bargain with Mephistopheles is the classic statement of the ironic condition. Having spent
his life seeking the key to nature's secrets—seeking the ideal, therapeutic union with nature—Faust feels himself to have reached the absolute limits of (fallen) human ability to unite with the world through
knowledge (see, e.g., lines 360-64, 1544-71, 1587-606, 1746-49). At
the same time, however, the transcendent will not leave him (naively)
in peace (1583-90). Torn between a limited condition and an infinite
aspiration, Faust's pact with Mephistopheles is a measure born of
ironic despair (1746-50). He decides that rather than live the perpetually unsatisfying life this world offers, he would destroy himself in order to achieve through dissolution a negative accession to the Absolute:

> I told you, I am not concerned with pleasure.
> I crave corrosive joy and dissipation,
> enamoured hate and quickening despair.
> My breast no longer thirsts for knowledge
> and will welcome grief and pain.
> Whatever is the lot of humankind
> I want to taste within my deepest self.
> I want to seize the highest and the lowest,
> to load its woe and bliss upon my breast,
> and thus expand my single self titanically
> and in the end go down with all the rest.[24]

(1765-75)

24. Du hörest ja, von Freud' ist nicht die Rede. / Dem Taumel weih' ich mich, dem schmerz-
lichsten Genuß, / Verliebtem Haß, erquickendem Verdruß. / Mein Busen, der vom Wis-
sensdrang geheilt ist, / Soll keinen Schmerzen künftig sich verschließen, / Und was der ganzen
Menschheit zugeteilt ist, / Will ich in meinem innern Selbst genießen / Mit meinem Geist das
Höchst' und Tiefste greifen, / Ihr Wohl und Weh auf meinen Busen häufen, / Und so mein
eigen Selbst zu irhem Selbst erweitern, / Und, wie sie selbst, am End' auch ich zerscheitern.

for humankind may become eminently useful and active. Public topics of fear and hope . . . are those on which the Philanthropist would dilate with the warmest feeling. Because these are accustomed to place individuals at a distance from self; for in proportion as he is absorbed in public feeling, so will a consideration of his proper benefit be generalized. In proportion as he feels with, or for a nation or a world, so will man consider himself less as that centre, to which we are but too prone to believe that every line of human concern does, or ought to converge. (Ingpen and Peck, 5:253)

Like Diderot, and in accordance with the skeptic's dilemma outlined by Hume, Shelley is trying to find a language of political engagement or integration, within a basically aggregationist philosophy. The internal struggle is evident in the almost self-contradictory desire to "place individuals at a distance from self" and in the profusion of images no one of which seems quite able to do the job he wants: "dilation," "generalization," "sympathy," "warm feeling," and, most interestingly, a centrifugal movement away from the self-as-center toward "a nation or a world" conceived, implicitly, as circumference.

Wordsworth uses the image of the world as circumference to the self's center in his *Excursion* (1814), with an expressly political intent. In the context of a jingoistic tirade on England's divine mission to spread civilization and enlightenment throughout the world, Wordsworth's Wanderer exclaims, "Vast the circumference of hope—and ye / Are at its centre, British Lawgivers" (IX, 398–99). It is not surprising that we find Shelley quick to understand and respond to the ethical and political dimensions of this image, which, in Coleridge's use, are merely latent within its more purely metaphysical emphasis; indeed, in the "Speculations on Morals" Shelley uses it to define the keystone of ethical action: "The only distinction between the selfish man, and the virtuous man, is that the imagination of the former is confined within a narrow limit, whilst that of the latter embraces a comprehensive circumference" (Ingpen and Peck, 7:75). Again and again in Shelley's poetry and prose we find versions of this imagery describing the relationship of the self and the not-self and insisting on the moral value of dilating the former to embrace the latter.[28]

28. A partial list, not including those already cited, of Shelley's uses of this imagery, both those endorsing its therapeutic message and those disrupting it, would include *Adonais*, xlvii, 4; "To Jane: The Recollection," iv, 49; "The Witch of Atlas," xxiii, 7; "Peter Bell the Third," IV, vii, 2; *A Refutation of Deism* (Ingpen and Peck, 6:54), "The Assassins" (6:160); "On Life"

Both Milton Wilson and, more recently, Hoagwood have recognized the importance in Shelley's thought of a concept of identity that runs along a continuum from the self-contained center to dispersal at the circumference, but there are serious problems with each critic's account. Wilson identifies most of the important instances of Shelley's use of this imagery, gives an intelligent, if one-sided, account of its significance, and usefully relates it to Shelley's general theory of the self. Unfortunately, he is unaware of the post-Kantian origins of the image, and argues that it originates in the nineteenth century with Shelley's use; not unrelatedly, he overlooks its political import (155–67).

Hoagwood picks up on the image of the circle, but reads it exclusively as the "epistemological circle" bounding the skeptical self, beyond which we are incapable of certain knowledge, rather like Diderot's or Kant's "island" of knowledge (*Skepticism and Ideology*, 39). But while it is true that Shelley occasionally invokes the image of the self as bounded by a circle that cuts us off from other minds and from the deep truth of the world, far more frequently his emphasis is on a centrifugal impulse that is aimed at the breaking of boundaries rather than the passive acceptance of them. Shelley describes circles that, like Coleridge's, include other minds; by expanding our identity to the circumference of the circle we (therapeutically) dilate our being to a heightened self-consciousness; the individual self-consciousness is merely the self-conscious moment of an integral larger whole, ranging, in Shelley's imagery, from a pair of friends or lovers, through the state, to, at least in glimpses, the Absolute.

The poet's capacity to "measure the circumference and sound the depths of human nature with a comprehensive and all-penetrating spirit" (Reiman and Powers, 508) can hardly refer to an inevitable certainty of our knowledge within the "epistemological circle" (it is tautologous to say we have complete knowledge of everything we certainly know), nor can it refer to our equally inevitable surrender to the "facticity" of the "experiential circle." From the point of view of a strict relativism every individual's picture of the world is complete in itself, and therefore they have always filled their "circle of knowledge." To introduce new items is to "change their minds" in the Drummondian sense.

Hoagwood's reading of Shelley's "circular" imagery as a rigid delimitation of the boundaries of knowledge suggests that Shelley perversely

---

(Reiman and Powers, 476); "Essay on Christianity" (Ingpen and Peck, 6:230); "The Coliseum" (6:303–4); *A Philosophical View of Reform* (7:20); "Essay on the Devil, and Devils" (7:100); *A Defence of Poetry* (Reiman and Powers, 485, 503, 508).

opted to use an image that he knew to be central to a quite opposite political and epistemological philosophy deliberately to obscure the expression of his own. Shelley's "circles," however, are as much inclusive as exclusive. The example that most perfectly captures the delicate balance between the two tendencies comes from his unfinished story of 1818, "The Coliseum": "The internal nature of each being is surrounded by a circle, not to be surmounted by his fellows; and it is this repulsion which constitutes the misfortune of the condition of life. But there is a circle which comprehends, as well as one which mutually excludes, all things which feel. And, with respect to man, his public and his private happiness consist in diminishing the circumference which includes those resembling himself, until they become one with him, and he with them" (Ingpen and Peck, 6:303-4). This is the ironic condition; the individual is simultaneously aware of the fragmenting consequences of our fallen state ("the misfortune of the condition of life") and of an impulse toward the Absolute—the circle in which self-consciousness would be a self-consciousness of "ALL IN EACH" and we would know the other "even as also I am known."

In his complex, ironic "Essay on the Devil, and Devils" (1820) Shelley shows both how profound his understanding of the implications of the ironic condition is and how fully he understands the implications of Coleridge's brief reference in the *Biographia* to the "centrifugal and centripetal" forces of creation: "Shall we suppose that the Devil occupies the centre and God the circumference of existence, and that one urges inwards with the centripetal, whilst the other is perpetually struggling outwards from the narrow focus with the centrifugal force, and that from their perpetual conflict results that mixture of good and evil, harmony and discord, beauty and deformity, production and decay, which are the general laws of the moral and material world?" (Ingpen and Peck, 7:100). It is a measure of how deeply Shelley has thought through his reading of Coleridge that we find him here pulling together the *Biographia*'s plagiarized excerpt (from Schelling's *System*) on the contrary forces that generate the world of production and decay, the image of God (from the *Statesman's Manual*) as the circumference of a circle of which the individual is the center, and the allusion to "centrifugal and centripetal" forces already mentioned. By replacing Coleridge's individual (Christian) mind with Satan, Shelley is not just being mischievous. Satan appealed to the Romantic generation because his condition captures the elements of the Romantic Ironic predicament. As the rebellious angel who fell from the right hand of God, he represents our fall from the Absolute. Moreover, his fall—at least in Milton's version, the most important to the English Romantics—is precipitated by a sudden and inexplicable self-consciousness of his hitherto naively accepted blessedness.[29] Jealousy of God's power is an effect of this more primal cause; Satan can only be jealous of God once he is conscious of himself as a separate entity (Abdiel calls him, damningly, "alienate from God" [*Paradise Lost,* V, 877]), that is, once he is already fallen. Milton's Satan carries his hell within him: his own restless ambition to recapture his former glory. Like the Romantic poet, he strives self-consciously for a centrifugal expansion to an Absolute that was once his birthright. Like Schlegel, Satan can glory (or try to) in his *felix culpa:*

> I give not heaven for lost. From this descent
> Celestial virtues rising, will appear
> More glorious and more dread than from no fall,
> And trust themselves to fear no second fate.
>
>   (II, 14–17)

His importance to Shelley, and others, as a figure of irresistible revolutionary desire is rooted in this infinite (political) will to power, which, translated into poetic terms, will become the restless striving of Schlegel's "universal, progressive poetry."

Shelley is engaged in a subtle, complex exploration of the limits, rewards, and dangers of this therapeutic imagery.[30] This is most apparent in Shelley's use of Coleridge's image of the drop of dew that reflects the heavens. Shelley uses the image in his "Ode to Heaven" (published with *Prometheus Unbound* in 1820), which is a direct meditation upon therapeutic idealism, and specifically upon Coleridge's use of the image in the *Statesman's Manual.*

Shelley presents three successive views of the heavens,[31] each view a more philosophically complex position than the preceding. The first three stanzas, in the voice of the "CHORUS OF SPIRITS," are a naive (in the Schillerian sense) praise of this "Palace-roof of cloudless nights!" (1).

---

29. See Satan's long meditative soliloquy at the opening of book IV of *Paradise Lost,* in which the mystery of why he, and he alone, of the heavenly aristocracy achieved this self awareness is raised but left unanswered.

30. See Michael O'Neill's excellent discussion of Shelley's use of center/circumference imagery in "Adonais"; he argues that Shelley exploits these images in full consciousness that they are "no more than ingenious tropes" (280).

31. Here I am using the version of the poem with the headings ("A REMOTER VOICE" and "A LOUDER AND STILL REMOTER VOICE") that were dropped from the published version of 1820, probably without Shelley's authorization; see Chernaik, 220–23. They are not essential to this reading, but they do help to confirm the impression that each successive point of view brackets the preceding one(s).

The chorus has no consciousness of a possible separation from this "heaven":

> Which art now, and which wert then;
> Of the present and the past,
> Of the eternal Where and When,
>   Presence chamber, Temple, Home,
>   Ever-canopying Dome
>   Of acts and ages yet to come!
>
> (4–9)

Space and time ("Where and When") are naively accepted as immutable and unproblematic, the inevitable a priori frameworks of the "infinite ascent of Causes" and "interminable succession of Effects" ("acts and ages yet to come") beyond which Coleridge's dewdrop image is intended to make us see.

In the second section "A REMOTER VOICE" urges us to think again, in terms Coleridge would endorse. This voice has a sentimental-ironic appreciation that its relationship to the world is not quite as it seems. To it, the cope of heaven is "but the Mind's first chamber" (28), the product of the a priori structures of the mind. Like Coleridge seeking the "hidden mystery in every . . . form of existence," it dreams of a day when, beyond "the portal of the grave" (32), it shall see past the delusive forms of time and space and penetrate to the noumenal Absolute—"a world of new delights" (33) that reveals that this (fallen) world and the visible form of heaven are (as Werther argued) "But a dim and noonday gleam / From the shadow of a dream" (35–36).

The first two voices fall easily into the pattern of naive thesis and ironic antithesis, but the third voice abruptly refuses the expected role of synthetic resolution. It opens by dismissing both the preceding viewpoints as irrelevant: "Peace! the abyss is wreathed with scorn / At your presumption, Atom-born!" (37–38). It would be easy to see this as a skeptical refusal of a "dogmatic" decision—Demogorgon's abysm scorning once again to "vomit forth its secrets." The appellation "Atom-born" would then be read as an affirmation of the Lucretian aggregative flux against the integrated naiveté of the first voice(s) and the sentimental desire for integration of the second. But while the deep truth may be without images, this last "LOUDER AND STILL REMOTER VOICE" is willing to explore at least two: both rehearse and subtly disrupt the therapeutic strategies of synthesis, allowing neither skeptical atomism nor therapeutic idealism to stand unchallenged.

The first image is organic: "What is Heaven? and what are ye / Who its brief expanse inherit?" (39–40) asks the voice. The answer:

> What are suns and spheres which flee
>   With the instinct of that spirit
>   Of which ye are but a part?
>   Drops which Nature's mighty heart
>   Drives through thinnest veins. Depart!
>
>   (42–45)

The image is strongly therapeutic: we are all parts of one great spirit, which expresses itself—is "symbolized" in Coleridge's sense—in suns, spheres, and ourselves. Thus we are like the lifeblood of that mighty organism, nature. But Shelley's language sends a less reassuring message. Heaven's "brief expanse" and the "suns and spheres which flee" undercut the sense of organic persistence and stability by emphasizing the precariousness and evanescence of the world. Nature's "mighty heart" sounds more encouraging, but there is an impression of stress and force irreconcilable with a therapeutic organicism in the way it drives the "drops" (including us) "through thinnest veins." We are not surprised when the stanza culminates with a hostile "Depart!" quite at odds with the potentially soothing image it has developed.

Finally, in the last stanza Shelley returns to Coleridge's dewdrop:

> What is Heaven? a globe of dew
> Filling in the morning new
>   Some eyed flower whose young leaves waken
>   On an unimagined world.
>   Constellated suns unshaken,
>   Orbits measureless, are furled
>   In that frail and fading sphere
>   With ten million gathered there
>   To tremble, gleam, and disappear!—
>
>   (46–54)

This stanza gains a directly political edge when we recognize the source with which Shelley is entering into dialogue. As Chernaik notes, Shelley's "eyed flower" "suggests the perceiving mind" (124) and as such could be seen as an improvement on Coleridge's image, ensuring the connection between the dewdrop's reflection of the universe and the individual self-consciousness dilated to an absolute self-consciousness is understood; the dewdrop becomes the all-reflecting eye of the individual human "flower." But if for Coleridge the therapeutic impact of the image rests on the incomparable vastness of the heavens being reproduced on the minuscule drop of dew, Shelley has approached the same image from another point of view, and wants us to understand what that implies for both the individual and the "totality."

The flower, together with its delicate, nonorganic, "eye," is projected into time in a way Coleridge's dewdrop most emphatically is not. Its "young leaves waken / On an unimagined world"; in gaining its eye, it has gained a perspective on the world that has no relationship to its previous existence. This sudden irruption of a new mode of consciousness cannot be narrativized as a return from ironic division to absolute unity; there is no connection between "before" and "after." When the flower loses its eye, it will "disappear" as enigmatically as it came, a loss of contact with the Absolute that cannot be narrativized as a fall. There is an intertextual echo here within the poem's original context of consumption, the *Prometheus Unbound* volume; this "unimagined world" has sprung forth with the same absolute discontinuity with the past as the "arts, though unimagined, yet to be," that Prometheus projects into the postrevolutionary society. Like Drummond's native, the flower has not figuratively but literally "changed its mind" by gaining a new organ of perception.

This is the point of separating the human "flower" from the extraorganic "eye"; Shelley is posing the question whether our uncertain, fleeting visions of the Absolute are really a result of removing veils and "seeing clearly" or rather the possibly delusive fruit of a prosthetic graft, seeing through the borrowed eye of religion, nationalism, or philosophy. At the very least, he suggests that such a vision is not the final and absolute synthesis Coleridge desires. The world springs into being not only with no hermeneutical connection to its past but also, as Shelley insists, with an uncertain future. The dewdrop eye's "frail and fading sphere" is fated to disappear only too quickly, and, as the evocation of *Prometheus Unbound* suggests, there is a direct political significance in this. If Coleridge's dewdrop reflecting heaven is primarily an image of the mind in nature, it is also an image of the citizen in the state, and Shelley here is deliberately unsettling the way Coleridge's metaphysics invest the state with a naturalness and immutability Shelley finds politically unacceptable. Just as the dewdrop in *time* must fall and shatter its perfect reflection of the ten million constellated suns, any political system, in time, will lose the legitimating support of the individuals who compose it. When they no longer see themselves as integrated, organic parts of its wider whole, it too will "tremble, gleam, and disappear!"

We can find confirmation of this reading in Shelley's line "With ten million gathered there." The "ten million" sounds oddly precise (and incorrect) as a number for the stars, which we would expect to be "myriad" or "numberless" or even "millions." In fact, Shelley is no longer referring to the stars here. In Shelley's poetry "the million" and "the millions" is used frequently, and almost exclusively, to refer to the "masses" or to a large body of people.[32] Given Shelley's interest in contemporary debates about Malthus and population growth, he must have been aware that the 1811 census of England and Wales indicated a total population of ten million (10,488,000, to be precise, which Shelley correctly rounds down to the nearest million; Godwin, *Of Population*, 221). Shelley is forcing us to confront the political implications of Coleridge's image: the flower and dewdrop are the citizen who stands for, or "enunciates," the ten million inhabitants of the state.

By mentioning a precise number, and thereby evoking a specific state, Shelley achieves a complex of objectives. Most straightforwardly, he gives a concrete political thrust to his undermining of Coleridge's image: the dewdrop's inherent, nonnarrativizable instability becomes a way of directly challenging the (English) state's organic transcendence of time's vicissitudes. Unlike Coleridge's tree, which incorporates damage into its visible life history, England conceived as a reflection in a drop of dew is liable to sudden and absolute extinction. This is not jejune revolutionary hyperbole; the "state" as Coleridge understands it relies entirely on the individual's recognition for its existence. If I cease to perceive myself as representative of the state, the state becomes, at least for me, nothing more than a complex aggregation of distinct individuals. While Shelley could not imagine in a preatomic age the actual instantaneous annihilation of the "ten million," he recognized that Coleridge's "Spirit of the State" exists, if at all, only to the extent we perceive it to exist.

Moreover, by insisting on this immense number of individual people, Shelley emphasizes how fragile the *communitas* of state spirit can be. The discourse of therapeutic politics generally invokes the state as an abstract Notion, a disembodied spirit seeking embodiment in the indi-

---

32. Ellis, *Concordance*, 448, lists forty-five occurrences of "million," "millions," and some "million-" compounds. Of those, thirty-seven (not including the present example) refer to "the masses, the majority of the people," "large number of persons," "exceedingly populous [cities]," and "vast numbers of persons, myriads." There are three references to the heavens (though two of those are in fact the same, having been drawn from *Queen Mab* and the reworked verses from that poem, *The Daemon of the World*), but each refers, vaguely, to the "million" constellations and worlds.

vidual citizen. Shelley gives Coleridge an uncomfortable reminder here that the task of expanding the (self-)consciousness of ten million individuals—each with a will as liable to change as the dewdrop on the leaf is to fall—to a point where each perceives him- or herself as fully representative of the total is, if not in itself politically inconceivable, doomed to at best transient success before inevitable scission. Coleridge tacitly acknowledges this fact when, in his *On the Constitution of the Church and State,* he proposes to entrust the national consciousness to a "National Clerisy."

Shelley is trying to force Coleridge's image to take political change and revolution into account, yet he is not dismissing that image. The dissolution of English political society is not something to be glibly counterposed to Coleridge's "dogmatism," and Shelley gives his image its due; the "Constellated suns unshaken" and "Orbits measureless" furled in the dewdrop's reflective eye are rich, complex, and beautiful. Their fragility is emphasized, and provokes in us a desire to guard and protect them. By releasing the inherent transience in Coleridge's image, Shelley wants to make us honestly confront what is at stake in political revolution or, at least, in the refusal by a revolutionary consciousness to take responsibility for the state. The dewdrop must eventually fall—nature gives us no image of a final and lasting synthesis—and Shelley wants us to be aware of both the loss and the liberation this implies.

Before leaving the poem, we should also note that Shelley includes in it a subtle, and even gentle, reminder that Coleridge himself is not always so certain of nature's (and by extension the state's) benign integration with the individual. In this context the "Orbits measureless" must evoke the "caverns measureless to man" in "Kubla Khan." Shelley is suggesting that for Coleridge the poet, if not for Coleridge the lay political preacher, there is a nature that escapes from our reflecting minds, a nature that is vast, alien, and cannot be therapeutically reduced to the status of our "inorganic body."

NAIVE WORDSWORTH AND SENTIMENTAL COLERIDGE: "PETER BELL THE THIRD"

I

Coleridge, along with Wordsworth, was also the focal point of another aspect of Shelley's exploration of post-Kantian aesthetics. Even before reading the *Biographia* or the *Lectures on Dramatic Art and Poetry,*

Shelley was aware of the opposition between the naive and the sentimental-ironic—in substance, if not in name—in the opposition between Wordsworth and Coleridge. In his poems "To Wordsworth" and
"To—" ("Oh! there are spirits of the air") in the *Alastor* volume of 1816,[33]
Shelley shows that he well understood this distinction. Wordsworth appears there as the "Poet of Nature" (1), turning humanity's "common
woes" (5) into poetry. Coleridge, on the other hand, appears in a form
recognizable to readers of "Dejection: An Ode":

> With mountain winds, and babbling springs,
>   And moonlight seas, that are the voice
> Of these inexplicable things,
>   Thou didst hold commune, and rejoice
> When they did answer thee; but they
> Cast, like a worthless boon, thy love away.
>
>   (7–12)

Rejected now by the nature he had once naively communed with, Coleridge, Shelley suggests, can only ask:

> Ah! wherefore didst thou build thine hope
>   On the false earth's inconstancy?
> Did thine own mind afford no scope
>   Of love, or moving thoughts to thee?
>
>   (19–22)

If Shelley had not read the lines "I may not hope from outward forms to
win / The passion and the life, whose fountains are within" in the 1802
Morning Post version of "Dejection: An Ode," we must credit him with
exceptional insight here.

It is in "Peter Bell the Third" (1819) that Shelley shows most clearly
how fully he has understood the pertinence of the opposition between
the naive/classical and ironic/Romantic to the poetic programs of

---

33. I am accepting here Mary Shelley's suggestion that this latter poem was "addressed in
idea to Coleridge" (Hutchinson, 527). I see no reason for her to invent this; the idea of a
pendant to his "To Wordsworth," a poem to address the other great voice of the first Romantic
generation, would naturally suggest itself to Shelley, and there is nothing within the poem to
discredit the claim, and much to support it. His reluctance to name Coleridge probably stems
from what is either a shrewd guess or, more likely, his retailing of literary-world gossip in the
third stanza: "thou hast sought in starry eyes / Beams that were never meant for thine" (13–
14).

Wordsworth and Coleridge. At the same time, he marks, in this poem, his political discontent with both approaches. If "Peter Bell the Third" has not received the critical respect and attention it deserves in Shelley criticism (although this is changing), one of the reasons is that the terms of Shelley's attack on Wordsworth have not been clearly understood. Shelley is engaged in a sophisticated and informed attempt to situate Wordsworth as the "naive" ideal and to use that reading of him as a way of exploring the political limitations of that position.[34]

One of the things that immediately puzzles us about "Peter Bell the Third" is its basic premise. Placing Peter Bell/Wordsworth in hell, scattering references to original sin throughout the poem, singling out the notorious (and later suppressed) "All silent and all—damned!" stanza from Wordsworth's poem as an epigraph, while not completely unjustified in a satiric attack on Wordsworth, seem slightly beside the mark. Despite the powerful impact of the voice of the Methodist preacher crying "Repent!" in Wordsworth's *Peter Bell* (946, 951), the preacher is exhorting his auditors to repent and be blessed, not threatening them with brimstone. Wordsworth is notably unorthodox on the question of original sin (in *Peter Bell* he refers to his polygamous potter's becoming "gentle as an infant child, / An infant that has known no sin" [969–70]) and even in his later poetry emphasizes the rewards of union with God/nature far more than the penalties of disobedience. Shelley's portrait of Wordsworth as, in Reiman and Powers's phrase, "a Methodist Peter Bell, predestined to damnation" (322), might seem not only ungenerous but obtuse. Curran, for example, argues that "Peter Bell the Third" should be considered as one of the pointlessly cruel satires Shelley censures in his "Fragment of a Satire on Satires" (*Annus Mirabilis,* 152). Hogle's reading is similar, but he endorses this attack, conflating Wordsworth's "Methodism" and his "mimetic desire" as a legitimate target for Shelley's "radical transference."

This is to mistake Shelley's point, however. Shelley's Peter never fully embraces any form of Christianity, let alone a hellfire-and-damnation Methodism. At most he comes to "half-believe White-Obi" (552), and even after he completely sells out to the Devil, he is remarkable more for the utter confusion of his philosophy than for its uncharitable rigor:

> To Peter's view, all seemed one hue;
> He was no Whig, he was no Tory:
> No Deist and no Christian he;—

34. See Hogle, *Shelley's Process,* 138–46, and Steven Jones, *Shelley's Satire,* chap. 3, for two very different (and very interesting) recent readings.

> He got so subtle, that to be
> Nothing, was all his glory.

> (564-68)

It is as a result of this confusion, Shelley suggests (see 609ff.), that Peter becomes such a biddable hack writer for the state, writing "odes to the Devil" (634) whenever required.

The logic of the poem's diabolic machinery actually stems from Shelley's *praise* of Peter. The passages in "Part Fourth" and "Part Fifth" where Shelley characterizes what he found admirable in Wordsworth's early poetry—which might appear to us as more or less grudgingly "giving the Devil his due"—are in fact at the heart of the poem. Shelley describes Wordsworth in terms that show how thoroughly he understood Coleridge's and Schlegel's distinctions between the classical and Romantic poetics, which, for Shelley, figures as the distinction between Wordsworth and Coleridge. The ideal of a naive bond with nature is for Coleridge a goal for which to strive; for Wordsworth it is, at least punctually, an achieved epiphany. The poems in the *Alastor* volume identified this difference: Wordsworth is the "Poet of Nature" that Coleridge can only yearn to be.

In "Peter Bell the Third" Shelley develops this theme in his description of Peter:

> He had a mind which was somehow
>   At once circumference and centre
> Of all he might or feel or know;
> Nothing went ever out, although
>   Something did ever enter.

> He had as much imagination
>   As a pint-pot:—he never could
> Fancy another situation
> From which to dart his contemplation,
>   Than that wherein he stood.
> · · · · · · · · · · · ·
> Thus—though unimaginative,
>   An apprehension clear, intense,
> Of his mind's work, had made alive
> The things it wrought on; I believe
>   Wakening a sort of thought in sense.

> (293-302, 308-12)

We already know why the image of "circumference and centre" is so apt. Wordsworth as a "naive" poet lives the absolute unity of part-in-whole to which the Romantic Ironic poet aspires. He is the center of one circle of "all he might or feel or know," which in the ironic condition becomes two agonizingly separate circles. His "thought in sense" is the result of their unity, the original unity of mind and world, which in the post-Kantian aesthetic it is the role of the imagination to re-create. This is why Peter/Wordsworth has "as much imagination as a pint-pot"; what seems a gratuitous insult is actually a necessary deduction from Shelley's (and Wordsworth's) theoretical premises. Wordsworth has no imagination because, as a naive poet, he *needs* no imagination. It is only we who have fallen from the unity of circumference and center, thought and sense, knowledge and feeling, who require imagination as a (therapeutic) road to recovery.

What might appear to be the poem's most unkind swipe at Wordsworth is in fact acute criticism. Peter is described as

> a kind of moral eunuch
> He touched the hem of Nature's shift,
> Felt faint—and never dared uplift
> The closest, all-concealing tunic.

(314–17)

Shelley is pointing to that constitutional flaw of the naive which allows the fall into the ironic condition to be read as a *felix culpa*. The naive has an achieved unity with nature, but it is a stagnant bond. The naive poet can express the natural perfectly but is incapable of growth, birth, and change. It is not anachronistic to read this passage with reference to the shift from the Lacanian imaginary (one recalls from the *Statesman's Manual* Coleridge's evocation of the naive bond with nature as being like an infant suckling at its mother's breast with its "strange dream of obscure yet happy sensations") to the realm of the symbolic. It is not anachronistic, because Lacan's theory is merely the latest manifestation of this quintessential Romantic pattern: the fall from childhood reverie (which is necessary in order to gain the symbolic order of speech, reason, and "progressive universal" poetry, but which haunts our thoughts, as Coleridge says, with "guilt" and a nostalgic "aching melancholy") into the adult world of stable but ironically "dividuous" meaning. Peter is a "eunuch" because he has renounced his phallic "manhood" in order to indefinitely delay his weaning from nature's breast.

In "Part Fifth" we learn that Peter "remembered well," "though it was without a sense / Of memory" (423, 424), because it is only in a self-conscious, fallen state that we are aware of "remembering" as an act, or process; to the naive, memory is a state of being. "Peter's verse was clear," Shelley tells us (433). Its clearness reminds us of Coleridge's injunction that the "Self," striving to return to the breast of nature, should become "glorified by its own transparency."

We can see now that the poem's setting in hell, and language of damnation, do not stem from some supposed desire of Wordsworth's to "see us all damned," although Leigh Hunt's review of *Peter Bell,* which in part occasioned Shelley's poem, was mostly concerned with this point, a fact that has obscured Shelley's meaning (Reiman and Powers, 321). The issue of "damnation" is raised naturally by the theoretical framework in which Shelley has chosen to place Wordsworth. It is only from the point of view of a fallen world (and, for Shelley, Satan, rather than Adam, is the great exemplar of the fall from the Absolute) that the naive can be perceived as "an approach" to the natural; in the prelapsarian world it is not possible to become self-conscious about how we approach the world. Just as Coleridge, gazing on a peaceful landscape, is led to think simultaneously of an infant asleep at its mother's breast and of our own guilt ("from this state hast *thou* fallen"), so that he is afflicted with the "aching melancholy" of the ironic condition, Shelley, contemplating the Wordsworthian ideal of becoming the transparent medium through which nature expresses itself, is driven to ask the question of what that ideal means in a world in which we are always already divided from nature, from others, and within ourselves.

Far from suggesting that Wordsworth is hasty to see us damned, Shelley, by setting his action in London-as-hell, is saying, "Given that we are 'damned' (fallen), what will happen in a fallen world to someone who attempts to maintain a prelapsarian ideal?" Shelley and Coleridge would agree that the naive union with nature proposed and indeed practiced by Wordsworth is not unproblematically available to us in a "dividuous" world. Where Shelley marks his distance from Coleridge's sentimental-ironic position is on the question whether the naive should even be a goal for those of us who are aware, perhaps uncomfortably, of our "disengagement" from the natural world. In "Peter Bell the Third," Shelley suggests that the naive can be politically culpable. To be, in Coleridge's expression, "what the plant *is,*" Shelley suggests, is an inadequate response to the political realities of hell/London.

Wordsworth's problem is that he cannot insulate himself from the dividuous world of hell. This is the significance of the Devil's coming to drag Peter away from the rural retreat of Windermere in "Part First."

Peter can survive for a while on his remembering "without a sense of memory" the redemptive promise of his childhood ("in his thought he visited / The spots in which, ere dead and damned, / He his wayward life had led" [413-15]), but eventually the world will confront him with problems that are not solvable within the naive discourse. Shelley's criticism of the naive is that it does not provide its adepts with any political resources once that inevitable day arrives. Because the naive contains no conception of alternative discourses, it cannot be articulated with them critically. This monologism means that Peter/Wordsworth's only response when political dilemmas break the magic circle of his naive world (the "circumference" he seemed to fill so completely) is to abandon the naive with a baffled resignation, even those elements of it that could form the basis of a criticism of "diabolic" politics (the basis of Shelley's criticism of the first Romantic generation's overreaction to the failure of the French Revolution; see the discussion of the *Revolt of Islam* in Chapter 4). This is what is most painful for his admirers, including Shelley, and makes sense of the quasi-epitaph in the final couplet of "To Wordsworth":

> Deserting these, thou leavest me to grieve,
> Thus having been, that thou shouldst cease to be.

In "Peter Bell the Third," after Peter has been thoroughly confused by the Devil and become "Nothing," Shelley tells us that "His morals thus were undermined" (579):

> In the death hues of agony
>   Lambently flashing from a fish,
> Now Peter felt amused to see
> Shades, like a rainbow's, rise and flee,
>   Mixed with a certain hungry wish.
>
> (584-88)

This is, Shelley's footnote explains, a reference to the *Excursion* (VIII, 557-71), a poem that "contains curious evidence of the gradual hardening of a strong but circumscribed sensibility, of the perversion of a penetrating but panic stricken understanding" (Reiman and Powers, 342). The terms of this description merit careful consideration because this is a direct comment, outside the playfulness of the poem, on Wordsworth himself. Wordsworth's sensibility is "strong but circumscribed"—he is powerful within the circle of his naive world—but once that circle is broken (or perverted) he becomes helpless: "panic stricken." This last is a subtle pun. Wordsworth is stricken by Pan, the god of nature, unable to deal with those aspects of the world that fall outside his realm. Politically, the result of this is the ease with which he is co-opted as a propagandist for the Devil's party (634ff.), rationalizing any evil because incapable of finding a secure framework from which to judge it.

II

But if Shelley finds fault with the naive, he is equally hard on the Romantic Ironic as a possible basis for a politics. If being a plant is unhelpful, so is the desire to be a plant (although at least as a conscious desire it has the advantage of being a position from which one can mount a critique of the actual). Coleridge's appearance in the poem, which I have already discussed above, underlines this point: trusting "in shadows undiscerned" (386), he has "damned himself to madness" (387); the "aching melancholy" with which he yearns to return to the breast of nature, and the desire to become "all permeable to a holier power," although they allow him to criticize the present day and its subjection to the "Spirit of Commerce," set goals so lofty that it is impossible to imagine a concrete (political) practice that might take us from the modern dividuous condition to the absolute reconciliation with nature he proposes. This is the meaning of the description of Coleridge in "Peter Bell the Third":

> This was a man who might have turned
>   Hell into Heaven—and so in gladness
> A Heaven unto himself have earned;
> But he in shadows undiscerned
>   Trusted,—and damned himself to madness.
>
> (383–87)

Had Coleridge been able to bend his immense gifts to the task of concrete reform, Shelley suggests, he might have been able to turn, or help turn, the actual political world (London/hell) into something more nearly approaching a *political* heaven. Instead, he has focused his energies on the attempt to realize a metaphysical, and metapolitical, heaven (the "shadows undiscerned"), and thereby damned himself to the "madness" of ironic despair, and damned himself (and us) to continuing in this (politically) fallen world. As a result, despite the fact that Coleridge describes in intoxicating language a poetic power quite at odds with the sordid world of the Devil's reign (388–97), the Devil can entertain himself with Coleridge standing tamely behind his chair at his "petits soupers" (377, 374), knowing full well that these lofty sentiments have no revolutionary bite. The Romantic Ironic, if it does not promote political oppression, passively condones it: it is difficult to make the step from yearning to be one with nature to responding coherently to the Peterloo massacre (see 644ff.).

Finally, Shelley's most "post-Kantian" conception was his idea of the relationship of the poet to what he called "the spirit of the age"—poetry being regarded as the vehicle of that spirit. The expression was a favorite of Shelley's, and his may well have been the first written use of it in English.[35] Whether or not this is the case, the idea was central to the therapeutic politics and metaphysics that was evolving in the period. In A. W. Schlegel's characterization of the classical as opposed to the Romantic spirit, in Winckelmann's description of a coherent classical mentality, in Coleridge's Schillerian descriptions of our mechanistic society enslaved by the "Spirit of Commerce," even in Burke's organic paternalism, Shelley met again and again with arguments that took this narrativization of history for granted.

One finds this concept in Shelley's writing, but that he did not adopt it as an unquestioned premise of historiography and social theory is a telling example of Shelley's consistently critical approach to his sources. Shelley occasionally conceived of the true poet as a kind of world-historical individual, alive almost unconsciously to the "spirit of the age": "The great writers of our own age are, we have reason to suppose, the companions and forerunners of some unimagined change in our social condition or the opinions which cement it. The cloud of mind is discharging its collected lightning, and the equilibrium between institutions and opinions is now restoring, or is about to be restored" (Reiman and Powers, 134). This idea is one of the key themes of Shelley's *Defence,* and finds particularly confident expression in the rousing conclu-

---

35. The *OED* gives an 1820 letter of Shelley's as its earliest English use of the expression. In fact, he had already used it in his *Philosophical View of Reform* of 1819. He uses it on at least three other occasions in the letters (*Letters,* 2:127, 180, 304; see also 164). Abrams, listing English uses of the phrase in the early nineteenth century, gives Shelley's *Philosophical View* as the earliest ("English Romanticism: The Spirit of the Age," 45). Ann and John Robson note in their edition of J. S. Mill's *Newspaper Writings* (228) that Hazlitt had mentioned, though not translated, in the *Examiner,* 1 December 1816, the title of a work by Ernst Moritz Arndt, *Der Geist der Zeit* (1805), which they claim to be the earliest occurrence of the German expression (the *Dictionary of the History of Ideas,* under "zeitgeist," suggests that Schiller used the phrase in his *Aesthetic Education,* but I have been unable to trace it there). Shelley would have read this edition of the *Examiner,* and it is possible the phrase was common coin in the Hunt circle; Hazlitt's more famous use of it in 1825 tends to corroborate this.

sion to that essay: "Poets are the hierophants of an unapprehended in-spiration, the mirrors of the gigantic shadows which futurity casts upon the present, the words which express what they understand not; the trumpets which sing to battle, and feel not what they inspire: the influ-ence which is moved not, but moves" (Reiman and Powers, 508). Here the comparison to Hegel's "world-historical individuals," whose goals correspond to the providential narrative of the *Weltgeist*, seems quite close. These are people who appear at crucial moments when one form or "stage" of the world-Spirit's development is played out and a new one must be ushered in: "[W]hen Spirit has deserted the reigning form, it is the world-historical individual who shows the way to what all men in their depths aspire to." This new stage is irresistible "even for those who are inclined by their own interest or judgment against it, because deep down they cannot help identifying with it" (Taylor, *Hegel and Modern Society*, 99).

But in the quotation, above, from the conclusion to Shelley's *Defence*, I have stopped short of the final and most famous line: "Poets are the unacknowledged legislators of the World." It is the unsettling implica-tions of that line that so typically for Shelley emerge as an abyss or vacancy at the moment of seeming plenitude and certainty. Can poets *both* be vehicles of a Spirit which situates them and in which they fulfill themselves in furthering its but dimly perceived providential goals, *and* be "legislators" of the world, the very perpetrators of the "self-given laws" that Hegel thought could lead only to a "*fury* of destruction"?

4

Skepticism Versus Idealism:
An Old Problem Reconsidered

LOVE'S RARE UNIVERSE

I

To answer the question on which I finished the last chapter, one could argue that Shelley believed poets are unacknowledged legislators *because* of their access to the "eternal" and the "one," that they "legislate" to the world because, by giving a local habitation and a name to the universal truths of the *Weltgeist*, they make known *in* the world the immutable laws by which it must operate, regardless. This argument, although weighty, is almost certainly wrong. Shelley does want to empower individuals with the ability to change their political situations. He does, as we saw when exploring his skeptical revolutionism, want to release the kind of open-ended change that cannot be reconciled with a therapeutic-idealist politics and poetics. The Shelley who writes of poets as the mirrors of the shadows cast by futurity on the present seems incompatible with these goals. What I explore in this chapter and the next is how these two sides of Shelley's thought relate to each other.

I begin by returning to the question of the spirit of the age. Throughout Shelley's writing he is prone to shift with alarming suddenness from, say, a notion of inspiration as an external spirit entering and using the hardly conscious poet as a tool for expression—the model that obtains in much of the *Defence*—to an assertion in the same essay that the "power" of creation "arises from within, like the colour of a flower which fades and changes as it is developed, and the conscious portions of our natures are unprophetic either of its approach or its departure" (Reiman and Powers, 405), that far from being the unconscious and even unwilling vehicle of *Geist* a poet is "the happiest, the best, the wisest, and the most illustrious of men" (506) but totally alienated from society: "a nightingale, who sits in darkness and sings to cheer its own solitude with sweet sounds" (486).

We find this same apparent paradox in *Hellas* in the equivocation over whether Ahasuerus really conjures up an external/other-directed vision for Mahmud or Mahmud has an internal/self-directed hallucination "through the confusion of thought with the objects of thought, and the excess of passion animating the creations of imagination" (note to *Hellas;* Hutchinson, 479). Here Shelley's otherwise unaccountably labored explication of this minor point stems from his own deep-seated uncertainty over the possibility of real, externally generated inspiration of the kind for which the dramatic situation clearly calls. Not even poetic license could assuage Shelley's troubled and indecisive attitude toward this question.

But the problem goes further than simple indecisiveness. For Shelley, the whole idealist model of multeity-within-unity was at once the defining moral center of what he recognized as a functional politics, and was undermined as both conceptually improbable and—most troublingly—ethically repugnant. To understand why requires us to take another look at Shelley's seemingly most confident statements of therapeutic idealism. For example, this passage from the preface to the *Revolt of Islam* seems at first glance one more statement in line with Hegel's notion of the individual, who, in the formation of society's norms and ends, "brings them about through his activity, but as something which rather simply is": "[T]here must be a resemblance, which does not depend upon their own will, between all the writers of any particular age. They cannot escape from subjection to a common influence which arises out of an infinite combination of circumstances belonging to the times in which they live; though each is in a degree the author of the very influence by which his being is thus pervaded" (Hutchinson, 35).

On closer examination, however, Shelley's statement of the dialectic here seems too frank; he resists the appeal to a grounding, determining-in-the-last-instance pole in the dialectic that could weight and give a guarantee of continuity to the system. This loosening up of the dialectic leads to an emphasis on the course of literature through the ages, not as the regular progression of the developing spirit or one great poem or "revolutionary class" but as a nonfinite, or *atelic,* generation of new and different meanings. "All high poetry is infinite. . . . Veil after veil may be undrawn, and the inmost naked beauty of the meaning never exposed. . . . [A]fter one person and one age has exhausted all of its divine effluence which their peculiar relations enable them to share, another and yet another succeeds, and new relations are ever developed, the source of an unforeseen and an unconceived delight" (Reiman and Powers, 500).

This image of time as succession without story, as the continuous reinvention of the poem *ex nihilo,* is impossible to reconcile with the therapeutic idealism he seems to proclaim so confidently elsewhere in the *Defence.* Here we seem to have completely returned to the Shelley I described under the rubric of skeptical revolutionism.

How then to reconcile these two Shelleys? The question is hardly new; indeed, describing Shelley as "torn" between idealism and skepticism is one of the hoarier clichés of Shelley criticism. Like many clichés, however, it contains an element of truth that has not yet been ascertained. An earlier generation of critics was content to see Shelley as simply confused on this issue, drawing on "various traditions [that] remain imperfectly assimilated, so that one can discriminate two planes of thought in Shelley's aesthetics" (Abrams, *Mirror and the Lamp,* 126). Since C. E. Pulos's *Deep Truth,* however, the dominant trend of Shelley criticism has been toward establishing the coherence, consistency, and originality of Shelley's thought. Pulos himself suggested that Shelley had forged a "skeptical idealism" out of his divided intellectual inheritance, using Drummond's *Academical Questions* to find "a mode of reconciling the empirical and the Platonic traditions" (Pulos, 112). Wasserman, in his influential and erudite account in *Shelley: A Critical Reading,* preferred to see the two poles of Shelley's thought as representing an intellectual itinerary: from a skeptical, revolutionary youth to an idealist, visionary maturity (although Wasserman advances contradictory views on this point and never pretends that Shelley's thought is absolutely consistent at any time).

More recently, the "opposition" tends to have been cast aside as outmoded. More and more, Shelley critics have foregrounded Shelley's skepticism as the leading tendency in his thought. Although writers like Lloyd Abbey and Jerrold Hogle still refer to Shelley's "Platonic skepticism" or "skeptical idealism" (Hogle, *Shelley's Process,* 294),[1] the emphasis in both cases is heavily on the skepticism. The influence of de-

---

1. Hogle's actual expression is "an idealism so skeptical that it finds no single idea on which to rest and a skepticism so idealistic that it has to affirm the perpetual fall and rise from idea to idea."

constructionist criticism, and a reaction against the New Critical ideal of the poetic text, which had so thoroughly marginalized Shelley's poetry, have combined in the last two decades to make predominant an interest in the way Shelley's texts resist closure, subvert the "dogmas" of contemporary ideology, and call into question their own epistemological status. Rather than well-wrought verbal icons, Shelley's poems are increasingly seen as complex, uncentered works that refuse monologic coherence; such meanings as the reader tentatively constructs are always (already) threatened with sudden collapse.[2]

The striking thing about Shelley's texts, however, and the reason this debate has been so long-lived, is the way therapeutic and skeptical concepts seem to jostle each other within not just the same work but the same paragraph, or even sentence, of the same work. Trying to decide whether Shelley is "really" a skeptic or "really" an idealist, either absolutely or at any stage of his career, is a quixotic task.

Nowhere is this better exemplified than in his "On Life" of 1819. This remarkably complex text has long been a crux in Shelley criticism, and has been cited as evidence of Shelley's out-and-out idealism and of his radical skepticism. If we take a brief look at it, however, we will see that neither argument really holds. Consider this remarkable passage, whose relationship to therapeutic discourse does not need to be spelled out:

> The view of life presented by the most refined deductions of the intellectual philosophy, is that of unity. . . . The difference is merely nominal between those two classes of thought . . . ideas and . . . external objects. Pursuing the same thread of reasoning, the existence of distinct individual minds, similar to that which is employed in now questioning its own nature, is likewise found to be a delusion. The words *I, you, they,* are not signs of any actual difference subsisting between the assemblage of thoughts thus indicated, but are merely marks employed to denote the different modifications of the one mind.
>
> Let it not be supposed that this doctrine conducts to the monstrous presumption that I, the person who now write and think, am that one mind. I am but a portion of it. The words *I* and *you* and *they* are grammatical devices invented simply for arrangement, and totally devoid of the intense and exclusive sense usually attached to them. (Reiman and Powers, 477–78)

---

2. See Paul Hamilton, "'Old Anatomies': Some Recent Shelley Criticism," for a useful overview of this trend.

Nothing could seem more blatantly idealist: we transcend our habitual view of the spatial and temporal world of "time and place and number," with its aggregative manifold of individual minds, and rise to a point of view from which we can perceive our selves as a conscious portion of "one mind" composed of all minds.

We are immediately confronted with a paradox, however. Shelley describes this philosophy, appropriately, as the "intellectual system"; but then he suggests that "the most clear and vigorous statement of the intellectual system is to be found in Sir W. Drummond's Academical Questions" (476). A skeptical reading of Shelley, such as Hoagwood's, inevitably seizes upon this as proof that what appear to be Shelley's most unbounded flights of idealist enthusiasm are actually his idiosyncratic, perhaps deliberately subversive presentations of Drummond's brand of radical skepticism. The argument is cogent, but there are serious problems with it.

Hoagwood rejects any hint of idealism in Shelley's reference here to "one mind":

> Wasserman makes much of it by capitalizing two letters in a phrase that Shelley applies to a person ("one mind") and then transforming that phrase into a confession of virtually religious faith; this is the One Mind concept that Wasserman elaborates with impressive complexity but with almost total impertinence to Shelley's actual statements. In *On Life* (where the phrase "one mind" appears), Shelley is concerned to enclose the terms of the argument within epistemological and even linguistic limits; Wasserman, in contrast, lunges into a religious impulse and an assertion of x beyond y (Being beyond existence). (*Skepticism and Ideology*, 218 n. 53)

Citing Charles Robinson, Hoagwood suggests how this apparent idealism can (and ought to) be read in the light of Shelley's evocation of the *Academical Questions:* "Shelley uses the phrase 'one mind' to designate not the ontological unity into which all human minds are subsumed, but rather the epistemological unity of thoughts in an individual mind" (218; the reference is to *The Snake and the Eagle*)—or, in other words, the modifications of "the one mind" being modifications of one individual mind circumscribed within the "epistemological circle."

The argument is ingenious, but presents some grave problems. Most simply, it does not mesh with the sense of the passage. Shelley explicitly sets out to deny the "existence of distinct individual minds," a goal that is hard to reconcile with a confident reference to modifications of one such "distinct individual mind." The paragraph directly follows one in which he muses on children's ability in the state of "reverie" to feel "as if the surrounding universe were absorbed into their being. They are conscious of no distinction." It is hard, too, to understand what role the "unity" Shelley's "intellectual philosophy" announces is supposed to play in Hoagwood's schema.

Hoagwood is also being unfair to Wasserman in suggesting that "On Life" is the only place "where the phrase 'one mind' appears." Shelley uses the phrase, or similar expressions, in many different works, and always with an unmistakable impulse toward mental collectivity.[3] Even granting Hoagwood's distinction between Shelley's "philosophical" prose and unphilosophical poetry—a distinction Shelley dismisses as a "vulgar error" (Reiman and Powers, 484)—Shelley's prose is rich in collective minds,[4] proof that Shelley's political ideal could sometimes take the form of an absolute collectivity.

One passage commonly cited as proof that the "intellectual system" is skepticism follows shortly after the reference to *Academical Questions:* "What follows from this admission [that the "intellectual system" is irrefutable]? It establishes no new truth, it gives us no additional insight into our hidden nature, neither in action nor itself. . . . It reduces the mind to that freedom in which it would have acted, but for the misuse of words and signs, the instruments of its own creation" (Reiman and Powers, 477). There is nothing in this, however, incompatible with therapeutic idealism. Therapeutic politics are not generally radical politics; they do not seek to establish a new system, but to change the way the individual mind (but for the misuse of words and signs) conceives of its relationship to the system. The therapeutic imperative is to grasp the universal *in* the particular, not to make the abstract and revolutionary leap to the universal by abandoning the existent world of particular distinctions. Hegelians and Spinozists, just like the inhabitants of Hoag-

---

3. See, e.g., *Prometheus Unbound,* IV, 93-94, 394-95, 400-402; "The Daemon of the World," II, 539; "Lines Written Among the Euganean Hills," 316; *Revolt of Islam,* V: "Laone's Speech," 4, 13; VII, xxxi, 5.

4. Most notable, perhaps, is the reference in the *Defence* to the "co-operating thoughts of one great mind," which are responsible for the "great poem" of which all individual poems are merely portions. One could also point to the striking passage from the preface to *Prometheus Unbound,* which, nearly contemporary with "On Life," tells us that "the cloud of mind is discharging its collected lightning," or to his vision of the ideal society in the "Assassins," in which "all formed, as it were, one being, divided against itself by no contending will or factious passions" (Ingpen and Peck, 6:162).

wood's "experiential circle," jump out of the way of buses, even if they know that they and the bus are all, in some sense, one.

Schiller made this point in a passage sufficiently similar to the above quotation from "On Life" that it raises the question whether Shelley had read the *Aesthetic Education:* "Beauty gives no individual result whatsoever, either for the intellect or for the will; it realizes no individual purpose, either intellectual or moral; it discovers no individual truth, helps us to perform no individual duty" (101). But despite this apparent inefficacy, therapeutic "Beauty" is still the means to attaining "something infinite."

One can pursue this idealist reading of "On Life" quite far. The passing reference to Drummond is more ambiguous than has been realized. To what aspect of Drummond's work is Shelley referring? Might he not be picking up on Drummond's attacks on the integrity of the individual mind? Drummond's own pure fideism could be taken to assert an ultimate unity-in-God underlying the apparent chaos of the phenomenal world. Shelley's substantive definitions of the "intellectual system" bear no obvious relationship to the radical skepticism he seems, elsewhere, to have readily absorbed from Drummond, but we easily recognize the influence of Coleridge in the following: "Whatever may be his [man's] true and final destination, there is a spirit within him at enmity with nothingness and dissolution (change and extinction). This is the character of all life and being.—Each is at once the centre and the circumference; the point to which all things are referred, and the line in which all things are contained.—Such contemplations as these materialism and the popular philosophy of mind and matter, alike forbid; they are consistent only with the intellectual system" (Reiman and Powers, 476). Whatever Shelley intends by the "popular philosophy of mind and matter"—and he cannot mean therapeutic idealism—it is clear that aside from the reference to William Drummond, "On Life" presents no problems and every encouragement for anyone who wants to read the "intellectual philosophy" as a therapeutic idealism. When Shelley tells us that the "view of life presented by the . . . intellectual philosophy, is that of unity," he explains that this is the kind of unity-with-nature that a child appears to achieve in its state of "reverie" and that we adults, (fallen) victims of the apparent solidity of "impressions, planted by reiteration," have lost the ability to enjoy. We cannot mistake the echo of Coleridge's "aching melancholy" at the sight of the "beautiful infant" asleep at its mother's breast, smiling "in its strange dream of obscure yet happy sensations." Like him, Shelley seems to suggest that "from this state hast *thou* fallen! Such shouldst thou still become." To read the claim that we are all at once center and circumference as an argument that we are all isolated within our "epistemological circles" seems forced at best.

My point is not that we should abandon the skeptical reading of "On Life" and substitute for it an idealist one. It is, rather, that what makes "On Life"—and indeed all Shelley's writing—exciting, challenging, and politically effective is its genuine undecidability. Despite the emphatic moments of therapeutic prophecy in this piece, there is one undeniable moment of pure skeptical doubt, and significantly it follows directly the ringing confidence of his argument that he is but a "portion" of the "one mind": "It is difficult to find terms adequately to express so subtle a conception as that to which the intellectual philosophy has conducted us. We are on that verge where words abandon us, and what wonder if we grow dizzy to look down the dark abyss of—how little we know" (Reiman and Powers, 478). Once again the train of thought that leads Hegel to Absolute Knowledge finds Shelley peering into an abyss, contemplating vacancy.

II

Given this tight interweaving of apparently contradictory philosophies, attempts to read Shelley as entirely skeptical or entirely idealist inevitably give us an incomplete portrait of his thought. The exploration of the political implications of skepticism and therapeutic idealism in the last two chapters puts us now in a position to understand that this has particularly serious consequences for any attempt to describe Shelley's politics.

The "decentering" tendency in Shelley criticism appears eagerly to embrace the idea of opening his text out to the possibility of multiple meanings and multiple, even contradictory, discursive frameworks. The most interesting, most provocative, and most thorough statement of this argument is in Hogle's monumental *Shelley's Process: Radical Transference and the Development of His Major Works.* The impressive intellectual scope and power of this work make it something of a limit case. If we can find serious problems with his argument, they are likely to represent problems with this entire approach. Nor are they hard to find. Hogle's concept of "transference" (the term owes a great deal to Jean Hall's concept of "transformation" developed in *The Transforming Image*) maintains that Shelley's works open out to an endless, directionless, and constant free play of significance:

> "[T]ransference" . . . literally indicates any "bearing across" between places, moments, thoughts, words, or persons—while

adding the "conveyance" of any perception *without* total inversion into a location, figure, or moment not its own. If it is a
"center" for Shelleyan thought in this study it is the most decentered one that could possibly be imagined and is really more of a
rootless passage between different formations. It is a primordial,
preconscious shift, intimated in the movement of perception,
feeling, and language, always already becoming a different enactment of itself at another time and in conjunction with other elements. (15)

For Hogle, this aimless, unstoppable drift of meaning has a directly political relevance: "[W]hen such ['decentering'] frames are employed [in
reading Shelley's texts], I find that Shelley's writing fairly explodes with
revolutionary movements and implications hitherto unrecognized" (vii).
This "revolutionary" impact of Shelley's transferential drive stems from
the power of transference to disrupt the stable meanings on which oppressive, hierarchical systems depend: "The reader must construct the
new option, not just by composing the redefinitions of 'ruler' and 'subject' that are needed, but by accepting, in the new logic that he or she
makes, the incessant transformation of all the reworked terms by other
forms of them, the *illogic* (by most current standards) that is humankind's best hope for future equality, free development, and social justice" (197). The world of Shelley's texts, in Hogle's view, is a world of
mythopoeic associationism in which forms coalesce and decompose according to any principle that happens temporarily to predominate.
    There are two major, and related, problems with this. The first is that,
while individual readings of Shelley's texts can be exciting and apparently liberating, collectively the effect of reading through Hogle's text is
of a rigid monologism. Time after time we discover that Shelley's text
destroys all stable meanings and promotes transferential drift. It appears
that Shelley had only one song to sing, and sang it with relentless repeti-
tiveness. Although Hogle would be willing to accept that one can discern skeptical and therapeutic frameworks intermingled in Shelley's
work, it is impossible, within the terms of his argument, to make anything of this. In principle, each Shelley text can mean, will mean, has
meant, anything one cares to suggest. In the world of transferential drift
any meaning one proposes will instantly appear reflected in the work
one is reading. One cannot address the tension between any two tendencies in the work, because without relatively stable distinctions it is
impossible for any tension to be maintained. Indeed, Hogle, unlike
Hoagwood, recognizes the tendency in Shelley's later work to explore

the imagery of the collective "one mind," and even recognizes the influence of Coleridge in this tendency (296), but this turns out to be the "one mind" of universal transferential play. All is One because each is transferentially capable of becoming anything.

This is the most serious problem of the "decentering" approach to Shelley. Once a text has been opened up to mean everything, it becomes impossible for it to *mean* anything. The transferential text is a kind of hermeneutical "white noise," meaning everything and nothing. Hogle works so hard to show that every Shelley text is playful, destabilizing, and disruptive that he ends up making them sound completely interchangeable and ultimately—and most damagingly—boring. Why read a work that says nothing it does not instantly unsay? And if you have read one, why read another?

The second problem is a specific case of this general one. What is the political significance of the *soi-disant* "radical" transference? Consider this description of the transferential liberation effected by *Prometheus Unbound,* the liberation to mix and match "mythographs" (the elements of myth), and by implication all discourses, at will:

> For this poet there must be—and we should more consciously recognize that there is—a transpersonal level of sheer figures inhabited by all the world's mythographs irrespective of the systems they serve, in which each shape veers toward all the others it resembles (or would join to itself) without finalizing any combination until the conscious will calls one forth from its depths. Even syncretic mythography would be impossible without this pre-existent interplay, yet the latter puts the former in question by eventually dissipating all syncretic conflations. To be unbound from a domineering system, even from the Great Memory, is automatically to return (as Prometheus does) to this serene but teeming clearing house of figural potentialities. To be Prometheus (or Asia) as well as being unbound is to dissolve into being the many-shaped, almost invisible, energizer, channeller, and performer of this vast mythographic interplay. (204)

While it is true that this dissolution of structure implies a negation of "domineering systems," Hogle's polymorphic political pluralism is vulnerable to Eagleton's recent critique of poststructuralist politics:

> If there is a type of Kantian categorical imperative which Lyotard would be willing to accept, it would be: "One must maximise as much as possible the multiplication of small narratives." The

problem with this case is that it is a sentimental illusion to believe that small is always beautiful. What small narratives does Lyotard have in mind? The current, gratifyingly minor tributary of British fascism? Plurality, in short, as for post-structuralism in general, is a good in itself, quite regardless of its ethical or political substance. What is morally just is to generate as many language games as possible, all of them strictly incommensurable. (*Aesthetic*, 399)

This is a better critique of Hogle than of Lyotard. What Lyotard means by "small narratives" is narratives that do not seek to impose themselves upon other narratives. In that sense, fascism, no matter how small the number of its adherents, is a dominant narrative, with absolute claims that negate the claims to validity of all other narratives. The problem with Hogle's radical transference is that there seems to be no certain ground on which to make such a distinction; not only might he ask "qu'importe qui parle?" but "qu'importe ce qu'on dit?" The concept of a truly radical transference seems to deny the possibility of political action in any recognizable sense.

Hogle's attempts to describe a practical transferential politics forcibly recall Godwin's fireside chats, so resistant is he to any appeal to even transiently stable collectivities: "To be discussing reform in a centerless collective or to be working with another being to change both your characters toward greater sympathy with each other and others beyond you: these actions *are* universal transference in particular guises, in willed, practical reworkings of our deepest cultural and mental impulse" (*Shelley's Process*, 261). Eagleton, like Shelley in Godwin's case, would no doubt be inclined to ask how many capitalists are going to lose sleep over this?

What is lacking is Lyotard's notion of the *différend*: how can one engage in political struggle with that which one cannot, at any level, distinguish from oneself? Hogle, like many American deconstructionist-influenced critics, ignores the delicate balancing act between difference (the basis of our ability to mean anything) and the ever-present possibility of the subversion of difference (which is never absolutely realized) that lies at the heart of Derrida's concept of *différance*. The "break" that opens up the possibility of the iterative play of the signifier represents only an ever-present possibility "without it preventing the mark from functioning" ("Limited Inc," 202). There can be no point in subverting hierarchies if those hierarchies do not present at least a certain resistance to our efforts, which implies a degree of stability on their part.

It is difficult to understand what exactly Shelley's texts are supposed to free us from. The apparent ease with which Hogle's Shelley triumphs over oppression makes one wonder how it is possible that we have not been freed, or have not realized that we are already free, long since. Transference dances off Shelley's texts and rapidly installs itself in every imaginable discourse; it seems less a peculiar quality of Shelley's writing than the inherent structure, or antistructure, of language itself. If this is the case, if all language endlessly deconstructs itself, what need have we of, and where is the radicalism in, transferential poetry and deconstructionist critics?

Hogle assures us that, despite its loudly proclaimed rejection of telos, transference "is humankind's best hope for future equality, free development, and social justice." It may seem difficult to imagine what gives him the confidence to assert that this is the inevitable end point to which a radically decentered free play must tend. This brings us, however, to the most disturbing aspect of almost all these "decentering" readings of Shelley. There is, or should be, at least one genuinely radical aspect to Hogle's "transference," Hall's "transformation," Simpson's version of "Romantic Irony," Scrivener's "philosophic anarchism," Wright's "metaphoricity," and the like, and that is the unleashing of a politically efficacious negativity, even if it is one that seems too comprehensive to be part of any specific politics. These critics, however, refuse to accept the consequences of that negativity. Coleridge, who believed that "extremes meet," would have appreciated the irony of their solution. Again and again we find that this negation is in fact a negation of the negation. Shelley's "skepticism" is a kind of *via negativa* to an aimless, second-order idealism that reassures us that change can only ever be part of the gradual revelation of human unity.

This is implicit in Hogle's approach to the Shelleyan "One." He does not identify some negative, deconstructive power hitherto unnoticed in this idealist concept. Rather, the fact that he recognizes the One as essentially the same as his transferential universe reveals the extent to which the transferential ability of each particular text to reflect and embody any discourse is the return of the Coleridgean "ALL IN EACH": heaven in a drop of dew, or the particular as vehicle of the universal.

Take, for example, Hogle's reading of the role of Demogorgon in *Prometheus Unbound,* particularly as it relates to his deposition of Jupiter: "This shifting from old methods of retraction and repression to more productive yet related constructs that drag down their predecessors: this sequence is history's enactment of Demogorgon's 'nature.' In that sense it/he is, as he later claims [III, i, 52], the 'Eternity' in the process of time, the perpetual impulse bringing about the ideologies of the past, the present, and the future" (*Shelley's Process,* 189). If Demogorgon represents the transferential principle operating in the historical world, he must also represent a providential Absolute acting to bring about the salvation of the "One," which has fallen into division. How else to explain that this supposedly amoral and atelic transference is always toward "more productive . . . constructs"? How else to explain that a complete surrender to the transferential principle Demogorgon represents will guarantee us "future equality, free development, and social justice?" With Eternity watching over us to bring about a millennial order of equality and justice, it is not surprising that Hogle should draw on the most characteristic of therapeutic-idealist images to convey the nature of Shelley's transferential politics, here in a description of the *Philosophical View of Reform:* "He proposes a multiple, fluid, and ever expanding set of interactions between different interests and needs that lack an initial core of entirely fixed principles. This outreach from different groups of people toward more and more interrelations with others should work to fashion a series of common aims and projections that can draw even more thinkers into the group and still leave room for divergent desires, abilities, and means to ends. Such a conflation at its best can be unabashedly centripetal and centrifugal at the same time" (258).

This unconsciously presupposed idealism acts as a kind of safety net. Shelley might be the most daring of poetic trapeze artists, turning somersaults in the void between subject and object, cause and effect; but when he eventually drops (beating his luminous wings more or less in vain), he is not swallowed by the abyss; his most nihilistic disruptions of meaning always turn out to have a therapeutic import.

It is not difficult to find examples to demonstrate that this close connection between textual "decentering" and therapeutic idealism is not peculiar to Hogle. The abrupt and catastrophic endings of *Adonais* and *Epipsychidion,* where Shelley suddenly seems unable to continue, are not, Hall assures us, evidence of any crisis of confidence; having reached the "final rapture of universal fusion . . . the Shelleyan poem simply dies of its own happiness" (*Transforming,* 104). Hall's openended, uncontainable, "transformation," we learn, does have a final goal, although the quest for it can be constantly renewed. It is one familiar to readers of Schiller, Schelling, and Coleridge—a "universal fusion," or reconciliation of mind and world, achieved in the creative act: "the poet [by writing a poem] changes the world into an image of his ideal self" (104, 165).

Similarly, Simpson manages to conflate the skeptical critique of causality and his peculiar version of "deconstruction" into an ultimately therapeutic approach. He turns the skeptical critique of the very notion of cause and effect into the positing of a mystical unity of the two terms, a "con-fusion" that he explicitly relates to the Coleridgean fusion of subject and object (112–14). In his view, the attempt to ground epistemology on ontology, which is the essence of therapeutic idealism (all knowledge is basically self-knowledge), is also the hallmark of a deconstructive destabilization of meaning (113). Like Hogle, he implies that the deconstructive undermining of individual oppositions is predicated upon the possibility of a total collapse of differences into a primordial and undifferentiated Absolute (Hogle's "One," Simpson's "con-fusion").

For a final example we return to Hoagwood. The skeptical view of historical process is one that must deny the possibility of narrative recuperation or totalization; change is never development, the unfolding in time of a singular truth, but sheer and irreducible sequence. Like these other skeptical critics, however, Hoagwood is not willing to face the antitherapeutic consequences of pursuing this argument to its logical conclusions; he wants to find the reassurance of human values in history. We first sense this in his discussion of perfectibilism. In the "eternity" of the "process of ideological construction," which sounds much like Hogle's transferential "One" and its endless formation and deformation of mythographs, the unattainability of perfection ensures an endless process of improvement: "Perfection (finality) being unattainable, progress (or at least change) is and should be perpetual" (*Skepticism and Ideology*, 95). The same reasoning led to Friedrich Schlegel's description of Romantic poetry as "progressive universal poetry"; in the fallen world we can only crave the Absolute, not attain it. Within Hoagwood's skeptical and relativist perspective, however, the very notion of "progress" should be inconceivable, as he partly acknowledges in his parenthetical disclaimer: "or at least change."[5] Hoagwood is blurring what, in the terms of his argument, should be an absolute distinction. Only if I can hold past and present together and see their differences as stages in the development of a unitary truth can I say that the present represents progress over the past.

If he blurs this difference here, Hoagwood later completely subordinates the radical potential of atelic change to the humanist programma-

5. Hoagwood (*Skepticism and Ideology*, 181) denies any teleological overtones to Shelley's concept of perfectibility. Nonetheless he believes that the political innovations Shelley is advocating all represent "improvements" over the present, and he fails to explain what philosophical (rather than practical) difference there could be between a short-term teleology (the struggle for political goals) and a long-term teleology (the struggle to realize an ideal society).

tic of progressive spiritual travail: "To summarize: a statement of fact can be validated because it promotes human development. With the criterion of utility in its broadest intellectual sense, this validation can warrant an utterance. . . . Shelley's readers are enjoined to struggle toward certain objects of collective importance; Shelley calls this struggle a duty" (207). The "promotion" of "human development," the "duty" to "struggle" toward goals of "collective importance"—one might well be reading Schiller. "Enhancement" and "human development" should mean nothing to a relativist; neither "duty" nor "struggle" should make sense to the skeptic who dissolves the unity of duration into mere flux; Shelley's sure knowledge of what objects are of "collective importance" seems surprising for someone trapped within the "epistemological circle." Hoagwood, like Simpson, Hall, and Hogle, quietly assumes an optimistic humanism quite incompatible with his critical position.

The problem with this is not that the therapeutic idealism this criticism assumes is an illegitimate critical framework. The problem is that having it come in the back door in this way prevents us from properly confronting it. If in the past there was too easy an assumption that Shelley was basically idealist, it remained possible to try to understand his skepticism in relation to that idealism, either as a youthful phase or as simple confusion. The current wide consensus that his skepticism is the essence of his philosophy at once denies the possibility of reading any individual text in idealist terms but leaps to the assumption that globally his skeptical texts serve therapeutic purposes. Above all, this means that Shelley's own conscious struggle with these two approaches— its urgency, its rare triumphs, its frequent desperation—cannot be addressed. The elements of the struggle never meet: each work is contentedly skeptical, its effect miraculously and unproblematically therapeutic.

To acknowledge the conscious agon in Shelley's thought allows us to put in question the therapeutic assumptions of contemporary critical practice. Both the therapeutic-idealist and the skeptical approaches involve serious political difficulties: the first stifles political innovation and denies the possibility of a genuine *différend* between a political system and its individual members; the second seems unable to address the individual's sense of attachment to a wider social network and is therefore limited in its usefulness as the basis of any active politics. The question is whether Shelley simply alternates between these two positions, using each to criticize the limitations of the other, or is in fact operating within an entirely different conceptual framework in which some principled rapprochement of these apparently opposite viewpoints is possible.

Hegel's portrait, in the *Phenomenology,* of the skeptic as the incipient form of the Unhappy Consciousness suggests a third, less flattering
possibility:

> In Scepticism . . . the wholly unessential and non-independent
> character of this "other" becomes explicit. . . . [T]hought . . .
> annihilates the being of the world in all its manifold determinate-
> ness, and the negativity of free self-consciousness comes to know
> itself . . . as a real negativity.
>   . . . Scepticism corresponds to [the] *realization* [of "the *inde-*
> *pendent* consciousness which appeared as the lord and bonds-
> man relationship"—the relationship internalized in the Unhappy
> Consciousness] as a negative attitude towards otherness, to de-
> sire and work. . . . [T]his polemical bearing towards the manifold
> independence of things will . . . be successful, because it turns
> against them as a free self-consciousness that is already complete
> in its own self . . . the independent things in their differences
> from one another are for it only vanishing magnitudes. . . .
>   . . . Scepticism . . . *makes* this "other" which claims to be real,
> vanish. What Scepticism causes to vanish is not only objective
> reality as such, but its own relationship to it. . . . Through this
> self conscious negation it procures for its own self the certainty
> of its freedom, generates the experience of that freedom, and
> thereby raises it to truth. What vanishes is the determinate ele-
> ment, or the moment of difference . . . because the "different" is
> just this, not to be in possession of itself, but to have its essential
> being only in an other. (123–24)

This is an accurate description of the inadequacies Shelley saw in his
politics of skepticism, particularly the erasure of the other and the solipsistic certainty of the self. But it goes further, and herein lies the challenge of this description for our understanding of Shelley. Hegel's
description comprehends the skeptic's/Shelley's *awareness* of these
inadequacies, not only in the emphasis on the "self-conscious" nature of
the negation of the other in the quotation above, but also in the almost
desperate switch to seeking an ideal other beyond the self to save the
self from its confusion:

> [T]his consciousness [the Skeptic], instead of being self-identical,
> is in fact nothing but a purely casual, confused medley, the dizzi-
> ness of a perpetually self-engendered disorder. It is itself aware of

this; for itself maintains and creates this restless confusion. Hence it also admits to it, it owns to being a wholly contingent, single, and separate consciousness—a consciousness . . . which takes its guidance from what has no reality for it [i.e., the otherness of the world]. . . . But equally, while it takes itself in this way to be a single and separate . . . and a *lost* self-consciousness, it also, on the contrary, converts itself again into a consciousness that is universal and self-identical [Shelley's "switch" to idealism]. . . . This consciousness is therefore the unconscious, thoughtless rambling which passes back and forth from the one extreme of self-identical self-consciousness to the other extreme of the contingent consciousness that is both bewildered and bewildering. It does not itself bring these two thoughts of itself together. At one time it recognizes that its freedom lies in rising above all the confusion and contingency of existence [the centrifugal, idealist impulse], and at another time equally admits to a relapse into occupying itself with what is unessential. . . . Point out likeness or identity to it, and it will point out unlikeness or non-identity; and when it is now confronted with what it has just asserted, it turns round and points out likeness or identity. Its talk is in fact like the squabbling of self-willed children, one of whom says *A* if the other says *B,* and in turn says *B* if the other says *A,* and who by contradicting *themselves* buy for themselves the pleasure of continually contradicting *one another.* (124–26)

This is a challenge to us because we must ask if Hegel is not right. Can Shelley's thought be subsumed into Hegel's project, its difficulties and contradictions merely signs of its immaturity? Would time have led him from this inchoate paradoxy to a resolution of all problems in something similar to the Hegelian Absolute? Or, on the other hand, can we argue that Shelley does indeed "bring these two thoughts of [himself] together," that if he is "bewildered and bewildering" at times, it is because he is dealing with problems not only extremely complex in themselves but disruptive of the very possibility of a thoroughgoing therapeutic idealism? In other words, the question is whether Shelley-as-Hegel's-skeptic represents an antithetical moment in the development of the wide therapeutic consensus in which we still live, or an abyssal gap within Hegel's system from which one might begin to unravel it. Any such unraveling would have important consequences for our own critical practice.

Hegel subsumes the skeptic's problems within the overall progress of

Spirit. For him, skepticism eventually becomes conscious of the internal division in its thought (the Enlightenment "separation," or "disengagement") "and now knows itself to be a duality. Consequently, the duplication which formerly was divided between two individuals, the lord and the bondsman, is now lodged in one. The duplication of self-consciousness within itself, which is essential in the Notion of Spirit, is thus here before us, but not yet in its unity: the *Unhappy Consciousness* is the consciousness of self as a dual-natured, merely contradictory being" (126). The skeptic, in a movement "necessary" for Spirit's advance, progresses in the moment of the Hegelian *Aufhebung* into the Unhappy Consciousness. The skeptic's separation from the world will prove to be a *felix culpa,* a negation that can in turn be negated. Hegel sees the childish antics of the skeptic erased by the achievement of a higher stage of consciousness.

The question whether there is an alternative other than willful and disenabling nihilism to the therapeutic attempt to find the Infinite through the Finite, to think the fragment without recourse to a redemptive Absolute, recurs at every level of Shelley's thought and work. Can one conceive of humanity without God, of a revolutionary poet who is not a *representative* voice but merely an isolated and oppositional nightingale singing to cheer its solitude, of the poem as inherently and not adventitiously fragmentary, and of events as possessing a real negative power and not as destined to subsumption within a narrative "Whole." The philosophical and political ramifications of the achievement of such a conception would be considerable.

III

One of the few Shelley critics in recent years to make the case for Shelley's idealism is William Ulmer, in his *Shelleyan Eros.* Ulmer correctly focuses upon the centrifugal drive of Shelleyan *erōs,* its impulse toward an ever widening circle of consciousness that is not really compatible with the restrictive "epistemological circle" of a pure skepticism. He notes, however, that this drive of Shelley's seems to have as its ultimate destination a collapse into dissolution and death, which he relates, at length, to Freud's concept of the death instinct: "The allegorical subplot of Shelley's poetry gradually exposes the contradictions of his metaphorical idealism, its willed fictions and covert violence. With that exposure, Shelley's poems accept death as the telos of desire and gravitate increasingly toward a visionary despair" (18).[6]

6. A similar argument has been made by John Hodgson in his *Coleridge, Shelley, and*

Ulmer puts his finger on one of the paradoxes of idealist desire-as-ego-expansion—that the overcoming of all differences in perfect union seems to be indistinguishable from the undifferentiated absolute negation that is death:

> Heterogeneity is the truth of supplementarity between Shelleyan self and antitype, the truth of their incongruence. Desire continually struggles against this truth, resisting frustration by envisioning an origin in which all deferrals end. In *Alastor* this closure is death projected as the negative, or transposed, form of transcendence.
>
> Only the logic of Shelleyan idealism, then, makes the Poet ask, "does the dark gate of death / Conduct to thy mysterious paradise . . . ?" [211–12]. His longing for unmediated rapture makes him gravitate towards the ultimate realities that frame life as both "the beginning impulse and . . . ultimate end of being," defining death as the coincidence of origin and end, self and antitype. . . . Centered on the source, the poet's yearning for death is regressive, a backward impulse "to embark / And meet lone death" [304–5] in a reunion. . . . What the poet truly seeks is the reiteration of a prior event. As in Freud, repetition in *Alastor* performs a restorative, stabilizing function. Repetition is the (spuriously) temporalized mode of Sameness. . . . Desire's compulsion to repeat, its fascination with an idealized origin, commits Eros to Thanatos. (33; see also 61, 151)

Ulmer pursues this logic through all of Shelley's poetry, suggesting that Shelley posits death—as the ultimate collapse of all differentiation—as a *via negativa* out of the ironic contradictions of our fallen reality.

For Ulmer, who shares the "decentering" critics' political philosophy, this amounts to a debunking of any claims for Shelley's political sophistication. Shelley's intolerance of difference, even at the price of life, supposedly renders suspect any potential radicalism in Shelley's thought (see, e.g., 97, 107, 130, 147).

Transcendental Inquiry (72–79, 81–114), who finds Shelley's position to be an almost parodically value-reversed version of Coleridge's, with the death instinct figuring not as a transcendental fulfillment but as a negation of such a possibility. Ulmer's reading of the death instinct is more convincing; it seems difficult to make it a useful starting point for the kind of deconstructive play that Hodgson wishes to derive from it.

Ulmer is right that there is this potential risk in idealist multeity-in-unity, that it may become an undifferentiated totalitarianism indistin-guishable from the horror of change and difference associated with Freud's death instinct, and for this reason his analysis of Shelley's rela-tionship to the death instinct is preferable to its main rival in recent Shelley criticism, Hodgson's *Coleridge, Shelley, and Transcendental In-quiry.* Where he errs is in his assumption that Shelley's poetic associa-tion of *erōs* and death is entirely uncritical. A reexamination of Shel-leyan *erōs* is the ideal place to start an exploration of how Shelley critiques his "idealism" with his "skepticism," and vice versa, in order to arrive at an entirely new position.

We have seen that one of the chief objections to skepticism as politi-cal philosophy was Hume's pragmatic objection to "Pyrrhonian" isola-tionism. Echoing Spinoza's argument about the Bible, Shelley held that "[a]ll reformers have been compelled to practice . . . misrepresentation of their own true feelings and opinions," having been forced to "accom-modate" their "doctrines to the prepossessions of those whom [they] addressed" (Ingpen and Peck, 6:243, 242). But this is a paradox: on the one hand, one must obey the "idealist" impulse to solidarity ("speaking representatively" in Cavell's phrase) in order to have one's words en-gage with the social context at all; and on the other hand, one must maintain a skeptical "disengagement" from that context in order to be able to propose a radical critique. How can one, without pandering to the prejudices of a system one intends to change, be sufficiently a part of one's society to have one's writings actually heeded?

Ulmer believes that under the pressure of this paradox Shelley opts for an idealist solidarity that undermines any pretended radicalism in his poetry: "Shelley [in the end] displaced his radicalism into idealized myths capable of accommodating it only because his radicalism was a displaced idealism from the start" (24); Ulmer offers us an example of Shelley's adapting his words to the "prepossessions" of his audience, with supposedly dire consequences: "Despite his avowed feminism, for instance, Shelley accepted models of poetic creation that regard the author as 'a father, a progenitor, a procreator, an aesthetic patriarch whose pen is an instrument of generative power like his penis'" (23).[7] The key to answering this problem lies in a reexamination of Shelley's theory of the self, and the relationship of the self and the other. The therapeutic drive to reconcile the subject with the object can be read

---

7. Ulmer does not give any examples of Shelley's use of these models. In fact, Shelley's models of poetic creation are generally feminine or asexual (the "cave of the witch poesy," the Witch of Atlas as a "sexless bee," the non-gender-specific spirit who slept "on a poet's lips" in *Prometheus Unbound*, etc.).

simultaneously as a desire for a return to a prelapsarian unity with God and as a "totalitarian" unification of society. These two impulses are both readily apparent in Shelley's opposition to the "system of voting by ballot" (anonymous voting) on the grounds that it isolates the individual from the community: "The elector and the elected ought to meet one another face to face, and interchange the meanings of actual presence and share some common impulses, and, in a degree, understand each other" (*A Philosophical View of Reform,* Ingpen and Peck, 7:44). Shelley's evocation of 1 Cor. 13:12 in his emphasis on "face to face" communication serves to emphasize the epiphanic promise of this communication between self and other, and the quasi-divine status of this metaphysics of "actual presence." But Shelley's ultimate arguments for this kind of *Sittlichkeit* are never purely idealist. He proposes to embed revolutionary politics within the terms of existing discourses not for its own sake but in order to give that politics more powerful effects. Shelley's fear that "individuals acting singly with whatever energy can never effect so much as a society" (Ingpen and Peck, 5:256) is a purely practical doubt about the efficacy of individual action. He is so far from holding up unity per se as a political goal that in a series of "suggestions" he wished to append to the *Proposals for an Association of Philanthropists* (from which the last quotation is drawn), he elaborates a complex plan of "secession" whereby the danger of "fictitious unanimity" (*Letters,* 1:277) inherent in such an "association" would be averted: "[T]he minority whose belief could not subscribe to the opinion of the majority on a division in any question of moment & interest should secede. Some associations might by refinement of secessions contain not more than three or four members" (*Letters,* 1:267; Jones prints "recede" for "secede," which must, from the context, be an error).

The root of this instability lies in Shelley's complex theory of self.[8] Relevant here are two aspects of the theory: one, his distaste for self, and the other, the question of the boundaries and definition of the self. Shelley always saw "the dark idolatry of self" as the root of most social evils, whether too great a love or too great a hatred of self—as evidenced in the final speech of *Prometheus Unbound*'s third act:

> Self-love or self-contempt on human brows
> No more inscribed, as o'er the gate of hell,
> "All hope abandon, ye who enter here."

(III, iv, 134–36)

---

8. For a thorough discussion of this aspect of Shelley's thought, see Wasserman, *Shelley,* 109–22; Milton Wilson, 91ff., is also useful, as is McNiece, 162, 224.

In his earliest letters to Hogg he coined the term *aphilautia* to describe
the desired state of disinterest in self and wrote passionately against the
self's evil effects: "I cannot endure the horror the evil which comes to
self in solitude. . . . [W]hat strange being I am, how inconsistent, in
spite of all my bo[a]sted hatred of self—this moment thinking I could so
far overcome Natures law as to exist in complete seclusion, the next
shrinking from a moment of solitude, starting from my own company as
it were that of a fiend, seeking any thing rather than a continued communion with *self*" (*Letters,* 1:77–78).

But neither the skeptical nor the idealist traditions that Shelley in-
herits make it clear how one is to avoid being trapped within the self.
The "epistemological circles" of radical skepticism make other minds a
tricky proposition. If Drummond is correct in contending that as little as
a change of mind entails a change of existential state, then a truly other
mind would be existentially unavailable. From the idealist side, however, to *know* and to *be* become progressively confused; the idealist
seeks to overleap the artificial boundaries between subject and object,
mind and world, which are the product of our fall into self-division. In
Coleridge's words (which Shelley knew): "During the act of knowledge
itself, the objective and subjective are so instantly united, that we cannot determine to which of the two the priority belongs. There is here
no first, and no second; both are coinstantaneous and one" (*Biographia,* 1:255). Knowledge is a return to an original "identity of subject
and object" (1:279), and therefore the "other," once known, becomes
self: to know completely, which is the telos of all knowing and desiring,
is to "know even as also I am known."

This poses particular problems for our understanding of desire. Shelley's distinctive theory of the soul-within-the-soul can be read as an attempt to propose a model of an erotic dynamic within the constraining
terms of these intellectual frameworks. This is perhaps elaborated most
fully in his "On Love": "We dimly see within our intellectual nature a
miniature as it were of our entire self, yet deprived of all that we condemn or despise. . . . [A] soul within our soul that describes a circle
around its proper Paradise which pain and sorrow and evil dare not
overleap. To this we eagerly refer all sensations, thirsting that they
should resemble or correspond with it. The discovery of its anti-type;
the meeting with an understanding capable of clearly estimating the
deductions of our own . . . this is the invisible and unattainable point to
which Love tends" (Reiman and Powers, 474). Shelley is trying, here, to
overcome the solipsistic tendencies of Drummond's relativism and idealist knowing-as-self-consciousness, by creating a love object that is "inter-

nal" and yet maintains a degree of alterity. There is, however, an unresolved tension between this model and Shelley's earlier description of love in the same essay as "that powerful attraction towards all that we conceive or fear or hope beyond ourselves when we find within our own thoughts the chasm of an insufficient void and seek to awaken in all things that are, a community with what we experience within ourselves" (473). This version seems to suggest, not that we discover the "other" within the self, but that we seek others because of the insufficiency of the self.

This indecision is the sign of a profound discontent with the implications of both the skeptical and the idealist models of desire and knowledge. Consider once again Shelley's disavowal of solipsism in the midst of outlining his theory of the "one mind" in "On Life": "Let it not be supposed that this doctrine conducts to the monstrous presumption that I, the person who now write and think, am that one mind. I am but a portion of it." Shelley protests too much; his very vehemence betrays his anxiety over this tendency in the theory. His model of epiphany is continually contaminated by the model of the "soul within the soul," the other as projected self. The consequence is that love, "the great secret of morals . . . a going out of our own nature," becomes exactly the morally repugnant obsession with self Shelley sought all his life to avoid.

Once again we find the seeds of this thought in Shelley's earliest writings. A letter to Hogg in January 1811 says: "I am afraid there is selfishness in the passion of Love for I cannot avoid feeling every instant as if my soul was bursting, but I *will* feel no more! it is selfish—I would feel for others, but for myself oh! how much rather would I expire in the struggle" (*Letters*, 1:36). He goes on to ponder the merits of suicide. This is no doubt a callow piece of posing, but it serves to demonstrate to what extent these patterns of Shelley's thought formed the foundations, albeit highly unstable, upon which any subsequent, more fully articulated politics would have to be built, and therefore calls into question any easy identification of Shelleyan idealist *erōs*.

One way out of this paradox would be to posit an external other by an act of pure faith—Drummond's fideistic solution. But this option is not open to Shelley, because, as Abbey has argued, Shelley regarded faith as dogma, and dogma, because it is the idolatry of the mind's own ideas, as worship of the self. In this connection Abbey (47) aptly cites Shelley's lines from the *Revolt of Islam* on the origin of religion:

> " 'Some moon-struck sophist stood
> Watching the shade from his own soul upthrown

Fill Heaven and darken Earth, and in such mood
The Form he saw and worshipped was his own,
His likeness in the world's vast mirror shown.' "

(VIII, vi, 1–5)

At least one source for this idea Shelley would, ironically, have found in Drummond himself: "We seek to attach ideas to mere abstractions, and to give being to pure denominations. The dreams of our imaginations become the standards of our faith" (Drummond, 166). For Shelley, to have "faith" in the existence of an other that was not a projection of self would, paradoxically, be another form of unhealthy self-obsession.

This problem becomes one of the central knots in Shelley's poetry, the source of numerous hesitations or uncertainties. At the end of the chapter from which the above quotation was drawn, Drummond poses the question, "Is there not one, who perceives his own ideas, and calls them external objects; who thinks he distinguishes the truth, and who sees it not; who grasps at shadows, and who follows phantoms; who passes from the cradle to the tomb, the dupe and often the victim of the illusions, which he himself has created?" (167). Shelley devotes much of his poetry to exploring the terrible implications of such a situation. One example so apt as to suggest this passage of Drummond's served as its source is *Alastor.* One moment in that poem becomes in various forms a crisis repeated throughout Shelley's oeuvre. It comes when the "Poet or Visionary" (to use Wassermann's terms) who "lived . . . died . . . sung . . . in solitude" (*Alastor,* 60)—making him an exemplary version of the skeptical self alienated from the world of society-as-Spirit—encounters his visionary "veiled maid." Shelley gives full rein to the erotic power of the desire for the other in this first meeting:

He reared his shuddering limbs and quelled
His gasping breath, and spread his arms to meet
Her panting bosom: . . . she drew back a while,
Then, yielding to irresistible joy,
With frantic gesture and short breathless cry
Folded his frame in her dissolving arms.

(182–87)

Shelley had a profound reverence for the moment of sexual inter-course as the highest example and symbol of harmonious connection with the other. Inverting the conventional conceptual hierarchy, he called it "the one thing which made it impossible to degrade [people] below the beasts, which . . . separated . . . an anti-social cruelty, from all the soothing, elevating and harmonious gentleness of the sexual inter-course and the humanizing charities . . . which are its appendages" (*A Philosophical View of Reform,* Ingpen and Peck, 7:32). But in *Alastor,* having reached this pitch of sexual excitement and therefore, implicitly, of self-other epiphany, Shelley throws cold water on the scene as he abruptly introduces the disturbing possibility that the "veiled maid" is nothing but a "vision in which [the Poet] embodies his own imagina-tions" (preface, 69), and the Poet nothing but Drummond's "victim of the illusions, which he himself has created":

> Now blackness veiled his dizzy eyes, and night
> Involved and swallowed up the vision; sleep,
> Like a dark flood suspended in its course,
> Rolled back its impulse on his *vacant* brain.
>
> Roused by the shock he started from his trance—
> .   .   .   .
>   the *vacant* woods
> Spread round him where he stood. Whither had fled
> .   .   .   .
> The mystery and the majesty of Earth,
> The joy, the exultation? His wan eyes
> Gaze on the empty scene as *vacantly*
> As ocean's moon looks on the moon in heaven.
>   (188–202; my emphasis)

It is unclear if the passion of the two (if there *are* two) lovers is consummated. The numbing repetition of the word "vacant" and ana-logues such as "empty," "blackness," "Night," "sleep," "dark flood," and "trance," which elevate the Poet's solitude to an existential absolute, is abruptly introduced as the logic of desire drives us toward a climax of pure presence. The problem that has led to this abrupt crisis is spelled out for us, however: "as vacantly / As the ocean's moon looks on the moon in heaven." The Poet's "lover" may be no more than a reflection of the Poet's mind, a "psychidion" rather than an epiphany.

Ulmer would presumably agree with Wasserman that Shelley de-scribes here an "orgasmic merging with the perfect and mirrored Other until the finite self is absorbed into the infinite" (*Shelley,* 24). Wasser-man's admission that there is an element of "autoeroticism" in this vi-sion, and that Shelley's "orgasmic union" leads only to "vacancy" and death, would complete Ulmer's argument for the thanatological nature of Shelleyan *erōs*. But is there not something rather too abrupt in Shelley's collapse from plenitude to "vacancy"? Can we really believe that Shelley is proffering this autoerotic model uncritically, as the ideal expression of his ultimate hopes for *erōs?* The connection between perfect love and death need not be expressed so bleakly as this.

It is useful to consider Shelley's preface to *Alastor* in this context. Wasserman (40) is forced to read the preface as the uncomprehending voice of the Narrator, criticizing the Poet for his "self-centred seclusion" (Reiman and Powers, 69) without understanding the beauty of his quest for the Absolute. Wasserman's reading of the Poet's quest is similar to Schiller's reading of the most famous of all Romantic expressions of the idealistic *Todessehnsucht,* Goethe's *Werther,* which is interesting to compare to Shelley's preface, both for its similarities—which are striking enough to suggest the possibility of direct influence—and its differences, which call into question the easy assimilation of Shelley's vision to the therapeutic pattern represented by *Werther.* Schiller describes Werther as

> [a] personality who embraces the ideal with burning feeling and abandons actuality in order to contend with an insubstantial infinitude, who seeks continuously outside himself for that which he continuously destroys within himself, to whom only his dreams are the real, his experience perennial limitations, who in the end sees in his own existence only a limitation, and, as is reasonable, tears this down in order to penetrate to the true reality. (*Naive and Sentimental,* 137–38)

Shelley's preface describes his Poet as

> a youth of uncorrupted feelings and adventurous genius led forth by an imagination inflamed and purified through familiarity with all that is excellent and majestic, to the contemplation of the universe. . . . So long as it is possible for his desires to point towards objects thus infinite and unmeasured, he is joyous, and tranquil, and self-possessed. But the period arrives when these objects cease to suffice. His mind is at length suddenly awakened and thirsts for intercourse with an intelligence similar to itself. He images to himself a Being whom he loves. Conversant with speculations of the sublimest and most perfect natures, the vision in which he embodies his own imaginations unites all of wonderful, or wise, or beautiful, which the poet, the philoso-

pher, or the lover could depicture. He seeks in vain for a prototype of his conception. Blasted by his disappointment, he descends to an untimely grave. (Reiman and Powers, 69)

Werther's death is seen as a "reasonable," if extreme, solution to an
otherwise insoluble problem. Werther's death is the culmination of his
logic of desire because it allows him to "penetrate to the true reality" by
breaking down the artificial barriers of our (sentimental-ironic) fallen
condition. The death of Shelley's Poet is presented as a solution to his
problem neither in the preface nor (*pace* Wasserman) in the poem; it is
the tragic result of his pursuing an erotic logic that is inherently flawed.

The preface criticizes the Poet for this error. The Poet may succumb
to an "illustrious superstition," but it is still a superstition; the "Being" is
a delusion, and the Poet culpable for creating it: his "self-centred seclusion was avenged by the furies of an irresistible passion pursuing him to
speedy ruin" (69). There is an implicit assumption in the preface, which
is supported in the poem by such figures as the "Arab maiden" (129),
that other erotic dynamics are possible, and preferable, though how
these might work is not elaborated. The preface shares something like
Ulmer's perception of the dangers of idealist erotic logic; whatever
"voice" the preface represents, it is not the dupe of idealist paradoxy
Ulmer believes Shelley to be.

Wasserman's claim that the preface is in the voice of the "Narrator,"
and is not to be taken as "Shelley's" opinion of the Poet's career, depends upon his reading of the Poet's union with the "Being" as being an
at least potentially legitimate version of therapeutic union with the Absolute. If we do not start from that assumption, however, there is little
in the poem or preface that is likely to lead us to it. Wasserman's "Narrator" must be assumed to have chosen even the title of the poem, because his reading renders the "avenging demon" superfluous. It makes
more sense to assume that the preface represents Shelley's own reading
of his poem and that Shelley is undertaking a critique of idealist erotics
rather than retailing them through his poems.

If we return to my earlier distinction of a "tragic irony" (of which
Werther is a prime example) and a "comic irony," we can say that Shelley appears to be exploring here the consequences of tragic irony for
our model of erotic fulfillment—what we might call tragic *erōs*. Further,
we could say that Ulmer has mistaken this exploration of the erotic
drive to the Absolute for the general condition of "Shelleyan *erōs*," and
that what he posits as the "solution" to the problems of Shelley's erotic
dynamic, namely death, is what Shelley sees as the problem.

Tragic *erōs* is a possibility within any therapeutic erotic dynamic. If one posits as the telos of all desire a return to an absolute unity from which we have been sundered, and makes erotic desire a type of this fundamental drive, then absolute fulfillment becomes difficult to distinguish from absolute negation.[9] Shelley's exploration of *erōs* is a critique of the dream of absolute fulfillment, or of the belief that every fragment presupposes a whole.

In Shelley's poetry after *Alastor* the intimate association of the perfect fulfillment of desire with vacancy and death becomes habitual and gives Shelley's poetry one of its distinctive qualities. To penetrate to the heart of the mystery is to discover the emptiness at that heart; Demogorgon's "the deep truth is imageless" is possibly the best known of these moments, but there are many other examples. When Shelley begins to hear Liberty's car approach at the end of the "Ode to Liberty," and revolutionary desire seems on the verge of complete fulfillment:

> the spirit of that mighty singing
> To its abyss was suddenly withdrawn;
>
> . . . .
>
> My song, its pinions disarrayed of might,
>   Drooped; o'er it closed the echoes far away
> Of the great voice which did its flight sustain,
>   As waves which lately paved his watery way
>   Hiss round a drowner's head in their tempestuous play.
>
> (271–72, 281–85)

The moment at which the relationship of the individual poet to the "great voice" of the One Poem or One Mind seems to be bearing fruit, the relationship proves chimerical and disappears in one of Shelley's disturbingly frequent images of death by drowning. The highest pitch of desire collapses into death; *erōs* reveals itself to be Thanatos.

In *Epipsychidion*, Shelley expresses the therapeutic desire for "absolution" very clearly:

> Ah, woe is me!
> What have I dared? where am I lifted? how
> Shall I descend, and perish not? I know
> That Love makes all things equal: I have heard
> By mine own heart this joyous truth averred:

9. Paul Hamilton notes a similar dynamic in the poetry of Keats ("Keats and Critique," 124).

The spirit of the worm beneath the sod
In love and worship, blends itself with God.

(123-29)

The possibility of pure "joyous" transcendence of self in the epiphany of
the other is clouded even as he asserts it, however: "woe is me!" The
poem ends with a projected idyll on a "delicious isle," a "far Eden of the
purple East," where the narrator and his ideal love will live in a blissful
union, where "to love and live / Be one." But this "Eden" is not the
millennial seat of perfect consummated desire that he projects and that
we might expect from the theological framework of his desire. Shelley
makes explicit the reasons for the failure of this vision, confirming the
analysis above:

> We shall become the same, we shall be one
> Spirit within two frames, oh! wherefore two?
> One passion in twin-hearts, which grows and grew,
> 'Till like two meteors of expanding flame,
> Those spheres instinct with it become the same,
> Touch, mingle, are transfigured; ever still
> Burning, yet ever inconsumable:
> In one another's substance finding food,
> Like flames too pure and light and unimbued
> To nourish their bright lives with baser prey,
> Which point to Heaven and cannot pass away:
> One hope within two wills, one will beneath
> Two overshadowing minds, one life, one death,
> One Heaven, one Hell, one immortality,
> And one annihilation. Woe is me!
> The winged words on which my soul would pierce
> Into the height of love's rare Universe,
> Are chains of lead around its flight of fire. —
> I pant, I sink, I tremble, I expire!

(573-91)

Erōs, the therapeutic desire for "oneness," is revealed to be paradoxical
in the final despairing vision of "one annihilation. Woe is me!" What is
annihilated here is the lover's contact with the other: his self is all too
present in the claustrophobic confines of those four repetitions in the
final line "I . . . I . . . I . . . I . . ." What should be the triumph of *erōs* is
reduced, at the moment of maximal achievement, to the monotonous

iteration of the self: "Love makes all things equal." The promise of unity is revealed as a collapse into undifferentiated selfhood.

If the other becomes self in the achievement of desire, then all that can be achieved by the "centrifugal" impulse ("my soul would pierce / Into the heart of love's rare Universe") is meaningless self-aggrandizement, a unity-*sans*-multeity that is, for Shelley, neither heaven nor hell, but the denial of those "differences" between people which he held to be the basis of "moral knowledge" ("Speculations on Morals," Ingpen and Peck, 7:83) and hence all possible politics. Desire itself is erased and, in the sudden absence of the possibility of difference, becomes death: "I expire!"

It is clear, however, both from the despairing tone of this passage and from the fact that the lover announces his *own* death, that this death is not a final escape from the self but a dying into the self, a self without differences and without end. This is not Schopenhauer's *Todessehnsucht* as desire to escape from the world of will. This death-in-life reminds us of one of Shelley's oldest and most persistent fears, the fate of Ahasuerus. As he wrote in 1811 to Hogg: "For the immoral 'never to be able to die, never to escape from some shrine as chilling as the clay-formed dungeon which now it inhabits' is the future punishment which I believe in" (*Letters,* 1:35). In "On Love" Shelley writes, "So soon as this want or power [of Love] is dead, man becomes the living sepulchre of himself, and what yet survives is the mere husk of what once he was" (Reiman and Powers, 474). What *Epipsychidion* makes clear is that the dynamic of therapeutic *erōs* is such that its maximal gratification is precisely the elimination of "this want or power" and renders the *successful* lover a "living sepulchre."

As before, it is difficult to agree with Ulmer that Shelley accepts this as the necessary and desirable logic of *erōs*. The description of the devolution of therapeutic desire into thanatological collapse is too self-conscious. We find within the poem itself a direct criticism of the therapeutic-idealist logic of desire. The post-Kantian effort to reunite subject and object is often expressed in the imagery of marriage, yet in the *Epipsychidion* Shelley gives us his most famous antimatrimonial and antitherapeutic broadside:

> Narrow
> The heart that loves, the brain that contemplates,
> The life that wears, the spirit that creates
> One object, and one form, and builds thereby
> A sepulchre for its eternity.

(169–73)

The "sepulchre" relates to the passages from "On Love" and the letter to Hogg cited above, and describes the situation at the poem's end: therapeutic erotic union become thanatological annihilation.

IV

This is not to suggest that Shelley has from the start a fully formulated alternative to idealist tragic *erōs*. Throughout his poetic career Shelley explored ways in which the dilemmas of tragic *erōs* might be overcome. One of the most challenging and interesting of these is his explorations of the desire for the self-as-other—an autoeroticism that finds its most powerful form in the exploration of the symbolic significance of incest.

The Romantic poets are all intrigued by incest. In Peter Thorslev's influential argument about the nature of Romantic interest in incest, brother-sister incest is, for the Romantic hero, "the only love possible" because "[f]irst it symbolizes perfectly this hero's complete alienation from the society around him; and second, it symbolizes also what psychologically speaking we can call his narcissistic sensibility or, more philosophically speaking, his predilection for solipsism" (50). Thorslev attributes this to "the Romantic psyche's love affair with self" (5–6). This tone of disapproval is even stronger in Alan Richardson's reassessment of sibling incest in Romantic poetry, "The Dangers of Sympathy." Richardson emphasizes the connection between incest and death in Romantic thought, arguing that the frequency with which incestuous couples meet untimely ends demonstrates a residual guilt complex asserting itself to reclaim a conventional morality (744).

My reading of Shelley, however, suggests that the opposition on which these moralistic distinctions are based (love of "other" is good; love of "self" is bad) does not bear too close an examination. In Shelley's view, love of the other *becomes* love of self, and incest is therefore a figure for the attainment of therapeutic *erōs*. Lévi-Strauss makes a similar point in his *Elementary Structures of Kinship:* "[Parental and conjugal love] are both forms of love, and the instant the marriage takes place, considered in isolation, the two meet and merge; 'love has filled the ocean.'. . . But to intercross they must at least momentarily be joined, and it is this which in all social thought makes marriage a sacred mystery. At this moment, *all marriage verges on incest.* More than that, it is incest, at least social incest, if it is true that incest, in the broadest sense of the word, consists in obtaining by oneself, and for oneself, instead of by another and for another" (qtd. in Boon, 226; Boon's emphasis).

Nonetheless, Shelley's positive associations with incest seem to leave him open to Ulmer's criticism. When Shelley does give us an unarguably positive image of incest, however, in *Laon and Cythna,* he points out in

the preface that the aspect of incest that interests him is that it is a
"crime of convention," and he introduces it to "startle the reader from
the trance of everyday life" (Hutchinson, 886). This cannot inoculate us
against the other symbolic functions of this relationship, but it problematizes the assertion that Shelley saw incest as an ideal model of inter-
human relationship. As a blow against "Custom," incest in *Laon and
Cythna* is a blow against the therapeutic model of the state and its own
incestuous reproduction of the same.

Shelley's attitude toward incest was complex. He felt the attraction of
the idea of a perfect union, but he also recognized its dangers and its
relationship to Thanatos. He wrote, apropos of *The Cenci,* that incest
"like many other *incorrect* things [is] a very poetical circumstance. It
may be the excess of love or of hate" (*Letters,* 2:154). Even as "love" he
sees it as an "excess"; in *The Cenci,* where it appears as a form of hate,
we see just how much he was aware of its potential dangers. Count
Cenci is an absolutist tyrant. He denies that his family can have any
interests or claims that could stand against his supreme and unifying
will. Beatrice must be broken to his perception of the world because
her moral purity stands as a constant assertion of an alternative reality.
Shelley's exploration of the count's use of incest as a weapon to break
her will (see I, iii, 167; IV, i, 10–12, 43–44, 90) and break her sense of
self is both psychologically and symbolically acute. Here is a nightmare
image of the therapeutic dissolution of ego boundaries that underwrites
the absolutist state. In raping Beatrice, the count relies upon the logic of
therapeutic *erōs* to make this a merging of souls, so that she will "see /
Her image mixed with what she most abhors" (IV, i, 147–48).

Even in an early work like *Alastor,* Shelley uses the autoerotic implications of his imagery as a subtle critique of the Poet's quest for absolute
union. Consider the passage where the Poet wins through, after his
perilous sailing trip, to "One darkest glen . . . [which] invite[s] / To
some more lovely mystery" (451–54). This would seem to be a promise
of the imminent completion of his quest, but he is confronted, in a
moment of terrible irony, with a well that reflects back his own "treach-
erous likeness" (474). The Poet has tracked his dream to a symbolic
"source," only to discover himself.

In *Epipsychidion* Shelley uses a mythic version of the incest motif to
introduce what will prove to be the crisis and undoing of the projected
idyll in the final phase of the poem. The narrator describes the remote
island that will be their new Eden. Upon this island is a tower that

> for delight,
> Some wise and tender Ocean-King, ere crime

Had been invented, in the world's young prime,
Reared it, a wonder of that simple time,
An envy of the isles, a pleasure-house
Made sacred to his sister and his spouse.

(487–92)

This long-dead incestuous couple serves as a proleptic image of the ideal union of the poet and his lover. But the despairing collapse into self that ends the poem calls into question the idyllic promise of this passage. If incest must serve as the image of the perfect relationship (sister *and* spouse, in the knot that serves, paradoxically, to untie Lévi-Strauss's neat systems of kinship) of self to other, then once again that relationship is not a way out of the self, but merely a narcissistic reflection of it.

V

The real test of Ulmer's contention that Shelleyan *erōs* is a cover for idealist politics, however, is Shelley's idea of the relationship of the political reformer to society, or, in other words, the role of desire in political struggle. Is revolutionary *erōs* a mask for a furious attempt to establish therapeutic totality at any cost—which might be a version of either of Hegel's "two thoughts"—or is it an attempt to find some genuinely new understanding of the relationship of individual and society, part and whole? Shelley's vision of society with which he opens his most sustained exploration of the nature of the erotic drive makes it clear that the therapeutic ideal of the erasure of barriers within an absolute state has not yet been achieved, and that the obstacles to its achievement are real: "I know not the internal constitution of other men, or even of thine whom I now address. I see that in some external attributes they resemble me, but when misled by that appearance I have thought to appeal to something in common and unburthen my inmost soul to them, I have found my language misunderstood like one in a distant and savage land" (Reiman and Powers, 473).

This passage could be read to support an argument for either reading of Shelley, depending on whether we insist more upon his portrait of complete dissociation from society, which sounds like Hegel's portrait of the alienated skeptical consciousness, or upon his deep distress at being in that state, which sounds like an implicit longing for an idealist reintegration.

The *Revolt of Islam* is a sustained meditation upon these competing models of the relationship of the "revolutionary" to society. It is Shelley's most "idealist" attempt to find a reconciliation of the "two thoughts," although its political basis is thoroughly "skeptical." If we explore this attempt, we shall see that, for Shelley, its ultimate failure conveys the lesson that the therapeutic framework is unworkable for a truly radical politics. We shall see how clearly Shelley explores the different dynamics within which Ulmer believes him to be trapped.

THE *REVOLT OF ISLAM*

It is necessary, at the outset, to defend the decision to use the *Revolt of Islam* form of the poem rather than the version not subject to Shelley's self-censorship, *Laon and Cythna*. There are several good arguments for regarding *Laon and Cythna* as the canonical text for Shelley studies and relegating the *Revolt* to the status of a corrupt version, but other considerations have prevailed here. Shelley's act of misrepresentation is itself theoretically interesting. The altered text becomes itself implicated in the contradictions and tensions it aims to explore. A text about power and reactions to power and "Custom" is itself a product of an acquiescence to power and "Custom."

The *Revolt* is a good example of the complexity of the "context of production." The path from *Laon and Cythna* to the *Revolt* is a series of complex negotiations and compromises that involve competing, incompatible conceptions of the nature of that context (e.g., could it accept a story involving explicit brother-sister incest or not?), a complexity that radically problematizes historicist representativeness.

I

The opening images of the poem prepare us for a radical duality. In the first canto the poet witnesses the struggle between an eagle and a serpent with "many a check, / And many a change, a dark and wild turmoil" (I, xii, 1-2). When he speaks to the woman who receives the serpent into her bosom at the end of the fight, she explains that their struggle represents a Manichaean cosmology:

> "Know then, that from the depth of ages old,
>   Two Powers o'er mortal things dominion hold
> Ruling the world with a divided lot,
>   Immortal, all-pervading, manifold,
> Twin Genii, equal Gods—when life and thought
> Sprang forth, they burst the womb of inessential Nought."
>
> (I, xxv, 4-9)

Shelley proposes principles of good and evil, which we can match up with the terms of the politics of skepticism and idealism. But the series of Manichaean oppositions that he maps onto the basic opposition of good and evil are not consistently correlated. The Spirit of Evil, "whose name was Legion," is represented by "King, and Lord, and God" (I, xxviii, 9) as well as "Death," "Decay," "Winged and Wan diseases" ("an array / Numerous as leaves that strew the autumnal gale"), "Poison," "Fear," "Hatred," "Faith," and "Tyranny" (I, xxix, 1-9). The spirit's power is all pervasive:

> "His spirit is their power, and they his slaves
>   In air, and light, and thought, and language, dwell;
> And keep their state from palaces to graves."
>
> (I, xxx, 1-3)

The Spirit of Good can be detected

> "when mankind doth strive
> With its oppressors in a strife of blood,
> Or when free thoughts, like lightenings, are alive
>   And in each bosom of the multitude
> Justice and truth with Custom's hydra brood
> Wage silent war; when Priests and Kings dissemble
>   In smiles or frowns their fierce disquietude,
> When round pure hearts a host of hopes assemble,
> The Snake and Eagle meet—the world's foundations tremble!
>
> . . . .
>
>   when Hope's deep source in fullest flow
> Like earthquake did uplift the stagnant ocean
> Of human thoughts—mine shook beneath the wide emotion."
>
> (I, xxxiii, 1-9; xxxviii, 7-9)

We find many of the recurring themes of Shelley's poem in these passages. Power, law, custom, and authority are associated with death, oppression, and stagnation and are held to have powerful and wide-ranging effects: they dwell in air, light, thought, and language. They must therefore be combated by a total overthrow of the system; the "world's foundations" are at stake, and an "earthquake" in human thought is necessary.

Shelley's all-inclusive term for the nexus of ideas that meet in the Spirit of Evil is "Custom," which is expressly thanatological (see xxix, 1, 3, 5, 9; xxx, 3; xxviii, 8; restricting ourselves to just those lines quoted from above). We must, however, distinguish between two different symbolic values that Shelley ascribes to "death." The death Shelley associates with custom is the death-in-life of the "living sepulchre," death as the eradication of all possibility of change and novelty. This must not be confused with death as a figure for change in general, that "sea-change into something rich and strange" that is essentially a part of the process of life. An acceptance of this kind of death is part of the iconoclastic spirit of freedom, the "free thoughts" that, exempt from the constraints of custom, are "alive" and dispel the "stagnant" thoughts of the mind under the killing constraints of authority. This fundamental distinction between custom as death, in the form of stagnation, and freedom as change and growth runs through a range of other oppositions that are crucial to the poem's symbolism: age versus youth, cold versus ardent or impassioned, and continuity versus change. The forces of custom are "old," "cold," and cannot accept "change." These three words (far more than their complements) recur throughout the poem at key moments. Thus Laon, when denouncing the Tyrant's allies at the moment of surrendering himself to them, says:

> "O willing slaves to Custom *old,*
> Severe taskmistress! ye your hearts have sold.
> Ye seek for peace, and when ye die, to dream
> No evil dreams: all mortal things are *cold*
> And senseless then; if aught survive, I deem
> It must be love and joy, for they immortal seem.
>
> . · . · . · . · . · . · . · . · .
>
> It doth avail not that I weep for ye—
> Ye cannot *change,* since ye are *old* and gray,
> And ye have chosen your lot—your fame must be
> A book of blood . . ."
>
> (XI, xvii, 4–9; xxi, 1–4; my emphasis)

He continues by offering himself in return for Cythna's safe passage to America, where "There is a People mighty in its *youth* . . . / Where, though with rudest rites Freedom and Truth / Are worshipped" (XI, xxii, 1, 3–4; my emphasis).

This can be read in Painite terms of moldy parchments restraining youthful vigor. The emphasis on death as the hidden meaning of custom is, however, more explicit than it is in Paine. The "slaves" of the Spirit of Evil "keep their state from palaces to graves." This intimate connection between power and death is emphasized by the poem's "cold" imagery, which links the frozen rigidity of conservatism with the cold of the grave, giving a surprising power to the word's many occurrences in the poem. (Much of this imagery recurs in *The Cenci*, which similarly analyzes "age's firm, cold, subtle villainy" [I, iii, 175] and its rage for death.)

The more radical implications of this symbolism are Godwinian and Drummondian at base. This is best exemplified by Shelley's adoption of "change" as an end in itself. "Ye cannot change, since ye are old and grey" places no emphasis on the direction of change, merely on the necessity of change per se. This is more clearly seen in the stanza following the first of the two quoted above:

> "Fear not the future, weep not for the past.
> . . . .
>   . . . Want, and Plague, and Fear, from slavery flow;
>   . . . mankind is free, and . . . the shame
> Of royalty and faith is lost in freedom's fame!"
>
> (XI, xviii, 1, 7–9)

This passage is an echo of an earlier one describing the first day after the revolution:

> To hear, to see, to live, was on that morn
>   Lethean joy! so that all those assembled
> Cast off their memories of the past outworn.
>
> (V, xlii, 1–3)

The two passages together provide a skeptical model of radically discontinuous change, "brisant tout à coup le lien des souvenirs"; the moment of change severs us completely from a forgotten past. Shelley embraces the amnesiac society so feared by Burke and Hegel, inserting a "Lethean" rupture of memory into that continuity of social reproduction which Hume and Diderot recognized as the basis of sociopolitical identity.

When Laon finds the fallen Tyrant after the revolutionary forces have prevailed, he finds him immured in his "Imperial House" with Cythna's child. The word "change" recurs throughout the passage: "I . . . of his change compassionate, / . . . soothed his rugged mood" (V, xxv, 2–3); the child "a nursling of captivity / Knew naught beyond those walls, nor what such change might be" (xxvii, 8–9); "in the hearts of all / Like wonder stirred, who saw such awful change befall (xxviii, 8–9); "that lonely man / Then knew the burden of his change" (xxix, 6–7). The child's ignorance of the world "beyond those walls" is a symbol of the stultifying nature of custom. Nothing in its stagnant order has taught the child, or the Tyrant, how to adapt to the radical discontinuity of "change."

This is particularly emphasized in the case of the Tyrant:

> And he was troubled at a charm withdrawn
> Thus suddenly; that sceptres ruled no more—
>
> . . . .
> Such wonder seized him, as if hour by hour
> The past had come again.
>
> (V, xxviii, 1-2, 5-6)

He is unable to accommodate the new situation, endlessly repeating to himself the moments leading to the change, before that break in the continuities of custom of which he is unable to conceive. This helps us to make sense of Laon's accusation that the Tyrant and his allies "seek for peace, and when we die, to dream / No evil dreams," which seems harmless in itself. Shelley is accusing their entire conception of power and custom of being a thanatological repression of change and the possibility of change. The Tyrant's reaction to the revolution, to repeat compulsively the events leading to the trauma, reminds us of Freud's argument that repetition compulsion is an expression of the death instinct, the inherent conservatism of the organism that seeks to avoid new stimuli, or what Shelley, in his "Essay on a Future State," called the "desire to be forever as we are" (Freud, "Pleasure Principle").[10]

But this passage from the *Revolt* shows us how clearly Shelley understood the relationships between power, conservatism, death, repetition, and aggression, which are all linked in Shelley's concept of custom. Consider this speech of the Hermit to Laon:

>   "the Queen of Slaves,
>   The hoodwinked Angel of the blind and dead,
>   Custom, with iron mace points to the graves
>   Where her own standard desolately waves
>   Over the dust of Prophets and Kings.
>   Many yet stand in her array—'she paves
>   Her path with human hearts.'"
>
> (IV, xxiv, 2-8)

---

10. Ulmer draws out the relationship between that "desire" and Freudian *Thanatos* in full (10 n. 21).

The Tyrant's thanatological drive finds expression, and confirmation, in his revenge:

> his footsteps reel
> On the fresh blood—he smiles. "Ay, now I feel
> I am a King in truth!"
>
> (X, viii, 4–6)

All these thoughts come together in one charged stanza early in the poem, where the "so" in the sixth line reveals the causal link between custom and the thanatological suppression of change:

> old age, with its gray hair,
> And wrinkled legends of unworthy things,
> And icy sneers, is nought: it cannot dare
> To burst the chains which life forever flings
> On the entangled soul's aspiring wings,
> So is it cold and cruel, and is made
> The careless slave of that dark power which brings
> Evil, like blight, on man, who, still betrayed,
> Laughs o'er the grave in which his living hopes are laid.
>
> (II, xxxiii, 1–9)

This urgency and the belief that the evil of custom infects all aspects of thought, language, and life in the custom-based society underlie one of the most important of Shelley's arguments in the poem, that the revolution must eschew means that, even if they are necessary to its "success," would implicate it in structures of action that belong to the old order. The Hermit warns Laon, "If blood be shed [the method of custom], 'tis but a change and choice / Of bonds" (IV, xxviii, 1–2). This advice bears fruit when Laon saves the Tyrant from the vengeful crowd:

> "What do you seek? what fear ye," then I cried,
> Suddenly starting forth, "that ye should shed
> The blood of Othman?—if your hearts are tried
> In the true love of freedom, cease to dread
> This one poor lonely man. . . . "
>
> (V, xxxiii, 1–5)

Although this can be seen as the moment that dooms the revolution to failure (Foot, 171–72), Laon's actions are in accordance with the principles laid out in the preface, which ascribes the failure of the French

Revolution to the fact that "men who had been dupes and slaves for centuries were incapable of conducting themselves with the wisdom and tranquillity of free men so soon as some of their fetters were partially loosened." The problem, for Shelley, is a lack of sufficiently sweeping change, the inability to reject patterns of thought that have become hardwired: "If the Revolution had been in every respect prosperous, then misrule and superstition would lose half their claims to our abhorrence, as fetters which the captive can unlock with the slightest motion of his fingers, and which do not eat with poisonous rust into the soul" (Hutchinson, 33).

This passage, however, raises a problem. So far I have offered a reading of the *Revolt* entirely in keeping with my portrait of Shelley's "Politics of Scepticism." But the poem does not maintain this as a unified schema. Just as Paine turned from decrying the moldy parchments of the past to establishing constitutions to be revered for thousands of years, Shelley shifts, often abruptly and paradoxically, into concepts radically counter to the skeptical position that seems so firmly entrenched in the passages we have so far examined.

The argument that custom "eats with poisonous rust into the soul" is a backhanded acknowledgment of the idealist strain in Shelley's thought, a nightmare version of the concept of *Sittlichkeit* that acknowledges the power of social memory over Lethean discontinuity. A true Godwinian skeptic would argue, as Godwin does in a passage from the *Political Justice* to which Shelley's appears to be a rejoinder, that "the chains fall off of themselves, when the magic of opinion is dissolved" (1:99).

The preface contains a number of allusions to the concept of, if not the term, "the spirit of the age": "The year 1788 may be assumed as the epoch of one of the most important crises produced by ["a general state of feeling among civilised mankind"]. . . . the sympathies connected with that event extended to every bosom. The most generous and amiable natures were those which participated the most extensively in these sympathies" (Hutchinson, 33). This idea is strongly reminiscent of Hegel's world-historical individual. *Geist* takes the form of a "general state of feeling," and the world-historical spirits are those most fully representative of the *Zeitgeist*. Shelley refers later in the preface to the poets' "subjection to a common influence . . . belonging to the times in which they live" (Hutchinson, 35).

This concept also appears in the body of the poem; Laon and Cythna can be seen not as attempting to establish a radical discontinuity within the present order but as world-historical individuals acting in the service of the Notion as it realizes itself through history. Thus Laon, in his opening account of his education as a revolutionary, tells us:

> Such man has been, and such may yet become!
>   Ay, wiser, greater, gentler, even than they
> Who on the fragments of yon shattered dome
>   Have stamped the sign of power—I felt the sway
>   Of the vast stream of ages bear away
> My floating thoughts—my heart beat loud and fast—
>   Even as a storm let loose beneath the ray
> Of the still moon, my spirit onward past
> Beneath truth's steady beams upon its tumult cast.
>
> (II, xii, 1–9)

This stanza casts Laon as an agent of the "vast stream of ages" seeking a therapeutic return to a prelapsarian origin ("Such man has been"). Memory gains an entirely positive valuation now; there is no suggestion here of "casting off memories of the past outworn." The "stream of ages" returns to its origin, in a journey that revalues its "fall" from what "man has been" as a *felix culpa*. This appears to adumbrate the Hegelian progress of Spirit, a circle of "recollection" (*Erinnerung*) that ends at its beginning but "at a higher level" (Abrams, *Natural Supernaturalism,* 235), exactly as Laon hopes to bring humanity to its recollected great past, but "wiser, greater, gentler."

Cythna makes a similar claim in her attempt to make sense of the failed revolution and her and Laon's role in it:

> "Virtue, and Hope, and Love, like light and Heaven,
>   Surround the world.—We are their chosen slaves.
> Has not the whirlwind of our spirit driven
>   Truth's deathless germs to thought's remotest caves?"
>
> (IX, xxiii, 1–4)

Here, she suggests a role for herself and Laon isomorphic with that of the world-historical individual, emphasizing even more than Laon the extent to which the individual need not be a conscious actor to advance the designs of "the cunning of Reason." Her choice of words to express this—"their chosen slaves"—is particularly disturbing; almost everywhere else in the poem "slave" collocates with "tyrant." Shelley seems to be attempting to spread the safety net of a "higher order" to guarantee a continuity of values subtending the disjunction threatened by the revolution. There is a distinction between "good" and "bad" tyrannies, it would appear; not *all* resistances to "change" are evil.

These are not isolated moments in the poem. There is a recurrent association of memory and continuity with the forces of good within the poem, forces I have so far associated with discontinuity and an extreme distrust of the past. We might begin to examine these by asking ourselves what exactly Cythna means by "the whirlwind of our spirit"? We would expect it to be "spirits" if she were referring to Laon and herself, but in context and in the singular it seems to take on an indeterminate scope only anchorable on the vast forces of virtue, hope, and love—"tyrant" to their "slaves."

This "spirit" is identical with, or is close kin to, the Spirit of the peculiar "Temple of the Spirit," where Laon begins his story, recollecting the path by which he and Cythna arrived at that beginning; in good therapeutic manner, their story ends at its beginning and begins at its end with this *Erinnerung* of the Spirit's progress. The Temple of the Spirit turns history into narrative, the unfolding of the Notion through time. Given its structural prominence as a metacommunicative frame for the poem, it could be argued that this forces us to read the poem's skepticism as the unconscious "slave" of the Spirit's continuous development, unknowingly helping to generate the "necessary" result: the incorporation (internalization) of the story at its end (telos) into the timeless history of the Temple of the Spirit.

A reading of this nature would cite Shelley's description of the poem as "a succession of pictures illustrating the growth and progress of individual mind aspiring after excellence" (Hutchinson, 32) and would note that this description cannot refer to any one protagonist of the poem. But it would soon run into problems, problems that demonstrate how closely interwoven in the poem these contradictory discourses are (the skeptic's saying *A* to *B* and *B* to *A*?). The word "individual" problematizes the reading of the preface passage as a full-blown idealism, or at least suggests the collapse into self-obsession Shelley saw as one of its potentials. In the enigmatic Spirit of the Temple

> there lay
> Paintings, the poesy of mightiest thought,
>   Which did the Spirit's history display;
> A tale of passionate change, divinely taught,
> Which, in their wingèd dance, unconscious Genii wrought.
>
> (I, liii, 5–9)

This suggests—given that Laon and Cythna are, at the poem's end, inducted into this temple as a kind of world-historical hall of fame—that "the Spirit's history" is history per se. But the Burkean continuity this would seem to project onto history is surely undermined by the description of its progress as "passionate *change*"—a word that becomes highly charged in skeptical contexts in the poem—wrought by "*unconscious* Genii," an introduction of a Lucretian randomness completely destructive of the "cunning of Reason" essential to an idealist notion of historical process.

We find the same seemingly unconscious yoking of idealist and skeptical viewpoints in the poem's treatment of memory—that core of the therapeutic project. Memory, which we saw expelled in the revolution's "Lethean joy," we discover elsewhere to be essential to life. We learn, in the description of the evil aftermath of the revolutionary wars, that "Faith, Plague, and Slaughter, / A ghastly brood; [are] conceived of Lethe's sullen water" (X, xvii, 8–9). This collocation of custom's thanatological drive with forgetfulness is completely opposed to the radical skeptical argument.

In the first stanza of Laon's story he recounts his earliest childhood memories; in the second he tells us:

> In Argolis, beside the echoing sea,
>   Such impulses within my mortal frame
> Arose, and they were dear to memory,
>   Like tokens of the dead:—but others came
>   Soon, in another shape: the wondrous fame
> Of the past world, the vital words and deeds
>   Of minds whom neither time nor change can tame,
> Traditions dark and old, whence evil creeds
> Start forth, and whose dim shade a stream of poison feeds.
>
> (II, ii, 1–9)

This stanza inextricably weaves the concepts of death and memory in such a way that we cannot safely either oppose or link them. The seemingly innocent childhood memories (distanced by the peculiar Lockean formulation of lines two and three) are "tokens of the dead," an image that is thoroughly ambiguous. It can be read as revulsion against memory as the voice of death (the "living sepulchre" variety), as when Cythna—in "converting" the sailors who rescue her after her escape from the Tyrant's prison and in order to make it easier for them to cast off those fetters which eat with poisonous rust into the soul—tells them not to think of their past, servile lives: "The past is Death's" (VIII,

xxii, 7). Or it can be read as a comforting sense of continuity *with* the
dead, as in Burke's "partnership" of living and dead.

This second reading might seem to be reinforced (except for the contrastive "others came") by the cult of remembered heroes Laon celebrates in lines four to seven, but for the bizarre volte-face in lines eight
and nine, where the skeptical view of memory's chilling action in the
form of custom/tradition enters the sentence without even a full stop to
separate it from the celebrated heroes of the past, idealistically unassailable by time or change.

This uneasy, contradictory stanza helps us understand what is problematic in Laon's and Cythna's roles as orthodox heroes in the poem.
The problem is that of Paine's moldy parchments and lasting constitutions. Laon and Cythna decry "traditions dark and old" and memory's/
custom's "mortal chain" but in turn hope, at least at times, to be remembered as inspiring leaders for an eternity after the revolution. This indeed is one aspect of their induction into the Temple of the Spirit.

Heroes from the past play a significant role in the poem. The Hermit,
who rescues Laon in the third canto, provides us with a particularly rich
example. He is partly modeled, as Mary Shelley points out in her note
on the poem, on Dr. Lind, Shelley's mentor from his Eton days. Mary
Shelley would no doubt have considered it unwise, given the diplomatic
constraints under which these notes were written, to point out that he
is also modeled on Godwin, and in some respects on Paine as well. He
stands in relation to Laon as the past heroes of '90s radicalism did to
Shelley.

The Hermit himself is an anomalous figure. He is old and therefore
should, theoretically, be part of the Spirit of Evil's forces of death. He is
also "cold / In seeming" (IV, xvii, 3–4), an enjambment that speaks volumes. In Shelley's first, self-introductory letter to Godwin he tells him,
"I had enrolled your name on the list of the honourable dead" (*Letters,*
1:220), and this connection with death hangs over the Hermit:

> That hoary man had spent his livelong age
>   In converse with the dead, who leave the stamp
> Of ever-burning thoughts on many a page,
>   When they are gone into the senseless damp
>   Of graves;—his spirit thus became a lamp
> Of splendour, like to those on which it fed:
>   .   .   .   .
> But custom maketh blind and obdurate
>   The loftiest hearts:—he had beheld the woe

> In which mankind was bound, but deemed that fate
>   Which made them abject, would preserve them so;
>   And in such faith, some steadfast joy to know,
> He sought this cell. . . .
>
> (IV, viii, 1–6; ix, 1–6)

Shelley here draws on his ongoing dispute with Godwin over the efficacy of radical revolutionary action to develop once more the paradoxes inherent for him in the concepts of memory and continuity. Again, we can tease out the sudden reversals of thought through these stanzas. The first two lines emphasize the Hermit's age and the connection, almost perverse, that this establishes with death; but in line 3 "the dead's" thoughts prove to be eternally alive. The next three lines are thoroughly ambivalent. The "senseless damp of graves" implies the chilling effects of a "dead hand" on present thought. The Hermit's spirit as "a lamp of splendour" might seem to settle the issue in favor of memory, but "like to those on which it fed," with its internal rhyme back to the "dead" in the second line, to which it compares him, problematizes this. The old (read "dead," elsewhere) Hermit "feeds" on the dead to become like them. This gesture equates the *Erinnerung* of memory with a thanatological cannibalism of the past.

This corruption of *erōs* into autoeroticism finds an echo when Cythna describes being raped by the Tyrant:

> She told me what a loathsome agony
>   Is that when selfishness mocks love's delight,
> Foul as in dream's most fearful imagery
>   To dally with the mowing dead. . . .
>
> (VII, vi, 1–4)

Power, autoeroticism—rape's "selfishness" making it a masturbatory mockery of the mutuality of "love's delight"—and necrophilia combine to show us what lurks under the Hermit's reverence for past heroes.

This would not be a problem were it not for the fact that Laon and Cythna are themselves aiming to be the remembered heroes of the future. The poem shows this beginning to happen in the first moments after their execution. A man stands forth to proclaim that

> " '. . . to long ages shall this hour be known;
>   And slowly shall its memory, ever burning,
> Fill this dark night of things with an eternal morning.' "
>
> (XII, xxix, 7–9)

This is not an aberrant reaction; such eternalization is situated as a goal for Laon at the outset of his mission, when the Hermit tells him that he has raised the "lamp of hope on high, which time nor chance / Nor change may not extinguish" (IV, xvi, 7–8)—a rare but telling occurrence of "change" in a pejorative context—and even more tellingly in Cythna's speech to Laon that precipitates his self-sacrifice:

> "The good and mighty of departed ages
>   Are in their graves, the innocent and free,
> Heroes, and Poets, and prevailing Sages,
>   Who leave the vesture of their majesty
>   To adorn and clothe this naked world;—and we
> Are like to them—such perish, but they leave
>   All hope, or love, or truth, or liberty,
> Whose forms their mighty spirits could conceive,
> To be a rule and law to ages that survive."
>
> (IX, xxviii, 1–9)

The desperate irony of the final line of this stanza reveals the great difficulties posed by this conception of the role of the hero in the *Revolt;* the moldy parchments may have been replaced with "majestic vesture," but this kind of hypostatization and fetishization of the "law" is exactly the deadening effect of custom that prompted both Laon and Cythna to affirm at the peak of the revolution's success that one proof of the movement's failure would be "If our own will as other's law we bind" (V, xlix, 1). Here Laon and Cythna are striving for hegemonic domination.

Shelley must face the problem that to proclaim revolutionary action by "heroes" or "Poets" successful one must suggest that they acted with power, the power to change events. The most obvious form of power is always that employed by the structures one seeks to overthrow. "Heroes and Poets"—even those who eschew violent means—can implicate themselves in the systems of power they seek to overthrow by using any "powerful" form of resistance. I shall briefly explore the problem in its "heroic" form before examining in more depth the problem as it faces "Poets."

Cythna, after escaping from her prison cave, meets and converts to freedom's cause a group of "Mariners," slavers working for the Tyrant. The arguments she makes for their conversion are some of Shelley's finest passages against faith and power, and yet the moment of conversion is a bizarre reversal in which the proof of their commitment to "freedom" is an oath of allegiance that, as a reader of Godwin, Shelley would have known was part of the trappings of ideological obfuscation (*Political Justice,* 2:262ff.):

> "do ye thirst to bear
> A heart which not the serpent Custom's tooth
> May violate?—Be free! and even here,
> Swear to be firm till death!" They cried "We swear! We swear!"
>
> (VIII, xxvii, 6-9)

To swear to do something is an abdication of personal responsibility to an abstract hypostatization of power. This moment is echoed later in the poem; Laon asks the assembled forces of tyranny to whom he is surrendering himself to "Swear by the Power ye dread." "We swear, we swear!" they cry (XI, xxv, 7). Cythna's attempt to forge revolutionary solidarity is uncomfortably close to tyranny's wise prejudice.

The second case is more complex. The victorious revolutionary troops hail Laon as "The friend and the preserver of the free! / The parent of this joy!" (V, xviii, 3-4), and gather around "one whom they might call / Their friend, their chief, their father" (V, xiii, 5-6). The revolutionaries seem to be instantly re-creating the authority structure they have overthrown. Most problematic is the genealogical role ascribed to Laon. The word "father" makes few appearances in this poem, and none of them pejorative. It is a curious absence; we would expect "father" to join the litanies of Priest, King, Despot, Tyrant, God and so forth. Shelley subtly explores that relationship in his *Cenci* ("Great God, whose image upon earth a father is" [II, i, 17], and elsewhere), and Burke established the image of the good citizen as a dutiful child who tends to the father's ills with "trembling solicitude." Shelley had spent much of his own life fighting "tyranny" in the form of fathers (his own, Harriett Westbrook's, and Mary Wollstonecraft Godwin's).

Shelley's omission disguises his insertion of Laon into the order of power/custom/death in order to make him a viable "leader" of the revolution. He becomes a principle of order for a Burkean society-as-organic-partnership: "fraternal bonds," "a nation / Made free by love;—a mighty brotherhood" (V, xiii, 9; xiv, 3-4). To keep Laon's role as father of the revolution secure, Shelley is willing to perform a curious inversion of the actual chronological relationship between the Hermit and Laon (or the intellectual/chronological kinship relationship of Lind/Godwin/Paine to Shelley). The Hermit tells Laon that he has "been thy passive instrument": "thou hast lent / To me, to all, the power to advance" (IV, xvi, 1, 3-4).

II

The question of the role of "Poets" is even more interesting; not only are attitudes toward language an important meeting ground for these contradictory attitudes toward change and memory, but any theory of language, particularly poetic language, must reflect back on Shelley's aims and goals in his poetry and have implications for how he conceives the role of the poet in revolutionary practice.

Poets and language play a highly visible role in the poem. Laon is a poet, and in some ways his words are the efficient cause of the revolution. We learn of his poetry—"Hymns which [his] soul had woven to Freedom" (II, xxviii, 6)—in his first self-description:

> my song
> Peopled with thoughts the boundless universe,
> A mighty congregation, which were strong
> Where'er they trod the darkness to disperse
> The cloud of that unutterable curse
> Which clings upon mankind:—all things became
> Slaves to my holy and heroic verse.
>
> (II, xxx, 1-7)

Words here are seen as powerful tools to combat oppression, but the word "slaves" sets up disturbing resonances. The problem is the same as that faced by "heroes." Language is a problematic weapon, tending to reproduce the ideological tyranny it overthrows. Given that evil inhabits language itself (I, xxx, 1-3), the creation of a postcustom language is both imperative and impossible.

The trap is that language is itself part of custom. To speak truly originally is to be incomprehensible; to be understood is to be within some shared, custom-based language game. Laon tries to hide this in his description of the source of his inspiration:

> With deathless minds which leave where they have passed
> A path of light, my soul communion knew;
> Till from that glorious intercourse, at last,
> As from a mine of magic store, I drew
> Words which were weapons;—round my heart there grew
> The adamantine armour of their power.
>
> (II, xx, 1-6)

But his attempts to distract us from what is really happening—invoking the peculiar ahistorical nature of "magic" words that arrive from outside any tradition—fail if we compare this stanza to its echo in the description of the Hermit's "converse with the dead." Laon's "glorious intercourse" is revealed to be a textual necrophilia with those who "have passed," and we are not surprised that his heart should be frozen in the adamant of the "power" he elsewhere hopes to overthrow.

This paradox is recalled every time—and there are many—a reference is made to the revolutionary's use of "strong speech" (IX, vii, 1), "mighty eloquence" (IV, xi, 2), or "the strength / Of words" (IV, xviii, 4). We are uneasily forced to consider the revolutionaries as sharing in the forms of power they hoped to overthrow, forms of power adroitly and extensively used by the forces of evil themselves—such as the Iberian Priest, whose speech makes "each one / [see] gape beneath the chasms of fire immortal" (X, xl, 2-3), or the "grave and hoary men" "bribed to tell" how Athens "fell / Because her sons were free" and "that among / Mankind the many to the few belong . . . that age was truth . . . that the young / Marred with wild hopes the peace of Slavery" (IX, xiv, 1-8).

This argument, though, however philosophically valid, is politically disabling. If all uses of language are either part of the status quo or gibberish, then no forum for revolutionary activism could exist. We would be forced to say, "If *words* be used 'tis but a change and choice of bonds."

This problem of how power inhabits language is the problem of ideology, which is in many ways the central dilemma of Shelley's "two thoughts." Theories of ideology oppose custom and memory to revolutionary iconoclasm, but all the paradoxes of the skeptical and idealist political positions crystallize on this issue. To the extent that ideology is regarded as a real force and an inherent evil, the means used to fight it are simultaneously reduced in effectiveness (we are all "tainted" by ideology) and compromised in their nature (are we simply trading one ideology for another?). Traditionally, Marxists claimed a distinction between the "ideological" obfuscations of capitalist society and the "scientific truths" of Marxism, this argument resting heavily on Marx's theory of "inversion"; if ideology "inverts" our view of the world, this implies that there is a right-way-up to which it could be restored (Jorge Larrain is an indefatigable expositor and defender of such "inversion"). Since Gramsci, however, there has been a growing school of thought that questions this model. Ernesto Laclau and Chantal Mouffe's *Hegemony and Socialist Strategy* shows that the concept of "inversion" is itself a product of a hegemonic logic that attempts to establish Marxist analysis as a unitary and unassailable truth. They argue that to go beyond ideology is never a final step and that we need to accept a "radical demo-

cratic" politics that constantly seeks to undermine the hegemonic aspirations of the ideological frameworks that inevitably precipitate out of
any social system. They recognize, however, that this entails giving up
claims to "class consciousness" and universality, which have an undeniable political power:

> [T]he possibility of a *unified* discourse of the Left is . . . erased.
> If the various subject positions and the diverse antagonisms and
> points of rupture constitute a *diversity* and not a *diversification,*
> it is clear that they cannot be led back to a point from which
> they could all be embraced and explained by a single discourse.
> Discursive *discontinuity* becomes primary and constitutive. The
> discourse of radical democracy is no longer the discourse of the
> universal; the epistemological niche from which "universal"
> classes and subjects spoke has been eradicated, and it has been
> replaced by a polyphony of voices, each of which constructs its
> own irreducible discursive identity. This point is decisive: there
> is no radical and plural democracy without renouncing the dis-
> course of the universal and its implicit assumption of a privileged
> point of access to "the truth," which can be reached only by a
> limited number of subjects. (191–92)

In the *Revolt,* Shelley is unwilling to abandon the universalist scope
of his "words of power." He still seeks contact with some more-univer-
sal truth than that represented by custom, in order to ground his revolutionary attacks upon it in a subtending continuity. The *Revolt* draws the
same distinctions as Marx does between good and evil words, between
language that discloses and disrupts the discourse of power and language that is part of the mystification and reification of this discourse.
Cythna's "strong speech . . . tore the veil that hid / Nature, and Truth,
and Liberty, and Love," and the Hermit's "mighty eloquence" is used to
free Laon from his prison, thereby freeing him symbolically and actually
from the Tyrant's ideological discourse of power. But the "grave and
hoary men" speak "falsehood," and the Iberian Priest loathes and hates
the "clear light / Of wisdom and free thought" because it threatens his
"Idol" (X, xxxiii, 1–4). Language can be used either to liberate and disrupt ideological distortions or to create and preserve them.

One of the most interesting examples of this is Shelley's exploration
of "naming." David Simpson has already discussed the theory of "naming" in Romantic poetry in his *Irony and Authority* (68–81), and I base
this reading of Shelley's practice on his more general discussion. Simpson reads "naming" as a crux in Romantic poetry, an act that can be

either "a gesture of tyranny and limitation, or a saving necessity in the process of self-constitution" (70). To name something is either to hypostatize it within an ideological framework or to counterhegemonically *rename* it in such a way that it is broken out of that framework. A name is a label, which can make something (or someone) unavailable for certain ways of thinking.

The word "name" makes several intriguing appearances in the *Revolt*. During the Tyrant's rape of Cythna there comes a moment when he wavers and is "no longer passionless," but then he sees her as "a loveless victim," and "her words of flame . . . availed not; then he bore / Again his load of slavery, and became / A king, a heartless beast, a pageant and a name" (VII, v, 7–9). Cythna speaks "words of flame," a word that suggests both a disruption of the "cold" order of custom and a certain transience or evanescence. These words disrupt custom not by using its ideological techniques to create a countercustom but by genuinely eschewing the discursive patterns of the power nexus. The Tyrant, on the other hand, reveals the distortions of custom and power by his inability to escape his "load of slavery"—his complete "representativeness" of the structures of power he inhabits. He becomes finally and most damningly a mere "name" (which rhymes in ironic contrast with "flame" above), completely at one with the role in which custom ideologically imprisons him by naming him king. He is the slave of the language of custom, the language that in the mouth of the Iberian Priest "pierce[s] like ice through every soul" (X, xxii, 9).

What the Tyrant lacks is the "Courage of soul, that dreaded not a name" (IX, 72–73), of which Shelley writes in *Queen Mab:* the courage and will to challenge the way the world is "named." This is, for Shelley, where tyrant and slave become one, each abdicating his own will and responsibility to become part of a total system of oppression, oppression rooted in the reification of names:

> For they all pined in bondage; body and soul,
> Tyrant and slave, victim and torturer, bent
> Before one Power, to which supreme control
> Over their will by their own weakness lent,
> Made all its many names omnipotent.
>
> (*Revolt:* II, viii, 1–5)

What slave and tyrant, victim and torturer, share is a belief in Hegelian *Sittlichkeit;* they accept the fact that their roles in life must be defined by the given social order, even if that social order oppresses them. They legitimize it, and help reproduce it, by accepting the ideological labels

(names) that it imposes upon them, and upon the world. As Sheila Row-
botham puts it, "The power of naming is a real force . . . the false power
which avoids and actually prevents us thinking about the complexities
of what is happening by covering it up in a category" (qtd. in Ryan,
196). Hence the Tyrant's "passionless" rape of Cythna. To him she is the
"loveless victim" whose existence validates his tyrannical might—a category, not a person. Cythna's triumph is to refuse to accept this label.

This makes us all the more surprised at Cythna's description of her
captivity in the cave, when she discovers within her mind the therapeutic "One mind, the type of all, the moveless wave / Whose calm reflects
all moving things that are" (VII, xxxi, 5-6), from which discovery she
creates

> "signs to range
> These woofs, as they were woven, of my thought;
> Clear, elemental shapes, whose smallest change
> A subtler language within language wrought:
> The key of truths which once were dimly taught."
>
> (VII, xxxii, 1-5)

I call this "therapeutic," but Foucault argues that the "tâche fondamentale du 'discours' classique, c'est *d'attribuer un nom aux choses,* et *en
ce nom de nommer leur être*" (*Mots et les choses,* 136).[11] Once again
we are reminded that the Enlightenment project is not as dissimilar to
the post-Kantian one as it might appear. A language that names the
world absolutely, in all its details, is a language in which an absolute self-
consciousness of the world might express itself. Such a "pure" language
has interesting political implications. One of the first, and most influential, attempts in the modern era to eradicate metaphorical indeterminacy from language is that of Hobbes. Central to Hobbes's political
theory is his exclusion of metaphor from language in the attempt to
construct a language of pure reason. In his view the "authority of the
sovereign's law depends on the establishing of unambiguous proper
meanings for words. . . . Hobbes associates ambiguity, equivocation, and
improper metaphor with sedition. Such absolute meaning requires the
possibility of absolute knowledge, of a logos in which meaning and
word coalesce as law" (Ryan, 3).

A language where "meaning and word coalesce as law" would be a
language in which one could not avoid a "free conformity to law" in

---

11. "fundamental task of Classical discourse is *to ascribe a name to things, and in that
name to name their being*" (*Order of Things,* 120).

one's thought. A concrete language may seem a product of a purely "disengaged" mentality, but in fact promises the same reconciliation with the world that Schiller and Schelling see in poetry. The world and our language describing the world become one and same thing. Every word becomes simultaneously a token of its own pure representative embeddedness in the language and a token of our cognitive belonging to the world (and vice versa). The step from this to symbolic, or Christian, hermeneutics is probably inevitable; Marx described such an ideological version of language, writing, as Michael Ryan says, "in terms that seem to foreshadow Derrida": "[T]he whole problem of the transition from thought to reality, hence from language to life, exists only in philosophical illusion . . . our ideologists . . . [set] out in search of a word which, as a *word,* formed the transition in question, which, as a word . . . in a mysterious superlinguistic manner, points from within language to the actual object it denotes; which, in short, plays among words the same role as the Redeeming God-Man plays among people in Christian fantasy . . . thus the triumphant entry into 'corporeal' life" (54).

Cythna, in her prison-house language, has made a language of pure ideological concretization in which names can be substituted for things and presumably, therefore, the state of *things* cannot be changed at all. It is perhaps not surprising, then, that after her release she "frees" the mariners only to bind them to a new "faith" in "Liberty"—a "name" that has now been fully hypostatized: "they called aloud / On Liberty—that name lived on the sunny flood" (IX, iv, 8–9). Liberty, like the Tyrant, has dropped out of the indeterminacy of change and become "a pageant, and a name," though just a few stanzas before, Cythna has told the Mariners how the "Power's names" ("God's names" in *Laon and Cythna*)

> " 'are each a sign which maketh holy
> All power—ay, the ghost, the dream, the shade
> Of power—lust, falsehood, hate, and pride, and folly;
> The pattern whence all fraud and wrong is made,
> A law to which mankind has been betrayed.' "
>
> (VIII, x, 1–5)

A concise analysis of the power of ideology to rule "living" process with "dead" ("the ghost . . . Of Power") language, just as she is about to do herself.

III

Shelley's own role in writing this poem must be considered in the light of these problems. The contradictions within the poem play through his various attempts to describe his goals and methods in the preface. Shelley establishes a goal of writing "fearlessly," "with an utter disregard for anonymous censure," with "newness and energy," and without "the imitation of any style of language or versification peculiar to the original minds of which it is the character; designing that . . . what I have produced . . . be properly my own" (Hutchinson, 32)—a revolutionary language bent on change, therefore, anti-ideological "words of flame" to combat the forces of "misrule and superstition." But Mnemosyne is the mother of the muses with good reason; poetry, memory, and tradition are closely interwoven, and Shelley is not yet ready to say with Blake that "the Daughters of Memory shall become the Daughters of Inspiration" (*Milton*, preface).

After announcing his separation from tradition Shelley wonders: "How far I shall be found to possess that more essential attribute of Poetry, the power of awakening in others sensations like those which animate my own bosom, is that which, to speak sincerely, I know not." Nor indeed *can* he know this if his claim of "newness" is valid; he must accept his rupture with society, accept, as Laclau and Mouffe argue, that a true anti-ideological radicalism must renounce "the discourse of the universal." But he is loath to do so, wanting his poetry to have the social force promised by therapeutic "engagement." He begins with a minimal concession of a "resemblance, which does not depend upon their own will, between . . . the writers of any age"; progresses to a dialectic in which writers "cannot escape from subjection to a common influence," although "each is . . . the author of the very influence . . . by which his being is thus pervaded"; and finally announces "the universal and inevitable influence of [the] age." This gets Shelley step-by-step to the point where he can acknowledge a revealing contradiction to his claims to complete freedom from tradition: "I have adopted the stanza of Spenser" (Hutchinson, 35).

The word "adopted" is intriguing; it evades the actual "parental" relationship here much in the way the Hermit and Laon's relationship is inverted later. Shelley's relationship to Spenser is not his "adoption" of the orphan Spenser, but a sheltering in the security provided by the parental authority of Spenser's stanza and an inscription of his poem in the course of tradition. Shelley's relationship to Spenser goes beyond the merely technical matter of borrowed stanzaic form. The *Revolt*, like *The Fairie Queene*, is a romance.[12] Spenser writes his famous poem "to

---

12. See David Duff's excellent *Romance and Revolution* for an account of the significance of the poem's genre in relationship to its political goals.

fashion a gentleman or noble person in vertuous and gentle discipline." Shelley writes his to "awaken the feelings, so the reader should see the beauty of true virtue, and be incited to those inquiries which have lead to my moral and political creed, and that of some of the sublimest intellects in the world" (32). Both are appealing to a notion of social engagedness—poets as social instructors, who, as representatives of the society in which they are embedded, can insert their works into known and expected normative patterns of response.

Both see as central to their enterprises the epic scope and intent of their subject matter, its representation of the total social field of which they are a part and a self-conscious moment. Spenser cites Homer, Virgil, Ariosto, and Tasso as his models; Shelley, who had urged the French Revolution—"the master theme of the epoch in which we live" (*Letters*, 1:504; see also 508)—on Byron as the theme for an epic poem, seeks to have his poem judged "before the tribunal from which Milton received his immortality."

The problem with this is the inherent conservatism of the epic ideal—even as embodied in the epic romance. The aim of epic is to "embody the history and aspirations of a nation in a lofty and grandiose manner" (Cuddon, 225). Shelley is, therefore, lending his poem to the ideologizing and mythologizing of history, extracting it from the contingency and flux of revolutionary "change" and elevating it to an eternal truth. If he is to receive the "crown of immortality," he must presuppose an absolute standard of truth and beauty and a perpetual continuity of memory that negate the possibility of the total revolutionary change that Shelley's commitment to "newness" and contempt for "imitation" had seemed to announce.

IV

So far we have seen how Shelley's "two thoughts" run through the poem's content and poetic practice, frequently closely associated, but with little evidence of the possibility of bringing them together in any satisfactory resolution, let alone any attempt to do so. To some extent the poem remains divided against itself and "unreadable." But there are ways in which the poem does attempt to create a unity out of these contradictions.

One such way is through the symbolic value of incest, which, in the *Revolt*, leads a double life, running through both sides of most oppositions, yoking them together in a highly unstable unity. The explicit incest in *Laon and Cythna* was only partly suppressed in its transformation into the *Revolt.* Laon still speaks of his and Cythna's mutual passion based upon

> the youthful years
> Which we together passed . . .
> The blood itself which ran within our frames,
> That likeness of the features which endears
> The thoughts expressed by them, our very names . . .
>
> (VI, xxxi, 4–8)

Their names at this stage are almost identical, Cythna having taken the name Laone as a *nomme de guerre.* As this renaming suggests, the real significance of incest in the poem is as a symbol of interpersonal unity rather than as a specific act. Laon's description of his and "Laone's" mock marriage spells this out:

> There we unheeding sate, in the communion
>   Of interchangèd vows, which, with a rite
> Of faith most sweet and sacred, stamped our union.—
>   Few were the living hearts which could unite
>   Like ours, or celebrate a bridal-night
> With such close sympathies, for they had sprung
>   From linkèd youth, and from the gentle might
> Of earliest love, delayed and cherished long,
> Which common hopes and fears made, like a tempest, strong.
>
>   And such is Nature's law divine, that those
>   Who grow together cannot choose but love,
>   If faith or custom do not interpose.
>
> (VI, xxxix; xl, 1–3).

To love that which you do not know is impossible, and what does one know beyond the self? Biological relatedness is only one symbol of this a priori unity, as the emphasis on "close sympathy," "linked youth," and "grow[ing] together" makes clear. We can tease out of these lines all the oppositions that divide the poem, brought together under the theme of incest.

Incest also symbolizes Shelley's skeptical revolutionism. The last three lines quoted above hearken back to the canceled passage from the *Laon and Cythna* preface in which Shelley justifies the incest theme as helping to "break through the crust of those outworn opinions on which established institutions depend" by exposing incest as a mere "crime

. . . of convention" (Hutchinson, 886). This radical Drummondian insistence upon the constituted nature of our social institutions is exactly the kind of amnesiac revolutionism Burke feared. Throwing out "outworn" opinions finds a significant echo when the revolutionaries "cast off their memories of the past outworn."

But the same passage is strangely conservative in another reading; by suggesting that the multitude of "artificial vices" impedes the development of "real virtues," it suggests that beneath the purely "conventional" morality there is an absolute moral order that remains when the dross of contemporary custom is removed.

This equivocation has its counterpart in Laon and Cythna's curious mock marriage. Supposedly, in this moment, the two lovers are flying in the face of "outworn" customs, but can we not read this moment as fulfilling at its highest level the orthodox promise of marriage, making one flesh of the celebrants? Their ceremony has all the trappings of "communion," "interchanged vows," "a rite of faith" (a word used almost exclusively in a pejorative sense elsewhere in the poem), "union," and "bridal-night" celebration. Incest is seen as both a skeptical disruption of the customary forms of marital relationship *and* as the complete and more perfect realization (by stripping away delusions and getting down to "real virtues") of the unifying, therapeutic, promise of marriage.

"Incest," as something other than mere biological accident, is an affirmation of traditional kinship structures in general, even if it subverts them in the particular instance. Incest, per se, is only possible in a society that recognizes, remembers, and maintains traditional family relationships. The thoroughly promiscuous society, a stock bogeyman of antirevolutionary rhetoric, cannot recognize incest. Incest, then, can become an assertion of memory and continuity. Laon and Cythna's lovemaking occurs in a ruined building where "Memories, like awful ghosts . . . come and go" (VI, xxvii, 4), and its expression is as if "all the wingèd hours which speechless memory claims, / Had found a voice" (VI, xxxi, 9; xxxii, 1). In the "bridal-night" stanzas, love springs from "linked youth," "earliest love," and "common hopes and fears," and flourishes when people "grow together." Laon and Cythna find their true selves in a return to a grounding origin in a shared tradition, even if that tradition is shared by only two people.

The failure of incest satisfactorily to bring Shelley's "two thoughts" together is foreshadowed at the beginning of the poem, though we do not immediately realize it. In the "Dedication," which opens the poem, Shelley portrays his relationship to Mary Wollstonecraft Godwin as be-

ing just as "incestuous" as Laon's and Cythna's, but here the solipsistic
tendency of the relationship is more clear because the counterbalancing
outward connection to a revolutionary movement is taken away. Shelley,
before meeting Mary, "moved alone" in a world of "black despair" (dedication, vi, 5, 4). After she has joined him—in despite of "the mortal
chain / Of Custom" (dedication, vii, 4-5)—the situation seems to have
improved little:

>   Truth's deathless voice pauses among mankind!
>   If there must be no response to my cry—
>   If men must rise and stamp with fury blind
>   On his pure name who loves them,—thou and I,
>   Sweet friend! can look from our tranquillity
>   Like lamps into the world's tempestuous night,—
>   Two tranquil stars, while clouds are passing by
>   Which wrap them from the foundering seaman's sight,
>   That burn from year to year with unextinguished light.
>
>   (dedication, xiv, 1-9)

This echo of the Lucretian *suave mari magno* suggests that it is
tough luck for the foundering seaman. The Shelleys are unable to reach
out beyond their incestuous "partnership" of two. The problem lies in
what this suggests about the poem, which is very much a part of their
relationship ("these delights, and thou, have been to me / The parents
of the song I consecrate to thee" [dedication, ix, 8-9]). The poem,
seemingly aimed outward, according to the principle of *erōs,* toward an
engagement with the society it seeks to transform, instead is apparently
built upon the assumption that there "must be no response to my cry"
in a world where "Yet never found I one not false to me" (dedication, vi,
6)—a telling echo of Eccles. 7:28, which underlines the solipsistic
mood of the dedication, dismissing the world beyond the self as "vanity."

This supports James Boon's contention that, discursively, incest is a
principle of limitation, in this instance limiting discourse to the self
(227-28). This is counter to the epic inclusiveness of the poem's aspirations, but it fits well with the poem's nature as "private epic," aiming to
glorify Laon and Cythna and extract them from the process of history
"To be a rule and law to ages that survive." Moreover, it reveals that the
flaw in the epic concept is its autoerotic nature. Like *erōs,* epic proclaims itself as a transcendence of self, centrifugally and hermeneutically
reaching out to include everything in its context of production; but it
proves to be an obsession with self, a representation *of* tradition (of

which the self is heir and representative) for the pleasure of and consumption *by* tradition—an autoerotic circle, based on the *inclusiveness*
of epic as it seeks to insert the entire tradition back into the tradition in
the hypostatized form of epic. This model is symbolized in the poem by
the Hermit, who as product and representative of a written tradition in
turn feeds cannibalistically on that tradition, cannibalism serving here as
a symbolic form of autoeroticism.

This connection between incest and cannibalism is where the attempt to find a mediation between idealism and skepticism by means of
incest falls apart. The connection is only made irrefutably clear when
Laon, imprisoned by the Tyrant's men, has a "vision" ("I know not yet,
was it a dream or no" [III, xxiv, 6]) of four corpses being brought in and
hung up in his cell:

> Leaning that I might eat, I stretched and clung
> Over the shapeless depth in which those corpses hung.
>
> A woman's shape . . .
>   .   .   .   .
> Hung there; the white and hollow cheek I drew
> To my dry lips . . .
>   .   .   .   .
> Alas, alas! it seemed that Cythna's ghost
>   Laughed in those looks, and that the flesh was warm
> Within my teeth!
>
> (III, xxv, 8-9; xxvi, 1, 3-4, 6-8)

Here, the line between incestuous and cannibalistic desire is collapsed
in the grimly playful equivocation of "the white and hollow cheek I
drew / To my . . . lips," and we realize, retrospectively, that if the
poem's heroes succumb to this extreme implication of the discourse of
incest, then any resolution of the poem's contradictions under its auspices can lead only to, quite literally, a dead end. All reason for political
action is nullified in this economy of death, and all that is left is for us is
a solipsistic political quietism of the kind disturbingly adumbrated in
Shelley's "Dedication."

V

There is, however, a second way Shelley attempts to mediate the "two
thoughts," a way that addresses the fact of death without necessarily
being defeated by it. It is a theme in the poem we have as yet not
explored. It occurs throughout the poem but finds its major statement

at Cythna's summing up of her account of her actions and adventures in Laon's absence. This is a singular attempt in the poem to make sense of the progress of their story, establishing the principles upon which the rest of their actions are based.

Her speech in the ninth canto runs from the twentieth to the thirty-sixth stanza and is principally an attempt to reconcile their own inevitable deaths and the seeming failure of the revolution with the progress of liberty and the eventual freedom of humanity. The explanation she seizes on, making us retrospectively aware of its frequent significance in the poem to that point, is an extended seasonal metaphor that is important enough for us to unfold at length:

> "The blasts of Autumn drive the wingèd seeds
>   Over the earth,—next come the snows, and rain,
> And frosts, and storms, which dreary Winter leads
>   Out of his Scythian cave, a savage train;
>   Behold! Spring sweeps over the world again,
>
> . . . .
>
> "O Spring, of hope, and love, and youth, and gladness
>   Wind-wingèd emblem! brightest, best and fairest!
> Whence comest thou, when, with dark Winter's sadness
>   The tears that fade in sunny smiles thou sharest?
>   Sister of joy, thou art the child who wearest
> Thy mother's dying smile, tender and sweet;
>   Thy mother Autumn, for whose grave thou bearest
> Fresh flowers . . .
>
> . . . .
>
> "Has not the whirlwind of our spirit driven
>   Truth's deathless germs to thought's remotest caves?
>   Lo, Winter comes!—the grief of many graves
>
> . . . .
>
> Stagnate like ice at Faith the enchanter's word,
> And bind all human hearts in its repose abhorred.
>
> "The seeds are sleeping in the soil: meanwhile
>   The Tyrant peoples dungeons with his prey,
>
> . . . .
>
> . . . gray Priests triumph, and like blight or blast
> A shade of selfish care o'er human looks is cast.

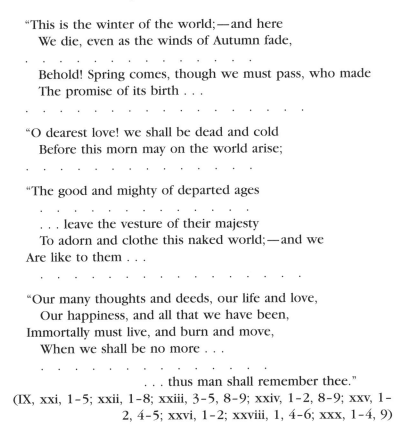

"This is the winter of the world;—and here
   We die, even as the winds of Autumn fade,
  .   .   .   .

   Behold! Spring comes, though we must pass, who made
   The promise of its birth . . .
  .   .   .   .

"O dearest love! we shall be dead and cold
   Before this morn may on the world arise;
  .   .   .   .

"The good and mighty of departed ages

  .   .   .   .
   . . . leave the vesture of their majesty
   To adorn and clothe this naked world;—and we
Are like to them . . .

  .   .   .   .

"Our many thoughts and deeds, our life and love,
   Our happiness, and all that we have been,
Immortally must live, and burn and move,
   When we shall be no more . . .

  .   .   .   .
            . . . thus man shall remember thee."
(IX, xxi, 1-5; xxii, 1-8; xxiii, 3-5, 8-9; xxiv, 1-2, 8-9; xxv, 1-
        2, 4-5; xxvi, 1-2; xxviii, 1, 4-6; xxx, 1-4, 9)

Much of this symbolism I have already explored, but this sustained attempt to place death, continuity, change, and life in a cyclical progression is something new, and asks us to reread as cyclical succession
what I proposed was a simple contradiction between "change" and
"memory." There is change and discontinuity, but it is comprehended
within a wider "seasonal" continuity. There is the stagnation and living
death of the custom/power nexus, but it is subject to necessary change.
   This pattern of imagery is associated throughout the poem with crucial moments of liberation and freedom from custom's wintry grip, serving to reclaim contradictions in the light of Cythna's more developed
argument. In the "Dedication" Mary's entry into Shelley's life is described in these terms: "Thou Friend, whose presence on my wintry
heart / Fell, like bright Spring upon some herbless plain" (dedication,
vii, 1-2). The Tyrant at the moment of his "awful change" is surrounded

by a "mighty crowd . . . like the rush of showers / Of hail in spring" (V, xxix, 1, 3-4), and the slave women Cythna frees after her own release from the Tyrant's cave have "brows as bright as spring" (VIII, xxix, 3). Laon and Cythna make love in the ruin where "The autumnal winds, as if spell-bound, had made / A natural couch of leaves" (VI, xxviii, 1-2), associating them with Autumn even before Cythna begins her speech.

The promise of vernal rebirth hidden within the "death" of autumn therapeutically recuperates loss, death, and fragmentation as intimations of a greater whole. This symbolism has always been easily incorporated in Christian mythology—many of Christ's attributes evidently being derived from pagan myths of death and resurrection connected with the seasons (Osiris, Adonis, Dionysis-Zagreus). To cast Laon and Cythna as types of Christ is one therapeutic "solution" to the problem of their skeptical/incestuous isolation from the world. They become pure representative beings, Coleridgean "symbols" of the "vast stream of ages"; as such, their deaths are recuperated by that stream, which negates the negation of their deaths and assures their eventual triumph. It is a comforting belief for an isolated poet with a "passion for reforming the world," but it is, as Shelley soon realizes, a problematic one as well.

The *Revolt* draws on the story of Christ in a quite straightforward way. The final three cantos of the poem—significantly, after Cythna's extended "seasons" speech—run more or less parallel to the betrayal and crucifixion of Christ, with Laon acting as his own Judas and both Laon and Cythna taking the place of Christ. They willingly sacrifice themselves for the advancement of the whole in accordance with the seasonal/Christian pattern. Even before this final apotheosis, however, Laon has been established as a type of Christ. When the crowd is about to murder Othman, Laon, in an evocation of Christ's response to the woman taken in adultery, cries out: "What call ye *justice?* . . . Are ye all pure? Let those stand forth who hear, / And tremble not" (V, xxxiv, 1, 3-4). Earlier, Laon steps before the spear aimed at one of the finally vanquished soldiers of the Tyrant. The spear pierces his arm, but Laon smiles and apostrophizes the wound as blood starts to "gush" from it:

>   "Oh! thou gifted
> With eloquence which shall not be withstood,
> Flow thus!"—I cried in joy, "thou vital flood,
> Until my heart be dry, ere thus the cause
> For which thou wert aught worthy be subdued—

. . . .
'Tis well! ye feel the truth of love's benignant laws."

(V, ix, 3-7, 9)

This dramatic episode enacts in miniature the core of the Christian myth; Laon takes the punishment for the sins of others and serves thereby to absolve them of their crimes. Interestingly, it is after this action that they all, revolutionaries and former enemies, gather around Laon as "Their friend, their chief, their *father*." We also find that central imagery of Christian devotion, the blood of Christ that washes us clean; the ambivalence of "vital flood" perfectly captures the central paradox of the Christian myth, that Christ dies (Laon loses his "vital" blood) so that we may live (the stream is "vital"—life giving—to us).

The Christ story allows us to read death as the prelude to a new life, to reread the revolutionary's alienation from the world as suffering Christlike rejection *by* the world ("men must rise and stamp with fury blind / On his pure name who loves them" [dedication, xiv, 3-4]), a rejection to be transcended in the resurrection, when the incestuous limitations of the profane are transformed into the all-embracing unity of divine *erōs*. By reading his apparently estranged, autoerotic revolutionaries as representatives of all humanity, whose love in fact expands to an erotic universality, Shelley appears to have reconciled his "two thoughts." Skeptical "death" as diasparactive discontinuity is redeemed and recuperated by the discovery that this death is a dying-into-the-whole, a negation that is negated by the Spirit's advance. Shelley has reconciled his opposing conceptual systems by linking them not in a paradigm of simultaneity but in one of succession and teleological growth. Hegel's criticism of the self-contradictory skeptic is circumvented by introducing a process of contradiction that is resolved in growth: not "If *A* then *B*, if *B* then *A*," but "Now *A*, then *B*, (then *C*)"; now through a glass darkly (autoeroticism), then face to face (divine *erōs*).

But just as incest as a resolution threatened to engulf the oppositions in a solipsistic skepticism, this threatens to vindicate Hegel by bringing the two thoughts together in therapeutic fashion—a process of thesis, antithesis, synthesis. Like Hegel, Shelley has made "the history of the world . . . the true *theodicaea,* the justification of God in History" and the "Calvary of Absolute Spirit" (qtd. in Abrams, *Natural Supernaturalism*, 189).

Hegel would seem to have been completely vindicated; the skeptic seeking to bring his two thoughts together finds that the only way is through the Hegelian *Aufhebung*. The seasonal process, as much as Christian eschatology, is a process dependent on preservation-through-destruction, and Cythna's insistence on the necessity of their death to bring forward spring's "paradise" (IX, xxvi, 5), which will be both their negation and an expression of their fullest triumph ("Spring comes, though we must pass, who made / The promise of its birth" [IX, xxv, 4–5]), fits this therapeutic pattern perfectly, explaining her apparently paradoxical insistence both that they (Laon and Cythna) will be forgotten (people will "Insult with careless tread, our undivided tomb" [IX, xxix, 9]) and that they will be remembered in the most determinist, constitutive sense (they will "be a rule and law to ages that survive" [IX, xxviii, 9]). Only this therapeutic confidence that the moment of defeat is the moment of victory and growth, that death heralds new life, and the apocalyptic belief that the "last days" before the accession to "paradise" will be the most catastrophic allow Shelley to read the order of death/custom as a (dialectically) necessary stage for even his heroes to go through in order to achieve the new revolutionary order.

Hence the otherwise incomprehensible claim in the preface that "the temporary triumph of oppression [in the French Revolution—"temporary" only in Shelley's vatic voice], [is the] secure earnest of its final and inevitable fall" (Hutchinson, 32). Winter promises spring, Passion promises resurrection, the triumph of custom promises the triumph of revolution.

VI

But it is not this simple. It is the question of teleology that proves the major sticking point for a straightforwardly therapeutic reading of Cythna's speech. Her speech is bracketed by two powerful skeptical statements that disrupt the therapeutic framework outlined above. It begins with the assertion "We know not what will come" (IX, xx, 1) and over its last five stanzas reverts to a powerful skepticism directed, at least in part, at the idealist synthesis discussed earlier. At the peak of her confident statements of the certainty of the immortal "preservation" of their political initiative in "fame," which, "sculptured" in "human hope," will "Survive the perished scrolls of unenduring brass" (IX, xxxi, 8–9), she falters: "we too . . . must depart, / And Sense and Reason . . . would bid the heart / That gazed beyond the wormy grave despair . . . ; no calm sleep . . . but senseless death—a ruin dark and deep!" (IX, xxxii, 1–9). A profound uncertainty has entered here, and she suddenly dismisses the idealist certainties she had so confidently stated before:

"These are blind fancies—reason cannot know
   What sense can neither feel, nor thought conceive;
There is delusion in the world—and woe,
   And fear, and pain—we know not whence we live,
   Or why, or how, or what mute Power may give
Their being to each plant, and star, and beast,
   Or even these thoughts . . .

. . . .

"Alas, our thoughts flow on with stream, whose waters
   Return not to their fountain—Earth and Heaven,
The Ocean and the Sun, the Clouds their daughters,
   Winter, and Spring, and Morn, and Noon, and Even,
   All that we are or know, is darkly driven
Towards one gulf.—Lo! what a change is come
   Since I first spake—but time shall be forgiven,
Though it change all but thee!"—she ceased. . . .
                (IX, xxxiii, 1-7; xxxv, 1-8)

"What a change is come" indeed. Time is no longer the providential seasonal scheme that tends inexorably to the goal of preserving their spirit for immortality, but a disruptive force which threatens to "change" everything and of which Cythna expects so little that she will "forgive" it if it minimally spares her beloved, which is to say, her alter ego. The seasonal system itself is now comprehended within a wider process, whose end is hidden from us: "Winter, and Spring" (now strangely unified as if their former opposition had collapsed) are "darkly driven" toward one of Shelley's skeptical abysses, the "one gulf"—an ironic displacement of the concept of the unified, immanent telos.

Most telling is the ironic echo of Laon's self-proclamation as world-historical spirit in the second canto: "I felt the sway / Of the vast stream of ages bear away / My floating thought"; Cythna's stream is more Lucretian flux than idealist *Weltgeist,* scattering their thoughts in its unforeseeable course. Disrupting the therapeutic movement of circular reconciliation and return, this stream's "waters / Return not to their fountain." Shelley emphasizes this point, which is a repetition from the first stanza of Cythna's speech where, denying a knowable telos to history ("We know not what will come") and speaking of "the homeless future's wintry grove" (5), she calls "steadfast truth, an unreturning stream" (IX, xx, 9).

The seasonal pattern is one of return, and in the short term posits a telos. But these skeptical passages force us to rethink the meaning of

the seasonal cycle, to consider that as much as winter's coming promises spring, spring's promises winter; this "return" is more like the
Nietzschean eternal return than Hegelian completion, a thanatological
repetition that is a suggestive contrast to the discourse of creation and
life seen on first reading (Freud, "Pleasure Principle," 22). Cythna suppresses this fact by studiously avoiding a mention of summer, which
would return us from "revolutionary" spring to "tyrannical" autumn. But
this absence is only made all the more noticeable in the repetition in
stanza after stanza of the incompleted cycle (a season being named at
xxi, 1, 3, 5; xxii, 1, 3, 7; xxiii, 5; xxv, 1, 2, 4; and xxvi, 6, 7), so that the
verse enacts the repetition Cythna suppresses.

Cythna's speech complicates any straightforwardly idealist reading of
this complex of imagery, too, in that it contains the sole statement of
necessitarian theory in the poem—in lines usually (and often) quoted
out of their surprising context:

> "One comes behind,
> Who aye the future to the past will bind—
> Necessity, whose sightless strength for ever
> Evil with evil, good with good must wind
> In bands of union, which no power may sever:
> They must bring forth their kind, and be divided never!"
>
> (IX, xxvii, 4–9)

The therapeutic essence of idealist providentialism, that the evil of our
fallen world is God's planned path to lead us to good, is irrevocably
shed here. Necessity is "sightless" and can bind evil only to evil and
good only to good. The "evil" death and disruption of autumn cannot be
the necessary cause of the "good" of spring. History cannot have a providential pattern or be the product of a dialectical cunning. By disrupting
the possibility of a final homecoming in the cyclical "progression" of
Spirit, and by removing the telos (immanent or transcendent) of the
progress, Shelley has made it impossible to state confidently that the
internal division of the skeptic will be resolved in the direction of the
Spirit's growth.

Shelley has not, however, simply overthrown the idealist structure
and replaced it with a skeptical one. Rather, he achieves a conceptual
palimpsest that generates a series of moments we must read in both
idealist and skeptical senses in order to make any sense of them at all,
and this is as close as he comes in the *Revolt* to bringing the "two
thoughts" together, a "syn-thesis" only in the etymological sense of "putting together." To an extent this must remain unparaphrasable, a di-

remption of our reading of the word "spring," for example, which cannot be synthesized into a unified self-identical significance. But despite this, as a general summation of the ways this internally divided discourse is actualized within the poem, we can argue that what Shelley retains from the idealist pattern is a process, or at least the ever-present possibility of a process, of the reclamation of death and discontinuity for a future good, but the skeptical insistence that this good cannot be predicted and that it is not predicated upon the present evil remains. The evil and good cannot be seen as different aspects of an absolute Notion.

Hence Cythna's insistence upon the finality of their deaths. There *may* be resurrection; indeed it is empirically observed in the seasonal cycle that winter's death feeds into spring's life, but the dying individual can only hope that *this* death will be part of such a cycle. Death is thus a meaningless, randomizing disruption ("We know not what will come," "we shall be dead and cold," "senseless death—a ruin dark and deep!") and potentially but unknowably also a moment in a process of growth. We are thus unable to foresee the change we hope our work will effect. Change is still "change from" rather than "change to." There is no triumphant arrival at closure, no apocalyptic fulfillment, but, without any dogmatic belief in idealist certainties, there is made available to the skeptically isolated individual a mechanism whereby individual action (and individual death) might have an effect. Skeptical disengagement from society, which attracted Shelley to idealist *Sittlichkeit,* might not be absolute if the (Christlike) sacrifice of self might lead to the advance of the whole.

This sounds like small comfort, but the distance between, say, the nihilistic futility of the Poet's quest to contact an other in *Alastor* and the doubt-ridden and anxious but nonetheless hopeful appeal for the poet's effort and death to "quicken a new birth" in "Ode to the West Wind" (64) is palpable. Hence the "autumnal tone" in the ode is "sweet though in sadness" (61) because the promise it brings of spring's possibility is at least as real as the certainty of present death, the reality of which all idealisms must suppress.

Shelley several times states the political implications of this argument, but nowhere in more appropriate terms than in his last letter to Southey (17 August 1820), where he is upbraiding him for the "rash judgment" generated by his dogmatic Christianity: "The immediate fruits of all new opinions are indeed calamity to the promulgators and professors; but we see the end of nothing, and it is in acting well, in contempt of present advantage that virtue consists" (*Letters,* 2:231). Shelley's model here is the Christ who meets calamity for innovating in contempt of

custom, but a Christ without supernatural assurance of eventual triumph—"an innocent and a persecuted man" (2:231), as Shelley describes himself, who sees the end of nothing. As he writes elsewhere,
the honest person in a corrupt system must be seen "as a kind of Jesus
Christ. . . . If faith is a virtue in any case it is so in politics rather than
religion" (2:191).

This compromise discourse, then, is a Trojan horse by which skepticism can invade idealism and maintain political validity, but it is not
without problems. The fact that Shelley has allowed himself to compromise with "tradition" leaves him still unable satisfactorily to resolve the
question of the nature of the poem itself and his duties as poet. In the
almost exactly contemporary "Essay on Christianity" he argues that
Christ, in order to overthrow contemporary doctrines, had first to get a
hearing for his innovative theories by giving them an assimilable form.
This is the "Trojan horse" idea, but although Shelley can make it sound
like harmless chicanery—"like a skillful orator . . . he secures the prejudices of his auditors, and induces them by his professions of sympathy
with their feelings to enter with a willing mind into the exposition of
his own" (Ingpen and Peck, 6:242)—there is an underlying epistemological insight with disturbing implications: "All reformers have been
compelled to practice this [self-]misrepresentation. . . . [I]t is deeply to
be lamented," but "truth cannot be communicated until it is perceived"
(243).

That is, without dressing novelty in forms recognizable by custom it
is not even visible. In theory, having put his innovations into the Trojan
horse of custom, "Jesus Christ proceeds to qualify and finally to abro-
gate the system of the Jewish law" (243). But this is problematic in the
light of Shelley's arguments that to use the forms of oppressive custom,
with however laudable an intent, is to replicate that oppression. In that
light, what can we make of Shelley's arguments for a political "faith" or,
more important, of the resurrection of Laon and Cythna and their elevation to the Temple of the Spirit? It is difficult to absolve Shelley of the
charge of assimilating his critique into structures that diffuse its innovative power.

Michael Ryan has also argued that a revolutionary movement must
eschew all conceptual frameworks associated with the status quo. He
recognizes, however, that a renunciation of existing forms of power can
seem politically disabling: "[A]n emphasis on plurality over authoritarian
unity . . . argu[ing] for the flawed . . . if not contradictory, nature of all
. . . absolute or total philosophic systems . . . consistently elicits accusa-
tions of "paralysis." How can one do anything if it is inevitably flawed, if

indeterminacy precludes absolute truth?" (Ryan, 213). But he concludes that despite this threat of disengaging radicalism from the structures it seeks to overthrow, this is a necessary risk because "the monolithic concepts of this organization, of the struggle, of values, and of the 'gradual' construction of socialism held by both leninism and the New Left's Right are untenable . . . in consequence one very important struggle is the one against our own drives (in part metaphysical) to adhere to such forms of power, forms that are not merely not prefigurative of socialism, but also are inimical to the material concept of socialism. And authority is one of those forms" (219–20). But what is at stake in this attempt to do without "authority"? For Ryan, it means a total break with the past, a renunciation of the determination of our identity by the authority of "tradition." He characterizes this as a renunciation of "filiation." Deriving his argument from Derrida and Adorno, he argues that filiation, which he defines as "the attempt to pin down an origin, an 'absolute ancestor,'" is a principle of authority and absolute identity, and Derrida and Adorno "[b]oth see pure identity as death" (77).

This concept of filiation allows us to understand a central moment of equivocation in the *Revolt,* which shows us that Shelley is not quite happy with his attempt to reconcile the "two thoughts." This is quasi-acknowledged in the poem by an awkward loose end that refuses to be tied up, an unreadable element that destabilizes his attempted solution. This is the child who is discovered by Laon with the Tyrant.

How are we to read this child? She is, ostensibly, the product of the Tyrant's rape of Cythna, and yet the child proclaims herself to be—whether literally or symbolically is unclear—Laon's (XII, xxiv, 4). We might be tempted to read this as an example of the kind of elective filiation that Ryan evidently proposes. The child may be produced by tyranny, but she is not doomed to be defined by, and to replicate the patterns of, tyranny. Shelley appears to have a crucial loss of confidence over this child, however. By having her die at precisely the moment Laon and Cythna do, so that she may join them in their voyage to the Temple of the Spirit, he ducks the questions his attempted "syn-thesis" of the "two thoughts" is unable to answer satisfactorily. What does the child owe to her parentage? To what extent is she forced to honor the "memory" of her father (whether Laon or the Tyrant)? Can she throw it in the "kettle of magicians," or must she approach it with fear and "trembling solicitude?" How much of her "identity" is inevitably "representative" of her "productive context," and how much of it can she freely re-create? What is the relationship of "text" to (ideological) "context"?

The child's death allows Shelley to avoid addressing the question of filiation, so that we cannot finally decide upon the meaning of his seasonal metaphors. The child cries out to be cast as the "seed" left behind after Laon and Cythna's death, which will lead to a glorious new spring of liberation—an idealist piece of filiation (at least matrilineal) that would tilt Shelley's unstable "syn-thesis" toward a conventionally therapeutic synthesis: tyrant and slave come together to produce this last, latest incarnation of the immortal spirit of Liberty. Alternatively, given Shelley's preoccupation with children who rebel against "tyrannical" fathers, we might have expected him to make the child simply the Tyrant's, won over to the revolution by moral suasion. This would represent a direct skeptical assault upon the principle of filiation. As it is, the child remains an enigma, which points to the unsatisfying irresolution of the *Revolt.*

The "decentering" school of Shelley criticism would argue that Shelley's poetry after the *Revolt* is an attempt to deny the filial tie of Cythna's child to any parents, to exploit the moments of indecision in that poem and explode the Burkean/therapeutic principle of filiation and its insistence upon grounding social, poetic, or conceptual innovation in a continuity that denies its power of novelty. But although this reading can give a persuasive account of Shelley's poetry of political protest, there are problems. We can see these problems perhaps more clearly in Ryan's attempt to marry deconstruction and Marxism in precisely the kind of "decentering" politics these critics ascribe to Shelley.

If the "incestuous" principle of filiation is to be overthrown, can this be achieved from a position radically exterior to the structures of the "endogamous" society? Or does a rush to proclaim oneself marginal actually support the status quo's attempt to exclude alterity from its self-same identity? Is it not rather ridiculous to suggest that poetry can be a more powerful weapon against oppression than "conventional" (that is, conventionally "powerful") revolution? Ryan acknowledges this occasionally, despite scoffing, as we saw, at suggestions that "paralysis" follows self-exclusion from "authority" (or logocentrism). In comparing Derrida and Adorno he argues that "[b]oth negative dialectics and deconstruction are imminent critiques of philosophies of identity and transcendence. These philosophies must be undermined from within, on their own ground and using their own principles. Both Adorno and Derrida see this strategy of subversion as an imposed necessity. Derrida says that the language of metaphysics is the only language available to him. He has no choice but to place it under erasure, effaced yet legible, so that it can be used against itself. For this reason, the post-critical text will be almost indistinguishable from the pre-critical one" (73–74). Shelley's use of incest in the *Revolt,* with its calculated subversion of "the crust of . . . outworn opinions on which established institutions depend," might serve as an example of this immanent critique, a use "against itself" of the incestuous order of custom/metaphysics. But the dangers are apparent in the fact that, like Derrida's postcritical text, Shelley's attempt to insert his critique into the structure he wants to overthrow has forced him, in the use of incest, to replicate that structure almost exactly, even to accentuate its problems. Is it not possible to read Derrida's contention that there is no "hors-texte" as an exclusive principle of textual endogamy, a textual *Geist* "almost indistinguishable" from Hegel's?

Ryan proposes an exogamous, dispersive socialism created instantaneously by a massive refusal of "filiation," similar to Hogle's "transferential" rejection of meaning. He proposes a formulation to which he returns several times (217, 219) and which reminds us of Hogle's "transferential One": "I will argue here that unity, rather than authority, is needed, and that at this point in history in North America, unity excludes authority. By unity, I mean the articulation of a diverse, differentiated plurality; unity or a whole or identity or a 'totality' is never anything but that anyway" (215). This "diverse unity" is Ryan's Hegelian conscience (via Marx) reintegrating contradiction endogamously within the system, having contradiction issue in the resolution of apocalyptic marriage—the mystery of the two made one. Ryan's "exclusion of authority" is, then, "almost indistinguishable" from Coleridge's idealist "multeity-in-unity."

To the extent that this insertion within the order it aims to subvert is, following Boon, a principle of textual incestuousness, then, following Derrida, we could say it concurs with the "incestuous" roots of Hegelian Absolute Knowing (see Ryan, 201). Cythna's child cannot commit incest in despite of convention unless she is conventionally filiated; transgression as conscious transgression presupposes and supports law. A poetic of "subversion," then, which is what Shelley's "decentering" metaphoricity is, would seem to be a textually incestuous/cannibalistic moment in Spirit's history when Absolute Knowing pretends not to be itself and sets about consuming itself as if it were another. To do this it pretends to be a liberated moment of life setting free the dead to a new, eternally joyful, transferential existence, but although it refuses to acknowledge its allegiance to death, it is inextricably bound to it. The "decentering" reading of Shelley's post-*Revolt* writing shies away from these problems, but still falls victim to Adorno's and Derrida's (and

Ryan's) "imposed necessity" of incestuous filiation. Subversive as this possibility may be, we have seen that the logic of subversion demands and supports the existence of the structure it "subverts."

"THE TRIUMPH OF LIFE"

I

Sometime after the completion of the *Revolt of Islam,* Shelley achieved a profoundly altered understanding of the relationship of his "two thoughts." In his last poem, "The Triumph of Life," Shelley returns to the problems of memory and death-as-disjunction, representativeness and atomization, revolutionary disjunction and filiation, which he explored in the *Revolt.* He makes of them something very different, however. In this section, I explore what the "Triumph" has to say on these issues, in order to show that the failed reconciliations of the "two thoughts" in the *Revolt* have given way, in the meantime, to a radically new relationship. Whether and how this new solution genuinely reconciles the "two thoughts" is the question I attempt to answer in Part Two.

The question of death is particularly relevant to how we approach the "Triumph," because it lies at the center of one of the recurrent cruxes in criticism of this poem. Shelley's own death, which left the poem "unfinished," has revealed the profound uncertainties in our cultural and critical attitudes toward death and authorship. On the one hand, there has been a tendency to look in the "Triumph" for "last words," not just those words that, as chance would have it, were the last Shelley could write, but words that give us a clue to the nature of Shelley's poetic enterprise, that at some level mark a closure or fulfillment (or recantation) of Shelley's life and oeuvre considered as a "whole." This is to read Shelley's death therapeutically as, in Dilthey's terms, that "last moment of a life" when "the balance of its meaning [can] be struck" (Dilthey, 74–75).

If we read Shelley's life as a narrative totality, the "Triumph" gains special significance as the moment when he looks back on his life and work and seeks to capture its essence. Hence the vehemence of the critical debates over whether the "Triumph" is a pessimistic palinode to Shelley's previously optimistic idealism, or a fulfillment of that vision in a bleaker register, or the pure extreme of his "decentering" poetics. Each critic is claiming not just that this one poem is or is not consistent with many of Shelley's earlier poems but that either by exemplification or by contrast this poem determines our reception of "Shelley" and all that means.

Ironically, the "fact" of the poem's unfinishedness is precisely what opens it up to so many competing interpretations. The attempt to force Shelley's life and death into a unity resolved at the moment of death is a clear case of what Foucault calls the author function: "a certain functional principle by which, in our culture, one limits, excludes, and chooses; in short, by which one impedes the free circulation, the free manipulation, the free composition, decomposition, and recomposition of fiction. . . . The author . . . marks the manner in which we fear the proliferation of meaning" ("What Is an Author?" 159). Poetic fragmentation may prompt us to attempt a reconstitution of the "whole" of which the text is a "part," but our inability to decide upon which "whole" we are to reconcile the text with neither eliminates the possibility of finding meaning in the text nor makes the text seem any more intractable to interpretation. As Foucault suggests, meaning proliferates in the absence of imposed "wholes"; it does not dissipate. The "Triumph"'s fragmentary nature is irreducible, and irresolvable. Shelley's death makes it infinitely debatable how he might have finished the poem. It is even possible to assert the poem's openness and read this as a kind of "closure" at the same time. When Marjorie Levinson, for example, writes of the poem's "(in)conclusion . . . imaginatively confirm[ing] the work's skeptical idealism" (*Fragment,* 129; see also 205), she confirms how impossible it is for us not to recuperate the accidental within essentializing narratives.

The question of the "unfinished" quality of the "Triumph" is, as Derrida has observed ("Living On," 103), neither innocent nor obvious. It is predicated upon numerous complex decisions about the relationships between the natures of author, text, and reader and the imputation to all of them of a coherence of identity (in the text's case founded upon its "filiation" to the grounding unity of the author's subjectivity), which Shelley himself called into question. The hypostatization of the identity of author and text requires the author's death. Shelley's identification of custom and its "freezing" of the potential plurality of signification as a thanatological discourse is supported by the embarrassment his own untidy death causes those trying to hypostatize his life and work in turn. Death creates the possibility of identity, or "identification." Immortality would leave open the eternal possibility of recantation—the embarrassment of the subject revealing his or her unselfsameness. Interpretation can always reconcile the contradictions in a life retrospectively, but an immortal subject would always be capable of retroactively upsetting any "final" reading of the life. Hence the younger Romantics' feeling that Wordsworth had lived too long: "thou leavest me to grieve, / Thus having been, that thou shouldst cease to be" ("To Wordsworth," 13-14). If he had died in 1800, he would not have complicated their reading of him as a precursor and an ally. Identity demands death-as-closure to turn the interval from birth to death into a narrative totality.

Shelley's death in midpoem (if it was) will not allow this closure. His death animates for us the distinction drawn earlier between death as thanatological "living sepulchre" and death as ultimate, unnarrativizable "change." Shelley's accidental disappearance from the scene brings home sadly to us the infinite, incommensurable potential of his life, a potential that defeats the possibility of hermeneutical closure. Hence the persistence of attempts to read the death either as an outright suicide or as a welcome end for a man who had drained life's cup to the dregs; we "fear the proliferation of meaning."

On the other hand, any reading of the poem, no matter how "faithful" to its metaphoric disruptions of "fidelity," reveals a certain hostility (the desire to kill off Shelley "neatly") to the openness and undecidability of the text, a point de Man notes at the end of his essay on the "Triumph" when he writes of the unavoidability of the "use" of texts "for the assertion of methodological claims made all the more pious by their denial of piety" ("Shelley Disfigured," 68).

II

Contemporary readings of the "Triumph" have focused upon the issues with which I am concerned. Hogle reads the poem as a criticism of Rousseau for his inability to enter into the world of absolute amnesiac transference offered to him in the nepenthe of the shape all light (*Shelley's Process,* 321-39). Two more-nuanced readings, which I briefly explore, offer radically different readings of the shape all light, but agree that memory, and the ability to erase memory, are key issues in the poem. These are de Man's "Shelley Disfigured" and David Quint's "Representation and Ideology in *The Triumph of Life.*"

De Man argues that the poem deconstructs the nature of "filial" language. He bases his argument on the role of light in the poem. He begins with an analysis of the role of the sun, which opens the poem by "springing forth." De Man reads this as a representation of the violent coming-into-being of figuration, an act of linguistic and cognitive positing that reveals itself as a "violent . . . light, a deadly Apollo" (64) and the act of figural positing as a purely "arbitrary act of language" by its clear lack of "natural" motivation: "The most continuous and gradual event in nature . . . is collapsed into the brusque swiftness of a single moment" (63).

He focuses on the "shape all light" as "the figure for the figurality of all signification" (62) in that she is that fundamentally paradoxical structure, a shape created from light, which is "referentially meaningless since light, the necessary condition for shape, is itself . . . without shape." In the poem this "shape" of light creates itself by reflection in "a mirror . . . that articulates it without setting up clear separation that differentiates inside from outside as self . . . from other" (55). Like figural language, then, the shape is problematic in being "message" created out of "medium" without clear distinction between the two, breaking the possibility of believing in the innocence of language/light as a purely transparent medium of a fixed world in which and by which it is grounded and motivated.

This "deadly Apollo," the positional language of figuration, seeks to obscure its violent origins and to seem "naturally given" (or "frozen," in Shelley's language): "[T]he appearance of the shape . . . is both a figure of specular self-knowledge, the figure of thought, but also a figure of 'thought's empire over thought,' of the element in thought that destroys thought in its attempt to forget its duplicity." This is seen in the shape's "trampling" of Rousseau's previous thoughts into the "dust of death." But this attempt at hiding its arbitrary origins is doomed to failure: "For the initial violence of position can only be half erased, for the erasure is accomplished by a device of language that never ceases to partake of the very violence against which it is directed. . . . the trampling gesture enacts the necessary recurrence of the initial violence: a figure of thought, the very light of cognition, obliterates thought" (65). And so the poem reflects the permanent revolution of metaphoric "decentering":

> The repetitive erasures by which language performs the erasure of its own positions can be called disfiguration. . . . metaphor, the bearer of light which carries over the light of the senses and of cognition from events and entities to their meaning, irrevocably loses the contour of its own face or shape. We see it happen when the figure [the shape all light] first appears as water-music, then as rainbow, then as measure, to finally sink away "below the watery floor" trampled to death by its own power. . . . *The Triumph of Life* warns us that nothing, whether deed, word, thought or text, ever happens in relation, positive or negative, to anything that precedes, follows or exists elsewhere, but only as a

random event whose power, like the power of death, is due to the randomness of its occurrence. (65-69)

What de Man is not interested in is the political expression of this attitude toward language. However, Quint has provided us with a neat and very persuasive political reading of the "Triumph"'s displacements of the dogmatic power of figuration. For him, "thought's empire over thought" is the power of ideology, the "shape" in the chariot representing the "*principle* of ideology, any representational shadow exalted into a god, into an absolute authority that exerts its tyranny over the mind and imagination" (643). He relates this fruitfully to Shelley's argument, in the essay "On Life," that the philosopher and the "reformer" have a "duty" to "leave, a vacancy . . . [to reduce] the mind to that freedom in which it would have acted, but for the misuse of words and signs, the instruments of its own creation" (Reiman and Powers, 477). This is perhaps the clearest single statement of Shelley's political investment in metaphorical displacement, the "decentering" of the mind from enslavement to dogmatically "misused" words and signs. Quint argues that what the "Triumph" reveals to us is the outcome of hypostatizing (de Man would say "monumentalizing" ["Shelley Disfigured," 69]) one's own mental/linguistic creations in an attempt to fill that "vacancy," the principle of cognitive undecidability that it is our "duty" to acknowledge.

He focuses on the moment when Rousseau, "between desire and shame / Suspended" (394-95), asks the shape to "Shew whence I came, and where I am, and why" (398). Her reply is the ambiguous "Arise and quench thy thirst" (400), which Rousseau does (or attempts to do) with disastrous consequences: "suddenly my brain became as sand" (405). Quint's useful analysis of this much-debated crux in the "Triumph" is that Rousseau, as representative Enlightenment philosopher, here falls by refusing to admit the necessity of the vacancy within; he creates the shape in his imagination ("misuse of words and signs" or the violence of figurality) and then seeks from his own creation answers to the necessarily unanswerable questions of life. This is then the moment of his enslavement to ideology, something he half realizes in his division between *desire* for closure and *shame* at enslaving his thought under the empire of custom's reified thought. The shape itself then wanes, as, paradoxically, this dogmatic belief in the products of the self's imagination (words and signs) in turn kills the imagination that produced them.

These readings by de Man and Quint together provide us with an analysis of the poem in terms of the politics and poetics of skeptical metaphoricity, both affirming the notion of permanent language-led revolution I set in opposition to the *Revolt's* attempts at a reconciliation of skepticism and idealist growth through the continuous reclamation of discontinuity.

The "Triumph," however, is a more complexly structured poem than these analyses allow. Perhaps the most telling sign of this is the considerable sympathy in the poem for Rousseau. He is not simply held up as an example for us in our unideologized correctness to shun and avoid. Indeed, the narrator asks Rousseau to answer for him much the same questions as Rousseau asks of the shape, and Rousseau's reply—"But follow thou, and from spectator turn / Actor or victim in this wretchedness, / And what thou wouldst be taught I then may learn / From thee" (305–8)—suggests that to understand Rousseau's fate we must share it, indeed, in the disturbing ambiguity of this injunction, that we must *teach* him his fate by our example ("what thou wouldst be taught I then may learn / From thee").

What is being put in question is the pristine separation of a revolutionary ethos from the ideologizing/monumentalizing process. To understand this moment requires us to understand Shelley's choice of Rousseau as guide. To see Rousseau as representing "the Enlightenment" is inadequate. Donald Reiman, one of the surprisingly few critics seriously to examine Shelley's reasons for choosing Rousseau as his guide,[13] argues that since Shelley primarily associated Rousseau with *Julie: Ou, la nouvelle Héloise*, Rousseau and the shape represent Saint-Preux and Julie, and that Shelley had little interest in the historical Rousseau (*Shelley's "The Triumph of Life"*). But this is debatable.

To understand Rousseau's significance in the "Triumph" we have to see how, in Shelley's reading of him and in his contemporary reputation, he is situated in all the lines of tension and contradiction that I have examined in Shelley's thought in the *Revolt.* He is, for Shelley, a perfect "thing to think with," a symbolic figure that allows him to explore, if not to resolve, the points of fracture in his own thought.

Rousseau was generally held responsible, in Shelley's time, for the French Revolution (Duffy, 84). In itself, this allows us to find a certain relevance for the *Revolt,* the "beau ideal" of that revolution, in anything that may be concluded about Rousseau in this poem. But the *Revolt* is more powerfully recalled in this poem than by this connection alone.

---

13. The fullest exploration of this issue is in Duffy, who relies largely on Voisine. De Man makes some interesting points about Shelley's choice, but his reading is not specifically historical.

Shelley performs a curious textual graft at the beginning of the "Triumph," picking up a line from the *Revolt* in a place that demands our attention. The narrator rises, as the sun hastens to "impose" (20) itself upon the world, from "thoughts which must remain untold" (21), to have a vision "rolled" on his brain (40). In the *Revolt,* Laon, chained to the rock by the Tyrant's forces under the sun's "shafts of agony" (III, xx, 3) watches the ship taking Cythna away "with such thoughts as must remain untold" (III, xvii, 9), and afterward, "two visions burst" upon him (III, xxiv, 2). It is a curious parallelism that has several effects, but that serves to bring the *Revolt* forcibly into the "Triumph" and suggests a series of parallels between Laon, Rousseau, the "Triumph"'s narrator, and Shelley.

Laon, as we have seen, was, or attempted to be, the revolutionary-as-Christ, taking upon himself an identity representative of the spirit of Liberty and dying for its advancement. The Rousseau of the "Triumph" is strongly reminiscent of the Rousseau of the *Rêveries,* which Mary Shelley tells us Shelley had read for the first time in 1815 (Hutchinson, 528). In 1816, in Switzerland, he read *Julie* for the first time, and then in 1817, he wrote *The Revolt of Islam.* This representative revolutionary ideal is intimately associated with Rousseau.

The promise of pure representative being—complete transparency between individual and society—was one of the more intoxicating promises of revolutionary *fraternité.* In the third book of the *Excursion* Wordsworth's Solitary recalls achieving therapeutic absolution in an apocalyptic marriage with "Society" at the height of the Revolution:

> Thus was I reconverted to the world;
> Society became my glittering bride,
> And airy hopes my children.—From the depths
> Of natural passion, seemingly escaped,
> My soul diffused herself in wide embrace
> Of institutions, and the forms of things;
> As they exist, in mutable array,
> Upon life's surface.
>
> (734-41)

Or, as he puts it a little later, he seeks to "stretch" "a web / Of amity . . . / Beyond the seas, and to the farthest pole" (746-47).

The Rousseau of the *Rêveries* is very much the Rousseau of the "Triumph," defeated, rejected, and resentful of life. But the rejection is of a specific type: "Me voici donc seule sur la terre, n'ayant plus de frère, de prochain, d'ami, de société que moi-même. Le plus social et le plus aimant des humains en a été proscrit par un accord unanime. Ils ont cherché dans les raffinements de leur haine quel tourment pouvait être le plus cruel à mon âme sensible, et ils ont brisé violemment tous les liens qui m'attachaient à eux. J'aurais aimé les hommes en dépit d'eux-mêmes" (3).[14] We cannot but hear an echo, here, of the "man of sorrows," "despised and rejected of men." It is a theme to which Shelley constantly returned in his own self-characterizations: "I have everywhere sought [sympathy], and have found only repulse and disappointment" (Reiman and Powers, 473); "If men must rise and stamp with fury blind / On his pure name who loves them" (*Revolt,* dedication, xiv, 3–4); "you have done ill in accusing . . . an innocent, and a persecuted man [meaning himself]" (*Letters,* 2:231). This *imitatio Christi* is made all but explicit by Rousseau when he says that all the world as it passes "[crache] sur moi, qu'une génération tout entière s'[ammuse] d'un accord unanime à m'enterrer tout vivant" (*Rêveries,* 4).[15] The phenomenon of *rêverie* is a moment of (Christlike) therapeutic expansion of the subject to become a moment of the entire world's self-consciousness; it is absolute *erōs* triumphant as the boundaries between subject and object are overthrown: "[I]l me semblait que je remplissais de ma légère existence tous les objets que j'apercevais. . . . je n'avais nulle notion distincte de mon individu" (17).[16]

It is moments like this that caused Shelley to give Rousseau a startling and unique prominence in his "Essay on Christianity": "Rousseau . . . is perhaps the philosopher among the moderns who in the structure of his feelings and understanding resembles most nearly the mysterious sage of Judæa" (Ingpen and Peck, 6:247).

This equation of Christ and Rousseau, which occurs in an argument that Christ's doctrines propose an egalitarian communism, owes a lot to these moments where identity collapses—moments like those experienced by Wordsworth's Solitary. We see its political attractions for Shelley in the same essay: "Once make the feelings of confidence and affection universal and the distinctions of property and power will vanish" (245). But Rousseau is, for Shelley, one of those borderline figures that

14. "So now I am alone in the world, with no brother, neighbour or friend, nor any company left me but my own. The most sociable and loving of men has with one accord been cast out by all the rest. With all the ingenuity of hate they have sought out the cruellest torture for my sensitive soul, and have violently broken all the threads that bound me to them. I would have loved my fellow-men in spite of themselves" (*Reveries of the Solitary Walker,* 27).

15. "[spits] upon [me], and that an entire generation . . . of one accord take[s] pleasure in burying me alive"(*Reveries of the Solitary Walker,* 28).

16. "[I]t seemed as if all I perceived was filled with my frail existence. . . . I had no distinct notion of myself as a person" (*Reveries of the Solitary Walker,* 39).

test the boundaries of the possibility of *erōs*. The *Rêveries* is a record of a withdrawal from humanity, the desire not to represent but to disengage oneself from society. Rousseau announces his project at the very beginning: "Mais moi, détaché d'eux et de tout, que suis-je moi-même? Voilà ce qui me reste à chercher" (3).[17]

Shelley's undoubted favorite among Rousseau's works was *Julie: Ou, la nouvelle Héloïse*. It may seem strange that Shelley admired this work so ardently; indeed, he himself called it "a book . . . in some respects absurd & prejudiced . . . yet the production of a mighty Genius" (*Letters*, 1:493). Yet it is concerned with exactly the problems of *erōs* and "endogamy" we have seen to be so central to Shelley's thought. Saint-Preux, Mary Shelley tells us, "in his abnegation of self, and in the worship he paid to Love . . . coincided with Shelley's own disposition" (Hutchinson, 536). The revolutionary potential of this selfless devotion to *erōs* was a standard focus for contemporary opinions of Rousseau, whether as revolutionary hero or villain. Burke above all had latched onto Saint-Preux and Julie's relationship as exemplary of the revolutionary disruption of the order of genealogical continuity: "The rulers in the National Assembly are in good hopes that the females of the first families in France may become an easy prey to dancing masters, fiddlers, pattern-drawers. . . . By adopting the sentiments of Rousseau they have made them your rivals. In this manner these great legislators complete their plan of levelling, and establish their rights of men on a sure foundation" (qtd. in Duffy, 40). Burke is distressed at the potential of real and metaphorical bastardization corrupting the frail "foundations" of filiation on which the current order rests, and Shelley would have had good reason to applaud this disruptive potentiality of (very literally) erotic dissemination.

But the irony is that Burke has chosen a poor target. The central problematic of *Julie* is Julie's question: "Veux-je suivre le penchant de mon coeur, qui préférer d'un amant ou d'un père?" (177).[18] Her decision is clearly to obey the word of the father: "[I]l faut immoler le bonheur au devoir" (291).[19] Everywhere the book makes the competition between an erotic-exogamous and an incestuous-endogamous order clear. Wolmar, Julie's eventual husband, represents a return to the incestuous order; he is her father's dearest friend, and Julie, in marrying him, is

17. "But I, detached as I am from them and from the whole world, what am I? This must now be the object of my inquiry"(*Reveries of the Solitary Walker*, 27).
18. "If I am to follow the inclination of my heart, whom should I give precedence to: a lover, or a father?" (my translation).
19. "It is necessary to sacrifice happiness to duty" (my translation).

"[l]iée au sort d'un époux, ou plutôt aux volontés d'un père, par une chaîne indissoluble" (319).[20] Her father places Wolmar *in loco parentis* by handing on to him the secret of her liaison with Saint-Preux, confirming his role as guardian of filial fidelity.

Julie's relationship with her father is consistently described in erotic terms. This is most marked in the scenes following his physical attack on her. Baron d'Etange feels his daughter has been defending Saint-Preux too strongly and attacks her in a fit of passion, "se livrant à son *transport*"—a word that is used repeatedly, and almost exclusively, elsewhere, to describe Saint-Preux and Julie's amorous intoxication (see, e.g., 15, 38, 58, 64, 70, 75, 76, 83, 90, 92, 113, 120, 122, 123). This quasi-rape is the incestuous mirror image of Julie's exogamous lovemaking with Saint-Preux. That encounter led to a pregnancy, which the Baron's correspondent attack causes to miscarry, thus reasserting the order of uncompromised filiation that Julie's revolutionary promiscuity threatened to undermine (160). Julie is fully reconverted; she tells us of "[u]ne certaine gravité qu'on n'osait quitter, une certaine confusion . . . mettaient entre un père et sa fille ce charmant embarras que la pudeur et l'amour donnent aux amants. . . . [L]'attendrissement . . . me gagnait . . . je penchai mon visage sur son visage vénérable, et . . . il fut couvert de mes baisers" (150).[21] A little further on she describes this scene ("nos *transports*," again) as "le plus délicieux moment de ma vie!"

Shelley would have appreciated this image of the father revealing the violence underlying filial continuity—his interest in the *Cenci* story can be read as an attempt to rewrite and revalue this episode—but Julie's evident approbation of this return to the autoerotic fold of "duty," with its thanatological exclusion of alterity (Julie's marriage "aux volontés d'un père" she describes as "une . . . carrière qui ne dois finir qu'à la mort" [319]),[22] must have horrified him. This was, for Shelley, the Rousseau of those *Confessions,* which he called "a disgrace to the confessor" (*Letters,* 1:84), Rousseau the exemplar of autoeroticism, or, as Spivak has called him, "that famous masturbator" (Spivak, introduction to Derrida, *Of Grammatology,* lxxxv).

In addition, Rousseau helps Shelley to become aware of his equivoca-

---

20. "bound to the destiny of a husband, or rather to the will of a father, by an unbreakable chain" (my translation).

21. "a certain gravity that one dare not abandon, a certain confusion . . . placed between a father and his daughter that charming embarrassment which modesty and love give to lovers. . . . Emotion . . . overpowered me . . . I moved my face over his venerable countenance and . . . it was covered in my kisses" (my translation).

22. "a . . . career that can only finish with death" (my translation).

tions over the role of writing in the orders of revolution and custom. In the *Rêveries* Rousseau is deeply suspicious of "le plaisier d'écrire . . . parce qu'orner la vérité par des fables c'est en effet la défigurer" (59).[23] Rousseau overcomes his mistrust of this promiscuous flux of metaphoric error by inscribing his own writing in an autoerotic, purely endogamous order: "[J]e n'écris mes rêveries que pour moi" (11).[24]

The word "défigurer" is interesting. The concept of disfiguration, together with the idea that writing is inevitably connected with it, allows us tentatively to sum up the significance of Rousseau's presence in the "Triumph." Central to this significance is the concept of "tragic irony." Rousseau is the quintessential "sentimental" writer, and *Julie* was the bible of European sentimentalism. The "ironic" and the "sentimental" are two sides of one coin. Rousseau's distrust of writing is a fundamental aspect of the ironic condition. His atavistic longing for a society in which "everybody knew everybody else" ("Essay on the Origin of Languages," qtd. in *Of Grammatology,* 168), so that all communication could take place in the immediacy of speech, is a longing for a purely endogamous community in which every conversation would be, as Derrida puts it, "auto-affection" (*Of Grammatology,* 166). Writing, with its imposition of a gap between production and consumption, is at once the mark of our fallen condition and that of our infinite striving for a return to the Absolute.

In the fallen world of irony no identity can long resist the forces of fragmentation, error, and promiscuous consumption. This is the "disfiguration" to which Rousseau knows all writing is subject because it is distanced from its creator and its context of production. The nihilistic "disfiguration" upon which de Man seizes ("Shelley Disfigured," 46) is one of Rousseau's deepest fears of what might result from purely exogamous dissemination of meaning—which the promiscuity of writing always threatens.

"Disfiguration" has a special significance in *Julie.* Saint-Preux's vision of the fallen, ironic world of Paris, that promiscuous, exogamous world where no voice can ever hope to speak directly to the whole, stands as a negative pole to the calm and order of the "naive" world of Clarens, the self-sufficient, endogamous retreat of Julie and Wolmar. The worst threat Paris poses is to the integrity of Saint-Preux's identity. Paris is a "chaos" (207), a "torrent" (221), a "flux et reflux" (210), where "tout change à chaque instant" and therefore "le spectacle exige une conti-

23. "the pleasure of writing . . . because to decorate truth with fables is in fact to disfigure it" (*Reveries of the Solitary Walker,* 80).
24. "I am writing down my reveries for myself alone" (*Reveries of the Solitary Walker,* 34).

nuité d'attention qui interrompt la réflexion" (222);[25] it threatens to "défigurer" the "divin modèle" of Julie that Saint-Preux carries within himself—the anchor of his being (233). In such a world there is no possibility of Christlike representativeness: "[C]hacun songe à son intérêt, personne au bien commun, et . . . les intérêts particuliers sont toujours opposés entre eux, c'est un choc perpétuel de brigues et de cabales, un flux et reflux de préjugés, d'opinions contraires, où les plus échauffés, animés par les autres, ne savent presque jamais de quoi il est question" (210).[26] No memory can survive this constantly erasing flux of particularizing "deaths," and Saint-Preux does "fall" into sexual infidelity, the ironic duplication/disfiguration of his "naive" love for Julie.

This world of ironic fragmentation and disfiguration is one model for the "perpetual flow" and "living storm . . . whose airs too soon deform" of the "Triumph." The final, nightmarish visions in the "Triumph" of the "phantoms" (482), the "dim forms" (483), of "Mask after mask [falling] from the countenance / And form of all" (535–36) to be "soon distorted" (531) and ultimately to self-destruct, are usually, and correctly, identified with the Lucretian simulacra. But as visions of contemporary society, they are equally drawn from Rousseau: "[J]e ne trouve qu'une vaine apparence de sentiments et de vérité, qui change à chaque instant et se détruit elle-même, où je n'aperçois que larves et fantômes qui frappent l'oeil un moment et disparaissent aussitôt qu'on les veut saisir. Jusques ici j'ai vu beaucoup de masques, quand verrai-je des visages d'hommes?" (*Julie*, 212).[27]

The Rousseau of the "Triumph" both represents and undermines all the above "Rousseaus." On the question of writing, for example, we have precisely the progressive-ironic model on which the *Revolt* is partly based; Rousseau tells us: "If I have been extinguished, yet there rise / A thousand beacons from the spark I bore" (206–7). This is a model that combines the ironic fragmentation and impermanence of the written word (Cythna's "words of flame") with seasonal-Christian re-

---

25. "the scene demands a continuity of attention that interrupts reflection" (my translation).

26. "Each thinks of his own interest, none of the common good; and . . . individual interests are always opposed to each other, it is a perpetual collision of plots and cabals, an ebb and flow of prejudices, of contrary opinions, where the most agitated, worked up by the others, almost never know what is going on" (my translation).

27. "I find nothing but a delusory appearance of feeling and truth, which changes at each moment, and destroys itself; I see only larvae and phantoms that strike the eye for a moment, and disappear as soon as one wishes to grasp them. Until now I have seen many masks; when will I see the faces of men?" (my translation).

demption via death and resurrection. But this is subsequently undermined:

>   "I
>   Have suffered what I wrote, or viler pain!—
>
>   "And so my words were seeds of misery—
>   Even as the deeds of others."
>
>   (278–81)

Here he expresses his hostility to the written word and his desire to
ground it in the immediacy of self-presence, refusing to accept the
ironic rupture between self and words that might allow the spark to
light new beacons after the original is extinguished. Thus his words—in
a bitter parody of the seasonal imagery of the *Revolt* ("The seeds are
sleeping in the soil")—can only be "seeds of misery."

    Similarly, for him there is neither the possibility to be the Laon-type
revolutionary Christ Shelley wished him to have been nor the possibility
to remove himself absolutely from the ironic "world of agony" (295) for
which he cannot be the Christ, in pure endogamous self-reference ("détaché d'eux et de tout, que suis-je moi-même? Voilà ce qui me reste à
chercher"). These issues come to a head in that part of the poem that
has drawn the most critical commentary, Rousseau's short "autobiography," which climaxes with his encounter with the "shape all light." It
has long been recognized that Rousseau's account of how he "wake[s]
to weep" (334), "Under a mountain" (312), beside a "cavern high and
deep" (313), invites a reading as an account of Rousseau's birth, though
just what kind of "birth" is intended has been disputed.[28] The "shape all
light" is the great crux of interpretation of this poem. Readings tend to
divide up into two broad camps that see the shape as either a Good
Thing or a Bad Thing.[29] Either we should be attracted by her evident

---

28. Bradley ("Notes on Shelley's 'Triumph of Life,'" 454) and Baker (*Shelley's Major Poetry*,
265–66) interpret the passage as representing Rousseau's literal birth. Bloom (*Shelley's Mythmaking*, 263–64) argues, instead, that it refers to a kind of spiritual rebirth, an argument that
is not dissimilar to Reiman's attempt to read this scene as Julie's "Elysée," and therefore as a
spiritual "awakening" of Saint-Preux. Hodgson, more recently, and originally, has argued that it
represents the reverse passage, from life to death ("The World's Mysterious Doom," 601–4).

29. Every critic who has written on the *Triumph* has had a kick at this can. What follows is
just a representative sampling to demonstrate the futility of trying to settle this problem on
either alternative. Bradley called her a "revelation of the ideal" (454), a reading followed by
Carlos Baker (264); for Cameron (*Golden Years,* 467) she represents a kind of liberating political rebirth; for Reiman (*"Triumph,"* 60ff.) she is both a figure of the poetic imagination and
Saint-Preux's Julie, in both cases a dangerous object of devotion but inherently good; for Hogle

beauty and her ambiguous promise to "quench" Rousseau's "thirst" for knowledge (400), or appalled by the apparently disastrous consequences when he tries to take her up on that promise ("And suddenly my brain became as sand" [405]). Too much ink has been spilt on this question to let us hope that this debate is resolvable. We need to try a new approach, admitting that the shape all light is inherently undecidable and asking why this should be.

One answer is to read the shape as standing for the very principle of irony, or ironic self-consciousness, that rules the world of the poem. This would account for the radically opposed responses that the shape generates. Those who read the shape as a (good) representation of the Ideal are perhaps not so far from those who read her as a representation of our (evil) estrangement from the Ideal. In the fallen, ironic world, as we have seen, consciousness of the Ideal is necessarily accompanied by consciousness of our fallen state; the more we strive to "touch with faint lips" the cup she raises, the more we are aware that our brains are made of fragmented "sand" (405). It is equally possible to see this as an eternally deferred, but ever renewed, promise of unity, or as a perpetual banishment from paradise.

There is good reason to read the shape in this way. De Man's reading of her as a representation of "figuration," and Reiman's as representing the reflection of "Ideal creativity" in the human imagination (*"Triumph,"* 63ff.), both make the same point from opposite sides, that she represents the ironic "breach" in naive perception of the world that doubles perception in self-conscious awareness of the fact of subjecthood. Rousseau's passage from the time he "wakes to weep" to the time he encounters the shape, is the passage from the "naive," unselfconscious bond with the world, which is the product of the Lethean stream's "sweet and deep . . . oblivious spell" (331), to a "sentimental," indirect perception of the world (the "figural" and "imaginative" deferral represented by the shape). That the newly awoken Rousseau's relationship with the world is one of naive immediacy is emphasized by a passage from the *Rêveries* that appears to have influenced this part of the poem. Rousseau comes to consciousness after an accident: "Je naissais dans cet instant à la vie. . . . Tout entier au moment présent je

---

she represents pure liberatory transference. For Bloom (*Shelley's Mythmaking,* 266ff.) the shape is the principal of ineluctable reality that destroys the possibilities of vision, or "I-Thou" relationship; for de Man she is the delusive principle of figuration; for Quint the oppressive constraint of ideological distortion; Hodgson (*Coleridge, Shelley,* 91–92) reads Rousseau's encounter with her as a necessarily failed epiphany, not unlike Bloom's; for Ulmer (173–74) she represents the death instinct.

ne me souvenais de rien; je n'avais nulle notion distincte de mon individu, pas la moindre idée de ce qui venait de m'arriver" (17).[30] Rousseau's encounter with the shape is the passage "back" to identity from
having "nulle notion distincte de mon individu."

We can see this in the questions Rousseau puts to the shape: "Shew
whence I came, and where I am, and why" (398). These are the questions of ironic self-consciousness, and mark Rousseau's "fall." The shape
does not answer the questions; it is she who, by making him aware of
figural representation, brings him to the point where he can ask them.
His "fall" is inevitable, but it is debatable what we are to make of it.

This reading is supported by a textual allusion in this passage that has
not, to my knowledge, been noticed before—Eve's account of her own
coming to consciousness in Milton's *Paradise Lost,* book IV:[31]

> That day I oft remember, when from sleep
> I first awaked, and found myself reposed
> Under a shade of flowers, much wondering where
> And what I was, whence thither brought, and how.
> Not distant far from thence a murmuring sound
> Of waters issued from a cave and spread
> Into a liquid plain, then stood unmoved
> Pure as the expanse of heaven; I thither went
> With unexperienced thought, and laid me down
> On the green bank, to look into the clear
> Smooth lake, that to me seemed another sky.
> As I bent down to look, just opposite,
> A shape within the watery gleam appeared
> Bending to look on me, I started back,
> It started back, but pleased I soon returned,
> Pleased it returned as soon with answering looks
> Of sympathy and love.
>
> (449–65)

"What I was, whence thither brought, and how"—these are the questions Rousseau puts to the shape. Moreover, the landscape where Eve
wakes (soon) to weep, with its "waters issu[ing] from a cave," is re-

---

30. "In this instant I was being born again. . . . Entirely taken up by the present, I could
remember nothing; I had no distinct notion of myself as a person, nor had I the least idea of
what had just happened to me" (*Reveries of the Solitary Walker,* 39).

31. Reiman, who assiduously notes Miltonic parallels in his study of the "Triumph," suggests
a comparison with Adam's coming to consciousness (60 n. 99), but the connection is merely
thematic.

markably like Rousseau's. Shelley's "cavern high and deep" has "a gentle rivulet" coming from it that keeps "for ever wet / The stems of the sweet flowers, and filled the grove / With sound" (316–18). The implication that it too forms a pool is shortly confirmed when he refers to the "well that glowed / Like gold" (346–47). Like Eve, Rousseau moves to the well, and gazing into it sees a "shape." Rousseau's lies "Amid the [reflected] sun . . . on the vibrating / Floor of the fountain" (349–51); Eve's, "within the watery gleam."

The parallels are too close to be ignored, and invite a new reading of the "shape all light" that is yet not so new. A "shape all light" has been dismissed as "referentially meaningless" (de Man, "Shelley Disfigured," 55), but what could better describe that insubstantial shape which is a reflection? The genesis of the "shape all light," whatever it *comes* to mean, is as Rousseau's reflection in the well (a return to the ironic nadir of *Alastor*), unrecognized by him before his complete accession to self-consciousness, just as Eve does not recognize her reflection until God warns her against her "vain desire" (*Paradise Lost,* IV, 466; "vain" meaning autoerotic—and therefore naive—as well as useless).

This reading adds depth to existing readings of the shape; it does not overturn them. The point is still reflection, reproduction, and self-consciousness. Rousseau, like Eve, "falls" into self-consciousness from a too-great desire to "know"; his apparently exogamous, erotic desire for the "other" is revealed, as in *Alastor* and *Epipsychidion,* to be an autoerotic longing for his reflection. Reiman has noted the similarity between Rousseau's disastrous encounter with the shape all light and Eve's eating the fruit of the tree of knowledge of good and evil (*"Triumph,"* 67). Milton, in the passage quoted above, proleptically figures Eve's ruinous thirst for knowledge, and Shelley, with perfect aptness, relates Rousseau's sentimental/ironic quest for (self-)knowledge to that of Eve—original author of the Fall. The disputes over the nature of the shape and the nature of world of the "Triumph" are yet other versions of the debate over whether our fall is a *felix culpa.*

In the ironic world of representation, the possibility of disfiguration, which is unknown to the naive consciousness, becomes an omnipresent threat. The curious fact about the "Triumph" is that the poem "itself" gives us few clues to what we are supposed to make of this threat. Neither of the "two thoughts" seems an adequate response to the world of the poem, and none of the attempts made in the *Revolt* to reconcile them now functions. There is, however, a directly political significance in our response to the world of the "Triumph." Both the narrator's and Rousseau's responses are similar to Burke's anxious fear of the "chaos of elementary principles," to which amnesiac revolution reduces society. Both seek a principle of memory and identity to hold up against this chaotic flux. When Bloom analyzes the encounter with the shape all light as a failed epiphany (*Mythmaking*, 220–75), he is on the right track; in this moment Rousseau is seeking to extend his identity to the completeness of Absolute Knowing (or "general will"), to become a Christ, or a representative self-consciousness. But in the ironic, disfiguring world of the "Triumph," this is not possible; he cannot incorporate the whole.

But if he cannot seek to become the moment of self-consciousness of Spirit (knowing "whence I came, and where I am, and why"), nor can he "forebear / To join the dance" (189) and fully exclude himself from what he could not transcend immanently. With echoes of important patterns of imagery in both *Julie* and the *Rêveries*, Rousseau recounts his entanglement in the dance of the chariot's captives:

> "I among the multitude
> Was swept; me *sweetest flowers* delayed not long,
>   Me not the shadow nor the *solitude*,
>
> "Me not the falling stream's Lethean song,
>   . . . .
>   . . . but among
>
> "The thickest billows of the living storm
> I *plunged*, and bared my bosom to the clime
>   Of that cold light, whose airs too soon deform."
>   (460–63, 465–68; my emphasis)

Here is Rousseau "overcome / By [his] own heart alone" (240–41), pulled away from his solitary botanical pursuits and, as he says of himself in the *Rêveries*, "[j]eté . . . dans le tourbillon du monde," where he "n[e] parviendrai[t] jamais à l'état dont [s]on coeur sentait le besoin" (26).[32] This "plunge" into the torrent of the world, which is also Saint-Preux's plunge into the "torrent" of Paris (Reiman, *"Triumph,"* 76), and the consequent deformation and erasure of identity are, as Duffy notes, a recurrent motif in Rousseau's writing (Duffy, 115–16). With deliberate irony, however, Shelley echoes here a slightly unusual form of the image from the *Rêveries*, where Rousseau is describing the therapeutic expansion of self to Christlike representativeness: Rousseau's wish is to "[se]

---

32. "Thrown into the whirlpool of life . . . [where he] would never attain the state to which [his] heart aspired" (*Reveries of the Solitary Walker,* 48).

jeter tête baissée dans ce vaste océan de la nature" (95; Duffy misses this one).[33] The attempt at therapeutic ego expansion is defeated by the disfiguring flux of the ironic world. Rousseau's dream of transparent representativeness, in a slightly different version of the dilemma of tragic *erōs,* fails in its very success. In the world of irony, there is no clear distinction between the expansion of identity and its dissolution.

On the other hand, a purely "skeptical" acceptance of sheer antirational transference is not apparently more useful. The dance that Rousseau enters is Dionysian; the people in the crowd "Throw back their heads and loose their streaming hair" (147)—both traditional iconic attributes of the maenad. But what is, in the "Ode to the West Wind" and the "Song of Pan," a positive and vital expression of the energy that overthrows the tyranny of custom/reason has become here the symbol of those who, "a captive multitude" (119), "Oft to new bright destruction come and go" (154); the Dionysian dance is "swift, fierce and obscene" (137) and does not seem to be a true "liberation" from the order of reason. De Man equates this dance with the "measure" (60) in the shape's trampling feet and proclaims this the rhythm of the poem itself, "the madness of words."

Such a "decentering" view of the poem argues that Rousseau's mistake is to seek eternal truths in a world where they are not available. Dionysus is himself a type of Christ, however. Just as the dissolution of identity involved in Rousseau's bid for representativeness undermines its therapeutic value, so the ego expansion implicit in a pure transference (the tendency that leads to Hogle's "transferential One") undercuts the radicalism of transferential "madness." Both approaches appear equally to be a denial of the reality of the ironic world; one attempts to transcend it, and the other attempts to embrace it so utterly that all disfigurations become restatements of the one, central truth of "madness." The maenad has an affinity with the revolutionary Christ; each seeks a transcendence that proves to be an ever-renewed destruction.

De Man's reading makes the dance akin to Hegel's "Bacchanalian revel in which no member is not drunk; yet because each member collapses as soon as he drops out . . . is just as much transparent and simple repose" (Hegel, *Phenomenology,* 27). If elsewhere Shelley hoped to displace this by activating the maenad's disruptive perspective, here neither Hegel's godlike perspective nor "decentering" metaphoric displacements are given priority:

33. "throw myself headlong into this great ocean of nature" (*Reveries of the Solitary Walker,* 112).

> Maidens and youths fling their wild arms in air
>   As their feet twinkle; now recede, and now
>
> . . . .
>
>   Kindle invisibly; and as they glow
> Like moths by light attracted and repelled,
>   Oft to new bright destruction come and go,
>
>
> . . . .
>
>   —Behind,
> Old men, and women foully disarrayed
>
>   . . . .
>
> Limp in the dance and strain with limbs decayed
>   To reach the car of light . . .
>
>   . . . .
>
>   But not the less with impotence of will
> They wheel, though ghastly shadows interpose
>   Round them and round each other, and fulfil
>
> Their work and to the dust whence they arose
>   Sink and corruption veils them as they lie—
> And frost in these performs what fire in those.
>   (149–50, 152–54, 164–65, 167–68, 170–75)

This bleak refusal of therapeutic narrative absolutism (Hegel's "transparent and simple repose") will not allow us to assert either the unity of the process (as *Geist*/Providence/redemption/"frost") or the disruptive pluralistic alterity of the dancers (madness/radical transference/"fire"). We should, bearing in mind the imagery of the *Revolt*, realize how significant it is for Shelley to see "frost" and "fire" as having the same effect. The maenadic dance that was to be beyond death and custom is now seen as essentially the same Christlike attempt to transcend death and discontinuity that motivated the idealism of the *Revolt*. Both are, in the view of the "Triumph," equally unsuccessful. The dance (radical transference/"skepticism") is trapped, as the sun (Absolute Reason/"idealism") is trapped, in a wider process we have yet to understand.

Rousseau subverts Shelley's problematic oppositions by being suspended "between desire and shame"; it is exactly this unresolved, unresolvable "suspension" that Shelley is seeking, an undecidability of *erōs* (desire) and autoeroticism (the *amour propre* of shame). The moment of sublation, the synthesis that would reconcile the oppositions contained in the figure of Rousseau, never comes; it is always approached only to become a new beginning—which is not a post-Kantian return to the beginning at a higher stage, because there is no *Erinnerung.* The poem's form disrupts the possibility of memory. Like "radical transference" the idealist structure of circular return is undermined as a possible form *of* the poem by being included *in* the poem, as both Hodgson and Ulmer note (Hodgson, *Coleridge, Shelley,* 91f.; Ulmer, 173f.). Rousseau voices this desire of circular fulfillment, in the aftermath of his failed moment of transcendence, when he talks of the "hope" "That his day's path may end as he began it / In that star's smile" (417-19). But it is a forlorn hope, ironically expressed as Rousseau's mind goes through a stunning series of aimless revolutions:

> "And suddenly my brain became as sand
>
> > "Where the first wave had more than half erased
> The track of deer on desert Labrador,
> > Whilst the fierce wolf from which they fled amazed
>
> "Leaves his stamp visibly upon the shore
> > Until the second bursts—so on my sight
> Burst a new Vision never seen before."
>
> >   (405-11)

A complete image (brain turned to sand) is not so much developed as re-created in each of the next six lines; sand as substance, sand as beach, sand as an erasable "writing" surface, and so forth. From line to line each transformation, each addition of information—"Labrador," "deer," "the fierce wolf"—"bursts" on the reader's consciousness like the "Vision" on Rousseau's, with a curiously detached, contingent relationship to what precedes and follows it.

   This sudden irruption of the vision into consciousness marks it as something "new," but just as the waves ceaselessly return on the beach, the vision is not new (at least not to us); it is a repetition, of sorts, of the triumphal progression that the primary narrator has already narrated to us and that—in a repetition of structure as well as content—Rousseau now narrates to him. This is the effect the poem as a "whole" has on us: a series of contingent "events" that, intuitively at least, seem to deny the orchestrated process necessary to idealist "growth" but that in their repetitions seem radically counter to the creative promise of pure skeptical metaphoricity.

Derrida has described well the sense of time's disconnection in the poem, and our uncertain relationship to it:

> *There is* the double narrative, the narrative of the vision enclosed in the general narrative carried on by the same narrator. The line that separates the enclosed narrative from the other—
>
>   . . . .
>
> And then a Vision on my brain was rolled.
>
> ─────────────
>
>   . . . .
>
> —marks the upper edge of a space that will never be closed. What is the *topos* of the "I" who quotes himself in a narrative {of a dream, a vision, or a hallucination} within a narrative, includ-ing, in addition to all his ghosts, his *hallucinations of ghosts,* still other visions within visions (e.g., "a new Vision never seen be-fore")? What is his *topos* when he quotes, in the present, a past question formulated in another sort of present {". . . 'Then, what is Life?' I said. . . ."} and which he narrates as something that presented itself in a vision, and so on? ("Living On," 85-86)

The "Triumph" insists on the extreme novelty of actions. The sun "springs" forth, the visions "burst," each new wave erasing what had gone before. Beside the Lethean stream Rousseau, in a sudden accession to consciousness without history or memory, "wake[s] to weep" (334), not knowing if his past life was "Hell," "Heaven," or anything at all; he trails no clouds of glory; his birth is a sheer event, allowing no continu-ity of filiation. We are never sure if at any given moment what has passed before is supposed to be recalled—just as, in theory, in an epis-tolary novel, the narration does not have a single perspective, either of time or of personal identity. In de Man's words: "Each of the episodes forgets the knowledge achieved by the forgetting that precedes it" ("Shelley Disfigured," 65).

Despite these disruptive new beginnings, the poem denies and under-mines their status (which de Man asserts) as original moments. A series of repetitions runs through the poem, including the basic repetition of the vision of the car's triumphal progress; the questions, "Whence cam-est thou and whither goest thou? / How did thy course begin . . . and why?" (296-97) recur with minor variations at lines 48, 178, 297, 398, and 544; even the language of the poem is often a repetition from Shel-ley's earlier poetry, as is, for example, the "thoughts which must remain untold." When Rousseau "wakes to weep," the world may be new to

him, but the moment itself has occurred before in "Charles the First,"
IV, 30; *Adonais,* III, 2; *Hellas,* 227; *The Revolt of Islam,* III, xxvii, 9; XI,
ix, 4; "Mutability," iii, 7; *Rosalind and Helen,* 775; and is repeated later
in the "Triumph" (430).

Almost at the outset, the narrator tells us that even the very first
vision and the sunrise that precedes it, which de Man felt so strongly to
be *sui generis,* are repetitions:

> I knew
>
> That I had felt the freshness of that dawn,
> Bathed in the same cold dew my brow and hair
> And sate as thus upon that slope of lawn
>
> Under the selfsame bough, and heard as there
> The birds, the fountains and the Ocean hold
> Sweet talk in music through the enamoured air.
>
> (33–39)

This poem is in a hall-of-mirrors universe, where nothing is definitely
reflection or origin. Its very verse structure mirrors this, terza rima being impossible really to "begin" or "end" without doing violence to the
structure (Shelley's death being one of the more radical ways to resolve
this structural dilemma).

The repetitions and the problematization of origins in the "Triumph"
have been noticed and analyzed before, but, as Bernard Beatty notices,
they remain problematic. Beatty reads the repetitions as both "horrific,"
uncanny intimations of figural alienation and, curiously, "lyrical" elements akin to variations on a theme. Several critics have related these
repetitions to the Freudian death instinct,[34] and it is this reading that is
most relevant here. The most detailed such reading is Ulmer's, who,
predictably, reads the "Triumph" as the culmination of "Shelleyan Eros";
trapped within the uncanny repetitions of erotic "new bright destructions," *erōs* reveals itself, once again, to be Thanatos: "the aim of all life
is death" (165).

This reading is plausible, and pertinent, but we may add some observations to Ulmer's account. Shelley himself had a keen awareness of the
"uncanny" nature of repetition. For example, in Shelley's short essay on

---

34. Leighton is the first to suggest that we read these repetitions as "uncanny" in the Freudian sense (*Shelley and the Sublime,* 159); the connection between repetition and the death
instinct is implicit in Hodgson's cycles of death-in-life in "The World's Mysterious Doom" and
all but explicit in his *Coleridge, Shelley, and Transcendental Inquiry,* 91ff.; Ulmer gives us the
most extended version of this argument in *Shelleyan Eros,* 158–82.

dreams, he tells us of seeing while on a walk a scene in itself inoffensive: "The effect which it produced on me was not such as could have been expected. I suddenly remembered to have seen that exact scene in some dream of long—" At this point Shelley left the essay, scrawling: *"Here I was obliged to leave off, overcome by thrilling horror"* (Ingpen and Peck, 7:67). The death instinct, as it appears in Freud's writings, is situated on very much those lines of tension that the figure of Rousseau draws together. Freud establishes the death instinct in a Manichaean struggle of opposition with "the libido of our sexual instincts [which] would coincide with the Eros of the poets and philosophers which holds all living things together" ("Pleasure Principle," 50). He speaks of "eternal Eros . . . in . . . struggle with his equally immortal adversary" ("Civilization," 145). Freudian Thanatos is, as it is for Shelley, inextricably related to the self, to autoeroticism: "[T]he ego-instincts . . . seek to restore the inanimate state" ("Pleasure Principle," 44), and it is only the remarkable individual who, like the Hegelian world-historical individual, transcends the self and works for the growth and progress of society. Significantly, Freud's model for this person "of overwhelming force of mind" is a Rousseau/Shelley/Laon/Christ, a man of sorrows "during their lifetime . . . mocked and maltreated by others and even despatched in a cruel fashion" ("Civilization," 141).

Most of us, according to Freud, are still licking our psychic wounds from "the prohibition against an incestuous choice of object . . . perhaps the most drastic mutilation which man's erotic life has in all time experienced" ("Civilization," 104). And herein lies the problem for Freud as for Shelley: *erōs* is not truly in opposition to Thanatos/autoeroticism; it is merely a perverted form of narcissism, or tragic *erōs,* the object libido only developing as the "[primary] narcissistic libido turns toward objects" (118); and therefore Thanatos has always already defeated *erōs*'s attempts to transcend it: the "guardians of life . . . were originally the myrmidons of death" ("Pleasure Principle," 39). *Erōs* is only an extension of Thanatos. One of Freud's Shelleyan conclusions to this Shelleyan equation is that we must "abandon the belief that there is an [erotic] instinct towards perfection at work in human beings, which has brought them to their present high level of intellectual achievement and ethical sublimation and which may be expected to watch over their development into supermen" ("Pleasure Principle," 42). Freud finds, as Shelley did, that to abandon the possibility of a pure fulfillment of *erōs* is to reject the notion of an "immanent teleology" in human affairs: "we see the end of nothing" (*Letters,* 2:231).

Freud sees as the basic principle of the death instinct a compulsion to

repeat. All matter, both organic and inorganic, "tend[s] towards the restoration of an earlier state of things" ("Pleasure Principle," 37–38);
therefore it shuns new stimulus and seeks to return to death by as repetitive a path as possible. Shelley, as Ulmer notes (10 n. 21), propounded
a similar view in his short essay "On a Future State": "This desire to be
for ever as we are; the reluctance to a violent and unexperienced
change . . . is common to all the animated and inanimate combinations
of the universe" (Ingpen and Peck, 6:209). It is clear, however, in context, that Shelley is criticizing this "desire to be for ever as we are" as a
prejudice against change that clouds our ability to think more clearly
about the processes of life and death in which we are engaged. He does
not posit this as the fundamental truth of our being, merely as one
inevitable aspect of our complex nature. We could contrast it directly
with that "spirit within . . . at enmity with nothingness and dissolution,"
which he praises in "On Life," and which he declares there to be "the
character of all life and being" (Reiman and Powers, 476).

Change and inertia, discontinuity and memory, are both "common to
all the animated and inanimate combinations of the universe," and this
is equally true of the world of the "Triumph." The problem with proposing Thanatos as the "key" to the repetitions of the "Triumph" is that,
once again, Shelley seems too conscious of this possibility; *unheimlich*
repetition is one part of the truth of the ironic world, but it is not the
whole story. Indeed, the one thing the "Triumph" does make clear to us
is that it is foolish to seek "the whole story" in a world of ironic fragmentation. If Ulmer's claim that the "whole story" is that "the aim of all
life is death" were correct, then Rousseau's baffling encounter with the
shape all light would make no sense. According to Ulmer's account, she
should have a satisfactory answer to Rousseau's questions ("whence I
came, and where I am, and why")—"death."

But if the shape all light does unleash death upon Rousseau in answer
to his questions, as Ulmer would be quick to point out, it is not death as
he and Freud envisage it. It is not death-in-life—the thanatological "living sepulchre"—but a series of "deaths," the multiple "deaths" of the
disjunctive stream of changes that invade Rousseau's brain become "as
sand," which cannot be totalized into a single truth or telos of life.
Rousseau himself, so desperate for a therapeutic Absolute with which to
harmonize the fragments of his existence, cannot find in the shape's
"answer" even this *via negativa* to representative existence. His fragmentary "deaths" do not add up to an intimation of universal and absolute Thanatos; they lead him to the dance of life. And even if this dance
should be read as a dance of death, note that here too Shelley refuses

therapeutic totalization: the dance is not Hegel's "simple repose"; it is a "*living* storm," which cannot be grasped as a simple whole. Rousseau's account of it is particular, subjective, and, above all, transitory.

If Shelley's "Triumph" can be read as a massive assault upon the stability of identity, this does not mean that all he leaves us with is a nihilistic Absolute, or identity-in-death. Neither repetition nor dissolution in this poem are absolute. Shelley's repetitions, as Hogle notes, are not the sheer repetitions of the death instinct; they are repetitions-with-a-difference (*Shelley's Process,* 334–36). His dissolutions always leave a residue of continuity. This is not an irreducible "core" of identity—any given aspect of Rousseau's consciousness is open to erasure, or "disfiguration"—but it creates a disjunctive chain of being that gives Rousseau a history "at enmity with nothingness and dissolution" even if he is unable to appreciate that.

Shelley has managed to bring into balance, in the "Triumph," the two defining tendencies of the "two thoughts": memory and change-as-death. In doing so, he returns the moment of negativity—the sheer negativity of the moment of erasure, or death in ironic "disfiguration"—to history; something that, as we have seen, a therapeutic historicism is unable to do. "Process" in the "Triumph" is simultaneously predicated upon repetition and change, endogamy and exogamy, and neither one of these is the secret "key" to which everything else may be reduced. There are profound implications in this for both Shelley's poetics and his politics.

Shelley's model of process, here, reconciles revolutionary disjunction with an element of "traditional" continuity. The essence of the ironic world is that each gives meaning to the other; the drive to the Absolute reveals the inevitability of fragmentation, and vice versa. One of the major implications of the model of "process" in the "Triumph" is that revolutionary change is both inevitable and incomprehensible—we cannot become world-historical spirits who witness and represent the birth of a new age. Change, when it occurs, affects us in the very essence of our being. This need not be a tragic reality, though Rousseau and the narrator clearly find it such. If "life"—including our political life—is like the "Triumph of Life," then it is at least endlessly fascinating. There is much that is horrific in the "Triumph," but we would not call the "Triumph" itself horrific.

I have merely touched, here, on the implications of this new "balance" of the "two thoughts" because I have yet to establish how this balance has been achieved. I am not yet in a position to be able to read the "Triumph" without putting to it the wrong kinds of questions. To find the right ones, we must go further into the question of what "death" and "memory" mean to Shelley, and explore the ways he approaches these concepts in his poetry between the *Revolt* and the "Triumph." What emerges from this is a profound rethinking of the epistemological underpinnings of therapeutic thought. When I have followed Shelley's attempt to construct an alternative to this thought, I shall be able to return the "Triumph" and finish the reading I have started here.

5

Death: Continuity and Contingency

THE PERSISTENCE OF MEMORY

The analysis, in the last chapter, of the "Triumph of Life" went a long way toward constructing a bridge between Shelley's "two thoughts." In the process, however, it has left us with a serious equivocation. Death and memory appear to be as much confused as correlated. Expanding on, and adding depth to, his equation of custom-as-social-memory and death in the *Revolt,* Shelley has generalized the connection between all forms of memory, in the form of the repetitions of the death instinct and the path to death. Yet, at the same time, a new form of death, fragmented, partial, even quotidian, has appeared as the enabling condition for change and innovation. Death, in this form, is our only escape from filiation, or the repetitions of memory. To clarify this apparent confusion is also to clear the way for a Shelleyan reconciliation of the "two thoughts."

It is possible to read Shelley's difficulties here as symptomatic of the "Romantic condition." Bloom's *Anxiety of Influence* proposes a neat diagnosis of these symptoms. The *clinamen* as a revisionary ratio is a kind of death, in this case a suppression of the memory of the past, posited as a form of escape from that memory. The generalization of death in Shelley's "Triumph," at each moment "brisant tout à coup le lien des souvenirs," would be, in the terms of Bloom's theory, nothing more than an attempt to escape the guilt of the oedipal desire to negate the father. In Bloom's Freudian agon, repetition of the past (memory) is a kind of death. Repetition is an erasure of the self in a world in which fathers and sons ("precursor poets" and "ephebes") are locked in a zero-sum battle for identity. Without the preemptive erasure, by means of the *clinamen,* of the father's legacy, we are prey to an "anxiety of influence" resulting from the pressures of filiation and the *unheimlich* iteration of the past.

The *clinamen* does not save us from anxiety, however. The internalization of guilt over the erasure of the father ensures the return of the repressed. In the terms of Bloom's analysis, Shelley's equivocation is no more than a tacit acknowledgment that the avoidance of memory by means of death is doomed to failure. The cycles of memory are unavoidable, and nothing is more déjà vu than youthful refusal to repeat the past. In this view, combating memory with death in the form of the *clinamen* would be nothing more than a manifestation of the manic version of the Romantic Ironic. The swerve of the *clinamen* recalls the intricacies of Friedrich Schlegel's arabesque. In both cases, the "anxiety" (which takes the form of exhilaration in Schlegel, and neurosis in Coleridge) bears witness to the inevitability of circular return—in this case, a return to the Absolute.

Reading revolutionary change as an oedipal gesture is not anachronistically post-Freudian. Burke characterizes the state as a grey-haired and wounded father, the revolutionaries as those who desire to "heal" those wounds by chopping him up and throwing him in the "kettle of magicians." The topos was established long before the Revolution itself. Saint-Preux represents an oedipal "revisionary" *clinamen* in the cycle of filiation. Intriguingly, just as Paine simultaneously decries our bondage to the "moldy parchments" of the past and envisages an everlasting polity founded upon the revolutionary constitution, Lord Bomston, who defends Saint-Preux's "noblesse" to the Baron d'Etange ("non point écrite d'encre en de vieux parchmins, mais gravée au fond de son coeur en caracteres ineffaçables" [Rousseau, *Julie,* 143]),[1] limits the revolutionary *clinamen* to a single event. After the marriage to Julie, Saint-Preux "sera le fondement et l'honneur de sa maison comme votre premier ancêtre le fut de la vôtre" (144).[2]

Both Paine and Rousseau tend to confirm the Bloomian model. The oedipal *clinamen* is always caught in this contradiction. The son's erasure of the father is never absolute; the son must revive the memory of

1. "not written in ink on old parchments, but engraved at the bottom of his heart in ineffaceable characters" (my translation).

2. "will be the foundation and honor of his house as your first ancestor was of yours" (my translation).

the father, with the resultant guilt and anxiety, because the son's wish is
to become the father, with the father's authority and power. The oedipal son does not want a generalized attack on the despotism of tyrannical fathers, or the despotism of memory; instead, he hopes that through
the oedipal *clinamen* he will be exempted from this particular father.
Saint-Preux's struggle with Baron d'Etange is for the possession and control of Julie, not an attempt to liberate Julie per se. The irony of the
oedipal cycle is that erasing the father is only a step in the cyclic re-
creation of paternal authority.

But if this is true of *Julie* and of some contemporary readings of the
French Revolution (Ronald Paulson details many more), it is not true of
the erasures that proliferate in the "Triumph of Life," or of the therapeutic responses to the Revolution. The "anxiety of influence" is a genuinely "Romantic" emotion, but Bloom is wrong to suggest that it is the
characteristic and defining element of the Romantic condition. At least
equally characteristic is a diametrically opposed anxiety, which we
might call an anxiety of insufficient influence, or an anxiety of amnesia.

If the typical Romantic move is to seek within the self a source of
creative expression, then the relationship to tradition can be figured
two ways. One, Bloom's, is to see it as a dangerous distraction—a het-
eronomy that overrides and obscures our access to the truth within: "I
may not hope from outward forms to win / The passion and the life,
whose fountains are within" (from Coleridge's "Dejection: An Ode").
But it is also possible, as the post-Kantians do, to see tradition as the
true source of the self, to see our connection to the past as the only
guarantee of a true understanding of our creative individuality. The
"anxiety of amnesia" fears a loss of the past conceived as an integral
element of self.

Burke's insistence that we should "make . . . reparation as nearly as
possible in the style of the building" (*Reflections,* 375), Coleridge's anxious recommendation of "the collation of the present with the past, . . .
the habit of thoughtfully assimilating the events of our own age to those
of the time before us" (*Lay Sermons,* 9), and Hegel's impassioned denunciation of revolutionary abstraction and negation all bear witness to
this "anxiety of amnesia." For these therapeutic Romantics, the *clinamen* is a threat, not a hope. The characteristic form of the therapeutic
vision of history—the circle of memory that binds the sequence of
events into an absolute unity—attempts to allay the fear that the process of history might be a sequence of aleatory disjunctions.

There may seem to be little anxiety in the post-Kantian vision of circular *Erinnerung:* "[T]here is in the external world a constant sequence
of changes, which do not, however, lose themselves in the infinite, but

are restricted to a specific circle, into which they constantly revert. This sequence of changes is thus at once both finite and infinite" (Schelling, *System,* 121–22). But despite this confident assurance that memory's law is unassailable, we must be impressed with the urgency and vehemence of Burke's, Coleridge's, and Hegel's exhortations to avoid the trap of amnesiac change. Change is at once unthinkable and inevitable. In practice, the circle of history is one of homeostatic error correction; Burke sets out to "repair" the building, which has suffered the inevitable ravages of time, in the "style" of the original.

If, in the "Triumph," the fear of death as "living sepulchre" seems to have found an equivocal solution in the generalization of death as *clinamen,* in the work of these therapeutic philosophers the fear of death as *clinamen* seems to have found an equivocal solution in the overcoming of death by repetition. Coleridge's "aching melancholy" at the sight of the baby at the breast helps us to see the thanatological implications of this. Freud bases the death instinct on a fundamental resistance to change in any organism—a resistance also remarked upon by Shelley; Coleridge's archetype of memory as a return to the mother's breast, his bitter self-reproof and desire to return to infanthood ("from this state hast *thou* fallen! Such shouldst thou still become" [*Lay Sermons,* 71]), both arise from a desire for return to the origin in whose terms growth and change—life itself—can only be read as a fall.

We can now understand why a Bloomian reading of Shelley's invocation of death against memory as oedipal "revision" is mistaken. The "Triumph" is a breeding ground for the *clinamen,* but these amnesiac assaults on the past have none of the characteristics of the oedipal *clinamen.* The "Triumph"'s erasures and recommencements avoid the double bind of the oedipal *clinamen*—the simultaneous erasure and reconstitution of past authority—and thereby circumvent the attendant guilt complex of the anxiety of influence.

Shelley enters into the anxiety of amnesia and explodes it from within by surrendering his poem to the *clinamen* completely. When we lose our past so thoroughly that we can only conjecture as to its qualities ("the heaven which I imagine"), when all memory is "trampled into the dust of death," it is impossible to retain a sufficient grasp on the past to be long troubled by an anxiety over its corruption in the process of reproduction (Rousseau's nostalgia for an imagined heaven is not part of the anxiety of amnesia; it is a projection onto the past of a purely imaginary divine order rather than an anxious attempt to prevent the dissipation of the present one). In the "Triumph," memory never succeeds in completing its homeostatic circle.

However, Shelley does not seem to escape from an inverted form of the paradox of the therapeutic philosophers' anxiety of amnesia; if they stand on guard against errors that theoretically should not occur, Shelley appears to be advocating a revolutionary *clinamen* that is in any case inevitable. We have returned to the problem of Hogle's generalized transference. If all thoughts are trampled, willy-nilly, into the "dust of death," there can be no meaning to political *struggle*, and the political effect of reading Shelley's poetry would be indistinguishable from that of reading a government press release or a packet of cornflakes.

We can clarify this point by turning to the antitherapeutic side of the "two thoughts" for an account of the relationship between death and memory. Gilles Deleuze, in his study of Foucault, suggests that the crux of Foucault's project is exactly "le choix entre la mort ou la mémoire."[3] "Peut-être," suggests Deleuze, "a-t-il choisi la mort" (106).[4] The death he chooses is of a type familiar to readers of the "Triumph": "une mort multiple" that transforms "la vie" into "la simple distribution dans le vide de morts 'partielles, progressives, et lentes' " (102).[5] Deleuze suggests that Foucault found a way out of the paradoxical political nullity of "choosing" a death that seems inevitable. Deleuze argues that Foucault doubles memory; there is a memory that stands in opposition to death and that is vulnerable to death, but there is another memory, "l'absolue mémoire," which is a "mémoire du dehors, au-delà de la mémoire courte qui s'inscrit dans les strates et les archives."[6] It is absolute in that it is not a memory *of* some particular thing, but the opening of the very possibility of both "la mémoire" and "l'oubli" (114, 115). "L'absolue mémoire" is the space within which the "non-lieu" of death as "l'oubli" can make sense; it is not a place but the precondition of both place and nonplace. Within *l'absolue mémoire* "la mémoire est coextensive à l'oubli. C'est cette coextensivité qui est vie, longue durée" (115).[7] Within this *longue durée*, the idea of "choosing death over memory" makes (political) sense because a link has been established between the two that, before, was unthinkable.

We can make this clearer by applying it to the "Triumph." The

---

3. "the choice between death or memory" (*Foucault*, 99).

4. "Perhaps he chose death" (*Foucault*, 99).

5. "life [into] the simple distribution within the void of 'slow, partial and progressive' deaths" (*Foucault*, 95).

6. "the 'absolute memory' or memory of the outside, beyond the brief memory inscribed in strata and archives" (*Foucault*, 107).

7. "memory is coextensive with forgetting. It is this coextensive nature which is life, a long period of time" (*Foucault*, 108).

multiplication of "deaths" within the poem can only take place within an absolute memory represented by the poem as a "whole." This is not to suggest that they are hermeneutically fused into a "deeper meaning"—absolute memory is contentless. The poem is the necessary precondition—"place," or Heideggerian "opening"—for Shelley's erasures. The precondition for erasure, however, is also the precondition for memory—the poem conceived as hermeneutical whole. Even if hermeneutical totality is not actually realizable, even if the *clinamen* is unavoidable, memory never ceases to reassert itself within the flux of process as an alternative realization of the poetic space. To "choose death" is a choice that must be made over and over again; it is a constantly renewed resistance to an affirmation of memory that can only lead to the debilitating anxiety of amnesia.

This schema would also clarify the relationship between thanatological death-as-living-sepulchre and death as amnesiac *clinamen.* Deleuze resolves this problem by a doubling of death to match the doubling of memory: "Ce qui s'oppose à la mémoire [absolue] n'est pas l'oubli, mais l'oubli de l'oubli, qui nous dissout au dehors, et qui constitue la mort" (115).[8] The *clinamen*-death is a form of "l'oubli" *within* "l'absolue mémoire," not of "l'oubli de l'oubli." Thanatological death forgets the possibility of forgetting and would create an equivalence between "l'absolue mémoire" and its negation.

This solution is problematic, however. For those who have "chosen death" and committed themselves to the flux of "l'oubli" and the *clinamen,* absolute memory should be a limit, the "opening" it represents not only the precondition of the flux but the precondition of conceptualizing from within the flux. Absolute memory could not be thought from within the processes of memory and forgetfulness that it, supposedly, makes possible. In other words, while this theory can account for Foucault's and Shelley's arguments, it cannot account for them within the terms of their own theories, or their commitment to "death." Deleuze requires a transcendence of the mutations of countermemory to achieve a perspective in which flux can appear a willed alternative to stability; he cannot explain how the individual within that flux is supposed to attain this transcendent perspective.

While Deleuze's argument is not directly useful to us, then, its failure does help us to clarify our problem and to determine what kind of

8. "Memory is contrasted not with forgetting but with the forgetting of forgetting, which dissolves us into the outside and constitutes death" (*Foucault,* 107-8).

solution would be acceptable. To conceptualize change as it operates within Foucault's counterhistories, or within the "Triumph," one must be able to construct a theory of change from a perspective immanent to the flux of process—a perspective that recognizes its own vulnerability to the vicissitudes of historical flux. Immersed in an aleatory process of disjunctive change, we are never presented, in the "Triumph," or in Foucault's work, with the confrontation between an absolute memory and an absolute forgetfulness. What Foucault describes is rather the confrontation of an unstable subject and relatively stable discursive structures within which the subject is constituted. Consider the conclusion to his *Les mots et les choses:*

> [P]armi toutes les mutations qui ont affecté le savoir des choses et de leur ordre . . . un seul, celui qui a commencé il y a un siècle et demi et qui peut-être est en train de se clore, a laissé apparaître la figure de l'homme. Et . . . c'était l'effet d'un changement dans les dispositions fondamentale du savoir. . . . Si ces dispositions venaient à disparaître comme elles sont apparues, si par quelque événement dont nous ne pouvons tout au plus pressentir la possibilité, mais dont nous ne connaissons pour l'instant encore ni la forme ni la promesse, elles basculaient, comme le fit au tournant du XVIIIᵉ siècle le sol de la pensée classique,—alors on peut bien parier que l'homme s'effacerait, comme à la limite de la mer un visage de sable. (398)[9]

Foucault describes the subject as a fragile construct at the mercy of random processes of "mutation" and "erasure." Yet despite this, large patterns of order and (again relative) coherence, the "arrangements of knowledge," do manage to emerge.

This is also true of the "Triumph," where Foucault's imagery of sand and sea is right at home. Despite the trampling of thoughts into the "dust of death," order constantly reemerges from atomic flux. The *clina-*

9. "[A]mong all the mutations that have affected the knowledge of things and their order . . . only one, that which began a century and a half ago and is now perhaps drawing to a close, has made it possible for the figure of man to appear. And that appearance . . . was the effect of a change in the fundamental arrangements of knowledge. . . . If those arrangements were to disappear as they appeared, if some event of which we can at the moment do no more than sense the possibility—without knowing either what its form will be or what it promises—were to cause them to crumble, as the ground of Classical thought did, at the end of the eighteenth century, then one can certainly wager that man would be erased, like a face drawn in sand at the edge of the sea" (*Order of Things*, 386–87).

men can only be recognized as a "swerve" or "death" if it supervenes upon a period, however brief, of continuity. Even in the delirious shifts of the "suddenly my brain became as sand" sequence, there are evanescent structures of continuity where memory (if only in the form of grammatical coherence) reasserts its prerogatives.

The paradox of "choosing" an inevitable death can be usefully rephrased here from an immanent perspective. What we need to explain is not a stark opposition of change-as-death and absolute memory but contrasting rhythms of change. Foucault is convinced that the "arrangements of knowledge" are impermanent, but they are sufficiently stable that it makes political sense to pit ourselves against them. What is hard to understand—given the forces of "mutation" (the *clinamen*), given that the "arrangements of knowledge" are merely faces in the sand that the flux of the sea will "erase"—is how any arrangement of knowledge can achieve even a relative permanence. Foucault and Shelley appear to have described systems that could not avoid a rapid descent into maximum entropy: atomic particles in a randomizing flux—Burke's "chaos of elementary principles."

Even more difficult to understand is how order *reemerges* from this flux once the process of "mutation" is under way. Deleuze showed us that one must be able to explain the continual reappearance of order from disorder to make sense of a "commitment" to countermemory in the form of death or the *clinamen.* It is just this question that Foucault leaves in abeyance. The reappearance of stability within flux is a premise of his work, but he does not explain it. Change remains, in this "antitherapeutic" philosophy, as inconceivable and inevitable as it is in a therapeutic one.

We now have two questions to take to Shelley for which we must seek an "immanent" solution. First, how do we account for the "persistence of memory"? In a world of constant entropic "disorganization" how can there be a negentropic maintenance of "arrangements of knowledge" or "custom's lawless law"? Second, how do we explain the spontaneous reappearance of structures of memory from the atomic disintegration that eventually defeats them? If, as he puts it in *Hellas* (1821), "the tempest shakes the sea, / Leaving no figure upon memory's glass" (130–31), what accounts for the reemergence of figures within an unstable flux?

The second problem points to a form of history that both the therapeutic and antitherapeutic approaches are forced to recognize but neither wants to claim—the incomplete memory, the circle with aleatory revision. The "Triumph" is rich in these; the erasures of memory, instead of giving rise to either a new world or an entropic flux, lead to repetition-with-a-difference.

DEATH

I

Let us begin to answer these questions by returning to the image of the trace in the sand. It is striking that both Shelley and Foucault use this image to capture the frailty of the structures of human knowledge. Direct influence is possible, but unlikely. One possible reason that this image suggests itself to both writers is that both are drawing on the antitherapeutic resources of the revolutionary Enlightenment. Foucault is greatly influenced by the work of a near contemporary of Shelley's, the French pioneer in pathological anatomy Marie-François-Xavier Bichat (Deleuze, *Foucault* [Minuit], 101ff.). Foucault's conception of a proliferation of plural "deaths" derives, in part, from his study of Bichat in *Naissance de la clinique*. There he writes that "Bichat a relativisé le concept de mort, le faisant déchoir de cet absolu où il apparissait comme un événement insécable, décisif et irrécupérable: il l'a volatilisé et réparti dans la vie, sous la forme de morts en détail, morts partielles, progressives et si lentes à s'achever par-delà la mort même" (147).[10] The attraction of this "perméabilité de la vie à la mort" (144)[11] for Foucault is that it undermines the integrity of human life considered as a hermeneutical totality. Foucault is wrong, however, to suggest that this view of death originates with Bichat. In *Le rêve de d'Alembert,* some thirty years before the publication of Bichat's work, Diderot had made the same argument:

> Et vous parlez d'individus, pauvres philosophes; laissez-là vos individus. . . . Qu'est-ce qu'un être? . . . la somme d'un certain nombre de tendances . . . Est-ce que je puis être autre chose qu'une tendence? . . . Non. Je vais à un terme . . . Et les espèces? . . . Les espèces ne sont que des tendances à un terme commun qui lear est propre . . . Et la vie? . . . La vie? une suite d'actions et

10. "Bichat relativized the concept of death, bringing it down from that absolute in which it appeared as an indivisible, decisive, irrecoverable event: he volatilized it, distributed it throughout life in the form of separate, partial, progressive deaths, deaths that are so slow in occurring that they extend even beyond death itself" (*Birth of the Clinic,* 144).

11. "the permeability of life by death" (*Birth of the Clinic,* 142).

de réactions . . . Vivant, j'agis et je réagies en masse . . . mort, j'agis et je réagis en molécules . . . Je ne meurs donc point . . . Non, sans doute je ne meurs point en ce sens, ni moi ni quoi que ce soit . . . Naître, vivre et passer, c'est changer de formes . . . Et qu'importe une forme ou une autre? (196; only the first ellipsis is mine, the others are in the original and indicate the disjointed speech of d'Alembert as he talks in his sleep)[12]

This appears to be concerned with our ability to find a materialist substitute for immortality beyond this life, rather than with the permeation of this life by death. To understand why this is not the case, we must recall the close etymological and semantic relationship between the atomic and the anatomic. To anatomize is to "cut up"; its logical tendency, and termination, is the "atom"—the indivisible, or that which cannot be cut. By anatomizing the human being Bichat splintered the presumed integrity of the "organism" into an aggregation of more or less independent, though cooperative, organic subsystems ("Les envelloppes successives de la vie se détachent naturellement, énonçant leur autonomie et leur vérité dans cela même qui les nie" [Foucault, *Naissance,* 145]).[13] Each of these "atoms" of the body is a site for a potential death that may be marginally or entirely independent of the death of those critical subsystems to which we typically refer to decide if "death" has occurred: brain and heart. Bichat has anatomized death into a myriad of atomic deaths. Foucault describes this myriad as the "présence fourmillante" of death in life. It is a short step from Foucault's ants ("fourmilles") to Diderot's parallel between the organism and the swarm of bees: each bee is an atom of susceptibility to death, but no atom's death necessarily provokes the dissolution of the whole (*Rêve,* 217). The quotation from Diderot above must be read with his atomistic model of the human being in mind. The swarm of bees, the "faisceau de brins," are images of "[l]'homme [qui] se résolv[e] en une infinité

12. "And then you talk of individuals, you poor philosophers! Stop thinking about your individuals. . . . What is a being? The sum of a certain number of tendencies. . . . Can I be anything more than a tendency? . . . No, I am moving towards a certain end. . . . And what of species? Species are merely tendencies towards a common end peculiar to them. . . . And life? A series of actions and reactions. . . . Alive, I act and react as a mass . . . dead, I act and react as separate molecules. . . . Don't I die, then? Well, not in that sense, neither I nor anything else. . . . To be born, to live and to die is merely to change forms. . . . And what does one form matter any more than another?" (*D'Alembert's Dream,* 181–82).

13. "The successive envelopes of life are detached naturally, enunciating their autonomy and truth in the very thing [that denies them]" (*Birth of the Clinic,* 143; with my modification).

d'hommes atomiques" (186).[14] The deaths that extend beyond the dissolution of the organism are simply the continuation of a process that
must equally, according to theory, characterize the period of "life." "Je
ne meurs donc point" because I am continually "dying." The atomic
generalization of death is also the erasure of the boundary of death. Just
as Bichat describes a proliferation of death within anatomized atomic
life, he also, like Diderot, notes that "longtemps encore après la mort de
l'individu, des morts minuscules et partielles viendront à leur tour disso-
cier les îlots de vie qui s'obstinent" (Foucault, *Naissance,* 144-45).[15]

Unlike Bichat, and anticipating Foucault, Diderot makes the political
implications of this atomism clear. His rejection of the "individual" as a
chimerical delusion of "pauvres philosophes" is a direct assault on the
conservative force of the organic metaphor; the dissolution of "man" as
an inevitable and natural totality, reread as "la somme d'un certain
nombre de tendances," is what Foucault intends by the erasure of the
face in the sand. Diderot's reduced-scale model of socialization, the
monastery that seeks to preserve and pass on its "esprit monastique"
(217), exists as a body on the same terms as the "individual" considered
as a society of atomic animalcules; each member of the society, each
atom, is a potential point of entry for death as *clinamen* or innovation.
The survival of the monastery depends upon an unstable dynamic equilibrium between a continual erosion by death and repair by memory/
custom.

The atomic dispersal of death equally erodes and blurs the boundaries
of the social form. Burke opposes the intact, integral body of the state-
father to the bloodthirsty, anatomizing desires of the revolutionaries;
Diderot anticipates and forestalls that argument by disintegrating the
father, reading him as an atomistic "faisceau" always already permeated
by death. Burke hoped to harness the conventional idea of death to
stigmatize social change with the fear and horror associated with that
"undiscovered country." Diderot allays the fear of social change by reducing the fear of death: "Si l'homme se résout quelque part en une
infinité d'hommes animalcules, on y doit avoir moins de répugnance à
mourir" (187).[16] That hypothetical "quelque part" proves to be here,

14. "[the] man [who] can divide himself up into myriads of microscopic men" (*D'Alembert's Dream,* 172).
15. "long after the death of the individual, minuscule, partial deaths continue to dissociate
the islets of life that still subsist" (*Birth of the Clinic,* 142).
16. "If there is a place where man can divide himself up into myriads of microscopic men,
people there should be less reluctant to die" (*D'Alembert's Dream,* 172).

where "[n]aître, vivre et passer, c'est changer de formes . . . Et qu'importe une forme ou une autre?"

Shelley's and Foucault's uses of the figure in the sand are indebted to
this model of society and the "individual," which allows them to conceptualize the vulnerability to change essential to their social theories.
The figure is an atomistic constellation that demonstrates the creation of
large-scale structures from atomic aggregation while admitting that each
atom, each grain of sand, is a potential site of death and a point of entry
for mutation. The evanescent figure in the sand helps us to overcome
the hermeneutic prejudice that all parts must be subsumed by and in
wider wholes. The atomistic generalization of death in Enlightenment
atomism allows Shelley to overcome organicist social determinism, or
filiation; he is no longer confined to the bleak option of parricide or
conformity offered by Burke and Coleridge. In the "Ode to Liberty,"
Shelley makes this explicit:

> O, that the free would stamp the impious name
>   Of KING into the dust! or write it there,
> So that this blot upon the page of fame
>   Were as a serpent's path, which the light air
> Erases, and the flat sands close behind!
>   Ye the oracle have heard:
>   Lift the victory-flashing sword,
> And cut the snaky knots of this foul gordian word,
>   Which weak itself as stubble, yet can bind
>   Into a mass, irrefragably firm,
>   The axes and the rods which awe mankind.
>
> (211–22)

The hypostatized "name" of "King" has ideological force only while it is
abstracted from the atomistic disintegration of social process so that it
gains hegemonic "irrefragibility." If social forms are traced in a sand of
which we are the grains, each of us becomes a potential *clinamen,* the
path of future mutations of those forms.

Shelley's "Ode to Heaven" gains new resonance in this context. By
introducing death, in the form of the vicissitudes of time, into Coleridge's reassuringly atemporal image of the therapeutic inherence of
part within whole, the drop of dew that reflects the universe, Shelley
restores to the "part" its (atomistic) particularity, its distinction from the
whole to which it "belongs." Shelley accepts the terms of Coleridge's
image but inverts the emphasis; whereas, for Coleridge, the dewdrop's

fragility and evanescence reinforce the need for therapeutic "absolution" within the totality, for Shelley they demonstrate the vulnerability of the therapeutic Absolute to a particulate *clinamen*. The death of the dewdrop precipitates the death of the whole. English society, like the trace in the sand, is an evanescent constellation of ten million "atom-born" individuals, ever vulnerable to their particular and *fourmillante* death.

A short, unfinished, and deceptively simple poem from 1820, "Death," emerges in this light as an astute, and remarkably complete, manifesto of the atomistic "perméabilité de la vie à la mort":

I.

Death is here and death is there,
Death is busy everywhere,
All around, within, beneath,
Above is death—and we are death.

II.

Death has set his mark and seal
On all we are and all we feel,
On all we know and all we fear,

.   .   .   .

III.

First our pleasures die—and then
Our hopes, and then our fears—and when
These are dead, the debt is due,
Dust claims dust—and we die too.

IV.

All things that we love and cherish,
Like ourselves must fade and perish;
Such is our rude mortal lot—
Love itself would, did they not.

A death that is "busy everywhere," including "within," a death that in some way constitutes us ("we are death"), even as living beings, can only be understood as particulate; like Bichat's, it has been "volatilisé et réparti dans la vie, sous la forme de morts en détail, morts partielles, progressives et . . . lentes."[17] When the debt falls due and "dust claims

---

17. "volatilized . . . [and] distributed . . . throughout life in the form of separate, partial, progressive [and slow] deaths" (Foucault, *Birth of the Clinic*, 144).

dust," there is an implicit suggestion that death itself is a kind of atomistic "dust."

This suggestion becomes a simple assertion in the "Triumph" when the shape tramples Rousseau's thoughts into "the dust of death." Atomistic erosion is rife in this poem. Not only Rousseau's brain but the poem itself becomes "as sand"; constellations emerge from the flow, but death constantly erodes their boundaries. Rousseau sees the people caught up in the car's procession as "atomies that dance / Within a sunbeam" (446-47). Order emerges from the dance, but it is always order inhabited by death and dissolution; a figure drawn in sand between two erasing waves. The "dim forms" (483) or "phantoms" (487) that prompt dreams of power and domination among earthly monarchs (493-505) temporarily organize the disordered flux of the atomic dance. The final result of this "rage for order" is only a proliferation of death as earth is turned into a "charnel" (505), a kingdom of the "old anatomies" (500).

Shelley's revival of this old word for "skeletons" picks up on its relationship to the dancing "atomies" (446). The body as "anatomy" is destined to anatomization, or atomistic dissolution. Burke argued from the integrity of the organism to the totality of the state-father. Shelley draws an inverse parallel; the dissolution of the hierarchical state is as possible as the anatomization of the human body. The organism and the organization are equally subject to this "perméabilité de la vie à la mort."

II

Shelley's preoccupation with death is too easily read as a curious psychological trait. By placing his work in relationship to Bichat's and Diderot's, we discover, in the light of Foucault's reading of Bichat, an urgent political relevance in this preoccupation. What is more, we broaden considerably the terms of Foucault's reading of Bichat. Where Foucault sees only a *sui generis* innovator, we now see, if not a "movement," a widespread attempt in the late eighteenth and early nineteenth centuries to rethink the meaning of death. Reading Shelley in relation to this directly political project, he emerges as a profound and original contributor to this little-understood strand of the radical Enlightenment opposition to the therapeutic ideology.

The atomistic fragmentation of death is most evidently an assault on the organicism of the therapeutic approach. This approach is premised upon, in Taylor's words, "an *a priori* unity of a human life through its whole extent" (*Sources of the Self*, 51; see also 288-89). This unity demands, logically, a punctual and absolute death as its complement. From Schelling through Dilthey to Taylor we repeatedly meet with this insistence upon death as narrative closure and a correspondent privileging of "the last moment of a life . . . [when] the balance of its meaning [can] be struck" (Dilthey, 74–75). The atomistic view of death blurs boundaries whose precision is vital to the therapeutic perspective; what unity can a human life or the life of a state have if one can never be sure quite where it starts and where it ends?

This diffusion of death in life must, however, be sharply distinguished from Wertherism, the Byronic *Todessehnsucht* with which Shelley's fascination with death has often been confused. *Todessehnsucht,* as much as therapeutic idealism, is a privileging of death. Byronic despair welcomes death as an absolute negation of life. The generalizing anatomy of death is also a banalizing of death; if it strips death of its terror, it also strips it of any mysterious seductiveness. The fragmented and fragmenting deaths that proliferate through the "Triumph" are not the grand renunciation of the delusions of the will that Schopenhauer finds in Byron. Rousseau remains "between desire and shame suspended" even as his brain becomes atomic sand; a fragmentary *fourmillante* death implies an equally teeming life that reasserts itself beyond any boundary we nominate as the "moment" of death.

ANTIORGANICISM IN LATE-EIGHTEENTH-CENTURY LITERATURE

I

I have described the antiorganicism, of which this reconceived death is part, as a widespread concern of the latter half of the eighteenth century. One reason we find it figuring so prominently in Shelley's thought is that it is particularly prominent in the literature of that period. Both the sentimental and the ironic are antiorganic—organicism being one of the essential attributes of the classical/naive. The self-consciousness of the sentimental or ironic author inevitably leads to a work that operates on a minimum of two incommensurable levels. For Friedrich Schlegel, the hallmark of ironic literature is the exploitation of this internal division to create a "chaotic" hybrid work of literature that multiplies indefinitely its conscious references to disparate elements of the literary tradition: "Irony is a clear consciousness of an eternal agility, of the infinitely abundant chaos" ("Idea" 69; *Dialogue,* 155). In Schlegel's view, this aesthetic of the "arabesque," of the deliberate cultivation of a knowing artistry without regard for the organic unity of the work, was the defining characteristic of the most exciting work of the period. Diderot's novels figured prominently among the works most often cited as evidence for this (along with works by Sterne, the prime exemplar of the sentimental, Jean-Paul, Schlegel's own *Lucinde,* and so forth). Both Bichat and Shelley, then, lived in a literary climate in which the option, markedly influenced by Diderot, of a certain antiorganicism provided a model for construction of a work out of disparate and disharmonious elements (what we might call aesthetic atoms), with little concern for absolute integration. If this did not directly put into question the "absolu" and "insécable" nature of death, it did provide a framework in which a multiple and "chaotic" death would make sense.

Although ignored by Schlegel, the contemporary genre that best exemplified his aesthetic was the Gothic novel, and we can identify its impact on Shelley's thought with more confidence. Shelley's relationship to the Gothic is too often read as a youthful indiscretion or as evidence of an aesthetic or temperamental weakness. The medievalism that increasingly occupied Friedrich Schlegel as the one true source of a creative aesthetic chaos and that becomes in Carlyle, Ruskin, and others the dominant (and dubious) legacy of European Romanticism in the nineteenth century was popularized by the rise of the Gothic in literature and design in the eighteenth. The affinities between the Gothic on the one hand and the sentimental and ironic on the other are not far to seek. Any reader of Radcliffe's *Mysteries of Udolpho* will be struck by the persistent echoes of *La nouvelle Héloise,* that *summum* of eighteenth-century sentimentality.[18] Inversely, Rousseau warns readers about the "gothique ton" of his collection of letters (4). The *Mysteries,* in accordance with the theory of the ironic, and as is typical of a work of Gothic literature, is a highly artificial, self-consciously "literary" and stylized work. It is also an aggregative hybrid, pulling together bits and pieces of Rousseau, *Werther,* Schiller's *Robbers,* Sterne, and a host of

18. The heroine's father, St. Aubert, is a positive caricature of the Rousseauist ideal, living in his country retreat, pursuing botany, and overflowing with paternal benevolence for his less fortunate neighbors. Emily herself is prone to spout Rousseauist platitudes at the drop of a hat. More concretely, Saint-Preux's sojourn in Paris is the model for Valancourt's corruption by the metropolis. Radcliffe does not stint herself on opportunities to point out the Rousseauist moral of this either: the supersophisticated pleasures that betray a false "civilization" are constantly held up, as in *Julie,* against the solid and healthy values of a tranquil rural lifestyle (Radcliffe, 293–94, 466, 471, 500, 507, 516, 584, 597).

other influences, with no effort to conform these atomistic chunks to a unified aesthetic goal.

A good example of this is the introduction into the "body" of Radcliffe's text, on the flimsiest of pretexts, the entirety of a "provençal tale" that one character happens to read (551ff.). This conforms perfectly to Schlegel's demand for a dialogic literature (à la Diderot, Sterne, and himself) able to incorporate different and not necessarily compatible voices and genres in a "many-sided" "hodgepodge" (*Dialogue,* 55, 95). For Schlegel, modern literature, that antiorganic, anticlassical, many-sided "arabesque," is "Romantic" because it descends from the medieval *Roman.*[19] Radcliffe's "provençal tale" emphasizes exactly those aspects of the *Roman* that make it central to Schlegel's theory, in particular its self-conscious artificiality. The blatant intrusion of the "provençal tale" serves as an ironic example of the very artificiality and deliberate exoticism the tale itself ascribes to the "romantic fiction" of the past (552). We might try to integrate the tale organically into the work as a "whole" by arguing that it is the "key" to the work's form. But if it is, it is a key that opens to us an ironic paradox: the essence of the Gothic, it tells us, is to be like the *Roman.* The essence of the *Roman* is to have no essence, to pull together whatever will serve to enhance its effectiveness. The Gothic, then, becomes a genre of shared and blatant conventions, highly wrought theatricality, and self-consciously "exotic" motifs, thrown together with little concern for unity of effect.

The general political affiliations of the Gothic novel are not clear. Radcliffe's *Mysteries* toys with some intriguing scraps of revolutionary rhetoric, although it is debatable how seriously we should take these. The Rousseauist denunciations of the corruptions of supersophisticated Paris, for example, were a standard part of revolutionary rhetoric in which Paris served as foil to the stoic restraint of republican *vertu.* The arbitrary power of the evil Montoni reminds one that "gothic" was a favorite revolutionary epithet for the feudal values of the *ancien régime,* a fact that gives an interesting cast to Emily's learning to "[despise] the authority, which, till now, she had only feared" (382). The impassioned attack on the *"Denunzie secrete,"* the arbitrary arrest and secret imprisonment of Venetian citizens on the basis of anonymous

---

19. The word is most often translated as "novel," which, as Eichner points out (*Friedrich Schlegel,* 52ff.), badly misrepresents Schlegel's intent. Schlegel's belief that the *Roman* is the necessary form of a modern literature in no way precludes the possibility of a *romantische* drama or poetry: Shakespeare was, indeed, the *romantische* writer par excellence.

accusation, is strongly reminiscent of prerevolutionary outrage at the *lettres de cachet.*

But whatever its explicit content, the Gothic's Rousseauist sentimentality and sublime discontinuity make it inherently "revolutionary," which explains why it attracted radical authors like Godwin and the young Shelley. Burke's *Reflections* had defined the Revolution as archetypally sublime. Radcliffe's *Mysteries,* published in 1794, embraces that sublimity as an aesthetic imperative: "To a warm imagination, the dubious forms, that float, half veiled in darkness, afford a higher delight, than the most distinct scenery, that the sun can shew" (598-99). Drawing on Schelling's distinction between the true narrative totality of "history" and a mere "series of events without aim or purpose," Coleridge had argued that the role of "narrative" was "to convert *a series* into a *Whole*"; we have seen that the political correlative of this therapeutic aesthetic is the attempt to "narrativize" historical process—Coleridge's attempt to find in "the collation of the present with the past" an "antidote to that restless craving for the wonders of the day," which he saw as the revolutionary sickness of his time (*Lay Sermons,* 9, 8).

The peculiar structure, or antistructure, of the Gothic novel, its constant openness to digression, its willful multiplication of "events without aim or purpose"—at least with regard to the advancement of the "plot"—place it in radical opposition to the aesthetic and political ideals of the therapeutic organicists. The Gothic novel is best defined negatively as an antiorganic, antitherapeutic antinarrative. Radcliffe seems embarrassed by having a plot at all; the majority of incident in the book bears no relation to it, and the little that does is treated in the most mechanical and conventional way. Digression in the *Mysteries* is elevated to the first principle of composition, the spurious intrusion of the "provençal tale" being a relatively minor example. The entire sojourn at Udolpho that gives the book its name, and all that castle's spurious "mysteries," could be excised from the novel without the reader missing a beat. The closer we examine parts of the novel, like the "provençal tale" or the sojourn in Udolpho, the more they seem to disintegrate from the whole and fold in on themselves. If we try to grasp the whole *as* a "Whole," we find nothing but a constellation of fragments in a void or a figure traced in the sand.

We are still a crucial step away from an explicit recognition of the pathological anatomy of narrative, although death, and a disturbingly nonfinal death at that, is a preoccupation of the Gothic. The step is taken decisively, however, in a work Shelley knew well: *Frankenstein.*

Mary Shelley's post-Gothic political fable makes clear the efficacy of an anatomical critique of Burkean organicism. In 1811, shortly after his expulsion from Oxford, Shelley, with his cousin, Charles Grove, attended with marked interest a course of lectures on anatomy at St. Bartholomew's Hospital (White, *Shelley,* 1:121). It is possible that he would have met directly with Bichat's work there at that time, but in any case the anatomical perception of the body as a community of different systems would have undermined the a priori assumption of organic unity. Mary's "Gothic" monster, perhaps in part influenced by Shelley's memories of this course, stages the creation of the Gothic work from the diverse "points of view" of the literary tradition as the creation of a new human body from the fragmentary remnants of many others. Burke's organic metaphor—the state as an integrated organic totality like the human body—is comprehensively subverted here in a way that takes us back to Diderot's atomism. The viability of Frankenstein's monster, his potential humanity, destroys the vehicle of Burke's metaphor: the human body is not an integrated totality; its parts have a life and death quite independent of the life and death of the whole. From the atomizing dust of death a new constellation of parts can emerge; no part is absolutely dedicated to its context. At the same time, we are asked to reread the tenor of the metaphor according to the new understanding of the vehicle: the state *is* like the human body; it is a constellation of atomic units, each vulnerable to an individual death, collectively composing an ephemeral figure in the sand.

Reading *Frankenstein* almost contemporaneously with Coleridge's *Statesman's Manual* and *Biographia Literaria* and A. W. Schlegel's *Lectures on Dramatic Art and Poetry* provided Shelley with a new understanding of the literary work of art. By casting the Gothic's relationship to tradition as the construction of a monster from bits of various corpses, Mary Shelley directly challenged the basis of the aesthetic organicism he encountered in Coleridge and Schlegel. Above all, she made it difficult for him not to perceive the isomorphisms between political and aesthetic organicism and their joint dependence on an "absolu" and "insécable" death. We can read the "Triumph" as a poetic version of Frankenstein's monster—not as a "Gothic poem" but as a post-Gothic product of and dramatization of the Gothic aesthetic. In Frankenstein's monster life reemerges out of the disassembly and reassembly of human bodies. In the Gothic, plots are disassembled and reassembled in the same manner, with the same mysterious reemergence of vitality from the dust of death. The "Triumph" internalizes this process, which occurs across the different works of the Gothic and romance genres; the poem, itself a "fragment," seems constructed of fragments. As we read, the poem disintegrates and reintegrates before us; from each disintegration bits and pieces—atoms of poetry—are salvaged and reused. As with popular cinematic representations of the monster, the "uncanny" in this process is concentrated in the "scars," those disquieting reminders that what seems to fit so well in the context in which we receive it was also once at home for us—*heimlich*—in quite another context.

II

What emerges from both the Romantic Ironic and the Gothic is a strong belief in aesthetic atomism; texts, plots, themes, and characters are vulnerable to a particulate death or dissolution, but will coalesce into new constellations of meaning. The problem is still how to account, in this perspective, for the second half of that process, the "persistence of memory" and the reemergence of order. After all, the reanimation of the sutured fragments of Frankenstein's monster is only made possible by the *deus ex machina* of "galvanism."

Once again, we run into Hegel's criticism of an antiorganic revolutionism, that it appears to have no way of instituting the creativity it promises, achieving nothing but a "fury of destruction." Shelley must have had some anxiety about this. Creation, in some sense, was his highest goal: *"Non merita nome di creatore, se non Iddio ed il Poeta"* (*Defence*, Reiman and Powers, 506). The Gothic's and the Romantic Ironic's playful pillaging and confounding of the literary tradition, while undeniably exhilarating, can also appear to be a radically finite game; transgression can only be meaningful while there are still boundaries to transgress.

Shelley's and Foucault's traces in the sand, it should be remembered, lie on the edge of the sea. As each wave comes in, the particles of sand are caught up in a radically destabilizing turbulent flux; the trace disappears in a randomizing chaos. As an image of the fragility of individual or societal identity, this appears conclusive; how can we possibly conceptualize the reemergence of an identity, no matter how transient, from such a radical disorganization? The atomistic aesthetic we have described here seems to be Hogle's radical transference: "a rootless passage between different formations . . . a primordial, preconscious shift, intimated in the movement of perception, feeling, and language, always already becoming a different enactment of itself at another time and in conjunction with other elements" (*Shelley's Process*, 15).

The aptness of Hogle's thesis for the whole antiorganic "movement" would seem to be borne out if we return to Diderot's *Rêve:* "[T]out est en un flux perpétuel . . . tout animal est plus ou moins homme; tout minéral est plus ou moins plante; toute plante est plus our moins animal. . . . Toute chose est plus ou moins une chose quelconque, plus ou moins terre, plus ou moins eau, plus ou mois air, plus ou moins feu; plus ou moins d'un règne ou d'un autre. . . . Donc rien n'est de l'essence d'un être particulier" (195; only the second ellipsis is mine).[20] (It is notable here, too, how close we are to the Gothic, with its own interest in the perpetual transgression of apparently stable boundaries: man and animal, dead and alive, and so forth.)

The optimistic version of radical transference holds that when these boundaries are blurred, meanings are "decentered" and we are "made aware that we in the West are poised between continued submissions to the 'One' of tyrannizing centers and new realizations that a 'One' of never-ending change may free us, if we accept it, from the oppressions of existing absolutes" (Hogle, *Shelley's Process,* 26). The problem with this, and the problem with late-eighteenth-century antiorganicism as I have so far described it, is identified by Diderot: "Qui sait si tout ne tend pas à se réduire à un grand sédiment inerte et immobile? Qui sait quelle sera la durée de cette inertie?" (*Rêve,* 190).[21] This idea haunted much of the scientific thought of Shelley's time. Herschel held that the cosmos was headed, inevitably, to a catastrophic gravitational collapse (Grabo, *Newton,* 84f.). In Erasmus Darwin's *Zoonomia* Shelley read an anticipation of the most dire implications of the second law of thermodynamics: "Without heat and motion, which some philosophers still believe to be the same thing, as they so perpetually appear together, the particles of matter would attract and move towards each other, and the whole universe freeze or coalesce into one solid mass. These therefore counteract the gravitation of bodies to one center; and . . . become . . . the causes without which life cannot exist" (qtd. in Grabo, 51).

Why shouldn't the tendency of this turbulent atomistic flux be a constant increase in entropy? Why shouldn't its ultimate result be not liberation or oppression but absolute indifference—maximum entropy?

Shelley's "Vision of the Sea" gives us such a nightmare vision of a transferential tempest in which "Death, Fear, / Love, Beauty, are mixed

20. "[A]ll nature is in a perpetual state of flux. Every animal is more or less a human being, every mineral more or less a plant, every plant more or less an animal. . . . Any given thing is a specific thing only in greater or lesser degree, more or less earth, more or less water, more or less air, more or less fire, more or less in one classification or another . . . so nothing is of the essence of a particular being" (*D'Alembert's Dream,* 181).

21. "Who knows whether everything is not tending to degenerate into the same great, inert, motionless sediment? And who knows how long this inertia will last?" (*D'Alembert's Dream,* 176).

in the atmosphere, / Which trembles and burns with the fervour of dread" (161–63). Tigers fight an unequal battle with the sea; sharks and dogfish eating the corpses of dead sailors are compared to the Jews receiving manna in the wilderness; a baby smiles and laughs at the destruction around it. This transgressive carnival of destruction is a world turned upside down that releases no surge of revolutionary creativity but transfixes us with the "terror of tempest" (1).

To find a way of conceiving the reappearance of order and the persistence of memory within the transferential flux, we have to turn to the source of Enlightenment atomism, who has been conspicuous by his absence from this discussion: Lucretius. We will find in him a basis for understanding how Shelley combats the threat of entropic indifference without recourse to therapeutic organicism.

PART TWO

THE PART EXCEEDS THE WHOLE

6

Lucretius: Toward a Chaotic Theory of Social Reproduction

The importance of Lucretius's influence upon Shelley has long been recognized, and there are excellent general discussions of the topic.[1] A new understanding of Lucretius has emerged in the past decade or so, however, in the light of broadly based developments in contemporary science that are commonly known, collectively, as chaos science, or the sciences of complex dynamics. This altered understanding of Lucretius offers us new insights into Shelley's use of him. Chaos science is part of the "peculiar relations" of our "age"; through its optic, Shelley's poetry reveals "an unforeseen and an unconceived delight" (*Defence,* Reiman and Powers, 500).

There is, fortunately, no need to give a general account of chaos science here—there exist a number of excellent ones[2]—but in this chap-

---

1. The classic paper on Lucretius's influence on Shelley is Paul Turner, "Shelley and Lucretius." Also worthy of note is Phillips, "Lucretian Echoes in Shelley's *Mont Blanc.*" Hogle also regards his transferential paradigm as Lucretian; this point is dealt with below.

2. The best short general outline of chaos science I know of, though it is now a little dated, is Crutchfield et al. Gleick's is an excellent book-length survey for the nonscientist; Nina Hall's collection of essays is another very useful guide for the nonspecialist. Hao Bai-Lin provides an excellent survey of papers ranging from the very technical to the introductory; Kim and Stringer's collection, *Applied Chaos,* is mostly highly technical; but Rössler's "Future of Chaos" is an interesting counterpoint to the view of chaos theory I propound here. There are a myriad of other introductions for the general reader, including Waldrop, Briggs and Peat, Ruelle (*Chance and Chaos*), Stewart, Cohen and Stewart, and Lewin, which are all more or

ter I discuss the immediately relevant concepts in enough detail to allow a reader who has not yet looked into chaos theory to follow the
argument. Drawing principally on the work of Michel Serres, I show
how these concepts relate to Lucretian physics, and then consider some
of the aesthetic implications of chaos theory and what light it sheds on
the paradoxes of the atomistic society and individual. In the next chapter, I turn to the question of how far such a reading reflects Shelley's
own conception of his poetic, and political, aims, and how far this can
be attributed to his reading of Lucretius. Finally, in Chapter 8, I return
briefly to the "Triumph," which I left paralyzed by contradictions, to
demonstrate the direct applicability of this approach.

Some of this has already been touched on by other Shelley critics.
Most notably, Hogle draws on both Serres's study of Lucretius and Jane
Phillips's paper on Lucretian echoes in "Mont Blanc" to suggest that
Shelley's "centerless transference" is, at base, a "Lucretian turbulence"
(*Shelley's Process*, 86, 74; see also 32–49, 74ff.). Hogle has, however,
misinterpreted the thrust of Serres's argument and the special nature of
Lucretian turbulence. Like many of those in the humanities who have
been attracted by the new sciences of complexity, Hogle has let himself
be carried away by the literary associations of the terminology. The
word "chaos" itself is the principal snare for someone from a literary
background. A good example of this is Katherine Hayles's *Chaos Bound;*
Hayles is well versed in chaos science, but her attempts to apply it to
literature are unconvincing, primarily because, when she turns to literary examples, she reverts to a concept of chaos more familiar to Hesiod
or Milton than to Edward Lorenz (a similar criticism could be applied to
some aspects of Patrick Brady's work). "Chaos" conjures up images of
either purely entropic nullity or Hogle's brand of infinitely transgressive
confusion and turmoil. The chaos of chaos science, and its turbulence,

---

less useful. Hayles, *Chaos Bound,* is the first book-length work on the application of chaos to
literary theory; Argyros, in his *Blessed Rage for Order,* gives a wide-ranging discussion of the
philosophical issue raised by chaos theory, although his approach is completely opposed to
mine; a useful shorter statement of Argyros's argument can be found in "Narrative and Chaos";
Brady has written a number of papers on the literary implications of chaos theory; Walker's
"Romantic Chaos" explores a chaos-theory approach to the writings of Novalis, an interesting
case to compare with Shelley; Reibling provides an excellent brief overview of the social and
political implications of chaos theory. Hayles has also edited a useful and suggestive collection
of articles on chaos and literature: *Chaos and Order.* Prigogine and Stengers is a work on
which I have drawn heavily for my own understanding of the wider philosophical implications
of chaos theory. Serres, *La naissance,* is the best study of the Lucretian roots of modern
physical theory. Unannotated remarks about chaos theory should be read as my own views
about chaos theory, based on a composite picture drawn from these works.

can best be described by Friedrich Schlegel's "Idea" 71: "Only that confusion out of which a world can arise is chaos" (*Dialogue*, 155).[3]

To be sure, Diderot's "tout est en un flux perpétuel" is a direct translation from Lucretius (*Nature of the Universe*, 179, 5.280), whose
physics is, as Serres puts it, premised on "une canonique de la fluence"
(*La naissance*, 63).[4] This flux is as much creative as it is destructive,
however: "The destructive motions can never permanently get the up-
per hand and entomb vitality for evermore. Neither can the generative
and augmentive motions permanently safeguard what they have created.
So the war of the elements that has raged throughout eternity continues
on equal terms. Now here, now there, the forces of life are victorious
and in turn vanquished" (Lucretius, 76–77, 2.569–76).[5] It is this realization that "un ordre, plusieurs ordres émergent du désordre" as much as
"le désordre émerge de l'ordre" (Serres, *La naissance*, 63)[6] that is the
central insight of chaos theory.

CHAOTIC CREATIVITY

Images of storm at sea recur throughout Lucretius's *De rerum natura*
and figure in several of its most famous passages on the inescapable
turmoil of life. Lucretius sees the turbulent interaction of the atoms that
constitute the physical universe as the result of storms in "this multi-
tudinous ocean of matter, this welter of foreign bodies" (76, 2.550). Yet
these storms are not like that in Shelley's "Vision of the Sea"; they are
not Hegel's "fury of destruction." Like Foucault's and Shelley's erasing
wave, Lucretius's turbulence can also be seen as a fury of creation: "The
human infant, like a shipwrecked sailor cast ashore by the cruel waves,
lies naked on the ground, speechless, lacking all aids to life, when nature has first tossed him with pangs of travail from his mother's womb
upon the shores of the sunlit world" (177, 5.222–25). This image—one

---

3. The German post-Kantians' interest in "chaos" is enticing for anyone interested in literary applications of chaos theory. Walker's "Romantic Chaos" offers some very intriguing parallels in the work of Novalis to the reading of Shelley I am offering here—most notably on the
issue of the intimate relationship between destruction and creation (44–45).

4. "a structured understanding of flow" (my translation).

5. All translations of the *De rerum natura* have been taken from the Penguin edition.
These have all been checked against the original, and book and line numbers are given for
each corresponding passage.

6. "an order, several orders, emerge from disorder [as much as] disorder emerges from
order" (my translation).

of the sources of Rousseau's coming to consciousness on the banks of the river Lethe in the "Triumph"—captures the dynamic balance of Lucretius's philosophy; the turbulent vicissitudes of life can oppress us and wear us down (just as Rousseau "wakes to weep," the infant here "fills the air with his piteous wailing" [177, 5.226]), but they can also produce new life and new order. The seashore, that liminal juxtaposition of turmoil and (relative) stability which produces the *suave mari magno,* is, in Lucretius as in Shelley and Foucault, a profoundly ambivalent space of creation and destruction.

The distinctive feature of chaotic systems is that they are nonlinear dynamic systems. Nonlinear systems are those which have at least an element of feedback or causal circularity in their development. In a linear system, the flow of causality runs only one way; with any given input, we have a predictable output. The state of a nonlinear system at any given time cannot be determined simply by our knowledge of the state of some exterior input; it will always be in part a function of its own preceding state. Every event in a nonlinear system feeds back into the future development of the entire system, or as James Gleick puts it: "Nonlinearity means that the act of playing the game has a way of changing the rules" (Gleick, 24).

Lucretius's storm at sea is a canonical example of the chaotic system. Weather is not the predictable end product of a given input; in fact, the input (the sun's heat and the earth's rotation) is fairly stable, but the output varies wildly—disorder emerges from order. This is because every effect within the atmosphere becomes, in turn, a cause of new effects. Arbitrarily small effects have a tendency to take on a life of their own under feedback amplification. This is the famous "butterfly effect," or sensitive dependence on initial conditions—the recognition that an event as minute as the flap of a butterfly wing might be the difference between the occurrence or nonoccurrence of a storm half the world and many iterations of the feedback loop away.

Classical, Newtonian science holds that we could master the unpredictability and destructive violence of weather if we could gather sufficient information about the current state of the atmosphere and the ocean so as to predict the development of the weather with the same accuracy that we predict the movements of heavenly bodies. The extreme version of this belief, championed in the eighteenth century by Pierre Simon de Laplace, was that with sufficient knowledge the future of the entire universe would become a simple sequence of inevitable consequences: "The present state of the system of nature is evidently a consequence of what it was in the preceding moment, and if we conceive of an intelligence which at a given instant comprehends all the relations of the entities of this universe, it could state the respective positions, motions, and general affects of all these entities at any time in the past or future" (qtd. in Crutchfield et al., 48). The insight chaos science gives us, however, is that our inability to predict the weather is not a reflection of our limited ability to gather relevant data, but a fundamental fact of nonlinear dynamic systems. No matter how precise our information about the current state of the system, our ability to predict its future development will be limited; significant information will always lie below the scale of our measurement. This is true even of such apparent areas of Newtonian triumph as the motion of the planets: "[A]n error as small as 15 metres in measuring the position of the Earth today would make it impossible to predict where the Earth would be in its orbit in just over 100 million years' time" (Carl Murray, 106). It is important to understand that this is an absolute fact about the system, not merely a mechanical limitation to the precision of measurement or, as Laplace assumed, a result of "the weakness of the human mind" (qtd. in Crutchfield et al., 48); any arbitrarily precise description of the state of the system will be an approximation, and in "rounding off" it will be forced to ignore significant differences that will soon dramatically and disproportionally affect the future history of the system (Rae, 105).

Another way of considering the same characteristic of such systems is that any complete description of their state at a given time would be fractal—that is to say, infinitely detailed. The finer the scale of the description, the more information would be revealed, with no convergence to a limit. The basic rationale of the scientific method is, if not exactly defeated, baffled here; "looking closer" or describing the phenomenon more precisely does not bring us proportionally closer to an ideal, "complete" understanding of the phenomenon but opens ever new realms of unassimilable data. Two meteorologists trying to decide if Tuesday a month from today will be a good day to go down to the shore to experience the Lucretian *suave mari magno* will get different answers according to the detail of their information. That is no surprise for traditional science, of course, but as they increase that detail, as their data collection occurs on finer and finer scales, their predictions will not tend to converge on an increasingly certain outcome; the storm will appear and disappear from the projected future histories of the weather system in a "chaotic" random sequence. More detail changes our understanding of the world; it does not necessarily refine it. A nonlinear world is one that is so complex that no two descriptions of it, even if they are commensurable, are likely to be identical.

One corollary of this infinite complexity is that it not only imposes a "rounding off" on our attempts to represent and understand the world, it imposes a "rounding off" even on real-world physical interactions.[7] Consider a classic example of complex interactions: a number of balls colliding on a frictionless billiard table. This system is nonlinear, despite the apparent linearity of this very Newtonian model, because, as the balls interact, circular paths of causality—pockets of turbulence—will be established as kinetic energy is eventually passed back to the ball that originally possessed it. Imagine that one starts with six blue balls at one end of the table and six red at the other end, and then simultaneously imparts to each ball a different velocity. It is not hard to imagine the result; blue and red balls will soon be randomly distributed over the whole surface of the table. According to Laplace's understanding of the world, if we instantaneously reversed the velocities of each of those balls—or, in other words, reversed the arrow of time in the physical equations describing their movement—we would eventually see all the blue and red balls separate from each other and gather (momentarily) at the opposite ends of the table in their original starting positions. Chaos science tells us that this is not what would happen. In the complex, nonlinear, interactions of the balls on the table, arbitrarily small errors would multiply through the system, sending the balls into the same entropic, randomizing flux into which they originally degenerated.

Error is unavoidable here because one ball colliding with another cannot possibly convey with *infinite* precision all the information of velocity and trajectory it "contains"; there will always be an element, no matter how minute, of approximation in any physical transmission of kinetic energy (at a subatomic level, quantum physics suggests that that energy exists in discrete units [quanta] that by definition cannot represent infinite degrees of variation; see Prigogine and Stengers, *La nouvelle alliance*, 293–320; Coveney, 210; Stewart, 295).[8] Classical physics' assumption of the arbitrariness of time's arrow in real-world physical interactions proves false. As Ilya Prigogine and Isabelle Stengers put it: "[P]our certains types de systèmes, l'idée d'une détermination infiniment précise des conditions initiales, nécessaire pour la définition d'une trajectoire, n'est pas seulement une idéalisation, mais encore une idéal-

---

7. This is not an uncontroversial claim—there are few in chaos science—and I should specify that in making it I am drawing principally on Prigogine and Stengers' arguments (see 295ff. and 400ff.). However, the example of the billiard balls that follows is suggested by Crutchfield et al. (48–49).

8. For a dissenting argument from a chaos theory perspective, see Cohen and Stewart, 251–60, and Ruelle, *Chance and Chaos*, chap. 18.

isation inadéquate. Dès ce moment, le fait que nous ne connaissions *jamais* une trajectoire mais un ensemble de trajectoires dans l'espace des phases n'est plus seulement une manière plus prudente d'exprimer les limites de notre connaissance, mais le point de départ d'une manière nouvelle de concevoir la description dynamique" (*La nouvelle alliance,* 321).[9]

This conception of the world can be seen as pessimistic. We have stumbled onto the second law of thermodynamics by an alternative route; information is constantly lost, entropy increases with time. No matter how well ordered the initial state of the system, the proliferation of error will ensure that that ordering information is eventually lost; the "far goal of time" appears to be Diderot's "grand sédiment inerte et immobile," or entropic heat death.

Within a system that is globally entropic, however, it is possible to find open-ended, negentropic subsystems that do not obey the second law of thermodynamics. Such systems are known as "dissipative systems" because their negentropic drive toward increased organization and complexity is fed by increasing the entropy of the total system. Life on earth, for example, which has become increasingly complex over millennia of evolution, can only do so through feeding on the dissipating energy of the sun; it is ultimately doomed to the same entropic goal as the sun, but in the meantime continues its negentropic process. Turbulence is such a dissipative structure. A turbulent flow is globally entropic—the system represented by the stable laminar flow that precedes turbulence is rapidly lost in a jumble of conflicting currents—but locally one can see the eddies and swirls of turbulence as creations of order, as the appearance of new, albeit unstable, systems. The same inevitable errors that deface and dissipate the initial conditions of the system also open a window for innovation. The same feedback loops that magnify and propagate errors also generate robust, if temporary, subsystems out of those initial deviations. Once again, Lucretius's storm is a good example. All "weather systems" are turbulence—quasi-independent subsystems within the global atmospheric system. The storm may be, from one perspective, an epiphenomenon of entropic decay, but that is not the perspective of those who experience it. For them, it

9. "[I]t can be shown that *for certain types of systems* an infinitely precise determination of initial conditions leads to a self-contradictory procedure. Once this is so, the fact that we never know a single trajectory but a group, an ensemble of trajectories in phase space, is not a mere expression of the limits of our knowledge. It becomes a starting point of a new way of investigating dynamics" (*Order out of Chaos,* 261).

is a positive *event* that, as Lucretius demonstrates, carries its own freight of meaning.

From this perspective, then, rather than lament the loss of initial information, it is possible to value the creativity of a chaotic system. The richness of the storm's symbolic freight in *De rerum natura* is a direct correlative of its chaotic unpredictability. This is the point around which crystallize most of chaos science's claims to mark a paradigmatic shift from the concerns of classical physics. In a Laplacean world—a world with no entropy—the absolute conservation of initial information also means that the system produces no information; once set up and running, a Laplacean system has nothing new to tell us, and a sufficiently well-informed observer in a Laplacean world would have no reason to keep observing that world. Present corresponds to past; future corresponds to present with absolute conservation of detail: "[L]a nature désignée par la dynamique classique est l'héritière de la puissance du Dieu créateur. Elle 'se connaît elle-même' avec une précision positivement infinie. Elle correspond à l'image insomniaque d'un musée monstrueux, incapable de produire la moindre distinction, d'oublier le moindre détail, répétition maniaque de ce qui a été dans ce qui est" (Prigogine and Stengers, *La nouvelle alliance,* 25).[10]

This world is Coleridge's infinite I AM, an elaboration through time of the single truth of the system's initial condition and its consequences. The "répétition maniaque," like the neurotic repetition compulsion Freud relates to the death instinct, is a denial of the possibility of innovation. Serres contrasts Lucretian science with a classical science whose "ordre des raisons est répétitif. Le savoir ainsi enchaîné, itératif infiniment, n'est que science de mort. Science de choses mortes et stratégie de mise à mort. L'ordre des raisons est martial. . . . Les lois sont les mêmes partout, elles sont thanatocratiques. Il n'y a rien à savoir, à découvrir, à inventer, dans le répétitif" (*La naissance,* 136).[11]

On the other hand, "a chaotic trajectory, from a given initial condition, is a nonrepeatable experiment" (Stewart, 289). "Chaos [is] the creation of information": "As the system becomes chaotic . . . strictly by

10. "Nature as understood by classical dynamics is the inheritor of the power of God the creator. It 'knows itself' with a positively infinite precision. It corresponds to the insomniac image of a monstrous museum, incapable of producing the least distinction, of forgetting the smallest detail, a maniacal repetition of what has been in what is" (my translation).

11. "order of reasons is repetitive, and the train of thought that comes from it, infinitely iterative, is but a science of death. A science of dead things and a strategy of the kill. The order of reasons is martial. . . . The laws are the same everywhere; they are thanatocratic. There is nothing to be learned, to be discovered, to be invented, in this repetitive world" ("Lucretius: Science and Religion," 100).

virtue of its unpredictability, it generates a steady stream of information. Each new observation is a new bit. This is a problem for the experimenter trying to characterize the system completely, 'He could never leave the room,' as Shaw said. 'The flow would be a continuous source of information' " (Gleick, 260). For Prigogine and Stengers, this condition of never being able to leave the room is the sign of a radically changed understanding of the role of the scientist vis-à-vis the natural world. The same infinite complexity and resultant erosion of information that leads to entropic indifferentiation is for them the guarantee of a continually surprising and undetermined future: "[L]'instant [est] la mémoire du passé, mais non pas sa mémoire intégrale car cette mémoire, comme toute description, n'articule que des informations de précision finie; corrélativement cet instant désigne un avenir essentiellement ouvert" (*La nouvelle alliance,* 25).[12] This means abandoning much of classical science's orientation toward predictive power as the hallmark of serious science. Chaotic indeterminacy introduces history to science: "La définition d'un état, au-delà du seuil d'instabilité, n'est plus intemporelle. Pour en rendre compte, il ne suffit plus d'évoquer la composition chimique et les conditions aux limites. En effet, que le système soit dans *cet* état singulier n'en est plus déductible, d'autres états lui étaient également accessibles. La seule explication est donc historique, ou génétique: il faut décrire le chemin qui constitue le passé du système, énumérer les bifurcations traversées et la succession des fluctuations qui ont décidé de l'histoire réelle parmi toutes les histoires possibles" (231).[13]

In Lucretius we find an atomistic understanding of both natural and historical process that is suggestive for extending the conceptual framework of chaos theory into areas of direct interest for the humanities. Serres asks us to reconsider the Lucretian *clinamen* not as Bloom's oedipal break with the past but as an acknowledgment of entropy. The *clinamen,* Serres argues, springs from the same reasoning that proposes the atom as a limit to our ability to divide matter. The *clinamen* is a deviation from a certain trajectory—most famously, the constant flow/

12. "Any given moment [is] the memory of the past, but not its complete memory—because that memory, like all descriptions, can only convey information of finite precision. Correlatively, the given moment indicates an essentially open future" (my translation).

13. "The definition of state, in far-from-equilibrium conditions, is no longer atemporal. To give an accurate account of it, it is no longer sufficient to describe the chemical composition and the limiting conditions of the system. In fact, that the system is in *this* particular state is no longer deducible from them; other states were equally accessible. The only explanation is therefore historical, or genetic: it is necessary to describe the path that constitutes the history of the system, to enumerate the bifurcations traversed and the succession of fluctuations that have decided the actual history among all the possible histories" (my translation).

fall of atoms that precedes the creation of the world. To define a trajectory with absolute precision, it must be possible to distinguish it from
any other trajectory. In reality, however, there is always a limit to our
ability to distinguish different trajectories as the difference between
them becomes very small. For Lucretius, the name of this limit is the
clinamen—the irreducible range of play or deviation in a flow of
atoms. Lucretius agrees with Prigogine and Stengers that "nous ne connaissions *jamais* une trajectoire mais un ensemble de trajectoires dans
l'espace des phases";[14] the crucial congruence with contemporary chaos
science is that this irreducible element of play in physical trajectories,
like the irreducible, *insécable* remnant of material that is the atom, is
not merely a limit to the precision of our perception or to our ability to
slice extremely small pieces of matter, but a recognition of the finite
precision of real physical processes. Neither *clinamen* nor atom is supposed to be a fundamental, measurable minimum. As Elizabeth Asmis
emphasizes in her *Epicurus' Scientific Method,* the *clinamen* represents
a deviation of "'no more than the least' (*nec plus quam minimum*)"
(279). It represents an arbitrary but ineradicable limit in real-world
physical precision (see Asmis, 278–80).

For Serres, the origin of this argument is in early Greek attempts to
develop an infinitesimal calculus (17ff.). The goal of such a calculus is to
define the angle of the tangent to a curve. It is a problem that naturally
raises the question of the limits of the precision with which we can
define an angle. As one comes arbitrarily close to the point at which the
tangent touches the curve, the two lines come ever closer, but anything
less than infinite precision—which means any real-world precision—
will leave an "atom" of difference (Davies, 218–19). For Lucretius, the
same reasoning applies to a physical trajectory; the *clinamen* represents
the inevitability of deviance without infinite and absolute conservation
of information.

We think of "going off on a tangent" as maximal error, as being as far
from the original trajectory as possible, but imagine attempting to move
in a perfect circle in the real world; it takes literally infinite precision to
distinguish the circle from the tangent at any given point. A very short
distance along the tangent, however, and one's error becomes dramatically obvious; one has moved into quite a different space. Circle, *clinamen,* and resulting tangent illustrate sensitive dependence on initial conditions. Arbitrarily small errors have consequences out of all proportion
to their magnitude.

14. "we never know a single trajectory but a group, an ensemble of trajectories in phase
space" (*Order out of Chaos,* 261).

In the therapeutic argument, memory takes the form of a circle—either the idealist hermeneutical circle of Absolute Knowing or the organic historical circle of Burke's social contract between past and future generations and Coleridge's collation of past and present. From this perspective, the *clinamen* must be read either as a self-deluded step in the oedipal circle of reiterating the past, which is how Bloom reads it, or as sheer loss, Hegel's unthinkable fury of destruction. On the other hand, the antitherapeutic decision to "choose death" takes the form of a tangential atomistic erasure and confusion of those mnemonic circles. In *De rerum natura* we move beyond this simple opposition for the first time, and find these two perspectives united. The Lucretian *clinamen,* like the antitherapeutic one we considered earlier, is an antioedipal one. It is a point of entry for death, as loss of information, into a system, and to that extent an assault on memory, not its unrecognized continuation. But at the same time, its most interesting and original properties depend upon its relationship to the constant creation and deformation of reiterative circles.

The Lucretian *clinamen* is, like chaotic entropy, not only a path to disorder, but, in conjunction with the turbulent cycles of nature, a motor for the creation of new order as well; indeed, according to the *De rerum natura,* the *clinamen* is the origin of life on earth, of anything more complex than the undifferentiated flux of atoms. Lucretius rejects a Laplacean world in which "all movement is always interconnected, the new arising from the old in a determinate order" (67, 2.251–52); such a "répétition maniaque de ce qui a été dans ce qui est" is, to him, sterile and uncreative. Without the "play" in the system represented by the *clinamen,* there is only the monotony of the infinitely predictable.

At the same time, however, Lucretius insists that the universe of atoms is a closed system. This means that the errors introduced by the *clinamen* must feed back into the development of the whole: "[Y]our finite class of atoms, if once you posit such a thing, [will] be scattered and tossed about through all eternity by conflicting tides of matter. They could never be swept together so as to enter into combination; nor could they remain combined or grow by increment" (76, 2.560–64). Being "swept together" so as to "remain combined" and "grow by increment" is chaotic creativity, the emergence of robust, negentropic dissipative structures within a globally entropic closed system. The *clinamen* emerges in the linkage of cause and effect, past and present, and causes the circle to deviate onto one of its tangents, but the reiterative, circular impulse remains. Causes are not totally divorced from their effects—the *clinamen* is not a ghost in the Laplacean machine—but no effect is the complete and only possible expression of its cause. The

260 Shelley and the Chaos of History

present still emerges from the past, only now with a constant accumulation of atomistic error. The *clinamen* does not disperse the stream of atoms but creates an eddy within it: "C'est l'angle minimum de formation d'un tourbillon, apparaissant aléatoirement sur un flux laminaire" (Serres, *La naissance,* 14).[15]

Lucretius's insight, increasingly corroborated by contemporary chaos science, is that natural cycles are rarely the balanced, homeostatic ones that underlie the organicist metaphors of therapeutic conservatism: "[S]i ces circulations sont des cercles parfaits, alors le mouvement trouve son équilibre, le monde est immortel, il passe à l'éternité. C'est le coup de génie de la physique des atomes: il n'y a pas de cercle, il n'y a que des tourbillons. Pas de bouclage exact, pas de circonférence pure, des spirales qui se décalent, qui s'érodent" (Serres, *La naissance,* 74; see 64ff.).[16] Hence Lucretius's interest in "meteors," those unpredictable phenomena like lightning and thunder, which, in their randomness and abruptness, "dramatisent la variable fondamentale de la physique."[17] The natural cycle and the meteoric deviation are "[d]eux temps pensés pour la première fois ensemble, équilibre et déséquilibre évalués pour la première fois l'un par rapport à l'autre" (110).[18] Serres points out that "au livre II, précédent immédiatement la description du *clinamen,* l'éclair et la foudre précipitent leur flamme et traversent les raies de la pluie de leur vol oblique (*transversosque volare per imbris fulmina, nunc hinc, nunc illinc,* ici et là)" (102 n. 1).[19] He notes elsewhere that the *nunc hinc, nunc illinc,* is immediately echoed in the description of the appearance of the *clinamen: incerto tempore, incertisque locis.* By yoking together the therapeutic circle and the antitherapeutic "physique des atomes," Lucretius offers us, in Serres's words, a "théorème du monde" that goes well beyond the simple oppositions we began with: "[N]i le néant ni l'éternité. Ni droite ni cercle. Ni écoulement laminaire ni cycle stable. La nature, c'est à dire la naissance, c'est à dire la mort, cst la

---

15. "It is the minimum deviation for the formation of an eddy, appearing in an aleatory manner in a laminar flux" (my translation).

16. "If these circulations are perfect circles, then the movement finds its equilibrium, the world is immortal, it passes on into eternity. This is the stroke of genius of atomic physics: there is no circle, there are only eddies; no perfect closure of the loop, no pure circumference; instead, spirals that are always offset, that continually decay" (my translation).

17. "dramatize the fundamental variability of physics" (my translation).

18. "two orders of time conceived for the first time together—equilibrium and disequilibrium evaluated for the first time in their relationship to each other" (my translation).

19. "in book II, immediately preceding the description of the *clinamen,* the lightning and the thunderbolt throw down their flame and cross the lines of rain with their oblique flight (*transversosque volare per imbris fulmina, nunc hinc, nunc illinc,* here and there)" (my translation).

droite inclinée par l'angle qui produit un tourbillon global, que l'usure du temps ramène à la droite. Ni cercle ni droite, tout est instable et stable à la fois" (74).[20]

"C'est à dire la naissance, c'est à dire la mort": Lucretius's turbulent world, our world, is one that tends constantly to decay, a world in which death atomistically erodes the most stable and vital structures. It is a world, as James Nichols puts it in his study of Epicurean political philosophy, that "is not something permanent and secure but is exposed—and we and all things are likewise exposed with it—to immense forces of destruction that will assail the world at some unforeseeable moment" (114). Serres points out that the cataclysmic plague in Athens that Lucretius describes in vivid detail at the end of his poem haunts the whole work as an entropic destiny for all the complex, unstable systems that chaotic creativity has thrown up. At the same time, however, the storm of turbulence throws out the infant child as the storm of sea throws the shipwrecked sailor on the shore—born from the waves like Venus, who, we are told at the very beginning of the poem, instills into the "breasts of one and all" a "passionate longing [to] reproduce their several breeds" (27, 1.19–20). Reproductive reiteration makes the *clinamen* as much creative spark as atom of death. Lucretian flux is Schlegel's chaos: "that confusion out of which a world can arise" (see Segal, 195–96).[21]

We can find an admirably lucid model for this optimistic, negentropic chaos in Diderot's *Rêve,* alongside his pessimistic fear of an entropic sediment. Dr. Bordeu extracts the kernel of truth from the "extravagante supposition" of the man who "se résout . . . en une infinité d'hommes animalcules": "Si l'homme ne se résout pas en une infinité d'hommes, il se résout du moins en une infinité d'animalcules dont il est impossible de prévoir le métamorphoses et l'organisation future et dernière. Qui sait si ce n'est pas la pépinière d'une seconde génération d'êtres séparée de celle-ci par un intervalle incompréhensible de siècles et de développements successifs?" (187).[22] All the elements of chaotic creativity

20. "Neither nothingness nor eternity. Neither the straight line nor the circle. Neither a laminar flow nor a stable cycle. Nature—which is to say birth, which is to say death—is the straight line deviating by the angle that produces an eddy in the entire system, which in turn is returned to the straight line by the vicissitudes of time. Neither circle nor straight line, everything is unstable and stable at once" (my translation).

21. Segal's *Lucretius on Death and Anxiety* offers an account of the role of death in the Lucretian physical world that is very similar to mine.

22. Man may not divide up into myriads of men, but at any rate he does break up into myriads of minute creatures whose metamorphoses and future and final state are impossible to foresee. "Who knows whether this is not the breeding-ground of another generation of beings separated from this one by an inconceivable interval of successive centuries and modifications?" (*D'Alembert's Dream,* 172–73).

are here: the infinite, fractal detail that ensures that significant differences fall below any scale of observation and makes it "impossible de prévoir le métamorphoses et l'organisation future et dernière"; the cyclic, venereal "développements successifs" that reiterate and multiply these microscopic, atomic differences to generate an unpredictable, macroscopic future; and the realization that nature's apparently homeostatic cycles, such as reproduction, are in fact open-ended, turbulent, and creative. It is not surprising that a recent study of Diderot's writings from the point of view of information circuits should remark upon the similarities between Diderot's vision of the natural world and that revealed in the writings of Serres and of Prigogine and Stengers (de la Carrera, 3–4).[23]

Diderot, however, seems not to have realized the equivalence of entropy and the creation of information. The infinitesimal, atomistic richness of detail that makes the human body a "seedbed" of future potential is the same chaotic confusion that guarantees the constant generation of error. The reproductive cycles that develop the animalcule into a complex species are also those which magnify and propagate errors throughout a system until it collapses into an inert sediment. Growth is error seen sufficiently close-up, the locally negentropic moment within the globally entropic system. This is the Lucretian solution to the problem of the reemergence of the "trace in the sand" from atomistic obliteration. The grains of sand within the wave, like atoms within turbulent flow, are swept into the semistable structures of turbulent cycles that produce local differences—and therefore traces, meaning—within the global chaotic erasure.

CHAOS IN HISTORY

The question that still remains is how we can apply this to social systems in general and to literature in particular. Lucretius has little to say on the latter subject, but he provides us with a suggestive sketch of the history of civilization that shows us how we can steer a course between the therapeutic and antitherapeutic versions of history.

The key issue is the role of error in history—error in the reproduc-

23. Lyotard (*The Inhuman*, 45–46) also points out the connections between Diderot, Lucretius, and the new understanding of "complexity in the universe."

tion of the past in the present. From the antitherapeutic perspective this is straightforward; error is not only inevitable but essential; the atomistic model of society ensures that death in the form of lost structural information pervades the social system, erasing the past by breaking the threads of continuity that bind us to it. From a therapeutic perspective the issue is more complex. In theory, error should not occur; the reproductive cycle of past and present should be conservative. In practice, we find writers such as Burke, Coleridge, and Hegel exhorting us to root out the errors that inexplicably infest the reproductive process; we think of Coleridge's advocacy of the "habit of thoughtfully assimilating the events of our own age to those of the time before us" and Burke's injunction to "make the reparation as nearly as possible in the style of the building" (*Lay Sermons,* 9; *Reflections,* 375).

Burke's image suggests that reproductive errancy is accidental—in the full sense of that word. Some error may be inevitable in this sublunary world, but the role of the historical cycle is perpetually to correct it; the cycle of historical reproduction, like the hermeneutical cycle, is homeostatic; the function of both cycles is to eliminate the accidental and confirm the essential. Lucretius also uses the example of repairing a building to demonstrate his model of history, although with a quite different intent. As Serres emphasizes, Lucretius constantly underlines the fragility and susceptibility of all human structures: "Je ne cesse de réparer le toit sous lequel j'habite, de redresser les failles et de le mettre hors d'eau" (*La naissance,* 110).[24] Error is not the accidental exception in Lucretius's world but the rule; houses are subject to a constant entropic pressure as they stand up to an equally constant meteorological assault: "[L]'édifice, la terre et le monde s'effondrent, la ville, ensemble de maisons construites, est détruite: c'est la peste d'Athènes. La fin prévue et prévisible, préparée dès la poutre qui pend du toit en ruines" (110).[25]

Nonetheless, in book 5 Lucretius describes a history of human civilization that pursues a markedly negentropic drive toward greater and greater complexity. The motor of this evolutionary trend is the very cycle of error-and-reparation that Burke hoped would prove homeostatic. Lucretius's realization is that "[l]es correctifs, les réparations, les contrepoids . . . manquent le plus souvent leur but de compensation"

24. "I never cease to repair the roof I live beneath, to fix its cracks, to keep it away from the water" (my translation).

25. "The building, the earth, and the world collapse; the city, a collection of constructed dwellings, is destroyed: it is the plague of Athens. The end that was foreseen and foreseeable, prepared for ever since that beam which hung from the ruined roof" (my translation).

(Serres, *La naissance,* 221).[26] In attempting to repair the building, we create something new; the error is picked up in the cycle of social reproduction, and the course of history is nudged onto a tangential course; the circle of history becomes a spiral:

> Cela ne fait pas cercle, puisque la solution est toujours originale et neuve, puisque le décalage est toujours là, puisque l'inclinaison réapparaît toujours, puisque le temps de la dérive est le fond de l'entraînement. Cela ne fait pas cercle, autrement l'équilibre serait rétabli, nous serions victorieux de la dérive, il n'y aurait pas d'histoire. Cela fait cercle, cependent, pour l'ensemble des processus de la causalité. Une circulation, cause-effet en retour, descend la pente du déclin, en élargissant ses voies de compensation et de chute; cela décrit une spirale sans cesse en écart sur elle-même, une turbination qui, en avançant, cherche et perd toujours l'équilibre. (222)[27]

This is what Serres calls the "*solution tourbillonaire* [to the problem of history] . . . rigoureusement isomorphe à la genèse naturelle à partir du chaos" (222–23).[28] As in the chaotic system, error in the cycles of historical reproduction is the ambivalent origin of both degradation and creativity. The progress of civilization from huts to palaces in book 5 of *De rerum* is a history of errors becoming essence. Huts are invented to supplement the crude "coverlet of leaves and branches" (200, 5.972) used by primitive, presocietal peoples to keep them warm at night. The huts, however, change the nature of the beings who inhabit them, generating new needs and a new degree of social complexity (202, 5.1011–27). It also "mellows" them, so that they need fire for warmth. Fire "and

26. "correctives, repairs, counterweights . . . most often fail to be exactly compensatory" (my translation). Serres' exposition of Lucretius's chaotic solution to the problem of history can hardly be improved upon, and I am drawing on it heavily here (*La naissance,* 214–26).

27. "This process does not form a circle, because the solution is always original and new, because the offset is always there, because the angle of error always reappears, because the basis of the process is time-as-deviation [time that produces error]. This process does not form a circle, otherwise equilibrium would be restored, we would be victorious over deviation [drift/error], and there would be no history. This process does form a circle, however, for the processes of causality considered as a whole. A circulation, cause-effect in return, descends the slope of the decline, broadening its paths of compensation and descent; this process describes a spiral constantly in diversion from itself, a vortex that, in its progress, perpetually seeks and perpetually loses equilibrium" (my translation).

28. "*vortical solution* [to the problem of history] . . . rigorously isomorphic with the natural process of creation from chaos" (my translation).

other new inventions" (205, 5.1106-7) in turn change their "old way of life" (205, 5.1105) so much as to lead to the institution of "kings" and the founding of cities (205, 5.1108-9). Kings in turn demand the building of "citadels" to defend their power and prestige (205, 5.1109). King-ship leads to tyranny, and tyranny to revolt: "So the kings were killed" (206, 5.1136). Revolt leads to mob rule, and disgust with mob rule to the founding of constitutions and "fixed rights and recognized laws" (206, 5.1143-44). At each stage the attempt to repair a perceived error in the present state of things leads, through a feedback loop, or spiral, of historical development, to a new "stage" of social complexity: *"La dérive produit la réparation qui produit la dérive"* (Serres, *La nais-sance,* 222).[29] Long before Darwin, Lucretius has discovered that the twin motors of evolution are mutation and reproduction: "Il découvre l'efficace de la fluctuation au hasard, et de l'écart à l'équilibre: un temps déborde l'autre, est débordé par lui. Lucrèce découvre la croissance de la complexité, lorsque l'écart réapparaît au cours des cycles de retour à l'équilibre" (223).[30] In Lucretius's words: "It is . . . discontent that has driven life steadily onward" (215, 5.1434-35): "For what we have here and now, unless we have known something more pleasing in the past, gives the greatest satisfaction and is reckoned the best of its kind. After-wards the discovery of something new and better blunts and vitiates our enjoyment of the old. . . . In this, I do not doubt, the greater blame rests with us. . . . [M]ankind is perpetually the victim of a pointless and futile martyrdom, fretting life away in fruitless worries through failure to real-ize what limit is set to acquisition and to the growth of genuine plea-sure" (214-15, 5.1412-33).

Lucretius's point is not that we "progress" to something "new and better" but that our interpretation of our mode of life is inherently un-stable; the hermeneutical and historical cycles never become homeo-static. Jean Salem makes the point that this history is neither "progres-sive" nor "regressive" (neither Condorcet nor Rousseau [199-202]). It is not a providential history that follows a narrative, but an evolutionary history of continual contingent change: "[À] tous les stades du devenir, l'humanité avance simultanément, même si c'est parfois d'un pas inégal, sur la voie du bien et sur celle du mal" (202).[31] There always appears to be

29. *"Deviation produces correction, which produces deviation"* (my translation).

30. "He discovers the efficacy of random fluctuations, and of the deviation from equilib-rium: one order of time overthrows the other, and is overthrown by it in its turn. Lucretius discovers the growth of complexity when the deviation reappears in the cyclical return to equilibrium" (my translation).

31. "At all stages of development, humanity advances simultaneously—even if sometimes

some error, some *écart,* that demands repair, but that repair never fully supplements lack: "Il découvre ceci que seul l'insuffisant est productif. Mais que la production ramène l'insuffisance" (Serres, *La naissance,* 223).[32] What emerges here is a fractal model of society; it is a recognition that the social or cultural "context" is so richly detailed that any two definitions of it—whether proffered by two different observers simultaneously or the same observer over time—will be significantly different. The "reparation" cannot be Burke's simple error correction because it is impossible to define with infinite, and therefore final, precision the boundaries of our "discontent." Any "solution"—the hut as a solution to the chill of the night, or the citadel as a solution to the security of the king—contains a *clinamen,* an "atom" of social practice whose significance is invisible until it enters into and is magnified by the cycle of social reproduction. As Salem puts it: "[C]haque progrès de techniques humaines est-il présenté par Lucrèce comme le fruit d'une *découverte,* bien plus que d'une *invention.* De même que les dieux eussent été radicalement incapables de desseins providentiels à l'égard de ce monde . . . la technique humaine prouve avec une parfaite constance qu'*on ne peut jamais avoir de notion que de ce qui existe*" (194–95).[33] The "solution tourbillonaire" to historical process, then, is chaotic creativity. The atomistic, fractal detail of social forms leads to an entropic erasure of initial conditions, but that loss of information becomes generative of a new system state as it feeds back into a reiterative, reproductive cycle.

We constantly attempt to reproduce the past in the present; every reaffirmation of a significant relationship (meaning anything from turning up at your job in the morning to nursing your baby), every social or political continuity (from the continued existence of the institutions of representative government in my country to the continued existence of the buildings that house them), far from being simple stasis, is a dy-

---

unevenly—along the path of good and that of evil" (my translation). See also Nichols, 127–28. For a very different account of Lucretian "social evolution," see Asmis, 57–60. For an argument that biological evolution is precisely a "narrative," see Argyros, "Narrative and Chaos," and for an interesting discussion of the question of "progress" from a chaos-science perspective, see Lewin, chap. 7.

32. "He discovers this: that only insufficiency is productive—but that productivity returns us to insufficiency" (my translation).

33. "Every technical progress made by humanity is presented by Lucretius as the product of a *discovery* far more than as that of an *invention.* In the same way that the gods had been radically incapable of providential planning with regard to the world . . . humankind's technical capacity proves with perfect consistency that *one can only conceive of what already exists*" (my translation).

namic equilibrium. From moment to moment a reproductive feedback cycle matching practice to memory and deriving memory from practice is in operation.

The problem, for those who desire continued social stability, is that there is always more "information" in a culture, or cultural practice, than we can accept, at any one time, as "significant." When we look at the past—which is to say, the present as it becomes memory—with the intention of reproducing it, we are confronted with too many raw, atomistic data to know where to begin. This is the problem of the fractal detail of lived experience; there is no end to the differences in our cultural and physical environment that *might* be invested with significance. In order to extract from this atomistic flux a recognizable "practice" with performable rules, it is necessary to limit the possibilities of meaningfulness, to "round off" or impose a "scale" according to which certain data are excluded as accidental "noise," while others are deemed essential. This is the process by which "one limits, excludes, and chooses" in a world of a "cancerous and dangerous proliferation of significations." Foucault's description of the role of the author function expresses this need for "a principle of thrift in the [atomistic] proliferation of meaning" ("What Is an Author," 159). Foucault's metaphor is particularly apt: a cancerous growth illustrates the principle of chaotic creativity. Information loss within a feedback loop, a *clinamen* in the reproduction of the complex DNA code, might be entropic from the perspective of the total organism, but only because of the negentropic vigor of the cancerous subsystem itself.

Burke would have endorsed the image of innovation as a cancer, a tumor to be removed in order to restore the body politic to health, just as a building is restored to its original form. In the chaotic creativity of social reproduction, however, there is no hard-and-fast distinction between the "tumors" and the "healthy organisms," between error and essence, or between parasite and host.

As Burke's and Lucretius's use of the image suggests, buildings, as relatively persistent cultural products, are an excellent example of the burden and legacy of the past. The conservation of the architectural heritage, and the resistance to radical architectural innovation—particularly at the expense of that heritage—are notable expressions in our contemporary society of the resistance to social change. Throughout architectural history, the return to the past has been a constantly renewed rallying cry of different architectural movements—from the "renaissance" of the classical ideal in fifteenth-century Florence to the scattergun approach to architectural allusion that constitutes part of contemporary postmodernism. That the richly detailed legacy of the past greatly exceeds any one attempt to define it, however, is demonstrated by the striking differences between the products of these different "revivals"; no one could mistake a Renaissance palazzo for an American neoclassical bank, and yet both would claim to be a "return" to classical sources. The definition of a "style" is an exercise in exclusion, like Foucault's author function; it is also perhaps the clearest example of the fractal nature of cultural "rules." If one wishes to do more than build replicas of extant classical buildings, one must select from all the different features of a range of roughly contemporary but very diverse buildings those features that one holds to be the essence of their common "style." This in turn allows one to generate a stylistic "language" with sufficient creative "play" that entirely new buildings can be created that are recognizably "in the same style." But while one critic may hold, like Ruskin, that "[o]rnamentation is the principal part of architecture" (*Lectures in Architecture* [1853], qtd. in Pevsner, 383) and therefore conceive the "return to the past" as the establishment of a stylistic lexicon of ornamental detail, another may argue, with Schopenhauer, that the "sole and constant theme" of architectural aesthetics is the honest expression of *"support and load"* and consequently conceive of the return to the past in terms of locating the ideal of structural legibility (2:411ff.). The buildings produced under each system will, in all likelihood, be radically different, though both may be "derived" from the same "style."

Another way of looking at the same point is that any attempt to generalize after the fact about a period or style in architecture—or for that matter in literature—is only valid at that particular scale of generality; no individual work from that period is able fully to exemplify it. In the aesthetic world, like the meteorological one, "looking closer" rarely settles arguments as much as it provides material for new ones; almost any aesthetic generalization will appear, on close examination, to be a law composed solely of exceptions, which does not prevent these laws-without-instances from being useful and usable at their proper scale.

The fractal excess of information or of potential significance over any possible reproductive "rule" that generates chaotic creativity is particularly visible in the eighteenth- and nineteenth-century appropriations of the Gothic aesthetic, heavily influential in the formation of both Romantic aesthetic theory in general and Shelley's antiorganicist aesthetics in particular. The popular taste for Gothic architecture in the eighteenth and nineteenth centuries particularly valued and strove to reproduce the quaint asymmetry of Gothic churches. The radically different towers of the Chartres cathedral façade constitute a familiar example. But this asymmetry, part of the "essence" of the Gothic for the enthusiasts of that period, was an "error" from the perspective of the twelfth-century designers of Chartres, who envisaged symmetrically balanced towers for the façade and could never have imagined the extravagant complexity of the Flamboyant north tower (an "improvement" from the perspective of its fifteenth-century builders).

Architecture is often such a palimpsest of stylistic *clinamina;* because of their persistence through time and their relatively slow realization, buildings often accumulate additions and alterations to their original design and are "finished" in a style different from that in which they were commenced. Humphrey Repton (1752–1818), the first "landscape gardener" to call himself such and also an architect, praised the "magnificent irregularity" of Gothic architecture on the grounds that it allowed for the vicissitudes that such "consumption" of a building over time visits upon the building as it issues from its context of production:

> When we look back a few centuries and compare the habits of former times with those of the present, we shall be apt to wonder at the presumption of any person who shall propose to build a house that may suit the next generation. Who, in the reign of Queen Elizabeth, would have planned a library, a music-room, a billiard-room, or a conservatory? Yet these are now deemed essential to comfort and magnificence: perhaps, in future ages, new rooms for new purposes will be deemed equally necessary. But to a house of perfect symmetry these can never be added: yet it is principally to these additions, during a long succession of years, that we are indebted for the magnificent irregularity and splendid intricacy observable in the neighbouring palaces of Knowle and Penshurst. Under these circumstances, that plan cannot be good which will admit of no alteration
> "Malum consilium est, quod non mutari potest."
> But in a house of this irregular character, every subsequent addition will increase the importance. (Repton, 215–16)

These "subsequent additions" are like the digressions of the Gothic novel, a "series of events" that are never transmuted by the organic miracle into a "Whole."[34] It might be easy, shortly after the addition or

34. It is important to distinguish here between the general understanding of the Gothic aesthetic and that of the more serious antiquarians who led the Gothic Revival. Pugin, for

alteration is made, to argue for its surgical removal on the model of Burke's simple error correction—"make the reparation as nearly as possible in the style of the building"—but as the palimpsest enters the cycles of history, the distinction between original and error becomes harder and harder to maintain; the "cancer" becomes the "body."

In the late nineteenth century churches would be "restored" to a state of aesthetic purity they had never attained in the past: "[Sir George Gilbert] Scott and his colleagues never minded replacing a genuine Perpendicular window by an imitation earlier one when they had to restore a church" (Pevsner, 384). As with Viollet-le-Duc's more famous "restorations" in France, the results could certainly be defended as "making a reparation in the style of the building," but many felt (and feel) that they were more innovation than renovation. As these "restored" buildings enter the cycles of architectural history and reproduction—particularly photographic reproduction—these alterations have become invisible to the majority, who assume that this is the way these buildings have always been. The nineteenth century's addition to the stylistic palimpsest comes to seem an integral part of the work; the restorer's "error" becomes "essence."

But errors-become-essence can as easily, and as unpredictably, become errors again; the example of the trashed Perpendicular window, valued by an earlier generation as an example of the Gothic's essential variety, demonstrates that. The development of architectural aesthetics is truly a history of chaotic creativity; each attempt to reproduce the past redefines what it is that should be reproduced. This applies not only to attempts to return to the distant past but, even more interestingly, to attempts to "continue on" from the work of one's more immediate precursors. The infinite information presented by an achieved work of architecture ensures a constant generation of "error" in the process of extrapolating rules for future conduct from any preexisting work.

Kirk Varnedoe has proposed a similar theory of chaotic creativity in his recent history of modern art (Varnedoe soft-pedals the relationship

---

example, who execrates the decorative appropriation of Gothic elements that typifies the Strawberry Hill style of Gothic architecture, in his 1843 *Apology* argues that a Gothic building must be conceived as an organic whole, a uniquely appropriate "expression" of a given program. He rails against his contemporary architects who "send two designs for the same building, of utterly opposed character and style, for the selection of the committee; as if it were possible for more than one principle to be a correct expression of the intended building" (2n). On the other hand, one of Ruskin's chief arguments in favor of Gothic over classical architecture in *The Stones of Venice* is precisely that the latter, constrained by rule and order, stifles creativity, while the former gives the architect creative freedom.

between his theory and chaos science, but he is aware of the parallels [see, e.g., 98–99]). Such an approach bypasses the traditional, and traditionally problematic, question of the "origins" of cultural innovation. Varnedoe's master metaphor for such innovation is William Webb Ellis's (probably apocryphal) "invention" of the game of rugby in 1823. Webb Ellis, "with a fine disregard for the rules of football as played in his time first took the ball in his arms and ran with it thus originating the distinctive feature of the Rugby game"—as the commemorative plaque at Rugby School has it (10). This is the chaotic *clinamen;* as Gleick puts it, nonlinearity means that "the act of playing the game has a way of changing the rules." Webb Ellis's gesture was not an external catastrophe that forced change upon a system; the soccer players of Rugby School did not suddenly grow arms and hands for the first time and have to find a way to incorporate them into their game. Rather, a universally shared capability—that of carrying the ball and running with it—which had been explicitly ruled out of the traditionally reproduced rules of football as an "error," was, through an inexplicable and undetermined *clinamen,* redefined and reproduced as "essence": "A gesture such as Webb Ellis's explains what followed from it a lot more convincingly than it is itself explained by what came before. Nothing we could know of the boy and his background, nor any account of the circumstances of the school, could independently suffice to rationalize the wonder at the core: a charmed moment of fertilization between a gesture that might otherwise have fallen on fallow ground and a receptive field that might otherwise have gone barren" (10). Innovation arises out of the infinite complexity of the tradition itself: "Almost any context, whether it is the intellectual field of nineteenth century science, or Darwin's ideas, or Paris in the 1880's—or for that matter, a given café at a given moment—offers an indefinably broad latitude for response. And any epoch's repertoire of available conventions of representation contains a similarly untidy variety of possible forms" (126).

A radically new understanding of the operation of memory begins to emerge here: memory as a motor for innovation in a complex system. We have been reading memory until now as an integral element in a rigid conservatism—social and otherwise. For such diverse thinkers as Deleuze, Freud, and Schlegel, memory represents a deathly repetition of the past, or the cycle of recuperative incorporation into a hermeneutical Absolute. But from a Lucretian perspective, memory is always as much productive as it is reproductive. The mistake of the antitherapeutic opposition to "memory" that takes the form of a liberation of consumption from the constraints of a context of production (Foucault's *qu'importe qui parle?*) is that it fails to realize that memory *is* consumption—in this case, the irreducibly errant consumption of "the tradition." The antitherapeutic "breach" between production and consumption is a misrecognized version of the Lucretian *clinamen*. What makes that breach important is not that it defeats memory—which it does only in the sense of an entropic approximation of detail—but that it diverts the cycles of memory onto a turbulent, chaotic path, a hermeneutical equivalent of the chaotic "strange attractor."

The strange attractor, also known as the "fractal attractor" because of the infinitely complex path it describes, is one of the key elements of chaos theory. It is a model of nonlinear creativity, the homeorhetic feedback cycle in which arbitrarily proximate trajectories rapidly and inevitably diverge, although confined within more or less stable, though unpredictable, parameters (hence "attractor"). The metaphor of homeostatic organicism that underlies therapeutic theories of hermeneutics is directly challenged by this, and nowhere more clearly than in our consumption of the literary work of art. If we accept the fact that texts are infinitely complex in the same way that "Darwin's ideas" or "a given café at a given moment" are—that the significance of texts is fractally dense, in other words—then the entry of the text into the cycles of memory, that cycle with which we are all familiar in the homeostatic hermeneutical version, should generate a homeorhetic strange attractor, a chaotic hermeneutics.[35]

The closest existing analogue for such a theory of interpretation is Lyotard's concept of *enchaînement*—expounded, principally, in his *Le différend*. This is not surprising; Lyotard proposes his theory as a first step in bringing our approach to language into conformity with the "révolution relativiste et quantique" in modern physics—the same "revolutions" that Serres, Prigogine, and others see founded in the physics of *De rerum natura* and intimately connected with the most dramatic implications of contemporary chaos theory. Quantum theory is the crucial blow to the Laplacean dream of an infinitely predictable world; it is the discovery, in the physical world, of "atomism" in the fully Lucretian sense, of an irradicable, and potentially entropic, degree of uncertainty in our most refined descriptions of the physical world. As David Albert

35. Argyros argues the contrary (*Blessed Rage for Order*, 307–22). He sees the robustness of the strange attractor as indicating a self-regulating permanence that redeems for us the idea of narrative totality. Moreover, he argues that the "progressive" nature of evolutionary process (what I have called "chaotic creativity") provides us with an organic analogue for literary narrative that establishes its coherence. In my view, he overstates the narrative coherence of evolutionary process, and the stability of chaotic systems, which is always unpredictable. I return to this point below.

argues, quantum theory tells us that there can be no scientific proof of
even a purely physical determinism (177).[36] The implication of the observer in all our measurements of physical states, in particular the role
of the observer in precipitating what is sometimes known as "collapse
of the wave function" (36–37), where multiple potential states of being[37]
must "collapse" into one observable reality, makes that reality an errant
history of absolute events. Alastair Rae, drawing on the work of Prigogine, makes the point that when we add the perspectives of chaos
theory to quantum physics, we see that only the irreversible event, only
the *absolute* "event," is truly part of the "fundamental reality" of our
world. That is, "fundamental reality is not . . . the existence of the
physical world, but the irreversible changes occurring in it—not 'being'
but 'becoming.' Reversible 'events' which by definition leave no permanent record are illusions—not just to us, but to the whole universe
which undergoes no irreversible change as a result of their 'occurrence' " (116–17). Lyotard wants to expand this acceptance of the genuine historicity of the world, of the inevitability of the *clinamen,* to the
realm of meaning.

What Lyotard has in mind is a hermeneutical analogy with the Heisenberg principle of indeterminacy. Such analogies have been attempted
before, but usually in the unconvincing form of a simplistic relativism.
What Lyotard observes is that meaning, the response to meaning, and
the production of new meanings in response to that response—the process that from the therapeutic perspective must be seen as an unbreakable cycle—is best understood, not as a linear transformation in which
the present state is a simple derivative of past conditions, but as a chain,
each link of which represents a moment of partial indeterminacy and
potential errancy. This could be described as a quantic theory of meaning, holding that meaning is not amenable to infinitely precise description. One can describe a range, or envelope, of possible "trajectories"
for it, even suggest which are more statistically probable, but one cannot determine its course with finality.

Lyotard describes this in terms of a conversation. This is a favorite
metaphor of ordinary-language philosophers, who hold that all cultural
pursuits can be understood as contributions to the continuing "conversation" a society embodies and enacts. Each contribution to the conversation can be judged as "successful" or "unsuccessful" ("happy" or "unhappy," to use Austin's words) depending on whether it keeps the

36. For a persuasive philosophical refutation of determinism, see Dupré, chap. 8.
37. Such as, most famously, the death or nondeath of Schrödinger's cat.

conversation alive. This would be considered maintaining, in Wittgenstein's phrase, a "form of life." Wittgenstein's model of socialization, and of all forms of learning, is learning "how to go on," how to join in and continue a conversation, or language game, already in progress. The therapeutic assumption underlying this is that each "happy" contribution to the conversation must maintain it; there can be no "happy" contribution that throws the conversation into entirely unexplored territory, because only those contributions conformable to the rules of the game "count." The rules, therefore, are constantly reinforced, and a "form of life" is perpetuated.

Lyotard calls all of this into question. For each "turn" in the cultural "conversation," he suggests, there are innumerable ways to respond—enchaîner—and each response diverts the course of the conversation relative to the other possibilities: "[I]l faut enchaîner, mais le mode d'enchaînement n'est jamais nécessaire" (Le différend, 52).[38] Language is not a totality that excludes all but "happy" contributions; it is a series of quasi-indeterminate, quantic, decisions, a fact with directly political implications: "[L]a politique consiste en ce que le langage n'est pas un langage mais des phrases" (200).[39] These atomistic phrases are so many potential sites for the clinamen, so many potential sites of revolution or political dispute, where the part (phrase) can overthrow the whole (langage): "Tout est politique si la politique est la possibilité du différend à l'occasion du moindre enchaînement" (201).[40]

In one very restricted sense, the view of the literary work of art as fractal has always prevailed in hermeneutical theory. Significantly, this is the sense in which "fractal" has caught the public imagination and is most readily being appropriated and understood beyond the scientific community: self-similarity across scales. Alexander Argyros's Blessed Rage for Order is a notable example; he uses self-similarity across scales to make chaos theory a chief support of a quasi-Hegelian philosophy that makes "information" a matrix for Absolute Knowing. Brady's "Rococo Butterfly meets the Butterfly Effect" similarly suggests that chaos theory allows us to discover a "concealed order" behind the apparently disordered (1535–36).[41] Certainly, this is the most dramatic aspect of

---

38. "It is necessary to link, but the mode of linkage is never necessary" (The Differend, 29).

39. "Politics consists in the fact that language is not a language, but phrases" (The Differend, 138).

40. "Everything is political if politics is the possibility of the differend on the occasion of the slightest linkage" (The Differend, 139).

41. Not that these theories are without support in the scientific community. There are "chaoticians" who see chaos as the next great "science of everything"; see, e.g., Rössler, "Future of Chaos."

fractal organization, the organization displayed by large numbers of natural objects and processes, from fern fronds to frost crystals to the bronchial tubes in the lung, in which the details, and the details of the details, are miniature versions of the structure as a whole. If taken to its logical extreme—the hologram is an oft-cited real-world example—this would mean infinite detail with infinite redundancy; the whole would be everywhere manifest in the minutest parts—like a human being composed of identical homunculi. Chaos theory becomes an alternative route to therapeutic idealism.

If we limit the analogy to certain very specific cases, it is possible to find in this kind of fractal organization a natural analogy with the therapeutic-organicist theory of the work of art. The analogy must, however, be restricted to those cases of fractal organization where the recession of scales is always subject to an evident hierarchy; there must always be an obvious "whole" that is reflected in the "parts," as in the case of a fern or a lung or a hologram. Such critical chestnuts as the claim that all of *Hamlet* is mirrored in its first few lines, or the whole of any poem, play, or novel in some one scene, speech, line, or even phrase, lend themselves to an analogy with fractal organization. The Gothic fragmentation implicit, as Diderot made clear, in a *Hamlet* composed of an infinitude of mini-*Hamlets* is kept at bay, in theory at least, by the total subordination of the parts to a clearly identified and integral whole. The details of the text are only important insofar as they "represent" the whole; otherwise they are easily dismissed as insignificant.

The necessity of combining a pronounced hierarchy of scales with the organicist metaphor is as old as the metaphor itself; when Aristotle attempts to describe the perfect organic plot, or "arrangement of parts," in his *Poetics,* he realizes that there must be some principle of limitation on his dictum that "the transposal or withdrawal of any one of them will disjoin and dislocate the whole": "Again: to be beautiful, a living creature, and every whole made up of parts, must not only present a certain order in its arrangement of parts, but also be of a certain definite magnitude. Beauty is a matter of size and order, and therefore impossible either (1) in a very minute creature, since our perception becomes indistinct as it approaches instantaneity; or (2) in a creature of vast size— one, say, 1,000 miles long—as in that case, instead of the object being seen all at once, the unity and wholeness of it is lost to the beholder" (*De Poetica,* 1462). There would be, according to this account, a point at which some parts become too small to worry about, their "transposal or withdrawal" a matter of indifference for the unity of the whole.

There are two closely related ways in which the nature of fractals must be artificially limited for them to serve as an analogy for therapeu-

tic organicism. First, self-similarity across scales is not a necessary feature of fractals; and even when self-similarity is present, it should not be
confused with self-identity; as John Briggs and David Peat point out,
although "[f]ractal self-similarity pervades the bodies of organisms . . . it
is not the blatant homunculus self-similarity that was imagined by earlier
science" (107). Second, true fractals do not permit any hierarchy of
scales. One of the most interesting and challenging aspects of the fractal
is that it allows *contradictions* between scales. Consider this account of
Mandelbrot's heuristic example of a ball of twine: "Then what is the
dimension of a ball of twine? Mandelbrot answered, It depends on your
point of view. From a great distance, the ball is no more than a point,
with zero dimensions. From closer, the ball is seen to fill spherical
space, taking up three dimensions. From closer still, the twine comes
into view, and the object becomes effectively one-dimensional. . . . And
on toward microscopic perspectives: twine turns to three-dimensional
columns, the columns resolve themselves into one-dimensional fibres,
the solid materials dissolve into zero-dimensional points" (Gleick, 97).
The answer to the apparently simple question, What is it? depends upon
how close we are standing; different scales of approach yield radically
different answers. Nor can it ever be obvious at what scale we are observing the "whole"; the ball of twine might be a part of some mega-
structure composed of other such balls; the "points" into which it dissolves may reveal similar complexity as we approach them. Like the
proverbial parasitic chain of fleas,[42] the recession of scales continues "ad
infinitum," and each scale is as significant, as rich in information, as any
higher or lower one.

Does such a model of literary significance actually resonate with our
experience of texts? It is certainly true of the writer's relationship to the
world. Aristotle bases his normative scale for the beautiful, unified
"plot" on an analogy with the supposedly self-evident "unity and wholeness" of the individual animal. But is there a natural and obvious scale at
which to observe an animal? As Edward Wilson puts it, "[I]n the fractal
world, an entire ecosystem can exist in the plumage of a bird" (198). A
student of animal behavior would argue that it is senseless to examine
the individual animal abstracted from its social group; from an evolutionary perspective it is the entire gene pool that is significant; from a
microbiologist's perspective the animal is a vast society of more or less
cooperating cellular organisms, most of which could live their lives in-

---

42. "Great fleas have little fleas upon their backs to bite 'em, / And little fleas have lesser
fleas, and so *ad infinitum*" (Augustus De Morgan, *A Budget of Paradoxes*, 1872).

dependent of that particular animal (the Frankenstein principle; Dupré, 44). No scalar recession has a necessary limit; one could move upward through wider and wider nets of ecosystems toward the Gaia hypothesis and beyond, or downward via Lyn Margulis's theory of individual cells as symbiotic communes of cooperative microbes toward the study of the molecular building blocks of those microbes (Margulis and Sagan; Lovelock). John Dupré makes this scalar recession both in time and space a key part of his argument for the necessity of a "promiscuous realism" in science, an argument that closely parallels my own with regard to literature. To examine the natural world from an ecological perspective is to put to it quite different questions from those one would pose if one were examining it from an evolutionary perspective. Not only the questions are different, but the very ontological stability of such categories as "species" or "genus" is put in question as one shifts from one perspective to the other (42–43).

The same is true of narrative "plot." The "unity" of events is imposed from outside; it is not inherent. What is the appropriate "scale" at which a story becomes "complete"? Is, say, an individual human life a "natural" scale? From the perspective of Fernand Braudel's *longue durée,* the period stretching from the fifteenth to the eighteenth century was remarkable for its "inertia" (*Structures,* 27) and can be described as one more or less continuous and homogeneous stage of world "civilization." The events of the millions of individual lives that occupied those four centuries are, for him, but the "dust of history," which must be strung into immense "chains" by "indefinite repetition" in order to add up to the great "constants" of material life that appear relevant at his scale of approach (560). On the other hand, the entire *A la récherche du temps perdu* emerges from the attempt to unpack all that is contained in the epiphanic "plaisir délicieux" derived from a crumbled madeleine in a teaspoon of tea: "[T]outes les fleurs de notre jardin et celles du parc de M. Swann, et les nymphéas de la Vivonne, et les bonnes gens du village et leurs petits logis et l'église et tout Combray et ses environs, tout cela qui prend forme et solidité, est sorti, ville et jardins, de ma tasse de thé" (Proust, *Du côté de chez Swann,* 47).[43] The atomistic "dust of history" turns out to be as rich in significance as the massive continuities of the *longue durée.*

43. "[A]ll the flowers in our garden and in M. Swann's park, and the water-lilies on the Vivonne and the good folk of the village and their little dwellings and the parish church and the whole of Combray and of its surroundings, taking their proper shapes and growing solid, sprang into being, town and gardens alike, from my cup of tea" (*Remembrance of Things Past,* 36).

The work of art, narrative or otherwise, also exhibits this recession of scale; there is no "natural" scale at which to approach it. For example, no one should object to a reading of Shelley's "Ode to the West Wind" as an integral and unified work of literature, but Neil Fraistat shows that one cannot automatically privilege such an approach. When he chooses to view the poem in relationship to the entire volume in which it first appeared, what had seemed a unified whole becomes, just as naturally, a fragment of a larger work (*The Poem and the Book; Poems in Their Place*). One can as easily imagine discussing Hamlet's "ontological soliloquy" in a book devoted solely to that topic as in a book on *Hamlet,* on Shakespeare's oeuvre, on Elizabethan and Jacobean drama, on English literature, on European literature, or on world civilization. No one of these could lay claim to a self-evidently integral unity to which all other approaches must be subordinated.

Most important, what is true at any one of these levels of generality will not necessarily be true for the levels above or below it; there is no necessary self-similarity across scales. Otherwise, a shift of perspective like that proposed by Fraistat would not offer us the new insights it undoubtedly does. If chaos theory offers nothing else to literary theory, it allows us to understand why so many of the controversies of critical debate are arguments at cross-purposes. Our habitual response to a proposition in literary criticism—so familiar and obvious that it never appears to us as a theoretically loaded gesture—is to shift scales in order to test the statement. In terms of the metaphor we are working with here, we "look closer" to see if the details (of the text, the *oeuvre,* or the period) support the "global" statement. Thus a claim about the nature of Romanticism will be attacked, and defended, by examinations of the oeuvres of individual Romantic authors. The organic assumption that parts must conform to the whole underlies this apparently "natural" shift, which is unavoidable, but inevitably misleading when made on the assumption of the necessary coherence of information across scales.

Anyone who has devoted any serious thought to literature—or any information-rich aspect of a culture—is familiar with the curious way apparently self-evident "truths" often vanish as we begin "looking closer" at the details that should flesh them out. Time and again we find ourselves in a position like that of the photographer in Antonioni's *Blow Up,* who, sure that he has accidentally photographed a murder victim in the background of one of his photos, makes enlargement after enlargement of the suspect area. At first, it does appear that the victim's body might emerge into clearer view; but at a certain point, before we can be sure of what we have seen, a threshold is crossed, and the image breaks apart into an apparently random soup of amorphous blobs; information that exists at one scale disappears at another. Dupré makes the same point with regard to reductionism in scientific observation: a phenomenon that is well established and ontologically valid at one level of observation (say, the phenotypic expression of certain genes) may simply become confused and unclear as we "look closer" (at, for example, the microbiological chemistry of DNA) (128–29).

In the same way, each time we shift scales, seeking confirmation of some claim made at a higher level, we find that the question does not apply at the new scale of approach. No individual author's oeuvre quite conforms to any blanket statement about the literature of the period. No one work quite conforms to statements about the oeuvre; and it is always possible to find passages in the text that are counterinstances for any generalization about the individual work. Deconstructive criticism has made us all realize that there is no limit to this recession and that the minutest details of a text can overthrow what seems to be the "obvious" meaning.[44]

Those who think deconstructive criticism irrelevant for just this reason could consider a far more traditional branch of literary scholarship that demonstrates the point even more dramatically: the editing of literary texts. Ironically, there is no better example than the case of Shelley's own poetry and prose (see Reiman, *Romantic Texts and Contexts,* for a thorough account of the tortuous history of Shelley's texts). The bitter acrimony of the disputes occasioned by some attempts to edit Shelley's texts would strike an uninterested observer as foolish; can dubious capitalizations and arguable commas really make that much difference? Surely the *ens* of Shelley's poetry is unchanged by such accidents of *substantia?* But this is true only at a sufficiently coarse scale; as soon as we approach the text with genuine attentiveness to its details, we discover the contrary to be true. A spurious capital or a misplaced comma could be a sufficient *clinamen* to divert us into an indefensible reading of an entire poem—and that poem distort our view of the entire oeuvre (for want of a comma, the line was lost . . .).

It is for this reason that no specialist is happy with a generalist description of their topic. It is also for this reason that works, or bodies of work, that generations of critics have contentedly dismissed as uninteresting and valueless are always ripe for rediscovery and reevaluation. This is a process whose effects cascade across scales: the reevaluation of

---

44. It might be more accurate to say that deconstructive criticism has simply reminded us of this fact, which William Empson propounded at length in *Seven Types of Ambiguity.*

a neglected work by a well-known author can profoundly alter our approach to the oeuvre; the reevaluation of an oeuvre (such as Shelley's) or genre (such as the Gothic) can alter our conception of an entire period; and such cases as the reevaluation of women's writing alter the entire canon.

The world of literature is "un véritable océan," like Paris in Balzac's description: "Jetez-y la sonde, vous n'en connaîtrez jamais la profondeur. Parcourez-le, décrivez-le! quelque soin que vous mettiez à le parcourir, à le décrire; quelque nombreux et intéréssés que soient les explorateurs de cette mer, il s'y rencontrera toujours un lieu vierge, un antre inconnu, des fleurs, des perles, des monstres, quelque chose d'inouï, oublié par les plongeurs littéraires" (*Le Père Goriot,* 34).[45] Balzac's oceanic Paris—agitated "par les tourbillons de la vie parisienne" (38)—is a descendent of the Lucretian *tourbillon* that tramples Saint-Preux's moral identity into atoms. Balzac's description of the literary imagination before the infinite complexity of Paris improves upon the model of fractal recession as I have so far described it. The vertiginous recession of scales from the *longue durée* down to an afternoon tea break is an oversimplification; it implies that we could simply agree to organize our approaches to literature according to their "degree of distance" from the text.

There is one more aspect of fractal "disorganization" that we must consider in order to be able to grasp the radical significance of the fractal nature of the literary work of art. The term "fractal" originally derives from the term "fractional dimensions," or dimensions that lie "between" the conventional orders of dimensionality, as, for example, the dimension of the ball of string when one can see it simultaneously as a two-dimensional string and a three-dimensional sphere. This straddling of dimensions means that fractal objects display characteristics of both the higher and lower dimensions between which they lie. This, in turn, allows for an interference and transmission of information *across* scales, as intimated above—the microscopic affecting the macroscopic, or what we have encountered elsewhere as "sensitive dependence on initial conditions," or the butterfly-wing effect. To speak of different scales of approach in terms of a spatial metaphor of proximity of viewpoint is misleading. The different "scales" are not fully isolable; they do

---

45. "[B]ut Paris is like the sea. Try to sound it, but you will never know its depth. Study it, write of it; but with whatever zeal you may study it and write of it, however numerous and eager may be the explorers of its ocean, there will always be an untrodden shore, an undiscovered cave, strange flowers, pearls and creatures unknown and forgotten to literary divers" (*Père Goriot,* 13).

not form so many distinct and complete worlds of meaning, which we can enter or leave at our pleasure and which need bear no relationship one to the other. When we approach a fractal object like the literary text, we find ourselves between scales, in situations of conflict and contradiction. The discrepancies between scales are thrust upon us as a problem that demands resolution, not as so many different options that we can adopt or discard at will: "[I]l faut enchaîner, mais le mode d'enchaînement n'est jamais nécessaire."[46]

Rather than this orderly sequence of scales from "the canon" or "a national literature" down to, say, a single word, each enclosed within and defined by the next like a series of Russian dolls, the interpretive frameworks we propose inevitably cut across each other. Where in the orderly sequence outlined above would one place such "scales" of interpretation as gender, ethnicity, or genre? Each overlaps with the other, and with all the other "scales" discussed above. The position of the consumer of literature is that of the observer before Aristotle's thousand-mile animal; no matter how apparently limited the object proposed for interpretive consumption, its infinite, fractal detail means that it always exceeds the consumer's vision. To attempt to make sense of the infinite proliferation of signification that confronts us, we are forced to propose heuristic frames that will at once control and make legible this turbulent torrent of information. Such a frame was the "author" identified by Foucault as "the principle of thrift in the proliferation of meaning." But these frames exist in an unstable and indeterminate space, a grey area between a hypothetical "whole," which never emerges from the fragments we actually experience, and atomistic "parts," which prove to be as richly detailed as the "wholes" in which we attempt to locate them. We cannot but be aware that our perspective is incomplete; whatever we attempt to examine through our chosen frame seems simultaneously too large and too small, or detailed, for the frame we have adopted; we see both ball and twine.

It is this that perpetually drives us to shift scales in critical practice. Foucault is wrong to see the "author function" as an almost insuperable fetish and a forcibly imposed normative scale of approach to literature. In fact, the author as a critical frame is always already problematic. We can hardly begin to use it to "limit, exclude, and choose" within the proliferating meanings of the field of literature without being forced to adopt different frames. The attempt to read an author's writings solely

---

46. "It is necessary to link, but the mode of linkage is never necessary" (Lyotard, *The Differend*, 29).

as more or less sublimated autobiography is one of the least interesting critical approaches. The question, Who is speaking?—in the sense of "what is the whole to which I shall refer this part?"—becomes, for all other readers, progressively more difficult to answer; the "parts" that appear within the frame divert any hermeneutical circle that tries to work them into a whole, referring the reader to other frames that cannot necessarily be brought into harmony with the first. The "author" is a Frankenstein's monster; if one is "close enough" to see the "whole" body, then one is also close enough to see the atomistic parts out of which the figure called "the author" is sutured together—the scattered fragments of more or less dubious evidence that any life leaves behind for the historian. As we move in to focus on those different parts—say, a specific text or an aspect of the life—they take on a life of their own, referring us to other frames, or other bodies, in which they are able to take their place. The poem *Hellas* may be seen as an "integral" part of the figure we call Shelley, but it is an equally integral part of Romantic Classicism, or of Western Ruin Sentiment, or the tradition of lyrical drama, or the literary response to the French Revolution, and so forth. These different frames, although they all overlap and therefore any one of them can divert us to any other, cannot be summed into a totality.

In the dynamics of consumption *all* literary texts, no matter how evidently their creators aspired to fulfill the organic therapeutic ideals of finality and redundancy, reveal a complexity of structure that can best be described as Gothic. The reader of any text, or group of texts, is like Emily exploring Udolpho's "proud irregularity" and the sublime uncertainty of the "changing scenery" of its Apennine setting:

> The grandeur of the broad ramparts, and the changing scenery they overlooked, excited her high admiration; for the extent of the terraces allowed the features of the country to be seen in such various points of view, that they appeared to form new landscapes. She often paused to examine the gothic magnificence of Udolpho, its proud irregularity, its lofty towers and battlements, its high-arched casements, and its slender watch-towers, perched upon the corners of turrets. Then she would lean on the wall of the terrace, and, shuddering, measure with her eye the precipice below, till the dark summits of the woods arrested it. Wherever she turned, appeared mountain-tops, forests of pine and narrow glens, opening among the Apennines and retiring from the sight into inaccessible regions. (Radcliffe, 245)

Emily's wandering through Udolpho is an image of the reader's course through the "proud irregularity" of *Udolpho*. The fractal nature of the literary work means that even the most tightly structured works become, in consumption, similarly sublime and irregular landscapes that "form new landscapes" when seen from "various points of view." The infinite openness to digression that I associated above with the Gothic text—the literary parallel of what Repton praised as the "magnificent irregularity and splendid intricacy" owed to the additive principle of Gothic architecture—proves to be a potential quality of all literature in consumption. The author may not intend to digress, but the reader is always at liberty to take an erratic, digressive course through the work, to create "new landscapes" by assuming "various points of view," to *enchaîne* in an unforeseen way, finding whole worlds of meaning in parts of the text the author never suspected could be given such emphasis. In the fractal text, we cannot help but "see a World in a Grain of Sand" if we choose to look closely enough at the grain. "*A* World," not "*the* World," just as Shelley is "an atom to *a* Universe," and not to "*the* Universe," in the *Defence* (Reiman and Powers, 505). This is not Coleridge's therapeutic discovery of heaven reflected in a drop of dew. The most apparently unified text is an atomistic *pépinière* of mutually inconsistent worlds.

Writing of Stendhal's *Le rouge et le noir,* Lyotard indicates what this suggests about the indeterminacy of the consumption of literary texts: "[L]e même nom supporte un repérage dans le monde des noms de la fiction stendhalienne et un autre dans celui des noms attestés par les moyens de la science historique sans léser l'une ni l'autre. Cet empiétement donne un bon exemple de différend: Napoléon empereur des Français, Napoléon Idéal de la raison politique pour Fabrice ou pour Julien?" ("Judicieux dans le différend," 226).[47] The answer is that he is both and neither. Each is a legitimate way for the reader to *enchaîne* upon the name of Napoleon, but each has a distinct set of implications that would lead to rapid divergences in interpretation; there is a "possibilité du différend à l'occasion du moindre enchaînement."

Curran, in his recent study of the attitudes of the British Romantics toward traditional genres, gives us a telling historical demonstration of this process that is all the more useful for us in that he is making an

---

47. "[T]he same name can provide one indicator in the world of names comprised by Stendhal's fiction and another in the world of names verified by historical science—and this without wronging either world. This entanglement provides a good example of a *différend:* is Napoleon the emperor of France, or is he the Ideal of political reason for Fabrice and Julien?" ("Judiciousness in Dispute," 54).

almost contrary theoretical argument. In the familiar historicist manner, he proposes the traditional genres as yet another neglected context of production that can provide a home and hearth for the disturbingly promiscuous texts of the Romantic poets. The poet who sits down to write a poem, Curran argues, inevitably thinks of writing a certain *type* of poem; as soon as this decision has been made, the poet is aware of being positioned within a defining tradition. "He" thinks of "the examples he knows within this genre, the conventions they share, the place of the genre within received critical categories, the cultural priorities assumed by the genre. . . . Before pen is put to page the poet will have cast himself into a particular mental framework that limits human options and prizes certain values above others. . . . [T]he generic choice has already committed him to . . . a mode of apprehension" (*Poetic Form*, 10–11). Consequently, Curran warns us to beware of "confusing the contexts of art with the lineaments of belief" in such a way that "an inherited generic order is confused with an author's own values" (11). Traditions apparently subsume the individual talent, the ideological imperatives of genre replicating themselves through their divers incarnations in the works of different individual poets.

Curran's historical evidence, however, demonstrates something altogether different. Again and again he shows us that the "tradition" contains the seeds of unpredictable innovation:

> Because the notion and therefore the nature of the ode alters with each succeeding epoch, it is all but impossible to write a normal history of the form. (63)

> [I]n Southey's adolescent experiment a Tory, reactionary, Anglican genre is transformed into one celebrating vernacular verse, uncouth folk, communal fellowship, democracy, and Methodist enthusiasm. Whatever the claims of the *Botany-Bay Eclogues* to high art, . . . Southey's pastorals constitute a watershed in the history of the genre. (99)

Sheer historical accident (in this case the "entropic" factor of simple historical ignorance) can divert the history of a genre onto unforeseen tangents:

> If literary history were written to the dictates of a retrospective simplicity, the subsequent development of the English ode would be inherent in [Jonson's "To the Immortal Memory and Friend-

ship of That Noble Pair, Sir Lucius Cary and Sir H. Morison" and
Milton's "Nativity Ode"]. But Abraham Cowley intervened and,
with much less Greek than either Milton or Jonson, reinvented
Pindar, necessitating the tactful correction of Congreve and other
successors, who nonetheless pursued a similarly spurious classicism. (64–65)

It is hard to see why we should be more impressed, as Curran urges us
to be (see, e.g., 84, 207ff.), by the empirically observable but quite
unpredictable elements of continuity within this evolutionary history
than by the startling reversals and random deviations that are its "essence." In the terms that I am exploring here, we could say that Curran
has settled on genre as the "natural" frame of reference within which to
approach literature, but his own historical work confirms the fractal
interference across scales I described above: information that falls below his normative scale (such as the extent of Cowley's knowledge of
Greek) can ultimately have drastic consequences for the history of an
entire genre.

Curran is right to denounce the post-Romantic myth that casts the
poet as an inspired genius creating works of pure originality *ex nihilo*. It
is useful, in response to that myth, to remind us that all art is created
with reference to the artists' conception of the tradition(s) that preceded them. But working from and in response to "tradition" need not
mean mere reiteration of its premises (or "constricting belief systems,"
as Curran puts it [209]).

Perhaps no clearer statement of this point could be found than that in
the preface to *Prometheus Unbound*. Poetry, Shelley reminds us there,
"creates, but it creates by combination and representation" (not, in
other words, *ex nihilo*). Poetry, in this sense, is determined by tradition;
but that determination, operating as it does through complex, nonlinear
interactions, generates an inherently indeterminable product: "A Poet, is
the combined product of such internal powers as modify the nature of
others, and of such external influences as excite and sustain these
powers; he is not one, but both. Every man's mind is in this respect
modified by all the objects of nature and art, by every word and every
suggestion which he ever admitted to act upon his consciousness [sensi-
tive dependence on initial conditions]. . . . Poets . . . are in one sense
the creators and in another the creations of their age" (Reiman and
Powers, 134–35). Poets are the creations of their age in that their "age"
offers them all the possible elements—including what survives of various artistic traditions, genres, and the like—out of which they might

construct their works; they are its creators because no two responses to those traditions—and the infinite complexity of "all the objects of nature and art . . . every word and every suggestion" within which each person acts and to which each person constantly adds—can possibly be the same. And no one response could hope to come close to a genuine *summa* of all these "fast influencings" that might reproduce it without entropic innovation.

In this way, the Lucretian account of a chaotically creative history moves us beyond the impasse of Deleuze's "choice" between "memory" and "death," which led us into problems on either side. From the vantage point of the Lucretian *clinamen,* memory and death are two aspects of the same phenomenon. To remember is always to create through error; each attempt at memory sees the death of a certain amount of systemic information. But each "death" is in turn picked up and reproduced in the cycle of memory; the "loss" becomes, through reiteration, a turbulent, negentropic "gain." The stark opposition between an idealist, therapeutic, mnemonic conservatism and a skeptical, disengaged, amnesiac revolutionism no longer appears tenable.

Chaotic creativity is a product of the union of death and memory, negation and affirmation; Prigogine and Stengers describe it as a reconciliation of Being with Becoming ("De l'être au devenir" is the title of book III of their *Nouvelle alliance*). From Wilson to Hall to Hogle, Shelley critics have affirmed Shelley's struggle to assert process against product. Milton Wilson's apologetic attempt to make room for Shelley's aesthetics within the New Critical reverence of the verbal icon is summed up in the comment that "[Shelley's] poems may mean; I doubt if they can be said to be" (39). Hall makes much the same point when she says: "His world is a world of relentless openness, in which truths constantly are being formulated but no final vision of Truth is possible" (*Transforming,* 166). Lucretius describes a flux of becoming, and it is this that makes Hogle willing to claim him as a significant precursor for Shelley's transferential poetry of process. But the flux Hogle has in mind is more Heraclitean than Lucretian; it is that amnesiac stream into which we can never step twice. The Lucretian flux, on the contrary, does return upon itself, if with a difference. As Michel Serres puts it: "[S]i je plonge dans un tourbillon, dans ce cycle local, je suis à peu près sûr de me baigner dans la même eau ou à peu près, ou dans l'eau maintenue" (*La naissance,* 189).[48] In the Lucretian flux "il y a des stabilités fines

48. "If I plunge into a whirlpool [eddy], into the local cycle, I am more or less certain to bathe in the same water, or more or less the same—or in water held more or less still" (my translation).

dans l'instabilité fluide" (189),[49] and these stabilities are the product of memory.

In this way, chaotic creativity takes us beyond the paradoxes of opposing death to memory's deathly repetitive stasis. The Lucretian *clinamen*, by giving us a way of conceptualizing death with memory, allows us to restate the terms of the problem. If we understand process as the product of death-within-memory, then we can oppose this to a modified form of Deleuze's "absolute memory." From a Lucretian or chaos-science perspective, Deleuze's "absolute memory" represents neither memory and death as they occur in the real world nor a transcendental "opening" within which that memory and death can operate; rather, it is the Laplacean dream of an infinitely conservative determinism. On the one hand we could find such an infinite conservation of information in Schelling's or Hegel's dream of the final triumph of memory in Absolute Knowing; on the other hand we could find it in the absolute inertia of Diderot's "sediment." It is not a question of choosing death or memory, then, but of realizing that "extremes meet."

In the real world we encounter neither absolute death nor absolute memory; such a nonentropic system would be entirely uncreative. Life and growth are negentropic dissipative by-products of an entropic decay—from an ideal Laplacean order, which was never in fact achieved, toward Burke's "chaos of elementary principles," which never (yet) arrives. As Charles Segal puts it, Lucretius "takes special pleasure in pointing out that even although the individual compounds undergo endless alteration and therefore death, the totality of the universe can never dissolve into nothingness: 'Something must survive intact, lest all things return to nothing and the abundance of things flourish as reborn from nothing'" (196; quoting Lucretius, *De rerum,* 1.672–74). We saw this same balance of decay and generation in Shelley's "Death":

IV.
All things that we love and cherish,
Like ourselves must fade and perish;
Such is our rude mortal lot—
Love itself would, did they not.

49. "there are subtle stabilities within fluid instability" (my translation).

7

The *Defence:* A General Theory of Chaotic Poetics

I

In this chapter we shall determine whether Shelley's own theoretical conception of his poetic practice corresponds to the model outlined in the preceding chapter and, if so, what consequences that has for his understanding of the relationship between his poetry and his political radicalism. The *Defence of Poetry* is Shelley's most sustained meditation upon the nature of poetic creativity and the sociopolitical role of poetry. The essence of Peacock's charge against poetry in *The Four Ages of Poetry* is that it is socially and politically useless. It is on this point that Shelley concentrates his *Defence,* which makes it an attempt to answer my principal question: in what way can poetry be understood as politically effective?

Shelley's first answer to this problem seems to be rather a cheat; he defines poetry, more or less, as anything that tends to generate political change: "All the authors of revolutions in opinion are . . . necessarily poets as they are inventors" (Reiman and Powers, 485). The breadth of his definition of poetry, which regards the distinctions between poetry and prose, or poetry and philosophy, as a "vulgar error" (484) and holds that "[l]anguage, colour, form, and religious and civil habits of action are all the instruments and materials of poetry" (483), allows him to argue that the "true Poetry of Rome lived in its institutions," and to hold that the "life of Camillus, the death of Regulus; the expectation of the Senators, in their godlike state, of the victorious Gauls; the refusal of the Republic to make peace with Hannibal after the battle of Cannae . . . are not the less poetry, *quia carent vate sacro*" (494). Easy enough, we might say, to argue that poetry is politically effective, if we define it as anything that proves to be so.

But this is not Shelley's aim. He is not so much redefining poetry as redefining our understanding of what we consider to be "political." He appears to move away from poetry, as if it hampered his claims to seriousness of purpose, but after making these sweeping claims about what might be called poetry, his concrete examples of the benefits brought to society by poetry are almost all based on what we usually call poems. The significance of this expansion of the usual definition of poetry runs in the other direction; he is not moving away from poems to the firmer ground of "real" political acts and more "important" social institutions; he is holding poetry up as a particularly clear case with which to demonstrate a general theory of cultural production and political change and asking us to realize that what is true of poetry, *stricto sensu,* is also true of these other sociocultural domains. This is in part what he means when he says we must learn to see "the poetry of life"; he wants to redefine our understanding of "moral, political and historical wisdom" and show us the "poetry in these systems of thought" (502).

The immediate occasion for the *Defence* was Peacock's *Four Ages of Poetry,* which had branded poetry as socially and politically worthless in our modern, utilitarian world. Behind this immediate attack Shelley, like his model Sydney, is grappling with the far weightier attack on poetry from one of his favorite philosophers, Plato. Plato had banned poetry from his ideal republic on the grounds that it was a corrupting appeal to base emotions over reason, which was not compatible with "orderly government": "For if you grant admission to the honeyed Muse in lyric or epic, pleasure and pain will be lords of your city instead of law and that which shall from time to time have approved itself to the general reason as the best" (bk. X of the *Republic,* 832). The ideal city is one united under the absolute law of reason. Plato's organic model for this unity would have inevitably prompted comparisons, for Shelley, with the therapeutic resistance to the "disengaged" radical Enlightenment:

> "Do we know of any greater evil for a state than the thing that distracts it and makes it many instead of one, or a greater good than that which binds it together and makes it one? . . .

"That city, then, is best ordered in which the greatest number use the expression 'mine' and 'not mine' of the same things in the same way. . . .

"And the city whose state is most like that of an individual man. For example, if the finger of one of us is wounded, the entire community of bodily connections stretching to the soul for 'integration' with the dominant part is made aware, and all of it feels the pain as a whole, though it is a part that suffers. . . .

". . . the best-governed state most nearly resembles such an organism." (bk. V, 701)

Like Burke, Plato is everywhere concerned with how to ensure the accurate reproduction of this ideal society, once established. His elaborate prescriptions for the recruitment and training of the guardians and rulers are designed to ensure the "condition of unchangeable constancy" that was Burke's ideal of organic reproduction. Everything must be measured against the "style of the building," and Plato does not shrink even from infanticide to eliminate "errors" that might corrupt the cycle of reproduction, or "filiation" (700).

Plato resents poetry because it dissolves the unified society, preventing the completion of this reproductive cycle. Poetry, and mimetic art in general, Plato argues, appeal to the subjective side of our minds; they deal with appearances, not with verifiable truths. The "best part of the soul" is "that which puts its trust in measurement and reasoning" (bk. X, 828), because it is then dealing with that which is accessible to all and to which our responses can be shared. For Plato, poetry has a kind of privative sublimity; it cuts us off from the shared, public realm of "general reason" and takes us into the shadowy, subjective realm of private "pleasure and pain" (see 828ff.). What makes this so dangerous—what Plato calls his "chief accusation against it"—is that it tends to propagate errors within the organic cycle of reproduction, "corrupt[ing], with rare exceptions, even the better sort," so that the absolute unity of the state, which is founded on the "beautiful" generality of reason, is dissolved into the sublime and fractured shadows of mimetic delusion: "Mimetic art . . . is an inferior thing cohabiting with an inferior and engendering inferior offspring" (828). Mimetic art cannot achieve true filiation.

Plato's banishment of the poet in the *Republic* is not absolute, however. He allows a hegemonic role for ideologically sound poetry—the "hymns to the gods and the praises of good men." He admits to feeling the "magic" even of dangerous, mimetic poetry, "especially when Homer is her interpreter," and calls for both poets and "lovers of poetry" to "[plead] her defence . . . and show that she is not only delightful but beneficial to orderly government and all the life of man," and assures these pleaders that "we shall listen benevolently, for it will be clear gain for us if it can be shown that she bestows not only pleasure but benefit" (832–33). It is this challenge that Shelley takes up in the *Defence*.

The *Republic* helps us to understand what is really at issue in the *Defence*. Peacock's utilitarian critique of poetry is not rich enough to have fully engaged Shelley's critical attention; even when he picks up its central issues—as, for example, in his criticisms of the effects of "an unmitigated exercise of the calculating faculty" (Reiman and Powers, 501)—it is clear that beyond Peacock he is responding to Plato's argument that the "best part of the soul" is "that which puts its trust in measurement and reasoning." This is part of Plato's impulse beyond the diverse appearances of the phenomenal world toward the ideal universal behind them, beyond the Many to the One, the same "pure moral impulse . . . directed at the Absolute" (Schiller, *Aesthetic Education*, 53) that underlies the post-Kantian therapeutic philosophy. Plato's organic ideal of the state's structure and reproductive dynamic, his vision of it as an absolute totality each part of which is a representative instance of the whole, and his fear of poetry as something that fragments that totality, dissolving the unified and intelligible into the disengaged and obscure, are vividly contemporary problems for Shelley, with clear parallels in the organicist politics of Burke and Coleridge.

The *Defence* poses two questions: to what extent can poetry be reconciled with society conceived as an organic totality; and to what extent ought society to be so conceived? The first question is the one that the *Republic* poses; the second goes beyond the parameters that Plato has established and calls into question the very criteria by which Plato would judge how "beneficial" poetry can be to "all the life of man." Shelley never ignores Plato's problematic, far from it. In the same year that he produced the *Defence,* he wrote a letter to Hogg asking him his opinion of the *Republic* and praising it warmly, "especially the sixth book of it": "His [Plato's] speculations on civil society are surely the foundations of true politics, & if ever the world is to be arranged upon another system than that of the several members of it destroying & tormenting one another for the sake of the pleasures of the sense, or from the force of habit & imitation; it must start from some such princi-

ples" (*Letters,* 2:360). There are times when Shelley's *Defence* appears
to be the very one the *Republic* calls for, one that reconciles poetry
with the "pure moral impulse" toward the "Absolute":

> The whole objection . . . of the immorality of poetry rests upon a
> misconception of the manner in which poetry acts to produce
> the moral improvement of man. . . . The great secret of morals is
> Love; or a going out of our own nature, and an identification of
> ourselves with the beautiful which exists in thought, action, or
> person, not our own. A man, to be greatly good, must imagine
> intensely and comprehensively; he must put himself in the place
> of another and of many others; the pains and pleasures of his
> species must become his own. The great instrument of moral
> good is the imagination; and poetry administers to the effect by
> acting upon the cause. (Reiman and Powers, 487–88)

Shelley turns around Plato's objection to poetry's concern with the subjective world of "pleasure and pain" to show that this is the key to a
genuine universality that binds the disparate parts of a society into a
unified whole. Plato's organic ideal of the state is one in which the
pains and pleasures of the part are shared by the whole, and vice versa:
"all of it feels the pain as a whole, though it is a part that suffers."

   Similarly, Shelley's attack on the "calculating faculty" does not challenge the ideal of absolute integration, but argues that the "poetic faculty" is better suited to realize this goal. The faculty of "measurement
and reasoning" is no longer concerned with the propagation and admiration of universal truths, but has become a tool to ensure that the "rich
. . . become richer and the poor . . . become poorer" (501). If "[t]hat
city . . . is best ordered in which the greatest number use the expression 'mine' and 'not mine' of the same things in the same way," then the
calculating faculty, almost entirely absorbed with questions of *meum et
tuum,* is an enemy of good order: "Poetry, and the principle of Self, of
which money is the visible incarnation, are the God and the Mammon
of the world" (503). The synthetic, comprehensive force of the poetic
imagination, closely related as it is to the "enthusiasm of virtue, love,
patriotism, and friendship," realizes the drive to the Absolute far more
fully than the analytical and divisive calculating faculty: "[W]hilst they
last, self appears as what it is, an atom to a Universe" (505).

   The attractions of therapeutic organicism for a political poetry are
readily apparent. If each part instantiates the whole, then poets and
their poems can lay claim to a certain representative force. "Ye are

many, they are few" can only be politically efficacious if the "many" can in some sense become "one"; "the pains and pleasures of his species must become his own." Shelley sketches a process that a Marxist would call the accession to class consciousness, or, in Hegelian terms, "species being."

Shelley has, however, experienced too much of the feeling of being "a nightingale, who sits in darkness and sings to cheer its own solitude with sweet sounds" (486), to think that this can be taken for granted. In its very construction, the *Defence* poses problems of the relationship of part to whole. The *Defence* is a fragment—a not completely settled version of the first part of a projected three-part work—and is itself composed of fragments. It is a product of a Gothic creative logic: Shelley cannibalized his own past writings to produce a Frankenstein's monster of a text, incorporating large portions of such texts as the *Philosophical View of Reform* and "On Life." Its most famous passage, the concluding, triumphant proclamation "Poets are the unacknowledged legislators of the World," is a particularly disturbing example of such textual suturing. Its privileged position and function as closure and summation of the "whole" suggest we should read it as a hermeneutical key to the meaning of the entire work. But if we have read the *Philosophical View* and know the different but equally "integral" role this "fragment" plays in that text, our attempt at organic totalization becomes unsettled. The "fragment"—which is only seen as a "fragment" once we know it has been dissected out of a previous text—suddenly reveals traces of its displacement (or scars). It seems no longer quite to "belong" in either the *Defence* or the *Philosophical View,* no longer able to be reliably related to either of the two (fragmentary) "wholes" that lay claim to it. The promiscuous ability of this famous passage to "belong" to two distinct works dis-integrates the texts; every part reveals the internal division that Derrida suggests is an inevitable consequence of the "iterability" of any utterance: "Every sign, linguistic or nonlinguistic, spoken or written (in the usual sense of this opposition), as a small or large unity, can be *cited,* put between quotation marks; thereby it can break with every given context, and engender infinitely new contexts in an absolutely nonsaturable fashion. This does not suppose that the mark is valid outside its context, but on the contrary that there are only contexts without any center of absolute anchoring" ("Signature Event Context," 320).

The relationship of part to whole, text to context, and the problem posed by iteration are central issues in the argument of the *Defence* as well as in the details of its construction. The iteration that Shelley is concerned with, however, is not that of the trace, or mark, but that of the context itself; his interest, like Plato's, is in the problem of social reproduction. The poet's and the poem's relationship to society—the *Defence's* principal subject—is a relationship of part to whole; it is also the relationship of text to the contexts of both production and consumption. Shelley's most "organic" conception of this relationship was the notion of the "spirit of the age." In the prefaces to *The Revolt of Islam* and *Prometheus Unbound,* and in the "unacknowledged legislators" passage common to *A Philosophical View of Reform* and the *Defence,* Shelley ponders the emergence of "a resemblance, which does not depend upon their own will, between all the writers of any particular age. They cannot escape from subjection to a common influence which arises out of an infinite combination of circumstances belonging to the times in which they live" (preface, *Revolt,* Hutchinson, 35). If, as Shelley's "Platonic" justifications of poetry's effect upon the imagination suggest, the role of poetry is to help us achieve a kind of species-being, then poetry would be an essential tool in the reproductive iteration of its productive context. This is an organic-hermeneutical process; the universal "spirit of the age" produces the individual poem, which, by means of its powers of consciousness-raising, generates the "spirit of the age."

Such a process need not, in theory, be incompatible with a degree of political change. A Marxist historicist critic like Cameron, reading the *Defence,* casts this in terms that are familiar to us from the Part One of this book. Shelley's argument, he suggests, is that the "literature of any age . . . both in content and form, is determined by its sociocultural roots" (*Golden Years,* 198). Poets are embedded or situated in a very specific productive context; their contribution to political change, in this view, is context determined; it emerges from their *Sittlichkeit:* "By means of his creative intellect, the poet is able to project the 'laws' underlying present historical conditions into the future, and to see, at least in general outline, the next forms of society. . . . The poet is able to foresee only in so far as he can understand the nature of the present" (195).

Although Cameron's historicist insistence upon this kind of groundedness is a useful corrective to Shelley's "decentering" critics, who make the break with any context, productive or consumptive, entirely unproblematic, it obscures a major theme in Shelley's critical theory, one that appears entirely incompatible with Plato's *Republic.* "The icy chains of custom" (*Queen Mab,* I, 127) are felt everywhere in Shelley's poetry and particularly in his prose, not as giving us a secure ground from which to envision the orderly development of social "progress," but as a force inimical to even the slightest change. "Custom" (= *Sitten*, cf. *Sittlichkeit*) is, in Shelley's view, the principal, and most redoubtable, agent of counterrevolution, "fetters . . . which . . . eat with poisonous rust into the soul." Social systems—and literary "styles"—tend to reproduce themselves blindly; the difficulty is not to integrate the particular individual into that process but to understand how any innovation can emerge from it. Cameron's (and Collingwood's) hope that at each stage of the reproductive cycle some naturally "emergent" (to use Williams's term) social form will offer itself and continue the constant march of "progress" collapses when we realize that, from the perspective of custom, any alteration is seen as amnesiac error.

This is as much a poetic as a political problem. In the *Defence*, the tension between the reproductive iteration of social institutions and the oppositional stance of the individual poet or poem is repeatedly emphasized. Poems (like revolutions) are the meteors that punctuate the self-reproductive cycle of literary "style" and political institutions. In the familiar Lucretian logic of the *clinamen*, their entropic cancellation of that cycle entails the negentropic benefit of the creation of information within it. "[E]very great poet," says Shelley, "must inevitably innovate upon the example of his predecessors" (Reiman and Powers, 484): "Their language is vitally metaphorical; that is, it marks the before unapprehended relations of things, and perpetuates their apprehension, until the words which represent them, become through time signs for portions or classes of thoughts instead of pictures of integral thoughts; and then if no new poets should arise to create afresh the associations which have been thus disorganized, language will be dead to all the nobler purposes of human intercourse" (482).[1] Wright describes this "disorganization"—here applied to those associations which, blunted by reiteration, have become lifeless or "inorganic"—as a process of "semantic entropy" (31). Although I might be expected to welcome that phrase, the word "disorganized" has misled Wright with regard to what is entropic in the system Shelley describes. Shelley uses the word ironically because his understanding of the nature of "organization" is radically at odds with that of most of his contemporaries. From a therapeu-

---

1. Critics like Wright, Hall, and Hogle, who are interested in Shelley's "decentering" play of metaphors, and others like Quint, Scrivener, and Hoagwood, who are interested in his struggles with "ideology," would argue that this metaphorical "disorganization" of words that stand for "classes of thoughts" must be read as an unmasking of ideological hegemony. Shelley's understanding of the nature of poetry raises problems for the concept of "hegemony," however; my argument is indebted to theirs, but distinct from it.

tic viewpoint, it is rather the poets, who forever "create afresh" associations that perforce become stale through reiteration in the mnemonic cycles of cultural reproduction, who entropically "disorganize" language that otherwise would be organically self-reproductive. Tasso's "bold and true word . . . *Non merita nome di creatore, se non Iddio ed il Poeta*," is applied by Shelley to this entropic "creation" of information through the diversion of the cycles of reproduction onto a new course. Poetry "purges from our inward sight the film of familiarity. . . . It creates anew the universe after it has been annihilated in our minds by the recurrence of impressions blunted by reiteration" (Reiman and Powers, 505–6). Shelley's poets are not in a battle with "semantic entropy"; they are willing to risk entropy for negentropic benefits.

The political effects, foreseen in the *Defence,* of unimpeded "reiteration" are those Shelley always associates with the stagnation and paralysis of custom, but now more clearly understood as the result of the power of reiterative redundancy to obliterate meaning, or information. Without the "disorganizing" force of poetry-as-*clinamen* the *Defence* would have no history to relate other than the infinitely predictable elaboration through time of the unavoidable consequences of the system's initial conditions. When "the antient system of religion and manners" threatened to fall into such a redundantly periodic cycle by "fulfill[ing] the circle of its revolution . . . the world would have fallen into utter anarchy and darkness, but that there were found poets among the authors of the Christian and Chivalric systems of manners and religion, who created forms of opinion and action never before conceived; which, copied into the imaginations of men, became as generals to the bewildered armies of their thoughts" (495). Shelley paints a stark portrait—which reminds us of Diderot's "sédiment inerte"—of the "heat death" of a society no longer able to produce such entropic disorganization: "For the end of social corruption is to destroy all sensibility to pleasure; and therefore it is corruption. It begins at the imagination and the intellect as at the core, and distributes itself thence as a paralyzing venom, through the affections into the very appetites, until all become a torpid mass in which sense hardly survives" (493)

I have been calling this logic "Lucretian"—which it is—but it is also, curiously, Platonic. Shelley is taking Plato's negative characterization of poetry as that which disrupts the organic totality and reproductive purity of his ideal city and redefining it as a virtue. Shelley's praise of the *Republic* to Hogg, cited above, may have seemed paradoxical in the light of what has just been said about the *Defence.* If we examine that statement more closely, however, we notice that he focuses his praise on "especially the sixth book of it."

In that book, Plato is concerned with the (Romantic Ironic) problem that always haunted Shelley: how we can make the transition from the corrupt present to the pure, or purer, future, when all our present means to bring about that change are, by definition, corrupt. Two of Shelley's favorite images are brought into play here. The first is what I have called the revolutionary Christ figure—like Laon, Lionel, Prometheus, or the Assassin—imagined to be suddenly transported to "civilized" society. Shelley's frequent self-descriptions as such a Christ figure, torn to pieces by an uncomprehending mob for his love of humanity, are a way of addressing the relationship between the pure part and the corrupt whole. The martyrdom of the Christ figure is an image of the hermeneutical erasure of error—making the reparation in the (corrupt) style of the building. But if, as Shelley suggested in his "Essay on Christianity," the canny reformer, like Christ, trying to avoid this fate, "accommodated his doctrines to the prepossessions of those whom he addressed. . . . [and] used a language for this view sufficiently familiar to our comprehensions" (Ingpen and Peck, 6:242), would she or he not become merely a link in the reproductive cycle of contextual iteration?

Plato also pictures a pure philosopher—Socratic rather than Christian—schooled "in the absence of corrupters," entering "the madness of the multitude," only to discover that "there is nothing . . . sound or right in any present politics, and that there is no ally with whose aid the champion of justice could escape destruction, but that he would be as a man who has fallen among wild beasts, unwilling to share their misdeeds and unable to hold out singly against the savagery of all, and that he would thus, before he could in any way benefit his friends or the state come to an untimely end without doing any good to himself or others." The only option open to this sage is an *ataraxia* expressed in terms that seem to have influenced Lucretius's Epicurean *suave mari magno:* "[T]he philosopher remains quiet, minds his own affair, and, as it were, standing aside under shelter of a wall in a storm and blast of dust and sleet and seeing others filled full of lawlessness, is content if in any way he may keep himself free from iniquity and unholy deeds" (*Republic,* bk. VI, 732).

But Plato shares Shelley's impatience with the political inadequacy of such autarchic isolation; what use, he asks, is a pure individual within a totality so corrupt that there can be no community of interests between them? "He would not have accomplished any very great thing . . . if it were not his fortune to live in a state adapted to his nature. In such a state only will he himself rather attain his full stature and together with his own preserve the commonweal" (732). In other words, with such a gulf between them, the part cannot fulfill its organic role of reproducing and preserving the whole. Instead, it is caught on the other side of the organic process; the corrupt totality is inclined not merely to ignore the wisdom of the "philosophical nature" but to bring about its "perversion and alteration; as a foreign seed sown in an alien soil is wont to be overcome and die out into the native growth" (733).

Plato is able to criticize this organic/hermeneutical process of "making the reparation in the style of the building," because he does not believe in the "wise prejudice" that demands that we construct our political ideals from the givens of our sociocultural context. He believes we can measure societies against "the heavenly model" (736). For Shelley, who does not share such a belief, this passage of the *Republic* amounts to an admission of the conservative limitations of the organic model of social reproduction by one of its most influential proponents.

The second of Shelley's "favorite images" to which Plato has recourse reinforces this admission. This is his advocacy of "change"—considered as an absolute, though not necessarily global, erasure of "initial conditions"—as a means of breaking the iterative cycle of social reproduction. In a letter to Hunt of 1820, Shelley picks up the theme and language of book VI of the *Republic* when he writes: "It is less the character of the individual than the situation in which he is placed which determines him to be honest or dishonest, perhaps we ought to regard an honest bookseller, or an honest seller of anything else in the present state of human affairs as a kind of Jesus Christ. The system of society as it exists at present must be overthrown from the foundations with all its superstructure of maxims & of forms before we shall find anything but disappointment in our intercourse with any but a few select spirits. This remedy does not seem to be one of the easiest" (*Letters,* 2:191). In seeking a way out of the redundantly reproductive cycle of "things as they are," Plato, too, is forced to suppose a moment of absolute disjunction, or revolution, when the old reproductive cycle is canceled and a new one inaugurated: "[The philosopher-rulers] will take the city and the characters of men, as they might a tablet, and first wipe it clean—no easy task. . . . And thereafter . . . they would sketch the figure of the constitution" (*Republic,* bk. VI, 736).

Shelley's "not . . . one of the easiest" may be a direct echo of Plato's "no easy task"; they both appear to be right. But Plato has already suggested in book III how this task might be accomplished: through poetry.

Trying to imagine how the citizens of the (present, corrupt) society will be persuaded to commit themselves fully to the new order—particularly in the difficult but reproductively crucial issue of giving up their children to be raised by the state—Plato suggests the rulers have recourse to a hegemonic myth that he calls a "noble lie":

> I hardly know how to find the audacity or the words to speak and undertake to persuade first the rulers themselves and the soldiers and then the rest of the city that in good sooth all our training and educating of them were things that they imagined and that happened to them as it were in a dream, but that in reality at that time they were down within the earth being molded and fostered themselves. . . . And when they were quite finished the earth as being their mother delivered them, and now as if their land were their mother and their nurse they ought to take thought for her and defend her against any attack and regard the other citizens as their brothers and children of the selfsame earth. (bk. III, 658, 659)

This poetic myth of organic totalitarianism is the means by which Plato's rulers will simultaneously erase the past and establish the future; he concedes that the present generation will never fully believe it, but "their sons and successors and the rest of mankind who come after" will (660). This is the logic of the *clinamen:* one reproductive cycle is canceled, and a new one begun. Plato's subsequent banishment of poetry seems to stem more from a fear that other poems might perform the same *clinamen* within the periodic iteration of his ideal society and its hegemonic poem/myth than from an absolute aversion to the perversion of the "truth."

This definition of poetry as a political and ideological *clinamen* lies at the heart of Shelley's *Defence*. Shelley takes this antiorganic and revolutionary "part" of Plato's text and allows it to "exceed" the iterative organicism of the "whole." But Shelley is not content with overturning Plato's text by highlighting its internal inconsistencies. The discovery of the platonic *clinamen* is itself a *clinamen* in the process of responding to Plato's request for a defense of poetry; from attempting to explain poetry's role in reinforcing and reproducing the organic solidarity of individuals within a social totality, the *Defence* is diverted to the task of accounting for poetry's ability to "disorganize" the context in which it is produced.

Plato's poetic *clinamen* is a solitary and foundational gesture, but the history related in the *Defence,* and Shelley's own poetic practice, demand a chain of such "cancellations." Shelley's response to Plato's hegemonizing revolution anticipates Laclau and Mouffe's strictures against the "foundational" pretensions of the classic Marxist theory of revolution (*Hegemony and Socialist Strategy,* 177–78). The overthrow of Platonic organicism allows Shelley to graft an elaborated Lucretian theory of the *clinamen* onto Plato's embryonic one. The Plato of the *Phaedrus,* who praises—in a passage particularly admired by Shelley—the indispensable "madness" of poetic inspiration as "bacchically inspiring" (*Letters,* 2:29 n. 4), here meets the Lucretius who makes this Bacchic dance the fundamental dance of matter and history. From their union, and by thinking through their relationship to the organicism of the *Republic,* Shelley develops a basis for a full-fledged chaotic theory of the politics of literature.

II

Despite the telling comment that singles Lucretius out as being, "in the highest . . . sense, a creator" (Reiman and Powers, 494), the *Defence* has not been read as a notably Lucretian work. It is true that it contains few straightforward allusions to the *De rerum natura,* but by the time Shelley wrote the *Defence,* he had so thoroughly absorbed Lucretius's work— which he had intensively reexamined just six or seven months before beginning (*Letters,* 2:479)—that he had gone beyond superficial allusions and assimilated what he wanted from Lucretius to the very structure of his thought. The *Defence* provides a "solution tourbillonaire" to the problem of poetic creativity and cultural and political innovation.

Everywhere in the *Defence* Shelley insists upon the constant reproductive pressure within all institutions of human society—that "desire to be for ever as we are," which he suggests elsewhere is the zero-degree telos common to all animate and inanimate structures. Without interruption, he suggests, this conservative iteration would reduce the world to a "torpid mass," an undifferentiated, endlessly redundant repetition of the same "mediocrity." This "torpid mass," like Diderot's "sédiment inerte," is only a hypothetical limit case; in reality poetical and revolutionary disorganization always does prevent the circle from falling back onto itself: "But corruption must have utterly destroyed the fabric of human society before Poetry can ever cease. The sacred links of that chain have never been entirely disjoined, which descending through the minds of many men is attached to those great minds, whence as from a magnet the invisible effluence is sent forth, which at once connects, animates and sustains the life of all. It is the faculty which contains within itself the seeds at once of its own and of social renovation" (Reiman and Powers, 493).

The two key words here are "chain" and "seeds." Ostensibly they seem to imply an organicist paradigm—the cyclic chain of birth, death, and regeneration with which he flirted in the *Revolt.* In fact, the chain is the irreversible historical flux that Lucretius derives from the constantly renewed *attempt* at reproduction. The image of the chain suggests how the cyclic generates the "progressive." When Shelley describes history as cyclic, he is referring only to this iterative impulse, not to the irreversible, entropic flow of empirically experienced history. Shelley defines the heroic moments of the history of the Roman republic as "episodes of that cyclic poem written by Time upon the memories of men" (494), but he intends us to understand the difference between a cyclic impulse and a circular *répétition maniaque.* The cyclic, conservative impulse of memory is the very mechanism by which error, or "innovation," is propagated through the system; when "*poets* among the authors of the Christian and Chivalric systems of manners" create "forms of opinion and action *never before conceived,*" it is their "organic" role as simultaneously offspring and midwives to the "spirit of the age" that ensures that this error/innovation, this *clinamen,* is "copied into the imaginations of men, [to become] as generals to the bewildered armies of their thoughts" (495). Error becomes essence; memory propagates death; the organic cycle "disorganizes" itself.

A preliminary answer to how and why this occurs can be suggested in exploring the significances of the word "seeds." Shelley is fond of seed imagery as the promise of a future social renovation (*The Revolt of Islam* and "Ode to the West Wind"), but the claim that poetry "is the faculty which contains within itself the seeds at once of its own and of social renovation" is an allusion to key moments in both the *Republic* and the *De rerum natura.* Shelley uses the latter to explode the former.

Plato compared the hapless philosopher unable to overcome the corruptive force of the social totality to "a foreign seed sown in an alien soil . . . wont to be overcome and die out into the native growth," an oppressive, organically "reparatory" relationship between whole and part that Shelley paraphrased in his letter to Hunt: "It is less the character of the individual than the situation in which he is placed which determines him to be honest or dishonest." In the *Defence,* the "seed" still refers to the egregious (or erroneous) part, but the seed that Plato imagines invariably falling on fallow ground is now understood to be a *clinamen,* a fertile source of "forms and opinions never before conceived," or "social renovation."

In the *De rerum natura* "seed" (and "generative particle") are two of Lucretius's most common names for what I have elsewhere called "atoms." The description of poetry as "the faculty which contains within itself the seeds at once of its own and of social renovation" takes on a new significance in the light of Lucretius's illustration of the proposition that "things consist of mixed seed [*res permixto semine constant*]" (80, 2.687) by an analogy with the mixing of letters that compose the words of his own verses (80, 2.688–99). Poetry promises to "renovate" society perpetually because it is prone to perpetual atomistic reorganization. We recall Diderot's Lucretian speculation that each person, considered atomistically as a community of "animalcules dont il est impossible de prévoir les métamorphoses et l'organisation future et dernière," might be a "pépinière" (seedbed) of future unimaginable beings separated from the present generation "par un intervalle incompréhensible de siècles et de développements successifs" (*Rêve,* 187).[2] Shelley is proposing a similar evolutionary model whereby the attempted reiteration of poetry—or any other cultural practice—as a context and model for future production leads, like those venereal "développements successifs," to "social renovation"—"reproduction" to creation. For Plato, mimetic art is "an inferior thing cohabiting with an inferior and engendering inferior offspring." Plato's anxiety at the potential for corruption that enters in with each reproductive step of this mimetic chain is vindicated, in its essentials, by the Lucretian model of venereal error as creation.

The modified Gothic definition of poetry in the *Defence* as that which "subdues to union under its light yoke all irreconcilable things" (Reiman and Powers, 505) can be compared to Repton's praise of the "magnificent irregularity" and infinite elasticity of Gothic architecture. It suggests the fractal complexity of poetry as an atomistic seedbed of potentially divergent paths of future development, depending upon which of these "irreconcilable things" will be incorporated into any attempt at reproduction. The *Defence* spells out the process that brings this renovation about; a combination of fragmentation and iteration in which the cyclic reiteration of cultural forms is subject to atomistic errancy, or chaotic creativity.

This is well illustrated in the thumbnail sketch of the impact of Chris-

---

2. "minute creatures whose metamorphoses and future and final state are impossible to foresee" (*D'Alembert's Dream,* 173). "By an inconceivable interval of successive centuries and modifications" (*D'Alembert's Dream,* 173).

tianity on European history at which we have already glanced briefly. It is a history that begins with "scattered fragments" that are mnemonically "preserved" by the writers of the Gospels, and makes no progress toward totality; fragmentation keeps reappearing at each stage as each period tries to appropriate the mingled legacies of the past. Shelley describes an ever-renewed round of atomistic, syncretic reshufflings of the deck offered by the different "traditions" feeding into any given historical moment; each society, or social system, is regarded as an atomistic constellation of parts, some, but never all, of which are successfully transmitted to the next generation of the system. Among those that survive will be those "seeds . . . of social renovation" which, in their new context, will revolutionize the society.

The message of Jesus exists for us only as "scattered fragments preserved to us by the biographers of this extraordinary person, [which] are all instinct with the most vivid poetry." Shelley's definition of poets as those who bring about "forms of opinion and action never before conceived" urges us to see these "scattered fragments" of "vivid poetry" as seeds of potential social renovation, or atoms of entropic errancy, each potentially a *clinamen* in the reproductive cycle of history, if the "seed" falls upon fertile soil. These atomistic "fragments," which already represent an error with respect to Christ's "original" message, are subject to error in the reiterative cycles of history; the word "scattered" emphasizes the aleatory aspects of the transmission into text, and thereby into the social "memory," of Christ's teachings. What is preserved in the Gospels is a textual "ruin" that testifies to the irretrievable erasure of "initial conditions." The aleatory "scattering" continues with each reproductive iteration: "[H]is doctrines seem to have been quickly distorted" (495).[3]

One particular distortion Shelley observes is the amalgamation of fragments of the Christian message with equally "scattered fragments" of Platonic doctrine: "[T]he three forms into which Plato had distributed the faculties of mind underwent a sort of apotheosis, and became the object of the worship of the civilized world" (495). This is a demonstration of the inevitable syncretism of history's atomistic reshuffling: "[I]t may be assumed as a maxim that no nation or religion can supersede any other without incorporating into itself a portion [cf. "fragment" and

3. A view that conforms to modern biblical scholarship. Robin Lane Fox describes our "Old Testament" as "only one late and arbitrary line, surviving from an earlier uncontrolled variety" (*Unauthorized Version*, 101). He records the history of the transmission of Judeo-Christian sacred texts as a perpetual evolutionary process of more or less random decimation and hybridization.

"seed"] of that which it supersedes." Even Christ's "original" message was partially composed of fragments of Platonic doctrine: "Christianity . . . became the exoteric expression of the esoteric doctrines of the poetry and wisdom of antiquity" (496). The disjunctive chain of syncretic "distortion" neither descends from nor tends toward the "pure" or the "undistorted."

Sometimes this entropic process leads to a negentropic amelioration of an oppressive situation: "[M]ark how beautiful an order has sprung from the dust and blood of this fierce chaos! . . . The poetry in the doctrines of Jesus Christ, and the mythology and institutions of the Celtic conquerors of the Roman empire, outlived the darkness and the convulsions connected with their growth and victory, and blended themselves into a new fabric of manners and opinion" (495). In the Middle Ages, the "principle of equality" inherent in both Platonic and Christian thought gained dominance within the syncretic "blend," and the "abolition of personal and domestic slavery, and the emancipation of women from a great part of the degrading restraints of antiquity were among the consequences of these events." The "poetry" in the Platonic/ Christian fragments, their ability to negate aspects of their contexts of production, operates upon slavery and the complete disenfranchisement of women. Shelley was not so deluded as to regard medieval society, or his own society, as an egalitarian, feminist paradise;[4] his point is to show that with time and the atomistic errancy of the iterative cycles of historical reproduction, what is produced in one context with the intent to "preserve" that context can eventually destroy it. In the eleventh century Shelley sees the point at which an egalitarian ideal began, however imperfectly, to emerge from "the poetry of the Christian and Chivalric systems" (496). This beginning is not a victory in itself, but it is the "seed" of a future we now inhabit.

The key to this new social order is a new understanding of love: Romantic "sexual love," which posits as an ideal, however falsified in actual practice, the physical, spiritual, and intellectual union of men and women as equal partners, and a generalized "everlasting love," which underlies an ideal of social mutuality and equality: "Love, which found a worthy poet in Plato alone of all the antients, has been celebrated by a

4. *Pace* Leighton, who throws this part of the *Defence* in the face of Shelley's "avowed feminism" ("Love, Writing, and Skepticism in *Epipsychidion*," 227). Glib dismissals of Shelley's feminism are *de rigueur* these days (see, e.g., Gelpi, "The Nursery Cave," 46), though Leighton's has the merit of going beyond the ad hominem reflex of sisterly solidarity with Harriett or Mary, or both. For an excellent discussion of the significance of "chivalry" in the age of Revolution, see Duff, *Romance and Revolution,* chap. 1, 136–37, 142–43.

chorus of the greatest writers of the renovated world; and the music has penetrated the caverns of society, and its echoes still drown the dissonance of arms and superstition." The "preservative," mnemonic efforts of the poets plant the "seed" in history's cycles: first the "Provençal Trouveurs," who establish the Romantic world of chivalry and courtly love; then Petrarch, whose works release a "gentleness and . . . elevation of mind" that renders men "more amiable, more generous, and wise, and lift[s] them out of the dull vapours of the little world of self" (497); then Dante, who is the first to elevate this new ideal into an epic cosmology. Each of these could be said merely to "express" the prevailing ideology of his context of production, but each expression acts as a *clinamen* within the cycle of social reproduction, exerting a pressure on society to conform in reality to the ideals it promulgates in theory. These expressions, in turn, enter a positive-feedback loop whereby each statement of the new ideal brings forth imitators and supporters whose added voices magnify and help propagate the message, while subtly changing it as well:

> At successive intervals, Ariosto, Tasso, Shakespeare, Spenser, Calderon, Rousseau, and the great writers of our own age, have celebrated the dominion of love, planting as it were trophies in the human mind of that sublimest victory over sensuality and force. The true relation borne to each other by the sexes into which human kind is distributed has become less misunderstood; and if the error which confounded diversity with inequality of the powers of the two sexes has become partially recognized in the opinions and institutions of modern Europe, we owe this great benefit to the worship of which Chivalry was the law, and poets the prophets. (497–98)

The word "trophy" descends from the same Greek root as the word "trope," and each of these "trophies" does represent a turning point where poetry-as-social-memory fulfills its double role as both destroyer and preserver of the social system.

It is this combination of atomistic errancy with cycles of reproduction that Shelley has in mind in the *Philosophical View of Reform,* in which he describes "Modern society" as an "engine assumed to be for useful purposes, whose force is by a system of subtle mechanism augmented to the highest pitch, but which, instead of grinding corn or raising water acts against itself and is perpetually wearing away or breaking to pieces the wheels of which it is composed" (Ingpen and

Peck, 7:10). Poetry breaks to pieces ("atoms," "seeds," "portions") the wheel of social reproduction; the "breach" between its moment(s) of production and its moment(s) of consumption allows it to become the means by which society "acts against itself," producing its own destroyer. In the essay "On Life" Shelley describes life as "an education of error" (Reiman and Powers, 477); in the *Defence,* he writes that "[e]very epoch under names more or less specious has deified its peculiar errors" (486–87). The "deification" is never successful; even those most committed to the reigning "errors" of the day sow the seeds of its erasure. Such a history conforms to Gleick's description of nonlinear dynamics where "the act of playing the game has a way of changing the rules" (24).

<h2 style="text-align:center">III</h2>

Several questions might be raised at this point, but the most pressing one is, Why should this be so? In particular, why should this be so with regard to poetry, especially poetry that does not in any way make a virtue of its "diasparactive" fragmentation?

Shelley devotes almost the last half of the schematic history of the impact of Christianity on European culture and literature outlined above to a discussion of Milton and Dante, the two greatest epic poets of the Christian era. If the schizophrenic nature of *The Revolt of Islam* was due, as Leigh Hunt suggested, to an attempt to serve two masters, Lucretius and Dante (qtd. in White 1:531), the *Defence* could be said to resolve that dilemma by providing a Lucretian description of the Dantean poetic. The dilemma of the *Revolt* was between an epic poetic and a poetic of revolutionary change. Epic poetry—perhaps none more so than Dante's—makes the most serious claim to being the complete reflection of its context of production, which the therapeutic philosophers see in all poetry; the epic is customarily "conceived as a repository of cultural knowledge . . . that contained all the known arts and sciences and set the rules for governance of homes and empires alike" (Curran, *Poetic Form,* 180). Shelley recognizes this totalitarian therapeutic aspiration: "Homer was the first, and Dante the second epic poet: that is, the second poet the series of whose creations bore a defined and intelligible relation to the knowledge, and sentiment, and religion, and political conditions of the age in which he lived, and of the ages which followed it, developing itself in correspondence with their development" (Reiman and Powers, 499). Both Milton and Dante, then, represent a limit case for the therapeutic resistance to atomistic entropy; if they can be shown to be subject to the same unstable decay as others, then the organicist hypothesis is in serious trouble.

Each of these poems, Shelley suggests, maintains a crucial distance from "the knowledge and sentiment and religion and political conditions of the age"—or, in other words, from its context of production. That distance creates a "sublime" discontinuity that allows our understanding of the poems in the context(s) of consumption to evolve independently of their relationship to the "defining totality" of any "cultural context." Shelley insists from the start that this disjunction between the work and the context it is supposed to "represent" need not necessarily result from a consciously oppositional stance on the part of a "revolutionary" author swept up in the "fury of destruction": "It is a difficult question to determine how far they [Milton and Dante] were conscious of the distinction which must have subsisted in their minds between their own creeds and that of the people" (498).

If the principal aim of each poet was to write a specifically Christian epic, a theodicy that would establish the literature and languages of the modern, Christian world as fit rivals for those of the classical world, they are, in Shelley's view, curiously notable for their heterodox opinions. Dante observes "a most heretical caprice in his distribution of rewards and punishments"; Milton's poem "contains within itself a philosophical refutation of" Christianity. The work of each poet, far from "developing itself in correspondence with . . . [the] development" of the system it embodies, is open to promiscuous consumption in unimaginable future contexts when the beliefs it is supposed to champion have succumbed to historical entropy: "[W]hen change and time shall have added one more superstition to the mass of those which have arisen and decayed upon the earth, commentators will be learnedly employed in elucidating the religion of ancestral Europe, only not utterly forgotten because it will have been stamped with the eternity of genius" (499). In Shelley's Lucretian model, "change and time" are synonymous; far from embodying for all eternity "the knowledge and sentiment and religion and political conditions of the age" in which they were written, *La divina commedia* and *Paradise Lost* will be consumed and enjoyed as works of "genius" even when the religion they attempted to put in "systematic form" is all but "utterly forgotten."

The real irony of this independence of part from whole is that it also manifests itself in the opposite direction. The most telling evidence of the radical unpredictability of the history of *Paradise Lost* in consumption is not its progressive disengagement from the Christian message but

its apparently complete incorporation by the eighteenth-century church
as a pillar of orthodox Anglicanism. To complete a quotation given only
in part above: "Milton's poem contains within itself a philosophical refutation of that system of which, by a strange and natural antithesis, it
has been a chief popular support."

The strange phrase, "strange and natural," is used to describe a "natural" but unpredictable evolution of what is "naturally" an unstable system. The phrase implies the necessity of a radically empirical stance in
the face of the turbulent fluctuations of the development of such a complex system. As in the phrase "strange attractor," what is considered
"strange" is a sudden alteration of state, with no apparent external cause
of sufficient magnitude to account for it, within a system that develops
through iterative reproductive cycles. In both cases the word is a consciously employed misnomer; the "strange" behavior is quite "natural,"
but it is a challenge to what we have previously assumed to be the
"natural," organic, course of development for such systems.

Part of the problem for both Dante and Milton is the very desire to
rival the productions of the classical world: "Dante and Milton were
both deeply penetrated with the antient religion of the civilized world;
and its spirit exists in their poetry probably in the same proportion as
its forms survived in the unreformed worship of modern Europe" (499).
Just as the New Testament was a Gothic mixture of Greek philosophy
and Judaic theology, these Christian epics could not help but preserve
what they set out to destroy, or at least eclipse, by reproducing in part
their classical models. By setting out with this reproductive logic, albeit
with a "corrective" intent, they inscribed their poems within the general reproductive errancy of Western cultural history, where each moment is an atomistic "disorganization," or remixing, of the preceding
one. As the poems, and the religion they aim to serve, start to fragment
under the critical gaze, the dissociation of the poems from their contexts of production seems to be inevitable.

An organicist critic would respond, however, that the complexity and
contradictions of the cultural contexts from which these poems emerged
is best represented by the complexity and contradictions within the
poems. The goal of therapeutic organicism is to produce an enduring
totality from the diasparactive fragments of reality. Shelley acknowledges the "eternity of genius" that is manifest in these poems; is this not
an admission of the organicist argument—atomistic fragments have
been melded into an "eternal" truth? Besides, the *Defence* is rife with
arguments that the poet "participates in the eternal, the infinite, and the
one" (483); how are we supposed to take these if not as intimations of

some higher, absolute truth that is manifest in the fragmented realities of individual poetic achievements?

To respond to this objection, we must take a closer look at Shelley's descriptions in the *Defence* of the nature of the poetic text as such in these two great exempla of epic poetry. One of the best readings of Shelley's theory of poetic language as outlined in the *Defence*, William Keach's, finds its chief problematic in just this opposition between competing visions of the nature of language. On the one hand, he argues, Shelley sees language as a divine "spark," a "mirror" that has the unique capability of reflecting the pure truth underlying the distorted surfaces of reality; and on the other, Shelley sees language as itself a distorting "veil," or smothering layer of "ashes," that falls between the poet's original conception and the poem's readers, robbing them of the force and perfection of the poet's initial, complete inspiration (*Shelley's Style*, 22–33). This opposition is analogous to that between Shelley's "two thoughts"; Keach describes it as a "linguistic skepticism" opposed to a Romantic conception of poetry as incarnation of a higher truth. For Keach, this is also a struggle between pessimism and optimism, a struggle that pessimism, or skepticism, wins: "[I]n the end the veil of language remains as evidence of 'the limitedness of the poetical faculty,' in spite of Shelley's wondrous capacity to make a virtue of that limitedness" (33).

But need we accept this view that the *Defence* is one more schizophrenic argument between an Enlightenment Shelley and his Romantic alter ego (a view recently repeated by Hall ["The Divine and the Dispassionate Selves"])? It is possible to see both veil and mirror, spark and ashes, as aspects of a single problematic. The key passage for Keach's argument is the culmination of Shelley's discussion of Milton and Dante, a description of the nature of Dante's poetic language:

> His very words are instinct with spirit; each is a spark, a burning atom of inextinguishable thought; and many yet lie covered in the ashes of their birth, and pregnant with a lightning which has yet found no conductor. All high poetry is infinite; it is as the first acorn, which contained all oaks potentially. Veil after veil may be undrawn, and the inmost naked beauty of the meaning never exposed. A great Poem is a fountain forever overflowing with the waters of wisdom and delight; and after one person and one age has exhausted all its divine effluence which their peculiar relations enable them to share, another and yet another succeeds, and new relations are ever developed, the source of an unforeseen and an unconceived delight. (Reiman and Powers, 500)

There are two arguments being made here, which I deal with separately, although they are so interdependent that it is impossible to dissociate them completely. The first involves a claim about the *structure* of poetic language; the second concerns the *dynamics* of poetic interpretation as determined by that structure. I deal with the structural question first, but before I begin, I wish to note one of the most striking "dynamic" claims Shelley advances. This is the final one, that "new relations are ever developed, the source of an unforeseen and an unconceived delight." There are, again, two radical claims being advanced here. The first is that a text will never be finally and completely "understood"; through time, it will continue to be interpreted and reinterpreted ad infinitum. The second is that what is new in each new reading is, at least sometimes, absolutely so. Different readings do not develop out of each other in an organic unfolding through time of a unitary truth; rather, they arrive "unforeseen" and above all "unconceived," which is to say that no matter how closely we read the text *now,* we shall be unable to determine within it the seeds of all its future forms. Strictly speaking, the hermeneutical history of the literary work of art is, Shelley is claiming, evolutionary—that is, contingent, irreversible, and chaotically creative; the critic's only stance in regard to the text's unfolding history of consumption is one of radical empiricism.[5] Or as Salem puts it in regard to the evolutionary Lucretian history of human technical "progress": "[O]n ne peut jamais avoir de notion que de ce qui existe" (195).[6]

Shelley has touched here upon one of the central problems of all hermeneutical endeavors—their interminability. As critics, we are all aware but rarely acknowledge that no matter how many readings of a text have been produced in the past, a return to the text is always liable to produce an "unforeseen and unconceived delight." It is impossible to "remember" a text without, to some extent, dismembering our previous understanding of it, but these revisionary readings—such as, for example, feminist or deconstructive readings today—often elicit suspicion and hostility; each generation intends its own revisionary readings to be the last in the sequence—the final veil withdrawn to reveal the "inmost naked beauty of the meaning." It is difficult, within the dominant Western *epistēmē,* to escape the feeling that if the disjunctive sequence of undrawn veils never comes to an end, or does not, at the very least,

---

5. There is a close affinity between what I am calling "radical empiricism" and the "categorical empiricism" argued for in Dupré's *Disorder of Things,* 80–84.
   6. "One can only conceive of what already exists" (my translation).

converge upon some final revelation, literary criticism's claims to "knowledge" will have been put in question. "Knowledge" should be final and absolute; if "chatter about books" can never be resolved, if interpretation, like analysis, is interminable, what use is there in continuing?

Keach's interpretation would spare us this discomfort. When confronted with this passage, he reads the "veils" as an infinite number of partial barriers that lie between the reader and an absolute, unitary truth, which we know, somehow, to be "there" despite the fact that it is never finally revealed. This truth is a hermeneutical asymptote toward which we tend endlessly without ever quite reaching it: "The infinite potential meaning of poetry is seen to depend upon the inability of words ever completely to conduct and therefore to discharge the mental energy they signify" (Keach, *Shelley's Style*, 28). The spark of "pure" inspiration lies covered in the ashes of poetic realization, which it is our (infinite) task to remove, piece by piece. With this reading, Keach is able to account for Shelley's apparent celebration of what, for the critic, seems instinctively to be an admission of interpretive defeat; Shelley "sets about transmuting an apparent limitation into a strength" (28). Shelley's position would then be the archetypal Romantic Ironic one of Schlegel's declaration in Aphorism 116 from the *Athenaeum:* "[Romantic poetry's] peculiar essence is that it is always becoming and that it can never be completed" (*Dialogue,* 141). This would be no more of a defeat for Shelley than for Schlegel; as Schiller puts it in his *Naive and Sentimental Poetry,* preferable to "the absolute achievement of a finite" is the "approximation to an infinite greatness," because "only the latter possesses *degrees* and displays a *progress*" (112–13).

Keach, however, is too good a reader of the *Defence* not to realize that this reading does not fit Shelley's many explicit statements of what I have been calling "entropy." Meaning, in the *Defence,* rarely has a constant, incremental drive to plenitude; rather, it seems often to turn awry and, ultimately, to become erased. Poetic inspiration is "a fading coal." For Keach to maintain his argument that Shelley posits a final and absolute truth that somewhere underlies the poem, he must read Shelley's veils as curtains that the poet uses almost willfully, initially to obscure and eventually to eclipse that truth. It is not hard for Keach to find passages in the *Defence* that appear to suit his argument:

> Few poets of the highest class have chosen to exhibit the beauty of their conceptions in its naked truth and splendour; and it is doubtful whether the alloy of costume, habit, etc., be not neces-

sary to temper this planetary music for mortal ears. (Reiman and Powers, 487)

Poetry. . . . arrests the vanishing apparitions which haunt the interlunations of life, and veiling them or in language or in form sends them forth among mankind. (505)

In Keach's view, when Shelley's pessimistic skepticism gets the better of him, this protective "tempering" becomes a nearly complete, and quite inevitable, betrayal of the original "naked truth and splendour." The clearest statement of that pessimism, he suggests, is the "fading coal" passage: "[W]hen composition begins, inspiration is already on the decline, and the most glorious poetry that has ever been communicated to the world is probably a feeble shadow of the original conception of the poet" (Keach, *Shelley's Style,* 29). The words that make up poetry are subtly transformed here, Keach argues, from divine sparks covered with the ashes of a given period's interpretive blindnesses, into ashes themselves that bury the spark of inspiration that prompted the poem. Despite the generally confident and celebratory tone of the *Defence,* Keach feels that it is this pessimistic view that, ultimately, prevails. If it were not for the inadequacy of words—specifically poetic words—we might be able to attain to the truths that they obscure. This then is a first "structural" answer to the "dynamic" problem of infinite interpretive renewal, and a fairly disastrous one; poetry's inherent obscurity makes it ultimately undecidable; one reader's guess is as good, or bad, as another's.

Keach's argument that Shelley attempts to save an "inmost naked beauty of the meaning" at the high price of conceding that we have no adequate tools with which to reach that meaning calls to mind an earlier attempt to deal with interpretive interminability by one of the most influential "interpreters" of this century: Freud's "Analysis Terminable and Interminable." The impossibility of establishing, in theory or in practice, a definite end point at which analysis can be said to have been "completed" was, and is, as much of an embarrassment for therapeutic psychoanalysis as for literary criticism, and for the same reasons; if the process produces no definite solutions, we suspect it of arbitrariness and artificiality, the problems that it addresses of being either entirely fanciful or else unstable epiphenomena of some misrecognized underlying problem (in the words of Jacques Lacan: "[N]ot only in the public mind, but still more in the most private feelings of each psycho-analyst, imposture looms overhead" [*Fundamental Concepts,* 263]). Freud's solution, like Keach's, is to accept a pragmatic limitation in the effectiveness of psychoanalytic practice as the price to pay for leaving its theoretical claims to scientific accuracy inviolate. Some nuts, Freud concludes, are just too tough to crack. Feminine penis envy, for example, and masculine "repudiation of femininity" render the subject incapable of properly submitting to the therapeutic situation ("Analysis," 250ff.). He concedes that even when therapy is "successful," the therapist's decision to terminate analysis is always more or less arbitrary, a matter for the practitioner's judgment: "[T]he termination of an analysis is . . . a practical matter. . . . The business of the analysis is to secure the best possible psychological conditions for the functions of the ego; with that it has discharged its task" (249–50). Although the intent of the passage is to reassure his readers that these decisions are relatively facile in practice, "best possible" is indeterminable; this is as useful as claiming that one abandons the analysis of a text when one has said everything significant there is to say about it.

An alternative to ascribing the interpretive dilemma to an imperfect world of obscure, "veiling" words and ultradefensive egos is proposed in Derrida's essay "My Chances/*Mes Chances*." Derrida finds in Freud's *Psychopathology of Everyday Life* a comparison between the interpretive stance of the psychoanalyst and that of the "superstitious man," who finds deep significance in the most minor phenomena of life. Both are resolved, Freud writes, "not to let chance count as chance but to interpret it" (qtd. in "My Chances," 22). This "hermeneutical compulsion," as Derrida labels it, has become, in the popular mind, a defining feature of the psychoanalytic approach, and one that underscores the close relationship between the critical and psychoanalytic endeavors. Just as the most common reproach of literary critics from "ordinary readers" is that they find too much significance in the most minor details of texts, the popular image of the psychoanalyst is as someone who "reads too much" into our least important, and apparently involuntary, gestures—an idea whose intimate association with the Freudian project gives us the term "Freudian slip." Freud, naturally, does not admit to being indistinguishable from the "superstitious man"; he even tells a complex tale in order to demonstrate the difference—an incident that the superstitious person would regard as full of obscure portent but that he accepts as "mere chance"—but as in "Analysis Terminable and Interminable," the boundaries he establishes are purely pragmatic. It may be that "sometimes a cigar is just a cigar," but the option of reading it as more than just a cigar is always open.

Derrida argues that Freud's unsuccessful attempts to find some princi-

ple upon which to rest the distinction between superstitious paranoia
and hermeneutical tenacity are based upon a misrecognition of the nature of meaning. Derrida argues that it is an error to think of meaning as
something stable, an "inmost naked beauty" that is won with difficulty
by diligent hermeneutical endeavor. Rather, meaning tends to proliferate
endlessly in the promiscuous iterability of the "trace," or "mark," an
understanding of meaning that Derrida describes as a reemergence of
the atomism of Democritus, Epicurus, and Lucretius. The promiscuity of
the mark is a function of the "*atomystique* of the letter" (10), its lia-
bility to an atomistic deviation or *clinamen.* The "Freudian slip" is such
a *clinamen;* Freud cannot determine an absolute difference between
the "true" or "significant" slip and the mere accident, because there is
none. This does not mean either that a cigar is never more than a cigar
or that it is always a phallus; rather, it means that the boundary between
cigar and phallus, chance and meaning, error and essence, is fluid. The
insatiability of the hermeneutical compulsion and the interminability of
the hermeneutical process are not, then, the result of a world that is
remarkably niggardly of grist to the hermeneutical mill (veiling words
and defensive egos), but one that is riven with an infinitude of
"chances," or *clinamina,* any of which can defensibly be taken as a
starting point for hermeneutical activity.

Returning, with Derrida's argument in mind, to Shelley's description
of the ever-renewed source of unforeseen and unconceived delight in
Dante's poetic language, we are struck by the Lucretian provenance of
his imagery: the combination of flux ("fountain," "effluence") and punc-
tuality ("burning atom," "spark")—the latter most tellingly represented
by the meteorological indeterminacy of the lightning awaiting its im-
previsible conductor—and the imagery of (venereal) generational iteration (the acorn that promises a succession of oaks, the sequence of
social contexts or "peculiar relations" that "succeed" one another in the
same generational rhythm) that nonetheless veers into innovation ("new
relations are ever developed, the source of an unforeseen and an unconceived delight").

Note that the image of the acorn that contains all future oaks should
not be read in the Coleridgean terms of organic multeity-in-unity, but
the Lucretian terms of disjunctive iteration. Shelley makes his understanding of its significance clear when he returns to it in a letter written
in 1822: "Have you read Calderon's *Magico Prodigioso?* I find a striking
similarity between Faust & this drama, & if I were to acknowledge Coleridge's distinction I should say, Göthe was the greatest philosopher &
Calderon the greatest poet. *Cypriano* evidently furnished the *germ* of

Faust, as Faust may furnish the germ of other poems; although it is different from it in structure & plan, as the acorn from the oak" (*Letters,* 2:407). Shelley thinks of the acorn as a "germ" (or "seed") in the Lucretian atomistic sense. Cyprian does not become Faust through organic necessity any more than the "other poems" to which Goethe's play may one day give rise can be foretold by inspecting the seeds that constitute the *pépinière* that is *Faust.* What strikes Shelley about the relationship between oak and acorn is not their organic unity but their striking dissimilarity in "structure and plan."

The image of the "veil after veil" that "may be undrawn and the inmost naked beauty of the meaning never exposed" does not, however, seem to be explicitly Lucretian. Keach's readings reflect the norm for interpretations of Shelley's veil imagery ("Lift not the Painted Veil"; *Prometheus Unbound,* III, iii, 113; iv, 190; *Epipsychidion,* 472; "Ginevra," 122; "Triumph of Life," 32, 413); it is seen either as Platonic in origin (the veils as the phenomenal manifold that reflects, and distorts, the Ideal) or skeptical (the veil standing for our epistemological limitations, like Hoagwood's confining "circles"). If we reconsider these veils in the light of their Lucretian context, however, they have quite different implications for our understanding of the reader's relationship to the text.

Lucretius does not use the word "veil," but it is a small step from Shelley's veils, which are constantly being "undrawn," to his *membranae,* "a sort of outer skin perpetually peeled off the surface of objects and flying about this way and that through the air" (131, 4.31–32). This is the much-derided theory of the *simulacra,* those images composed of an atom-thin outer layer being thrown off by all objects in a constant stream, images that are the medium of sight and that, in their deformed versions, are the basis of occult visions, hallucinations, and dreams. We know from the nightmare vision of "Mask after mask" (cf. "veil after veil") that "fell from the countenance / And form of all" (536–37), which closes the "Triumph of Life," that Shelley was struck by this feature of Lucretian physics (Turner, "Shelley and Lucretius," 281–82). Critics who dutifully note the debt to Lucretius in the "Triumph" passage cannot, however, find much significance in this apparently outmoded, even silly, hypothesis of Lucretian science. Paul Turner, whose primary interest is Shelley's debt to Lucretius, disowns this one; he argues for a violent divorce between tenor and vehicle: "[T]he thought is Platonic, but the image is Lucretian" (281).

An answer to the problem can be found in Serres's revisionary reading of *De rerum natura.* Serres—who calls the *simulacra* "voiles invisibles"—reads them as a way of conceptualizing the infinitesimal limits to

the precision with which we can define any physical object. They are
not so much real as virtual objects that symbolize a mathematical truth
that is revealed to us by the transformations of the appearance of an
object relative to the vantage points from which it is viewed, a truth
that springs from the early attempt at an infinitesimal calculus, which
Serres argues forms the mathematical underpinning of Lucretian
physics.[7] If we recall the definition of an atom as the arbitrary but always significant limit to our ability to define the difference between a
curve and a tangent to that curve, then Serres's reasoning here is easy to
follow: "Les tuniques volantes sont les bords fluctuants, et les super-
ficies des limites. *Summo de corpore.* Les simulacres se détachent des
choses comme en leur traitement infinitésimal. Il s'en détache autant
qu'on veut. Chaque objet devient source d'une infinité d'enveloppes. La
vue est aussi rigoureuse que la méthode mathématicienne. Or, comme
tout objet n'a pu être produit que part et dans un tourbillon, ou dans un
spirale, c'est la turbulence comme telle qui devient émettrice de ses
enveloppes" (*La naissance,* 129).[8] "Il s'en détache autant qu'on veut";
"veil after veil can be undrawn"; arbitrary degrees of precision always
leave room for error, for the atom-*clinamen* of significant difference. As
we encounter, view, and attempt to determine the nature of any object,
what it presents to our gaze—what, for us, it *is*—is its border, its "skin."
The definition we make to ourselves of the nature of that skin posits a
certain "envelope" within which the "real" object must exist. But the
envelope is always too large. Just as no real-world trajectory can be
determined with sufficient precision to exclude tangential deviation,
there is always an infinite number of other possible envelopes between
the one we posit and the "real" object. That "border" of envelopes represents a fractal coastline of infinite complexity: "*Les formes idéales de
la géométrie ne sont pas transparentes, invariantes et vides, elles sont
denses et compactes,* pleines presque à saturation, d'un tissu complexe,
*et recouvertes, sur les bords, de voiles invisibles et que permettent de
les voir,* de limites infinitaires et qui pourtant sont là" (130).[9]

---

7. Asmis (chap. 15) offers an interesting account of Epicurean interest in the concept of
the "limit."

8. "The flying envelopes are fluctuating borders, the surface as it approaches its limit.
Summo de corpore. The *simulacra* detach themselves from things as in an infinitesimal calculation. As many can be removed as one wishes. Each object becomes a source of an infinite
number of envelopes. Sight is as rigorous as the mathematical method. Now, as all objects are
produced from and within a vortex [eddy], or in a spiral, it is turbulence itself that becomes
the emitter of its own envelopes" (my translation).

9. "*The ideal forms of geometry are not transparent, invariant, and empty, they are
dense and compact,* full almost to saturation, of a complex tissue, *and their borders are*

Shelley, then, in drawing on this image in the *Defence,* is proposing a theory of the text as a hermeneutical fractal. He regards the literary text as *infinitely* detailed: "All high poetry is infinite." McFarland quotes that line as an affirmation of the Romantic drive to the Absolute (*Forms of Ruin,* 28), but he has missed Shelley's point; like the Lucretian object presented to the eye, the literary text, ever revealing new meanings/veils in the light of the "peculiar relations" of its context of consumption, never appears twice in exactly the same way. Any one reading of the text is a "veil" that may conform more or less adequately to the "reality" of the text but that always leaves room for an infinite number of other "veils"—other valid descriptions of the work.

Shelley's veils are not something that stands *between* the reader and the work's "meaning"; they are all there is of meaning in the literary work of art. The "inmost naked beauty of the meaning" is never revealed because there is no such thing; Shelley's celebration of the "unforeseen and unconceived delights" offered by poems each time we reread them is not *faute de mieux,* as Keach implies, nor is it paradoxical, as Keach states; the veils do not represent an endless deferral of the "real meaning," but a perpetually renewed succession of "meanings," each as real as the next.

Shelley was fascinated by the erasure of scalar hierarchies, those moments in which "the part exceeds the whole." As early as his notes to *Queen Mab,* we find him expanding upon a Godwinian perfectibilian theme to this effect: "Time is our consciousness of the succession of ideas in our mind. . . . If . . . the human mind, by any future improvement of its sensibility, should become conscious of an infinite number of ideas in a minute, that minute would be eternity. . . . [T]he number of ideas which . . . [the human] mind is capable of receiving is indefinite" (note to *Queen Mab,* VIII, 203–7, in Hutchinson, 825). In the *Defence,* this kind of scalar indefiniteness characterizes the structure of Dante's poetry. This is what Shelley means by calling "each word" of that poetry "a burning atom of inextinguishable thought." The phrase is picked up from an earlier passage of the *Defence* that makes its meaning clear: "The parts of a composition may be poetical, without the composition as a whole being a poem. A single sentence may be considered as a whole though it may be found in a series of unassimilated portions; a single word even may be a spark of inextinguishable thought" (Reiman

---

covered with invisible veils that allow them to be seen, with infinitesimal limits that nonetheless are there" (my translation).

and Powers, 485–86). Each scalar level is potentially as compelling, as rich in significant detail, as any of the others. Shelley may appear to propose the individual word as a final limit to this fractal descent, but we should remember that the "atom" (or "spark") in this Lucretian framework represents only the arbitrary limit to our ability, or willingness, to make distinctions. Shelley's model for the proposition that words are the "atoms" of poems is Lucretius's example of letters as the atoms of words, a regression that implies the existence of ever finer scales of atomistic particularization. Shelley insisted upon the arbitrary and conventional nature of words as signs;[10] taken in isolation as "semantic units," or "building blocks" of literary significance, individual words would be quite meaningless. To reduce our analysis to the scale of individual words returns us to the infinite detail of the entire linguistic field in which words become meaningful, much as looking up a word in a dictionary can only refer us to a host of other words. This is why each word, each "particle" of a poem, covers an inexhaustible and "inextinguishable" wealth of information, or "thought."

I have so far been dealing primarily with Shelley's structural claim about the nature of poetry, that "veil after veil may be undrawn and the inmost naked beauty of the meaning never exposed." It is now time to turn to the second part of his statement, the dynamic prediction that "after one person and one age has exhausted all of its divine effluence which their peculiar relations enable them to share, another and yet another succeeds, and new relations are ever developed, the source of an unforeseen and an unconceived delight."

The critical consequences of the literary text's fractal nature, which I described in the previous chapter, might make us see this passage as advocating a simplistic relativism. It is not, and for two reasons. Although the text's "meaning" varies radically with our approach to the text, it is nonetheless possible, within this model, for us to communicate with each other about texts we understand quite differently. While we have no means of predicting, and are in practice constantly surprised by, what other readers make of a text, it is usually possible for us to identify, a posteriori, those parts of the text to which the reader has responded, to reconstitute the chain of *enchaînements*. Typically, our a posteriori certitude leads to the mistaken assumption that an a priori deduction should have been possible. What we confront here is our

---

10. See, e.g., the *Defence*: "[L]anguage is arbitrarily produced by the Imagination and has relation to thoughts alone" (Reiman and Powers, 483); or "On Love": "These words are inefficient and metaphorical—Most words so—No help" (Reiman and Powers, 474 n. 2).

inability to grasp the irreversibility of time; we assume that if a causal pathway can be traced backward from the present, it must, at least ideally, have been possible to trace it forward from the past.

Moreover, we can confidently declare some readings to be mistaken. It is true that there is no "inmost naked beauty of the meaning," but this is not to say that, in Paul Feyerabend's sense, "anything goes." This is not a version of Hogle's absolutely transgressive transferential flux; nor is it a "skeptical" position, in the proper sense of that word. The distinctive nature of a chaotic system is that it "is deterministic, but you can't say what it is going to do next" (Gleick, 251). A descriptive "envelope" or "veil" for a given text can be proposed that does not "fit"; some *enchaînements* are non sequiturs. The "Triumph of Life" is not a love lyric; *La divina commedia* is not a socialist-realist novel. For any "envelope" or "veil" that is proposed, however, there will remain a degree of "play" between it and the text, and that play is always significant.

Comparing two readings of the same text at radically different scales is like comparing two good translations of the one source text. Each is recognizably "determined" by the "same" causal matrix—the original text—but each will respond to something quite different within it; "il faut enchaîner, mais le mode de l'enchaînement n'est jamais nécessaire." The system "is deterministic, but you can't say what it is going to do next"; it operates, like quantum mechanics, according to a principle of indeterminacy.

The second, and more important, difference is that relativism is based upon a linear input-output model; it assumes that a given reader produces certain predictable kinds of reading. Shelley's fractal conception of the text is quite different. We are now in a position to understand why Shelley replicates the elements of the organicist paradigm so fully in the *Defence,* to the point where it can seem that he is, like Sydney, mounting his defense on Plato's terms. Like the organicists, he is fascinated by the relationship between part and whole, and like them again, he places whole and part into historical and hermeneutical feedback cycles—nonlinear cycles. The fractal complexity of the text explains why the results that he describes—"new relations are ever developed, the source of an unforeseen and an unconceived delight"—and that we can empirically corroborate in our experience of reading are so different from the "unchangeable constancy," or dynamic equilibrium, by which Burke characterized the ideal organic cycle. The key to Shelley's understanding of the history of the fractal text in consumption—the text in which "a single word even may be a spark of inextinguishable thought," that "spark" a "burning atom . . . pregnant with a lightning which has yet found no conductor"—is in those crucial lines from *Epip-sychidion* from which I have already quoted a part, but of which we can now understand the full significance:

> If you divide suffering and dross, you may
> Diminish till it is consumed away;
> If you divide pleasure and love and thought,
> Each part exceeds the whole. . . .

(178–81)

The therapeutic approach acknowledges that no one description of a text can be more than partial; but it is the role of the hermeneutical circle to recuperate these partial perspectives and use them to work toward totality. In McFarland's terminology, the Infinite can only be approached via the diasparactive, the *ens* via the *substantia*. Shelley's idea that each age has its "peculiar relations," which only allow it to grasp certain aspects of a given text, is central to the anthropological historicism analyzed in the first part of this book, but the goal of therapeutic hermeneutics is always to synthesize these partial perspectives into an Absolute; the fragments we encounter are always fragments of a single "Whole." Gadamer happily admits that "[e]very age has to understand a transmitted text in its own way" (261), but it is in the higher totality of the "Tradition" that these partial perspectives are summed into an abiding truth. Time "is not a yawning abyss, but is filled with the continuity of custom and tradition, in the light of which all that is handed down presents itself to us. . . . Everyone knows that curious impotence of our judgement where the distance in time has not given us sure criteria" (164–65). The real, absolute significance of the text is progressively revealed through time; reading is a homeostatic process in which errors are steadily eliminated as each generation refines its approach to the text. The telos of this process is the revelation of the text's, and the "culture's," narrative totality, or "plot," in the organic Aristotelian sense.

Shelley's fractal work of art has no plot in this sense; it has plots, but not "a plot"; parts, but no "Whole"; *substantia,* but no *ens.* Each "veil" is an attempted plot, but what it ignores (the "atoms" of detail that fall below any scale of description) is not insignificant detail that a later reading will recuperate into the main cycle of interpretation, but "sparks," "burning atoms of inextinguishable thought," "lightning which has yet found no conductor"—parts that exceed the whole. Each individual reading is at best a "preservation" of "scattered fragments" of the text, and the fragments that are missed will prove central to some future, perhaps radically different understanding of the text.

IV

It may appear that I am confusing two related but distinct arguments here. On the one hand, I am suggesting that the history of poetic *production* is chaotically creative over time, as poets respond to, and diverge from, the preceding efforts in their chosen genre; and on the other hand, that readers' *consumption* of texts is chaotically creative from reading to reading. Such a confusion is inevitable and legitimate, but it does mean that the directly political significance of the *Defence* as a solution to the political dilemmas of the "two thoughts" takes some teasing out. If, as Shelley suggested, poets are at once the creations and the creators of their age, they are its creations only insofar as they are its consumers. The chaotic creativity of poetic production is dependent upon the chaotic creativity inherent in the consumption of literary texts. On the other hand, without a tradition of poetic production the chaotic creativity of textual consumption would be merely a curious end product, without further consequences for literary history. It is the creative indeterminacy of the "individual talent's" response to an inherited tradition that ensures the constant innovation that characterizes the evolution of traditions; ironically, however, this innovation can only be effected if and when the "individual talent" attempts to add to the tradition. Lyotard makes this point particularly well: "Quand Cézanne prend son pinceau, l'enjeu de la peinture est questionné, Schönberg se met à son piano, l'enjeu de la musique, Joyce saisit sa plume, celui de la littérature. Non seulement de nouvelles stratégies pour 'gagner' sont essayées, mais la nature du 'succès' est interrogée" (*Le différend*, 201).[11] The rules of the game are altered by playing it; the "unhappy" speech act becomes "happy." This is what is missing from Wittgenstein's account of learning to "continue the language game," the possibility that part can overthrow whole, individual talent divert the tradition. In Shelley's words: "every great poet must inevitably innovate upon the example of his predecessors" (Reiman and Powers, 484). This was the moral of Varnedoe's story of William Webb Ellis. Varnedoe's own account of how "artists grasped new possibilities from within established games, and

---

11. "When Cézanne picks up his paint-brush, what is at stake in painting is put into question; when Schönberg sits down at his piano, what is at stake in music; when Joyce grabs hold of his pen, what is at stake in literature. Not only are new strategies for 'gaining' tried out, but the nature of the 'success' is questioned" (*The Differend*, 139).

transformed what was known into the seeds of something new" (23), makes art history just as much a history of consumption as of production.

The foregoing argument helps to explain, and is in turn illuminated by, an earlier passage in the *Defence* that had hitherto puzzled us; that is Shelley's apparently organicist encomium of the unifying power of the imagination: "A man, to be greatly good, must imagine intensely and comprehensively . . . the pains and pleasures of his species must become his own." If we continue the passage, we can see that Shelley is conscious of the limits to the possibility of realizing this totalitarian species-being: "Poetry enlarges the circumference of the imagination by replenishing it with thoughts of ever new delight, which have the power of attracting and assimilating to their own nature all other thoughts, and which form new intervals and interstices whose void forever craves fresh food" (Reiman and Powers, 488). The "ever new delight" here is the same as the "unforeseen and unconceived delight" in the "veil after veil" passage. Shelley concedes that there is a constant attempt to complete the hermeneutical cycle; he admits the mnemonic *impulse* toward totalization, but suggests that in practice it is constantly defeated by the fractal complexity of poetry and "pleasure and love and thought." The "thoughts of ever new delight" that are furnished by poetry initiate the hermeneutical attempt to synthesize a whole; these "thoughts" suggest to us a frame with which to approach the text, which has "the power of attracting and assimilating to [its] own nature all other thoughts"; in terms of hermeneutical theory, we could say that this frame posits a whole into which we can "attract and assimilate" the parts that will confirm, with minor modifications, our understanding of the whole. We have seen, however, that with a fractal text those parts will exceed the whole into which they are to be assimilated. As each new proposed "whole" attracts and assimilates "parts," those parts, in turn, suggest new "wholes" quite incommensurable with the first. This is what Shelley means by the "new intervals and interstices whose void forever craves fresh food"; an unbridgeable gap constantly reappears between parts and the wholes into which we would assimilate them, a sublime "void"—that irreducibly significant, arbitrarily small gap between the interpretation and the text as its hermeneutical asymptote— whose "food" is the "veil after veil" of successively ruined interpretations.

This helps us understand how Shelley reconciles his "two thoughts" of death (or negation) and memory in order to account for both change and continuity in literary and political history. The text's role as *clina-*

men in the mnemonic cycles of cultural reproduction means that the part not only exceeds, but partially negates, the whole, threatening it with the kind of atomistic disintegration—the proliferation of interstices or void space between part and whole—that Burke's rhetoric of organic totalitarianism was designed to overcome. Shelley insists upon this destructive capacity of the part relative to the whole; the textual atom is a "spark, a burning atom of inextinguishable thought" and "pregnant with . . . lightning"; literature, as an atom of the cultural "whole" that attempts constantly to reproduce itself, permanently threatens destruction to that "whole": "Poetry is a sword of lightning, ever unsheathed, which consumes the scabbard that would contain it" (491). The "scabbard," stands for any would-be organic totality that would enlist poetry as its mnemonic tool or organ of reproduction.

This imagery carries a deliberate echo of the sparks scattered from the "unextinguished hearth" of the "Ode to the West Wind." The revolutionary destination of the "sparks" in that poem is clear, as it is when Shelley returns to the imagery in the "Triumph of Life," where Rousseau in his capacity as principal propagator of the ideals that brought about the French Revolution tells him that the "spark I bore" gave birth to "a thousand beacons" (207); society's consumption of Shelley's words/ atoms/sparks spells, he hopes, its consumption by the ensuing revolutionary fire. But in the *Defence,* what was, in the "Ode," a purely personal, and almost despairing, desire for revolutionary capability has become a calm assurance that "all high poetry" inevitably contains the "sparks" that will unwrite the present, and rewrite the future.

Lightning, apart from its Lucretian associations, was an image popularly associated with liberty and revolution; the enormous popularity of Benjamin Franklin, the "Electrical Ambassador," in prerevolutionary France was based in part on what was perceived to be a direct relationship between the mastery of lightning and the advent of liberty (Schama, 44). Franklin's popularity may in part explain the widespread adoption of the Promethean myth as a symbol of revolutionary aspiration, as Turgot's epigram *"Eripuit Coelo Fulmen, Sceptrumque Tyrannis"* suggests (qtd. in Schama, 44; he translates: "He seized fire from the heavens and the sceptre from tyrants").

But that Promethean image of revolution is merely the age-old oedipal model; it resolves itself into the question of who has the thunderbolt/ phallus. As such, it returns us to the "revolutionary" stasis of Bloom's anxiety of influence. In that model we can overthrow the burden of memory only by submitting to it so completely that we replicate it, becoming the father/Jupiter in our turn. Nothing could be further from the "unforeseen and unconceived delight" promised by Shelley. The anxiety of influence makes no sense in a world of ceaseless, chaotic creativity. Shelley's great advance in revolutionary theory—the lesson that he hoped would revive revolutionary enthusiasm from the general despair over the disappointed expectations of the French Revolution— is to offer us a non-oedipal revolutionism, one that predates Deleuze and Guattari's by a century and a half.

Laclau and Mouffe describe "the classic concept of revolution" as one that "implied the *foundational* character of the revolutionary act, the institution of a point of concentration of power from which society could be 'rationally' reorganized" (176). Shelley's revolutionary poetic lightning also has a dual nature; the destructiveness of the poetic text, its entropic capacity to destroy the context in which it is produced, is matched by its creativity, its negentropic capacity to produce a constant stream of "unforeseen and unconceived delight." However, this double-ness reconciles, rather than paradoxically fuses, the "two thoughts" of death and memory.

This mutuality of entropy and negentropy can only be understood in terms of the Lucretian system in which death and memory can be grasped simultaneously, where they are, in Serres's words, "[d]eux temps pensés pour la première fois ensemble, équilibre et déséquilibre évalués pour la première fois l'un par rapport à l'autre" (*La naissance,* 110).[12] One *temps,* the cyclic, organic time of absolute memory, leads, if it is allowed to dominate to the exclusion of the other, to the infinite redundancy of perpetual repetition; in Shelley's words, the "universe" is "annihilated in our minds by the recurrence of impressions blunted by reiteration." "Le savoir ainsi enchaîné, itératif infiniment," argues Serres, "n'est que science de mort. . . . Il n'y a rien à savoir, à découvrir, à inventer, dans le répétitif. . . . C'est le zéro de l'information, la redon-dance" (136).[13] The cyclic impulse of therapeutic organicism devolves into the thanatological "desire to be for ever as we are" that Shelley sees as the basis of our belief in a life after death: "*Le Même, c'est le Non-Etre*" (137).[14]

The other *temps,* that of death, ruin, and disequilibrium, "le temps

12. "two orders of time conceived for the first time together—equilibrium and disequilib-rium evaluated for the first time in their relationship to each other" (my translation).

13. "The train of thought that comes from [the order of reasons], infinitely iterative, is but a science of death. . . . There is nothing to be learned, to be discovered, to be invented, in this repetitive world. . . . It is information-free, complete redundance" ("Lucretius: Science and Religion," 100).

14. "*The Same is Non-Being*" ("Lucretius: Science and Religion," 100).

. . . qui use l'horloge . . . [et] ruine la maison" (110),[15] is equally inconceivable, for Shelley, as an absolute; maximum entropy and the infinite
conservation of information would in *effect* be identical—an infinitely
redundant, undifferentiable totality.

Shelley's dictum that poets "are in one sense the creators and in another the creations of their age" shows that, like Lucretius, he understood "les processus en causalité circulaire ou semi-circulaire" (223);[16]
but these circles never quite return on themselves without the appearance of "new intervals and interstices whose void forever craves fresh
food": "Il découvre l'efficace de la fluctuation au hasard, et de l'écart à
l'équilibre: un temps déborde l'autre, est débordé par lui. Il découvre la
croissance de la complexité, lorsque l'écart réapparaît au cours des cycles de retour à l'équilibre" (223).[17] Shelley's "intervals and interstices"
are equivalent to Serres's ever recurrent "écart à l'équilibre"; it is the
perpetually renewed "lack" or "discontent" that Lucretius makes the
motor of history:

> *La dérive produit la réparation qui produit la dérive. . . . Le
> désir est l'effet de la dégradation et il en est la cause;* ou *la
> dégradation est cause du désir et elle en est l'effet. . . .* Cela ne
> fait pas cercle, puisque la solution est toujours originale et
> neuve, puisque le décalage est toujours là, puisque l'inclinaison
> réapparaît toujours, puisque le temps de la dérive est le fond de
> l'entraînement. Cela ne fait pas cercle, autrement l'équilibre ser-
> ait rétabli, nous serions victorieux de la dérive, il n'y aurait pas
> d'histoire. Cela fait cercle, cependent, pour l'ensemble des pro-
> cessus de la causalité. . . . [C]ela décrit une spirale sans cesse en
> écart sur elle-même, une turbination qui, en avançant, cherche et
> perd toujours l'équilibre. Voilà, en précision, *la solution tour-
> billonnaire:* elle est rigoureusement isomorphe à la genèse natu-
> relle à partir du chaos. (222–23)[18]

---

15. "time . . . which wears out the clock . . . [and] ruins the dwelling" (my translation).

16. "the processes of circular or semicircular causality" (my translation).

17. "He discovers the efficacy of random fluctuations, and of the deviation from equilibrium: one order of time overthrows the other, and is overthrown by it in its turn. Lucretius
discovers the growth of complexity when the deviation reappears in the cyclical return to
equilibrium" (my translation).

18. "*Deviation produces correction, which produces deviation. . . . Desire is both effect
and cause of the decay; or decay is both cause and effect of desire. . . .* This process does not
form a circle, because the solution is always original and new, because the offset is always
there, because the angle of error always reappears, because the basis of the process is time-as-
deviation [time that produces error]. This process does not form a circle, otherwise equilib-

In this *solution tourbillonnaire* Shelley manages to reconcile his "two thoughts." Memory and death, reproduction and error, no longer appear as the absolute opposites that they seemed necessarily to be in Foucault's analysis. Instead, the fractal nature of the literary text makes memory, no matter how "faithful" it attempts to be, inevitably creative, which is to say, inevitably destructive of the past it attempts to preserve.

Shelley accepts, then, that poetry is a key moment in the reproductive, reiterative cycles both of the wider society and of the individual's interpretation of the self's relationship to the world. He fully acknowledges the role poetry plays in the mechanisms of social reproduction central to the organicist theory, and equally acknowledges their predominance in social practice. But he has learned from Lucretius that, in an infinitely complex world, memory is, perforce, an agent of innovation as much as of conservation. Memory is indeed a "quaint witch," as he calls her in his "Letter to Maria Gisborne" (132). In Shelley's model, it is memory itself that propagates death. This is what he means when he says in the *Defence* that poetry "makes familiar objects be as if they were not familiar; [because] it reproduces all that it represents" (Reiman and Powers, 487). Mimetic representation, the mnemonic function of poetry, cannot help but be a re-production, or re-creation, that introduces some degree of error into the "original." Or, as he says elsewhere in the same work, poetry has the power to make "us the inhabitants of a world to which the familiar world is a chaos. It reproduces the common universe of which we are portions and percipients, and it purges from our inward sight the film of familiarity which obscures from us the wonder of our being. . . . It creates anew the universe" (505). Each revolutionary "death," each *clinamen*-meteor that disrupts the reproductive iteration of the social context, introduces innovation into the reproductive cycle. And it is only because the text mnemonically, and "organically," "reproduces the common universe of which we are portions and percipients" that it also has the power to revolutionize and "create anew" that universe through accumulated entropy.

What, then, is the meaning of Shelley's claim that a poet "participates in the eternal, the infinite, and the one" and of these other similar statements from the *Defence*:

---

rium would be restored, we would be victorious over deviation [drift/error], and there would be no history. This process does form a circle, however, for the processes of causality considered as a whole. . . . this process describes a spiral constantly in diversion from itself, a vortex that, in its progress, perpetually seeks and perpetually loses equilibrium. This is, precisely, the *vortical solution*—rigorously isomorphic with the natural process of creation from chaos" (my translation).

A Poet participates in the eternal, the infinite, and the one; as far as relates to his conceptions, time and place and number are not. The grammatical forms which express the moods of time, and the difference of persons and the distinction of place are convertible with respect to the highest poetry without injuring it as poetry. (483)

A Poet therefore would do ill to embody his own conceptions of right and wrong, which are usually those of his place and time, in his poetical creations, which participate in neither. (488)

Few poets of the highest class have chosen to exhibit the beauty of their conceptions in its naked truth and splendour; and it is doubtful whether the alloy of costume, habit, etc., be not necessary to temper this planetary music for mortal ears. (487)

[Poetry] arrests the vanishing apparitions which haunt the interlunations of life, and veiling them or in language or in form sends them forth among mankind. (505)

Every epoch under names more or less specious has deified its peculiar errors. . . . But a poet considers the vices of his contemporaries as the temporary dress in which his creations must be arrayed. (486–87)

Veil after veil may be undrawn, and the inmost naked beauty of the meaning never exposed. (500)

On the one hand there appears to be some absolute poetic quiddity, or *ens,* with which the poem has a privileged, although unclear, association; but on the other hand, that *ens* appears to be necessarily, and permanently, veiled and obscured by the *substantia* in which it is embodied.

We saw above that Keach reads this as the tragic condition of poetry; it is derived from a pure source, but is inevitably corrupted by the impurity of the language from which it must be constructed. Such an argument is an extension of Plato's imagery of the cave, with poetry as the delusive shadows cast upon the cave wall by the light of Truth. Keach's belief that Shelley is frustrated and oppressed by the necessity of dealing with the "temporary dress" of permanent truths echoes Plato's belief that it is foolish to watch the delusive shadows if one can explore their source instead.

Shelley himself was taken with the imagery of Plato's cave; in *Adonais,* for example, the "dome of many-coloured glass" that "Stains the white radiance of Eternity" is derived from it, and so are his various injunctions not to lift "the painted veil which those who live / Call life." The *Defence* being a direct response to Plato's *Republic,* it would surprise us if that book's most famous passage had left no mark on the *Defence*'s thought and imagery. Keach believes that Shelley resents the obscuring veils of language in which poems must be dressed; but in the quotations given above, we learn only that such "veiling" is *necessary,* not that it is inherently desirable or undesirable. It is "the temporary dress in which [the poet's] creations must be arrayed." Keach argues that Shelley is putting a brave face on his inner turmoil, but this seems to be begging the question. Our analysis of the "veil after veil" passage suggests that this necessity is not something toward which one can really *have* an attitude; the veils, delusive and temporary as they are, are all we know of any reality. The sonnet "Lift not the painted veil" assures us that the "one who had lifted it" failed to find "truth" (14); the speaker in *Adonais* has not as yet tried the experiment.

It must strike every contemporary reader of Plato's allegory of the cave how nearly Plato appears to have anticipated the situation of viewers in a cinema. From Shelley's point of view, the movement from poetic *substantia* to existential *ens* would make as much sense as for the viewer of a film to gaze directly into the beam of the projector to find the "essence" of the insubstantial shadows on the screen. The "white radiance of eternity" must be "stained" if it is not to be an infinitely redundant *non-être.*

"THE WITCH OF ATLAS"

But what, then, of poetry's, and the poet's, relationships to "the eternal, the infinite, and the one"? An answer, as well as a general corroboration of our reading of the *Defence,* can be found by turning to one of Shelley's poetic meditations on the role and nature of poetry, "The Witch of Atlas." The Witch, whether or not she is supposed to be identified with that of "the still cave of the witch Poesy" ("Mont Blanc," 44), seems to represent poetry, or at least its effects; her cave holds "Visions swift and sweet and quaint" (161), which she visits inconstantly upon humanity.

The word "quaint" is interesting; not one of Shelley's favorite adjectives, it seems reasonable to wonder if he has in mind that other witch of his, the "quaint witch Memory" from the "Letter to Maria Gisborne." The very least one could say of this poetic Witch's relationship to Mnemosyne is that it is "quaint." She herself is a poet: "All day the wizard lady sate aloof . . . broidering the pictured poesy . . . upon her growing woof " (249-53). The poetry she writes and represents is of the kind described in the *Defence*—a deeply playful "disorganization" of normal hierarchies of oppositions and values. While she writes, a fire burns in her hearth:

> Men scarcely know how beautiful fire is—
> Each flame of it is as a precious stone
> Dissolved in ever moving light, and this
> Belongs to each and all who gaze upon.
> The Witch beheld it not, for in her hand
> She held a woof that dimmed the burning brand.
>
> (259-64)

Shelley rediscovers here the radical notion of "words of flame" from the *Revolt,* and reinvents it. Fire is entropy—the dissipation of heat—made visible; the purely evanescent beauty of flame is a negentropic dissipative structure dependent upon that entropic dissolution; as such it defeats both the appeal to any noumenal *ens* and the absolute restrictions of property that are its capitalist counterpart, creating a radically democratic, utterly promiscuous beauty that belongs, unlike the "precious stones" it rivals, to "each and all" (see 262).

The Witch's poetry is even more insubstantial, or insubstantiating, than the fire; her poetic "woof" has all the beauty and entropic, revolutionary potential of the Lucretian lightning/*clinamen* awaiting its conductor. The Witch accordingly is an atelic prankster seeking to subvert "all the code of custom's lawless law" (541), wreaking havoc among all the structures of state power (church, court, army, and family respectively in stanzas lxxiii-lxxvi). She is always one step removed from the world, aloof, unwilling to treat as necessarily real and present the hypostatized forms of custom's lawless laws, which are "Written upon the brows of old and young" (542). "[L]ittle did the sight disturb her soul" (545), Shelley tells us.

The Witch, and the "Witch," pose starkly for us the problem of poetry's relationship to the amnesiac order of change and its putative eternal verities. On the one hand, the Witch is strongly associated, in the poem, with meteorological imagery—Lucretian shorthand for contingent indeterminacy. Her mother, after being impregnated by Apollo, runs through a (neg)entropic series of metamorphoses—"dissolv[ing] away" (64) into a "vapour" (65), "then into a cloud" (66), "then into a meteor" (69), and lastly into an asteroid (71-72). This *clinamen*-ridden career sets the pattern for the Witch's own history. She herself is constantly associated with Shelley's habitual meteorological pyrotechnics: her ministering thoughts "Cloth[e] themselves or with the Ocean foam, / Or with the wind, or with the speed of fire" (211-12); her boat moves "like a cloud / Upon a stream of wind" (369-70); her troops of "ministering Spirits" emblazon their merits on "meteor flags" (459, 462); "Ofttime" she "Follow[s] the serpent lightning's winding track [perhaps an allusion to *De rerum*, 2:213-15] . . . laugh[ing] to hear the fireballs roar behind" (485-88); and to her eye, "the constellations reel and dance / Like fire-flies" (269-70).

The Witch subverts oppositions in accordance with the *Defence*'s poetic principle of "yok[ing] all irreconcilable things"—such as the fire and snow she kneads together to create the hermaphrodite, a figure who disrupts in turn the stability of sexual difference. The hermaphrodite is the Witch's only "child" and, like Cythna's child in the *Revolt,* is a *clinamen* in the order of generational filiation. The Witch herself is a "sexless bee / Tasting all blossoms and confined to none" (589-90)—an affirmation of the disruptive *jouissance* of sexuality over its inscription in the order of custom as generational "reproduction."

In the Witch's dealings with "those who were less beautiful" (618)—the apparently circumlocutory phrase for "evil" or "wicked" people is a careful avoidance of hypostatization—Shelley returns to one of his favorite images of entropic, atomistic erasure to describe the way the Witch, as the principle of revolutionary poetic amnesia, makes

> All harsh and crooked purposes more vain
>   Than in the desart is the serpent's wake
> Which the sand covers.
>
>   (619-21)

A reshuffling of the atomistic order that maintains the trace in the sand obliterates it completely; information is lost irretrievably, and revolutionary innovation enters by the same door.

Above all there is the structure of the poem itself, or rather its antistructure. It begins logically enough with the Witch's conception, but after that it is motivated by sheer narrativity-without-narrative or peripeteia-without-plot, dazzling us, like the democratic art of the fire, with ephemeral verbal pyrotechnics. Mary Shelley calls it, in terms that set

the tone for nearly all subsequent criticism both hostile and apprecia-
tive, "wildly fanciful," "a brilliant congregation of ideas," and "abstract
and dreamy" (Hutchinson, 388–89). This is true as far as it goes, and the
phrase "congregation of ideas" is particularly shrewd—identifying the
structural principle on which the poem is based as Gothic constellation
rather than "organic" interdependence. But "abstract and dreamy,"
which inevitably comes to the ear with a flurry of luminous wings beating vainly and ineffectually in the void, is definitely misleading. The
verse impels us forward; thirty of the poem's seventy-odd stanzas begin
with "And," imparting a marked narrative urgency to the poem (And
then . . . and then . . .).

This simulacrum of narrative drive is purely ironic, however; the
poem subverts the concept of the unified, Aristotelian plot by being a
purely contingent sequence of absolute events; it "tell[s] no story, false
or true" (4). The insistently repeated "and" throughout the poem is
merely the trace, or scar, of the suturing that has brought these disjunctive narrative elements together.

The poem is a deliberate affront to the therapeutic-organic drive to
narrative absolutism. As in Shelley's "Triumph of Life," one is forced to
respond to the poem empirically as a series of "unforeseen and unconceived" events; one is never quite sure what any given part of the poem
"remembers" of what has gone before. The poem's parts cannot help
but exceed a whole that can never be identified. The poem's "ands" are
as much disjunctions as conjunctions, moments of *enchaînement* in
Lyotard's sense; their insistent repetition flaunts the Gothic aggregative
principle that underlies the poem's construction. The Witch's "story" is
a chain of digressions, each of which leads only to a new digression—or
clinamen—and never back to the "main" story; it is a series of atomistic *phrases* rather than *un langage* (see Lyotard, *Le différend,* 200).

This digressive, disjunctive sequence of events—none of which builds
upon preceding ones, although one event does sometimes inherit certain things from its predecessors (the Witch herself, the hermaphrodite,
et cetera)—comes to no resolution. The poem ends with an entropic
collapse familiar to all readers of Shelley's poetry (see, e.g., "Julian and
Maddalo," *Prometheus Unbound,* the "Ode to Liberty," and "Mont
Blanc"); the narrator suddenly leaves off with secrets still in his (or her?)
possession:

> . . . what she did to sprites
> And gods . . .
>   .   .   .   .

> I will declare another time; for it is
>   A tale more fit for the weird winter nights
> Than for these garish summer days, when we
> Scarcely believe much more than we can see.

(666–72)

Shelley's endlessly digressive and centerless narrative mounts an assault on our concepts of identity. It is imperative for the therapeutic approach to be able confidently to ground notions of personal identity in an assertion of narrative totality: we "understand ourselves inescapably in narrative," writes Taylor, because we seek a "meaningful unity" in our lives, grounded upon the "a priori unity of a human life through its whole extent" (*Sources of the Self,* 51). What is it, in the rarely used "name" Witch—actually a descriptive label—or the far more frequently employed personal pronoun "she," that guarantees to us the continuity of the Witch's identity through the amnesiac string of incidents in which "she" figures? These unnarrativizable incidents in Shelley's poem are best described by Derrida's Lucretian definition of "events" in "My Chances/*Mes Chances*": "[T]here are those of us who are inclined to think that unexpectability conditions the very structure of an event. Would an event that can be anticipated and therefore apprehended or comprehended, or one without an element of absolute encounter, actually be an event in the full sense of the word? . . . [A]n event worthy of this name cannot be foretold" (6).

Taylor, or any other therapeutic philosopher who wants "the future to 'redeem' the past" (*Sources of the Self,* 50–51), cannot allow the possibility of an event in this sense. The truly unpredictable—what I have elsewhere called the "irreversible"—is always, in Burke's sense, sublime; it creates a discontinuity in the "unchangeable constancy" of organic auto-reproduction. Any "event," in Burke's world, amounts to a revolution, and Shelley's Witch *is* a revolutionary, although an entirely non-oedipal one; she converts the army of "king Amasis" to pacifism and liberates his political prisoners (stanza lxxv), but establishes no alternative power structure in his place. Her revolution is an "and" added to a sociopolitical order that was premised upon the abolition or the permanent suspension of the possibility of an "and." Her "and" announces both the (partial) erasure, or supersession, of that old order and the inevitability of change and innovation.

The insecurity of the Witch's identity, the chaotic creativity with which her career develops, and the necessity for the reader to adopt a radically empirical approach to her wholly irreversible history all find their counterparts in the *Defence*'s conception of poetry as that which removes "veil after veil" but of which the "inmost naked beauty of the meaning" is never revealed. The Witch, of course, is also veiled: "Light the vest of flowing metre / She wears" (37–38); her vest/veil is "light," but not lightly to be removed:

> If you unveil my Witch, no Priest or Primate
> Can shrive you of that sin, if sin there be
> In love, when it becomes idolatry.
>
> (46–48)

Keach uses the Witch's "vest of flowing metre" as further evidence of Shelley's belief in the unfortunate necessity of "clothing or veiling . . . thought in language" (*Shelley's Style,* 182). He does not address these later lines, however. Not only does Shelley here explicitly confirm our understanding that the removal of "veil after veil" is never an unveiling per se, he also reasserts in only half-playful terms what he had already implied in his sonnet "Lift not the painted veil"—that the attempt to find the "inmost naked truth," which we assume, or hope, lies behind the painted veil, is not only delusive, but a "sin."

The nature of that "sin" is made clear to us by the contrast Shelley draws between the Witch's light robe and Peter Bell's "looped and windowed raggedness" (40). To strip Peter of his poetic "veil" is all too easy; the arras of poetic *substantia* in Wordsworth's didactic fable is woven for the sole purpose of disclosing the "universal," Christian *ens* that lurks behind it. In Shelley's opinion, this is not poetry, the anti-essential essence of which is to "tell no story, false or true" (4), but to "leap and play . . . Till its claws come" (6–7). In the words of the *Defence:* "A poet . . . would do ill to embody his own conceptions of right and wrong, which are usually those of his place and time, in his poetical creations, which participate in neither." The attempt to so embody Wordsworth's "own conceptions of right or wrong" leads him, in Shelley's view, to shut his poetry off from its true sources of "unforeseen and unconceived delight," the infinitely complex and endlessly changeable "vest of *flowing* metre" that is poetry's *substantia*-without-*ens.*

In place of this, so to speak, profound superficiality, Wordsworth has opted for a superficial profundity—the therapeutic organicist's desire to move above the flux of process to an Absolute that in Shelley's view is merely infinite redundancy. This is "Hell's hyperequatorial climate" (42), the same inhabited by the "dead and damned" Peter Bell the Third. In both cases, the emptiness of their pretensions to transcendence, of their claims to see "beyond the bottom . . . Of truth's clear well" ("Peter Bell the Third," 539-40), is the death of true poetic creativity; Peter is "hardly fit to fling a rhyme at" ("Witch," 44), because Wordsworth has attempted to sacrifice the fractal multiplicity and complexity of his text, and the joyful processual flux of the world, to the hollow ideal of an eternally selfsame noumenal *ens,* which in Shelley's view is where death, memory, poetry, and all are reduced to nonbeing.

Shelley's strictures against didacticism have drawn much ironical comment, starting with Claire Clairmont's mordant comment on "Shelley's three aversions, God Almighty, Lord Chancellor and didactic Poetry" (Clairmont journal, 8 November 1820; qtd. in White, 2:602 n. 63). The denunciation of didacticism from the *Defence* quoted above is among the six passages quoted earlier to illustrate Shelley's apparent commitment to an ideal of poetic "eternity," several of which are drawn from similar attacks on poetic didacticism. This would appear to undermine our understanding of the basis of Shelley's condemnation of Wordsworth's "sin." Perhaps didacticism is wrong because it is too much concerned with the ephemeral, and too little with the eternal and unchanging?

We come now to the second aspect of the Witch that makes her useful for thinking the relationship between poetry's ephemerality and its eternal "truths." The Witch appears to draw a sharp distinction between herself and the entropic world she inhabits. When the "Ocean-Nymphs and Hamadryades, / Oreads and Naiads" (217-18) sue to "live forever in the light / Of her sweet presence" (223-24), she replies, "This may not be," because she cannot tolerate their ephemerality:

> "The fountains where the Naiades bedew
> Their shining hair at length are drained and dried;
>   The solid oaks forget their strength, and strew
>   Their latest leaf upon the mountains wide;
>   The boundless Ocean like a drop of dew
> Will be consumed—the stubborn centre must
> Be scattered like a cloud of summer dust—
>
> "And ye with them will perish one by one—
>   If I must sigh to think that this shall be—
> If I must weep when the surviving Sun
>   Shall smile on your decay—Oh, ask not me
> To love you till your little race is run;

I cannot die as ye must . . . over me
Your leaves shall glance—the streams in which ye dwell
Shall be my paths henceforth, and so, farewell!"

(226—40)

This is the portrait of a world caught in that entropic "storm / Which with the shattered present chokes the past" (*Epipsychidion,* 211-12), a world in which not just the individual "eyed flower" but the "boundless ocean" is "a drop of dew" waiting to be consumed. The question is what we are to make of the Witch's relationship to that atomistic (272), entropic flux? Why is she apparently not a part of it, and if she in some way represents the revolutionary force of poetry, what does that mean for poetry's own relationship to the "storm of time"?

One answer would be to argue that the Witch has attained the therapeutic totalitarian view of a world "eterne in mutabilitie." As such she would represent a sort of constant derivative of the world's geometric rate of change; this is what Hogle has in mind when he makes her embody his "transferential One"—the only possible *ens* of his diasparactive world, the principle of the interchangeability of all signs become an endless, universal I AM, or "Great Memory" (*Shelley's Process,* 217). In support of such a reading one could cite the Witch's apparent access to a world

beyond the rage
Of death or life, while they were still arraying
In liveries ever new, the rapid, blind
And fleeting generations of mankind.

(613-16)

This is where she hides "those she saw most beautiful" (593), after she steals them from the grave to restore them to a strange kind of suspended animation. Reading the Witch as an allegory of poetry, we could then argue that poetry is the eternal Absolute that arises from a world of error when that world is stripped of its delusive veils, vests, and "liveries ever new."

In a recent paper in the same "decentering" vein as Hogle's work, Hall has revived Bloom's argument that the Witch represents a pure autarchic alterity that challenges our capacity for imaginative transcendence of our everyday world of mutability and error ("Poetic Autonomy"; see 259 n. 1). Hall cites the passage I am considering here, to prove that there is no point of contact between the Witch and the mutable world inhabited by the naiads, which is, of course, our world (209). She equates this passage with two other passages in the poem: one, which I have already quoted, that follows her speech to the naiads— "All day the wizard lady sate aloof . . . broidering the pictured poesy . . . upon her growing woof" (249-53)—and one, which precedes it, in which the Witch, realizing that her beauty has noxious effects upon those who gaze upon it, weaves "a subtle veil . . . A shadow for the splendour of her love" (151-52). Hall argues that this implies a dualism between the Witch as transcendent, absolute *ens* and our world of mutable *substantia*. For the transcendent to be perceived in our fallen world, it must disguise itself in mortal form, in this case the Witch's veil.

But such a reading—apart from "sinning" against Shelley's injunction not to seek to unveil his Witch—struggles to account for the Witch's actual behavior in the poem. Despite renouncing contact with the nymphs, her period of sitting "aloof" seems to last indeed but a "day" (249). The corpses she reanimates might lie "age after age / Mute, breathing, beating, warm and undecaying / Like one asleep" (609-11), but she herself lives emphatically in the present; not rising above the world, but moving on with it; not only caught up in the turbulent flow of the world's transient events, but actively adding to that turbulence. She cannot bear to love the rapid, blind, and fleeting generations of mankind, but she can bear to tease, subvert, and revolutionize them.

If we return to the Witch's speech to the naiads, however, we see that what the Witch is claiming there is not the power to become a transcendental representative of all these myriad acts of mutability; rather, she claims the power of forgetting:

> "If I must sigh to think that this shall be—
> If I must weep when the surviving Sun
>   Shall smile on your decay—Oh, ask not me
> To love you till your little race is run;
>   I cannot die as ye must . . ."

If the Witch must remain attached to the past, *if* she must "sigh" and "weep" for each entropic loss, *then* she refuses to love the passing forms of the world. The figure that hovers behind this speech, and particularly in the line "I *cannot* die as ye must," is the sibyl, whose enchainment to memory and the past makes a mockery of her immortality. The sibyl "wants to die" because her world has been reduced to an infinitely redundant world of absolute and inalterable memory. The Witch, however, chooses to sacrifice the claims of memory in order to perpetuate the possibility of love; she "tast[es] all blossoms" but is "confined to none." She maintains her fierce enjoyment of the world's catastrophic career by claiming the Olympian right of a near total indifference to its fate, past and future; little does any "sight disturb her soul." This is not to say that she is, like the sibyl, indifferent to the world per se, far from it; rather, her radically empirical approach to the world breaks the chains that would tie her, futilely, to loss. She overcomes her eternity by becoming eternally contemporary. Only those rare few "most beautiful" can penetrate her unconcern, and the dubious immortality she bestows upon them says more of the limitations of her devotion to what is past—and the limitations on the efficacy of that devotion—than of its intensity.[19]

This amnesiac capacity makes it impossible for her to subsume the chaotic flux of events into an Absolute. The flux is her element; nothing in her transcends its entropic powers of erasure. This is the importance of the poem's undermining of identity. To call the Witch immortal implies that there is some irreducible *ens* that persists through all her transformations and lies beneath all her infinite veils. The Witch, however, is not a "character" but a prosopopoeia of the principle of the inescapability of change. Her "immortality," her so-called inability to die, is actually an openness to "death" so constant and complete that no moment can be singled out as "her death." She escapes from death as it is understood in the therapeutic tradition—a moment of narrative closure that withdraws the veil to reveal the secret unity of all that preceded it.

It is true, as Hall points out, that we do see the Witch "weaving" her own "veil" to shelter mere mortals from the glory of her beauty, and that this is a venerable metaphor of the necessarily oblique manifestations of the divine in our mortal world. In such an avowedly playful

19. This reading of the Witch's relationship to the naiads goes against the more usual interpretation. Both Richard Cronin (*Shelley's Poetic Thoughts,* 67) and, more recently, Jean Hall ("Poetic Autonomy," 209, 215) state the opposite case powerfully. Hall sees the Witch as "autonomous because she is perfect and immortal" (209), and therefore inhuman, while Cronin argues that her "power is contingent on her remaining abstracted from any personal relationship with transient beings" (67). If they are right, the Witch would then become a self-sufficient, autonomous philosopher. That argument can be made, but only on the grounds that the portrait is deliberately ironic, and designed to show us that such a position is untenable. Otherwise it is difficult to account for the fact that the Witch is so constantly engaged with the petty details of the lives of "transient beings." The Witch, as she is shown in the poem, is neither "autonomous" nor autarchic; rather, she is the epitome of the "leaky vessel," Plato's model for the futile life of constantly assuaging desires that are as continually renewed ("tasting all blossoms yet confined to none"). She is a "dissipative structure," feeding off the perpetual entropic strife of a world whose constant sustenance she clearly needs.

poem, however, the venerability of the image should be enough in itself
to alert us to the fact that Shelley may not be using it straightforwardly.
At line 145 onward, the Witch weaves a "subtle veil" out of "three
threads of fleecy mist, and three / Long lines of light" and "As many star-
beams" (146, 147, 149) and cloaks herself in it; but when, at line 249,
she "sits aloof" to weave her "pictured poetry" (252), we learn that she
does so upon a "growing woof" (253) that can only be a continuation of
the "subtle veil" already commenced.

The Witch, then, has "veiled" herself in poetry. But the Witch, if she
can be said to "be" anything, *is* "poetry." She has veiled herself in herself. To remove the Witch's veil is always to find another, and yet another; it is an endless play of unforeseen and unconceived delights that
yields us no constant derivative that can be presented as the changeless
essence of the process. What could be less an *"ens"* than the purely
entropic, fugitive substances from which she weaves her veil? Richard
Cronin rightly mocks the more abstruse allegorizations of the materials
in this passage as misdirected and overserious. But he errs on the side of
frivolity in reading it as nothing more than a collection of "tongue
twisters" and deliberately ridiculous images (*Poetic Thoughts,* 65). The
fragility and evanescence of these materials is what makes the Witch's
ability to "weave" them into the veil of poetry miraculous; the obvious
comparison is to the poet in *Prometheus Unbound,* who creates "Forms
more real than living man, / Nurslings of immortality," from equally insubstantial materials (see I, 737–51).

As for the "divine" beauty of the unveiled (or "preveiled") Witch, a
second reading of Shelley's language in describing the state of those
who gaze upon it reveals that they are not a lucky few to have gained
access to the One that lies behind the Many; rather, *they* are the deluded ones, natives of Peter Bell's "hyperequatorial climate" "betrayed"
by the hunt for a chimerical *ens,* who cannot see the beauty in our
"bright world" and its "fleeting images," the "world so wide" and its
"circling skies," and seek an unchanging One, which, to Shelley, means
only nonbeing:

> For she was beautiful—her beauty made
>   The bright world dim, and every thing beside
> Seemed like the fleeting image of a shade:
>   No thought of living spirit could abide—
> Which to her looks had ever been betrayed,
>   On any object in the world so wide,

On any hope within the circling skies,
But on her form, and in her inmost eyes.

(137–44)

This is the only "immortality" possible in a world that operates on the entropic principles that Shelley sets out in the very first stanza of the poem proper, when he refers to "those cruel Twins, whom at one birth / Incestuous Change bore to her father Time, Error and Truth" (49–51). This playful mythic cosmogony sums up with remarkable precision the Lucretian principle of chaotic creativity that we have pursued through Shelley's *Defence*. It is a mythologized sketch of a strange attractor. It establishes the inevitability of error, or the unavoidability of the *clinamen,* which is both the condition and the result of the Witch's madly fanciful career. *Change* is the daughter of Time; this is a comment on the inevitability of change—the inevitability of decay, which is also growth—but it is more; it is an acknowledgment of the constant, and general, attempt to establish continuity within time, and its necessary defeat. Change is the *daughter* of Time; the flux of time is a reproductive flux, a reiterative one. It is just that it is never quite successful in its attempt at reproductive continuity; Time produces Change, and Change in turn produces the "Twins" Error and Truth. No Truth without Error—there can be no reproduction without innovation, but no Error without Truth—how could we find delight in what is "unforeseen and unconceived" if *nothing* could be foreseen and *nothing* came to fruition from a prior conception. Shelley makes it clear that he is not asserting the absolute transferential equivalence of all signifiers. For there to be information, there must be both order and disorder, Error *and* Truth. This is a world, in short, that demands a stance of radical empiricism, a world in which the past cannot be preserved for long before it is obliterated by accumulated errors, a world in which consciousness must live, like the Witch, in the eye of that storm which chokes the past with the shattered present—a world in which one must delight in the strange beauty of ruins, and learn to accept the limitations of memory and "reparation."

What, then, does this mean for poetry—above all for a *soi-disant* "political" poetry? If the Witch represents poetry, are we to assume that Shelley thought that poetry should be indifferent to the world—that it should find little in it to "disturb its soul"? Such a finding seems counter to Shelley's own poetic practice and political aspirations, and counter to our hopes of what poetry can be for us.

That it seems so is a measure of how "natural" it has become for us to understand a text's political force in the terms of a therapeutic historicism. Like Mary Shelley, we distrust a poem, like "The Witch of Atlas," that "leap[s] and play[s]," "tasting all blossoms and confined to none." We seek an authenticity of utterance within a specific sociopolitical context that makes the text seem truly "committed" to the political juncture of its context of production. We seek the genuine "speech act" that momentarily instantiates, and crystallizes, all the rules and conditions of its appearance. We seek the part that incarnates the whole. What "The Witch of Atlas" shows us, however, is that when Shelley argues, in the *Defence,* that poetry "participates in the eternal, the infinite, and the one," or that a "poet . . . would do ill to embody his own conceptions of right and wrong, which are usually those of his place and time, in his poetical creations, which participate in neither," he is arguing for a radically different conception of the political role of poetry, not that poetry should be politically irrelevant. The "Witch" also shows us that poetry's "eternity" and "infinity" need not imply its ineffability or its abstraction from, or synthesis of, the flux of events.

Poetry is "eternal" in the same way the Witch is: it is eternally contemporary. Like the Witch, poetry must choose between the ability to continue loving the world—to continue its urgency for the world, its political relevance—and memory, its dedication to the conditions that originally called it forth. A poem that could only speak "authentically" within the "peculiar relations" of its context of production—that could, in other words, only be one genuine "speech act"—would be a poetic sibyl without the gift of prophecy, a withered relic only "alive" enough to make us conscious of its affinity with the dead. This is what Paul Hamilton has usefully identified as Shelley's "futuristic reception aesthetic . . . which tries to make room for a revolutionary, not a liberal culture" ("Old Anatomies," 307).[20] The only partial exception to this rule is poetry's ability to preserve in memory the deeds and thoughts of "the Wise, / The great, the unforgotten" ("Triumph of Life," 208-9), those heroes and heroines whose names recur as touchstones in Shelley's prose and poetry: Bacon, Plato, Lucretius, Dante, Milton, and so forth. It is this function of poetry that Shelley has in mind in the Witch's peculiar suspended animation of "those she saw most beautiful." The limitations of the Witch's powers indicate the limitations of poetry's purely mnemonic capacity; a very few names from the past can be

---

20. McGann refers to "Shelley's Futurism," but in his usage this implies a prophetic foreclosure of the future, rather than an openness to many possible futures (quoted in Allen, 253).

"kept alive" by poetry, but only poetry itself continues to live. Homer is nothing but a name to us; Hector and Achilleus live and change. We must not be fooled by the poet's ability to use real people as the starting point for the creation of poetic characters. Shakespeare's Richard the Third, Tolstoy's Napoleon, Plato's Socrates—these may help "keep alive" the names of the historical characters whose names they share, but their vitality, their richness, their challenge are all their own. The historical Socrates is a subject of academic debate; Plato's creation is a living, and therefore changing, presence.

To say that poetry "participates in neither" the place nor the time of the poet is not to say that it transcends place or time; "the alloy of costume, habit, etc . . . [is] *necessary* to temper [poetry's] planetary music for mortal ears"; "a poet considers the vices of his contemporaries as the temporary dress in which his creations *must* be arrayed" (Reiman and Powers, 487; my emphasis both times). This "temporary dress" is not one eventually to be shucked off to reveal the unchanging *ens* that lies behind it: "[A]fter one person and one age has exhausted all of its divine effluence which their peculiar relations enable them to share, another and yet another succeeds, and new relations are ever developed, the source of an unforeseen and an unconceived delight." If poetry is veiled, it is, like the Witch, veiled in itself; the work of the critic is not to "strip" the poem, to move from veil to revelation, *substantia* to *ens,* but to join in on the poem's own terms in its endlessly provocative dance of veils. The poem, like the Witch "tasting all blossoms, and confined to none," belongs to all contexts and to none; but it can only exist *for* us within the veils of "place and time," within our "peculiar relations," our particular consumptive context.

On the other hand, poetry's continuing relevance and power are dependent on its ability to "exceed the whole," to exceed its context of production and continue in its eternal renewal of consumptive creativity—"unforeseen and unconceived delight." Poetic "immortality," then, is premised on the very revolutionary sublimity to which it seemed to be in paradoxical opposition. Poetry is "immortal" because it is always dying, just as its negentropic effects on its readers result from its constant entropy, and just as its amnesiac powers are dependent upon its mnemonic function.

Shelley's strictures against "didactic poetry" are not an attempt to depoliticize poetry; on the contrary, they are an attempt to make us recognize the greatest political power of the poem. The poem that "participates in neither" its time nor its place is the text that by virtue of that negativity can revolutionize all contexts in which it is consumed; it is poetry that eternally applies Pound's dictum "Make it new" both to itself and its context of consumption; it is the part that always exceeds the whole. This is the poetry of which he writes: "[I]t is a strain which distends, and then bursts the circumference of the hearer's mind, and pours itself forth together with it into the universal element with which it has perpetual sympathy" (485). It is poetry that has the capacity to break us free from the narrow circles of thought "blunted by reiteration" that define, at any given moment, the poet's context of production and the readers' context(s) of consumption, and give us a "perpetual[ly renewed] sympathy" with a universe in becoming.

8

Spectators Become Actors:
The Politics of Temporality

POETRY IN EVOLUTION

I

The belief in the infinite complexity of the literary text—or its infinite "richness"—is not new. It is central to the Romantics' belief that literature could be a path to the Absolute. But in this lies a crucial difference, also. The therapeutic Romanticists did look for "the world" in a grain of sand. When they admired the con-fusion of the Gothic cathedral they were admiring its "multeity-in-unity," its ability to synthesize diverse elements into a unified conception of the Absolute. What is at stake between the therapeutic and chaotic descriptions of the role of memory in social reproduction is their diametrically opposed understandings of the relationship between part and whole. In the therapeutic argument, memory recuperates—"redeems" would not be too strong a word—the apparently atomistic and "disengaged" elements of what should be a social "totality." Historicist hermeneutics is designed to reconcile the apparently disparate elements of historical action with a wider narrative totality; Dilthey's and Collingwood's interest in biography is grounded in this attempt to anchor the individual in the universal. From a chaotic perspective, however, the "breach" that opens every time we return to the tradition—like Webb Ellis or Dante—is proof of the irreducibly atomistic nature of society. Society has more "parts" than memory can synthesize into a whole: the problem of fractal detail. Memory, through its unpredictable reproduction of certain parts at the expense of others, drives a wedge between part and whole; the *clinamen* within a mnemonic cycle allows the part, like a cancerous growth, to develop in opposition to the "whole" that gave it birth, and eventually to overthrow and replace it. And the essence of fractal organization is that any "part," at whatever scale, is itself composed of equally nonintegral and potentially oppositional "parts." Each "part" is potentially a new departure point, or bifurcation, in an errant history before which, like the scientific experimenter unable to leave the room, we can maintain only a radical empiricism: "[I]l faut décrire le chemin qui constitue le passé du système, énumérer les bifurcations traversées et la succession des fluctuations qui ont décidé de l'histoire réelle parmi toutes les histoires possibles" (Prigogine and Stengers, *La nouvelle alliance,* 231).[1] Far from cementing a political or aesthetic conservatism, memory, in Lucretian terms, is the motive force of a permanent revolution; in *De rerum natura,* the daughters of memory are also the daughters of inspiration.

This is why it is necessary for Burke and Hegel to insist upon the absolute sterility of revolutionary discontinuity. Real error, for Burke, brings the reproductive cycle of history to a crashing halt. His "great primaeval contract of eternal society," that therapeutic and hermeneutical circle "linking the lower with the higher natures" that, in Laplacean fashion, "holds all physical and moral natures, each in their appointed place" (*Reflections,* 195), cannot allow for a part that might define itself in opposition to the whole. Above all, error must be allowed to have no significant—which is to say, evolutionary—consequences in the course of history. If error could become essence, revolutionary disengagement—the consumptive "breach" that argues society as produced can be defined in opposition to its conditions of production—would become an ever-present possibility lurking within every element of society. The hermeneutical task of the cycle of memory is, as his building metaphor implies, reparative; major errors are erased, minor ones corrected. For Burke, to break society into atomic units is a patricidal anatomy, "rashly to hack . . . [our] aged parent in pieces"; to hope for subsequent life from these units is as foolish as to wish, like Frankenstein, that putting those pieces in the "kettle of magicians" will "renovate . . . [our] father's life" (194). Such a social atomism is a "chaos," but

---

1. "[I]t is necessary to describe the path that constitutes the history of the system, to enumerate the bifurcations traversed and the succession of fluctuations that have decided the actual history among all the possible histories" (my translation).

not Schlegel's "confusion out of which a world can arise": "The municipal corporations of that universal kingdom [the social contract] are not morally at liberty at their pleasure, and on their speculations of a contingent improvement, wholly to separate and tear asunder the bands of their subordinate community, and to dissolve it into an unsocial, uncivil, unconnected chaos of elementary principles". (195)

A Lucretian, or chaotic, theory of sociocultural reproduction does "dissolve" Burke's organic, integral "corporations" into atomistic figures in the sand. With Frankenstein, it holds that such a dissolution can be a prelude to recomposition and continued life. Unlike Deleuze or Foucault, however, it need not hope for some mysterious galvanic action to bring about the reemergence of a figure from atomic flux; to their thoroughly amnesiac society it opposes a new understanding of the reproductive, reiterative cycle of memory that provides us with a nonreductive account of historical change.

To understand the implications of this, we must understand how completely Shelley's "révolution quantique" runs counter to epistemological and ethical theories so deep-rooted in Western thought that it is difficult for us even to see them as "theoretical"; they form part of the very fabric of our commonsense understanding of the world and our place in it. The common denominator of these "theories"—the assumption that underlies all the different philosophical stances to which I have appended the grab-bag label "therapeutic"—is an assumption so basic that it sounds banal, even trite, to state it baldly:[2] understanding is a movement from the partial to the total; to understand completely (which is always the *telos* of rational inquiry) is to understand the relationship of every part to the whole.

This assumption (which, despite appearances, is not—or not yet—hermeneutical philosophy, but that which makes that philosophy so persuasive), despite being radically counter to the basic tendency of Lucretian physics, makes a memorable appearance in the *De rerum natura,* or at least in the common reading of one its most famous passages, the *suave mari magno:* "But this is the greatest joy of all: to stand aloof in a quiet citadel, stoutly fortified by the teaching of the wise, and to gaze down from that elevation on others wandering aimlessly in a vain search for the way of life" (60, 2.7–10). The Epicurean sages' *ataraxia* abstracts them from the turbulent flux of time and allows them to grasp it as whole, neutralizing the effect of flux by a perspective that looks

2. Although this is precisely what the "categorical empiricism" and "promiscuous realism" of Dupré's *Disorder of Things* are designed to combat.

beyond the confusion of the surface to its eternal basis. This is not to say that they grasp every detail of its motion; that is impossible. Rather, the aleatory character of the flux of events is simply accepted as the transient, circumstantial surface of an eternal order.

This, at least, is one way of reading this passage. It is the way Serres reads it: "[L]'ataraxie est un état physique, l'état fondamental de la matière; sur ce fond se forment les mondes. Troublés de circonstances. La morale, c'est la physique. La sagesse accomplit sa révolution. Elle remonte la volute vers cet état premier, l'ataraxie est l'absence de tour-billons. *L'âme du sage est étendue à l'univers global.* Le sage est l'uni-vers. Il est, apaisé, le pacte lui-même" (*La naissance,* 162; my empha-sis).[3] This is the same "second-order idealism" we encountered in Hogle's theory of the "transferential One," a world "eterne in muta-bilitie" that can be grasped, even identified with, as a totality if we practice a pragmatic "wise acceptance" of its inevitable turbulence/transference. The sage, in other words, can *comprehend* the universe (in both senses) from a sufficiently exalted perspective.

As a dry epistemological truism (the more we see, the more we com-prehend), it may seem an unlikely starting point for a demonstration of the political significance of Shelley's theories of poetry, but its ramifica-tions are far wider than that. I have already explored in some depth, especially in the first part of this book, the ethical and political signifi-cance of the importation of this epistemological tenet into our attempts to understand our personal and collective histories. The impulse to gain the "view from the citadel" becomes the providentialist belief that all actions must be understood as part of an absolute order, which in turn encourages the symbolic interpretation of all phenomena as expressions of that order; or that impulse becomes the historicist hermeneutics that demands that every product of a given society be read as characteristic of "the culture"; or it becomes the ordinary-language philosopher's be-lief in a "form of life" embodied in a set of conventions, or "language" in the widest sense, to which all "meaning events" can be referred and with reference to which they can all be understood.

It is a short step, if a step at all, from these "providentialist" versions of the impulse toward the whole to a series of directly ethical, and hence political, claims with which we are also familiar: that our lives

3. "Thus, ataraxia is a physical state, the fundamental state of matter; on this base, worlds are formed, disturbed by circumstances. Morality is physics. Wisdom completes its revolution, going back up the helix toward this first state of things; ataraxia is the absence of vortices. *The soul of the wise man is extended to the global universe.* The wise man is the universe. He is, when pacified, the pact itself" ("Lucretius: Science and Religion," 121; my emphasis).

should be lived as far as possible in accordance with what we understand of the Divine Plan; that every action that obscures or erases the conventions that define our "form of life," or the state, is *ipso facto* an evil. The extreme political version of this position is the totalitarian State of Hegel's *Philosophy of Right*, with reference to which, as an all-encompassing Absolute, we must define every aspect of our lives. Nor is it a great step to specifically poetic concerns. The overriding concern of the same post-Kantian attempt to reconcile the subject with the world that culminates in the Hegelian reconciliation of subject and State is to show us that art, and specifically poetry, is the key to achieving the desired self-conscious understanding of our position in the providential order of the whole. Taylor's exposition of the quasi-religious role of art (and particularly literature) in the nineteenth and twentieth centuries demonstrates how natural it has become for us to identify the fundamental role of literature with a drive to a vision of the Absolute (*Sources of the Self,* 419ff.). Hence McFarland's urgent and repeated insistence that to resist the movement from the "diasparactive" fragments toward a transcendental totality is not just a critical but a moral failing (*Forms of Ruin*). Hence, too, the moralizing tone with which New Historicist critics are wont to reprove those who fail to consider the "historical context" in their critiques. The belief in the duty of the poet to reconcile us with the Absolute is closely related to the belief in the duty of the poet to reconcile us with the prevailing political order; the Wordsworth of *The Prelude* and the Wordsworth of the *Sonnets upon the Punishment of Death* have at least this "providential" impulse in common.

The foundation of this ethical *parti pris* in favor of reference to a universal order has been subjected to a searching critique by Martha Nussbaum in her *Fragility of Goodness;* it is possible to build directly on her findings in this part of my argument. Nussbaum is all the more useful in that she describes her own task as a "therapeutic" one, enlisting "philosophy to show us the way back to the ordinary" (260). The neo-Aristotelian flag under which she marches would apparently place her in the same broadly defined camp as the many "therapeutic" ordinary-language philosophers and historicist critics to which I have generally opposed Shelley's chaotic proclivities. In exploring, here, the extent to which we can reconcile Nussbaum's "tragic ethics" with Shelley's chaotic creativity, we can elucidate Shelley's areas of both agreement and disagreement with the therapeutic position.

Nussbaum recognizes that she is calling into question the dominant tradition of Western ethics by putting the superiority of the "view from the citadel" on trial. Her attempt to propose an alternative ethics founded upon an understanding of the ethical significance of tragedy enables us to see the common ground underlying the apparently disparate traditional approaches that reject that significance. From her perspective, the common theme in Western ethical understanding from Plato to Kant and beyond is the ultimate appeal, for all ethical judgments, to a universal, superhuman ethical order. Whether, as in the case of the Platonic "real above" (Nussbaum, 138), we have direct access to this supersensible realm or, as in the case of the Kantian categorical imperative, must deduce its nature from an immanent critique of lived experience or, as in the case of the Hegelian *Begriff* or the Coleridgean symbol, must discover the supersensible universal in and through the sensible particular, there is still, explicitly or implicitly, an appeal to a "standpoint that is more than human, one that can look on the human from the outside" (138), a standpoint on the citadel from which the apparent storm of human action resolves itself into a universal order.

The question, for Nussbaum, is whether the complex and contradictory contingencies of real life can be usefully related to such a universal order. Tragedy is the genre in which we ponder ethical dilemmas that strike us as at once deeply interesting and difficult to resolve, and yet Nussbaum demonstrates that from the standpoint of the citadel it is impossible to conceive of a truly tragic situation. The tragic character is often an apparently good person rendered morally suspect or evil by a concatenation of circumstances to which he or she is unable to find an uncompromising response. If all ethical decisions could be referred to a universal, internally coherent order, however, no individual could be essentially compromised by the sheer force of contingent circumstance. In the view from the citadel, the illusion of tragedy is a product of a restricted perspective; the appeal of tragedy is a sign of our limited metaphysical intelligence. Hence Plato's decision to ban tragedy from his republic. For him, the contingent sequence of "diasparactive" events is always amenable to a redemptive ethical hermeneutics that will reconcile it to the universal ethical verities; it can never challenge our allegiance to these verities: *fiat justitia, et pereat mundus.*

Although Nussbaum does not draw the parallel herself, it is useful to consider the similarities between Plato's myth of Er and Kant's "transcendental ought," which is the solution to his antinomy of pure reason, in order to understand how these philosophies reject the ethical significance of contingent events. In Plato's myth of Er at the end of the *Republic,* souls that are waiting to be born are allowed to choose their next lives. These lives "of every variety" offered to the souls come replete with a series of contingent circumstances: "wealth and poverty and sickness and health and the intermediate conditions" (bk. X, 842). The point of this is that only a foolish soul chooses a life based upon these inessential factors, without regard for the transcendent and eternally fixed matter of its moral worth (which determines the length of that soul's sojourn in purgatory after death). Plato is at pains to assure us that the "blame is his who chooses. God is blameless" (841). In other words, every aspect of our lives, no matter how much it may appear to be part of a train of circumstances beyond our control, can be held as representative of our essential moral condition, as willed in a moral intention that precedes and transcends any detail of circumstance.

Kant makes the same point when he turns to the apparent contradiction between a transcendent, categorical moral imperative and our total immersion in a Newtonian universe of inexorable cause and effect. One solution to this contradiction is the utilitarian morality of Hume, Godwin, and Bentham, but that simply abandons freedom of the will, and therefore real ethical responsibility, to a world ruled by necessity. Kant seeks to "reconcile nature and freedom" (*Pure Reason*, 369), a desire in which we recognize the fundamental therapeutic imperative, reconciling the subject (freedom) and the world (nature). His answer, which he recognizes "may seem extremely subtle and obscure" (369), is the same as Plato's. A subject must be considered both phenomenally and noumenally; phenomenally, its actions may appear determined by contingent events over which it has no control and for which it cannot be responsible; but noumenally—a perspective that transcends the categories of time, space, and causality—its actions pertain directly to the *Ding an sich* and cannot be excused by a chain of phenomena that has no noumenal significance: "In its empirical character . . . [the] subject, as a phenomenon, would submit, according to all determining laws, to a causal nexus, and . . . would be nothing but a part of the world of sense. . . . In its intelligible character, however, . . . the same subject would have to be considered free from all influence of sensibility, and from all determination through phenomena" (370–71).

Nussbaum, claiming to follow Aristotle in this (240ff.), renounces access by any means to a noumenal solution of ethical dilemmas; she insists upon restricting herself to an ethical empiricism, an exploration of the real, lived content of complex human lives. Two central aspects of her argument emerge from this: one is an emphasis on luck (or *tuchē*); the other is a belief in the "fragility of goodness."

In Nussbaum's view, human beings have multiple, potentially incompatible ethical commitments that cannot be reconciled within a universal ethical order. This is not, in her view, inherently an evil thing. It does, however, render our ethical commitments vulnerable to "bad luck." For most of us, most of the time, it is possible to serve our incompatible ethical commitments without their incompatibility becoming a crucial problem, but sometimes circumstances force us to make impossible choices between apparently equal claims. Antigone's duty to her dead brother and her duty to the city, Agamemnon's duty to his daughter and his duty to his men and allies, for example. At such (tragic) moments, we become suddenly, and catastrophically, aware of the impossibility of settling such conflicts by appealing to a universal hierarchy of value.[4]

Traditionally, those who do admit of such an appeal have argued that the ideal human life is one that is invulnerable to the vicissitudes of *tuchē*. The degree to which we are so vulnerable is, for them, a measure of our alienation from the unchanging ethical verities. They propose living life according to a *technē,* a rational plan for ordering one's life in conformity to the universal truths of the moral order (89–91). The Platonic doctrine that no one who fully understood the consequences of and alternatives to their actions would ever commit a wrong, like the Kantian doctrine that the categorical imperative is always accessible to the reflecting mind, is a prerequisite for an ethics that vaunts the power of *technē* over *tuchē* (113–14). If our ethical goal is to live our lives in conformity to reason, it must be demonstrated that reason is always capable of determining for us an ethically sound course of action.

The desire to impose a rational order upon our lives so as to free us from the slings and arrows of outrageous *tuchē* inevitably carries us beyond the mere regulation of our individual ethical lives to a political regulation of the life of the community; it is only possible to live a life according to the precepts of reason if the communal context of that life also conforms to reason's laws. The state itself becomes a *technē* for the elimination of the irrational—a goal that informs most political treatises from Plato's *Republic* to Godwin's *Political Justice* and culminates in the Hegelian therapeutic State as an embodiment of *Sittlichkeit*—Kant's aesthetic "free conformity to law" become a political free conformity to Absolute Reason. Nussbaum identifies the Hegelian State as the ultimate expression of the state-as-*technē;* a *technē* so completely internalized by the members of the state that there is no longer any felt opposition

4. This is an ethical equivalent of Dupré's "promiscuous realism"; our ethical lives, just like the natural world in which we live, are simply too complex to be adequately described by one grand narrative.

between reason and desire, and consequently no possible role for *tuchē* and no possibility of tragedy (see 53, 63, 67, 74–75, 353).

It is easy to understand the appeal of a life from which the possibility of tragedy has been eliminated, and it is one of the major strengths of Nussbaum's account that she never discounts the real attractiveness of this position. Nevertheless, she does reject it as a viable goal for a human community. Nussbaum makes two closely related arguments, both of which, as we shall see, can be found in Shelley's own political and ethical theories, and both of which are essential for bridging the gap from his theories of poetry to his politics. The first is that human values *cannot* in fact be harmonized into a coherent whole, or, in other words, that they are *essentially* "diasparactive." Second, even if they could be so harmonized, we would not wish them to be; she argues that the cost of "harmonizing" our ethical commitments is simply too high. To protect our lives from *tuchē* it is necessary to renounce a whole range of values that most of us would consider to be essential to our humanity; above all, those relating to *erōs* and *philia:*

> Aristotle's city refuses to eliminate risk. . . . [I]n his good city the possibility of contingent conflict of values is preserved as a condition of the richness and vigor of civic life itself. . . . Plato he aptly says, tried to make the city a unity in the way that a single organic body is a unity: with a single good, a single conception of "one's own," a single pleasure and pain. Aristotle argues . . . that this sort of conflict-free unity is not the sort of unity appropriate to the *polis.* . . . A city is by nature a plurality of separate parts. To make it one in the Platonic way is to eliminate the bases of political justice and of *philia,* two of its central goods. (353)

Nussbaum's objection to the Platonic and Hegelian states is not that they deny the claims of *erōs;* rather, it is that they offer us the absolute fulfillment of those claims. Her argument is essentially one of scale; an eternally harmonious, unified ethical order is simply incompatible with the "quick, tense splendour" (342) of needy human lives, and yet it is this that the Platonic and Hegelian states offer us as a complete fulfillment of erotic desire. Nussbaum discovers the same paradoxical relationship between the fulfillment and the negation of desire that manifests itself in Shelley's poetry as what I have labeled "tragic *erōs*": "*Erōs* is the desire to be a being without any contingent occurrent desires. It is a second-order desire that all desires should be cancelled. This need that makes us pathetically vulnerable to chance is a need whose ideal outcome is the existence of a metal statue, an artefact" (176). In our limited and necessarily finite human lives, to be saved from chance, error, and death—all the things that intervene between desire and fulfillment—is to be "saved" from all that makes a human life meaningful (this was the argument of Shelley's "Death"). It is to move to a scale at which human values could no longer be cherished, where we could no longer recognize such beings as human: "[T]he value of certain constituents of the good human life is inseparable from a risk of opposition, therefore of conflict. To have them adequately is to have them plural and separate; to have them in this way is to risk strife. But to unify and harmonize, removing the bases of conflict, is to remove value as well. The singleness of Creon's simplification or even Hegel's synthesis—even if successful—impoverishes the world" (353).

Luckily for us, the Hegelian synthesis cannot be successful, and this because human values betray a complexity that invites comparison with Shelley's fractal poetics. Just as the poetic text resists any attempt to "harmonize" its disparate features into a stable and coherent totality, a richly meaningful human life resists attempts to harmonize its ethical commitments: "[T]he richer our scheme of values, the harder it will prove to effect a harmony within it. The more open we are to the presence of value, of divinity, in the world, the more surely conflict closes us in. The price of harmonization seems to be impoverishment, the price of richness disharmony. It looks, indeed, like an 'unwritten law,' that 'nothing very great comes into the life of mortals without disaster'" (75).

Or, at least, the potential for disaster. The ethical commitments of a rich human life are incommensurable; the same kinds of scalar, and intrascalar, confusions pertain to any attempt to interpret this area of our lives as to the attempt to interpret poetic texts. One can imagine the subject caught in an ever-widening ring of allegiances to self, spouse, family, friends, employer, class, province, state, race, religion, gender, and so forth, but this invites a simplifying response of the kind "The greatest good to the greatest number." In practice, to be caught in a situation in which one's felt duty to any one of these allegiances is in conflict with any other—and for most of us this is, to some degree, always true—is to be presented with an insoluble equation involving incomparable goods. The advocates of *technē* propose one normative scale at which all apparent ethical dilemmas can be resolved into a choice between measurable quantities of an identical value.[5] The citizen

---

5. See Dupré, 85-171, for a comprehensive refutation of all such reductionist claims.

of the Hegelian State described in the *Philosophy of Right* refers all such dilemmas to the overriding question of the good of the State. The good Kantian imagines himself or herself as a universal human being establishing laws for all humankind. But if we consider for a moment the real complexities of our various ethical allegiances, we see how arbitrary such a procedure is: arbitrary and violent in the case of Hegel, where competing claims are simply swept aside for the sake of clarity; arbitrary and pointless in the case of Kant, because any description of a real ethical dilemma that poses it in terms sufficiently general to be imagined as a universal law is bound to exclude the detail that makes it problematic.

This is particularly true, as Nussbaum shows in her analysis of "relational goods" (343–72), of the relationships of *philia* and *erōs*. Their irreducible specificity resists any attempts at generalization. The fact that I love *this* person in *this* way cannot be postulated as a potentially universal condition, nor can the specific qualities of this love be weighed on a universal scale of value against the specific nature of my love for my country, and so on (343–44). This specificity makes *tuchē* a truly radical agent. The hazards of luck in human lives engender a sensitive dependence on initial conditions in human lives. "Love is not love that alters when it alteration finds" is only a livable maxim for a god. Not only does love alter when it confronts a constantly altering world, but human identities themselves are vulnerable to genuine and irrevocable change as a result.

This is the most radical claim for her ethics that Nussbaum is prepared to entertain, and she admits that it forces us to "ask ourselves whether we really think we live, and whether we really wish to live, in this Aristotelian world." The claim emerges from her reading of Euripides' *Hecuba,* which emphasizes its ethical, and implicitly political, radicalism. "This alarming story of metamorphosism," writes Nussbaum, "arouses and explores some of our deepest fears about the fragility of humanness, and especially of character, which might seem to be the firmest part of humanness" (399). The play does not allow us to take refuge in the notion of a "fatal flaw" in Hecuba's character that the blows of fate merely "reveal." If Hecuba, a noble, brave, and good person, can be so thoroughly transformed by the force of circumstance that her former "character" is not merely obscured or distorted but simply erased, then accident can affect essence, and the possibility of a political *technē* that would contain *tuchē* is denied.

We are very close to the central tenets of Shelley's chaotic creativity. At times Nussbaum's imagery can be strikingly similar to Shelley's; like him, and like Lucretius, she offers us a picture of "sailors, voyaging unsafely" (421), as an image of human life and the fragility of human meaningfulness. Like Shelley and Lucretius, again, she offers the unpredictable, devastating power of the lightning bolt as a metaphor for the unforeseeable destructive power of luck and love in human erotic interaction: "A lightning bolt strikes all at once, unpredictably, usually allowing no hope of defence or control. It is at one and the same time a brilliance that brings illumination and a force that has the power to wound and to kill" (193; see 192f.). This essentially unpredictable force, which is at once "Destroyer and Preserver," we meet in numerous guises in Shelley's poetry and prose. Just as Shelley finds he must adopt a radical empiricism in the face of fundamental poetic indeterminacy, Nussbaum's "ethical empiricism" is the only response to the radically transformative power of *tuchē*.

Radical empiricism is the key to understanding the political implications of Shelley's chaotic poetics, but it is also the most problematic area of overlap between Nussbaum's work and Shelley's. Before we can explore the full significance of Shelley's radical *political* empiricism, we must explore the curious, and very revealing, contradictions that haunt Nussbaum's concept of empiricism. In this way I hope to show that Shelley's empiricism is something quite opposed to our conventional—largely Baconian—notion of the aims and possible achievements of empirical inquiry.

Nussbaum does not claim to be an empiricist; in fact she resists the label. For her, empiricism is essentially Baconian, and she wants to correct what she sees as a persistent misreading of Aristotle as a proto-Baconian empiricist (240–63; see esp. 243ff.). She is, however, expressly basing her approach on those aspects of Aristotle's method that have traditionally been labeled empirical—specifically, his claim that the attempt to "set down the *phainomena*" is the basis of philosophical endeavor. Nussbaum distinguishes this from Baconian empiricism by arguing that *phainomena* (literally "appearances") should not be taken to mean "theory-neutral data." Rather, she sees Aristotle's attempt to "save the appearances" as making him a precursor of ordinary-language philosophers. The Aristotelian exploration of the *phainomena* is an exploration of a "form of life." Like Wittgenstein or Cavell, Aristotle is seeking a coherent but unapologetically anthropocentric account of "what we believe," rather than a Platonic account of the "really real" that would exist independently of any human inquirer.

The ordinary-language philosopher and the therapeutic historicist are empiricists to the extent that they deny the possibility of a philosophy that would directly describe the noumenal "real above." Instead, they work from empirical observations of what people actually do and say toward a description of the "form of life" that renders those acts and speech acts intelligible. That is the limit of this empiricism, however; we cannot call it a "radical empiricism," because it ultimately accepts the virtual possibility of a "view from the citadel." "The culture," "the language game," and "the form of life" all become fixed orders that generate and guarantee meaning in our lives. The possibility that mere "events" might alter these defining contexts cannot be seriously entertained, and therefore apparent "empiricism" becomes, on the one hand, an anxious redemptive effort to reconcile all the diasparactive "appearances" of a "culture" to the master narrative, or plot, and, on the other, the dogmatic exclusion of anything that threatens the stability and unity of this "plot" from the realm of human significance.

Nussbaum's brand of empiricist ethics is unique among the ordinary-language approaches with which she claims kin, in that it seriously entertains the possibility that speech acts might alter language games, texts contexts, in the chaotic pattern with which we have become familiar. If "goodness" is "fragile," just as poetic meaning is, then all human meaning might be: "[I]t is in the nature of political structures to change, and in the nature of personal friendship that the confidence man should be indistinguishable from the trustworthy man—sometimes even to himself. In this sense, nothing human is ever *worthy* of my trust: there are no guarantees at all, short of revenge or death" (419). Like Shelley, she chooses to accept the risks and costs of a multitude of atomistic "deaths" and discontinuities rather than succumb to the thanatological "desire to be forever as we are" that lies behind a "guarantee" of absolute order. Her analysis of the ethical significance of "tragedy" shows that it is impossible to reconcile all the productions of a given "form of life" with a coherent "language game." With Lyotard, she acknowledges that a real *différend* exposes a potentially tragic conflict between incommensurable schemes of values. Taken in its most uncompromising form, such an assertion invalidates the redemptive and hermeneutical thrust of the therapeutic project. The diasparactive, or fractal, fragmentation of meaning will not admit of totalization.

It is, however, unclear how far Nussbaum is willing to take these propositions. She is aware of the conservative tendency of the anthropocentrism—and ethnocentrism—of her Aristotelian/ordinary-language approach, but her attempts to dissociate her approach from it are not entirely convincing. At times, indeed, she seems to embrace and defend that conservatism. Her empiricism can assume both the redemptive and the protective roles of the therapeutic approach. She claims, for example, that "if we are each led singly through the best procedures of practical choice, we will turn out to agree on the most important matters, in ethics as in science" (11n). This implies that there is, after all, a universal rational order, or "real above," which empirical inquiry merely makes apparent to us. Such a statement is hard to reconcile with her contention that tragedy is not merely a case of misperception; if she is right, then all tragic *différends* should be, in principle, resolvable if the participants are capable of achieving a clear view of the situation. This implies that there is a citadel from which the eternal unity of our mortal storm becomes apparent. Or, more disturbingly, she can succumb to the Burkean "anxiety of insufficient influence": "We can have truth only *inside* the circle of the appearances, because only there can we communicate, even refer, at all" (257). This being the case, we must, it appears, preserve at all costs the "circle of appearances," the "language games," that constitute our "culture"—no matter what their content—because any erasure of that circle delivers us up to the abyss of utter meaninglessness, or the "chaos of elementary principles" feared by Burke. In this connection she approvingly quotes Aristotle's injunction to "join in by persuading oneself that the ancient beliefs deeply belonging to our native tradition are true," because, she writes, such beliefs have "survived so many changes of social and political belief of a more superficial nature" (257). This is an extraordinary argument for a committed feminist to make—what "social and political belief" has been more durable than that in women's inferiority to men?—and one is not reassured by her rather wistful assertion that "a feminist opponent of Aristotle's conservative view about the social role of women could try to show Aristotle that a progressive position actually preserves certain deep human beliefs about the equal humanity of other human beings better than his own political theory does" (258). This reminds us of those spurious appeals in the 1790s to "that magnanimous government which we derived from our Saxon fathers, and from the prodigious mind of the immortal Alfred" (Thompson, 95), or the attempts to dress the French Revolution up in classical garb, both designed to disguise and ground innovation as a return to the hitherto obscured heart of the tradition. It is, moreover, begging the question: "equal humanity" is what the "feminist opponent" hopes to prove; so far as we know, Aristotle considered it self-evident that the genders were unequal.

Like Burke, Nussbaum insists that this conservative preference for the traditional need not, in theory, eliminate innovation: "The method does not make new discoveries, radical departures, or sharp changes of position impossible, either in science or in ethics" (258). But, again like Burke, it is hard to imagine any *actual* innovation that would not be greeted as a catastrophe: "[K]nowing that humans heed merely human authority best in conditions of stability or slow change, we should not quickly alter our rules, even to improve them" (305). Ultimately, the concern for preserving the community and the tradition that guarantee stability of meaning justifies the same hostility to difference that we remarked in Cavell's *Claim of Reason:*

> So if the person [who disagrees with principles of rational con-
> duct that we hold to be fundamental] does not speak, he ceases
> to be one of us, and we are not required to take account of
> him. . . . Sometimes the opponent will not listen. "Some need
> persuasion, others need violence," Aristotle remarks somewhat
> grimly. . . . Philosophy, at the level of basic principles, seems to
> be a matter of bringing the isolated person into line, of dispelling
> illusions that cause the breakdown of communication. Some-
> times this can be done gently, sometimes only with violence; and
> sometimes not at all.
>
> (Nussbaum, 253)

The possibility that there might be a salutary "breakdown in communi-cation"—that, as Shaw argued, "progress" may depend upon the "unrea-sonable [man who] persists in trying to adapt the world to himself," rather than the "reasonable man [who] adapts himself to the world"—is not considered.

This apparently self-contradictory hostility to discontinuity stems from a similar equivocation within Aristotle's own "empiricism," an equivocation that has important consequences for the tradition of West-ern science and epistemology. Nussbaum overstates Aristotle's empiri-cist acceptance of *tuchē,* and the thoroughness of his renunciation of the "real above." In the preceding chapter, I used Aristotle's concept of "plot" as a foil to Shelley's chaotic poetics, and it is useful to bear Aris-totle's commitment to the unity of plot in mind as a model of his thera-peutic resistance to *tuchē.* Nussbaum's Burkean defense of "deep" cul-tural traditions can be described in Aristotelian dramatic terms as a defense of the unity and coherence of a culture's "plot."

The *Poetics* is not—or, at least, not simply—a work of science, ethics, or politics, however. It is possible to imagine enjoying the total-ity of an organically coherent plot as an aesthetically pleasing *contrast* with an everyday life admitted to be *tuchē*-dependent. Aristotle's *Meta-*

physics, however, shows how closely his poetics imitates his scientific epistemology. One of his chief concerns in the *Metaphysics* is to limit the potential significance of *tuchē,* his principal opponents, significantly, being Lucretius's atomistic precursors, Democritus, Empedocles, and Anaxagoras.

In the *Metaphysics,* the equivalent to the concept of plot is the concept of potentiality. The history of the world is a history of potential becoming actual; the apparently disjunctive nature of the appearances and disappearances, births and deaths, that threaten to dissolve our world into incoherent fragments can be redemptively reconciled into an inherent oneness if we recognize that beneath the diasparactive fragmentation of the actual lies the continuous unity of potential: "[E]verything changes from that which is potentially to that which is actually. . . . [A]ll things come to be out of that which is, but is potentially, and is not actually. And this is the 'One' of Anaxagoras [for Anaximander]; for instead of 'all things were together'—and the 'Mixture' of Empedocles and Anaximander [for Anaxagoras] and the account given by Democritus—it is better to say 'all things were together potentially but not actually'" (873).[6] From the perspective of the "One" the realm of significance of *tuchē* must be severely restricted: "[T]hat there is no science of the accidental is obvious; for all science is either of that which is always or of that which is for the most part. (For how else is one to learn or to teach another?)" (781).

Aristotle relegates chance to a second and inessential regime of causality as an inevitable, and inconsequential, degree of play in the basic process of the potential becoming actual: "Everything, therefore, that will be, will be of necessity; e.g. it is necessary that he who lives shall one day die; for already some condition has come into existence, e.g. the presence of contraries in the same body. But whether he is to die by disease or by violence is not yet determined, but depends on the happening of something else. Clearly then the process goes back to a certain starting-point, but this no longer points to something further. This then will be the starting-point for the fortuitous, and will have nothing else as cause of its coming to be" (782). This curtailing of the causal

---

6. The names of Anaximander and Anaxagoras appear to have been transposed in this passage. Anaximander was a younger contemporary of Thales who proposed, as did Thales, that the world was really one substance (the "One" of which Aristotle speaks and with which he identifies Anaximander, correctly, elsewhere [see, e.g., *Physics* 187a, 20f.], where Anaxagoras is also correctly identified with his "infinite" elements); Anaxagoras was, like Empedocles, a pluralist. Aristotle's meaning is clear enough whether the theories and names match up correctly or not.

chain either side of the accidental (it comes from nothing and leads to nothing—nothing essential, at least) we can read as an attempt to eradicate a sensitive dependence on initial conditions. It is a preemptive foreclosure of the possibility of the *clinamen* and the reproductive proliferation of error it entails. For Aristotle, error may be present in the actual and the individual, but the genus rises above that possibility; the genus is a "continuous generation of the same kind" (776)

The movement of Aristotelian empiricism, then, is from the *phainomena* to the "really real" (or "real above"—*pace* Nussbaum) of the potential that those *phainomena* strive to realize. The actual is to be treated as a series of clues for an underlying order, with its accidental properties edited out. Aristotelian science moves from the individual to the species, from the species to the general, from the part to the whole. Error cannot proliferate across these scales, and only affects the finer ones: "In general, it is absurd to make the fact that the things of this earth are observed to change and never to remain in the same state, the basis of our judgment about the truth. For in pursuing the truth one must start from the things that are always in the same state and suffer no change" (859).

It is often said that modern science is born from a repudiation of the Aristotelian tradition, at least in its scholastic form, and on many specific issues—such as theories of motion, gravitation, and so forth—this is true. But in this basic epistemological bias, which is simply another manifestation of the "view from the citadel," Aristotle's empiricism is more closely related to Baconian empiricism than either its champions or its detractors maintain. Bacon quotes the *suave mari magno* passage approvingly in his essay "Of Truth," explicitly associating the position of the scientist with regard to nature with that of the observers on the seashore and in the citadel. The achievement of such a view is, he claims, "heaven upon earth" (Bacon, 48). We may be sure that phrase is not an idle one. Bacon had a profoundly held belief that the mission of the New Science was literally providential. The increase of knowledge by scientific and explorative discovery was "a plant of God's own planting . . . [which] by a special providence, was appointed to this autumn of the world" (qtd. in McKay, 117). Ultimately, this would not only restore us to our "prelapsarian dominion over nature" (McKay, ii)—the highest achievement of which would be an earthly victory over death (259)—but it would be a fulfillment of divine prophecy; the "advancement of learning" was nothing less than part of God's providential scheme to usher in the millennium (117-19).

Baconian empiricism, then, like the Aristotelian variety, works on the assumption that the "appearances" of the world will reveal a coherent underlying "plot." That assumption has deeply influenced the subsequent history of Western science. The highest ideal of Western science since Bacon has been the aspiration of physics to classical status—that is, to be a universal, coherent account of the behavior of all the phenomena in the universe from creation to annihilation or, in the intriguingly Hegelian formulation of Stephen Hawking, "a complete *understanding* of the events around us, and of our own existence" (169; see also 155–69). The Laplacean "demon" is, as Hawking acknowledges (53–55), the theoretical embodiment of that aspiration. Laplace "has no need of that hypothesis [God]," because in his account the natural world has become God: *deus sive natura.* A *total* science is inevitably a theology, and indeed a theodicy. It makes the "plot" of the providential order clear to us and reconciles us to this best, because only, possible world.

The apparently opposed traditions of post-Kantian therapeutics and the scientific Enlightenment share a debt to Aristotelian empiricism, making the Laplacean "demon" and Hegelian Absolute Knowing parodic versions of each other, united at least in their redemptive and totalitarian conviction that every part, every fragment, finds its place in the whole. Nussbaum attempts to draw an absolute contrast between the ordinary-language approach of Aristotle and Hegel's ultimate recourse to Absolute Knowing; on this opposition she bases the contrasting politics and ethics she derives from the two philosophers. But Hegel expressly acknowledges his debt to Aristotle. In the preface to *The Phenomenology of Spirit* he relates his conception of reason as "purposive activity" to Aristotle's definition of "Nature as purposive activity" (12). As Taylor suggests, Hegel takes from Aristotle his concept of "internal teleology," which makes the universe "something analogous to a text in which God says what he is" (Taylor, *Hegel,* 88; see also *Hegel and Modern Society,* 16–17). The purposiveness of reason, which expresses itself in nature, is the basis of the Hegelian model of the constant realization of the Notion (*Begriff*), which we now see is a version of the Aristotelian actualization of the potential. In both cases, the providentialist turn that empirical inquiry takes is inevitable, as Taylor's analogy demonstrates; we move from the empirically diasparactive text to the coherent "real above" of the providential "plot."

Hegel also, like Aristotle, developed a doctrine of dual causality both to account for and to neutralize the importance of *tuchē* in his autotelic world. There is the true teleological causality that springs from the *Begriff,* and the negligible, inconsequential causality of error and accident in the realization: "The state is no ideal work of art; it stands on earth and so in the sphere of caprice, chance, and error, and bad behaviour may disfigure it in many respects. But the ugliest of men, or a criminal, or an invalid, or a cripple, is still always a living man. The affirmative, life, subsists despite his defects, and it is this affirmative factor which is our theme here" (*Right*, 279). If the State exists in a world of error, it is implicated in a historical process of error correction. Hegel's history is homeostatic reproduction. Historical process can be likened to adding branches to a tree—each branch serves only to make the tree more fully in accordance with its concept: "Any code could be still better—no effort of reflection is required to justify this affirmation; we can think of the best, finest, and noblest as still better, finer, and nobler. But a big old tree puts forth more and more branches without thereby becoming a new tree; though it would be silly to refuse to plant a tree at all simply because it might produce new branches" (273).

This last metaphor helps us determine the degree of similarity between Hegel's understanding of politics and Nussbaum's. Her own central metaphor, with which she opens the *Fragility* and to which she constantly reverts, is also a tree (1). Unlike Hegel, her emphasis is on the vulnerability of a growing plant to disaster, and the real possibility that because of luck it may be unable to flourish. But there are aspects of the metaphor that betray her unwillingness to follow through on the more radical implications of her acceptance of *tuchē*. To describe human character as a plant is to ascribe to it an "internal teleology" (character as plot, or master narrative). The effect of *tuchē* is limited to, at most, masking the full expression of this preexistent potential; unless it obliterates that potential entirely, we will still be able to reason from the fragmentary empirical evidence to the anterior ideal. A lightning-blasted oak, as Coleridge realized, is still recognizably an oak, not a pear or a peach. The metaphor, moreover, makes all *tuchē* seem a threat to the integrity of individual character.

If we apply the metaphor to a *community*, then the anxious patrolling of that community for heterogeneous elements, and the exclusion of those elements as "insane" or irrelevant, as proposed by Aristotle, Cavell, and Nussbaum, constitute an inevitable corollary. It is more logical to describe a community as being a forest, comprising many different types of plant, all competing for limited resources. A forest, however, is like Diderot's *grappe d'abeilles:* its identity is fluid, and the elements that compose it have no necessary relation to that identity. That is to say, a forest is Gothic, a Frankenstein's monster knit together of parts that, to an extent, live and die independently. To imagine a human community, with all its competing, incompatible factions, ideals, beliefs, and principles, as a single plant, is to state a political ideal.

The key to this politics is representativeness, the other side of Taylor's "expressivism." In a tree-community each branch of the tree is an expression, or representative, of the ideal that animates the whole. In Hegel's words: "Since the state is mind objectified, it is only as one of its members that the individual himself has objectivity, genuine individuality, and an ethical life." Therefore, "this final end has supreme right against the individual, whose supreme duty is to be a member of the state" (*Right,* 155–57). For the State-tree, discontinuity is dissolution, radical political change a chain saw. The only acceptable political effort is redemptive.

The movement from fragmentary *phainomena* to an essential underlying order is easily put into Christian language. The Baconian scientist enjoys "heaven upon earth" in the ultimate victory of his empiricism; the expansion of scientific knowledge is an *imitatio Christi* in which the divine Word is incarnated in the mind of the scientist; the view from the citadel is also the view from the cross. The logic of Baconian empiricism is essentially symbolic, in Coleridge's sense; it gives us a vision of "the Eternal through and in the Temporal" (Coleridge, *Lay Sermons,* 30). Coleridge unwittingly underscores the continuity of thought from Bacon to post-Kantian philosophy when he proposes the symbol as a necessary element in natural science: "God is the only solution, God, the one before all, and of all, and through all!—True natural philosophy is comprized in the study of the science and language of *symbols.* The power delegated to nature is all in every part: and by a symbol I mean, not a metaphor or allegory or any other figure of speech or form of fancy, but an actual and essential part of that, the whole of which it represents" (79). The movement of Hegelian politics is to make everyone a Christ, everyone a self-conscious incarnation of the "absolutely rational" that is the State. By this means, death and discontinuity can be reinterpreted as *Aufhebung,* in which the transience of the part merely confirms the continuity of the whole.

There is perhaps no clearer statement of the logic of this process than Hegel's account of the nature of war, an account that is deeply indebted to Aristotelian distinctions between essence and accident:

> War is not to be regarded as an absolute evil and as a purely external accident. . . . Here as elsewhere, the point of view from which things seem pure accidents vanishes if we look at them in the light of the concept and philosophy, because philosophy knows accident for a show and sees in it its essence, necessity. It

is necessary that the finite—property and life—should be definitely established as accidental, because accidentality is the concept of the finite. From one point of view this necessity appears in the form of the power of nature, and everything is mortal and transient. But in the ethical substance, the state, nature is robbed of this power, and the necessity is exalted to be the work of freedom, to be something ethical. The transience of the finite becomes a willed passing away, and the negativity lying at the roots of the finite becomes the substantive individuality proper to the ethical substance. (*Right*, 210)

Every incipient fragmentation of the whole becomes a confirmation of McFarland's claim that there are no fragments without "also the conception of a whole from which it is broken off" (*Forms of Ruin*, 50). Every dead soldier becomes a Christ, whose death confirms the spiritual reality of the State for which he dies. War, which we might have thought the worst of the storms that threatened the survival of the fragile plant, is a glorious confirmation of its essential integrity. Death, in a familiar Christian paradox, is an accession to eternal life.

The threat to the state, in Hegelian political logic, is not, in fact, from outside. This is perhaps why Nussbaum can contemplate the external blows of *tuchē* with equanimity; ultimately, those blows confirm, rather than threaten, the identity of her unacknowledged "real above," the community. The real threat is internal dissociation—revolution—the amnesiac erasure of the plant's "internal teleology," which could cause it to develop into a monster. Hence the real work of a therapeutic politics is simultaneously educational, interpretive, and purgative. The diasparactive fragments of the state must be constantly made self-consciously aware of their representativity; divisions, both real and apparent, within the state must be explained to the state's members in such a way as not to destroy their confidence in the state's fundamental unity. Class, religious, and racial divisions must not be allowed to prevail as the primary allegiance of any citizen's self-consciousness. Elements that cannot be made representative of the "form of life" must be neutralized or eliminated. The political role of poetry in a therapeutic philosophy is restricted to the first two functions, both of which could be described as a form of consciousness-raising.

II

Shelley's ethics, and consequently his politics, are based upon a willingness to take *tuchē* seriously. This entails a thoroughgoing critique of the representational politics of the state-as-*technē*. Shelley's Lucretian "metaphysics" (to use Shelley's own word), however, allow him to reject Aristotelian/Baconian empiricism in favor of a radical empiricism that in turn allows him to handle the ethical implications of *tuchē* without Nussbaum's complications, so that he is able to do justice to the appeal of community without subordinating all *tuchē* to its preservation.

To understand this we need to return in more depth to a topic we have encountered before, evolution. Indeed, a shorthand description of Shelley's Lucretian politics, which indicates how radically they diverge from what had hitherto been the mainstream of Western ethics and epistemology, is to call them "evolutionary," even Darwinian *avant la lettre.* The theory of natural selection represents a watershed in the history of Western thought, a "revolution in thought more far-reaching than that ushered in by Copernicus" (Goudge, 294). Although Shelley died some thirty-seven years before the publication of the *Origin of Species,* his intellectual interests ran in areas that would prove influential upon Darwin's theory. Lucretius, most notably, but also Buffon, Cuvier, Diderot, Erasmus Darwin, D'Aubuisson, and James Parkinson all contributed to turn Shelley's thoughts to questions of the prehistoric history of life on earth. Desmond King-Hele suggests that Shelley, despite being heavily influenced by Erasmus Darwin, did not pick up his evolutionary theories ("Shelley and Erasmus Darwin," 131ff.). King-Hele calls this Shelley's "worst failure in the field of ideas" (132). King-Hele is being too literal-minded here, however; he is only interested in biological evolution (which, even so, Shelley hardly ignores; see *Prometheus,* IV), and fails to see that Shelley was struck by the political and epistemological implications of the evolutionary idea. In the next chapter, I explore some of the manifestations of this interest in Shelley's poetry, such as the extraordinary passage in *Prometheus Unbound,* act IV, where the "cancelled cycles" of prehistoric monsters are unveiled by the penetrating beam from the forehead of the Spirit of the Earth.

My interests here, though, are not in the details of biological evolution but in the more general implications of evolutionary theory. If Lyotard was right to say that the "révolution quantique" is yet to take place in literary criticism, it would be as true to say that the impact of the Darwinian revolution is yet to be fully felt. There can be no proper understanding of the significance of one without the other. This is perhaps the principal reason why Shelley remains "a voice not understood." If Darwinism is the "shortest way" to describe Shelley's politics, it is also the most dangerous.

The most remarkable quality of therapeutic philosophies is their ability to incorporate, and make thoroughly theirs, the most apparently hostile philosophical and critical positions. This is true of Darwinian evolution, which in the popular mind, and even in much scientific and philosophical thought, was soon perverted into a species of Hegelianism. Despite the theological controversy that raged about Darwinism, it has been almost impossible for people to imagine evolution without imputing to the process an "internal teleology" that obscures its most radical implications. The *bellum omnium* of "natural selection" becomes—especially in the metaphors of social Darwinism—like Hegel's idea of war, a progressive stripping away of the "accidents" (unsuccessful, and hence inferior, species) to reveal the "essence,"[7] those successful species that represent the supreme expression of nature's "plan"; Nazi propagandists used this kind of social Darwinism as a justification for their euthanasia programs. To allow "unfit" human beings to survive was to meddle with nature's own "intentions."

It is not new to suggest that Shelley's politics are "evolutionary." Kenneth Cameron called Shelley's "theory of historical evolution" the "main inspirational force in Shelley's work," and made Shelley's evolutionary politics his key "proto-Marxist" contribution to political theory ("Social Philosophy," 512; see also *Golden Years,* 131ff.). But for Cameron, Shelley's "historical evolution" is a bridge from Godwinian perfectibilism (which, as a progressive approximation to reason through human history, has its own implicit "internal teleology") to Marxist dialectical materialism, which Cameron casts in its most teleological, and Hegelian, form as an inexorable, though unconscious, progress from "primitive capitalism" toward "communism" (*Golden Years,* 131).

Cameron's idea of evolution leaves no role for *tuchē* but to be gradually eliminated. The essence of the Darwinian revolution, however, was that for the first time in Western science, *tuchē* could be taken seriously. This is another way of saying that with Darwin history entered modern science for the first time. Or, rather, *reentered* science, because Darwinism is also in part a rediscovery of Lucretian evolution (Winspear, 2ff.; Lowenstein, 13–14; Beer, 14). What direct influence there was is hard to say, but the evolutionary hypothesis did not spring into Darwin's head fully formed; the idea of evolution crops up throughout eighteenth- and early-nineteenth-century thought—including, notably, as an *idée fixe* in the work of Darwin's famous grandfather. Many of those whose adumbrations of Darwinism are most striking, such as Di-

7. The most sustained recent version of this reading is in Argyros's *Blessed Rage for Order.* His "Narrative and Chaos" continues this firmly teleological reading of biological evolution.

derot, Kant, and Erasmus Darwin, are deeply influenced by *De rerum natura.*

This is not, as it might appear, an issue separate from Lucretius's relationship to contemporary physics and chaos theory. Argyros, indeed, makes evolutionary process the center of his literary and philosophical appropriation of chaos theory, although his reading of evolution as narrative "progress" or "self-organization into increasingly complex configurations" is closer to Cameron's than Darwin's (*Blessed Rage for Order,* 307–23). Argyros's belief in "progress" and attempt to discover "human cultural universals" (209–24) place him firmly in the therapeutic tradition. Curiously, he does note that Stephen Jay Gould's theory of evolution, if correct, would invalidate his own, but he dismisses this point, without argument, in a footnote (351 n. 1). This is unfortunate because Gould has been heavily influenced by chaos theory and his reading of evolution strongly supports the version of chaotic creativity advanced here, as we shall see.

The most radical implication of the Lucretian *clinamen* is "irreversibility," the fact that information is lost in the flux of physical interactions and that therefore events eventually "forget" their initial conditions and are cast adrift in a history of absolute events. The discovery of "time's arrow" in contemporary physics, which is intimately connected to the "révolution quantique" and Heisenberg's uncertainty principle, is, according to Prigogine—one of its principal expositors—in part derived from the attempt of Ludwig Boltzmann, in the nineteenth century, to provide a mechanical explanation of entropy. Prigogine and Stengers describe Boltzmann's solution as "en quelque sorte accomplir en physique la démarche de Darwin";[8] by realizing, more or less intuitively, what would become the fundamental element of the quantum revolution—that the behavior of complex interactions of large numbers of molecules can only be treated stochastically—Boltzmann institutes "[u]n principe d'évolution moléculaire" (*La nouvelle alliance,* 273, 275; see also Briggs and Peat, 146, 148).[9] Moreover, they point out that Boltzmann was conscious of his debt to Darwin and of the relationship between Darwinian evolution and the second law of thermodynamics (Prigogine and Stengers, *La nouvelle alliance,* 273n).

The implications of Darwinian evolution for our understanding of history, time, entropy, and chaotic negentropy are explored by Stephen Jay

---

8. "tantamount to accomplishing Darwin's feat, but this time in physics" (*Order out of Chaos,* 241).

9. "A principle of molecular evolution" (*Order out of Chaos,* 242).

Gould in his book *Wonderful Life: The Burgess Shale and the Nature of History*. He makes clear both Darwin's destruction of the therapeutic concept of history and his relationship to the central concepts of chaos science. It is indicative of the hold that the epistemological reference to a "view from the citadel" still has over us that Gould's book is largely a plea that science and intellectual culture in general learn to take history, "irreducible history" (277), seriously. The "scientific method" as usually understood has no models for dealing with contingent events, and yet evolutionary theory suggests that real history is a disjunctive chain of such events, of *tuchē*, which is not accessible to scientific *technē*. "Our most precious hope for the history of life," he notes, "a hope that we would relinquish with the greatest reluctance, involves the concepts of progress [i.e., teleological change] and predictability." And yet, the lesson of the fossil record "is a worst-case nightmare for this hope of inevitable order. . . . [O]ur origin is the product of massive historical contingency" (233).

The lesson of the Burgess Shale, an unparalleled collection of extremely detailed fossils of very early animal species, is one that is familiar to us: sensitive dependence upon initial conditions and the entropic erasure of information. The organisms of the Burgess Shale display a dazzling diversity of form: "When I say that one quarry in British Columbia houses more anatomical disparity than all the world's seas today, I am talking of a *small* quarry" (69).[10] This early diversity calls into question Argyros's claim that evolutionary history provides us with a clear pattern of increasing complexity, or "progress." The bizarre creatures of the Burgess Shale are among the "losers" of the evolutionary game of Russian roulette; they lived alongside the species that eventually bequeathed their physical structures to the modern world's major phyla, but at some point they or their offspring ceased to be viable. The abundance and the diversity of these animals, however, argue that it would be impossible to predict the "losers" and the "winners" beforehand. The results of evolution are "unforeseen and unconceived."

Gould's metaphor for this errant creativity is the replaying of "life's tape." He asks us to envision life as a videotape that we wind back to the time of the Burgess Shale organisms and then allow to play forward again. The therapeutic assumption, which is also the classical assumption of the "scientific method," is that the story will unfold more or less as it did before, that evolutionary history must have some "internal tele-

10. For a radically opposed interpretation of the Burgess Shale organisms, however, see Edward Wilson, 180–81.

ology" that tends, ultimately, to produce creatures like us. Gould argues, however, that

> the reconstructed Burgess fauna, interpreted by the theme of re-playing life's tape, offers powerful support for . . . [a] different view of life: any replay of the tape would lead evolution down a pathway radically different from the road actually taken. . . . [T]he divergent route of the replay would be just as interpret-able, just as explainable *after* the fact, as the actual road. But the diversity of possible itineraries does demonstrate that eventual results cannot be predicted at the outset. Each step proceeds for cause, but no finale can be specified at the start, and none would ever occur a second time in the same way, because any pathway proceeds through thousands of improbable stages. Alter any early event, ever so slightly and without apparent importance at the time, and evolution cascades into a radically different channel. (51)

One result of this "determinate indeterminacy" is to undermine the possibility of Aristotelian empiricism, or the Hegelian inclination to ad-duce the history of the world as evidence of a particular ontology. The observer of evolutionary history must be like the Shelleyan reader of poetry, or the observer of the chaotic unfolding of a strange attractor— a radical empiricist, unable to "leave the room" as the system errs through its chaotic history. The organisms of the world are like Shel-leyan poetic texts in another way, too; they betray a fractal density of detail from which an infinite number of possible evolutionary pathways may unfold. The profusion of life-forms within the "*small* quarry" of the Burgess Shale may be read as a biological equivalent of the poetic part exceeding the whole; every fragment of life contains an infinity of po-tential evolutionary futures, none of which is necessarily compatible with wider "wholes" of which the fragment is a part. An evolutionary world is inherently diasparactive, with each of its parts threatening to overthrow the whole: "Suppose that only a few will prevail, but all have an equal chance. The history of any surviving set is sensible, but each leads to a world thoroughly different from any other" (233). We have encountered this idea as the Gothic principle of the *pépinière*, or seed-bed, advanced by Diderot (*Rêve*, 187), which, as de la Carrera points out, erodes "the causal links between the present and the past" (139).

Diderot's *Lettre sur les aveugles* (1749), which Shelley almost cer-tainly would have read, makes precisely Gould's point in its brief sketch of a theory of evolution. Diderot proposes his own version of a theory of natural selection in which those primitive organisms survive "où le mécanisme n'impliquait aucune contradiction importante, et qui pouvaient subsister par elles-mêmes et se perpétuer" (104-5).[11] He immediately realizes how fortuitous this makes the eventual domination of *Homo sapiens*. Had it not been for remarkable luck "le genre humain . . . eut été enveloppé dans la dépuration générale de l'univers; et cet être orgueilleux qui s'appelle homme, dissous et dispersé entre les molécules de la matière, serait resté, peut-être pour toujours, au nombre des possibles" (105).[12]

Gould "challenge[s] any paleontologist to argue that . . . without the benefit of hindsight" (188) it would be possible to pick out, from the profusion of viable animals in the Burgess seas, those which are the ancestors of contemporary life. The survivors are the seeds, or atoms, that chance preserves from the turbulent river of time. They are the equivalent of the "scattered fragments" of biblical texts, of which Shelley writes in the *Defence,* that have by historical accident prevailed into and shaped contemporary society. About these early versions of scripture Robin Lane Fox makes a point that is the precise equivalent of Gould's point about the proliferation of equally viable lifeforms: "In the time of Jesus, scriptures were not standardized, and there was no reason to believe that the text familiar to us would dominate, drive out the others and be venerated as holy scripture" (102).

Above all, a proper understanding of evolution forces us to accept the reality of *tuchē* in our lives. Not merely that we ourselves—meaning the human species—are a product of *tuchē* ("Replay the tape a million times from a Burgess beginning, and I doubt that anything like *Homo sapiens* would ever evolve again" [Gould, 289]) but that events may be, as Gould writes, "just history," which is to say, sheer events (283). The irreversible time of real history invalidates the explanatory, hermeneutical apparatus of the "view from the citadel," and the incessant drive to harmonize the story of life—the stories of our individual lives, as well as the stories of the social systems of which they form a part—into a coherent totality.

This is not, as Gould emphasizes, to say that the concept of causality,

---

11. "whose mechanism was not defective in any important particular and who were able to support and perpetuate themselves" (*Diderot's Early Philosophical Works,* 112).

12. "the human race . . . would have been still merged in the general depuration of the universe, and that proud being who calls himself man, dissolved and dispersed among the molecules of matter, would have remained perhaps forever hidden among the number of mere possibilities" (*Diderot's Early Philosophical Works,* 112).

and causal explanation, is overthrown, or that our lives become random chains of inexplicable events; it is to say that the sequence of events only makes sense to us in retrospect; we cannot *foresee* the consequences of our actions beyond a very short term, and are therefore constantly reacting on an ad hoc basis to unforeseen circumstances: "Contingency is both the watchword and lesson of the new interpretation of the Burgess Shale. The fascination and transforming power of the Burgess message . . . lies in its affirmation of history as the chief determinant of life's directions" (288). The hermeneutical effort to harmonize our lives into coherent totalities can only be brought to bear upon the trail of past events. Although it can knit them into a plausible whole, that "whole" must be constantly, and sometimes radically, revised to incorporate the unforeseeable *tuchē* of the future; it gives us no guide to what we *are* or what we *shall* be, only what we have been: "We can explain an event after it occurs, but contingency precludes its repetition, even from an identical starting point" (278).

But what are the political implications of this? Gould claims that they are liberating, and empowering:

> Historical explanations are . . . in many ways more intriguing to the human psyche than the inexorable consequences of nature's laws. . . . [B]oth ends of the usual [Aristotelian] dichotomy—the inevitable and the truly random—usually make less impact on our emotions because they cannot be controlled by history's agents and objects, and are therefore either channelled or buffeted, without much hope for pushing back. But, with contingency, we are drawn in; we become involved; we share the pain of triumph or tragedy. When we realize that the actual outcome did not have to be, that any alteration in any step along the way would have unleashed a cascade down a different channel, we grasp the causal power of individual events. . . . Contingency is a license to participate in history, and our psyche responds. (284-85)

This is a common theme in the literature surrounding chaos theory. The idea that a "determinate indeterminism" opens a window of opportunity for "free will" without resort to an "extremely subtle and obscure" transcendental solution like Kant's is naturally attractive (see, e.g., Ruelle, *Chance and Chaos,* 33; Davies, 221). Moreover, sensitive dependence on initial conditions potentially grants the individual enormous powers (Argyros, *Blessed Rage for Order,* 347). In Gould's terms, "Contingency is the affirmation of control by immediate events over destiny, the kingdom lost for want of a horseshoe nail" (284). The microscopic can prevail upon the macroscopic. We do not beat our butterfly wings in vain; on the other side of the world, perhaps, tyrants cower beneath the storm we unleash.

This sense of being granted a relevance to the world that no previous science or philosophy has ever offered is what Serres means by the "nouvelle alliance" and what generates the almost millennial tone of Prigogine and Stenger's book of that title. For Prigogine and Stengers, the new sciences of complex nonlinear dynamics can be described as a combination of "Carnot et Darwin," entropy and evolution. The discovery of the irreversibility of time in the complex dynamical systems of nature and society generalizes to all sciences a version of the Heisenberg uncertainty principle—the *revolution quantique* and the Darwinian revolution hand in hand again. This is not a crude relativism but a discovery that the world exceeds in complexity any single attempt to describe it. The wave-particle duality of subatomic particles means that we can know *either* the position *or* the momentum of a microparticle, but not both at once: "[T]he *most* we can know of a microparticle is its *partially* defined state—that is, its 'contribution' to an irresolvable ensemble" (Hanson, 43). As Prigogine and Stengers are at pains to point out, this is not the result of a merely technical limitation on our ability to know something that is in principle knowable; it is an irreducible element of *tuchē* in the world, "an inevitable consequence of the laws of nature" (Rae, 105). This represents a fundamental challenge to the epistemological assumptions behind the Laplacean demon; that is, it is the final nail in the coffin of the "view from the citadel":

> Le physicien ne découvre pas une vérité donnée, que taisait le système, il doit choisir un langage, c'est-à-dire l'ensemble des concepts macroscopiques en termes desquels il sera demandé au système de répondre. C'est précisément cette idée de choix que Bohr exprimait avec le principe de complémentarité. Aucun langage, c'est-à-dire aucune préparation du système qui permet de le représenter par une fonction propre de l'un ou l'autre opérateur, ne peut épuiser la réalité du système; les différents langages possible, les différents points de vue pris sur le système, sont *complémentaires;* tous traitent de la même réalité mais ils ne peuvent être réduits à une description unique. Ce caractère

irréductible des points de vue sur une même réalité, c'est très
exactement l'impossibilité de découvrir un point de vue de sur-
vol, un point de vue à partir duquel la totalité du réel serait simultanément visible. (Prigogine and Stengers, *La nouvelle alliance,* 313)[13]

The choice of "languages" is not arbitrary, and what the world tells us in
each language is not arbitrary; but no one language exhausts all the
reality of the world, and no language can be entirely translated into
another. This is what Dupré usefully labels "promiscuous realism," a
belief that "there are many equally legitimate ways of dividing the world
into kinds" (6, 7), that the world is of such "complexity and variety"
that "only a pluralistic approach is likely to prove adequate for its investigation" (53). Shelley had indeed initiated the *révolution quantique* in
literature: "[A]ll high poetry is infinite. . . . after one person and one age
has exhausted all of its divine effluence which their peculiar relations
enable them to share, another and yet another succeeds, and new relations are ever developed, the source of an unforeseen [uncertain] and
an unconceived delight" (Reiman and Powers, 500): "[T]oute propriété
macroscopique est inséparable de l''éclairage' que nous choisissons de
projeter sur la réalité, et . . . celle-ci est trop riche, . . . ses reliefs sont
trop complexes pour qu'un seul projeteur puisse l'éclairer dans sa totalité" (Prigogine and Stengers, *La nouvelle alliance,* 313).[14]

 Prigogine and Stengers talk of a "reenchantment" of a world that the
traditional scientific approach had disenchanted: "Le savoir scientifique,
tiré des songes d'une révélation inspirée, c'est-à-dire surnaturelle, peut
se découvrir aujourd'hui en même temps 'écoute poétique' de la nature
et processus naturel dans la nature, processus ouvert de production et
d'invention, dans un monde ouvert, productif et inventif" (393).[15] This

---

13. "[The physicist doesn't discover a given truth that the system was hiding; he] has to
choose his language, to choose the macroscopic experimental device. Bohr expressed this
idea through the principle of complementarity. . . . No single theoretical language articulating
the variables to which a well-defined value can be attributed can exhaust the physical content
of a system. Various possible languages and points of view about the system may be complementary. They all deal with the same reality, but it is impossible to reduce them to one single
description. The irreducible plurality of perspectives on the same reality expresses the impossibility of a divine point of view from which the whole of reality is visible" (*Order out of
Chaos,* 225; with my modification).
 14. "Every macroscopic property is inseparable from the 'light' that we choose to throw on
reality, and . . . reality is too rich . . . its contours too complex for a single lamp to be able to
light it in its totality" (my translation).
 15. "Science, waking from its dreams of an inspired, or supernatural, revelation, can at the
same time discover itself to be a 'poetic attention' to nature and natural process in nature—an

"écoute poétique" is another name for what I have been calling "radical empiricism." It suggests that we "listen" to the languages of the world, but that the very act of listening is a creative one. Prigogine and Stengers quote, with approval, Deleuze's theory of empiricist creativity: "L'empirisme n'est nullement une réaction contre les concepts, ni un simple appel à l'expérience vécue. Il entreprend au contraire la plus folle création de concepts qu'on ait jamais vue ou entendue. L'empirisme. . . . traite le concept comme l'object d'une rencontre, comme un ici-maintenant, ou plutôt comme un *Erewhon,* d'où sortent, inépuisables, les 'ici' et les 'maintenant' toujours nouveaux, autrement distribués" (*Différence et répétition,* qtd. 388).[16]

There is another implication in the rejection of a simple determinism, however, that aids in this "reenchantment" of the natural world. Within the nonlinear dynamic systems of the natural and social worlds, microscopic indeterminacy leads, rapidly, to macroscopic chaos: "Les chemins de la nature ne peuvent être prévus avec certitude, la part d'accident y est irréducible . . . : la nature bifurquante est celle où de petites différences, des fluctuations insignifiantes, peuvent, si elles se produisent dans des circonstances opportunes, envahir tout le système, engendrer un régime de fonctionnement nouveau" (361).[17] Nature as conceived according to the traditional scientific outlook is "étrangère à l'homme qui la décrit" (356).[18] In an irreversible world of determinate indeterminacy, where a change in our point of view, or the smallest of our actions, might change the world irrecoverably, the scientific myth of the "disinterested observer" cannot be maintained; there is no longer any distinction between "acteurs et spectateurs" (368ff.): "Ainsi la science s'affirme aujourd'hui science *humaine,* science faite par des hommes pour des hommes. Au sein d'une population riche et diverse de pratiques cognitives, notre science occupe la position singulière d'écoute poetique de la nature—au sens étymologique où le poète est un fabri-

---

open process of production and invention in a world that is open, productive, and inventive" (my translation).

16. "Empiricism is in no way a reaction against concepts, or a simple appeal to lived experience. On the contrary, it undertakes the most frenzied creation of concepts that has ever been seen or heard of. Empiricism . . . treats the concept as an object that it encounters, as a here-and-now, or rather as an *Erewhon,* from which emerge, inexhaustibly, ever new 'heres' and 'nows,' always differently disposed" (my translation).

17. "The paths that nature will follow cannot be predicted with certainty, the role of the accidental is irreducible. . . . bifurcating nature allows little differences, insignificant fluctuations—if they are produced in opportune circumstances—to invade the entire system, to engender a new paradigm of operation" (my translation).

18. "foreign to the people who describe it" (my translation).

cant—, exploration active, manipulatrice et calculatrice mais désormais
capable de respecter la nature qu'elle fait parler" (373-74).[19]

This "nouvelle alliance" between the human observer and the natural
world is implicitly ethically and politically radical—placing free human
creativity at the center of human understanding of the world—as Prigogine and Stengers are well aware: "[A]u'delà des fausses classifications, des interdits, des contraintes culturelles, politiques et économ-
ique, les sciences n'ont, en droit, pas d'autre limite que celle de la
créativité humaine" (432).[20] The rapid turnover of "concepts" that Deleuze sees as characteristic of a radical empiricism suggests a kind of
"permanent revolution" in our frameworks of knowing; each attempt to
know the world will ultimately be exploded from within; to play the
game of science is constantly to change the rules by which we play:
"L'histoire des sciences . . . est toujours susceptibles de revenir en ar-
rière, de retrouver, au sein d'un paysage intellectuel transformé, des
questions oubliées, de défaire les cloisonnements qu'elle à constitués, et
surtout, de dépasser les préjugés les plus profondément enracinés,
même ceux qui semblent lui être constitutifs" (381).[21]

Regarding the directly political significance of this world of "irreducible history," Prigogine and Stengers content themselves with making a
few general suggestions. As for Gould, the central thrust of these is the
empowering implications of sensitive dependence on initial conditions:
"Nous ne savons qu'une chose: la présence d'interactions non linéaires
dans une population détermine la possibilité de modes d'évolution particuliers (effets boule de neige, propagations épidémiques, différencia-
tion par amplification de petites différences), et cela, quelle que soit la
populations" (259).[22]

19. "Thus science today declares itself to be a *human* process, science performed by human beings and for human beings. At the heart of a rich and diverse population of cognitive
practices, our science occupies the singular position of a poetical attention to nature—in the
etymological sense of 'poet' as 'maker'—an active exploration, manipulative and calculating
also, but henceforth capable of respecting that nature which it makes speak to us" (my translation).

20. "Beyond false classifications, interdictions, cultural, political, and economic constraints,
science, by rights, has no other limit than that of human creativity" (my translation).

21. "The history of science . . . is always capable of a sudden reversal of direction, of
rediscovering forgotten questions in the heart of a transformed intellectual landscape, of
breaking down the partitions it has created, and above all of going beyond the most deeply
rooted prejudices, even those which seemed fundamental to its enterprise" (my translation).

22. "We only know one thing: the presence of nonlinear interactions in a population determines the possibility of particular modes of evolution (snowball effects, epidemic propagations, differentiation through the amplification of small differences), and this holds true regardless of the type of population" (my translation).

The apparent "empowerment" of this "butterfly-wing effect" is illusory, however, and depends upon an appeal to a perspective that the other implications of chaos theory render illegitimate. It is true that "sensitive dependence upon initial conditions" implies that minute actions can have great consequences, but it is also true that these minute "initial conditions" are irrecoverable if we try to trace backward from the consequences to the causes. Moreover, the consequences are not predictable at the time of the actions. A butterfly in New Zealand may cause a storm in Montréal, but only a god or a Laplacean demon, abstracted from the "eddying flood" of contingent consequences, could ever be aware of the actual chain of determination. The storm will mean nothing to the butterfly, and the butterfly will mean nothing to Montréal.

Gould is correct that "for want of a nail" a battle may be lost, and perhaps the battle may decide the fate of many nations. This does not mean, however, that hiding nails becomes a deadly new military initiative. If every conceivable act of ours, no matter how banal, has an infinite array of dramatic potential consequences, many of which are incompatible, the "butterfly-wing effect" is no guide to effective political action. As David Ruelle cautions: "Un éternuement peut être la cause d'un cyclone quelques mois plus tard dans une autre partie du monde. Mais attention, *les mêmes raisons que donnent á un éternuement ce pouvoir exorbitant empêchent qu'on puisse en prévoir l'effet ou le mesurer après coup*" ("Hasard et déterminisme," 158).[23] We might say, adapting Baudelaire, that "ses ailes de papillon l'empêchent de marcher."

In an isolated fragment of uncertain date incorporated with the rather fluid collection of metaphysical and ethical reflections given the title "Speculations on Morals" by Mary Shelley, and probably composed sometime between 1817 and 1821, Shelley gave us a rather different, and more useful, account of the implications of a "fractal ethics." It is necessary to quote at length from this passage, which probably owes a debt to Mary Wollstonecraft's argument against Burke's *Reflections,* in her *Vindication of the Rights of Men,* that "[w]e should be aware of confining all moral excellence to one channel, however capacious" (38). Shelley here directly addresses our concerns with the relationship between individual agency and the "defining context":

23. "A sneeze may be the cause of a cyclone several months later in another part of the world. But it is important to note that *the same principle that gives the sneeze this exorbitant power makes it impossible that one could ever predict the outcome or trace the sequence of cause and effect backward*" (my translation).

[L]et us visit, in imagination, the proceedings of some metropolis. Consider the multitude of human beings who inhabit it, and survey in thought the actions of these several classes into which they are divided. Their obvious actions are apparently uniform: the stability of human society seems to be maintained sufficiently by the uniformity of the conduct of its members, both with regard to themselves, and with regard to others. The labourer arises at a certain hour, and applies himself to the task enjoined him. The functionaries of government and law are regularly employed in their offices and courts. The trader holds a train of conduct from which he never deviates. The ministers of religion employ an accustomed language, and maintain a decent and equable regard. The army is drawn forth, the motions of every soldier are such as they were expected to be; the general commands, and his words are echoed from troop to troop. The domestic actions of men are, for the most part, undistinguishable one from the other, at a superficial glance. The actions which are classed under the general appellation of marriage, education, friendship, &c., are perpetually going on and, [to] a superficial glance, are similar one to the other.

But, if we would see the truth of things, they must be stripped of this fallacious appearance of uniformity. In truth, no one action has, when considered in its whole extent, an essential resemblance with any other. Each individual, who composing the vast multitude which we have been contemplating, has a peculiar frame of mind, which, whilst the features of the great mass of his actions remain uniform, impresses the minuter lineaments with its peculiar hues. Thus, whilst his life, as a whole, is like the lives of other men, in detail, it is most unlike; and the more subdivided the actions become; that is, the more they enter into that class which have a vital influence on the happiness of others and his own, so much the more are they distinct from those of other men. . . .

We consider our own nature too superficially. We look on all that in ourselves with which we can discover a resemblance in others; and consider those resemblances as the materials of moral knowledge. It is in the differences that it actually consists. (Ingpen and Peck, 7:81–83)

These correspondent increases of "subdivision" and of "distinction" are a remarkable adumbration of fractal complexity; the microscopic proves to be every bit as detailed as the macroscopic, and more important, the microscopic proves to be just as significant as the macroscopic. It is the most minutely detailed aspects of our moral lives that "have a vital influence on the happiness of others" and ourselves.

Shelley does not deny the existence, or the importance, of what we might call the "cultural context," but he indicates that its apparently overwhelming importance is a product of our choice of scale of observation, our choice of "éclairage." If we choose to look more closely, we find that there is a disjunction between the macroscopic and the microscopic; individual human lives are not representative (or "expressive") of an atemporal totality that they make temporally incarnate.

This belief in fractal specificity has ethical and political implications. It opens the door for *tuchē* in human lives, and delivers us to the possibility of tragedy. The fractal "individual" (Shelley's endless sequence of *divisions* does not stop at the scale of "individuals") cannot avoid what Lyotard calls *le différend* and Shelley calls "differences." Because Shelley does not seek to ground identity, either of human beings or human values, with reference to any encompassing order, he opens himself up to the really radical implications of this fractal ethics in a way that Nussbaum cannot. Shelley is willing to accept the implications of moving this fractal relationship between society and the individual into time, with evolutionary results.

Shelley argues that there are "two classes of agency," which relate, respectively, to the "social and individual man." We may compare these complementary but incommensurate agencies to the wave-particle duality of quantum mechanics. "Almost all that which is ostensible submits to that legislature created by the general representation of the past feelings of mankind—imperfect as it is from a variety of causes"; they can "no more escape it, than the clouds can escape from the stream of the wind." On the other hand, they are no more determined in their shape than clouds are by the stream of the wind: "Internally all is conducted otherwise; the efficiency, the essence, the vitality [of actions,] derives its colour from what is no wise contributed to from any external source" (Ingpen and Peck, 7:82–83). This disjunction between the two "agencies" is the door through which contingency enters; the details of individual lives are not fully determined by their defining situation, and therefore the already "imperfect" "legislature . . . of the past feelings of mankind" is condemned to constant, even if unintended, erosion as those "feelings" undergo mutations that do not derive from the reproductive institutions of society.

I have considered the ravages of the *clinamen* in social self-reproduction; what interests me here are the implications of this for the "individual." What does it mean to live with *tuchē*; what are the ethical and (small-scale) political consequences of accepting our existence within irreversible time? A short answer is that given that the individual fractally reproduces the same scalar disjunctions as the society, the fate of the individual is to be, like society, "a system of subtle mechanism. . . . [which] is perpetually wearing away or breaking to pieces the wheels of which it is composed" (Ingpen and Peck, 7:10). If, as Shelley says elsewhere in the "Speculations," our "identity" is merely an intuitive sense of a "connection in the train of our successive ideas," the internal "subdivisions" of our nature must erode that connection over time, and the "past feelings" of the individual will be progressively alienated from present ones. The divided "individual" succumbs to a permanent revolution of "character."

This, however is too facile an answer; it tells us nothing of the real details of such a process or what they might imply for the quality of our ethical life as it is lived. A slightly longer answer would be to say that to accept our lives, our values, and our characters all as immersed in irreversible time, and all therefore subject to *tuchē,* is to make us deeply aware of the power of *enchaînement* over representativity. Clearly this answer needs some elucidation.

Lyotard's concept of *enchaînement* focuses us on the virtual "moment" when contingency enters the stream of events by opening up a range of possible evolutionary pathways, of which we can only choose— or be chosen by—one and whose consequences are all radically different. We do not usually consciously make these "choices," nor, when we do, are we aware of their ultimate consequences. In retrospect, however, we can see the curiously aleatory nature of the course of our lives: the options that opened at random; the possibilities that were forestalled before we were even aware of their existence; the roads not taken that make all the difference. Every act, every moment, is an *enchaînement* onto the entire history that has preceded it, and it opens and closes the doors to an infinity of different futures. Those who believe in representativity, on the other hand, do not accept this aleatoriness. Fate, either in the form of character, the cunning of history, or God, determines the choices we make. Wherever we are placed, our "real nature" will "express" itself. Providence unfolds itself in the world, and we make incarnate its plan.

III

Shelley pursues this question throughout his poetry, and it is there that we best see the implications of his ethical inquiries being tested. In *Alastor,* Shelley examines with some sympathy a life that aspires to representativity. The *Alastor* Poet has a vision of the Absolute, a vision of a perfect love beyond the reach of *tuchē,* beyond entropy, beyond mortality. He seeks to make his life a complete embodiment of that absolute ideal; he will accept nothing partial, nothing mortal, after his glimpse of absolute fulfillment. To a certain extent he succeeds in extracting himself from the flux of world; but the cost, Shelley suggests, is terrible.

The Poet's career is best approached by comparing him to those philosophers described by Nussbaum who attempt to make themselves stoically impregnable to the *tuchē* of the world by living according to an autarchic *technē.* Socrates, in Plato's *Gorgias,* insists upon the futility of seeking the good life through satisfying our never-to-be-satisfied appetites, and argues that to live well is to live beyond the reach of need and desire, which pierce the boundary between the soul, which dwells with eternal Forms (citadel), and the body, which inhabits the world of appearances (flux). Shelley must have appreciated, as Nussbaum does, the wisdom of Callicles' response: "In that case stones and corpses would be living superlatively well" (Nussbaum, 142, 144).

Plato scornfully characterizes the life that Callicles praises—a life spent fulfilling ever-renewed desires—as filling a leaky vessel or as being like that of a type of bird that constantly eats its own excrement (144), but the central thrust of Nussbaum's argument is that "need can be constitutive of beauty," the "quick, tense splendour" of fragile human beauty and goodness (342). The life that tries to ground itself only on eternal, unchanging, and unassailable verities will not be a fully human life. Or, in the words of a modern chaos theorist, "[If a] system ever does reach equilibrium, it isn't just stable. It's dead" (Waldrop, 147).

Alastor's preface (if we bracket for the moment any questions about whose voice it is supposed to be [Wasserman, *Shelley,* 39])[24] makes this relationship quite clear. The Poet, who leads an almost purely intellectual life, lives a life abstracted, as much as possible, from everything vulnerable to *tuchē:* "So long as it is possible for his desires to point towards objects thus infinite and unmeasured, he is joyous, and tranquil, and self-possessed." Above all, he is safe from *tuchē* because he has no interpersonal relationships, no *philia.* Suddenly, however, he falls into desire, and his mind "thirsts for intercourse with an intelligence similar to itself." He refuses, however to risk such intercourse with a real, vulnerable, changeable person: "He images to himself the Being whom he

---

24. Wasserman makes his "Narrator" too concrete by ascribing the preface to him. The skeptical *isostheneia* that Wasserman wishes to extract from the opposition between the narrator and the visionary/Poet is better reflected in the preface than the narrator's supposedly one-sided interpretation of the visionary's career.

loves. Conversant with speculations of the sublimest and most perfect natures, the vision in which he embodies his own imaginations unites all of wonderful, or wise, or beautiful, which the poet, the philosopher, or the lover could depicture" (Reiman and Powers, 69). "Blasted by disappointment, he descends to an untimely grave." Shelley does not find this "illustrious superstition" entirely blamable, but he does see it as a "self-centred seclusion" that is appropriately "avenged by the furies of an irresistible passion." He compares the Poet's crime to that of those ascetic souls who follow the stoic *technē,* described and abjured by Nussbaum, of abstracting themselves from the dangerous, entropic world of desire—in which the soul becomes a leaking vessel ever seeking replenishment—because its risks are too great. These are the people, Shelley writes, who, "loving nothing on this earth, and cherishing no hopes beyond, yet keep aloof from sympathies with their kind, rejoicing neither in human joy nor mourning with human grief; these, and such as they, have their apportioned curse. They languish, because none feel with them their common nature. They are morally dead. They are neither friends, nor lovers, nor fathers, nor citizens of the world, nor benefactors of their country" (69–70).

The Poet has been led into this crime by a "generous error" and a "sacred thirst of doubtful knowledge," but at base it is unmistakably the same refusal to open himself to *tuchē* that thereby cuts him off from everything most valuable in human life (the list of friends, lovers, fathers, citizens, and benefactors of their country is, apart from its androcentric nature, a fairly comprehensive list of the possible forms of human *philia*).

The poem bears out this failure. The thanatological impulse underlying the resistance to *tuchē* (*vide* "They are morally dead," above) is emphasized by the Poet's search for the "infinite and unmeasured," the absolute and unchanging, being revealed as a search for death. The Poet, however, is notoriously hedged about with contingent possibilities of *enchaînement* into the flux of our irreversible world. Shelley wants to make it clear to us that the denial of *tuchē* is a life-destroying effort of will, a voluntary blindness to opportunities that are perpetually abundant. Most obvious is the "Arab maiden" (129), who represents a possibility of an *enchaînement* into earthly love, with all its risks and rewards, which the Poet, tragically, ignores.

Equally important is the symbolic representation of *tuchē* in the landscape through which the poet passes. The Poet is always on the edge of chaos—literally—and yet never fully alive to the precariousness of his situation:

Seized by the sway of the ascending stream,
With dizzy swiftness, round, and round, and round,
Ridge after ridge the straining boat arose,
Till on the verge of the extremest curve,
Where, through an opening of the rocky bank,
The waters overflow, and a smooth spot
Of glassy quiet mid those battling tides
Is left, the boat paused shuddering.—Shall it sink
Down the abyss? Shall the reverting stress
Of that resistless gulph embosom it?
Now shall it fall?—A wandering stream of wind,
Breathed from the west, has caught the expanded sail,
And lo! with gentle motion, between banks
Of mossy slope, and on a placid stream,
Beneath a woven grove it sails. . . .

                                                        (387–401)

This passage might seem ludicrously unmotivated given that the boat arrives safely after all. But the indeterminacy of this moment, almost comic and strangely exhilarating in its sheer contingency, forms an ironic commentary on the Poet's deathly abstraction from the world. The curiously thrilling beauty of this moment is lost on him, and we feel the perversity of his quest after the Absolute in a world where life hangs upon "a wandering stream of wind."

A proper understanding of the role of *tuchē* also helps us to understand the moral seriousness of a point in "Julian and Maddalo" that has disappointed many of its readers. When Julian declares that if he had only been an "unconnected man," he might have carried out a plan to restore the Maniac to sanity, many commentators have regarded this as a rather lame excuse for abandoning the character who has impressed his sufferings upon Julian, and upon us, so powerfully.[25] Julian is blamed for being too ensconced in his own social world, too wrapped up with his own philosophical preoccupations, to fully connect with the Maniac and follow through on his airily idealistic plans of amelioration.

---

25. The classic statement of this point of view is Wasserman, *Shelley,* 80–82. The same case has been made by Hirsch ("A Want of That True Theory") and more recently, and vehemently, by Hogle (*Shelley's Process,* 121). See also Rzepka, "*Julian and Maddalo* as Revisionary Conversation Poem," 136, for a similar view. Stuart Curran maintains the opposite case in *Annus Mirabilis,* though from a perspective rather different from mine.

The basis of this condemnation is an ideal of moral representativity, which we can relate back to the Platonic and Kantian argument that acts must be judged in isolation from the stream of events in which they occur. This is the representativity of "character," by which we are led to believe that an individual's every act springs from a moral essence that is prior to any conjuncture in the lived reality of that individual. This is generally true of the characters in novels and poems; their acts can all be knit up into a fundamentally unified "plot" that gives them meaning and that they bear out, both at the level of their individual "characters" and at that of the work as a whole. Judging from that perspective, we find it easy to condemn Julian, because he forgoes a chance to act well that the poem has elaborated in detail, pleading other duties that the poem has not discussed at all.

But it is only a Julian reduced to the two-dimensionality of a conventional fictional character who can be so judged. Such a Julian would indeed be an "unconnected man." As such his life would be a version of the pathologically simplified lives of those "morally dead" Shelley condemns in the *Alastor* preface. If we grant Julian the (fractal) complexity of a real ethical life, this criticism becomes smug and absurd. Julian's inability to help the Maniac is not tragic per se, but it springs from the same implications of *tuchē* in an irreversible world that make tragedy possible. Only in a world without incompatible claims and incommensurable allegiances, a providential world where appearances can all be related to an underlying Absolute, could Julian be reasonably blamed for passing up this possible *enchaînement* into a different life. Julian is not an unconnected man, and the allegiances of *philia* and *negotium* (564, 582) that he asserts against the contingent option of nursing the Maniac are fully valid. We are all, as Julian makes clear, surrounded by different possibilities of *enchaînement,* different possible, and incompatible, futures between which the merest chance may decide. When Julian describes these "dreams of baseless good [that] / Oft come and go in crowds or solitude / And leave no trace" (578–80), we recognize a mental, and moral, version of the boat hovering indeterminately on the edge of the eddy in *Alastor.*

Throughout this poem, Julian is looking back to a recognizable moment of contingency that has shaped his life, much as Gould looks back at the Burgess Shale as a "moment" of evolutionary contingency. The Maniac represents a point of bifurcation where an alternative line of development presented itself but was not followed. This has vital implications for our understanding of the rest of the poem. This moment of pure contingency is an answer, of sorts, to Julian and Maddalo's debate at the beginning of the poem. What is at stake in Julian's *enchaînement* is not just the *setting* of his future development, but the very "essence" of who "Julian" is. A Julian who stayed in Venice, and stayed "day by day" (568) with the Maniac, would live, like the Julian who left, through "many years / And many changes" (583–84); they would be no more (and no less) the "same" Julian than a whale and a dog are the "same" because of their common evolutionary heritage. And is this not the issue of Julian and Maddalo's argument? Julian argues that

> ". . . it is our will
> That thus enchains us to permitted ill—
> We might be otherwise—we might be all
> We dream of happy, high, majestical.
> . . . .
> . . . It remains to know
> . . . and those who try may find
> How strong the chains are which our spirit bind;
> Brittle perchance as straw. . . . "
> (170–73, 179–82)

Maddalo presses "the darker side," arguing that our corrupted natures bind us to a life of woe; his is the argument of representativity, that evil acts bespeak essentially evil "characters." Ironically, by "failing" to attempt the cure of the Maniac, Julian, in retrospect, proves he was at least partly right; the "chains" that bind our spirit to a given form of life *are* brittle as straw. If we are "enchained" to a life of ill, other *enchaînements* are open to us.

It is doubtful, however, whether we can "choose" to be "happy, high, majestical." The future is open, and not fully determined by the past, but we cannot see very far into the consequences of our choices. In an irreversible world, we must continually renew our choice of life, even if, as Julian does when he returns to London, we choose to continue as before. Sometimes, as Nussbaum demonstrates, no "good" choice may be open to us, the result being genuine tragedy. Shelley's *Cenci* is a profound study of the tragic implications of contingency and the ethics of representativity. I do not wish to add more ink to the gallons already spilled on the issue of how far Beatrice is exonerated for her crimes by the circumstances that force her to commit them. Suffice it to say, as Wasserman does, that the extent of the controversy proves that Shelley has indicated a fault line in our ethical discourse (*Shelley*, 120–21).

One could make much the same argument about Beatrice as Nussbaum makes about Hecuba. Shelley insists upon Beatrice's purity of
"soul" at the beginning of the play, and we see her degenerate into a
murderer and a liar under the blows of *tuchē*. Shelley goes out of his
way to insist upon the contingent nature of her fate. Orsino's treach-
erous refusal to present her petition, the bizarre deaths of her brothers,
the deeply ironic arrival of the papal legate to arrest the count shortly
after his murder are developments that appear to cut off any *enchaînement* for Beatrice that would be both helpful and blameless.

The aspect I focus on here, however, is the issue of representativity
and personal identity. Wasserman has provided us with an excellent account of the *Cenci*'s contributions to Shelley's theory of self. Throughout his life, Shelley attributed much of the evil of the world to what he
called "the dark idolatry of self" (*Revolt*, VIII, xxii, 3). "Self-contempt" in
such poems as *Queen Mab* (IV, 185), *Adonais* (xxxvii, 7), *The Revolt of
Islam* (VIII, xxi, 3), and, above all, *Prometheus Unbound* (I, 8; I, 510;
II, iv, 25; III, iv, 134) is the hallmark of the tyrannic mind—both tyrant's
and slave's—the opposite of the "self-esteem" ("Hymn to Intellectual
Beauty," IV, 1) and "self-content" (*Prometheus Unbound*, I, 487) of the
liberated mind. As Wasserman, among others (e.g., Milton Wilson, 90ff.;
McNiece, 162, 224), suggests, Shelley argued, with his customary psychological acuteness, that hatred and contempt of others usually arises
out of hatred and contempt of the self:

> Self-hatred, or the belief that one's own nature is evil, makes one
> the slavish, will-less recipient of evil and thus necessarily the
> doer of evil to others. . . . Therefore the first principle of Shel-
> ley's moral solution is, in the words of Cythna's sermon to the
> sailors,
>
> > Reproach not thine own soul, but know thyself
> > Nor hate another's crime, nor loathe thine own.
>
> For self-reproach is self-contempt. . . . Self-knowledge therefore is
> the opposite of self-reproach; it is the knowledge that human
> nature is not inherently evil, that evil is not the "creation" of the
> will. (*Shelley*, 110; see 109–22)

Wasserman goes on to locate evil in a "continuously potential transcendent force," which is little improvement over a tainted will, but the rest
of his analysis is extremely acute. The concept of representativity sheds

much light on this theory of Shelley's, and on our responses to *The Cenci*.

The belief in a representative character is a denial that *tuchē* has any part in forming the self. Our actions, and the events that befall us, cannot shape our character; they can only "express" it, or provide an occasion for us to express it. If we subscribe to such an ideal, we will anxiously anatomize our actions for clues to our "real" identity, and, conversely, we will act as much as possible in conformity with what we have "learned" of who we are: to thine own self be true.

Orsino's soliloquy in *The Cenci* spells out this conservative cycle:

> 'tis a trick of this same family
> To analyse their own and other minds.
> Such self-anatomy shall teach the will
> Dangerous secrets: for it tempts our powers,
> Knowing what must be thought, and may be done,
> Into the depth of darkest purposes:
> So Cenci fell into the pit; even I,
> Since Beatrice unveiled me to myself,
> And made me shrink from what I cannot shun,
> Shew a poor figure to my own esteem,
> To which I grow half reconciled.
>
> (II, ii, 108–18)

Orsino's mistake, in Wasserman's words, is "the "moral error" of believing the "mask" of circumstances to be essential" (*Shelley*, 117). Believing himself to be "essentially" evil because he has learnt that he has *been* evil, Orsino makes himself blind, as Maddalo does, to alternative, contingent possibilities in his future; the only *enchaînements* he can recognize are more "characteristically" evil ones. This is true of Count Cenci as well, whose self-conscious certainty of his "monstrosity" informs all his actions.

The pernicious effects of a dedicated commitment to representativity can be seen in Beatrice as well as in Orsino and the count. In Beatrice, as in the *Alastor* Poet, we see the most sympathetic rendering of the desire for pure representativity. Shelley is showing us in both instances that the problem is not a particular *type* of representativity, but the refusal to admit the power of *tuchē* in general. Whatever we feel about the justifiability of Beatrice's "crime," readers are almost unanimous in finding her behavior after the crime unsympathetic. Why does she not boldly acknowledge the deed, and claim that it was justified, if she believes it was? The answer is that she has too much invested in her own myth of moral purity. She cannot accept that circumstances may have driven her to act "uncharacteristically"; the "evil" of her action is something she cannot absorb into her personal ideal of her character, which, she claims shortly before her death, "Though wrapped in a strange cloud of crime and shame / Lived ever holy and unstained" (V, iv, 148–49). Hence her bland, absolute, and frustrating denials of a reality that seems plain to us.

Hence, too, her fundamental "error," which, as Wasserman argues persuasively, is to believe that her father has the power ineradicably to dishonor her, a belief that empowers him with a force he would not otherwise have (94ff.). This belief may appear paradoxical, but we can see that it is the equivalent, on the level of personal "character," of the "anxiety of insufficient influence" characteristic of therapeutic representativity. She does grant one possible power to *tuché,* and that is the power of sheer annihilation, a dissolution of her soul. Certainly this is what Count Cenci hopes to achieve. "[T]he greater point" of his plan is "To poison and corrupt her soul" (IV, i, 44–45); he boasts that he shall force her to "become . . . to her own conscious self / All she appears to others" (85, 87–88). Shelley held that, as he says in the preface to *The Cenci,* "no person can be truly dishonoured by the act of another" (Reiman and Powers, 240). Only if we believe that we have been so dishonored and, making that "fact" the center of our self-definition, act "representatively," do we confirm the "tyrant's" power to degrade us.

If Beatrice could escape from her commitment to an ethical "essence" that serves merely to cow and disable her—if she could see, as Shelley puts it in the preface, that the "crimes and miseries in which she was an actor and a sufferer are as the mask and the mantle in which *circumstances* clothed her for her impersonation on the scene of the world" (242; my emphasis)—she might be able to escape from her bondage to Count Cenci's distorted version of reality and open herself to a sense of possibility, of a reinvention of her "self" that would render the count powerless.

Of course, she also might not. The count does have the power of life and death over her, and he can constrain her opportunities of *enchaînement* so drastically that no livable option appears to her. As such, it may be that she does have no choice but to murder him. Having done so, however, and by refusing to accept that her actions were a necessary though unfortunate consequence of contingent circumstances, she traps herself into an anxious self-justificatory preservation of the boundaries of her hypostatized self-image. In her complete, unearthly inflexibility in the face of her family's suffering, the torturing of her hired killers, and so on, she commits the same ethical error that Nussbaum ascribes to Aeschylus's Agamemnon: "Even if we say that the agent chose and acted under situational constraint, and so may bear a diminished guilt for his or her bad action, this is not the end of the question of praise or blame. If there is much that he cannot help, there is much, nonetheless, that he apparently can: his emotional responses to the dilemma, his thoughts about the claims involved. . . . A proper response . . . would begin with the acknowledgement that this is not simply a hard case of discovering truth; it is a case where the agent will have to do wrong" (42). Even after Count Cenci's death, Beatrice does not seem to have been liberated from his power. Her inability to face, and then move beyond, her responsibility for his murder appears to trap her in a dynamic of his creating.

The proper contrast with Beatrice's response to tyranny is, as is usually pointed out, Prometheus. Prometheus, of course, is immortal, and has rather longer to meditate his response than does Beatrice. The central, liberating act of *Prometheus Unbound* is Prometheus's renunciation of his curse against Jupiter. Prometheus suddenly forgoes representativity; he is willing to risk an *enchaînement* from his old version of the "self," entirely predicated upon an "eyeless" hatred of Jupiter (I, 9), to a new version who "wish[es] no living thing to suffer pain" (I, 305). It is an old complaint about *Prometheus Unbound* that it has no "drama" because the crucial reversal of the story occurs in Prometheus's mind either some time shortly before the play begins or imperceptibly in the first few minutes; Prometheus does not visibly struggle to gain his new perspective. But this is Shelley's point. Dramatic "struggle" to achieve a new understanding of the world is predicated upon the necessity of reconciling the new position with the old; one must reconcile the contemplated change with deep continuities of personal identity, and prove that the new position is fully representative of one's "character." Prometheus, however, "changes his mind," in Drummond's sense. For no definable reason—Shelley pointedly refuses to account for the change in Prometheus that all his supporters find so terrifying—Prometheus abandons his stultifying commitment to definition by the past, and opens himself up to an evolution into an unforeseeable future.

IV

With Prometheus, we have moved from the issue of "character," which I have so far been pursuing, back to a wider sense of the political. We return, however, with some new answers to old questions. Above all, we begin to understand why an individual would choose to live with the uncertainty and risk of Shelley's politics rather than the apparent security of the therapeutic position. Let us consider from the point of view of the individual agent the implications of a therapeutic politics. What does it mean to live "representatively"?

To answer that question let us return to Burke's metaphor of making repairs to a building as nearly as possible in the style of the original. This implicitly transgenerational injunction to continue to represent the essence of the past speaks to a central concern of all therapeutic philosophy: how to make each new act "part of" a "form of life"; how to defeat the irreversibility of time, so that we can reason backward perfectly from the act to the "form of life" that inspired it. It is natural that education, or acculturation, is a key concern of so much therapeutic philosophy; from Aristotle's description of those in fundamental disagreement with him as "apaideusa" (meaning "lacking in acculturation" [Nussbaum, 152]) to Wittgenstein's account of learning how and when to play the appropriate language game.

Consider Wittgenstein's celebrated metaphor of our language, and our language games, as an old and complex city: "Our language can be seen as an ancient city: a maze of little streets and squares, of old and new houses, and of houses with additions from various periods; and this surrounded by a multitude of new boroughs with straight regular streets and uniform houses" (8; sec. 18). The problem with this is that while, like Burke and his constitution/building, Wittgenstein is more than happy for change, addition, and corruption to have occurred in the remote past and, in principle, for additions to be made in the future, he does not provide any model of how such changes could occur. Learning a language game is learning a preexistent "formula," learning "how to go on" as others have "gone on" before (59–61; secs. 151, 154). The only *enchaînements* Wittgenstein imagines are those that replicate preexistent language games. If they do not, they are erroneous, and of no more interest than the errors Aristotle allows to creep into our sublunary world. In Austin's formulation, each performative *enchaînement* is either "happy" or "unhappy," and if "unhappy," it is inconsequential (133).

Wittgenstein resists the reduction of learning to a *process* in which certain concepts are more or less successfully conveyed to a learner by a teacher. This is welcome, but it means that an almost mystic holism takes its place. One moment we are baffled, and the next moment we cry, "Now I know how to go on!" (160; sec. 154). We learn by imitation, and we learn absolutely or not at all. The process seems to be insulated from *tuchē*. There is no possibility of a *clinamen* where every error is without issue, no possibility of evolution when every mutation is sterile. Every "meaning event" can be related to a known language game; every act is fully *representative* of a form of life: "Our mistake is to look for an explanation where we ought to look at what happens as a 'proto-phe-nomenon.' That is, where we ought to have said: *this language-game is played*" (167; sec. 654).

But consider what it actually means to learn from the past and to reproduce that past in the future. Imagine an architect who wants to add a building to a preexisting city, a city like the one in Wittgenstein's metaphor. Each building can be considered as a "repair" to the fabric of the city, a repair that must be made as much as possible "in the style" of the preexisting city that is its context and defines our idea of what a building should be. How do you add a building that is fully "representa-tive" of the "essence" of that city? How do you add a building that does not, even in a minor way, revolutionize the city, introducing a muta-tion—however slight—that future additions and repairs might magnify by reproducing? How do you just "go on?"

This will be easy enough in a city where every building is perfectly identical; but would not such a city be a perfect metaphor for the state-as-*technē*, which Nussbaum argues is too poor in meaning for a fully human life? That the "price of harmonization seems to be impoverish-ment" would be only too evidently true in such a city. Nor is this the city that Wittgenstein (or, implicitly, Burke) imagines us to inhabit. It is the rich complexity of our inheritance from the past, of our form of life, that each seeks to preserve. One could seek, as much contemporary postmodernist architecture does, to establish a "dialogue" with the built environment, "quoting" aspects of surrounding buildings (a lancet win-dow here, a gabled roof there, an Ionic portico for good measure); but such a solution, as we see all around us, produces a finished product that looks like none of its models and has already become an identifiable "style" with a name of its own, which may one day give birth to a "neo-postmodernist" movement.

One could choose a particular style from those of the buildings in the city and nominate it as the clear and true expression of the "essence" of the "national character." But as in the case of neo-Gothic architecture in nineteenth-century England—which was so regarded—this brings in its train insurmountable difficulties. If the decision prevails and every new building is built in that style, the city will become unrecognizable. This is unlikely to happen, however, because the movement will never agree upon what constitutes "going on," even in that "one" style. Does one

copy early, middle, or late examples of the style? Does one copy the
buildings as they have come down to us, with additions of different
periods and "instant aging" of the appearance, or does one build what
one imagines to have been the pure "intent" of the original builders?
Either way, one creates a "style" that never existed before. Error becomes essence, or "restoration" becomes invention. In the words of
Serres: "Apprendre lance l'errance" (*Tiers-instruit*, 28).

One might try to simplify things by demolishing every building that
did not conform to one's ideal of the "essential" style of the city. This
"aesthetic cleansing" we could call the genocidal road to aesthetic clarity. Once again, however, revolution will merely have been masked by a
rhetoric of "purification." The city will not be what it once was, and
will, moreover, have become inhumanly simplified.

In a world of fractal complexity—and such is the city of language and
language games that Wittgenstein describes—reproduction leads inevitably to evolution. There is no simple contrast of "happy" and "unhappy" performances in the language games of real life. To play these
games is constantly to revise their rules. Our "architect"—who could
stand for anyone attempting to "produce" anything with reference to his
or her "form of life"—must be resigned to being, in however minor a
way, a revolutionary, whose *enchaînements* do not *quite* buckle the
cycle of "cultural reproduction."

If, however, one cannot abandon the ideal of perfect representativity,
of a *Sittlichkeit* that is fully transparent to Absolute Reason, the price
one pays is a paralytic anxiety—specifically, an anxiety about the future.
Every act opens a myriad of potential, contingent futures, so every act
must be restlessly scrutinized to make sure it is not an *enchaînement*
into an unforeseen and unconceived future. There can be no joy in a
representative world, at best a grim satisfaction that the Notion has not
(yet) been completely defaced, at worst a thanatological obsession with
the elimination of "error." The "rapturous exaltation not to be confined"
belongs only to those who are willing to risk their identity to evolutionary
tuchē. They are alive to the sense of futurity and possibility, and therefore
have that sense of hope which is the hallmark of Shelley's politics.

V

Shelley's sharpest portrait of the opposing characters of the representative "Christ" and the evolutionary is to be found in the competing "Song
of Apollo" and "Song of Pan." Apollo is a complete portrait of the representative ideal:

Whatever lamps on Earth or Heaven may shine
Are portions of one spirit; which is mine.

. . . .

I am the eye with which the Universe
Beholds itself, and knows it is divine.

(23–24, 31–32)

He is anxiously obsessed with the stability of his identity. His song is a monomaniacal monologue in which in thirty-six lines the words "I," "me," "my," and "mine" appear, collectively, twenty-four times (compared with "Pan"'s ten times in as many lines). Apollo's song is a song to the stable self-identity of "the sovereign reason which 'knows' the world from a singular, selfsame point of view" (Ryan, 153). Apollo regards himself as the embodiment of reason, and as such it is his duty to eradicate "error."

The sun as the light of reason extirpating error was a favorite Enlightenment trope. Even in his early writing, Shelley reads an implicit violence into this, however; in the *Revolt* the agony of the baking sun on Laon in his captivity is linked to Apollo-the-archer's divine propensity for slaughter: "the Sun / Its shafts of agony kindling through the air" (III, xx, 2–3). For Shelley, the "light of reason," could hide as much as it revealed, extinguishing the more valuable "stars" of imagination, which fade into the light of common day. The universality of sunlight obliterates those crucial "differences" in which "moral knowledge" consists.[26]

The two "Songs" should be read with not only their own mythic context in mind (Apollo inflicts asses' ears upon Midas for finding Pan's music superior), but other related aspects of Apollo's story as well. The flaying of Marsyas, for example, is a closely related example of Apollonian "reason" resorting to thanatological violence to eradicate potential divergence. The story of Niobe's children is particularly important. Shelley wrote the longest of his "Notes on Sculptures in Rome and Florence" on her famous statue. He makes of her not a victim of her own hubris but someone fighting against the tyranny of an abstract rationality she cannot comprehend. Niobe's response is selfless; she has no time for the obsessive self-consciousness of "her omnipotent enemy" as she tries to shield her children from his wrath: "There is no selfish shrinking from personal pain; there is no panic at supernatural agency— there is no adverting to herself as herself" (Ingpen and Peck, 6:331).

---

26. Compare "Bright Reason will mock thee / Like the Sun from a wintry sky" ("When the lamp is shattered," 27–28).

With this background, the enjambment of the first two lines of the third stanza of the "Song" strikes us as particularly pointed:

> The sunbeams are my shafts with which I kill
>   Deceit, that loves the night and fears the day.
> All men who do, or even imagine ill
>   Fly me; and from the glory of my ray
> Good minds, and open actions take new might
> Until diminished, by the reign of night.
>
> (13-18)

In sharp contrast to Apollo's obsessive, thanatological defense of the stability and rationality of his identity, Pan's song is a riot of playful indeterminacies that seeks to undermine Apollo's through "the [fractal] inscription of the other in the selfsame" (Ryan, 153). Shortly before writing these poems Shelley had written in his "On Life": "The words *I*, and *you* and *they* are grammatical devices invented simply for arrangement and totally devoid of the intense and exclusive sense usually attached to them" (Reiman and Powers, 478). Pan's "Song" is the active assertion of this fluidity of identity against Apollo's attempt to "kill" all threats to the unity and sovereignty of his (Marsyas, Niobe, Midas).

Pan's "Song" is the antithesis of Apollo's. Where Apollo's is in a rigid, stately, repeatable form, Pan's is full of lyric inventiveness, playing at patterns only to subvert them; where Apollo's "Song" is unified, timeless praise of the "intense and exclusive" self with no external reference, Pan's is written in a dialogic voice of inclusive, indistinct identity—"From the forests and highlands / We come, we come" (1-2). Pan refers directly to his auditors (11, 23, 35), eschewing Apollo's pretensions to timelessness and embedding his song in the contingency of the present occasion. Where Apollo's "Song" sticks to its simple goal of praising in a unified voice a unified subject, Pan's is seemingly a description of some unspecified past occasion, a "then" to the auditors' "now":

> And then I changed my pipings,—
> Singing how down the vale of Maenalus
> I pursued a maiden and clasped a reed.
> Gods and men, we are all deluded thus!
>
> ("Song of Pan," 29-32)

There is a radical undecidability here in terms of the speaker's (speakers'?) identity and what Bakhtin calls "chronotope." Before "I changed my pipings" the poem is in the first person plural and the present tense ("we come, we come"); moreover, "I changed my pip-

ings," which seems to refer to some past event analogous to the present
occasion, also enacts what it describes; the mood of the "Song" changes
dramatically. The poem has no unified subject, in either sense, and we
cannot answer those central questions of the metaphysics of identity:
Who is speaking, where, and when? What and where are they speaking
of? What language game is being played? The multiple possible *en-chaînements* disjunctively dissipate identity: "Gods and men, we are all
deluded thus!"

Pan's "Song" does not deny the danger that *tuchē* poses for us. There
is a "sorrow in [his] sweet pipings" (36), and it stems directly from our
willingness to live with error in this "dædal [fractally complex] earth"
(26). But commensurate with that "sorrow" is the evanescent but ever
recurrent beauty and joy that emerges from "Love and Death and Birth"
(28)—desire, entropy, and venereal creativity—in a world of irreversible time. Pan shrewdly attributes Apollo's inability to weep in sympathy
with Pan's loss (34–36) to the "envy or age" that has "frozen" his
"blood" (35). Apollo envies Pan's openness to the future at the same
time as he fears it. Apollo cannot feel sympathy for Pan's sorrow, because that would be to admit that *tuchē* matters and cannot be "killed."
Unable to feel Pan's sorrow, he is equally unable to feel his joy in the
"dancing stars" (25; see *Prometheus,* IV) and the "dædal earth," which
to him are, on the one hand, "portions of one spirit; which is mine"
("Song of Apollo," 24), and, on the other, "to my embraces bare" (12).
Apollonian *erōs* is not threatened with "delusion," but absolute fulfillment, in Shelley's view of *erōs,* is "vacancy."

Pan's "Song" establishes the true spirit of Shelley's evolutionary politics. We may live in a world "where evil and good are inextricably entan-
gled and where the most admirable tendencies to happiness and preservation are for ever baffled by misery and decay" ("Essay on the Devil,
and Devils," Ingpen and Peck, 7:89), but Shelley chooses, most of the
time, to see this as a reason for celebration; no matter how evil our
contemporary situation may be, it is, usually, possible to find some admixture of good onto which to connect our *enchaînements* into the
future. It is not *always* possible; pure transferential transgression is not
possible in Shelley's world; we can only build from what we receive.
"Mind cannot create, it can only perceive," the skeptical credo of the
young Shelley, remains a partial truth even for the mature one. But the
"dædal earth" is so complex that perception becomes creativity. We do
respond to contexts, but our responses are so wildly divergent that the
context is eventually destroyed even by those who aim to reproduce it.
Memory becomes death.

It may seem that this undermines the very meaning of "political action" by encouraging a quiescent response to political oppression: "this too shall pass." But this is to miss the central thrust of Shelley's evolutionary solution to the dilemma of the "two thoughts." Shelley's acknowledgment of *tuchē* in human life is an acceptance both of life's temporality and its temporariness; it is these that give meaning to our ethical and political lives. The sweepingly skeptical nihilist who holds all social forms and political structures to be irrelevant because necessarily impermanent is in accord with the most dogmatic idealist in one thing: they both hold that the "really real" is the eternally real; the skeptic merely disputes our ability to satisfy that criterion. It is true that nothing in human life does, but the demand ignores the real scale of human lives. A chaotic world may be one where "nulle organisation, nulle stabilité n'est, en tant que telle, garantie ou légitime" (Prigogine and Stengers, *La nouvelle alliance*, 392),[27] but there are eddies within the flux of disorder, "dissipative structures" that for an unpredictable duration maintain a certain negentropic coherence and continuity of structure by increasing the entropy of the whole. One model of such a system is Plato's derisive metaphor for the finite, desiring life from which his *technē* was designed to save us, the "leaky vessel" that is ever refilled (Serres, *La naissance*, 86–89; see Nussbaum, 144; Lucretius, 126–27, 3.1008–10; 217–18, 6.9–23). Serres points out that Lucretius provides us with a dramatically different reading of the significance of this leaking vessel. To Lucretius, we are all such cracked vases, which can "never by any possibility be filled" (217, 6.21). Serres reads this as an image of a dissipative structure, the kind of "open system" that buys time against the second law of thermodynamics by trading local negentropy against global entropy (*La naissance*, 87ff.; "Ainsi le modèle hydraulique poreux est localement homéostatique et globalement homéorrhétique. Ce que je voulais démontrer" [89]).[28] The vase leaks, it is constantly "dying," but it is perpetually refilled; this dynamic equilibrium—this life—is predicated upon a capacity for dissolution: "Le vase et son fluide perdent. Mais ils sont stables pour un temps. Ils peuvent différer, une courte durée, le terme prévu par la loi de dissolution. Preuve alors que des flux y entrent pour équilibrer ceux qui sortent. . . . [L]e corps, système ouvert, est le lieu ou le siège d'un échange de flux; ils y entrent, ils en sortent. Mais ces flots sont, unitairement, de nourriture et de boisson, d'éros ou de perception, et d'information intellec-

---

27. "no organization, no stability, is, per se, guaranteed or legitimate" (my translation).
28. "Thus the porous hydraulic model is locally homeostatic and globally homeorhetic. QED" (my translation).

tuelle" (88).[29] This openness is not without risk, of course, and even an inevitable prospect of eventual failure. Death will come eventually; but without being open to the flux of the world, death would not be a "risk"; there would be no life for it to menace. Platonic autarchy is thanatocratic: our vulnerability to disaster is an essential part of our humanity. What Nichols says of Lucretian political philosophy is equally true of Shelley's: "His reasoning leads to the conclusion that the best life for man must be led according to nature, unconsoling though his view of nature is" (181).

Dissipative structures are "localement homéostatique et globalement homéorrhétique" (Serres, *La naissance,* 89).[30] Without such local homeostasis, there would be no meaning in life. There could be no perception of the inevitable deformation of identity, because there could be no identities to deform. Evolution can be observed only because it produces the relatively stable identity of species.[31] For the finite desiring life of a human being to make any moral sense, we need both the leak and the vase, which is to say, both erasure and memory. Similarly, there are local political continuities against which we can struggle as if they were as timeless and stable as they consider themselves to be. Throughout his life, Shelley reasonably and coherently attempted to organize and encourage resistance to a government and a political and social system he considered iniquitous despite, indeed aided by, the certain knowledge that they must eventually be trampled into the dust of history. The fact that a shark is the product of evolutionary contingency does not make it illogical to defend oneself from it, nor does the fact that sharks will one day be extinct; from the perspective of a single human life, that is only of interest once you are back in the boat.

Some political iniquities will almost certainly outlive us as they outlived Shelley. But the secret of Shelley's radical political hope, the secret that keeps Prometheus from yielding to Jupiter, is the evolutionary indeterminacy of the future. Living in a chaotic world, we are seldom justi-

---

29. "The vase loses its fluid, but this system is stable for a time. The vase and the fluid can defer, briefly, the end determined by the law of dissolution. This is proof then that a sufficient flow enters to balance that which comes out. . . . The body, an open system, is the site or seat of an exchange of flows; they enter, and they are emitted. But these flows are, taken individually, those of food and drink, those of sex or perception, and those of intellectual information" (my translation).

30. "locally homeostatic and globally homeorhetic" (my translation).

31. Or, perhaps, evolution can be observed only because we use "species" as one possible, though fairly arbitrary, way of dividing up the world. Dupré makes the point that evolution is not conceivable from the point of view of microbiology and can only make sense at a sufficiently "macroscopic" scale of analysis (134).

fied in abandoning hope for a better world or in assuming that we are powerless to help bring it into being. Like the experimenter who "cannot leave the room," the political subject who perceives the world in evolutionary terms sees it as incessantly generating new possibilities of *enchaînement* into alternative futures, a vision that strips political systems of their most powerful ideological weapon, their aura of inevitability.

Historical impermanence has always been cited by revolutionaries against the existing regime. From Volney's *Ruins* through Paine's "moldy parchments" to Marx's historical dialectic, political radicals have comforted themselves with the inevitability of the oppressor's downfall. Shelley's originality is to eschew the concept of revolution as "foundational" (Laclau and Mouffe, 177) and to recognize that the same lesson of impermanence applies to the new order as much as to the old. This too might seem to undermine political struggle: why fight for change if even the greatest victory will soon be followed by cumulative defeats? Again, the answer is that the question is posed at the wrong scale; only an immortal, unchanging being could make sense of fighting for an immortal, unchanging order. We need mortality to make desire and joy meaningful, and this is as true of the individual as it is of a political entity, no matter what its size.

This is the meaning of Shelley's unwillingness to specify the future form of a just society, his belief in "open-ended change," as I called it earlier, that manifests itself in the "negative forms" of *Prometheus Unbound,* for example, or his instructive misreading of the American constitution:

> [T]he founders of the American Republic . . . looked upon the past history of their species and saw that it was the history of his mistakes, and his sufferings arising from his mistakes; they observed the superiority of their own work to all the works which had preceded it, and they judged it probable that other political institutions would be discovered bearing the same relation to those which they had established which they bear to those which have preceded them. They provided therefore for the application of these contingent discoveries to the social state without . . . violence and misery. (*A Philosophical View of Reform,* Ingpen and Peck, 7:12)

This is the voice of an evolutionary politics. Each attempt to reproduce the system introduces changes—"errors," "contingent discoveries"— that eventually lead to its overthrow.

Unlike a thoroughgoing skepticism, this position allows that we can, with temporary success, and sometimes should, struggle against change; some of the things lost in the irreversible flux of time are valuable, even essential, to our well-being. Such losses are part of the inevitable admixture of evil in a finite world. But change is inevitable, the most dedicated attempt to reproduce the world will contribute to revolutionizing it. This is why "[p]oets are the unacknowledged legislators of the World," because their work is the perfect example of the inevitability of a creative response to context. This is made most clear in the original version of this passage in *A Philosophical View of Reform,* from which the passage about the American Republic also comes. This version includes the claim that "whatever systems they may [have] professed by support, they actually advance the interests of Liberty" (Ingpen and Peck, 7:20). Poetry is an essentially mimetic art, and poets, as historicist critics never tire of demonstrating, do produce works that reflect their "cultural contexts." But, as Shelley observes, to "reproduce" a fractally complex reality is to project a new one, possibly equally complex in its turn, and to contribute to the erasure of the "system" that one intended to memorialize.

To maintain the struggle against change beyond a certain point is to risk the paranoid anxiety of Apollo and to lose the possibility of creative joy. Life, Shelley says in "On Life," is "an education of error," and to insist on the eradication of error is to fail to profit from the sublime and ridiculous truth that "to . . . [the] principle of the mind overshooting the mark at which it aims, we owe all that is eminently base or excellent in human nature" ("Essay on the Punishment of Death," Ingpen and Peck, 6:189).

From a human perspective within the turbulent flood of events, the political promise of a chaotic world is not the self-aggrandizing (and self-delusory) one of flapping an arm and bringing down a government; it is the promise of being at home in a world of constant becoming, of the ability to define ourselves against the status quo and to hope realistically that the status quo will change in our lifetimes. Above all, it is to turn us toward the future with a capacity for wonder and joy at this "source of . . . unforeseen and . . . unconceived delight."

"THE TRIUMPH OF LIFE"

The clearest portrait of this "world of constant becoming" is in Shelley's "Triumph of Life," to which I now return to complete the reading of it I

started earlier. The "Witch of Atlas" showed us that Error and Truth are
the twin born children of Time, but the "Triumph" shows us what it is
like to live this as a reality. Above all, it shows us the implications of
accepting the finitude of our lives, our necessary temporality. The "Triumph" shows how fully Shelley understood the implications, for political action, of his "révolution quantique" in the theory of historical process. Quantum theory destroys the scientist's self-image as Laplacean
demon, or isolated observer of a self-contained world open, ideally, to a
single, comprehensive examination, by revealing the extent to which
our perception of the world is a product of our approach to it. Similarly,
the Shelleyan actor must acknowledge the limitedness of his or her
"point of view" in this "common universe of which we are portions and
percipients" (Reiman and Powers, 505).

In the "Triumph," Shelley renounces his ideal of Rousseau as a potential revolutionary Christ, and instead casts him into a shifting, atomistic,
amnesiac world in which aspirations to representativity are immediately
undercut by the erosion of any and all orders. That the world of the
"Triumph" is Lucretian is evident. The often remarked evocation of the
Lucretian *simulacra* (482ff.) is joined by such Lucretian elements as the
"perpetual flow" (298) of the "great stream / Of people" (44–45) in
life's parade; the "whirlwinds" (144) in which the dancing people are
enwrapped; the light that "drops" "veil by veil" from the morning star
(413); or the victims of life's chariot who "Seemed in that light like
atomies that dance / Within a sunbeam" (446–47; the movement of
motes of dust in a sunbeam is one of Lucretius's proofs of the constant
indeterminate movement of atoms [63–64, 2.125–32]). Lucretius describes clouds as *simulacra* that "[i]n their fluidity never cease to
change their form, assuming the outline now of one shape, now of another" (134, 4.141–42); and Shelley describes his *simulacra,* which
"the car's creative ray / Wrought . . . / As the sun shapes the clouds"
(533–35), in the same way, emphasizing, as Lucretius does, the rapidity
with which they are deformed, and ultimately transformed, by the errant flux of process.

The "Triumph" has always been a crux in Shelley criticism: critics
have divided sharply on the issue of whether the poem is a despairing
vision of the pointlessness of life's ridiculous pageant or a grim warning
that nonetheless leaves open the possibility of avoiding the "dance" if
we take the right approach to life. One of the chief delights of the
"Triumph" is that each time we read it, we seem to discover it anew.
Any reading that argues that the poem's portrait of a life in perpetual
flux, where we "to new bright destruction come and go" (154), is

purely pessimistic conflicts with the joy and pleasure we derive from the poem itself, which "destroys" itself as frequently as any of the "atomies" in the dance of life. While no reading of the poem can, or should, hope to be definitive, a reading should be able to acknowledge the poem's beauty.

The key to a proper understanding of the "Triumph" is to throw into question the status of the voices in the poem in a way that does not seem to have been done before. So many of Shelley's major poems are written in the borrowed voice of more or less elaborately constructed personae (*Alastor,* "Julian and Maddalo," *Epipsychidion,* "Peter Bell the Third") that it is odd that this possibility has not, to my knowledge, been considered in criticism of the "Triumph."[32]

It is, perhaps, the desire for "last words" that makes us read this poem as Shelley's direct and unmediated vision of life. Many critics, however, have argued that we are to find Rousseau at fault in the poem, and any of the more optimistic readings of the poem have to assume that an engagement with life's career more successful than Rousseau's is possible. The poem's narrator, however—about whom no information is given that allows us to identify him with Shelley, or anyone else—shares Rousseau's viewpoint and, for the duration of the extant fragment of the poem, is subject to his tutelage. Should we trust what the narrator sees?

The "Triumph of Life" is a criticism, not of life, but of a certain way of looking at life. It is a criticism of the attempt to achieve the "view from the citadel." At the time of writing the "Triumph," Shelley's early enthusiasm for Rousseau had been tempered by a more critical appraisal of his achievement; in the *Defence* he lists Rousseau, with some reservations, with Locke, Hume, Gibbon, and Voltaire, as one of those votaries of abstract reason the loss of whose works would not represent an incalculable blow to humanity (Reiman and Powers, 502, 502 n. 8). Rousseau, in his aspiration to representative self-consciousness, is a form of Shelley's Apollo; in the "Triumph," he is an Apollo who is no longer capable of believing in his own myth of an eternal, absolute order, but who still cannot reconcile himself to the mutable world he inhabits.

Apollo does figure in the "Triumph," in the form of the sun. The sun's rising at the poem's opening, which obliterates "the stars that gem / The cone of night" (22–23), is related to the vision that visits the narra-

---

32. Jones notes the curiously "detached" nature of the narrator and Rousseau in the "Triumph" (*Shelley's Satire,* 161–63), but from his perspective they are insufficiently "detached" to achieve true satiric distance. He does not seem to consider the possibility that they are to be criticized for their detachment.

tor. Shelley's sun is the sun of "reason," but reason seen in the coercive, ideologically restrictive form of the "Song of Apollo" or the "calculating faculty" of the *Defence*. This is a reason that insists that all data must be related to a single point of view; as such, Yeats was right to identify the sun in the "Triumph" as "the being and source of all tyrannies" (qtd. in Bloom, *Mythmaking*, 270). The narrator leaves the visionary realm of night, in which the multivocal stars shine forth, for the "single vision" of the sun:

> before me fled
> The night; behind me rose the day, the Deep
>
> Was at my feet, and Heaven above my head.
>
> (26–28)

The narrator's viewpoint merges with Apollo's;[33] his point of view becomes the all-embracing "view from the citadel" of Enlightenment reason, commonly symbolized by the sun. But the result is not Absolute Knowing. A "strange trance" (29) comes over him, the trance of reason itself. The trance represents the inability of this monological reason to perceive the complexity of a reality that it insists upon reducing to a unified story.

Under the tyrannical spell of this reason, the narrator has a vision of life. Who better to guide him than the man popularly identified as the foremost of the Enlightenment philosophes? Rousseau is an inspired choice because he was also so tempted by the irrational. He becomes, for Shelley, a gateway figure who allows us to imagine the possibility, within the poem, of a point of view different from that which is proposed to us.

Almost everywhere else in Shelley's writing the Lucretian vision of a world in a constant state of becoming is celebrated, as it is in the "Witch of Atlas," but in the "Triumph" it takes on a nightmare quality: why? The answer can be found, as David Quint suggests, in Rousseau's and the narrator's response to this world. They both search obsessively for guarantees of identity in the face of flux (177–79, 199, 208, 300–304, 543). The most dramatic example of this is Rousseau's response to

---

33. It is unclear whether the narrator's viewpoint has *become* Apollo's or merely approximates to it. In a poem that is quite cautious about the sun's whereabouts, the very uncertainty of this passage suggests the former. The night apparently "flees" him as it would the sun, and to say that "day" rises "behind" him (not the "sun") may be an iconic representation of causal sequence: first there is night, then comes the sun, and "subsequently" there is "day."

the shape all light, to which he turns for a certainty that proves to be delusive:

> " 'Shew whence I came, and where I am, and why—
> Pass not away upon the passing stream.' "

(398–99)

Shelley models this moment on another work he was reading (and translating) at the time of writing the "Triumph," a work he admired greatly: Goethe's *Faust*. According to Faust's pact with Mephistopheles, Faust's soul will be forfeit if he should ever tell the passing moment, "Oh stay! You are so beautiful!"[34] (1700). We know the passage struck Shelley, and was in his mind at the time of writing the "Triumph" (*Letters*, 2:436).

Rousseau's error is to fight against the inevitable forces of change and deformation in the world; he refuses to open himself to the future, and attempts to single out a particular moment of ideal beauty and fix it as a reference point forever: "Pass not away upon the passing stream." Like Faust, his "damnation" follows swiftly upon this attempt to transcend the flux of time in a moment of epiphany. As the shape offers to let him "quench his thirst" in the cup of nepenthe, a flood of atomistic change rushes through his brain, which becomes "as sand" and leaves him mourning the passing of the shape (which fades "veil by veil" [413] in perfectly Lucretian manner) in an unrecognizably transformed world.

Saint-Preux's career in *Julie: Ou, la nouvelle Héloïse* forms an ironic parallel to Rousseau's in the "Triumph." Saint-Preux inhabits a world of Lucretian flux when he is in the "torrent" of Paris, and much of the imagery of the "Triumph" comes from this part of Rousseau's novel. Paris is a place where one undergoes a constant "forgetting of initial conditions"; the "disfiguration" de Man notes in Shelley's poem is a key word, as well as a constant process, in Saint-Preux's Paris, a world where the faces of men are "masques" (212) that they discard at will, and where "tout change à chaque instant" in the "flux et reflux" of this "chaos."

Saint-Preux learns to loathe Paris, and looks back on it from the security of Julie's Elysée—which stands for the Epicurean Garden, a tranquil citadel removed from the flux of the world—as a place of horror. When he is in Paris, however, he is seduced by the "ivresse où cette vie agitée

---

34. "Verweile doch, du bist so schön!"

et tumultueuse plonge ceux qui la mènent" (*Julie,* 232).[35] This "ivresse" haunts the "Triumph" as an alternative to Rousseau's cynical despair in response to its giddying flux. Central to realizing this alternative is a piece of advice Shelley puts into Rousseau's mouth:

> "But follow thou, and from spectator turn
>   Actor or victim in this wretchedness,
>
> "And what thou wouldst be taught I then may learn
>   From thee."
>
>   (305–8)

This advice stands rather oddly in the poem. Rousseau offers it, but immediately launches into his account of the encounter with the shape all light. The narrator does not act upon it, and Rousseau does not seem to expect him to. It stands as a contingent point of bifurcation, a road not taken that invites us to inquire what it might mean if the narrator did "turn actor or victim" in the dance of which they remain decidedly abstracted "spectators." We are particularly struck by the ambiguity of Rousseau's "what thou wouldst be taught I then may learn / From thee." Does this mean that the narrator would only then be able to state clearly what he wants to learn from Rousseau; or, more intriguingly, does Rousseau mean that he would then learn from the narrator what the narrator would have learned by entering the dance? If the latter reading is correct, this would be an implicit acknowledgment on Rousseau's part that he does not know the meaning of the spectacle before them.

The move from "spectator" to "actor" is central to the implications of chaos theory. "Acteurs et spectateurs" is the title of a section of Prigogine and Stengers's *La nouvelle alliance* (368), which I have discussed above. The implications of the "révolution quantique" are that all "spectators" inevitably become "actors"; the old pretense of a science abstracted above the flux of phenomena is shattered, and all knowledge exists at a finite human scale, not a divine or eternal one. Rousseau's advice—"from spectator turn / Actor"—is borrowed by Shelley from Saint-Preux, who also discovered the radical implications of being "portions and percipients" of an infinitely complex world in the irreversible, chaotic flux of Paris. This was the discovery that led to the "ivresse" he would later read as a fall: "Je trouve . . . que c'est une folie de vouloir

---

35. "giddiness into which that agitated and tumultuous life plunges those who lead it" (my translation).

étudier le monde en simple spectateur. Celui qui ne prétend qu'observer n'observe rien. . . . On ne voit agir les autres qu'autant qu'on agit
soi-même; dans l'école du monde comme dans celle de l'amour, il faut
commencer par pratiquer ce qu'on veut apprendre" (*Julie,* 222).[36] The
parallel between "amour" and "le monde" is particularly striking, because in the pageant of life it is love, above all, that the narrator and
Rousseau as abstract spectators seem least able to comprehend:

> Maidens and youths fling their wild arms in air
>   As their feet twinkle; now recede and now
> Bending within each other's atmosphere
>
>   Kindle invisibly; and as they glow
> Like moths by light attracted and repelled,
>   Oft to new bright destruction come and go,
>
> Till like two clouds into one vale impelled
>   That shake the mountains when their lightning's mingle
> And die in rain,—the fiery band which held
>
>   Their natures, snaps . . . ere the shock cease to tingle
> One falls and then another in the path
>   Senseless, nor is the desolation single,
>
> Yet ere I can say *where* the chariot hath
>   Past over them; nor other trace I find
> But as of foam after the Ocean's wrath
>
>   Is spent upon the desert shore.—Behind,
> Old men, and women foully disarrayed
>   Shake their gray hair in the insulting wind,
>
> Limp in the dance and strain with limbs decayed
>   To reach the car of light which leaves them still
> Farther behind and deeper in the shade.
>
>   (149-69)

This is the equivalent of Plato's view of the desiring life as an ill to be
avoided by recourse to a suitable *technē.* There is nothing "incorrect" in

36. "I find . . . that it is foolish to wish to study the world as a simple spectator. He who
claims merely to observe, observes nothing. . . . One can only see how others act to the extent
that one acts oneself; in the school of life as in that of love one must begin by practicing what
one wishes to learn" (my translation).

this portrait of human desire and aging; it simply leaves out everything that gives them meaning. The problem is one of scale; from the detached, eternal viewpoint of the narrator's and Rousseau's citadel, human *erōs* becomes a bad joke, of which the inexorable advance of age and death is the punchline.

But what if we follow Rousseau's advice, which is also the heart of Prigogine and Stengers's "nouvelle alliance" with the world, and from spectators turn actors in this dance? What if we adapt our knowledge to the finite and irreversible reality of human lives? What if we accept the inevitability of *tuchē* in our lives, and open ourselves to the chance and change of an unforeseeable and inconceivable future? From such a scale—the scale of Pan's inclusive, multivocal "we," not Apollo's uniperspectival "I"—it is the knowledge that death is the inevitable outcome of their erotic minglings that makes real the intense fragile beauty of these "new bright destructions." This is that "quick tense splendour of human excellence" that, as Nussbaum points out, even the immortal Gods envy us (342). Rousseau and the narrator are looking at life through the wrong end of the telescope, and are therefore unable to see the beauty that rises out of its constant disfigurations. Rousseau's constant efforts to find a still point of unchangeable identity from which to stand and view the world blind him to its possibilities. Like Apollo, he can only condemn and execrate the "errors" that constantly deform the world around him.

If we return to the "Triumph of Life" and, turning actor not spectator, avoid Rousseau's mistake of demanding a value that is not at risk in the flux of process, then we find the apparent nightmare of life's dance is a product of incorrect seeing, or choosing an inappropriate scale. The beauty within the "living storm" does not register at the scale of Rousseau's and the narrator's hunt for eternal verities. The image of the "dance of life" is a clue that the perspective of the "spectators"—Rousseau and the narrator—is to be distinguished from that of the poet. The "maniac dance" (110) is modeled on the maenadic fury of the followers of Dionysus. The maenad is for Shelley a positive image of the poetically inspired. The self-portrait of Shelley carrying the thyrsus in *Adonais* (291) indicates his perspective as that of an actor in, and not a spectator of, the maenad's maniac dance.

Similarly, the *simulacra,* which Rousseau can see only as fitting inhabitants of Dante's *Inferno,* produce, among many who lead the tragic lives of the victims of *tuchē,* "others" who

"like elves
Danced in a thousand unimagined shapes
Upon the sunny stream and grassy shelves."

(490-92)

This, with its echoes of the Witch of Atlas's free creativity, or the dancing hours of *Prometheus Unbound*'s fourth act, or the "unforeseen and
unconceived delight" of poetic creativity (compare "unimagined
shapes"), which in *Prometheus* figures as "arts, though unimagined, yet
to be" (III, iii, 56), is too evidently a positive image in Shelley's imaginative world to allow us to share Rousseau's horrified repugnance.

Abandoning Rousseau's demand for stable, self-identical values, we
can even appreciate the beauty of the moment that is, for him, a nadir,
his encounter with the shape all light. Most readers would agree that
this passage is the most compelling in a poem of remarkable power. I
read this moment, earlier, as Rousseau's "fall" into the ironic world of
figuration. But if we take a "Shelleyan" attitude toward this passage, and
not Rousseau's, we are freed to appreciate the ephemeral beauty of the
shape's appearance. Even the rapid transitions of Rousseau's brain-be-
come-as-sand take on an exhilarating energy that is only frightening if
we demand, as Rousseau does, a rigid continuity of identity.

Hogle, who suggests that the shape represents the principle of radical
transference, argues that Rousseau's error is that he merely "touched
with faint lips" (404) her cup of transferential nepenthe, failing to drink
unreservedly and enter into pure and joyful amnesiac transference (*Shelley's Process,* 329-30). I agree with Hogle that Rousseau's vision is distorted because he demands absolute certainty in a world that does not
offer this, and that Rousseau's error is in too great an attachment to the
"past" (321-39). It is important to emphasize the differences, however.

Carlos Baker was the first to suggest that the phrase "touched with
faint lips" meant that Rousseau did not actually drink the nepenthe, but
merely touched his lips to the cup (264-65). One must agree with
Bloom, however, that this is a perverse reading: "If Shelley meant to
indicate that Rousseau did not drink, he would surely have made so
important a point a bit clearer. As it is, he employs an idiom, to touch a
cup with one's lips, which means that one drinks" (*Mythmaking,* 269);
in the *Revolt,* Laon tells us how he was nursed by the Hermit, saying
that "a potion to my lips / At intervals he raised" (III, xxxii, 1-2);
Baker's reading would suggest either that the Hermit was teasing his
patient or that the "potion" was a treatment for chapped lips.

Rousseau does drink of the shape's nepenthe, and the partial amnesia that follows is Shelley's view of ordinary, entropic process, the principle of evolutionary change that the shape represents. The absolute transferential amnesia that Hogle believes the cup to contain would, in Shelley's view, be an annihilation of meaning, which would eliminate any possibility of joy and hope along with regrets for the past. The shape is not a purely comforting figure, as Hogle wishes her to be. Some of what she "tramples into the dust of death" we are right to regret; Shelley does not attempt to replace the oversimplifications of the therapeutic Absolute with an equally oversimplified transferential Absolute. The world of *tuchē* is a world in which tragedy is possible, and to allow the possibility of genuinely negative political action as a normal part of political process is also to admit that we are exposed to considerable dangers.

When Shelley writes that the shape tramples our thoughts "As Day upon the threshold of the east / Treads out the lamps of night, until the breath / Of darkness reillumines even the least / Of heaven's living eyes" (389–92), we cannot but agree with the majority of commentators that this must be read as a lamentable obliteration of "differences," and this may appear to be fatal for the reading I am constructing here. Although this image is, as we have seen, a common one in Shelley's poetry, which usually indicates the obliteration of poetic inspiration by the "light of common day," Reiman is right to point out that here Shelley is in part echoing Saint-Preux's description of Julie: "Ne te vis-je pas briller entre ces jeunes beautés comme le soleil entre les astres qu'il éclipse?" (81; see Reiman, *"Triumph,"* 66).[37] It is unlikely that Shelley regards Julie as a purely destructive force to be shunned at all costs. Rather, this seems persuasive evidence that Rousseau's error is in how he approaches the shape. The world of ironic division that the shape represents is not inherently "evil"—no more than is Julie—but it obliterates us and all possibility of joy and love in us if we refuse to accept its limitations, and demand that it reveal an underlying therapeutic Absolute. Similarly, Julie is fatal to Saint-Preux only because he makes his love for her an absolute principle of his identity, so that he is incapable of responding usefully to the unfortunate *tuchē* that makes their happiness impossible. The ironic world contains the potential for tragedy; we recognize that the shape represents both the entropic and negentropic aspects of evolutionary process and that we should fear her, at the same time as we recognize that without her there is neither hope nor beauty.

---

37. "Do I not see you shining among those young beauties like the sun among those stars that he eclipses?" (my translation).

Everywhere, in fact, in this exceptionally lovely poem, there is beauty to be found. Rousseau and the narrator cannot get beyond their horror at the fact that the beauty is so ephemeral that it is always poised on the brink of destruction:

> "the crew
> Seemed in that light like atomies that dance
> Within a sunbeam.—Some upon the new
>
> "Embroidery of flowers that did enhance
> The grassy vesture of the desart, played,
>   Forgetful of the chariot's swift advance;
>
> "Others stood gazing till within the shade
>   Of the great mountain its light left them dim.—
> Others outspeeded it, and others made
>
> "Circles around it like the clouds that swim
> Round the high moon in a bright sea of air,
>   And more did follow, with exulting hymn,
>
> "The chariot and the captives fettered there,
>   But all like bubbles on an eddying flood
> Fell into the same track at last and were
>
>   "Borne onward. . . . "
>
> (445–60)

But cannot we, knowing that we too will be carried away by this turbulent "eddying flood" whether or not we fight against its current, choose to live as fully as possible the moments when we "dance / Within a sunbeam" or play upon the "Embroidery of flowers," whose "quick, tense splendour" owes everything to the "chariot's swift advance"?

PART THREE

SHELLEY'S ENTROPIC POETRY

9

Shelley's Lucretian Imagination

This part concentrates upon Shelley's poetry. Part Two considered only Shelley's more fully developed statements of his theory of chaotic creativity, without providing the context from which they emerged, and without showing how pervasive these ideas are in his poetic writing. Here, I flesh out and solidify some of the assertions of the previous section, not only about Shelley, but about Lucretius and his significance to the thinkers of the Enlightenment. This entails some inevitable repetition of theoretical points made earlier, but with a thinker as many-sided and unsystematic as Shelley it is important to show not only that a given philosophy can be found in his writing, but that it is recurrent and pervasive, before we can claim it as a truly characteristic aspect of his thought. Part Three, then, considers Shelley's changing relationship to Lucretius—and through Lucretius to his "two thoughts"—taking examples from *throughout* his poetic career. These are not reviewed in chronological sequence, but in thematically related groups.

Above all, I hope to show how much of Shelley's "two thoughts," which have alternately dominated Shelley criticism for so long, is in fact a misrecognized form of his "Lucretianism." This chapter therefore has two principal sections, one of which explores Shelley's "skepticism" and its relationship to Lucretius and his influence upon the skeptical Enlightenment, and the other of which takes the same questions to Shelley's "idealism."

I said above that Shelley's debt to Lucretius is well recognized in Shelley criticism and has been ably documented. It is not my intention to add greatly to the lists of specific borrowings and allusions in Shelley's works that have been compiled by Turner, Phillips, and others. Instead, I shall show that Serres's reading of Lucretius in the light of chaos theory gives us a new understanding of what Shelley's Lucretianism might mean. A broader definition of what is Lucretian in some of the most characteristic features of Shelley's imagery, and some of the most persistent of his intellectual concerns, not only deepens our understanding of both, but allows us to bring into relationship apparently opposed and even contradictory aspects of Shelley's thought.

Shelley encountered Lucretius's work early in his life and drew on it at every stage of his poetic career. It is not always obvious what that work meant to him, however, especially in his early years. One of the most important clues to its later significance in his work is to be found in his early attempts to mark his own corrective distance from certain Lucretian "errors." While Lucretius's poem gives him one of the epigraphs to *Queen Mab,* appears in its notes, and, as Turner demonstrates, is echoed in many places in the poem (269–70), Lucretian physics accord rather poorly with the poem's hard-line necessitarianism. This is particularly clear when Shelley observes the kind of turbulent flow central to Serres's reading of Lucretius:

> "No atom of this turbulence fulfils
> A vague and unnecessitated task,
> Or acts but as it must and ought to act."
>
> (VI, 171–73)

These often-quoted lines are more or less a translation of part of the passage from Holbach's *Système de la nature* that is attached to them in the notes. Holbach's atomistic materialism is in obvious ways indebted to Lucretius, but in this quoted passage he is clearly setting out to "repair" Lucretius's principle "error"—the *clinamen.* To do this he realizes he must reopen the question of turbulence, and he does so by evoking, and correcting, Lucretius's favorite image of turbulent flux: "[D]ans la plus affreuse tempête excitée par des vents opposés qui soulèvent les flots,—il n'y a pas une seule molécule de poussière ou d'eau qui soit placée au *hasard,* qui n'ait sa cause suffisante pour occuper le lieu où elle se trouve, et qui n'agisse rigoureusement de la manière dont elle doit agir" (Hutchinson, 809).[1] Shelley quotes this approvingly. The as-

---

1. "[I]n the most frightful tempest, excited by contrary winds, when the waves roll high as mountains; there is not a single particle of dust, or drop of water, that has been placed by CHANCE; that has not a sufficient cause for occupying the place where it is found; that does not

pect of Lucretius that is important to him in *Queen Mab* is, as Turner argues, the Epicurean *suave mari magno* (it is that famous passage he cites in the notes), the Olympian detachment from the turmoil of this world attained by the true disciple of necessitarianism.

Holbach's real interest, however, is not in demonstrating a simple material determinism in the arbitrarily small details of physical interaction; in his post-Newtonian age, that was pushing at an open door. Holbach is entering a dispute between Condorcet and d'Alembert about the hypothetical limits of the determinist hypothesis (Hahn, 14–18). Both of those writers were concerned with understanding God's providence and human free will in the light of the apparent explanatory power of Newtonian mechanistic models, which appeared to leave no room for the arbitrary. Holbach wants to demonstrate that these apply as fully to the moral and political realm as to the physical. Not just the "tourbillon de poussière" but the "tourbillon moral" must display a rigorous, non-entropic reversibility: "Dans les convulsions terribles qui agitent quelquefois les sociétés politiques, et qui produisent souvent le renversement d'un empire, il n'y a pas une seule action, une seule parole, une seule pensée, une seule volonté, une seule passion dans les agens qui concourent à la révolution comme destructeurs ou comme victimes, qui ne soit nécessaire, qui n'agisse comme elle doit agir, qui n'opère infailliblement les effets qu'elle doit opérer, suivant la place qu'occupent ces agens dans ce tourbillon moral" (Hutchinson, 809).[2] Condorcet had posited such a complete determinism two years earlier, in his *Lettre sur le système du monde et sur le calcul intégral* (1768), but only as a working hypothesis for the natural scientist. In that work he proposed a hypothetical "[i]ntelligence who would know the state of all phenomena at a given instant and the laws to which matter is subject, as well as their effect at the end of any elapsed time" (qtd. in Hahn, 16). This was the origin of the Laplacean demon, that "intelligence qui, pour un instant donné, embrasse tous les rapports des êtres de cet Univers." As Roger Hahn puts it, Laplace "borrowed Condorcet's guarded statement

---

[act rigorously] after the manner in which it ought to act" (Holbach, *System of Nature*, 1, 91; with my modification).

2. "In those terrible convulsions, that sometimes agitate political societies, shake their foundations, and frequently produce the overthrow of an empire—there is not a single action, a single word, a single thought, a single will, a single passion in the agents, whether they act as destroyers, or as victims, that is not the necessary result of the causes operating; that does not act as, of necessity, it must act, from the peculiar essence of the beings, who give the impulse, and that of the agents who receive it; according to the situation these agents occupy in the moral whirlwind" (Holbach, *System of Nature*, 1, 91–92).

of determinism, but stripped it of its conditional tense" (17). Hahn is wrong, however, to suggest that in this "daring feat" Laplace "took the final and crucial step towards an ideology of total determinism." Holbach had preempted him in the passage that Shelley incorporates in his notes.[3] Moreover, he had done so in a specifically ethico-political sphere. He posits a political science equivalent of the Laplacean demon observing not the abstract "rapports des êtres de cet Univers" but a political revolution. The absolute determinism of the moral world, he argues, "paraîtrait évident pour une intelligence qui sera en état de saisir et d'apprécier toutes les actions et réactions des esprits et des corps de ceux qui contribuent à cette révolution" (Hutchinson, 809).[4]

Holbach confirms the closely isomorphic relationship between the Laplacean and therapeutic versions of absolute memory; this hypothetical "intelligence" is a close cousin of the idealist absolute self-consciousness. What is more, he allies this to the Lucretian *suave mari magno;* like the Epicurean sage, Holbach's demonic "intelligence" is an absolute spectator of this world's turmoil, so exalted in perspective that, like the expanded idealist self-consciousness, it is able to grasp that turmoil as an inevitable, providential totality against which or within which it is foolish to struggle.

On the other hand, the connection that Holbach establishes between a physical and a political atomism is more explicit than any to be found even in Lucretius's own poem. Holbach feels safe in doing this, because he has discarded the Lucretian conception of the atom as a limit to the possibility of distinction, and with it the *clinamen* as an equivalent limit to the definition of a trajectory. Holbach's atom, like Coleridge's dewdrop, is infinitely informed of its relationship to the whole, and so "revolutionary" turmoil can never become entropic confusion. The "Ode to Heaven" shows us, however, just how precarious this "correction" of Lucretius the physicist by Lucretius the Epicurean sage could be. One has only to reintroduce the *clinamen* for Coleridge's dewdrop to follow "la loi de la pente extrémale" (Serres, *La naissance,* 46)[5] and "tremble,

---

3. Holbach's *Système de la nature* dates from 1770, whereas the paper that contains Laplace's most famous statement of absolute determinism, *Recherches sur l'integration des equations différentielles aux différences finies et sur leur usage dans la théorie des hasards,* was read to the Académie Royale in 1773, and published in 1776 (*Oeuvres complètes,* vol. 8). Shelley also refers to Laplace in his notes, and had evidently read his *Système du monde* (Hutchinson, 809).

4. "This could be evidently proved by an understanding capacitated to seize, to rate all the action and re-action, of the minds and bodies, of those who contributed to the revolution" (Holbach, *System of Nature,* 1, 92).

5. "the law of the inclination at the extreme" (my translation).

gleam, and disappear." If Shelley's "eyed flower" succumbs to the "écart à l'équilibre" within and by which, according to Serres, "[t]out est, tout est pensé, parlé ou travaillé" (33),[6] then, by the logic of Holbach's own analogy, the operation of the atomic components of social processes will prove to be something quite other than the infinitely ordered dance Holbach describes and more like the world described by Serres: "Le monde, les objets, les corps, mon âme même sont, dès le temps de leur naissance, à la *dérive*. A la dérive, au long de la descente du palier incliné. Cela signifie, comme il est usuel, qu'irréversiblement ils se défont et meurent. Le *De rerum* ne cesse pas d'indiquer la mortalité. Mais leur naissance même est dérive" (46).[7] Holbach's specific identification of atomic turbulence with political revolution begs to be reinterpreted in the light of a new understanding of atomic flux; if the atom is defined in opposition to the "totality" that contains it, revolutionary turbulence will appear to be the result of atomic indeterminacy and not the limit case of absolute determinism.

When Shelley called the doctrines of *De rerum natura* "yet the basis of our metaphysical knowledge" in the preface to the *Revolt of Islam* (1817) (Hutchinson, 36), he was acknowledging the pervasiveness of Lucretius's influence upon the rationalist spirit of the scientific enterprises of the preceding two centuries.[8] Pervasive, but never uncomplicated. Throughout the seventeenth century, Lucretianism was associated by both its detractors and its champions with the rise of the New Science (Hadzsits, 284–316; Spencer); no less a figure than Francis Bacon, after all, quoted the *suave mari magno* passage as a model of ultimate epistemological certainty in his essay *Of Truth* (Bacon, 48). In the eighteenth century, his materialism, his assaults on superstition and religion, and his defense of the freedom of thought and inquiry made him central to the concerns of the age. It was inevitable that he should find many champions, among them such characteristic figures as Voltaire, Diderot, Buffon, Chénier, Kant—whose early work *The Theory of the Heavens* is, as Serres shows (47–48), thoroughly Lucretian—Cuvier, and Erasmus Darwin (Fusil, "Lucrèce et les philosophes" and "Lucrèce

---

6. "everything is, everything is thought, spoken, or worked upon" (my translation).

7. "The world, objects, bodies, my soul even are, from the time of their birth, errant. Erring along the slope of an inclined plane. This means, as is usual, that they decay and die irreversibly. The *De rerum* never ceases to point out their mortality. But their very birth is errancy" (my translation).

8. See Fusil, "Lucrèce et les philosophes du XVIIIe siècle" and "Lucrèce et les littérateurs poètes et artistes du XVIIIe siècle"; Hadzsits, 317–31; Fleischmann; and Spencer, "Lucretius and the Scientific Poem in English."

et les littérateurs"; Hadzsits, 317-31; Spencer, 150-52). When Cardinal
Polignac wanted to launch a broadside against the growing tide of the
Enlightenment, in the form of a poem attacking the scientific presumptions of the age, it made sense to him and, presumably, to his audience
to entitle it *Anti-Lucrèce* (1749; English translation 1766), allowing Lucretius to stand as the figurehead of the godless materialists, including
Hobbes, Locke, Newton, Gassendi, and Spinoza (Hadzsits, 321, 322 n.
24).

Polignac's choice was a canny one, because Lucretius made even his
supporters uneasy, making this a characterization they could neither
completely deny nor defiantly embrace—this for obvious reasons if they
were Christians, such as James Thomson, whose *Seasons* is replete with
rather awkward attempts to anglicize Lucretian circumlocutions ("finny
tribes" and the like) but whose "Lucretian enthusiasm" in *Sacred to the
Memory of Sir Isaac Newton* (1727) concludes, "as is usual in the eighteenth century," according to T.J.B. Spencer, in an "anti-Lucretian" appeal to the soul's immortality (137-39). It was also common practice in
the seventeenth century; in the essay *Of Truth,* Bacon notes that Lucretius "beautified that sect that was otherwise inferior to the rest."
Wolfgang Fleischmann notes that in the first half of the eighteenth century, "every major thinker . . . had something to say on the subject of *De
Rerum Natura*" (172), but although the accusation of "Epicureanism"
was commonly made, no one was willing to admit themselves to be a
disciple of Lucretius. Even for the philosophes he was a dangerous ally;
many were content to use his writings without making specific reference to him. Thus Voltaire's *Candide* is a Lucretian reply to Leibniz that
never mentions Lucretius; Diderot helped Holbach translate the *De rerum natura* in 1768, one year before completing his *Rêve,* but that
work, while thoroughly Lucretian in content, contains no direct reference to Lucretius (Furbank, 324); Rousseau, as C.-A. Fusil points out,
repeatedly paraphrased Lucretius in his history of the growth of civilization, but never acknowledged these borrowings ("Lucrèce et les littérateurs," 169-70).[9]

Much of the reason for this reticence was the apparently ludicrous
concept of the *clinamen.* Even in the pre-Newtonian world, an ardent

---

9. It is interesting that, given this universal reticence, Shelley should have come across
Lucretius early in his life and continued to read him with enthusiasm. Oxford University, for
example, did not, in Shelley's day, normally include Lucretius in a student's course of studies
(Gordon, 20). It is interesting to note that "Flogger" Keate, master of the Lower School while
Shelley was at Eton, was an enthusiast for Lucretius (Gordon, 19). Perhaps it was he, rather
than Dr. Lind, who steered the young Shelley toward the *De rerum natura* in those years?

Lucretian such as Montaigne had seen the *clinamen* as the most egregious of "asneries" (Fraisse, 177). In the age of the New Science, Pierre Bayle—whom, incidentally, Shelley criticized for his "obliquity" (*Letters,* 1:432)—set the tone for the contemptuous mockery of this concept that prevailed throughout the eighteenth century (Hadzsits, 323; Fleischmann, 39-40, 203-7). Voltaire, responding to Cardinal Polignac's *Anti-Lucrèce* in his *Dictionnaire philosophique,* mocks him for confounding the self-evidently absurd notions of Lucretius with the all-conquering rationality of Newton. Ironically, the Christian and the philosophe were both worried by the same aspect of Lucretian physics, his attack on the notion of providence.[10] Fleischmann's *Lucretius and English Literature, 1680-1740* demonstrates that although the New Science of the late seventeenth century drew hostile attacks as neo-Epicureanism, both "divines" and "scientists" (notably Robert Boyle) were united in their opposition to the "atomistic denial of providence" (24; see 22-25). Nothing shows more clearly the affinity between the rationalist Enlightenment ideal of a horizontal tabulation of knowledge in which every part finds its place with reference to an absolute whole (that "*taxinomia* dont la grande nappe universelle s'étalait en corrélation avec la possibilité d'une *mathesis* et qui constituait le temps fort du savoir—à la fois sa possibilité première et le terme de sa perfection" of which Foucault writes [*Les mots et les choses,* 263])[11] and the therapeutic search for a providential Absolute than the attempts of the Enlightenment philosophers to "correct" Lucretius's dangerous error.

Like Bacon, Holbach could appreciate the *suave mari magno* as an image of the ideal position of the scientific observer; the world seen from the security of the quiet citadel becomes tabular, spread out before the anatomizing eye of the philosopher, who is then able to see how all parts take their place in the totality. Bacon—in a comment that immediately follows his quotation of the *suave mari magno*—makes it clear at the outset that this position is also that of God—or of a demigod such as the Laplacean demon: "Certainly it is heaven upon earth to have a man's mind move in charity, rest in providence, and turn upon the poles of truth" (Bacon, 48). Two centuries later, in the waning days of the Enlightenment, the same thought recurs in Godwin's *Political Justice.*

---

10. Voltaire's *Temple du goût* (1731) "describes a critical debate between Lucretius and the Cardinal de Polignac" (Fleischmann, 41). In this work, Lucretius apparently concedes philosophical but not poetic defeat to the cardinal (211).

11. "*taxinomia,* whose great, universal expanse extended in correlation with the possibility of a mathesis, and which constituted the down-beat of knowledge—at once its primary possibility and the end of its perfection" (*Order of Things,* 251).

Godwin's belief in a world that, in principle, if not always in practice, is perfectly accessible to and absolutely consistent with the impartial eye and incontrovertible rigor of reason is, like the "répétition maniaque" of Laplace's infinitely conservative world, a logical extrapolation from Baconian providentialism (on which, see McKay). Baconian scientific method requires a belief in an absolute order, even if it denies us the possibility of an immediate apprehension of that order. The experimental, inductive method is based on the assumption that each fragment of knowledge helps us discover, because it makes sense only as an exemplar of, a fixed and constant natural law. The Laplacean demon or angelic spectator need not, of course, work from example to law but can grasp the law and its exempla as a single, absolute totality, which it sees as such from its exalted position. It is toward that position that Godwin urges us in the *Political Justice* with reference to the world of political action: "[T]he soundest criterion of virtue is, to put ourselves in the place of an impartial spectator, of an angelic nature, suppose, beholding us from an elevated station, and uninfluenced by our prejudices, conceiving what would be his estimate of the intrinsic circumstances of our neighbour, and acting accordingly" (1:133). The contingent indeterminacy of the *clinamen* is anathema to this project.

Shelley's engagement with Lucretius's poem is simultaneously an exploration, at a fundamental level, of the most important and diverse aspects of his intellectual inheritance. When we start to look at Shelley's relationship to Lucretius in this way and not as an adjunct to other and "more essential" issues, it appears that one of the reasons the opposition between a "skeptical Shelley" and an "idealist Shelley" has proven sterile, and the two aspects so difficult to reconcile usefully, is that this opposition is based upon a misrecognition. Many of the things we label "skeptical" or "idealist" in Shelley's thought are the different sides of his response to Lucretius—a development of the opposition implicit in *Queen Mab*—and a return, within a Lucretian framework, to the principal dilemma of his debt to the radical Enlightenment.

LUCRETIAN "SKEPTICISM"

I

Shortly after writing *Queen Mab*, Shelley began to put in question the strict necessitarianism it ostensibly champions. In the "Essay on the Vegetable System of Diet" of 1814, for example, he returns to one of the themes of *Queen Mab*—vegetarianism as a panacea for virtually all the world's ills—but adds, among other things, an apology for attributing such importance to an apparently trifling issue:

> A popular objection which never fails to be opposed to every reasoning of this nature is, that it is incorrect to ascribe such mighty effects to causes so comparatively trivial. Such nevertheless are the laws of the world which we inhabit. A spark well kindled will consume the most sumptuous palace: some slight derangement in the association of a Monarch's ideas may involve his subjects in a long and sanguinary war. The dream of a frantic woman has lighted the piles of persecution in every corner of the civilized globe.—Man is an whole the complicated parts of which are so interwoven with each other, that the most remote and subtle springs of his machine are connected with those which are more gross and obvious, and reciprocally act and react upon each other. (Ingpen and Peck, 6:337)

It would be easy to overread this startling passage. It is a perfect description of sensitive dependence on initial conditions, and even suggests the role positive feedback loops ("reciprocally act and react upon each other") play in the magnification of initial errors to the point that they can overthrow the system. But Shelley did not, at this stage, have an elaborate theory of chaotic creativity. The goal of the "Essay" is to establish a perfectly homeostatic society of pacific vegetarians through the elimination of "derangements" and "frantic dreams." Nonetheless, it is remarkable what a distance he has moved from Holbach's position toward those aspects of Lucretian process that so disturbed the Enlightenment philosophes. It is not that minute events have an impact on the development of the system as a whole that is remarkable—that is also true in a necessitarian system, which conserves ad infinitum the consequences of any action by the least of its components—it is the nature of these events, and our relationship to them. We have moved from the legible horizontality of Holbach's atomic choreography, in which all events, no matter how small, are equally important to the order of the whole, to Foucault's "verticalité obscure" (*Les mots et les choses*, 263), in which the crucial originating event recedes from us into a vanishing perspective of atomistic indeterminacy. In Holbach's providential order, every moment has a preceding cause and a succeeding effect, and the chains of causality can be traced forward and backward without interruption as far as one wishes. In Shelley's, causes appear to suffer from a kind of inverse square law, rapidly becoming indistinct as one moves back from the present. Events are caused, but these causes are inaccessible to us.

Most interesting is the "slight derangement in the association of a monarch's ideas" that leads to war. The theory of the association of ideas was for Hume and Godwin the linchpin of the generalization of necessitarianism to human action. The association of ideas was supposed to be, in the realm of human action, something akin to Newton's law of gravitation in the realm of planetary motion; it made it possible for Godwin to conceive of a thoroughly rational social organization, as ordered as the Newtonian solar system, in which all misery and injustice would be eliminated, or minimized, by a thoroughly scientific understanding of the principles of human action. Now, suddenly, Shelley allows a slight, arbitrary, and unaccountable "derangement" of the chain of associations, with consequences commensurate with those we might expect in the world of planetary motion if we were to allow arbitrary "derangements" of the gravitational field.

This "derangement" is, consciously or unconsciously, a reintroduction of the Lucretian *clinamen* he had been at pains to deny in *Queen Mab*. It is an atomistic error, in the sense of being a residual limit to our ability to distinguish causal trajectories, that represents an entropic loss of information, or death, within the associational transmission of ideas (a loss that in turn becomes a "creative" moment in the history of a nation). One of the most characteristic themes of Shelley's poetry and prose is the erosion of order through time and change. Shelley evokes in his writing a world "pavilioned upon chaos" (*Hellas*, 772),[12] constantly under siege by entropic forces; there is an ever-present threat either of cataclysmic disorganization (storms, volcanoes, earthquakes, floods) or of gradual erosion (ruins, death, decay, fragmentation, and dissolution). What is distinctive about this rage for disorder is that Shelley is at pains to show that, as in the king's mental "derangement," real errors proliferate within process; initial conditions are effaced and information is lost, not simply complicated by disorganization.

By 1818, when Shelley writes "Lines Written Among the Euganean Hills," this hint has become a fully blown theory of sensitive dependence on initial conditions and the entropic erosion of paths of causa-

---

12. Shelley is fond of the word "chaos," and often uses it in ways that are suggestive for a critic acquainted with chaos theory. He does not, however, use it with the same meaning that has recently been attached to it in chaos science. Shelley's understanding of "chaos" is relevant to a reading of his poetry in a Lucretian/chaotic framework, but only, as here, as an image for the inherent instability, or entropic mutability, of the world.

tion. Shelley compares the defunct University of Padua, in its role as fosterer of the modern revival of antique learning, to an extinct "spark" (275) lying beneath the feet of a "Norway woodman" (269) around whom "the boundless forest shakes" (272) with the forest fire it started. The extinct spark represents the atomistic limit of our ability to trace the causal chain back to its "origin."

This loss of knowledge about the world, both potential and real, is easily and often mistaken for an aspect of his skepticism. In fact, Hume, the most important skeptical influence on Shelley, had no place in his system for such arbitrary and cumulative errors. In his view, we could as safely choose to ignore their possibility in the realm of mental association as the Newtonian physicist ignores the remote epistemological limitations of the inductive method. Shelley's interest in the "derangement" and erosion of order has as little to do with any absolute epistemological circumscription as Lucretius's assertion that "everything is gradually decaying and nearing its end, worn out by old age" (95, 2.1173–74); on the contrary, both are based on the assumption that we *can* know the world and that one of the things we know about it is that it tends toward disorder. Information about the world is not epistemologically unavailable, but it is constantly being effaced.

Again and again, when we look at examples of Shelley's "skeptical" portrayal of a world of unstable flux, we do not find the skeptic's *epochē* or *akatalepsia,* or even a straightforward "transferential" delight in the subversion of an established order, but a Lucretian vision of a world constantly losing structural coherence. Many of the most characteristic and recurrent images in Shelley's writing gain a new resonance in this regard. The fascination with ruins, for example, relates to both Burke's and Lucretius's understanding of the building as image for the legacy of the past. Burke called for repairs to be made as close as possible to the style of the original structure, but Shelley, like Lucretius, describes a world where "l'édifice, la terre et le monde s'effondrent" (Serres, *La naissance,* 110).[13] Dissolution and decay are so constant and pervasive that reparation would have to be (creative) guesswork.

Much has been written about the "ruin sentiment" that supposedly enters Western thought in the Renaissance and reaches a climax in the age of Romanticism (Goldstein; McFarland, *Forms of Ruin;* Rose Macaulay). Shelley shares his fascination with ruins with almost all the important writers, artists, architects, landscape gardeners, and aesthetic theorists of his time and the preceding century, but to cite Shelley as a

---

13. "the building, the earth, and the world collapse" (my translation).

typical proponent of this common enthusiasm obscures a crucial distinction. There are two broad streams of ruin sentiment in the eighteenth and early nineteenth centuries. We might call them the "optimistic Enlightenment" stream and the "melancholic Romantic" stream. The first stream is perhaps best represented by Volney's *Ruins of Empire.* Petra, for Volney, serves to point a moral about what is lasting and what is not in the history of humanity; and what last, and with time become increasingly clear and certain, are the eternal and universal verities of reason. Petra conjures up, via a predictable sequence of associations, a known past with a legible message, a past that represents an "error" with respect to the "essential" Enlightened Man gradually emerging from "the dust of creeds outworn." Petra's present ruined condition is a negation of the negation, or a reparation of a supervenient error. In this vein, Uvedale Price remarks, in his *Essays on the Picturesque* of 1794, that England's Gothic ruins "are the pride and boast of this island; we may well be proud of them, not merely in a picturesque point of view — we may glory that the abodes of tyranny and superstition are in ruin" (366).

The second stream also sees ruins as a reminder of the downfall of past systems, but, by way of contrast, sees in that catastrophic past an intimation of the inevitable decay and dissolution of the present. The best example, perhaps, is Byron standing in the Coliseum, "a ruin amidst ruins," meditating on decay. It is this view that lies behind the anxiety of empire described by Laurence Goldstein. The knowledge that modern Europe could now rival, and even surpass, the ancient empires in scientific achievement, technical competence, and geopolitical importance prompted the self-confident appropriation of the artistic, architectural, and literary trappings of imperial Rome that characterizes the new "Augustan Age"; but the classicist garb of the spirit of the age was imbued with a premonitory memory of "decline and fall." Paintings of the Louvre or the Bank of England as overgrown "classical" ruins (Rose Macaulay, 38) testify to this melancholic sense of imperial *vanitas;* the logic of the translation of empire would ensure future ascendancy to the most unpromising and backward of places: "[S]ome traveller from New Zealand shall, in the midst of a vast solitude, take his stand on a broken arch of London Bridge to sketch the ruins of St. Paul's" (Thomas Macaulay, 455).

This "anxiety" cannot be taken at its face value, however. As Goldstein shows, this form of ruin melancholy was more reassuring than distressing. At a simple level, the knowledge that one will leave ruins similar to those left by Rome and Greece, while it poses no immediate threat to the contemplator, is a pleasant reassurance that one belongs to the "club" of great imperial powers. More important, it exalts us to a more comprehensive and "providential" perspective from which to view the unfolding of history. As in the first "stream," we are uplifted from the temporal to the eternal, be it God's providential order or the Inexorable March of Progress. Byron finds in Rome "an immaculate charm which cannot be defaced" (*Childe Harolde,* IV, xxvi, 9).

The real source of anxiety in the ruin is the threat of irrecoverable loss; the ruin posits an absence that questions the coherence and completeness of our world. In both these streams of ruin sentiment, genuine loss is minimized; they both move, irresistibly, from the disturbing fragment to some reassuring totality. While the objects they are concerned with are physically ruined, their associational values are intact; the information they represent has not so much been lost as translated to a different—higher—level. Thomas Whately, in his description of Tintern Abbey in 1770, in which he proposes it as a (generic) model for "fictitious ruins" (follies), shows that the only ruin that makes aesthetic sense in these frameworks is one that allows us, in imagination at least, to make the necessary "reparations": "Nothing is perfect; but memorials of every part still subsist; all certain, but all in decay; and suggesting at once every idea which can occur in a seat of devotion, solitude, and desolation. Upon such models fictitious ruins should be formed; and if any parts are entirely lost, they should be such as the imagination can easily supply from those which are still remaining" (qtd. in David, 17–18). A genuinely enigmatic ruin holds no interest for Whately; while the ideal ruin speaks of loss, we are meant to know what has been lost and to be able to understand our position in relationship to that loss.

This is in accord with McFarland's therapeutic logic of the ruin, which he generalizes to all the Romantics: a belief that the ruined and the "diasparactive" always presupposes, and leads to, totality. McFarland makes the ruin a form of the Romantic Ironic *felix culpa;* for him, there is no fragment "unless there is also the conception of a whole from which it is broken off" (*Forms of Ruin,* 50). In this fallen, ruined world, we perceive only fragments, but the spirit's drive is always to restore these fragments to totality—to move *through* the fragment to the whole in a hermeneutical movement from error to essence, from the ruined and fragmented part to the perfect and absolute totality, from the individual to the universal. "Without faith [in some ultimately defining Absolute]," he suggests, "diasparactive awareness would be horror" (44).

Shelley did occasionally use ruins in these conventional ways, as the line quoted above from *Prometheus Unbound* suggests; his most famous ruin poem, "Ozymandias," is almost purely Volneyan. But more typical of Shelley are ruins whose associational significance has been eroded by "le temps . . . qui use l'horloge . . . [et] ruine la maison" (Serres, *La naissance,* 110).[14] The ruins in "The Assassins," *Alastor* (116–28), *The Revolt of Islam* (VI, xxii ff.), "The Coliseum," "Ode to the West Wind" (32–36), and *Epipsychidion* (483–512) do not serve to reconstruct in our minds a known past and assert the continuity of the historical development from that past; instead, they "[flash] like strong inspiration" (*Alastor,* 127) into the present, objects of consumption whose temporal and hermeneutical ties to contexts of production have been irreparably, though not absolutely, eroded.

In "The Assassins" and *Epipsychidion* the irretrievable erasure of the past is insisted upon; the "legend" "sculptured in mystic characters on the rocks" of Bethzatanai, the valley to which the Assassins escape, "once so beautiful and perfect, so full of poetry and history," is now "unintelligible" (158); the "lone dwelling" (484) to which the lover hopes to retire with Emily in *Epipsychidion*—"not a tower of strength" (486)—has succumbed to the atomistic erosion of time's "storm of change" (*Queen Mab,* VI, 160) to the point that "all the antique and learned imagery / Has been erased" (498–99). The "dwelling, built by whom or how / None of the rustic island people know" (484–85), is disengaged from any known human history: "It scarce seems now a wreck of human art" (493).

Even when the ruins have easily identifiable ties to a known history, however, as in "The Coliseum" and the "Ode to the West Wind," the emphasis is on the information lost rather than associational reconstitutions. The eroding force of "le temps . . . qui use l'horloge" is in the process of de- or recontextualizing the ruins, cutting them adrift from the "clock" of historical time and the initial conditions of their contexts of production. "Time has thrown its purple shadow athwart this scene [of the Coliseum]," Shelley tells us; no "recollection of the use to which it may have been destined" can "interfere with these [our present-day] emotions" (Ingpen and Peck, 6:303 n. 1).[15] The Coliseum, with its "great

14. "time . . . which wears out the clock . . . [and] ruins the dwelling" (my translation).

15. Shelley argues, in respect to the atrocities of Roman society, that "[w]e do not forget these things" but that in the eroding process of time we are no longer able to relate the Coliseum as it now appears to us to this history. It is as if the Coliseum and the contiguous facts of social history at the time of its construction were so many atoms in a turbulent cycle. However tightly they are knit together at the start, the turbulence of history's feedback cycles will eventually separate them. See Timothy Clark's excellent "Shelley's 'The Coliseum' and the

wrecked arches . . . overgrown with the younglings of the forest, and more like chasms rent by an earthquake among the mountains, than like the vestige of what was human workmanship . . . [is a] nursling of man's art, abandoned by his care, and transformed by the enchantment of Nature into a likeness of her own creations, and destined to partake their immortality!" (6:302-3).

Similarly, in the "Ode to the West Wind," the underwater ruins of Baiae's bay near Naples have suffered a sea change, becoming a fantastic dream architecture, "Quivering within the wave's intenser day" (34). They are no longer windows into the past, but surreal phantasms that the Mediterranean sees "in sleep" (33). The close connection between ruins and the erosive, amnesiac flux of the ocean's waves underlines their atomistic disengagement from the narratives of human history. The connection was established in Shelley's mind before he ever visited Naples, however. In the valley of Bethzatanai, there are "[p]iles of monumental marble" that lie "in heaps beside the lake" and are "visible beneath its transparent waves" (Ingpen and Peck, 6:157). And later, in "The Coliseum," he wonders if, "were the sea to overflow the earth, the mightiest monsters of the deep would change [the Coliseum's "great wrecked arches"] into their spacious chambers" (6:302).

The connection comes to him from *De rerum natura*. In book 5, in the midst of a discussion of the four elements, their interrelationships, and their mutability, Lucretius has a short comment on ruins, whose influence is manifest in each of the above passages: "Look about you and you will see the very stones mastered by age; tall towers in ruin and their masonry crumbling; temples and images of the gods defaced, their destined span not lengthened by any sanctity that avails against the laws of nature. The monuments of the great seem to ask us why we look there for immortality" (180, 5.306-12).[16] Immediately following this, Lucretius generalizes the vulnerability to "the stark strength of immeasurable age" (182, 5.378-79) to the fragile dynamic balance of elemental

---

Sublime" (the only sustained reading of Shelley's "Coliseum") for a related but contrastive reading.

16. Cf. "tall towers in ruin" and *Epipsychidion*'s "not a tower of strength"; "temples and images of the gods defaced" and, from "The Assassins," "temple dedicated to the God of knowledge and of truth," with its "unintelligible" legend, *Epipsychidion*'s "erased" "antique and learnèd imagery," the "Coliseum's" apparently heterogeneous speculations about "[s]olemn temples" and "[s]uperstitious rites" (Ingpen and Peck, 6:303 n. 1), and *Alastor*'s "ruined temples" (116), where "dead men / Hang their mute thoughts on the mute walls around" (119-20). The comment upon the "monuments of the great" is a précis of "Ozymandias."

strife. He wants us to acknowledge the four elements "to be children of time" susceptible to "death" by atomistic erosion: "[T]he doorway of death is not barred to sky and sun and earth and the sea's unfathomed floods. It lies tremendously open and confronts them with a yawning chasm" (182, 5.373–75). "[C]ivil strife rages among the world's warring elements" (182, 5.380–81); each wears away the other in a constant, entropic struggle for dominance (see Segal, 195). At present, this appears to be a dynamic equilibrium, but that equilibrium is precarious and susceptible to catastrophic, or chaotic, collapse: "[I]t may be that their long battle will some day be decided" (182, 5.381–83). On the one hand, it may be that "the sun and heat will overpower the rivers and drink their waters dry"; on the other, "the rivers . . . threaten . . . to deluge everything from the deep reservoir of the ocean" (182, 5.383–87).

This "battle" between Earth and Ocean becomes a staple of Renaissance figures for mutability—Spenser's, Shakespeare's, and Montaigne's being perhaps the most well-known examples[17] —and Shelley is drawing at once on that tradition and on the *De rerum* to generalize the import of this image and to show us that the "stark strength of immeasurable age" brings an entropic, atomistic "death" not only to human structures but to the very ground on which they are built as well. What sets Shelley apart from this tradition—which leads to Volney, Byron, Whately, Macaulay, and so forth—is his apparent acceptance of time's ravages. While Spenser, in his *Ruines of Time,* has the personification of the once prosperous and now "forgotten" city *Verlame* "mourne [her] fall with dolefull dreriment," Shelley, like the old man in "The Coliseum," seems happier with what the disengaged ruin offers for our current imaginative consumption than with the "original" object hidden behind time's "purple shadow" (see Clark, "Shelley's 'The Coliseum,'" 227).

Epipsychidion may appear to contradict this; there, a truce has been called in the battle, and Earth and Ocean "sleep in one another's arms"

17. See *The Faerie Queene,* V, ii, 37, 4–7; Shakespeare's sonnet no. 64, 3–12. Spenser's Giant, who seeks to weigh earth and sea in his "ballance" so as to "restore" them to their proper measures, intends to do the same with each of the elements (V, ii, 30–37). See also the "Mutability Canto," VII, vii, 17–26. The image was widely known from Ovid's version in book XV of *Metamorphoses* (340ff.), but Ovid, despite his curious and inaccurate ascription of the image to Pythagoras, is reworking Lucretius's material. It is possible Spenser is directly under Lucretius's influence (Greenlaw, 455ff.; Davis, *Edmund Spenser,* 231). Montaigne was under the direct influence of Lucretius, from whom he quotes frequently. See Simone Fraisse for an excellent discussion of the Lucretian influence upon Montaigne (one of Shelley's favorite authors).

(510). This truce is precarious, however, and serves, ultimately, to bring the inevitability of the battle into relief. Shelley uses the apparent détente to emphasize the "Elysian," dreamlike nature of this projected idyll and its fragile irreality. As long as Earth and Ocean sleep, then the island and the lover's dream of absolute unity and perfect bliss can continue. But just as the ideal of perfect unity must collapse into the despairing "one annihilation" (587) that is the only possible outcome of the tragic logic of Shelleyan *erōs*, we know from the "Ode to the West Wind" that Earth and Ocean are foredoomed to hear the clarion call that "didst waken from his summer dreams / The blue Mediterranean" (29–30). The Elysian dream expires along with all others in the abrupt collapse that, characteristically, ends the poem.

This brings us to a crucial difference between Shelley and the Renaissance tradition of mutability. If Spenser and Shakespeare believed that "nothing stands but for [Time's] scythe to mow" (Shakespeare, sonnet no. 60, 12), both poets firmly held to the Horatian *aere perennius;* poetry itself, the record of this all-but-universal erasure, was emphatically exempt from its depredations. Shakespeare's sonnet number 60, from which I have just quoted, ends with the couplet "And yet to times in hope, my verse shall stand / Praising thy worth, despite [Time's] cruel hand." Spenser's *Ruines of Time* claims that poetry is the one refuge from universal decay:

> Prouide therefore (ye Princes) whilest ye liue,
> That of the *Muses* ye may friended bee,
> Which vnto men eternitie do giue.
>
> (365–67)

The paradox of Spenser's poem—the paradox that remains in Whately's ruin-without-loss—is that it denies the obliteration it laments, guaranteeing that the "forgotten" city of Verlame shall be remembered after the Thames has long since run dry.

Shelley, on the other hand, recognizes not only that he himself is subject to the amnesiac wave of time, but that his poetry is as well. In *Adonais* Shelley even identifies himself with that wave, appearing among the mourners as "a dying lamp, a falling shower, / A breaking billow;—even whilst we speak / Is it not broken?" (xxxii, 6–7). There is a play on the word "broken" here, signaled by the unexpected syntax of that final half line; the wave "breaks"—presumably to break again—but as the poet speaks, something is "broken"; this is entropic decay, like the dying lamp and falling shower, a falling into ruin of the poetic voice.

It is a fitting accident of history that so many of Shelley's poems, including his last and greatest, are fragments—wrecks of human art. This is notoriously true of all the Romantic poets, but what sets Shelley apart is that so often his "finished" poems, *Epipsychidion* among them, seem to end by breaking down or collapsing. Wordsworth's and Coleridge's fragments of the *Recluse* and the *magnum opus*—fragments that, in Wordsworth's case, include his greatest poetic achievement—represented to their authors the scattered remnants of an absolute vision; their incompleteness was evidence of a failure to arrive at totality. Shelley nowhere suggests that he regards the catastrophic collapses that terminate, rather than "finish," so many of his poems as the unfortunate result of falling short of a different goal.

Shelley's poems often end with a catastrophic "breaking," or break down, at the "end"—the privileged point of narrative synthesis for a therapeutic hermeneutics. The abrupt failure, or withdrawal, that marks the endings of poems such as "Julian and Maddalo" ("the cold world shall not know" [616-17]), the "Ode to Liberty" ("the spirit of that mighty singing / To its abyss was suddenly withdrawn" [271-72]), "The Witch of Atlas" ("what she did to sprites / And gods . . . I will declare another time" [666-67, 669]), *Epipsychidion* ("winged words . . . Are chains of lead . . . I pant, I sink, I tremble, I expire!" [588, 590-91]), *Adonais* ("I am borne darkly, fearfully, afar" [482]), and *Hellas* ("Cease! drain not to its dregs the urn / Of bitter prophecy" [1098-99]) seems to bear witness that the work of the muses is as much subject to entropic vicissitudes as that of the architect and the builder (see Levinson, *Fragment*, 139).

The "Ode to Liberty" is of particular interest because it invokes, among its images of entropic decay used to describe the collapse of the poet's song, the same that Shelley later identified with his alter ego in *Adonais*. The "fading lamp" is prefigured by the "far taper" that also "fades" (279); the "falling shower" by the "summer clouds [that] dissolve, unburthened of their rain" (278); the "breaking billow" by the "waves which . . . Hiss round a drowner's head in their tempestuous play" (284-85). These images are all part of Lucretius's stock-in-trade, and all are closely associated with the passage on ruins, mutability, and decay in book 5 of *De rerum natura*.

There, Lucretius collapses the examples of rain and fading light onto each other, arguing that the sun, like "earthly lights that illumine the night," is "a lavish fount of liquid light" that "drenches the sky unwearyingly with fresh effulgence." Like pouring rain, however, this effulgence represents a constant, entropic loss from the source: "This is how you should picture sun and moon and stars—as showering their splendour in successive outbursts and for ever losing flash after flash of flame, not as enduring essences untouched by time" (180, 5.302-5; Shelley also describes the sun and moon this way: *Revolt*, XI, iii; "Letter to Maria Gisborne," 69-70). Lucretius is making a similar point about the essential mortality of natural processes when he reminds us, shortly afterward, that "the doorway of death is not barred" to "the sea's unfathomed floods" (182, 5.373-74). The breaking (and broken) billow and the tempestuous waves that torment the drowner—the one an image of the poet, the other of the poem dissolving, like the ruins of Baiae's bay, into the quivering flux of process—represent the two ways, equally common in *De rerum natura*, of reading the sea's "mortality." On the one hand, travel by water is symbolic of the vulnerability of human life to *tuchē*; death at sea comes unpredictably, suddenly, and often inescapably. On the other hand, this uncertainty is a product of the sea's own turbulent inconstancy, its own inherent "mortality" as expressed in the ever-renewed "deaths" of order in its turbulent flux, from the broken billow to the tempest.

Shelley's own death by water, and the spuriously prophetic quality it retrospectively gives to his remarkable interest in the topic,[18] should not make us shy of recognizing the importance of this passage in the "Ode to Liberty"—as indicated by his reprise of its themes with such a personal application in *Adonais*. Nor, however, should it distract us from the fact that Shelley's interest in the "mortality" of the sea, even in the numerous cases where it directly threatens a human life, is predominantly rooted in the latter of the two forms discussed above. Of all the Lucretian images of the proliferation of disorder, those associated with the sea and the rivers that feed it are the most pervasive in Shelley's writing. The passage from *De rerum* that I have been focusing on here is written, in part, to illustrate the "established fact that everything is in a perpetual flux" (179, 5.280). This is a metaphor whose vehicle is the self-evident mortality of the "original" flux: the turbulence of flowing water. Everything in Shelley's world, as in Lucretius's, threatens to dissolve and to be carried away by the flux of "Heaven's ever-changing shadow" (*Prometheus*, I, 28), including his own poetic voice. The drowner at the end of the "Ode to Liberty," like all Shelley's drowners and potential drowners, is one of those on the verge of "dissolving" like

18. A partial list of poems in which Shelley contemplates death by drowning includes *Alastor, The Revolt of Islam*, "Julian and Maddalo," "Stanzas Written in Dejection," "Ode to Liberty," "Time," *Adonais*, and the "The Triumph of Life."

the "summer clouds" and succumbing to the flux of process. The passage from the *Tempest* chosen as Shelley's epitaph would have been an
apt choice with reference only to his poetry, no matter how he had
died; the "sea change" is a basic modality of process in the world of that
poetry. Death so often takes the form of drowning in Shelley's verse
because death, for him, is a process of erosion or dissolution, not a
narrative closure; it is for the same reason that he insistently compares
death with sleep, which "steals" upon us slowly (the word is from
"Stanzas Written in Dejection, December 1818—Near Naples" [33],
where the connection between the two images of death is explicit [30-
36]).

    "Everything is in a perpetual flux"; Jane Phillips has shown that the
opening of "Mont Blanc"—where "The everlasting universe of things /
Flows through the mind" (1-2) and the individual mind brings its "trib-
ute" (5) of waters to that flow—is a statement of this Lucretian flux of
mutability. In a recent paper, Hogle has also read the poem in the light
of its Lucretian derivation.[19] We can see how closely related in Shelley's
mind were the ideas of processual flux and entropic decay in the reappearance, which Phillips notes, of the universal "flow" in the form of
the deceptively stable glacier. At first he describes this in static terms as
"a city of death" (105), but he soon realizes that despite its domes,
pyramids, pinnacles, towers, and "wall[s] impregnable of beaming ice"
(106), it is

> not a city, but a flood of ruin
>   . . . that from the boundaries of the sky
> Rolls its perpetual stream.
>
>   (107-9)

---

19. Hogle reads the poem in the light of its Lucretian affiliations as a revisionary critique of
Coleridge and Wordsworth ("Shelley as Revisionist"). Hogle's paper makes an argument similar
to the one I am making here, but the differences are crucial. He sees Shelley's position as a
kind of skeptical idealism; "Mont Blanc" teaches us that there is nothing in the universe but
thoughts that act upon other thoughts in various transformational ways (112). Thought is the
"Power" that comes down, in this case, in the "likeness" of the Arve, but that can sweep
through the mind in any and all forms it happens to adopt. This is a version of his "transferential One," and despite his attempt to link this to the *De rerum natura*, it is profoundly different from Lucretius's philosophy; the *clinamen* is a genuine "swerve"; it destroys some information and creates in its place new information that is entered into the memory of a system
and has serious consequences for its fate. Hogle's transferences are entirely playful; they remove all notion of consequence from thought's capricious career. The ultimate tendency of
his theory is Platonic, as his theory of the "transferential One" demonstrates; we eventually
become tired of observing the intricate dance of the inconsequential shadows, and seek the
sun that brings them into being.

The effect of this liquid "stream" of "ruin" is to erase information:

> The dwelling-place
> Of insects, beasts, and birds, becomes its spoil;
> Their food and their retreat forever gone,
> So much of life and joy is lost. The race
> Of man, flies far in dread; his work and dwelling
> Vanish, like smoke before the tempest's stream,
> And their place is not known.
>
> (114–20)

In different forms, this obliterating flow appears again and again in Shelley's writing. Like the Lucretian sea to whom "the doorway of death is not barred," it is an image of process as both product and producer of a proliferation of atomistic deaths or erasures. It appears as the "stream of thought" in *Alastor* (644), that stream with "searchless fountain, and invisible course" (507) "[w]hose source is inaccessibly profound" (502–3); it takes myriad forms in *The Revolt of Islam,* where Cythna's revolutionary eloquence, wreaking "living change" (V, liii, 8) upon its auditors, is likened to "a mountain-stream which sweeps / The withered leaves of Autumn to the lake" (1–2), and where "thoughts flow on with stream, whose waters / Return not to their fountain" (IX, xxxv, 1–2) and in whose entropic expenditure "All that we are or know, is darkly driven / Towards one gulf" (4–5; see also III, i, 5; IX, xx, 9); in the "Witch of Atlas," the Witch's boat is "the lightest . . . / Which ever upon mortal stream did float" (xxxi, 7–8)—the "mortal stream" nicely capturing the two senses of the sea's "mortality" in Lucretius, and the ability of the boat to "float" above it emphasizing the ambiguity of the Witch's position in relationship to a mortality she at once celebrates and denies; in the *Defence* it appears as "the poisonous waters which flow from death through life" (Reiman and Powers, 505); and in the "Triumph" it receives its most sustained and complex treatment in Shelley's poetry, appearing as the "Lethean" (463) rivulet beside which Rousseau awakens, a "passing stream" (399) upon which the shape all light treads without entering—a close cousin of the "mortal stream" upon which the Witch of Atlas floats in her boat. The Lethean stream proves to be a model for both the principal theme and the form of the poem, the vision of life being likened to "a great stream" (44), a "mighty torrent" (53), a "living sea" (113), "this perpetual flow" (298)—a direct translation from Lucretius (Phillips notes how often Lucretius collocates *fluere* and *perpetuo* [82])—"bubbles on an eddying flood" (458), and the "bil-

lows" of a "living storm" (466), while the poem is itself a "passing
stream" with "searchless fountain, and invisible course," with events,
images, and words that appear, disappear, and reappear like "bubbles on
an eddying flood."

Like Lucretius (Phillips, 83–84), Shelley constantly extends the application of words like "flow" and "stream" beyond the literal; in Shelley's
poetry, light, wind, "force," "woe," the notes of the skylark and the
impassioned poetry he wishes it would inspire, time, "Wisdom," nature,
and death all "flow,"[20] and a similarly diverse range of phenomena become "streams."[21] Like Lucretius, and in this anticipating contemporary
chaos science, he is particularly interested in the ways atmospheric phenomena can be likened to hydrostatic ones. Very frequently, he describes the wind as a stream or as "streaming"[22]—an image that is found
in Lucretius. Shelley's self-proclaimed "love [of] waves, and winds, and
storms" ("Song: Rarely, rarely, comest thou," 33) is a love of a transele-
mental, entropic flux.

Shelley is perhaps the most "meteorological" of English poets. That
Shelley had some scientific interest in meteorological phenomena is evident, but whatever the state of his knowledge, it neither accounts for
nor helps us to interpret his employment of aerial imagery and his passionate longing to become the wind: "Be thou, Spirit fierce, / My spirit!
Be thou me, impetuous one!" ("Ode to the West Wind," 61–62). The
only science Shelley needed to complete the "Ode to the West Wind,"
"The Cloud," and his other "meteorological" poetry was almost two
thousand years old: the "whole mass" of the "vast ocean of air," writes
Lucretius, in the passage on "perpetual flux" in book 5, "undergoes
innumerable transformations hour by hour" (179, 5.273–74); "the doorway of death" confronts the sky as much as the sea with its "yawning
chasm," which forces us to "acknowledge them to be children of time"
(182, 5.376–77).

The sky, and the clouds in it, are, for Shelley, visible emblems of the
playful amnesiac changefulness personified by the Witch of Atlas. The
Cloud tells us that, like her, "I change, but I cannot die" (76):

20. *Revolt*, V, xlviii, 6; VIII, xv, 8–9; XI, xxii, 9; "A Vision of the Sea," 117; *Epipsychidion*,
517; Lines: "The Cold Earth Slept Below," 5; "Lines Written Among the Euganean Hills," 232;
"To a Skylark," 85, 104; *Hellas*, 32; and *Alastor*, 533, 653.

21. *Revolt*, I, xlii, 3; xlix, 4; II, xii, 5; xxix, 1; "Ode to the West Wind," 15; *Prometheus
Unbound*, IV, 505; "Lines Written Among the Euganean Hills," 312; *Hellas*, 837. This is not an
exhaustive list.

22. The *Concordance* has a special section for these references under "stream" and "streaming."

I silently laugh at my own cenotaph,
    And out of the caverns of rain,
Like a child from the womb, like a ghost from the tomb,
    I arise, and unbuild it again.—

(81-84)

The equation of birth and death in the penultimate line—insisted upon in the internal rhyme of "womb" and "tomb"—is fundamentally Lucretian; it is the structure of the *clinamen,* which can always be read simultaneously as an entropic death or erasure and as a birth of new order. This duality is reinforced by the "unbuild" in the last line—a negative expression of a positive event; the cloud's appearance in the sky "unbuilds" the empty "blue Dome of Air" (80).

Entropic "unbuilding" is what the stream of "the steep sky's commotion" ("Ode to the West Wind," 15) constantly threatens us with; and this is not just the Cloud's tricksterlike playfulness. The "storm of change" (*Queen Mab,* vi, 160), the "storm of death" (*Alastor,* 609), and the "storm of time" ("Charles the First," iv, 52) are all aspects of that entropic "living storm" (461), into which Rousseau plunges in the "Triumph," "whose airs too soon deform" (468). Death in *Adonais* appears as the "storm" that breaks the lily (54), a manifestation of "the law / Of change" that "o'er his sleep the mortal curtain draw[s]" (72). The "wild West Wind" that Shelley invokes with such passion is also the wind that despoils the trees and sea blooms of their leaves, sings the "dirge / Of the dying year" (23-24), and announces to Shelley his own mortality (55-58). As in "The Cloud" and *De rerum natura,* however, death and birth are here two sides of one coin; mortality has the double-sidedness of the *clinamen;* the entropic Wind, both destroyer and preserver, "scatters" Shelley's "dead thoughts" into a debris of atomistic "ashes and sparks" (67), but this death promises in turn "to quicken a new birth" (64); they are "preserved" inasmuch as they enter the turbulent flux of process.

That word "turbulence," whose Latin root (*turba,* and cognate forms) is so central to *De rerum natura* (see Serres, *La naissance,* 37ff.) and which is now so central to chaos science, is an absent presence in the "Ode," tying together diverse aspects of its imagery. Lucretius habitually uses the word metaphorically to characterize the disorder and confusion of "the steep sky's commotion"; for example, in book 5 he refers to "the air's tempestuous tumult [*turbantibus aeris auris*]" (186, 5.502) and to the "lower regions" being "tossed to and fro by veering squalls [*incertis turbare procellis*]" (186, 5.504). The Wind in the "Ode" is characterized as a maenad in Shelley's favorite image of uncontrollable, amnesiac changefulness (see *Adonais,* xxxiii; "Triumph," 137–75). Excellent classical scholar that he was, Shelley must have been aware that, as Serres notes, the Greek root of the Latin *turba, turbē,* "se dit aussi des danses folles aux fêtes de Bacchus" (Serres, *La naissance,* 38).

Shelley's maenadic imagery reveals a new face to us here, one that also seems to speak of a constant, atomistic, loss of ordering information. In *Adonais* the destructive power of the west wind unites with the openness of the poet-as-maenad-as-breaking-billow to destruction. Both can now be seen as aspects of the entropic *turba* that Lucretius sees as the fundamental nature of the universe. As such they are, perhaps, less the triumphant achievement of an arduous struggle against the forces of custom and cold reason than the inevitable results of "the law of change." That law can manifest itself in ways other than the constant incremental deformations of the "flood of ruin," however. If Shelley is a "meteorological poet" in the modern sense of that term, he is also one in an older and more fully Lucretian sense. Shelley's constant evocation of nature's more spectacular "special effects" has traditionally been seen as a weakness in his verse, betraying a febrile and ineffective striving for effect as an end in itself. The "meteorological" book 6 of *De rerum natura,* however, makes the connection between these phenomena apparent. There, Lucretius deals in turn with such Shelleyan themes as thunder, lightning, thunderbolts, whirlwinds (or waterspouts), the formation of clouds, raindrops, earthquakes, the dynamic equilibrium of the sea's volume, volcanoes, the flooding of the Nile, Avernian lakes, fluctuations in the temperature of well water, magnetism, and, finally, epidemics—ending with the apocalyptic description of the plague of Athens.

Serres finds the common ground of these phenomena in their irreducibly contingent nature; they exemplify and symbolize the *clinamen* as entropic tendency to ruin: "Les météores dramatisent la variable fondamentale de la physique, cet écart à la ruine ou déclinaison [*clinamen*]" (Serres, *La naissance,* 110). It is this lesson in the entropic disjunction of causality writ large in natural phenomena that Shelley seized upon and made his own. In Shelley's poetry these "meteors" (in this expanded Lucretian sense) represent the unforeseeable and unqualified *events* that punctuate, imprevisibly (*nunc hinc, nunc illinc*), the smooth flow of "Time's fleeting river" ("Ode to Liberty," 76).

Two nearly contemporary poems, "The Cloud" and the "Ode to Liberty," serve as examples, in the first case, of Shelley's debt to Lucretius in this area and, in the second, of his own extension of the implications of the imagery. "The Cloud" (curiously ignored by Paul Turner) is Shelley's most directly Lucretian poem, an attempt to present an account of a natural phenomenon in poetic form. King-Hele (*Shelley: His Thought and Work*, 219–27) and others are wrong, however, to see this poem as growing out of an interest in contemporary scientific writing on clouds. Reiman and Powers's notes to the poem indicate the problems with that approach. To the line "I bind . . . the Moon's [throne] with a girdle of pearl" (59–60) they solemnly append a discussion of "cirrostratus nebulosus clouds . . . [which] produce the halo phenomenon when the sun or moon shines behind them," and to his "Sunbeam-proof, I hang like a roof" (65), a description of "low gray sheet stratocumulus opacus." By the same token, one could remark that certain cumolonimbus clouds do indeed look "very like a whale," and speculate upon Shakespeare's technical interest in cloud classification.

Shelley's poem shows no interest in classifying different characteristic cloud forms; his concern is entirely with the cloud's infinite mutability. The only "scientific" claim made in the poem is that the cloud is a step in the cyclic career of water on the planet, so that its destruction is also preparatory to its creation. This is not very up-to-the-minute science, however, being integral to Lucretius's account of cloud formation and to his account of the sea's failure to increase in volume, in book 6 (see, e.g., 6.607–38). Shelley's "Cloud" is in many ways a pocket digest version of that book. Consider a list of the natural phenomena that are common to both: cloud formation, the cycle of water, thunder, lightning, rain, hail, snow, earthquakes, volcanoes, and whirlwinds. While the first seven elements of that list are perhaps unsurprising, the last three are not so obvious. It is particularly telling that a relationship of equivalence is posited between the cloud and the earthquake (31–38), a relationship that seems forced unless we have followed Lucretius's accounts of the formation of clouds and the generation of earthquakes from the combined effects of wind and water, which announce to us that, like the cloud that dissolves in rain, the earth is likely to disappear one day "in a wild chaotic welter" (234, 6.607; see 231–35, 6.451–607).

We are also struck by the collocation of volcanoes and whirlwinds (61–62), which is not only to be found here (see, e.g., *Prometheus Unbound*, I, 86–90, 231–32, 526–27). It is hard to imagine what connection they have in Shelley's mind other than the fact that in his description of Mount Etna Lucretius tells us that "the flames sometimes shoot out in . . . a tornado [*turbine*, from *turbo*; whirlwind] through the throats of *Mount Etna*" (236, 6.639–41; Serres glosses this line as meaning that the lava flows from the crater in "volutes énormes" [*La naissance,* 102], though *turbine* is used figuratively to mean simply "stormy" or "tempestuous"), and then shortly afterward offers the whirlwind as a supporting example of the evolutionary generation quite "by chance" (*forte;* 6.672) of such mighty, fearful effects as the eruption of Etna (237, 6.665–69; along with the volcano and the whirlwind Shelley says "the stars reel and swim" ["The Cloud," 61]: Lucretius's third example with the whirlwind and the volcano is *flammescere caelum* [6.669] "the heaven to burst in a blaze").

Shelley's Cloud claims to "pass through the pores, of the ocean and shores; / I change, but I cannot die" (75–76). Lucretius is always at pains to emphasize the interpenetrability of the atomic particles in flux; water and air "atoms" in particular have a tendency to flow rapidly through all substances. These atoms sweep through the universe at incredible speed, "envelop[ing] seas and lands [compare "ocean and shores" above]" and passing "through every pore in the great world's cuticle" (232).[23]

Lightning is the "pilot" (18) of Shelley's cloud, and as Serres suggests (102 n. 1), lightning's character as unqualified event, falling "now this way, now that [*nunc hinc, nunc illinc*]" (66, 2.214), makes it a model of the purely contingent *clinamen,* which occurs "incerto tempore . . . incertisque locis" (2.218–19). The absolute unpredictability of lightning is, for Lucretius, a proof of the impossibility of an omniscient and omnipotent deity: "*[N]ature is free and uncontrolled by proud masters.* . . . Who can be in all places at all times, ready to darken the clear sky with clouds and rock it with a thunderclap—to launch bolts that may often wreck his own temples, or retire and spend his fury letting fly at deserts with that missile which often passes by the guilty and slays the innocent and blameless?" (92–93, 2.1090–91, 1099–104). In the same way, the uncontrollable and irresistible mutability of nature that is everywhere manifest in Shelley's "Cloud" defeats the therapeutic desire to "rule the sum total of the measureless" (92–93, 2.1095).

In the "Ode to Liberty," Shelley establishes a direct analogy between these exempla of entropic *clinamina* drawn from the natural world and events in the human, political, world. In his paper "A Volcano's Voice in Shelley," G. M. Matthews correctly identifies the volcanic activity

---

23. The original has *magni circum spiracula mundi,* which need not be translated as "pores" (Rouse gives "breathing-channels"), though it suggests the idea. Adam Walker, in his lectures at the Syon House academy, which White and others take to be the basis of Shelley's "scientific" interest in things meteorological, describes air as "so subtil that it pervades the pores of all bodies" (quoted in White, *Shelley,* 1:24). Both Walker's phraseology and his "science" seem suspiciously Lucretian.

(181ff.) in this and others of Shelley's poems as a symbol of revolutionary activity and of the catastrophic disruption of the social structure that a revolutionary "eruption" promises. The strength of the poem, however, does not lie in such one-to-one correspondences, but in the cumulative force of its nature imagery, which once again strikingly parallels the sixth book of *De rerum natura*.

Burke and Coleridge argued that political evolution must be a "natural" process and that the evil of revolution is its "unnatural" attempt to found a rational society; Shelley's "Ode to Liberty" accepts the possibility of drawing an analogy between natural and political change, but marshals an impressive array of examples of a profoundly different, Lucretian kind of "nature"—one in which the entropic, amnesiac "law of change" predominates over the organic inherence of part in whole.

What this has to say about the nature of political change is less reassuringly optimistic than Matthews suggests. Liberty's car is a "cloud charioted by flame" (260), in which it is not hard to recognize the cloud piloted by lightning of "The Cloud"; Liberty herself is "The lightning of the nations" (2; see also 142, 165). The "progress" of Liberty in the poem has all the tricksterish uncertainty of the ultramutable cloud. Athens ("a city such as vision / Builds from . . . battlemented cloud" [61–63]) may persist in "Time's fleeting river" (76), but the "spirit" of Liberty that animates it "makes chaos ever new" (89) elsewhere; lightning, thunder, tempest, rain, whirlwind, volcano, and earthquake accompany and provide the model for her unaccountable appearances and disappearances: *nunc hinc, nunc illinc; incerto tempore, incertisque locis.*

This holds both a promise and a threat. The promise is that, even in times of apparent political stagnation and repression, liberty, or revolution, may be about to burst, unannounced, upon the scene, like the "avalanche" that results when a "mass" of ideas piled "thought by thought" in "Heaven-defying minds" is suddenly, and unaccountably, dislodged by the loosening of a "great truth" in *Prometheus Unbound* (II, iii, 37–42).[24] Lightning's ability to confound the pretensions to omniscience of god or scientist makes it an equally apt symbol of the vanity of pretensions to absolute political power:

24. It is very interesting to compare this with Václav Havel's "Dear Dr. Husák," written in 1975, where he writes prophetically of a moment when "[t]he machine that worked for years to apparent perfection, faultlessly, without a hitch, falls apart overnight. The system that seemed likely to reign unchanged . . . is shattered without warning." This is quoted in Reibling, 186, precisely as an example of chaotic errancy in a political system.

> Ha King! wilt thou chain
> The rack and the rain,
> Wilt thou fetter the lightning and hurricane?
> The storms are free.
>
> (*Hellas*, 671–74)

The entropic flux of historical process has the potential literally to anni-
hilate the repressive institutions within which we live; if the free were
to write the "impious name / Of KING" ("Ode to Liberty," 211–12) in the
dust, it would be "as a serpent's path, which the light air / Erases, and
the flat sands close behind!" (214–15). This information-destroying, atomistic turbulence is, perhaps, one meaning of the "Wild Bacchanal [cf.
turbē] of truth's mysterious wine" (200).

On the other hand, the threat is that Liberty can disappear as easily
and inexplicably as she arrives; Liberty's car-cloud is introduced in the
penultimate stanza, but, in the final stanza, becomes the "summer
cloud" that dissolves in rain as a symbol of the poet's ruined inspiration.
The poet is left like one who drowns as waves crash round his head,
being erased by a turbulent flux like the name of king written in the
sand. Shelley takes the unpredictability of the volcanic eruption more
seriously than Matthews realizes. Although the "Ode to Liberty" is often
read as a prophecy of Liberty's inevitable triumph, Shelley's "law of
change" does not allow positive prophecy. Like Prometheus, the only
secret we can bear against tyranny is that it must end sometime; we
cannot know what that time will be: "the future is dark, and the present
is spread / Like a pillow of thorns for thy slumberless head" (*Prometheus Unbound*, I, 562–63).

In the face of an inherently turbulent political process we are "reduced" to a radically empirical observation of the evolution of that process: "the Fame / Of what has been, the Hope of what will be" ("Ode to
Liberty," 264–65). Like Benjamin's "angel of history," whose wings are
caught in a storm blowing from paradise, we ride the blast of the entropic "Storm / Which with the shattered present chokes the past" (*Epipsychidion*, 211–12); our faces must, like the angel's, always be "turned
toward the past," which appears as "one single catastrophe which
keeps piling wreckage upon wreckage and hurls it in front of his feet"
(*Illuminations*, 257):

> . . . wolfish Change, like winter howls to strip
> The foliage in which Fame, the eagle, built
> Her aiëry, while Dominion whelped below.

The storm is in its branches, and the frost
Is on its leaves, and the blank deep expects
Oblivion on oblivion, spoil on spoil,
Ruin on ruin.

(*Hellas,* 872-78)

In the end, we can only ask of Liberty, "Comes she not?" (261), and at this point the song must collapse because there is nothing to sustain it further.

II

One question I have not yet directly approached, although I have touched on the subject above, is how Shelley applies this Lucretian model of chaotic creativity to his own poetic practice, and what the implications of that would be. *Prometheus Unbound,* IV, for example, makes a direct, though still obscure, connection between entropic decay and the rapturous exaltations of its lyric outpourings. The insistence upon the entropic vulnerability of the poet and the poetic voice in *Adonais* (the "breaking billow") and the "Ode to Liberty" (the waves that "Hiss round a drowner's head") implicitly posits some connection between that vulnerability and the poet's creativity.

That connection lies at the heart of an image that in different forms haunted Shelley's imagination throughout his poetic career, the relationship between a greater and a lesser light (often the sun and stars), or between darkness and a faint or fading light (such as night and the stars). In the "Hymn to Intellectual Beauty," for example, Intellectual Beauty provides "nourishment" to "human thought," "Like darkness to a dying flame!" (44-45); similarly, in the fragmentary "To Mary—" of 1818, Shelley writes to Mary, "I am not well whilst thou art far; / As sunset to the sphered moon, / As twilight to the western star, / Thou, beloved, art to me" (11-14); in the "Ode to Liberty" the collapse of poetic inspiration is likened to "a far taper [that] fades with fading night" (279); the skylark in "To a Skylark" is described as "unseen" "like a star of Heaven, / In the broad daylight"; in *Adonais,* when the sun sets, we are told, "the immortal stars awake again; / So is it in the world of living men" (256-57); and in the "Triumph of Life," the way the shape all light tramples Rousseau's thoughts into the "dust of death" is compared to the way "Day upon the threshold of the east / Treads out the lamps of night, until the breath / Of darkness reillumines even the least / Of heaven's living eyes" (389-92). As these varied examples show—and this is not an exhaustive list—Shelley never settled on a

single meaning for this image; but there is a common theme. In each of
these examples an outflowing of creative or emotional energy is premised upon "darkness" or the maximally entropic negation of energy.

We can contrast this with his use of the image in *Queen Mab,* where
"Religion" sheds "a glare that fades before the sun / Of truth, and shines
but in the dreadful night / That long has lowered above the ruined
world" (VI, 143–45). Here, "night" and "ruin" are seen as purely negative, in contrast to the positive virtue of "truth," but in the formulation
of the "Hymn to Intellectual Beauty" and the examples that follow it
above, nothing is so clear-cut. Creativity seems to be the result of the
complex interplay of entropic conditions. For Lucretius, in an image
that Shelley also uses, light is, by definition, "dying"; it drains from its
source as a liquid stream of light-atoms. The "dying flame" and "fading
taper" of poetic creativity is, these images suggest, a negentropic "dissipative system" parasitically dependent upon entropic flux in order to
shine forth.

In the *Defence,* Shelley writes that "the mind in creation is as a fading
coal which some invisible influence, like an inconstant wind, awakens
to transitory brightness" (Reiman and Powers, 504), and also that poetry
is "a sword of lightning, ever unsheathed, which consumes the scabbard
that would contain it" (491). Both suggest that poetic creation is, like
the *clinamen* the lightning signifies, premised equally upon negation
and memory. Such a reading asks us to think again about the preface to
Prometheus Unbound and its statement that "the cloud of mind is discharging its collected lightning" (134), which we have hitherto discussed under the rubric of Shelley's "idealism." What we have since
seen of "clouds" and "lightning" in Shelley's thought problematizes any
simple idealist reading of this image. If the "great writers of our own
age are . . . the companions and forerunners of some unimagined
change in our social condition or the opinions which cement it" (134),
the irreducible unpredictability of the cloud and the lightning are the
signs of the unavoidable historical empiricism that makes this change
"unimagined."

The question, then, is not whether but how Shelley relates decay to
creation in the poetic world. To begin to answer this we can return to
Shelley's interest in ruins. I discussed this above in terms of his entropic
cosmology, but that was only half the story. Ruins, for Shelley, do not
merely provide evidence of the constant entropic tendency of the
world; they also have profound hermeneutical implications. The first
question we must ask is what role entropic erasure plays in the generation of their significance; how do we "read" atomistic fragmentation? I

use the word "read" quite literally. Shelley's ruined structures of a forgotten past are more than merely symbolic of literary texts whose ties to their contexts of production have been eroded by the hermeneutical *clinamen;* they are, in an important sense, "textual" objects.

In "The Assassins" (1814) we learn that in the valley of Bethzatanai, among the ruins left by the undefined "men of elder days" who had "inhabited this spot," was a "temple dedicated to the God of knowledge and of truth," where the "lore of ancient wisdom was sculptured in mystic characters on the rocks. The human spirit and the human hand had been busy here to accomplish its profoundest miracles. . . . There was deep and important meaning in every lineament of its fantastic sculpture" (Ingpen and Peck, 6:158). Our first assumption is that this temple of knowledge and truth will be a school of political liberty for the Assassins who escape from Roman domination into this valley, but this is not the case: "The unintelligible legend, once so beautiful and perfect, so full of poetry and history, spoke, even in destruction, volumes of mysterious import, and obscure significance" (158). This remarkable passage appears to affirm the richness of the legacy of the past, but actually denies both the reader and the Assassins access to it. The legend was once "beautiful and perfect," but now it is quite literally "lost information."

This "information" is "textual." In *De rerum natura* Lucretius makes a direct comparison between atoms and letters: "Consider how in my verses, for instance, you see many letters common to many words; yet you must admit that different verses and words are composed of different letters. Not that there is any lack of letters common to several words, or that there are no two words composed of precisely the same letters; but they do not all alike consist of exactly the same components. So in other things, although many atoms are common to many substances, yet these substances may still differ in their composition" (80, 2.688-98). Atomistic constellation is a form of codification; Shelley makes this point in the essay "On a Future State," where he describes thought itself as subject to atomistic erasure: "It is probable that what we call thought is not an actual being, but no more than the relation between certain parts of that infinitely varied mass, of which the rest of the universe is composed, and which ceases to exist so soon as those parts change their position with regard to each other" (Ingpen and Peck, 6:207). One of the lessons of chaos theory is that redundancy is essential in the transmission of any code because error, absolute and irrecoverable error, will inevitably invade transmission (see, e.g., Gleick, 256-58). If we think of buildings as analogous to linguistic codes—or "what we call thought"—we understand Shelley's insistence upon the absolute disjunction between the ruin in the context of consumption and the building as it appeared in the context of production. There is no continuum from legibility to illegibility for individual code elements; either one can read them, or they are absolutely and irrecoverably lost; they "[cease] to exist so soon as those parts change their position with regard to each other."

Information is atomistic; the expression "not an atom of difference" describes absolute redundancy, or the absence of information. Information, in Gregory Bateson's classic definition, is a "difference that makes a difference"; it is conveyed by atoms of difference, discrete units of difference—such as letters or the myriad on/off switches of a computer microchip—that are legible as such and "make a difference" to some receiver. If entropic disorganization confuses these differences, the lost information cannot be retrieved, it can only be replaced by a duplicate. From such a perspective, Burke's hermeneutically homeostatic "style" that guides the repair and replacement of missing parts can be properly understood as simple code redundancy, a surplus of information that does not deny the inevitable presence of entropic erasure within memory's cycles but is premised upon it. The "unintelligible legend" represents such an entropic loss within the reproductive transmission of the atomistically encoded lessons of the past into the present. The entropic decay and atomistic ruination of human and natural structures can also be understood as the result of a constant tendency to error in the code transmission of the reproductive cycles of history. The ruin is simultaneously a product of memory and loss; it is, quite literally, a textual *clinamen.*

But perfect redundancy is, as one would expect, an annihilation of information by its very "preservation." If information is "difference," perfect redundancy means the eradication of difference. What is striking is that the Assassins, permanently isolated in the consumptive context of the present by this erosive *clinamen,* still find the very loss and "destruction" of the past creative and enriching. Without "errors" there is ultimately no information. The effaced message speaks "volumes of mysterious import and obscure significance"; this seems to mean not merely that the remnant of the legend that has survived "destruction" is still a source of richness, but that the very destruction itself has opened up a potential for significance that is more than just a depleted version of the original. It is not so much that the deep truth is imageless as that the imageless apparently contains, or releases, a deep truth. What that truth is, the unfinished "Assassins" does not tell us.

III

The image of effaced, monumental inscriptions stayed with Shelley, however, and returns among the ruins in *Epipsychidion* (1821). There, the ruined "lone dwelling" (484) to which the lover hopes to retire with Emily is even more emphatically divorced from any connotative historical/productive context than the ruins in Bethzatanai. It was "built by whom or how / None of the rustic island-people know" (484-85). The lover does ascribe a sketchy origin to the building—the "pleasure-house" (491) of some "wise and tender Ocean-King" (488), "Made sacred to his sister and his spouse" (492)—but the extratemporal and extralegal location of this "history," in a "Titanic" (494) period "ere crime / Had been invented" (488-99), suggests that this history, though significant as such, is the lover's invention. The erosion of the ruin's ties to human history is so complete that it "scarce seems now a wreck of human art," appearing, rather, as a spontaneous and ahistorical product of "the heart / Of Earth" (494-95) and "living stone" (496):

> For all the antique and learned imagery
> Has been erased, and in the place of it
> The ivy and the wild-vine interknit
> The volumes of their many twining stems.
>
> (498-501)

As in "The Assassins," the erasure of information takes the form of an absolute annihilation of the "learned" lessons of the past, a forgetting of initial conditions. But *Epipsychidion* takes us further toward understanding the "volumes of mysterious import and obscure significance" contained in, or rather liberated by, these effaced signs. Reading takes on a new significance here, that of an active supplementing of certain absences or withholdings. The "learned imagery" is replaced by "volumes" of ivy and wild vine; Hillis Miller notes this rather pointed pun ("Critic as Host," 241), which insists upon the textual application of the image. (It also echoes the "volumes of mysterious import" of the "Assassins," and suggests the Lucretian "volutes," or errant cycles.) Miller reads the passage as epitomizing the logic of the parasite; it continues:

> Parasite flowers illume with dewy gems
> The lampless halls, and when they fade, the sky
> Peeps through their winter-woof of tracery
> With Moon-light patches, or star atoms keen,

> Or fragments of the day's intense serene;—
> Working mosaic on their Parian floors.
>
> (502-7)

The parasite, he argues, is Shelley's figure for the "genetic trace" (Miller, "Critic as Host," 237, 243), the residue of the inevitable failure, or ruin, of Shelley's poetic and idealist aspirations, from which he must "start the cycle" over again:

> Shelley's poetry is the record of a perpetually renewed failure. It is a failure ever to get the right formula and so end the separate incomplete self, end lovemaking, end politics, and end poetry, all at once, in a performative apocalypse in which words will become the fire they have ignited and so vanish as words, in a universal light. The words, however, always remain, there on the page, as the unconsumed traces of each unsuccessful attempt to use words to end words. The attempt must therefore be repeated. The same scene . . . is written by Shelley over and over again from *Queen Mab* to *The Triumph of Life* in a repetition ended only with his death. This repetition mimes the poet's failure ever to get it right and so end the necessity of trying once more with what remains. (237)

Miller is right that Shelley is providing a model of poetic creativity in this passage, and that it is based upon a cycle of entropic ruin and negentropic renovation. That cycle, however, is not the Sisyphean, thanatological cycle of an ever-renewed and ever-frustrated attempt to triumph over language. It is not true to suggest that *Queen Mab* is essentially the same "scene" as, say, "The Witch of Atlas"; nor could the "Witch of Atlas" be described as attempting to "end lovemaking, end politics, and end poetry, all at once, in a performative apocalypse," as *Queen Mab,* with its encyclopedic pretensions, could. The preface to the "Witch" renounces any such "permanent" goals as foolish delusions; its "visionary" beauty is premised upon its willingness to accept, at the outset, that it is its "doom to die" (13).

Shelley's cycles of creativity do not debar him from genuine innovation—quite the opposite, as the image of the "parasite flowers" makes clear. These flowers are not produced, as Miller's model would demand, from the residue of the ruined building; they have opportunistically occupied the space created by the erasure of the "antique and learned imagery." As such they represent an attempt, not to "start again" with ever the same material, but to "start anew." The old cycle is canceled, and a new one starts from a different position. The same is true of the projected mosaic on the "Parian floors" that replaces the parasite flowers "when they fade" (503). That mosaic of "Moon-light patches, or star atoms keen, / Or fragments of the day's intense serene" (505–6), owes nothing to the withered flowers except the evolutionary opportunity presented by their disappearance.

This chain of opportunistic replacement suggests a "parasitic" logic at work quite different from that proposed by Miller. It is closer to the one Serres proposes in his *Parasite,* as described by Eric White: "The term 'parasite' is . . . equivalent to Lucretius's *clinamen,* whose stochastic swerving produces novelty. The parasite is defined as 'a differential operator of change' that enables the stochastic emergence of islands of negentropy. It renews decaying systems and is therefore on the side of life. Thanatocratic systems accordingly seek to expel parasites. For instance, by chasing every parasite the Cartesian ego was able to constitute modern rationality, technology, mastery, and possession, 'the proliferation of a certain type of sameness' " (274, quoting from *The Parasite,* 196, 180). The parasite flowers and mosaics of projected light exemplify the death-is-birth duality of the *clinamen;* they are "islands of negentropy" in an entropic flux, which succeed each other in a disjunctive chain as each in turn succumbs to entropic decay.

But Serres also differs in an important way from Shelley. Serres himself evokes the "chain" metaphor when he contrasts the "parasite" to the mythic "producer" who is "an archangel because he bears information, news, novelty, and because he is necessarily at the head of the line in relation to the parasitic chain" (qtd. in White, 275). This "producer," of course, never exists: "The 'producer' is always already a parasite occupying an entirely relative position on the parasitic chain" (White, 275). This is the *mise en abîme* of Derridean *différance* and its endless deferral of the origin, which underlies Miller's account of Shelley's perpetually renewed but "always already" doomed attempt to defeat language once and for all.

It is true that Shelley's parasitic *clinamen* chain consigns the productive origin to an abyss of infinite deferral. But rather than constantly repeat, with gloomy self-satisfaction, the only too predictable "discovery" of this absence of origin, Shelley focuses his interest on the benefits we reap from its entropic erasure. Shelley's perpetually leaking and perpetually replenished vessel is always half-full rather than always half-empty. *The New Shelley,* a recent collection of papers by leading Shelley scholars, shows that the deconstructive and "decentering" bent in recent Shelley criticism is making Miller's perspective a commonplace, however.

Hogle, for example, yokes together two separate comments from Shelley's "On Life" to construct this paraphrase of his argument: "[E]very apparent 'object of thought' is always 'a thought upon which [an]other thought is employed' in a process whereby the latter relates the former to 'a train of [further] thoughts' ("Shelley as Revisionist," 112). Similarly, Tilottama Rajan takes a passage from the opening of the *Defence* that describes imagination as being able to compose from thoughts "as from elements, other thoughts, each containing within itself the principle of its own integrity" ("Web of Human Things," 86), arguing that Shelley is asking "[w]hether one can find meaning in the web of differences and displacements that constitutes speech, life, and all systems of representation" (107). Such views do admit of the possibility that thoughts can be affected by entropy, but they fail to explain how that fact can lead to the possibility of future creativity. Thoughts grow, rather interchangeably, from the husks of previous thoughts, each ruin presenting the same ever-renewed and ultimately hopeless task to the thinker.

What Shelley's parasite flowers show us is that thoughts develop out of thoughts, yes, but this does not suggest an ultimate equivalence of all thoughts in a "transferential One." Shelley's "On Life" makes this clear: "By the word *things* is to be understood any object of thought, that is, any thought upon which any other thought is employed, *with an apprehension of distinction*" (Reiman and Powers, 478). *Pace* Rajan, Shelley never worries about "whether we can find meaning" *tout court;* it is individual meanings whose mortality he describes, accepts, occasionally celebrates, and occasionally mourns. When errors enter the transmission of these thoughts from generation to generation, the world is no longer the same place it once was; old "distinctions" are lost, but, crucially, new ones are created. The mutability of thoughts is not equivalent either to their interchangeability or their meaninglessness.

Shelley does not mourn, or pretend to mourn, our "fallen" condition, but, accepting that we are "fallen," looks out for what rewards can be found outside the "bounds" of paradise, or the autarchic Epicurean "garden." In the passage from *Epipsychidion* above, Shelley insists upon a poetry of fragments in which, in that extraordinary phrase from earlier in the poem, "Each part exceeds the whole" (181). The ruined fragments cannot be subordinated to an absolute hermeneutical imperative. The sky working *"mosaic"* upon the Parian floor does so with "moon-light *patches*," "star-*atoms* keen" and "*fragments* of the day's intense serene."

The poetics of entropic ruination and the Gothic are brought together here and redefined. The poem becomes a Frankenstein's monster, or "mosaic" of aggregated fragments, each grafted onto a "whole" that they in turn reinvent. Progressive ruination through time inserts the static Gothic model into time's and memory's (canceled) cycles. The Gothic, at least as (mis)understood in the late eighteenth and early nineteenth centuries, is a form that aggressively renounces redundancy. As a nonorganic antistructure to which new fragments can be sutured, in principle, ad infinitum, the Gothic novel or the Gothic building is reinvented, in its details, with each example. No part can suggest the whole, because almost any part of the "series without aim or purpose" might be incorporated into any "Whole"; no one could deduce the nave of St. Denis from the ambulatory, or the remainder of *The Mysteries of Udolpho* from Emily's sojourn at Udolpho. The Gothic maximizes the creation of information by minimizing redundancy.

Burke's maximally redundant concept of "style," on the other hand, in which every part is dedicated to a precise location in a given whole, conforms, ironically, to the classical ideal of beauty as defined by Alberti: "the harmony and concord of all the parts, achieved in such a manner that nothing could be added, taken away or altered" (qtd. in Hartt, 223). This is an architectural version of Aristotle's organic totality of "plot": "a complete whole, with its several incidents so closely connected that the transposal or withdrawal of any one of them will disjoin and dislocate the whole" (*Basic Works*, 1463). Such a work can be conceived, but would never be built; it is, to put it simply, too dull, too information-poor to engage the creative urge. A building built in absolute conformity to Vitruvian rules could be reconstructed in its entirety from the scantiest fragments, but it is a telling fact that such a purely redundant "creation" has never been wrought.

This "code redundancy" also underlies Burke's definition of the beautiful in his *Philosophical Enquiry into the Origin of Our Ideas of the Sublime and Beautiful*. Burke's beautiful is the world seen from the height and security of the "quiet citadel" of the *suave mari magno*. His criteria of beauty stem from a desire to be able to take an object in as a whole, with every part clearly subservient to that whole. The beautiful object is "*comparatively* small" (we are at a sufficient distance from it to be able to comprehend it as a whole); it is "smooth" (it does not have any troubling discontinuities); if it has a "variety in the direction of the parts," nonetheless "those parts [are] not angular, but melted as it were into each other" (117). We love the beautiful, he argues, because it "submits to us" (113) and to the controlling gaze of the citadel.

The Burkean sublime, on the other hand, is the world seen in the thick of the storm of change. Its dominant emotion is "terror" caused by an "obscurity" that prevents us "know[ing] the full extent of any danger . . . [and] accustom[ing] our eyes to it" (58).

Anything that hinders our ability to understand something as a total-ity—"vastness," "infinity," and so forth—contributes to this terror. The Lucretian *clinamen*-meteor is definitively sublime; "everything sudden and unexpected" is terrifying, as is anything "intermitting" (cf. *nunc hinc, nunc illinc*) (83). The absences that haunt the fragment and the ruin are terrifying: "All *general* privations are great, because they are all terrible; *Vacuity, Darkness, Solitude* and *Silence*" (71). The sublime leaves us guessing, unable to make a "reparation" that would synthesize the disjunctive parts into a fully intuitable, determining whole.

This is enthusiastically embraced as an aesthetic ideal by the Gothic novelists: "To a warm imagination, the dubious forms, that float, half veiled in darkness, afford a higher delight, than the most distinct scen-ery, that the sun can shew" (Radcliffe, 598–99). Inserted into the cyclic dynamics of time and memory that they ceaselessly destroy and renew, these absences and disjunctions become a motor for a constantly cre-ative stream of new information and new sensations—"parasite flow-ers" that emerge from the entropic indeterminacies of the sublime's fragments to bring us their "higher delight." At its least compelling, this "stream," or "series of events," could be represented by the constant struggle of the sensationalist Gothic novel to outdo its forebears in spec-tacular and grisly effects; the absurdities of Shelley's *Zastrozzi* and *St. Irvyne* are typical of such empty "novelty." At its most interesting, it takes us into a realm where the poetic refusal of redundancy merges almost imperceptibly into political revolution.

When Burke says that "[g]ood order is the foundation of all good things" (*Reflections,* 372), he is making the rule-bound redundancy of his aesthetic of the beautiful into a political principle. We have encoun-tered this principal before, in the guise of the aesthetic "free conformity to law" that underlies the therapeutic politics of the first-generation Ro-mantics and the post-Kantian philosophers in general.

There was a well-established Romantic therapeutic model for dealing with absences—or, to use Burke's word, "privations"—and *Epipsychid-ion* is one of many poems in which Shelley pointedly invokes and di-verges from this "received" Romantic version. The origin of the ortho-

dox model is, like so much of the therapeutic tradition, to be found in
Kant's *Critique of Judgement*. Kant refers admiringly to Burke's theory
of the sublime and the beautiful (130–31), but criticizes it as limited by
Burke's empirical method. For Kant, the therapeutic imperative insists
that he recuperate the Burkean sublime that cuts us adrift from the
world, and find a way of taming its terrors—as Burke seeks to do with
its political equivalent. He does this, significantly, by resorting to the
suave mari magno. Not only must "we . . . see ourselves safe in order
to feel this soul-stirring delight" (112), but from the safety of our transcendental citadel, we turn our initial terror at the immensity or disjunctive disintegrity of the sublime object or event into a rapt admiration for
the "supersensible faculty within us" that permits us to go beyond our
empirical inability to "estimat[e] the magnitude of things of the world
of sense" and reconcile them with the demand of reason for "absolute
totality" (97): "The sublime is that, the mere capacity of thinking which
evidences a faculty of mind transcending every standard of sense" (98).
Such a transcendental faculty places us firmly in the "quiet citadel," giving us the therapeutic power of "estimating that might [of the sublime]
without fear, and of regarding our estate as exalted above it" (114).

   Via Coleridge, and as part of the general therapeutic attempt to see all
"parts" as finite expressions of an infinite "whole," this idea becomes a
recurrent theme in Wordsworth's poetry; the sublimity of privation is
one of the chief springs of its philosophical passages, and therefore a
principal element in Shelley's "idealist" legacy from the first-generation
Romantics. Like Kant, Wordworth's goal is to overcome the mere empirical sense of loss and find in the mind's response to that loss evidence of
a higher, spiritual totality. Sublimity is transformed into a *felix culpa*, a
moment of "diasparactive" vacancy through which the poet is led to
totality, a death that is the gateway to a higher life. The Christian, redemptive schema is insisted upon. In the 1815 *Essay, Supplementary to
the Preface*, he argues:

> The commerce between Man and his Maker cannot be carried on
> but by a process where much is represented in little, and the
> Infinite Being accommodates himself to a finite capacity. In all
> this may be perceived the affinity between religion and poetry;
> between religion—making up the deficiencies of reason by faith;
> and poetry—passionate for the instruction of reason; between
> religion—whose element is infinitude, and whose ultimate trust
> is the supreme of things, submitting herself to circumscription,
> and reconciled to substitutions; and poetry—ethereal and tran-

scendent, yet incapable to sustain her existence without sensuous incarnation. (*Prose Works,* 3:65)

The poet "establish[es] that dominion over the spirits of readers by
which they are to be humbled and humanised, in order that they may
be purified and exalted" (*Prose Works,* 80–81).

This is the totalizing goal of the poet's "comprehensive soul," as he
calls it in the preface to the *Lyrical Ballads* (Bloom and Trilling, 601).
Poetry "takes its origin from emotion recollected in tranquillity" (608);
in other words, from the *ataraxia* of the citadel the poet is able to
place the turbulent emotional experience into a "comprehensive," or
providential, framework. The theory of the "spots of time" in the *Prelude,* book XII, exemplifies this. These fragmentary moments of inexplicable affective power become, from the perspective of the tranquil citadel of recollection, symbolic gateways by which we gain access to "the
spirit of the Past / For future restoration" (*Prelude,* XII, 285–86). Just as
Kant holds that the sublime empirical privations of the world throw
into relief our transcendent mental capacities, the "*creative* soul" (XII,
207) that supplements absences with an understanding of the whole,
Wordsworth's "spots" contain an "efficacious spirit" that gives "Profoundest knowledge to what point, and how, / The mind is lord and master—outward sense / The obedient servant of her will" (221–23).

In the *Prelude*'s description of the crossing of the Alps, when the
travelers' minds are presented with a sudden, catastrophic privation—
the disappearance of crossing the Alps as dream and goal—Wordsworth
contrasts his initial response of baffled astonishment with a retrospec-
tive "reparation" that allows him to use this absence as a mirror in
which to glimpse the mind's "infinitude" (VI, 592–605). In this version
of the connection between the entropic ("the light of sense / Goes out"
[600–601]) and the negentropic ("but with a flash that has revealed /
The invisible world" [601–2]), the negentropic reaction is a transcendental movement that ensures that the discontinuity is not allowed to
threaten the therapeutic Absolute within which it must be made to
make sense. Entropy is rendered only apparent—a challenge to which
the comprehensive soul of the poet is always equal.

Not surprisingly, Wordsworth finds a very different significance in ruins than does Shelley. Ruins, for Wordsworth, are what they were for
Whately in his description of Tintern Abbey: "[M]emorials of every part
still subsist; all certain, but all in decay." In the *Prelude,* "the widely
scattered wreck sublime / Of vanished nations" (VIII, 614) may be "sublime" in its fragmentary discontinuity, but no fragmentary "part" is al-

lowed to exceed or disturb the "whole"; this wreckage all serves as "evidence" (612) of Wordsworth's belonging to a "human nature" (608) that is "not a punctual presence, but a spirit / Diffused through time and space" (610-11). The only ruin that prompts something like Burke's sublime terror or Shelley's disjunctive *clinamen* is one "not by reverential touch of Time / Dismantled, but by violence abrupt" (IX, 468-69). "Abruptness" is a feature of both aesthetic and political sublimity for Burke, and this convent sacked in revolutionary violence awakens in Wordsworth that anxiety of insufficient influence which haunts all therapeutic arguments as an unconscious recognition of their fragility.

None of the above-mentioned passages from the *Prelude* were available to Shelley, but the "Boy of Winander" episode (V, 364-97), published as a separate poem in *Lyrical Ballads* (1800), was. Again, in this passage, a sudden privation, the failure of the owls to give their expected reply to his "mimic hootings" (V, 373), shocks the Boy into an apprehension of a totality of which he was before an unconscious part:

> sometimes, in that silence while he hung
> Listening, a gentle shock of mild surprise
> Has carried far into his heart the voice
> Of mountain torrents; or the visible scene
> Would enter unawares into his mind,
> With all its solemn imagery, its rocks,
> Its woods, and that uncertain heaven, received
> Into the bosom of the steady lake.
>
> (381-88)

The "uncertain heaven" reflected as a whole in the "steady lake" is an image of the Boy's suddenly receptive heart receiving the totality of the environing scene—the lake's tranquillity standing here for the *ataraxia* of the sage for whom the uncertain developments of the storm of change are also resolved into a whole.

The central event of *Alastor,* also, is the encounter with a sudden privation, or, in the poem's favorite word, "vacancy." The disappearance of the "veiled maid" (151), swallowed by night and the "dark flood" of sleep that rolls across his "vacant brain" (191), opens a rift in the Poet's understanding of the world that he spends the rest of the poem seeking, unsuccessfully, to repair. Earlier in the poem, the Wordsworthian hermeneutical model is upheld; among the fragments of the "ruined temples" (116) the Poet gazes upon "The Zodiac's brazen mystery" (119) until these fragments fall into place as a hermeneutical totality in his "vacant mind" (126). Shelley invites us to draw a parallel between the successfully supplemented absences of the ruined temples and the disappearance of the "veiled maid" by echoing the "vacant mind" at line 126 with the "vacant brain" at line 191. Now, however, the privation refuses to be reduced, and vacancy does not open the door to a higher totality. Standing in the "vacant woods" (195), "His wan eyes / Gaze on the empty scene as vacantly / As ocean's moon looks on the moon in heaven" (200–202). What, in the "Boy of Winander" passage, is a model for the comprehensive understanding of the sage's reflective *ataraxia* is here reduced to a model of empirical phenomenalism. The lake or sea that *reflects* the "uncertain heavens" does not *comprehend* them; it merely mirrors them, "vacantly."

In *Alastor,* Shelley is trying to weigh the attractions of the therapeutic model against a growing suspicion that some cancellations and privations are not only irreparable, but necessary. He writes in the preface to the poem: "Among those who attempt to exist without human sympathy, the pure and tender-hearted perish through the intensity and passion of their search after its communities, when the vacancy of their spirit suddenly makes itself felt. All else, selfish, blind, and torpid, are those unforeseeing multitudes who constitute, together with their own, the lasting misery and loneliness of the world. Those who love not their fellow-beings live unfruitful lives, and prepare for their old age a miserable grave" (Reiman and Powers, 70).

The attempt to "exist without human sympathy" is the attempt to achieve the invulnerability to *tuchē* of the truly autarchic life. Shelley throws Wordsworth's own words into his face to close the preface and point its application: "The good die first, / And those whose hearts are dry as summer dust, / Burn to the socket!" Only a willingness to risk the sublime chances of the *clinamen* amid the inevitable fragmentation of real life over the ideal of life as absolute redundancy, the mortal "Arab maiden" over the autoerotic wish fulfillment of the "veiled maid," can save us from "burning to the socket" in the stale paradises of our autarchic gardens.

LUCRETIAN "IDEALISM"

I

It is just here, however, that a radically different perspective on the "storm of time" opens up to us. If Shelley's "skepticism" can be traced to his Lucretianism, so can his "idealism." So far, the "skeptical" image of a perpetual, entropic flux seems little different from the transferential flux of the "decentering" critics. Yet there is another side to Lucretius that we have yet fully to explore, which also makes itself felt in Shelley's writing; this is a desire to rise above the devastating flux of the world, to oppose the creative values of "life-giving Venus" to the destructive ones of "brutal" Mars, and to find the still point in this turning world. The key text here is also the *suave mari magno,* but with the emphasis on the *ataraxia* of the stable viewpoint of the observer and not the observed flux. This is the "view from the citadel" we encountered in Part Two, a view that implies a therapeutic "comprehension" of the flux of events as a "transferential One."

Paradoxically, this union with the world is achieved by a renunciation of the world, or rather a willingness to abandon the attempt to achieve a global understanding of the world. Serres argues that we must re-nounce the martial impulse to control the world and to master its flux of events. The sage retires into the Epicurean "garden" and "unties" all connections to the outside world. It is only through an absolute "letting go" that one can achieve the untroubled magnanimity of *ataraxia;* any engagement with the world beyond the garden is "a vain search for the way of life" (60, 2.9–10):

> [P]our le jardin, fermé, *du local au global l'inférence est tou-jours problématique.* Elle pose toujours des questions à resoudre singulièrement. . . . [The Epicurean sage] est autarcique, entouré de quelques amis, retiré au jardin du bruit que répand le forum dans une sécession sereine, dissident, séparé, autonome, sage dif-férentiel. Pas de système, pas d'univers, pas de totalité, de con-cordance ni de conspiration, tous concepts intégraux, global. Le seul infini est le vide, et les semences du réel sont distribuées atomiquement. . . . Déliés, séparés, nous serons nous-mêmes des dieux dans notre isolat partitif. L'infini échappe, monde par monde, aux causes totalisatrices, l'histoire échappe, lieu par lieu, à un régard ou à une force globale. L'espace est une distribution de jardins. Atomisme. (Serres, *La naissance,* 231–32)[25]

25. "For the garden, closed off from the world, *the inference from the local to the global is always problematic.* It always poses questions that must be answered individually. . . . [The Epicurean sage] is autarchic, surrounded by a few friends; he has retired to the garden from the noise of the forum in a secession that is serene, dissident, separated, autonomous, a wise differential. No system, no universe, no totality, concordance, or conspiracy: all integral, global concepts. The only infinity is emptiness, and the scattered seeds of the real are distributed atomistically. . . . Disconnected, separated, we shall ourselves be gods in our particulate isola-

This is similar to Hogle's argument in favor of an ideological *laissez-faire* as a *via negativa* to an absolute "serenity": "To be unbound from a domineering system, even from the Great Memory, is automatically to return . . . to this serene but teeming clearing house of figural potentialities. To be Prometheus (or Asia) as well as being unbound is to dissolve into being the many-shaped, almost invisible, energizer, channeller, and performer of this vast mythographic interplay" (*Shelley's Process*, 204). Hogle's *ataraxia* seems politically disabling, however, and Serres's "garden" is hardly a significant advance. Serres's "autarcique" sage might better be described as "autistic." With each of us separated into our own little paradise, shunning all contact with the world as a contagion by "martial values," it is impossible to imagine a coherent basis for political action, for literature, or for the love that is supposed to rule the "garden." Serres suggests we have "quelques amis" with us in our garden, but such complex "molecular" structures do not seem compatible with the absolute atomistic dislocation he describes. "Déliés, séparés, nous serons nous-mêmes des dieux dans notre isolat partitif"; but perhaps we might prefer some company in the "vain search for the way of life" to godhead at the price of isolation? "To stand aloof in a quiet citadel" (60, 2.8) seems a more apt image for this "autarchic" state than sharing a garden with friends.

Serres's model, however, is easy to trace in the Enlightenment appropriations of Lucretius that were important to Shelley. We have seen Holbach's use of the *suave mari magno* as a model for an "absolute knowing" of the turbulent flux of political process, and Shelley's appropriation of this in *Queen Mab*. The *Encyclopédie* itself is a "citadel, stoutly fortified by the teaching of the wise," from whose exalted perspective the mass of "choses particulières" is revealed in its underlying, taxonomic coherence—the coherence of a rational materialism that proclaims the essential therapeutic conformity of mind and world. We recall d'Alembert's variation on the *altitudo* of the *suave mari magno*: "[T]he universe, to someone who could embrace it from a single point of view, would be so to speak only a single fact and one great truth" (qtd. in Darnton, 204). Lucretius tells us, in a development of the image of the citadel that has profound resonances in the eighteenth century: "All life is a struggle in the dark. . . . This dread and darkness of the mind cannot be dispelled by the sunbeams, the shining shafts of day,

---

tion. The infinite escapes, world by world, from totalizing causes; history escapes, place by place, from a global vision or force. Space is a distribution of gardens. Atomism" (my translation).

but only by an understanding of the outward form and inner workings of nature" (61, 2.54, 2.59–61). For the Enlightenment, the step from the clear apprehension of the natural world as law-bound matter to a deist—and providentialist—sublimation of god-in-nature was as short as the distance between the two sides of Spinoza's *deus sive natura*.

The idea of the Epicurean "garden" as a retreat from the world's turbulent *negotium* was picked up by two Enlightenment philosophers who had a great deal of direct and indirect influence upon Shelley: Rousseau and Voltaire. Voltaire was one of the eighteenth century's great admirers of Lucretius. Although he ostensibly rejected the doctrine of the *clinamen* and accepted the absolute conservation of information through the pathways of cause and effect, in practice he took the lessons of Epicurean ethics to heart. *Candide* pits Pangloss's dogmatic Leibnizian belief in the "nécessité absolue" (190) of all phenomena against a distinctly entropic world in which very Lucretian disasters (earthquakes, plagues, shipwreck, and war) fall unpredictably, and catastrophically, into Candide's life, making it anything but an orderly development from first principles. Although it is possible to read Candide's wildly improbable adventures as a demonstration of chaotic creativity—without the entropic negation of Candide's early station in life, after all, he would never be able to marry Cunégonde or visit Eldorado—the moral Voltaire offers us is more purely Epicurean; "il faut cultiver notre jardin" (259). The retreat to the garden—which Voltaire himself practiced at *Les Délices*—is a renunciation of a world that refuses to make any coherent sense. A fortiori it is a renunciation of politics; the Turkish "bon vieillard" who teaches the heroes to cultivate their gardens announces that "je ne m'informe jamais de ce qu'on fait à Constantinople; je me contente d'y envoyer vendre les fruits du jardin que je cultive" (258).[26]

Rousseau's plunge into the "thickest billows of that living storm" in the "Triumph" is a reference to a persistent strain of imagery in Rousseau's writing that describes the complex interactions of modern urban existence as an obliterating torrent. Shelley would have been aware that Rousseau's "imagery of *torrent* and *tourbillon*" (Duffy, 115–16) is derived from the Lucretian imagery of *turba* and *turbo* (Serres, *La naissance,* 37ff.). Rousseau drew heavily on *De rerum natura* in his writings (Fusil, "Lucrèce et les littérateurs," 169–70), and its traces can be found everywhere in those works that most impressed Shelley.

---

26. "I never bother myself about what happens in Constantinople. I send my garden stuff to be sold there, and that's enough for me" (*Candide,* 142).

Although there was much that separated Voltaire and Rousseau, the Epicurean retreat from the confused *negotium* of the city to the security of the garden is a theme common to both. Paris in *La nouvelle Héloise,* for example, is described as a "chaos" (207, 222; as it is in *Candide* also [228]), a "torrent" (221), a "désert" (207), in which there reigns a kind of moral atomism: "[L]es intérêts particuliers sont toujours opposés entre eux, c'est un choc perpétuel de brigues et de cabales, *un flux et reflux* de préjugés, d'opinions contraires . . . le bon, le mauvais, le beau, le laid, la vérité, la vertu, n'ont qu'une existence locale et circonscrite" (210).[27] Like the air, "whose whole mass undergoes innumerable transformations hour by hour" (179, 5.273-74), in the turbulent flux of Parisian society "tout change à chaque instant."[28] This "mobilité des objets" results in a constant entropic decay: "ils s'effacent mutuellement avec rapidité" (*Julie,* 222).[29] The most frightening result of this entropic tendency is to erase the boundaries of personal identity: "Je vois ainsi défigurer ce divin modèle que je porte au dedans de moi, et qui servait à la fois d'objet à mes désirs et de règle à mes actions; je flotte de caprice en caprice . . . je ne puis être sûr un seul jour de ce que j'aimerai le lendemain."[30] Rousseau recognizes that this entropic generation of information demands a radical empiricism that, to him, is the unfortunate result of the impossibility of achieving the reflective heights of the citadel of reason: "On ne peut pas non plus voir et méditer alternativement, parce que le spectacle exige une continuité d'attention qui interrompt la réflexion" (233).[31] He is like the scientific observer of a chaotic system who "cannot leave the room."

But if the chaotic inferno of Paris is one pole of the moral universe of Rousseau's *Julie,* the other pole is the bucolic, rational utopia of Wolmar and Julie's Clarens; and the heart of that utopia is its literal paradise, Julie's "Elysée." Inside the walls of that garden, where nature has been *revue et corrigée* by human reason and even the windings of the streams are products of human art (456-57), "la paix règne." Here Saint-

27. "Individual interests are always opposed to each other, it is a perpetual collision of plots and cabals, an ebb and flow of prejudices, of contrary opinions . . . the good, the bad, the beautiful, the ugly, the truth, virtue, have only a local and circumscribed existence" (my translation).

28. "everything changes at each moment" (my translation).

29. "they mutually destroy each other with rapidity" (my translation).

30. "Thus I see the divine image that I carry within myself, and that served at once as the object of my desires and as a curb to my actions, disfigured; I float from caprice to caprice . . . I cannot be sure for a single day of what I will crave for tomorrow" (my translation).

31. "One cannot observe and meditate alternatively either, because the scene demands a continuity of attention that interrupts reflection" (my translation).

Preux spends "deux heures auxquelles je ne préfère aucun temps de ma vie"; everything in this "quiet citadel," this refuge from the turmoil of the exterior world to which only the select few—family and the closest of friends—are admitted, "portât dans [s]on âme un calme préférable au trouble des passions les plus séduisantes."[32] Like the stream tamed by art, Saint-Preux finds the simple harmony of the spot capable of eliminating his own mind's tendency to error, a kind of anti-*clinamen* that "rectifiât en [lui] les écarts de l'imagination" (470).[33]

The garden returns him to a self-mastery, an "autarcique" autonomy, in marked contrast to his Parisian dissolution. In Paris, the "ivresse où cette vie agitée et tumultueuse plonge ceux qui la mènent" takes him "au point d'en oublier quelques instants ce que je suis et à qui je suis" (233).[34] "[F]lott[ant] de caprice en caprice" he loses self-control to the extent that—being tricked into literal "ivresse" by a group of equally dissolute soldiers—he sleeps with a prostitute (275–76). In the "île déserte" (469) of the Elysée, on the other hand, he finds his atomistic insularity reinforced to the point that he is finally able fully to master his passion for Julie and accept the fact of their separation: "Je me disais: 'La paix règne au fond de son coeur comme dans l'asile qu'elle a nommé'" (470).[35]

The same pattern is found in the *Rêveries,* where the turbulent *monde* is opposed to the peaceful contemplativeness of the botanical pursuits of the autarchic "promeneur solitaire" of the title. Withdrawal from the world lends a perspective from which the "chaos of elementary principles" that demands and defeats our constant attention is revealed as a unity of sorts. Severance from the world allows one's ego simultaneously to expand indefinitely in identification with it in the state of reverie. Serres may be influenced by Rousseau's "ravissemens inexprimables . . . à m'identifier avec la nature entiére" (qtd. in Duffy, 109) when he talks of Lucretian *ataraxia* as that "absence de tourbillons" when "[l]'âme du sage est étendue à l'univers global. Le sage est l'univers" (*La naissance,* 162).[36]

32. "brought into his soul a calm preferable to the agitation caused by even the most seductive passions" (my translation).

33. "rectified in [him] the errors of the imagination" (my translation).

34. "giddiness into which that agitated and tumultuous life plunges those who lead it [takes him] to the point of forgetting for several moments what I was, and whose I was" (my translation).

35. "I said to myself: 'Peace reigns at the bottom of her heart as it does in the refuge she has named'" (my translation).

36. "The soul of the wise man is extended to the global universe. The wise man is the universe" ("Lucretius: Science and Religion," 121).

Given its currency in the Enlightenment sources most important to him, it is not surprising that we find this complex of ideas in Shelley's poetry. *Queen Mab* does not only refer in passing to Holbach's Enlightenment appropriation of the *suave mari magno;* it is premised upon a similar appropriation. Ianthe's spiritual journey up and out of the world is so much gain in perspective; from the distance of Mab's—and reason's—quiet citadel "Eternal Nature's law" (II, 76) is clearly legible. The force of Mab's political message lies in the fact that she inhabits the ideal position of the classical *epistēmē,* as so defined by Bacon, Holbach, Laplace, and Godwin; she has risen above the need for inductive reasoning because the universe lies "stretched" out (II, 70) in tabular form before her, its laws manifest as d'Alembert's "single fact and one great truth." There is nothing more characteristic of the Enlightenment retreat to the Lucretian citadel than Mab's constant injunctions to the Spirit to "Behold!" (e.g., II, 109, 111, 112, 134; III, 22, 57; IV, 229). Political abuses are abstracted from the confused flux of process to become self-evident facts, directly revealed to the Spirit's eye in their distinctive character, so that she immediately understands their role in the universal order of necessity:

> The Fairy pointed to the earth.
> The Spirit's intellectual eye
> Its kindred beings recognized.
> The thronging thousands, to a passing view,
>   Seemed like an anthill's citizens.
>   How wonderful! that even
> The passions, prejudices, interests,
> That sway the meanest being, the weak touch
>   That moves the finest nerve,
>   And in one human brain
> Causes the faintest thought, becomes a link
>   In the great chain of nature.
>
> (II, 97–108)

Queen Mab is an early poem, but the pattern persists even in the later poetry. In a world of flux and turbulent decay, Shelley maintains a longing for a quiet citadel beyond the reach of the storm. This drive is the link between the Enlightenment mathesis and the Idealist *esprit de système.* In Shelley's writing, atomistic fragmentation often prompts an antithetical assertion of desire for the exalted perspective from which to observe that "The One remains" even if "the many change and pass"

(*Adonais*, 460). That confident statement comes from *Adonais*, although his own "spirit's bark" is there committed to the tempest, and driven "darkly, fearfully, afar" (492). Death "tramples" life's "dome of many coloured glass" to "fragments" (462, 464), but rather than leave us with a residue of inert sediment, this atomistic decay merely reveals the "white radiance of Eternity" (463) in all its glory; at the end of the poem the bark aspires, at least, to cross the void between the tempestuous present world and that radiance (487-95). Similarly, while the "storm of time" piles ruin on ruin in *Hellas,* some higher force appears to be at work to counteract its effects:

> If Greece must be
> A wreck, yet shall its fragments reassemble
> And build themselves again impregnably
>   In a diviner clime
> To Amphionic music on some cape sublime,
> Which frowns above the idle foam of Time.
>
> (*Hellas,* 1002-7)

Here, the reassembly of fragments seems less a project for Victor Frankenstein than a bodily resurrection that translates the historical city-state into a "quiet citadel" beyond the reach of the storm.

The most characteristic manifestation of Shelley's desire to reach the tranquil realm of the "Star above the Storm" (*Epipsychidion,* 28) is a Rousseauist one. Throughout Shelley's life and writing he repeatedly returns to the idea of a small community of the elect, like the community of the Assassins in the isolated valley of Bethzatanai. Like Julie and Wolmar's Clarens, this community is to be a calm and rational "île déserte" from which to observe the "vain search" of those lost on the turbulent sea of human action. The Lucretian affinities of the idea are readily apparent in this version from the dedication to *The Revolt of Islam:*

> —thou and I,
> Sweet friend! can look from our tranquillity
> Like lamps into the world's tempestuous night,—
> Two tranquil stars, while clouds are passing by
> Which wrap them from the foundering seaman's sight,
> That burn from year to year with unextinguished light.
>
> (xiv, 4-9)

"Tranquillity"—the literal meaning of *ataraxia*—is also the goal in *Epipsychidion,* where the island "Beautiful as a wreck of Paradise" (423) to which the poet hopes to escape with Emily "is an isle 'twixt Heaven, Air, Earth, and Sea, / Cradled, and hung in clear tranquillity" (457-58), permanently exempt from storms (465-56), which thereby avoids a very Lucretian triad of woes: "Pestilence, War and Earthquake" (462).

Star, valley, island, paradise: all are symbols of separation and retreat—atomist autarchies from whose tranquil vantage point we grasp the eternal behind the transient. Much of Shelley's supposed "idealism" takes the form of this opposition of storm and citadel; the question is whether an idealist reading is the most compelling way to understand the significance of this persistent motif. It would only be partly to the point to argue that its Lucretian affinities suggest that Shelley's critics have confused idealist ego expansion with an *ataraxia* that is actually about withdrawal from the world; that "confusion," if it is one, was well established before Shelley wrote, and is still current in Serres's reading of Lucretius. What we must ask ourselves is how Shelley understood the relationship of the citadel to the storm.

II

In *Prometheus Unbound,* Prometheus projects a postrevolutionary retreat with Asia to

> a Cave
> All overgrown with trailing odorous plants
>
> . . . .
>
> Where we will sit and talk of time and change
> As the world ebbs and flows, ourselves unchanged.
>
> (III, iii, 10-11, 23-24)

This "cave" is another version of the atomistic, idyllic refuge from the world of "time and change," one that apparently demands to be read in relation to some version of Hogle's transferential *Aufhebung,* especially if we take the play in its original three-act version. The negation of the principle of negativity as represented by Jupiter allows Prometheus and his small community of the revolutionary elect to transcend the finite and mutable world and grasp the eternal, superordinate totality it constitutes. Prometheus's cave, in such a reading, would represent what Hogle calls the "transferential One": the world changes ("What can hide man from mutability?" [III, iii, 25]), but change itself is eternity's secret truth.

Shelley takes care to make Prometheus and Asia's cave an antitype of Lucretian images of entropic change. Earth's description of the cave includes a number of these—the maenads, an ancient temple beside a lake, "torrent streams," and waves—but all in negative form, like the negatives at the end of the Spirit of the Hour's description of the post-revolutionary world that follows shortly after. The cave lies "beyond the peak / Of Bacchic Nysa, Maenad-haunted mountain" (III, iii, 153–54), and beyond "torrent streams" (156) of the Indus. We realize that this "beyond" implies a transcendence of the maenadic world of irrational *turba* when we find the cave:

> Beside [a] windless and chrystalline pool
> Where ever lies, on unerasing waves,
> The image of a temple, built above,
> Distinct with column, arch, and architrave
> And a palm-like capital, and overwrought,
> And populous most with living imagery—
> Praxitelean shapes, whose marble smiles
> Fill the hushed air with everlasting love.
> It is deserted now, but once it bore
> Thy name, Prometheus.
>
> (III, iii, 159–68)

One needs to be familiar with Shelley's almost automatic association of antique structures and water with ruin and erasure to feel the full force of this remarkable passage. "Unerasing," a neologism occurring nowhere else in Shelley's poetry (or elsewhere, to my knowledge), would draw attention to itself even if it were not coupled oxymoronically with "waves." As it is, the explicit exclusion of either of Shelley's almost ubiquitous "streams" ("windless" [159]) indicates that this cave represents an absolute transcendence of flux—an indication confirmed by what might appear a curiously pedantic description of the temple and its history (169ff.) if we were not aware what a *lusus naturae* an unruined abandoned temple with an intact and fully known history is in Shelley's imaginative world. The enumeration of "distinct" (and "everlasting") parts is in implicit opposition to a world where no part retains its integrity, where all distinctions are liable to transgression, and where "column, arch, and architrave" are liable to become indistinguishable ruins quivering within the wave's intenser day.

The postrevolutionary world that is imagined here is one that does not negate change, but, imaginatively at least, transcends it. The Spirit of the Hour tells us that "man" has not escaped "chance, and death, and mutability" but is "ruling them like slaves" (III, iv, 201, 200). If "ruling chance" is not simply self-contradictory, it presumably means that the postrevolutionary imagination achieves a "wise acceptance" of the flux it unavoidably inhabits.

The problem with this reading is that Shelley was not content with ending the play at act III. Absolute Knowing, or absolute *ataraxia,* should be the "far goal of time," the telos of the revolutionary dialectic. The fourth act of *Prometheus Unbound* has always seemed a critical embarrassment because it is so obviously "tacked onto" what appears a fully realized work of art. Even its defenders accept its superfluity. For a recent example, see Stuart Curran (*Poetic Form,* 202), who reads it as a gratuitous, if pleasing, "celebration" of what has passed before. It is, however, its very "superfluity" that lends it its power. In the fourth act, Shelley abandons and undercuts the rhetoric of revolutionary consummation by returning political action to the world of time and change. The mere existence of a fourth act after the apparently complete resolution offered by the third calls into question the possibility of aesthetic or political finality in a world where there is always an "and then."

More specifically, the fourth act returns us dramatically from the citadel, or the garden, to the storm; everywhere, the flux that had been carefully negated at the end of the third act has burst into life again:

> Bright clouds float in Heaven,
> Dew-stars gleam on Earth,
> Waves assemble on Ocean,
> They are gathered and driven
> By the Storm of delight, by the panic of glee!
> They shake with emotion—
> They dance in their mirth.
>
> (IV, 40–46)

The "Spirits of the human mind" (81) paint a picture of the postrevolutionary mind radically different from that offered by the Promethean temple and its eternal reflection in "unerasing waves"; they have not been freed *from* the meteorological flux of the sixth book of *De rerum natura,* but freed to delight in its "mystic measure" (77) to the full:

> We join the throng
> Of the dance and the song
> By the whirlwind of gladness borne along.
>
> (83–85)

Wearing "sandals of lightning" (90), their minds "an Ocean / Of clear emotion . . . [in] mighty motion" (96–98), they accept the givenness to temporality these meteors symbolize, not in the spirit of stoic resignation suggested by Prometheus's "What can hide man from mutability?" (III, iii, 25), but as a Bacchic frolic with the Hours with whom they "Weave [a] dance on the floor of the breeze" (IV, 69).

This maenadic dance continues throughout the act, with different participants weaving in and out. The eternal calm of Prometheus's paradisal retirement home is recast here as stagnation, the inert sediment of maximum entropy, which must be constantly whirled into motion by meteoric energy. That stagnation is identified as the worst effect of Jupiter's rule; the Earth rails at the "Sceptred curse" (337) who attempted to "batter" and "blend" "All I bring forth, to one void mass" (343) "stamped by thy strong hate into a lifeless mire" (349). By contrast, the spirit of the new postrevolutionary consciousness is best expressed in Earth's rapturous exclamations:

> The joy, the triumph, the delight, the madness,
> The boundless, overflowing bursting gladness,
> The vapourous exultation, not to be confined!
>   Ha! ha! the animation of delight
>   Which wraps me, like an atmosphere of light,
> And bears me as a cloud is borne by its own wind!
>
> (319–24)

"Boundless, overflowing bursting . . . vapourous exultation" refers not only to the "cloven fire-crags, sound-exulting fountains [that] / Laugh with a vast and inextinguishable laughter" (332–33), to which Earth refers shortly afterward, but to the whole panoply of "uncontrollable" meteoric effects. The force behind this joy and madness is "love," or revolutionary *erōs*—an infinitely transgressive force that Lucretius describes as "the guiding power of the universe," without which "nothing emerges into the shining sunlit world to grow in joy and loveliness" (27, 1.21, 1,22–23). Revolutionary *erōs* creates connections that breach the walls of the autarchic garden and the Promethean cave, bringing life to Jupiter's "lifeless mire" and "void annihilation":

>   from beneath, around, within, above,
>   Filling thy void annihilation, Love
> Bursts in like light on caves cloven by the thunderball.
>
> (353–55)

This is the significance of the erotic duet of Earth and Moon. The proverbially chaste moon's planetary isolation is a symbol of atomistic autarchy; for all that we sublunary creatures are under its changeable sway, the moon itself has traditionally been held to be the boundary marker that separates us from the eternal order of the heavens. It is, then, an image for the citadel of the *suave mari magno,* tranquil above the storm (*Epipsychidion,* 315–18). Revolutionary *erōs* breaks down this isolation by meteoric transgression:

> It interpenetrates my granite mass,
> . . . .
> It wakes a life in the forgotten dead,
> . . . .
> And like a storm, bursting its cloudy prison
> With thunder and with whirlwind, has arisen
> Out of the lampless caves of unimagined being,
> With earthquake shock and swiftness making shiver
> Thought's stagnant chaos . . .
>
> (370, 374, 376–80)

Once the light of "imagination" is let into the Promethean cave, the flux that had been so assiduously frozen must start to move again. The Moon's orbit around the earth becomes not a simple mechanical product of a clockwork universe, but the dance of "a most enamoured maiden" (467) who "Like a Maenad" (473) "must hurry, whirl and follow" (477) her brother-lover. The Moon sings:

> The snow upon my lifeless mountains
> Is loosened into living fountains,
> My solid Oceans flow and sing and shine.
>
> (356–58)

This suggests that it is quite incorrect to read the closely following description of "Man's" "one harmonious soul of many a soul . . . / Where all things flow to all, as rivers to the sea" (400, 402) as an image of the Platonic "One Mind"; that "flow" is a transgressive and entropic one, and such "harmony" as it produces is not the stagnant and lifeless mire of an absolutely transparent self-consciousness, but rather like the "unquiet Republic of the maze / Of Planets, struggling fierce towards Heaven's free wilderness" (398–99).

The Earth's "joy" and "madness" are produced by the unleashing of creative powers that Jupiter's "stagnant" reign had kept repressed. This was also part of the projected postrevolutionary state at the end of act III (iii, 56), but there is a crucial difference that speaks volumes about how we are to understand the relationship of citadel to storm. In act III, creativity is unleashed by the revolution, but under the auspices of Prometheus's controlling gaze:

> And lovely apparitions
> .   .   .   .
> Shall visit us, the progeny immortal
> Of Painting, Sculpture and rapt Poesy
> And arts, though unimagined, yet to be.
> The wandering voices and the shadows these
> Of all that man becomes . . .
>
> (III, iii, 49, 54–58)

Mutable humanity is free to abandon itself to a transferential flux, apparently in defiance of memory and order, because "all that man becomes," within this Promethean epoch, is guaranteed a *post facto* unity. Entropy is sublimated here and becomes, for the mutable individual, a misrecognized form of Promethean absolute memory. In act IV, however, this heirarchized dualism is overthrown. No "star above the storm" can be imagined in a world where the transgressive force of love refuses to allow any atomistic autarchy; when "all things flow to all," the Promethean pretension to transcendence can only be read as a withdrawal from process that has no consequences other than simple disappearance. Prometheus's absence from act IV underlines that point; he is "lost information" from the perspective of the action there.[37]

The most striking difference between the two acts lies in the readmittance of the entropic destruction of information in act IV, even with regard to the political gains of the revolution. Demogorgon's closing speech affirms that "Eternity, / Mother of many acts and hours," might "free / The serpent that would clasp her with his length" (565–67). He

---

37. Wasserman's idealist reading, which prefigures Hogle's, accounts for this disappearance rather differently: "[W]hen Prometheus enters his cave with Asia the possibility of narrative has ended because he has passed beyond the limits of imagery and language. Only now he is truly the One Mind, and therefore he must disappear from the play" (*Shelley*, 360). Wasserman does not explain how we, *ici-bas*, are supposed to know this is what has become of Prometheus. Absolute identification with the universe, Shelley suggests, simply renders one meaningless. Kelvin Everest, on the other hand, would read this as an aspect of the artistic failure of the poem, its "unsatisfying untidiness" ("Mechanism," 244). Everest's reading has the great merit of taking the poem's disjunctions seriously, and not simply trying to explain them away. We simply disagree about how aesthetically "unsatisfying" such "untidiness" is.

must remind us of the ways to battle Jupiter, whose return, in the inherently unpredictable flux of historical process, remains an open possibility.

This speech comes as no surprise after Panthea's description of what is revealed by the Spirit of the Earth's unconscious x-ray probing of the earth's hidden secrets. The "whirling" (275) beams that emanate from the star upon the Spirit's forehead (270) are "sunlike lightenings"[38] (276) whose description awakens some interesting Lucretian echoes; they are "perpendicular now, and now transverse" (277), a reference to the lightning that appears to provide a model to Lucretius for the atomic *clinamen:* "transversosque volare per imbris fulmina cernis: nunc hinc, nunc illinc" (2.213–14; "Note again how the lightning flies through the rainstorms aslant . . . now this way, now that" [*Nature,* 66]). They "pierce and pass" through the "dark soil" (278) just as Lucretius describes the lightning passing "[t]hrough many substances . . . because its fluid fire slips through the gaps" (228, 6.348–49). The world they reveal is one thoroughly subjected to the entropic flux the lightning typifies:

> the beams flash on
> And make appear the melancholy ruins
> Of cancelled cycles; anchors, beaks of ships,
> Planks turned to marble, quivers, helms and spears
> And gorgon-headed targes, and the wheels
> Of scythed chariots, and the emblazonry
> Of trophies, standards and armorial beasts
> Round which Death laughed, sepulchred emblems
> Of dead Destruction, ruin within ruin!
> The wrecks beside of many a city vast,
> Whose population which the Earth grew over
> Was mortal but not human; see, they lie,
> Their monstrous works and uncouth skeletons,
> Their statues, homes, and fanes; prodigious shapes
> Huddled in gray annihilation, split,
> Jammed in the hard black deep; and over these
> The anatomies of unknown winged things,
> And fishes which were isles of living scale,
> And serpents, bony chains, twisted around
> The iron crags, or within heaps of dust

---

38. Shelley made no differentiation in spelling "lightening" and "lightning," although his editors usually do. The *editio princeps* has this as "lightnings."

To which the tortuous strength of their last pangs
Had crushed the iron crags;—and over these
The jagged alligator and the might
Of earth-convulsing behemoth, which once
Were monarch beasts, and on the slimy shores
And weed-overgrown continents of Earth,
Increased and multiplied like summer worms
On an abandoned corpse, till the blue globe
Wrapped Deluge round it like a cloak, and they
Yelled, gaspt and were abolished; or some God
Whose throne was in a Comet, passed, and cried—
"Be not!"—and like my words they were no more.[39]

(287–318)

This astonishing evolutionary torrent of annihilated, abandoned, wrecked, and ruined forms—atomistic *disjecta membra,* flotsam and jetsam of the "storm of time"—is a key to understanding the entire act. It is based in part on Cuvier's "catastrophe theory," which attempted to account for the rapidly accumulating and widely debated fossil evidence of extinct and unrecognizable animal species by positing an alternating "series of natural creations and destructions."[40] It does away with the simplistic mythic history proposed in acts II and III (see Asia's speech to Demogorgon, II, iv, 32ff.), which makes revolution a return to a Saturnian golden age, via a *felix culpa* that bought us knowledge at the cost of a period of Jupiterean misrule. The "mortal, but not human" past revealed by the Spirit's probing beams takes us out of this static, mythic chronotope and throws us into a torrent of entropic change, with the clear implication that we shall be, for some future age, as inexplicable a remnant of the past as these wrecks and fossils are to us. In such a context, revolution loses its epochal status and becomes a moment in *evolution:* the dramatic and sudden expression of a constant

39. Goldstein quotes this passage but sees it as a mere elaboration of the triumph over death and ruin announced at the end of act III. He sees the exposure of the layers and layers of previous ruined civilizations in Volneyan optimistic terms; these are errors that are being cast out, not portents for the future (206–7). Nowhere in act IV, however, does Shelley suggest that this constantly renewed cycle of creation and ruination has been overthrown.

40. Cameron, *Golden Years,* 553, 656–57 n. 47. See also Jeffrey. Grabo shows Shelley's debt to James Parkinson's *Organic Remains of a Former World* for an account of this theory (*Newton,* 179). Cameron blandly discounts the importance of Cuvier's theory for its "incorrectness" (*Golden Years,* 657 n. 47), although it adumbrates recent developments in evolutionary theory.

tendency to change. Like the Lucretian elements to whom the "doorway of death" is always open, we must now acknowledge ourselves, and our political actions, to be "children of time."

But the object of this fourth act is not simply to invert the solution of act III to the problem of reconciling the "two thoughts," to reduce memory to "dead Destruction" as act III had reduced flux to an "unerasing wave." This is Shelley's first sustained attempt to think the "two thoughts" simultaneously, without subordinating one to the other. As such, it represents the fruits of a breakthrough in Shelley's political and poetic thought around 1819–20, when Shelley first clearly perceived the negentropic benefit from entropic decay. This is perhaps most bluntly evident in the apparent non sequitur of the Earth's speech immediately following Panthea's "melancholy" catalogue of ruins above. As her voice falls under the absolute negation of the entropic comet-God's "Be not!" and is erased like the "cancelled cycles" of the past, the Earth's voice emerges, commencing the interplanetary epithalamium with the Moon with his rapturous effusion: "The joy, the triumph, the delight, the madness, / The boundless, overflowing bursting gladness." Shelley has realized that the negation of entropic flux at the end of act III was also a negation of revolutionary joy and creativity.

The love between Earth and Moon generates a flood of meteorological effects because, like the transgressive force of love itself, the "boundless, overflowing" creativity of the meteor is premised upon destruction; the "vast and inextinguishable laughter" of the volcano receives its echo from the "clouds and billows" (337) of "The Oceans and the Deserts and the Abysses / And the deep air's unmeasured wildernesses" (335–36), those self-erasing media of atomistic flux to which the "doorway of death" stands perennially open.

Shelley expressed particular admiration for Lucretius's discussion of love in book 4 of *De rerum natura* (*Letters*, 1:545). There, love is described as a "wound" inflicted on the lover by the beloved: "For the wounded normally fall in the direction of their wound; the blood spurts out towards the source of the blow; and the enemy who delivered it, if he is fighting at close quarters, is bespattered by the crimson stream. So, when a man is pierced by the shafts of Venus . . . he strives towards the source of the wound and craves to be united with it. . . . His speechless yearning is a presentiment of bliss" (162–63, 4.1049–52, 4.1055–57). Love must destroy in order to be able to create. This was one of the most important lessons of the tragic erotic conundrum of *Alastor* and *Epipsychidion:* that for love to lead beyond the "autarchic," and ultimately sterile, world of the self, the self must be willing to endure an irreversible "wound" to its atomistic integrity. As Nussbaum argues, the value of *erōs* and *philia* is in part dependent upon their vulnerability to *tuchē*.

It is this logic that accounts for the febrile and exultant tone of the Earth and the Moon's love song. Their explosive rapture is premised upon the "mortality" of their situation. The Earth describes himself to Demogorgon as "a drop of dew that dies" (523), while the Moon says she "is a leaf shaken by thee!" (528)—images that are common coin in Shelley's poetry for a susceptibility to entropic decay (see, in particular, the drop of dew on the "eyed flower" in the "Ode to Heaven," and the autumnal leaves of the "Ode to the West Wind," poems that were published with *Prometheus Unbound* in 1820). To bridge the distance between them requires a willingness to unleash a transgressive flux of potentially destructive forces from which they cannot guarantee their exemption:

> O gentle Moon, thy chrystal accents pierce
> The caverns of my Pride's deep Universe,
> Charming the tyger Joy, whose tramplings fierce
> Made wounds, which need thy balm.
>
> (499–502)

This allusion to the Lucretian passage cited above goes one better than Lucretius by making the "balm" for the erotic "wound" itself a transgressive "piercing" of the beloved's boundaries.

To be "pierced" by desire is to breach the walls of one's autarchic paradise; it is to "overleap the bounds," in those words of Milton's that Shelley reprises in *Alastor* to describe the Poet's sudden vulnerability to the illusory "veiled maid" (207: the reference is to *Paradise Lost,* IV, "Argument," 181–83; see Heppner, 101). As the Miltonic echo suggests, this is to risk an entropic "fall" to which the securely walled Epicurean "garden" could be considered invulnerable. The dominant tradition in Western thought has always placed a high premium on the integrity of personal boundaries—one need only think of the literal meanings or etymological derivations of words such as "corruption," "adultery," "contamination," "dissolution." The cracked vase is a traditional symbol of the fallen woman: no longer "intact," and therefore impure. Not only impure, but incorrigibly so; the broken vessel is a symbol of inexorable entropy.

Lucretius, however, celebrates the cracked and leaking vessel as an image for the kind of "dissipative system" that generates all life—local negentropy stolen from a globally entropic process. He rewrites Plato's fastidious rejection of the desiring life as endlessly filling a "leaky vessel" by accepting and revaluing its implications. All life, even the Platonic philosopher's, depends upon an entropic influx of food, thought, *erōs,* and *philia* to be sustained. To ward off risk by keeping this influx to a minimum, to maintain boundaries against it wherever possible, is to deny one's inevitable temporality, one's givenness to a world in evolution. Ultimately, it is to refuse all joy, because every joy is an opening to the flux of life and death, an exposure to *tuchē.*

Such "boundless," or boundary-defying, fluxes make it impossible to establish securely the rigorously dualistic approach to the flux of the world suggested in the *suave mari magno.* Shelley provides a "corrected" version as an image of the Moon's love for the Earth immediately before the "wound" image above:

> O gentle Moon, the voice of thy delight
> Falls on me like thy clear and tender light
> Soothing the seaman, borne the summer night
>   Through isles for ever calm.

(495–98)

The sage's citadel is no longer "wrap[ped] . . . from the foundering seaman's sight," as in the *Revolt of Islam;* rather than an autarchic *ataraxia,* the ideal here is an active concern that bridges the distance between observer and observed and has, as the "wound" image that follows makes clear, an entropic impact upon each party. The citadel is returned to the storm of change from which it sought exemption by the transgressive flux of revolutionary *erōs.*

At the same time, the "joy and madness" that this flux inspires are the product of successfully crossing a divide that is real enough and persistent enough to make that crossing a triumph. For the transgression of a boundary to give us joy, the boundary must have some solidity. The "nunc hinc, nunc illinc," of the meteor is only remarkable in a reasonably continuous stream of action, which these sheer events punctuate. Similarly, for the piercing "wounds" of love to give us joy, there must be some continuity of identity—meaning memory—in order for there to be an *experience* of joy or love. In a dualistic reading of the *suave mari magno,* it is from the eternal perspective of the citadel of the "transferential One" that we are able to appreciate the joyfulness of an unbounded, undifferentiated, and infinitely transgressive flux; but with such an option ruled out, it can only be in the "wounded" themselves that this continuity—which is perhaps best described as a continuous openness to discontinuous change—can exist.

This returns us to the creativity of the Lucretian *clinamen*. In order for the *clinamen*'s negation of information to be creative, we saw that it must itself have consequences that are preserved in a cycle of memory, even though that cycle is—and, if a *clinamen* has occurred within it, must be—vulnerable to further erasures and discontinuities that will send it turbulently off course. The *clinamen* stands on the threshold of the "doorway of death," allowing order to die into disorder, and new order to emerge from that disorder. It is implicit in the voice of the "happy Dead" (534), who answer Demogorgon's speculation, that their "nature is that Universe / Which once [they] saw and suffered" (536–37), with the claim that "as they / Whom we have left, we change and pass away" (538–39). Here, Shelley counters a view of death as an absolute narrative closure and a translation to another realm—in this case a transcendent identification with the "universe" that we recognize as the discarded version of the *suave mari magno*—with a reading of death as a continuation of a creative process of change that is not, in principle, different from the one we call life and growth.

More explicit is the "whirling" dance of the semichorus of the Hours, which entwines itself with "the enchantments of earth" (162):

> We encircle the Oceans and Mountains of Earth
> And the happy forms of its death and birth
> Change to the music of our sweet mirth.
>
> (172–74)

Death and birth, entropy and negentropy, are casually united here as twin aspects of the "happy" process of change on earth that the "circling" Hours keep constantly alive.

Wasserman suggests that the "Dance of the Hours is . . . a recognizable commonplace. . . . their circular dance represented the harmoniously periodic movement of time" (*Shelley*, 364). The cycle is the basic form in which we understand the continuity of memory in time. This is particularly true of organic continuities; the cycle of the seasons, the diurnal revolution of the earth, and the reproductive cycle are the models to which Burke appeals when he talks of "preserving the method of nature in the conduct of the state": "Our political system is placed in a just correspondence and symmetry with the order of the world, and with the mode of existence decreed to a permanent body composed of transitory parts; wherein, by the disposition of a stupendous wisdom, moulding together the great mysterious incorporation of the human race, the whole, at one time, is never old, or middle-aged, or young, but in a condition of unchangeable constancy, moves on through the varied tenour of perpetual decay, fall, renovation, and progression" (*Reflections,* 120). In Wasserman's view, the cyclic imagery of act IV conforms to Shelley's idealist resolution of the revolutionary dilemma. Like Burke, he argues that the circularity of time "is the emblem of the totality of time": "In the world of nature, which freely and passively admits the Power and its law of Necessity, time both passes and is preserved, for it is a perpetually repeated circle without beginning or end. . . . [E]ternity in that domain is the *moving* circle, the whole possible course of events perpetually renewing itself. . . . Life is a circle that ends where it begins, not a line that abandons one point for another"[41] (*Shelley,* 371).

But this is to miss Shelley's point, which is most clearly stated in Panthea's description of the "ruin within ruin" revealed by the Spirit of the Earth's probing beams as "the melancholy ruins / Of cancelled cycles" (288–89). The cyclic, or reproductive, impulse of past history is here acknowledged, but that impulse is understood to be deflected. History is not "perpetually repeated," nor does it generate "unchangeable constancy"; there is no absolute conservation of information, despite our "desire to be for ever as we are"; history is "cyclic," but irreversible. This is not a paradox: Shelley's alternatives are not *either* a therapeutic cycle of narrative completion *or* absolute linear disjunction in the "transferential" mode; rather, he aims to think the "deux temps" of cycle and disjunction simultaneously, placing amnesiac erasure within the context of a constantly renewed attempt at memory—or, in other words, evolution.

The contemporary scientific debates that attracted Shelley's attention confirmed Lucretius's intuitive grasp of the self-destructive tendency of organic cycles. Herschel's theory of the universe as "finite and evolving," moving from a catastrophic birth to a catastrophic death (Grabo, *Newton,* 84), Erasmus Darwin's evolutionary theory that in the "millions of ages before the commencement of the history of mankind . . . all the warm-blooded animals have arisen from one living filament . . . with the

41. Wasserman is writing specifically of the image of Eternity as "the circular serpent, tail in mouth," which he suggests Shelley is invoking at IV, 567–69, and II, iii, 95–97. In fact, neither of these images describe the Ouroboros; it is only by assuming the point he hopes to prove— that time is circular for Shelley—that the snake that "would clasp [eternity] with his length" can be made to be circular. Similarly, the "snake-like Doom" is described as "coiled," which implies being ready to strike, not "looped," impotently, into a circle.

chaos; and may again by explosions produce a new world; which in process of time may resemble the present one, and at length again undergo the same catastrophe!" (Grabo, *Newton,* 44). This catastrophic cosmic cycle of "Ruin and Renovation" (*Hellas,* 718) is related to Cuvier's Lucretian catastrophic theory of evolution; both might be glosses on the "self-destroying swiftness" of Shelley's spheres.

We must read the description of this sphere in conjunction with the passage on "cancelled cycles," for which it prepares the ground, if we are to understand its imagery. Throughout Panthea's description, we see the cyclic being diverted into the maenadic volute, the apparently continuous being described simultaneously as discontinuous; the sphere exists in, and expresses, the conjunction of the "two thoughts," or the "deux temps." It is a sphere—an image of absolute, autarchic containment—and yet it transgresses that perfect integrity. It is atomistic, composed of a "thousand spheres" with "a thousand motions" (247), but at the same time it is "Solid as chrystal" (239)—solid, "yet through all its mass / Flow, as through empty space, music and light" (239-40). As it "slowly, solemnly roll[s] on" (250), it kindles simultaneously "Intelligible words and music wild" (252), the voices of memory and maenadic inspiration yoked together. That slow and solemn "roll," the Spirit of the Earth's cyclic regeneration, is deceptive; inside the sphere everything "whirls" (236, 246, 253, 275 [twice]) "with the force of self-destroying swiftness" (249)—the cyclic becoming *turba* through "self-conflicting speed" (259).[46] The "mighty whirl" (253) that "Grinds the bright brook into an azure mist" (254) is an allusion to Lucretius's description, in the "meteorological" book 6, of the *"presteres,"* or waterspouts, which are produced by the "eddying whirlwind [*versabundus turbo*]" dropping down into the sea (230; see 6.438ff.). The "elemental subtlety, like

46. Compare Wordsworth's use of the word "self-destroying" in his description of London in *The Prelude,* VII, 770 (1850). Wordsworth's description of London is influenced by Rousseau's description of Paris in *Julie,* but the therapeutic idealist, "Living amid the same perpetual whirl / Of trivial objects" (725-26; "whirl" replaces the 1805 *Prelude*'s "flow"), regarding the "endless stream of men and moving things" (151), where "Pleasure whirls about incessantly" (70), relies upon his ability to see "the parts / As parts, but with a feeling of the whole" (735-36), to make emerge from the apparent flux an intimation of eternity:

> This did I feel, in London's vast domain.
> The Spirit of Nature was upon me there;
> The soul of Beauty and enduring Life
> Vouchsafed her inspiration, and diffused,
> Through meagre lines and colours, and the press
> Of self-destroying, transitory things,
> Composure, and ennobling Harmony.   (765-72)

light" (255) to which the brook is "ground," is also a nod to Lucretian atomic physics. But in contrast to this catastrophic meteor, which "drowns the sense" (261), we find cradled peacefully within the sphere, "Like to a child o'erwearied with sweet toil . . . / The Spirit of the Earth . . . laid asleep" (263, 265).

These apparent contradictions are summed up in the very first description of the sphere rushing in "with loud and whirlwind harmony" (237). The sphere unites the "harmony" of the attempt at cyclic continuity with the uncontrollable, contingent destructiveness of the meteor. Shelley's account of the apparition emphasizes the paradoxical nature of "whirlwind harmony" while at the same time making the idea conceivable. This prepares us for the revelations of the world's history that immediately follow. The "self-destroying swiftness" of the whirling dance of the spheres, the short step, via the *clinamen,* from cycle to volute, makes the peculiar combination of constant entropic ruin within a "progressive" history that is suggested by the "melancholy ruins / Of cancelled cycles" conceivable. We understand that it is possible to "cancel" a cycle without abandoning the cyclic impulse.

The summation of this attempt to link the "two thoughts" is the "God / Whose throne was in a Comet" (316–17), whose annihilating injunction "Be not!" stands as an emblem of the entropic "cancellation" of past cycles (and of Panthea's poetic voice). Here we have a direct association of negation and cycle in the form of the comet, which, like the whirlwind, is a cyclic, or circling, meteor. The comet's regular orbit ("répétition maniaque de ce qui a été dans ce qui est"), the proof and understanding of which was one of the triumphs of Newtonian science, is yoked here to a meteoric negativity to provide a symbol of the cyclic negation that drives the contradictory processes of history. The comet-God's "Be not!" is a meteoric *clinamen* that prevents the cycles of history from quite completing themselves, thereby sending historical "progress" turbulently eddying forward in the form of "cancelled cycles," or chaotic volutes, rather than being able to settle into the "perpetually repeated circle without beginning or end" that Wasserman's idealist reading of the poem claims to find.

Grabo points out that Shelley's immediate source for the image is probably Humphrey Davy's account of scientific attempts to explain the same evidence of catastrophic evolution that prompted Cuvier's catastrophe theory. Leibniz and Whiston, notes Davy, attributed the cataclysm—identified with the biblical Flood—to the agency of a comet. Although Grabo does not comment on it, it cannot have escaped Shelley's notice that Davy refers to the cataclysm as "this great revolution" (qtd. in Grabo, *Newton,* 176). Revolution, as both cycle and disjunction, is what is at stake in this passage. Such a combination of reiteration and error, the "desire to be for ever as we are," confronted with the inevitability of atomistic "ruin" and erasure, is the recipe for "chaotic creativity." Hence the apparent paradox of having a "God," whose sole action is negation, of a historical status quo or of Panthea's poetic voice. A meteoric *clinamen*-God—the impersonal force behind the "cycle" of creation and destruction in Cuvier's catastrophic theory of evolution— creates by negating, allowing for new, revolutionary events to take the place of the past's canceled cycles just as the Earth's song of joy, triumph, delight, and madness usurps the void left by Panthea's silence.

III

Shelley continues his interest in the chaotically creative "cycles" of history after completing *Prometheus.* One of his most sustained meditations on the theme is to be found in *Hellas.* Wasserman reads this too as an expression of the idealist Absolute. He finds in *Hellas* a close approximation of Hegel's philosophy of history: "*Hellas* assumes that man is defined by the persistent active presence in him of the universal Spirit and that Spirit can develop through man's mastery of time's cycle. . . . Shelley's . . . teleological philosophy of history has affinities with Hegel's in proposing a progressive, not a sporadic or even apocalyptic, self-realization of Spirit, whose essence is Freedom: the collective human soul approaches more nearly, cycle by cycle of the time to which it is bound, the Absolute from which it derives, until the difference between time and the atemporal is infinitesimal" (*Shelley,* 411). If Wasserman is correct, this would be a blow to the argument advanced here that Shelley's aim is to insist upon the difference between "time and the atemporal," seeing an inability to accept the evolutionary temporality of our lives as a positive evil.

It is difficult to discern a "mastery of time's cycle" in *Hellas,* on the part of either Mahmud or the Greeks. Nor is the reader left with a feeling of achieving such mastery through penetration to a self-conscious as "universal Spirit"; the final lines of *Hellas* ("Oh, cease! must hate and death return?" [1096; see 1096–101]) are an antiteleological rejection of the possibility of finding a comforting narrative closure in historical time ("The world is weary of the past, / O might it die or rest at last!" [1100–101]). Although Hassam, Mahmud's servant, refers to the "Cycles of generation and of ruin" (154) that Ahasuerus has survived, and Mahmud refers to the "old world['s] . . . cycles / Of desolation and of loveliness" (746-47), Wasserman is too hasty in assuming that these statements imply that time, considered as a totality, pursues a stable and predictable cyclic "plot."

The images of "Time," per se, that the poem offers suggest quite the opposite. It is not necessary to spell out the Lucretian origins of such entropic images as Mahmud's "torrent of descending time" (350), or the chorus's more elaborate version:

> Worlds on worlds are rolling ever
> From creation to decay,
> Like the bubbles on a river
> Sparkling, bursting, borne away.[47]

(197-200)

The familiar range of meteorological effects and atomistic, fluxile erasures feature in the chorus's account of the progress of Liberty (648-737), with the emphasis once again on their uncontrollable, punctual nature ("Ha king! wilt thou chain / The rack and the rain, / Wilt thou fetter the lightning and hurricane? / The storms are free" [671-74]).

᠁e to the flux of time is a "frost" that is equated with "Slavery" ᠁. Only Athens is not "swallowed . . . as the sand does foam" (688-᠁)) by the "rushing wind" (720), "ocean foaming" (721), and "thunder[ing] . . . earthquake" (722) that reduce all other cities and states to "Ashes, wrecks, oblivion" (687). A god named "Destiny" (712) presides over this process, but her name is ironic; the course she sets as "The world's eyeless charioteer" (711) is pointedly ateleological. Her "earthquake-footed steeds" deal out meteorological destruction to "faith" and "empire" (713) in her blind course, and, like the comet-God of *Prometheus Unbound,* the only "creation" she can bring about, conforming to the logic of the *clinamen,* is premised upon destruction; it is the "renovation" that "rolls behind" the flitting shadow of "Ruin" (716-18).

47. It might be objected that it is unfair to stop short of lines 201-6, which seem to imply a leap to the unchanging perspective of the *suave mari magno.* But Shelley is careful to stress in the notes to the poem that that part of the chorus's song is merely a pleasing poetic fiction, the problem of the soul's immortality being one for which the solution "in our present state . . . is unattainable by us." The close relationship between "creation" and "decay" is central to our theory of chaotic creativity. This could be read in Neoplatonic terms; specifically, Paracelsus's version of the Neoplatonic doctrine of creation through decay (Abrams, *Natural Supernaturalism,* 158-59). But Shelley has evoked the Neoplatonic framework in order to emphasize his differences from it. By placing the "cycles" of creation and decay *within* a turbulent and irreversible temporal continuum, he makes them incompatible with any redemptive eschatology.

Ruin, indeed, is the fundamental movement of the entropic storm of time; as the phantom of Mahomet the Second puts it to Mahmud, in a speech that recalls Panthea's "ruin within ruin" speech:

> wolfish Change, like winter howls to strip
> The foliage in which Fame, the eagle, built
> Her aiëry, while Dominion whelped below.
> The storm is in its branches, and the frost
> Is on its leaves, and the blank deep expects
> Oblivion on oblivion, spoil on spoil,
> Ruin on ruin.
>
> (872–78)

When Mahmud suggests that the Islamic empire is waning like the crescent moon that is its symbol, Hassan tries to comfort him by appealing to the therapeutic regularity of natural cycles: "Even as that moon / Renews itself—" (347–48). Mahmud does not let him finish the sentence, and interjects: "Shall we be not renewed!" (348). In the entropic storm of time, there seems little probability that any cycle will be able to turn perfectly back upon itself without error, divergence, and consequent negation.

Wasserman, however, argues that Mahmud's comment represents an ironic misrecognition of "the inexorable cycle of time" (388). This cycle, he suggests, is the basis upon which Shelley concludes from the present "desolation" a "coming and inevitable 'loveliness'" (389) that must ensure the eventual victory of the cause of Liberty. This, however, is explicitly denied by Shelley in his note to the final "prophetic" chorus: "The final chorus is indistinct and obscure, as the event of the living drama whose arrival it foretells. Prophecies of wars, and rumours of wars, etc., may safely be made by poet or prophet in any age, but to anticipate however darkly a period of regeneration and happiness is a more hazardous exercise of the faculty which bards possess or feign" (Hutchinson, 479). There is no "inexorable cycle"; war and rumor of war, destruction and ruin, are, in any age, more statistically probable than "a period of regeneration" or "loveliness."

Nonetheless, this begs the question: what is the meaning of the "Cycles of generation and of ruin" and "cycles / Of desolation and of loveliness" already referred to, or Ahasuerus's apparent assertion of cyclic repetition in history:

                                              The Past
          Now stands before thee like an Incarnation
          Of the To-come?

                                                              (852–54)

Why should the final chorus cast the "possible" coming of Liberty in the
future as a return to a golden age: "The world's great age begins anew"
(1060)? The answer lies in understanding the nuances of scale in these
different visions of temporal and historical process. The image of "The
world's eyeless charioteer" clarifies this. Time itself is not cyclic; the
unpredictable course of events is ruled over by "eyeless," aimless Destiny. The "cycles" of ruin and regeneration occur *within* time; that is,
the objective course of history reveals to us periods of destruction followed by periods of regeneration, each, according to the logic of the
clinamen, predicated upon the other. These are the "Ruin and Renovation" that "roll" behind Destiny's chariot. As in *Prometheus Unbound,*
IV, the cyclic, reproductive impulse of historical action generates an
irreversible temporal "torrent" within which turbulent cycles appear
and disappear, locally homeostatic but globally homeorhetic, themselves
subject to the laws of ruin and renovation that they embody:

                    Worlds on worlds are *rolling* ever
                       From creation to decay,
                    Like the bubbles on a river
                       Sparkling, bursting, borne away.

     The cycles of desolation and loveliness belong to "this low sphere, /
And all its narrow circles" (749–50); they are the "cancelled cycles" of
reproductive evolution, turbulent eddies in the wake of Destiny's blind
course, not a predetermined course for her to follow.
     Mahmud's vision of the "Past" as an incarnation of the "To-come," can
only be understood correctly if we understand its "scale"; Ahasuerus
refers only to the inevitability of the eventual collapse of empire, not to
the manner or the timing of that collapse. Shelley's notes are anxious to
make us understand this, "disclaiming all pretension, or even belief, in
supernatural agency" on Ahasuerus's behalf (Hutchinson, 479). Ahasuerus himself is uninterested in the details of earthly history and
whether its course is circular or linear; for him, "The future and the past
are idle shadows / Of thought's eternal flight—they have no being"
(783–84).
     Shelley's own views are somewhat different. Ahasuerus is often taken

to speak for Shelley, but his voluntarist relativism is quite distinct from Shelley's views. Moreover, there is a marked, if subtle, difference between Ahasuerus's approach and that expressed in the choruses, which are more likely to represent the "authorial" voice. The inspirational enthusiasm in the final chorus for that "possible and perhaps approaching" period when "the world's great age begins anew" is undermined by Shelley's notes, which insist that we read this as a product of poetic license. But even with this license, Shelley chafes against the cyclic regeneration he describes; the catastrophic creativity of the *clinamen* reasserts itself throughout the final chorus in the face of its supposedly harmonious and organic cycles ("earth doth like a snake renew / Her winter weeds outworn" [1062-63]). The "return" of the "golden years" is premised upon the wreck of the present: "Heaven smiles, and faiths and empires gleam / Like wrecks of a dissolving dream" (1064-65). The renewed Hellas is not the old one returned; it is "A brighter Hellas" (1066), which launches "A loftier Argo" (1072) and produces "Another Orpheus" (1074) and "A new Ulysses" (1076). Reiteration has led to innovation. The perfections of this new Hellas are premised not only on the erasure of the intervening history between the old Hellas and the present, but on the erasure of major components of that old Hellas itself:

> O, write no more the tale of Troy,
>   If earth Death's scroll must be!
> Nor mix with Laian rage the joy
>   Which dawns upon the free;
> Although a subtler Sphinx renew
> Riddles of death Thebes never knew.
>
>   (1078-83)

The apparent paradox in the last two lines of a "renewal" of riddles that "Thebes never knew" expresses the logic of chaotic creativity; nonlinear "renewal" leads to irreversible evolution. When Shelley tells us that "Another Athens shall arise" (1084), he means a different Athens, just as the "new Ulysses" and "Orpheus" will travel routes and sing songs unimaginable to their namesakes. This new Athens will not stand as the completion and closure of an absolute narrative cycle begun with the founding of Athens. The entropic work of the *clinamen* will ensure that it shall

>   to remoter time
> Bequeath, like sunset to the skies,

The splendour of its prime,
And leave, if nought so bright may live,
All earth can take or Heaven can give.

(1084–89)

The eddying torrent of history will continue, incorporating "all earth can take" from the wreck of the new Athens, into its irreversible current, just as the scattered fragments that the decay of the historical Athens left to the error-ridden cycles of history were incorporated into the complex patchwork of modern cultures.

CONCLUSION

I

We have now arrived at Shelley's poetic of ruin and regeneration from two opposite directions: first, from the "skeptical" and "entropic" one of atomistic fragmentation, decentering and disjunction; second, from the "idealist" and "negentropic" one of the therapeutic attempt to recuperate fragments into a totalizing mnemonic cycle. Each of these approaches is confounded in turn. Shelley has opened the prospect of a new understanding of the creative process—in both the poetic and political realms; one based upon a permanently unresolved interaction of memory and obliteration. Let me briefly sum up some of its implications.

To begin with, we should observe that it is nothing like Chernaik's, Hall's, or Hogle's solipsistic and amnesiac creativity—a willful projection into the void whose mnemonic content is purely elective.[48] As the post-Kantian/Wordsworthian genealogy of Shelley's poetry of ruin demonstrates, the constant attempt at completing the cycle of memory is essential to it.

During the Shelley-Byron summer of 1816, which produced both the "Hymn" and "Mont Blanc," Shelley, in Byron's words, "dosed" him repeatedly with Wordsworth—with a marked effect upon the third canto of *Childe Harold's Pilgrimage* (White, 1:451)—but, as Phillips notes,

---

48. Curran also argues that Shelley's philosophy is at base radically relativist, that "the mind creates the reality in which it exists" (*Annus Mirabilis,* 201–2). Paradoxically, Curran and Hogle—and, to a lesser extent, Chernaik—are all believers in Shelley's almost superhuman powers of mythic syncretism. Perhaps this is a case of extremes meeting; if one can be "anything," then one can also be "everything."

shortly after returning from his trip to Chamouni, he was immersed in *De rerum natura* (93; see White, 1:457). Both are equally important to the understanding of Shelley's new concept of poetic creation. Ruination in the form of the *clinamen* intervenes upon and prevents the completion of the Wordsworthian cycle, pushing the cycle into the volute.

This is not an arbitrary imposition by the poet. "Mont Blanc"'s section V is a response to the flood of ruin in section IV, which in turn is a poetic response to an empirical observation of glacial destruction; the terminal question is a response to the "vacancy" that obstinately reappears in that supposedly culminating and comprehensive vision. At each (dis)junction, both memory and erasure, Wordsworth and Lucretius, are at work; each "parasite flower" grows out of the wreckage of the last, attempting, with incomplete success, to fill the silences, solitudes, and vacancies generated by that wreck.

Shelley accepts the empiricism of Burke's aesthetic response to the sublime, in that he does not assume a priori that all privations will be recuperated by the hermeneutical cycle. If mental "creation" is defined in Chernaik's and Hogle's solipsistic terms, Shelley can be said to subscribe, aesthetically, to the dictum that "mind cannot create, it can only perceive." However, by retaining the cyclic impulse—which means no more than admitting the inevitability, though not the comprehensiveness, of memory—Shelley calls into question the terror-stricken assumption that such an empiric "perception" of sublime privation can only issue in a catastrophic, and purely entropic, cul-de-sac. For Burke, the "chaos of elementary particles" has no issue, aesthetically or politically; only beauty, which is primarily understood as sexual beauty (see, e.g., *Philosophical Enquiry*, 115, 117), is generative. The political counterpart of its "continuity" is the "unchangeable constancy" that Burke extolled as the chief virtue of the organic model of social/sexual reproduction (compare Hegel's ideal State as a political expression of the Kantian beautiful "free conformity to law"). *Alastor* could be described as an affirmation of Burkean empiricism against Wordsworthian and Coleridgean idealism; when poets are confronted with the privative sublimity of the "vacancy of their spirit," they are impelled toward a search for community, at the end of which they are destined to "perish."

In his essay "On Love" of 1818, on the other hand, Shelley premises the erotic—or rather, in Lucretian terms, the venereal—reproductive impulse upon the discovery of a sublime vacancy within the human mind's imaginings: "the chasm of an insufficient void" that we perpetually rediscover "in our own thoughts" impels us toward "the invisible and unattainable point to which Love tends" (Reiman and Powers, 474). Privation and ruination have become generative; the empirical discovery of a void leads to the quasi-therapeutic attempt, as in "Mont Blanc," to recuperate it, but this goal is recognized as "unattainable"; the chasm of an insufficient void will open again within the response to the "initial" void, simultaneously canceling and regenerating the *enchaînements* of supplementary, or parasitic, reproductive cycles.[49] In this sense, the mere "perception" of the void *is* creative, not because it calls on us to projectively "half create" a supplementary totality, but because the void breaks us out of the redundant, self-confirming interpretive cycle and into a perpetual (re)generation of sublimity that amounts, according to Burke's political/aesthetic logic, to a perpetual revolution.

Like Lucretius's venereal evolution, this reiteration of revolutionary disjunction does not resolve itself into a redundant periodicity, however, but is instead an ever-renewed source of new information operating through the catastrophic ruination of the poetic voice. The end of "Mont Blanc" is the prototype of the sudden, unpredictable collapse, or *clinamen,* that catastrophically generates poems as particulate fragments rather than organic wholes.[50]

II

Shelley's poems are radically fragmentary; the defensive attempt in Shelley criticism of the 50s, 60s, and 70s to demonstrate their deeper unity and coherence is in some ways a less valid response to his poetry than the blank incomprehension and outrage variously manifested by Leavis and Eliot—those champions of the "Organic Society" and "The Tradition"—and, to a lesser degree, by the American New Critics. They, at least, like Burke, recognized revolutionary discontinuity when they saw it. But like Burke, too, they were mistaken in supposing that this discontinuity meant a purely entropic dead end. The poem as sublime fragment is "disengaged" from its context of production—it forgets its initial conditions—and becomes free to enter the atomistic logic of

49. Although there are affinities between Derrida's chain of supplements and Shelley's chaotic creativity, "supplementary" should not be read as an allusion to Derrida's theory (see *Of Grammatology,* 157, 141–64).

50. Hughes, in his "Coherence and Collapse," notes the tendency of Shelley's poetry to lead to sudden collapse, but his response to this is firmly in the post-Kantian therapeutic tradition: "[T]he imagistic progression is wholly organic and under some kind of overarching control, even when the particular passage seems to complete itself in a thematic or emotional (*not* formal) collapse" (Hughes, "Potentiality in *Prometheus Unbound,*" 108). My argument is that it is precisely formal collapse that interests Shelley.

Shelley's revised Gothic poetic. Just as the sublime dilapidation of the Coliseum liberates it from its context of production so that the old man can imaginatively turn its giant arches into gigantic, submarine caverns—or the erasure of the history of the ruins in *Epipsychidion* calls forward, and creates room for, the fanciful history of the "Ocean-King" and his sister-spouse—the "insufficient void" that prevents Shelley's poems from folding back onto themselves in a self-confirming cycle opens them out to a perpetual reinvention in consumption. We take the atomistic fragment and suture it into the Frankenstein's monster that is our own context of consumption: the ruined arches with an imagined cataclysm, the ruined palace with the narrator-poet's desire for an "incestuous" union. This monster, in turn, is fissured—or scarred—with other "insufficient voids" that invite a perpetual redefinition and rearrangement of these parts, which always exceed any whole into which they are incorporated.

This is the poetic form of the unstable joy and madness of revolutionary *erōs* that Shelley describes in *Prometheus Unbound,* IV. In the third act of that poem, Shelley attempts to close the redemptive cycle in the therapeutic totality of Promethean *ataraxia.* But, as in "Mont Blanc," a void opens up at the moment of fulfillment. Out of this void emerges the "parasite flower" that is act IV, a *clinamen* fragment that destroys, like lightning, or like a meteor, the redundant organic cycle.

Shelley's last bid for epic stature, *The Revolt of Islam,* he described as "a genuine picture of my own mind" (*Letters,* 1:577), "a work of which *unity* is one of the qualifications aimed at by the author," which should not, therefore, be seen "in a disjointed state" (1:536). Shelley's poetry of ruins renounces the normative power of epic stature in favor of a more ephemeral and unpredictable power of perpetual contemporaneity. Shelley's poems are "timeless" in a way quite opposed to epic timelessness; they are timeless because, unable to be read in anything other than a "disjointed state," we can never regard the task of responding to their sublime fragmentation as finished or resolved. Infinitely, though not absolutely, accessible as "parts" for the Gothic "wholes" we are currently attempting to create, they will always exceed those wholes, opening voids as they reproduce themselves through time and start the whole mad and joyful process over again as the latest incarnation of Frankenstein's monster dissolves in atomistic flux.

This is the power of privation-within-memory, the creative power of the perception of vacancy. Milton Wilson's comment, "[Shelley's] poems may mean, I doubt if they can be said to be" (39), is an acknowledgment that the only critical response to such a poetic is an equivalent of the radical empiricism Prigogine and Stengers suggest we must assume before the chaotic evolution of the world. The constant redefinition of the poem as its disintegrating parts are incorporated in different atomistic constellations[51] within the ever-changing context of consumption subjects its meaning to a chaotic hermeneutic analogous to Heisenberg's uncertainty principle. We become aware of the poem's current "meaning" only at the moment of its (self-)destruction—a destruction that diverts the reproductive trajectory of the poem's context onto an unpredictable new path that will lead to a reconstellation of the poem's fragments, and a new, and equally ephemeral "meaning."

51. There are close affinities between Shelley's fragmentary poetics and Benjamin's and Adorno's theories of the "constellation." (See Eagleton, *Ideology of the Aesthetic,* 330ff., for a good general account of this attempt to subvert the aesthetic drive to totality.)

Bibliography

Shelley Texts

Cameron, Kenneth Neill, and Donald Reiman, eds. *Shelley and His Circle, 1773–1822.* 8 vols. Cambridge, Mass.: Harvard University Press, 1961–.

Chernaik, Judith. *The Lyrics of Shelley.* Cleveland, Ohio: Press of Case Western Reserve University, 1972.

Clark, David, ed. *Shelley's Prose; or, The Trumpet of a Prophecy.* Albuquerque: University of New Mexico Press, 1954.

Ellis, F. S. *A Lexical Concordance to the Poetical Works of Percy Bysshe Shelley.* London: Bernard Quaritch, 1892.

Hutchinson, Thomas, ed. *Shelley: Poetical Works.* Revised by G. M. Matthews. Oxford: Oxford University Press, 1970.

Ingpen, Roger, and Walter E. Peck, eds. *The Complete Works of Percy Bysshe Shelley.* 10 vols. New York: Gordian Press, Julian Edition, 1965.

Jones, F. L., ed. *The Letters of Percy Bysshe Shelley.* Oxford: Clarendon, 1964.

Reiman, Donald. *Shelley's "The Triumph of Life": A Critical Study.* Urbana: University of Illinois Press, 1965.

———, ed. *The Bodleian Shelley Manuscripts.* New York: Garland, 1986.

———, ed. *Percy Bysshe Shelley.* New York: Garland, 1985.

Reiman, Donald, and Sharon Powers, eds. *Shelley's Poetry and Prose.* New York: Norton, 1977.

Shelley, Percy Bysshe. *Zastrozzi and St. Irvyne.* Edited by Stephen Behrendt. Oxford: Oxford University Press, 1986.

Shelley, Percy Bysshe, and Mary Shelley. *History of a Six Weeks Tour Through a Part of France, Switzerland, Germany and Holland: With Letters Descriptive of a Sail Round the Lake of Geneva, and of the Glaciers of Chamouni.* [1817.] Oxford: Woodstock Books, 1991.

Other Primary Material: Shelley's Contemporaries, Near Contemporaries, and Sources

Aristotle. *De Poetica.* Edited by W. D. Ross. In *The Basic Works of Aristotle,* edited by Richard McKeon, 1455–87. New York: Random House, 1941.

———. *Metaphysica.* Edited by W. D. Ross. In *The Basic Works of Aristotle,* edited by Richard McKeon, 689–934. New York: Random House, 1941.

Bacon, Francis. *A Selection of His Works.* Edited by Sidney Warhaft. Toronto: Macmillan, 1965.

Balzac, Honore de. *Le Père Goriot*. Paris: Gallimard, 1971.

———. *Père Goriot*. Translated by Jane Minot Sedgwick. New York: Holt, Rinehart & Winston, 1964.

Barcus, James, ed. *Shelley: The Critical Heritage*. London: Routledge & Kegan Paul, 1975.

Bentham, Jeremy. *Bentham's Political Thought*. New York: Barnes & Noble, 1973.

Berkeley, George. *Principles, Dialogues, and Philosophical Correspondence*. Indianapolis: Bobbs-Merrill, 1965.

Blake, William. *Complete Writings*. Edited by Geoffrey Keynes. London: Oxford University Press, 1974.

Bloom, Harold, and Lionel Trilling, eds. *Romantic Poetry and Prose*. New York: Oxford University Press, 1973.

Brett-Smith, H.F.B., ed. *Peacock's Four Ages of Poetry; Shelley's Defence of Poetry; Browning's Essay on Shelley*. Oxford: Basil Blackwell, 1953.

Burke, Edmund. *A Philosophical Enquiry into the Origin of Our Ideas of the Sublime and the Beautiful*. London: Routledge & Kegan Paul, 1958.

———. *Reflections on the Revolution in France and on the Proceedings in Certain Societies in London Relative to That Event*. Edited by Conor Cruise O'Brien. Harmondsworth, Middlesex: Penguin, 1969.

———. *A Vindication of Natural Society*. Indianapolis: Liberty Classics, 1982.

Clairmont, Claire. *The Journals of Claire Clairmont*. Edited by Marion Stocking and David Stocking. Cambridge, Mass.: Harvard University Press, 1968.

Coleridge, Samuel Taylor. *Biographia Literaria*. 2 vols. Edited by W. J. Bate and J. Engall. Vol. 7 of *The Collected Works of Samuel Taylor Coleridge*. Bollingen Series, no. 75. Princeton: Princeton University Press, 1983.

———. *Lay Sermons*. Edited by R. J. White. Vol. 6 of *The Collected Works of Samuel Taylor Coleridge*. Bollingen Series, no. 75. London: Routledge & Kegan Paul, 1972.

———. *On the Constitution of the Church and State According to the Idea of Each and Lay Sermons*. Edited by H. N. Coleridge. London: Pickering, 1839.

———. *Poetical Works*. Edited by E. H. Coleridge. Oxford: Oxford University Press, 1969.

Cowper, William. *The Poetical Works of William Cowper*. London: Wark, Lock & Co., 1912.

Diderot, Denis. *Diderot's Early Philosophical Works*. Edited and translated by Margaret Jourdain. Chicago: Open Court, 1916.

———. *Le neveu de Rameau et autres dialogues philosophiques*. Paris: Gallimard, 1972.

———. *La rêve de d'Alembert*. In Diderot, *Le neveu*, 179–238.

———. *Pensées philosophiques: Addition aux pensées philosophique* and *Lettre sur les aveugles: Additions à la lettre sur les aveugles* and *Supplément au voyage de Bougainville*. Paris: Garnier-Flammarion, 1972.

———. *Prospectus de l'encyclopédie*. Vol. 13 of *Oeuvres de Denis Diderot*. Paris: Brière, 1921.

———. *Rameau's Nephew* and *D'Alembert's Dream*. Translated by Leonard Tancock. Harmondsworth, Middlesex: Penguin, 1966.

Drummond, William. 1984. *Academical Questions*. Delmar, N.Y.: Scholars' Facsimiles & Reprints.

Fichte, Johann Gottlieb. *Addresses to the German Nation*. New York: Harper, 1968.

――――. *The Science of Knowledge: With the First and Second Introducti[ons]*. Translated by Peter Heath and John Lachs. Cambridge: Cambridge University Press, 1982.

Godwin, William. *Caleb Williams*. New York: Norton, 1977.

――――. *The Enquirer*. New York: A. M. Kelley, 1965.

――――. *Enquiry Concerning Political Justice and Its Influence on Morals and Happiness*. [1798] Edited by F.E.L. Priestly. 3d ed. 3 vols. Toronto: University of Toronto Press, 1946.

――――. *Of Population*. [London: 1820.] New York: Kelley, 1964.

Goethe, Johann Wolfgang. *Autobiography: Truth and Poetry, from My Own Life*. Translated by John Oxenford. 2 vols. London: H. G. Bohn, 1881–84.

――――. *Faust: First Part*. Original text with translation by Peter Salm. Toronto: Bantam, 1985.

――――. *Faust: Part Two*. Translated by Philip Wayne. Harmondsworth, Middlesex: Penguin, 1959.

――――. *The Sorrows of Young Werther*. Translated by Michael Hulse. Harmondsworth, Middlesex: Penguin, 1989.

Hazlitt, William. "Essay on the Principles of Human Action." [1805.] In *Complete Works of William Hazlitt*, edited by P. P. Howe, 1:1–91. London: Dent, 1931.

――――. *The Spirit of the Age; or, Contemporary Portraits*. New York: Chelsea House, 1983.

Hegel, G.W.F. *The Philosophy of History*. Translated by J. Sibree. New York: Dover, 1956.

――――. *Philosophy of Right*. Translated by T. M. Knox. London: Oxford University Press, 1967.

――――. *The Phenomenology of Spirit*. Translated by A. V. Miller. Oxford: Clarendon, 1977.

Hogg, Thomas Jefferson. *After Shelley: The Letters of Thomas Jefferson Hogg to Jane Williams*. Edited by Sylva Norman. London: Oxford University Press, 1934.

Holbach, Baron d'. *The System of Nature: Of Laws of the Moral and Physical World*. New York: Burt Franklin, 1970.

[Holbach, Paul-Henry Thiry, Baron d']. *The System of Nature; or, the Laws of the Moral and Physical World*. 2 vols. 3d ed. Translator anonymous. London: Sherwood, Neely & Jones, 1817 (this edition wrongly attributes the work to "M. de Mirabaud").

Hume, David. *Enquiries Concerning the Human Understanding and Concerning the Principle of Morals*. Oxford: Oxford University Press, 1970.

――――. *Inquiry*. Indianapolis: Bobbs-Merrill, 1955.

――――. *Essays, Moral, Political, and Literary*. Edited by E. F. Miller. Indianapolis: Liberty Classics, 1985.

――――. *History of England from the Invasion of Julius Caesar to the Revolution in 1688*. 5 vols. London: Longman, Green, 1864.

———. *Hume's Political Essays.* Edited by C. W. Hendel. New York: Liberal Arts, 1953.

———. *A Treatise of Human Nature.* Edited by L. A. Selby-Bigge and P. H Nidditch. Oxford: Clarendon, 1978.

Jones, F. L., ed. *Maria Gisborne and Edward E. Williams: Shelley's Friends: Their Journals and Letters.* Norman: University of Oklahoma Press, 1951.

Kant, Immanuel. *The Critique of Judgement.* Translated by J. C. Meredith. [1928.] Oxford: Clarendon, 1952.

———. *Critique of Practical Reason.* Translated by L. W. Beck. New York: Macmillan, 1956.

———. *Critique of Pure Reason.* Translated by F. M. Müller. New York: Anchor, 1966.

———. *Grounding for the Metaphysics of Morals.* Translated by James W. Ellington. Indianapolis: Hackett, 1981.

Keats, John. *Complete Poems.* Edited by Jack Stillinger. Cambridge, Mass.: Harvard University Press, Belknap Press, 1982.

Lewis, M. G. *The Monk: A Romance.* London: Oxford University Press, 1973.

Locke, John. *Essay Concerning Human Understanding.* Edited by P. H. Nidditch. Oxford: Clarendon, 1975.

———. *The Second Treatise of Government.* Indianapolis: Bobbs-Merrill, 1952.

Lucretius. *De rerum natura.* With an English translation by W.H.D. Rouse. Revised by Martin Ferguson Smith. 2d ed. Cambridge, Mass.: Harvard University Press Loeb Classical Library, 1982.

———. *On the Nature of the Universe.* Translated by R. E. Latham. Harmondsworth, Middlesex: Penguin, 1951.

Malthus, Thomas. *An Essay on the Principle of Population.* London: Everyman, 1958.

Mill, John Stuart. *Newspaper Writings: December 1822–July 1831.* Edited by Ann Robson and John Robson. Toronto: University of Toronto Press, 1986.

Milton, John. *Paradise Lost.* Edited by Alastair Fowler. Harlow: Longman, 1971.

Montaigne, Michel de. *Essays.* Translated by J. M. Cohen. Harmondsworth, Middlesex: Penguin, 1958.

Paine, Thomas. *The Political Works of Tom Paine.* Chicago: Belfords, 1879.

Peacock, Thomas Love. *Headlong Hall* and *Nightmare Abbey.* London: Dent, 1961.

———. *Memoirs of Shelley and Other Essays and Reviews.* Edited by H. Mills. London: Hart-Davis, 1970.

Plato. *The Collected Dialogues of Plato, Including the Letters.* Edited by Edith Hamilton and Huntington Cairns. Bollingen Series, no. 71. Princeton: Princeton University Press, 1961.

———. *Republic.* In *Collected Dialogues,* 575–844.

———. *The Symposium.* Harmondsworth, Middlesex: Penguin, 1951.

Radcliffe, Anne. *The Mysteries of Udolpho.* Oxford: Oxford University Press, 1980.

Redpath, Theodore. *The Young Romantics and Critical Opinion, 1807–1824: Poetry of Byron, Shelley, and Keats As Seen by Their Contemporary Critics.* New York: St. Martin's, 1973.

Repton, Humphrey. *Sketches and Hints on Landscape Gardening* [1795] and *The*

Theory and Practice of Landscape Gardening [1803]. Reprinted as *The Art of Landscape Gardening.* Cambridge, Mass.: Houghton, Mifflin & Co., 1907.

Rousseau, Jean-Jacques. *Confessions.* Harmondsworth, Middlesex: Penguin, 1954.

———. *Julie: Ou, la nouvelle Héloïse.* Paris: Garnier Frères, 1960.

———. *Rêveries du promeneur solitaire.* Paris: Garnier Frères, 1960.

———. *Reveries of the Solitary Walker.* Translated by Peter France. Harmondsworth, Middlesex: Penguin, 1979.

———. *The Social Contract and Discourses.* London: Dent, 1973.

Schelling, F.W.J. *System of Transcendental Idealism (1800).* Translated by Peter Heath. Charlottesville: University Press of Virginia, 1978.

Schiller, Friedrich. *Naive and Sentimental Poetry* and *On the Sublime.* Translated by J. A. Elias. New York: Frederick Ungar, 1966.

———. *On the Aesthetic Education of Man in a Series of Letters.* Translated by Reginald Snell. [1954.] New York: Continuum, 1965.

———. *The Robbers* and *Wallenstein.* Translated by F. J. Lamport. Harmondsworth, Middlesex: Penguin, 1979.

Schlegel, August Wilhelm. *A Course of Lectures on Dramatic Art and Literature.* Translated by John Black. London: n.p., 1815.

Schlegel, Friedrich. *Dialogue on Poetry* and *Literary Aphorisms.* Translated by Ernst Behler and Roman Struc. University Park: Pennsylvania State University Press, 1968.

———. *The Philosophy of Life and Philosophy of Language in a Course of Lectures.* Translated by A. J. Morrison. New York: Harper & Brothers, 1848.

Shelley, Mary. *Frankenstein; or, The Modern Prometheus.* Oxford: Oxford University Press, 1969.

———. *The Journals of Mary Shelley, 1814–1844.* 2 vols. Edited by Paula R. Feldman and Diana Scott-Kilvert. Oxford: Clarendon, 1987.

———. *The Last Man.* London: Hogarth, 1985.

———. *The Letters of Mary Wollstonecraft Shelley.* Edited by Betty T. Bennett. 3 vols. Baltimore: Johns Hopkins University Press, 1980–88.

Smith, Adam. *An Inquiry into the Nature and Causes of the Wealth of Nations.* Oxford: Clarendon, 1976.

———. *The Theory of Moral Sentiments.* Oxford: Clarendon, 1976.

Spenser, Edmund. *The Faerie Queene.* London: Longman, 1977.

Spinoza, Benedict. *The Chief Works of Benedict de Spinoza.* Translated by R. H. Elwes. New York: Dover, 1955.

Staël, Mme de. *De l'allegmagne.* 2 vols. Paris: Garnier Flammarion, 1968.

Thomas à Kempis. *Of the Imitation of Christ.* Translated by J. McCann. New York: Mentor, 1957.

Trelawny, E. J. *Records of Shelley, Byron, and the Author.* Edited by David Wright. Harmondsworth, Middlesex: Penguin, 1973.

Volney, Constantin. *Ruins; or, Meditations on the Revolutions of Empires.* Boston: Gaylord, 1835.

Voltaire. *Candide or Optimism.* Translated by John Butt. West Drayton: Penguin, 1947.

———. *Candide, ou l'optimisme.* In *Romans et contes,* edited by R. Pomeau, 179–262. Paris: Garnier-Flammarion, 1966.

————. *The Portable Voltaire.* New York: Viking, 1963.

Winckelmann, Johann. *Writings on Art.* Edited by D. Irwin. London: Phaidon, 1972.

Wolfe, Humbert, ed. *The Life of Percy Bysshe Shelley As Comprised in the Life of Shelley by Thomas Jefferson Hogg; The Recollections of Shelley and Byron by Edward John Trelawny; Memoirs of Shelley by Thomas Love Peacock.* London: Dent, 1933.

Wollstonecraft, Mary. *An Historical and Moral View of the Origin and Progress of the French Revolution and the Effect It Has Produced in Europe.* Delmar, N.Y.: Scholars Facsimiles & Reprints, 1975.

————. *Mary and the Wrongs of Woman.* Oxford: Oxford University Press, 1976.

————. *A Vindication of the Rights of Men.* Gainseville, Fla.: Scholar's Facsimiles & Reprints, 1964.

————. *Vindication of the Rights of Woman.* Harmondsworth, Middlesex: Penguin, 1972.

Wordsworth, William. *The Borderers.* Edited by Robert Osborne. Ithaca: Cornell University Press, 1982.

————. *The Poems of William Wordsworth.* Edited by John Hayden. New Haven: Yale University Press, 1981.

————. "Preface to the Lyrical Ballads (1802)." In *Romantic Poetry and Prose,* edited by Harold Bloom and Lionel Trilling. New York: Oxford University Press, 1973.

————. *The Prelude: A Parallel Text.* Edited by J. C. Maxwell. Harmondsworth, Middlesex: Penguin, 1971.

————. *The Prose Works of William Wordsworth.* Edited by W.J.B. Owen and Jane Worthington Smyser. 3 vols. Oxford: Clarendon, 1974.

————. *The Salisbury Plain Poems of William Wordsworth.* Edited by Stephen Gill. Ithaca: Cornell University Press, 1975.

————. *William Wordsworth.* Edited by Stephen Gill. Oxford: Oxford University Press, 1984.

Other Works

Abbey, Lloyd. *Destroyer and Preserver: Shelley's Poetic Skepticism.* Lincoln: University of Nebraska Press, 1979.

Abrams, Meyer H. *The Correspondent Breeze.* New York: Norton, 1984.

————. "English Romanticism: The Spirit of the Age." In *The Correspondent Breeze,* 44–75.

————. *The Mirror and the Lamp: Romantic Theory and the Critical Tradition.* London: Oxford University Press, 1953.

————. *Natural Supernaturalism: Tradition and Revolution in Romantic Literature.* New York: Norton, 1971.

Adorno, Theodor. *Negative Dialectics.* Translated by E. B. Ashton. New York: Continuum, 1973.

Aers, David, et al. *Romanticism and Ideology: Studies in English Writing, 1765–1830.* London: Routledge & Kegan Paul, 1981.

Albert, David Z. *Quantum Mechanics and Experience*. Cambridge, Mass.: Harvard University Press, 1992.

Allen, Graham. "Transumption and/in History: Bloom, Shelley, and the Figure of the Poet." *Durham University Journal* 85 (1993): 247-56.

Allott, Miriam, ed. *Essays on Shelley*. Totowa, N.J.: Barnes & Noble, 1982.

Althusser, Louis, and Etienne Balibar. *Lire le capital*. 2 vols. Paris: François Maspero, 1969.

Argyros, Alexander J. *A Blessed Rage for Order: Deconstruction, Evolution, and Chaos*. Ann Arbor: University of Michigan Press, 1991.

———. "Narrative and Chaos." *New Literary History* 23 (1992): 659-75.

Arthur, R. Anthony. "The Poet as Revolutionary in the *Revolt of Islam*." *Xavier University Studies* 10, no. 2 (1971): 1-17.

Asmis, Elizabeth. *Epicurus' Scientific Method*. Ithaca: Cornell University Press, 1984.

Attridge, Derek, et al., eds. *Post-Structuralism and the Question of History*. Cambridge: Cambridge University Press, 1987.

Austin, J. L. *How to Do Things with Words*. 2d ed. Cambridge, Mass.: Harvard University Press, 1975.

Bai-Lin, Hao, ed. *Chaos II*. Singapore: World Scientific, 1990.

Baker, Carlos. *Shelley's Major Poetry*. Princeton: Princeton University Press, 1948.

Baker, K. M. *Inventing the French Revolution: Essays on French Political Culture in the Eighteenth Century*. Cambridge: Cambridge University Press, 1990.

Bakhtin, M. M. *The Dialogic Imagination: Four Essays*. Edited by Michael Holquist. Translated by Caryl Emerson. Austin: University of Texas Press, 1981.

———. *Speech Genres and Other Late Essays*. Edited by Michael Holquist and Caryl Emerson. Translated by Vern W. McGee. Austin: University of Texas Press, 1981.

Bakhtin, M. M., and P. N. Medvedev. *The Formal Method in Literary Scholarship: A Critical Introduction to Sociological Poetics*. Translated by Albert J. Wehrle. Cambridge, Mass.: Harvard University Press, 1985.

Bandy, Melanie. *Mind Forg'd Manacles: Evil in the Poetry of Blake and Shelley*. Tuscaloosa: University of Alabama Press, 1981.

Barrell, John. *Shelley and the Thought of His Time: A Study in the History of Ideas*. New Haven: Yale University Press, 1947.

Bartel, Roland. "Shelley and Burke's Swinish Multitude." *Keats-Shelley Journal* 18 (1969): 4-9.

Barthes, Roland. "La mort de l'auteur." In *Le bruissement de la langue*, 61-67. Paris: Editions du Seuil, 1984.

———. *The Pleasure of the Text*. Translated by Richard Miller. New York: Hill & Wang, 1975.

———. *Writing Degree Zero*. Translated by Annette Lavers and Colin Smith. New York: Hill & Wang, 1968.

Bate, W. J., and J. Engall. Editors' introduction to Coleridge, *Biographia Literaria*, xli-cxxxvi.

Bateson, Gregory. *Steps to an Ecology of Mind: Collected Essays in Anthropology, Psychiatry, Evolution, and Epistemology*. London: Granada, 1973.

Beatty, Bernard. "Repetition's Music: *The Triumph of Life.*" In Everest, *Percy Bysshe Shelley,* 99-114.

Beer, Gillian. *Darwin's Plots.* London: Routledge & Kegan Paul, 1983.

Behrendt, Stephen. "The Exoteric Species: The Popular Idiom in Shelley's Poetry." *Genre* 14 (1981): 473-92.

Belsey, Catherine. "Richard Levin and In-different Reading." *New Literary History* 21 (1990): 449-56.

Benjamin, Walter. "The Author as Producer." In *Reflections: Essays, Aphorisms, Autobiographical Writings,* translated by Edmund Jephcott, 220-38. New York: Schocken Books, 1978.

———. *Illuminations.* Edited by Hannah Arendt. Translated by Harry Zohn. New York: Schocken Books, 1969.

Bennett, Tony. *Formalism and Marxism.* London: Methuen, 1979.

Blank, G. Kim. *The New Shelley: Later Twentieth-Century Views.* New York: St. Martin's, 1991.

———. ed. *Wordsworth's Influence on Shelley.* New York: St. Martin's, 1988.

Bloom, Harold. *The Anxiety of Influence: A Theory of Poetry.* New York: Oxford University Press, 1973.

———. *Poetry and Repression: Revisionism from Blake to Stevens.* New Haven: Yale University Press, 1976.

———. *Shelley's Mythmaking.* New Haven: Yale University Press, 1959.

———. *The Visionary Company.* Rev. ed. Ithaca: Cornell University Press, 1971.

Bloom, Harold, et al. *Deconstruction and Criticism.* New York: Continuum, 1979.

Boon, James. *Other Tribes, Other Scribes: Symbolic Anthropology in the Comparative Study of Cultures, Histories, Religions, and Texts.* Cambridge: Cambridge University Press, 1982.

Bostetter, Edward. *The Romantic Ventriloquists: Wordsworth, Coleridge, Shelley, Keats, Byron.* Seattle: University of Washington Press, 1963.

Boulton, James. *The Language of Politics in the Age of Wilkes and Burke.* London: Routledge & Kegan Paul, 1963.

Bradley, A. C. "Notes on Shelley's 'Triumph of Life.'" *MLR* 9 (1914): 441-56.

Brady, Patrick. "The Rococo Butterfly Meets the Butterfly Effect: A Chaos Theory Approach to Art and Literature." *Studies on Voltaire and the Eighteenth Century* 305 (1992): 1534-38.

Brailsford, Henry. *Shelley, Godwin, and Their Circle.* New York: Holt, 1913.

Braudel, Fernand. *The Perspective of the World.* Translated by Sian Reynolds. Civilization and Capitalism: Fifteenth to Eighteenth Century, vol. 3. New York: Harper & Row, 1984.

———. *The Structures of Everyday Life: The Limits of the Possible.* Translated by Sian Reynolds and Miriam L. Kochan. Civilization and Capitalism: Fifteenth to Eighteenth Century, vol. 1. New York: Harper & Row, 1981.

———. *The Wheels of Commerce.* Translated by Sian Reynolds. Civilization and Capitalism: Fifteenth to Eighteenth Century, vol. 2. New York: Harper & Row, 1982.

Brett, R. L. "The Philosophy of Romanticism." *Critical Survey* 3 (1968): 235-42.

Briggs, John, and F. David Peat. *Turbulent Mirror: An Illustrated Guide to Chaos Theory and the Science of Wholeness.* New York: Harper & Row, 1989.

Bristol, Michael. *Shakespeare's America, America's Shakespeare.* London: Routledge, 1990.

Burckhardt, Jacob. *The Civilization of the Renaissance in Italy.* Translated by S.G.C. Middlemore. 2 vols. New York: Harper & Brothers, 1958.

Butter, Peter. *Shelley's Idols of the Cave.* New York: Haskell House, 1969.

Cameron, Kenneth Neill. "The Political Symbolism of Prometheus Unbound." *PMLA* 58 (1943): 728-53.

———. "Shelley as Philosophical and Social Thinker: Some Modern Evaluations." *Studies in Romanticism* 21 (1982): 357-66.

———. "Shelley, Cobbett, and the National Debt." *Journal of English and Germanic Philology* 42 (1943): 197-209.

———. *Shelley: The Golden Years.* Cambridge, Mass.: Harvard University Press, 1976.

———. "Shelley and Marx." *Wordsworth Circle* 10 (1979): 234-39.

———. "Shelley and the Reformers." *ELH* 12 (1945): 62-86.

———. "The Social Philosophy of Shelley." In Reiman and Powers, 511-19.

———. *The Young Shelley.* New York: Macmillan, 1950.

Campbell, Olwen Ward. *Shelley and the Unromantics.* London: Methuen, 1924.

Campbell, William R. "Shelley's Philosophy of History: A Reconsideration." *Keats-Shelley Journal* 21-22 (1972-73): 43-63.

Carothers, Yvonne M. "*Alastor:* Shelley corrects Wordsworth." *MLQ* 42 (1981): 21-47.

Caudwell, Christopher. *Studies and Further Studies in a Dying Culture.* New York: Monthly Review Press, 1971.

Cavell, Stanley. *The Claim of Reason: Wittgenstein, Skepticism, Morality, and Tragedy.* Oxford: Clarendon Press, 1979.

———. *Must We Mean What We Say? A Book of Essays.* Cambridge: Cambridge University Press, 1976.

———. "Politics as Opposed to What?" In Mitchell, 181-202.

———. " 'Who Does the Wolf Love?' Reading *Coriolanus.*" In Greenblatt, *Representing,* 197-216.

Clark, Timothy. "Shelley's 'The Coliseum' and the Sublime." *Durham University Journal* 85 (1993): 225-36.

Clemit, Pamela. "Shelley's Godwin, 1812-1817." *Durham University Journal* 85 (1993): 189-202.

Cohen, Jack, and Ian Stewart. *The Collapse of Chaos: Discovering Simplicity in a Complex World.* Harmondsworth, Middlesex: Penguin, 1995.

Collingwood, R. G. *The Idea of History.* London: Oxford University Press, 1946.

Coveney, Peter. "Chaos, Entropy, and the Arrow of Time." In Hall, *Guide to Chaos,* 203-10.

Craig, David. *Marxists on Literature: An Anthology.* Harmondsworth, Middlesex: Penguin, 1975.

Cronin, Richard. "Shelley's Language of Dissent." *Essays in Criticism* 27 (1977): 203-15.

———. *Shelley's Poetic Thoughts.* New York: St. Martin's, 1981.

Crutchfield, James P., J. Doyne Farmer, Norman H. Packard, and Robert S. Shaw. "Chaos." *Scientific American* 225, no. 6 (1986): 46-57.

Cuddon, J. A. *A Dictionary of Literary Terms.* Rev. ed. Harmondsworth, Middlesex: Penguin, 1979.

Culler, Jonathan. *On Deconstruction: Theory and Criticism After Structuralism.* London: Routledge & Kegan Paul, 1983.

Curran, Stuart. "Percy Bysshe Shelley." In *The English Romantic Poets: A Review of Research and Criticism,* 4th ed., edited by John Clubbe et al., 593-663. New York: Modern Language Association of America, 1985.

———. *Poetic Form and British Romanticism.* Oxford: Oxford University Press, 1986.

———. *Shelley's Annus Mirabilis: The Maturing of an Epic Vision.* San Marino, Calif.: Huntingdon Library, 1975.

———. *Shelley's Cenci: Scorpions Ringed with Fire.* Princeton: Princeton University Press, 1970.

Darnton, Robert. *The Great Cat Massacre and Other Episodes in French Cultural History.* New York: Vintage, 1984.

David, Terence. *The Gothick Taste.* Newton Abbot, Devon: David & Charles, 1971.

Davies, Paul. "Is the Universe a Machine?" In Hall, *Guide to Chaos,* 213-21.

Davis, B.E.C. *Edmund Spenser: A Critical Study.* Cambridge: Cambridge University Press, 1933.

Dawidoff, Robert. "History . . . But." *New Literary History* 20 (1990): 395-406.

Dawson, P.M.S. *The Unacknowledged Legislator: Shelley and Politics.* Oxford: Clarendon, 1980.

de la Carrera, Rosalina. *Success in Circuit Lies: Diderot's Communicational Practice.* Stanford: Stanford University Press, 1991.

Del Prado, Wilma. "The Philosophy of *Prometheus Unbound.*" *St. Louis University Research Journal of the Graduate School of Arts and Sciences* 1 (1970):716-22.

Deleuze, Gilles. *Foucault.* Paris: Les Éditions de Minuit, 1986.

———. *Foucault.* Translated by Seán Hand. Minneapolis: University of Minnesota Press, 1988.

Deleuze, Gilles, and Felix Guattari. *Anti-Oedipus: Capitalism and Schizophrenia.* Translated by Robert Hurley, M. Seem, and H. Lane. Minneapolis: University of Minnesota Press, 1983.

———. *Capitalisme et schizophrénie: Mille plateaux.* Paris: Les Éditions de Minuit, 1980.

de Man, Paul. *Allegories of Reading: Figural Language in Rousseau, Nietzsche, Rilke, and Proust.* New Haven: Yale University Press, 1979.

———. *The Resistance to Theory.* Minneapolis: University of Minnesota Press, 1986.

———. "The Return to Philology." In *Resistance to Theory,* 21-26.

———. "Shelley Disfigured." In Bloom et al., 39-74.

Derrida, Jacques. *De l'esprit: Heidegger et la question.* Paris: Éditions Galilée, 1987.

———. *Limited Inc.* Evanston, Ill.: Northwestern University Press, 1988.

———. "Limited Inc: a b c . . ." In *Glyph,* 2:162-254. Baltimore: Johns Hopkins University Press, 1977.

————. "Living On • Border Lines." In Bloom et al., 75-176.

————. *Margins of Philosophy.* Translated by Alan Bass. Chicago: University of Chicago Press, 1982.

————. "My Chances/*Mes Chances.*" In *Taking Chances: Derrida, Psychoanalysis, and Literature,* edited by Joseph H. Smith and William Kerrigan, 1-32. Baltimore: Johns Hopkins University Press, 1984.

————. *Of Grammatology.* Translated by G. C. Spivak. Baltimore: Johns Hopkins University Press, 1976.

————. "Signature Event Context." In *Margins of Philosophy,* 307-30.

————. *Spurs: Nietzsche's Styles/Eperons: Les styles de Nietzsche.* Translated by Barbara Harlow. Chicago: University of Chicago Press, 1979.

Dilthey, Wilhelm. *Meaning in History: W. Dilthey's Thoughts on History and Society.* Edited and translated by H. P. Rickman. London: George Allen & Unwin, 1961.

Dollimore, Jonathan, and Alan Sinfield, eds. *Political Shakespeare: New Essays in Cultural Materialism.* Ithaca: Cornell University Press, 1985.

Donovan, John. "Incest in *Laon and Cythna:* Nature, Custom, Desire." *Keats-Shelley Review* 2 (1987): 49-90.

Drakakis, John, ed. *Alternative Shakespeares.* London: Methuen, 1985.

Droz, Jacques. *Europe Between Revolutions, 1815-1848.* London: Collins, 1967.

Dudley, D. R., ed. *Lucretius.* New York: Basic Books, 1965.

Duerksen, Ronald. *Shelley's Poetry of Involvement.* New York: St. Martin's, 1988.

————. "Shelley's Prometheus: Destroyer and Preserver." *Studies in English Literature, 1500-1900* 18 (1978): 625-38.

Duff, David. *Romance and Revolution: Shelley and the Politics of a Genre.* Cambridge: Cambridge University Press, 1994.

Duffy, Edward. *Rousseau in England: The Context for Shelley's Critique of the Enlightenment.* Berkeley and Los Angeles: University of California Press, 1979.

Dupré, John. *The Disorder of Things: Metaphysical Foundations of the Disunity of Science.* Cambridge, Mass.: Harvard University Press, 1993.

Eagleton, Terry. *The Ideology of the Aesthetic.* Oxford: Basil Blackwell, 1990.

————. "Literature and History." *Critical Quarterly* 27 (1985): 23-26.

Easterlin, Nancy, and Barbara Riebling, eds. *After Poststructuralism: Interdisciplinarity and Literary Theory.* Evanston, Ill.: Northwestern University Press, 1993.

Edwards, Paul, ed. *The Encyclopedia of Philosophy.* 8 vols. New York: Macmillan, 1967.

Eichner, Hans. *Friedrich Schlegel.* New York: Twayne, 1970.

Empson, William. *Seven Types of Ambiguity.* New York: New Directions, 1947.

Engels, Friedrich. *The Origin of the Family, Private Property, and the State.* New York: Pathfinder, 1972.

Enright, D. J. *The Alluring Problem: An Essay on Irony.* Oxford: Oxford University Press, 1986.

Evans, Frank B. "Shelley, Godwin, Hume, and the Doctrine of Necessity." *Studies in Philology* 37 (1940): 632-40.

Everest, Kelvin. "'Mechanism of a Kind Yet Unattempted': The Dramatic Action of *Prometheus Unbound.*" *Durham University Journal* 85 (1993): 237-46.

———. ed. *Percy Bysshe Shelley: Bicentenary Essays.* Cambridge: D. S. Brewer, 1992.

———. ed. *Shelley Revalued: Essays from the Greynog Conference.* Leicester: Leicester University Press, 1983.

Feyerabend, Paul. *Against Method: Outline of an Anarchistic Theory of Knowledge.* London: Verso, 1978.

Flagg, John S. "Shelley and Aristotle: Elements of the *Poetics* in Shelley's Theory of Poetry." *Studies in Romanticism* 9 (1970): 44-67.

Fleischmann, Wolfgang Bernard. *Lucretius and English Literature, 1680-1740.* Paris: A. G. Nizet, 1964.

Foot, Paul. *Red Shelley.* London: Bookmarks, 1984.

Foucault, Michel. *The Archaeology of Knowledge.* London: Tavistock, 1972.

———. *The Birth of the Clinic: An Archaeology of Medical Perception.* Translated by A.M. Sheridan Smith. New York: Pantheon, 1973.

———. *Discipline and Punish.* New York: Vintage Books, 1979.

———. *The History of Sexuality.* Vol. 1, *An Introduction,* translated by Robert Hurley. New York: Vintage, 1980.

———. *Language, Counter-Memory, Practice: Selected Essays and Interviews.* Edited by Donald Bouchard. Translated by Donald Bouchard and S. Simon. Ithaca: Cornell University Press, 1977.

———. *Les mots et les choses: Une archéologie des sciences humaines.* Paris: Gallimard, 1966.

———. *Le souci de soi.* Vol. 3 of *Histoire de la sexualité.* Paris: Gallimard, 1984.

———. *Naissance de la clinique: Une archéologie du regard médical.* Paris: Presses Universitaires de France, 1963.

———. "Nietzsche, Genealogy, History." In *Language, Counter-Memory, Practice,* 139-64.

———. *The Order of Things.* New York: Vintage Books, 1970.

———. *Power/Knowledge: Selected Interviews and Other Writings, 1972-1977.* Edited by C. Gordon. New York: Pantheon, 1980.

———. "Qu'est-ce qu'un auteur?" *Bulletin de la Société Française de Philosophie* 64 (1969): 73-104.

———. *The Use of Pleasure.* Vol. 2 of *The History of Sexuality,* translated by Robert Hurley. New York: Vintage, 1986.

———. "What Is an Author?" In *Textual Strategies: Perspectives in Post-Structural Criticism,* edited by Josue Harari. Ithaca: Cornell University Press, 1979.

Fox, Robin Lane. *The Unauthorized Version: Truth and Fiction in the Bible.* New York: Knopf, 1992.

Fraisse, Simone. *L'influence de Lucrèce en France au seizième siècle.* Paris: A. G. Nizet, 1962.

Fraistat, Neil. *The Poem and the Book: Interpreting Collections of Romantic Poetry.* Chapel Hill: University of North Carolina Press, 1985.

———. *Poems in Their Place: Intertextuality and Order of Poetic Collections.* Chapel Hill: University of North Carolina Press, 1986.

Freud, Sigmund. "Analysis Terminable and Interminable." In *Standard Edition,* 23:209-53.

———. "Beyond the Pleasure Principle." In *Standard Edition,* 18:7–66.

———. "Civilization and Its Discontents." In *Standard Edition,* 21:64–148.

———. *The Standard Edition of the Complete Psychological Works of Sigmund Freud.* Translated by James Strachey. 24 vols. London: Hogarth Press, 1953–74.

Fruman, Norman. *Coleridge: The Damaged Archangel.* New York: George Braziller, 1971.

Fuller, David. "Shelley and Jesus." *Durham University Journal* 85 (1993): 211–24.

Furbank, P. N. *Diderot: A Critical Biography.* London: Secker & Warburg, 1992.

Furst, Lillian. *Fictions of Romantic Irony in European Narrative, 1760–1857.* London: Macmillan, 1984.

Fusil, C.-A. "Lucrèce et les littérateurs poètes et artistes du XVIIIe siècle." *Revue d'Histoire Littéraire de la France* 37 (1930): 161–76.

———. "Lucrèce et les philosophes du XVIIIe siècle." *Revue d'Histoire Littéraire de la France* 35 (1928): 194–210.

Gadamer, Hans-Georg. *Truth and Method.* New York: Crossroad, 1988.

Gallant, Christine. *Shelley's Ambivalence.* New York: St. Martin's, 1989.

Geertz, Clifford. "History and Anthropology." *New Literary History* 20 (1990): 321–55.

———. *The Interpretation of Cultures.* New York: Basic Books, 1973.

Gelpi, Barbara Charlesworth. "The Nursery Cave: Shelley and the Maternal." In Blank, *New Shelley,* 64–148.

Gill, Stephen. *William Wordsworth: A Life.* Oxford: Oxford University Press, 1990.

Gleick, James. *Chaos: Making a New Science.* New York: Penguin, 1987.

Goldberg, J. "Making Sense." *New Literary History* 21 (1990): 457–62.

Goldstein, Laurence. *Ruins and Empire: The evolution of a Theme in Augustan and Romantic Literature.* Pittsburgh: University of Pittsburgh Press, 1977.

Gordon, Cosmo Alexander. *A Bibliography of Lucretius.* London: Rupert Hart Davies, 1962.

Goudge, T. A. "Darwin, Charles Robert." In Edwards, 2:294.

Gould, Stephen J. *Wonderful Life: The Burgess Shale and the Nature of History.* New York: Norton, 1989.

Grabo, Carl. *The Meaning of the Witch of Atlas.* Chapel Hill: University of North Carolina Press, 1935.

———. *A Newton Among Poets: Shelley's Use of Science in Prometheus Unbound.* Chapel Hill: University of North Carolina Press, 1930.

Gramsci, Antonio. *Selections from the Prison Notebooks.* Edited and translated by Quintin Hoare and Geoffrey Nowell Smith. New York: International Publishers, 1971.

Greenblatt, Stephen. "Capitalist Culture and the Circulatory System." In Krieger, 257–73.

———. *Renaissance Self-Fashioning: From More to Shakespeare.* Chicago: Chicago University Press, 1980.

———. *Shakespearean Negotiations: The Circulation of Social Energy in Renaissance England.* Berkeley and Los Angeles: University of California Press, 1988.

———, ed. *Allegory and Representation.* Baltimore: Johns Hopkins University Press, 1981.

————, ed. *Representing the English Renaissance.* Berkeley and Los Angeles: University of California Press, 1988.

Greene, Gayle, and Coppélia Kahn. *Making a Difference: Feminist Literary Criticism.* London: Methuen, 1985.

Greenlaw, Edwin. "Spenser and Lucretius." *Studies in Philology* 17 (1920): 439–64.

Guinn, J. P. *Shelley's Political Thought.* The Hague: Mouton, 1969.

Gutschera, Deborah. "The Drama of Reenactment in Shelley's *The Revolt of Islam.*" *Keats-Shelley Journal* 35 (1986): 111–25.

Hadzsits, George. *Lucretius and His Influence.* New York: Cooper Square Publishers, 1963.

Hahn, Roger. *Laplace as a Newtonian Scientist.* California: UCLA, William Andrews Clark Memorial Library, 1967.

Hall, Jean. "The Divine and the Dispassionate Selves: Shelley's *Defence* and Peacock's *The Four Ages of Poetry.*" *Keats-Shelley Journal* 41 (1992): 139–63.

————. "Poetic Autonomy in *Peter Bell the Third* and *The Witch of Atlas.*" In Blank, *New Shelley,* 204–19.

————. "The Socialised Imagination: Shelley's *The Cenci* and *Prometheus Unbound.*" *Studies in Romanticism* 23 (1984): 339–50.

————. *The Transforming Image: A Study of Shelley's Major Poetry.* Urbana: University of Illinois Press, 1980.

Hall, Nina., ed. *The* New Scientist *Guide to Chaos.* Harmondsworth, Middlesex: Penguin, 1992.

Hamilton, Paul. "Keats and Critique." In Levinson et al., 108–42.

————. "'Old Anatomies': Some Recent Shelley Criticism." *Durham University Journal* 85 (1993): 303–10.

Hanson, Norwood Russell. "Quantum Mechanics, Philosophical Implications of." In Edwards, 7:41–49.

Hartt, Frederick. *A History of Italian Renaissance Art: Painting, Sculpture, Architecture.* London: Thames & Hudson, 1980.

Haswell, Richard H. "Shelley's *Revolt of Islam:* 'The Connection of Its Parts.'" *Keats-Shelley Journal* 25 (1976): 81–102.

Hawking, Stephen. *A Brief History of Time: From the Big Bang to Black Holes.* New York: Bantam, 1988.

Hayles, N. Katherine. *Chaos Bound: Orderly Disorder in Contemporary Literature and Science.* Ithaca: Cornell University Press, 1990.

————, ed. *Chaos and Order: Complex Dynamics in Literature and Science.* Ithaca: Cornell University Press, 1991.

Heidegger, Martin. *Basic Writings.* Edited by D. F. Krell. New York: Harper & Row, 1977.

————. *Being and Time.* Translated by John Macquarrie and E. Robinson. Oxford: Blackwell, 1967.

Hendrix, Richard. "The Necessity of Response: How Shelley's Radical Poetry Works." *Keats-Shelley Journal* 27 (1978): 45–69.

Heppner, Christopher. "Alastor: The Poet and the Narrator Reconsidered." *Keats-Shelley Journal* 37 (1988): 91–109.

Hill, Christopher. *The World Turned Upside Down.* Harmondsworth, Middlesex: Penguin, 1975.

Hirsch, Bernard. "'A Want of That True Theory': *Julian and Maddalo* as Dramatic Monologue." *SIR* 17 (1978): 13-34.

Hoagwood, Terence A. *Prophecy and the Philosophy of Mind: Traditions of Blake and Shelley.* Tuscaloosa: University of Alabama Press, 1985.

————. *Skepticism and Ideology: Shelley's Political Prose and Its Philosophical Context from Bacon to Marx.* Iowa City: University of Iowa Press, 1988.

Hobsbawm, Eric. *The Age of Revolution: Europe, 1789-1848.* London: Cardinal, 1962.

Hobsbawm, Eric, and Terence Ranger, eds. *The Invention of Tradition.* Cambridge: Cambridge University Press, 1983.

Hodgart, Patricia. *A Preface to Shelley.* London: Longman, 1988.

Hodgson, John A. *Coleridge, Shelley, and Transcendental Inquiry: Rhetoric, Argument, Metapsychology.* Lincoln: University of Nebraska Press, 1989.

————. "The World's Mysterious Doom: Shelley's *The Triumph of Life.*" *ELH* 42 (1975): 603-4.

Hogle, Jerrold E. "Metaphor and Metamorphosis in Shelley's *The Witch of Atlas.*" *SIR* 19 (1980): 327-53.

————. "Shelley as Revisionist: Power and Belief in *Mont Blanc.*" In Blank, *New Shelley,* 108-27.

————. "Shelley's Poetics: The Power as Metaphor." *Keats-Shelley Journal* 31 (1982): 159-97.

————. *Shelley's Process: Radical Transference and the Development of His Major Works.* New York: Oxford University Press, 1988.

Hohne, Horst. "The Poet's Despair: On the Interpretation of Shelley's Last Poetry." *Zeitschrift für Anglistik und Amerikanistik* 30 (1982): 311-24.

Holmes, Richard. *Coleridge: Early Visions.* London: Hodder & Stoughton, 1989.

————. *Shelley: The Pursuit.* New York: Elisabeth Sifton Books, 1974.

Hone, J. Ann. *For the Cause of Truth: Radicalism in London, 1796-1821.* Oxford: Oxford University Press, 1982.

Horkheimer, Max, and Theodor Adorno. *Dialectic of Enlightenment.* Translated by John Cumming. New York: Continuum, 1986.

Houston, Ralph. "Shelley and the Principle of Association." *Essays in Criticism* 1 (1953): 45-49.

Howard, Jean. "The New Historicism in Renaissance Studies." In Kinney and Collins, 3-33.

Hoy, David Couzens. "Must We Say What We Mean?" In *Contemporary Literary Hermeneutics and Interpretation of Classical Texts,* edited by Stephanus Kresic, 91-106. Ottawa: Ottawa University Press, 1981.

Hughes, D. J. "Coherence and Collapse in Shelley, with Particular Reference to *Epipsychidion.*" *ELH* 28 (1961): 260-83.

————. "Potentiality in *Prometheus Unbound.*" *SIR* 2 (1963): 107-26.

Hughes, Daniel. "Shelley, Leonardo, and the Monsters of Thought." *Criticism* 12 (1970): 195-212.

Hunt, Lynn. *Politics, Culture, and Class in the French Revolution.* Berkeley and Los Angeles: University of California Press, 1984.

Jameson, Frederic. *The Political Unconscious: Narrative as a Socially Symbolic Act.* Ithaca: Cornell University Press, 1981.

502 Bibliography

————. *The Prison-House of Language: A Critical Account of Structuralism.* Princeton: Princeton University Press, 1972.

————, ed. *Aesthetics and Politics.* London: Verso, 1980.

Jeffrey, Lloyd. "Cuverian Catastrophism in Shelley's *Prometheus Unbound* and *Mont Blanc.*" *SCB* 38 (1978): 148–52.

Jones, F. L. "Shelley and Milton." *SP* 49 (1952): 488–519.

Jones, Steven E. *Shelley's Satire: Violence, Exhortation, and Authority.* DeKalb: Northern Illinois University Press, 1994.

Keach, William. "Radical Shelley?" *Raritan: A Quarterly Review* 5 (1985): 120–29.

————. *Shelley's Style.* London: Methuen, 1984.

Kelly, Gary. *The English Jacobin Novel, 1780–1805.* Oxford: Clarendon, 1976.

Keohane, Nannerl, Michelle Rosaldo, and Barbara Gelpi, eds. *Feminist Theory: A Critique of Ideology.* Chicago: University of Chicago Press, 1982.

Kim, Jong Hyun, and John Stringer, eds. *Applied Chaos.* New York: Wiley & Sons, 1992.

King-Hele, Desmond. *Shelley: His Thought and Work.* 2d ed. London: Macmillan, 1971.

————. "Shelley and Erasmus Darwin." In Everest, *Shelley Revalued,* 129–47.

Kinney, Arthur F. and Dan S. Collins, eds. *Renaissance Historicism: Selections from English Literary Renaissance.* Amherst: University of Massachusetts Press, 1987.

Klapper, M. R. *The German Literary Influence on Shelley.* Salzburg: Institut für Englische Sprache und Literatur, Universität Salzburg, 1975.

Knapp, Steven, and Walter Benn Michaels. "Against Theory." *Critical Inquiry* 8 (1982): 723–42.

Kramnick, Isaac. "On Anarchism and the Real World: William Godwin and Radical England." *American Political Science Review* 66 (1972): 114–28.

Krieger, Murray, ed. *The Aims of Representation: Subject/Text/History.* New York: Columbia University Press, 1987.

Krupnick, Mark, ed. *Displacement: Derrida and After.* Bloomington: Indiana University Press, 1987.

Kurtz, B. J. *The Pursuit of Death: A Study of Shelley's Poetry.* New York: Octagon, 1970.

Lacan, Jacques. *The Four Fundamental Concepts of Psycho-Analysis.* Edited by Jacques-Alain Miller. Translated by Alan Sheridan. New York: Norton, 1981.

Laclau, Ernesto, and Chantal Mouffe. *Hegemony and Socialist Strategy: Towards a Radical Democratic Politics.* Translated by Winston Moore and Paul Cammack. London: Verso, 1985.

Larrain, Jorge. *Marxism and Ideology.* London: Macmillan, 1983.

Leighton, Angela. "Love, Writing, and Skepticism in *Epipsychidion.*" In Blank, *New Shelley,* 220–41.

————. *Shelley and the Sublime: An Interpretation of the Major Poems.* Cambridge: Cambridge University Press, 1984.

Lentricchia, Frank. *Criticism and Social Change.* Chicago: University of Chicago Press, 1983.

Levin, Richard. "Unthinkable Thoughts in the New Historicizing of English Renaissance Drama." *New Literary History* 21 (1990): 433–47.

Levinson, Marjorie. "The New Historicism: Back to the Future." In Levinson et al., 18–63.

———. *The Romantic Fragment Poem: A Critique of a Form.* Chapel Hill: University of North Carolina Press, 1986.

Levinson, Marjorie, Marilyn Butler, Jerome McGann, and Paul Hamilton. *Rethinking Historicism: Critical Readings in Romantic History.* Oxford: Basil Blackwell, 1989.

Lewin, Roger. *Complexity: Life at the Edge of Chaos.* London: Phoenix, 1993.

Lovelock, J. E. *Gaia: A New Look at Life on Earth.* Oxford: Oxford University Press, 1979.

Lowenstein, O. E. "The Pre-Socratics, Lucretius, and Modern Science." In Dudley, 1–18.

Lukàcs, Georg. *History and Class Consciousness: Studies in Marxist Dialectics.* Cambridge, Mass.: MIT Press, 1971.

Lyotard, Jean-François. *The Differend: Phrases in Dispute.* Translated by Georges Van Den Abbeele. Manchester: Manchester University Press, 1988.

———. *The Inhuman: Reflections on Time.* Translated by Geoffrey Bennington and Rachel Bowlby. Cambridge: Polity Press, 1991.

———. "Judicieux dans le différend." In *La faculté de juger,* 195–236.

———. "Judiciousness in Dispute, or Kant After Marx." In Krieger, 23–69.

———. *Le différend.* Paris: Les Éditions de Minuit, 1983.

———. *The Postmodern Condition: A Report on Knowledge.* Translated by Geoffrey Bennington and Brian Massumi. Minneapolis: University of Minnesota Press, 1984.

———, ed. *La faculté de juger.* Paris: Les Éditions de Minuit, 1985.

Macaulay, Rose. *The Pleasure of Ruins.* New York: Thames & Hudson, 1953.

Macaulay, Thomas. "Von Ranke, October 1840." In *The Works of Lord Macaulay,* edited by Lady Trevelyan, vol. 6. London: Longmans, Green, 1866.

Macherey, Pierre. *Pour une théorie de la production litteraire.* Paris: Maspero, 1974.

———. *A Theory of Literary Production.* Translated by Geoffrey Wall. London: Routledge & Kegan Paul, 1978.

Macpherson, C. B. *The Political Theory of Possessive Individualism.* Oxford: Oxford University Press, 1962.

Maddox, Donald L. "Shelley's *Alastor* and the Legacy of Rousseau." *Studies in Romanticism* 9 (1970): 82–98.

Marchand, Leslie. *Byron: A Portrait.* London: Futura, 1971.

Marcuse, Herbert. *The Aesthetic Dimension: Towards a Critique of Marxist Aesthetics.* Boston: Beacon Press, 1978.

———. *Eros and Civilization: A Philosophical Inquiry into Freud.* New York: Vintage, 1955.

———. *One-Dimensional Man: Studies in the Ideology of Advanced Industrial Society.* Boston: Beacon Press, 1964.

———. *Reason and Revolution: Hegel and the Rise of Social Theory.* Boston: Beacon Press, 1960.

Margulis, Lyn, and Dorion Sagan. *Microcosmos.* New York: Summit Books, 1986.

Marx, Karl. *Capital.* Vol. 1. Translated by S. Moore and E. Aveling. New York: International Publishers, 1967.

———. *Early Writings.* Edited by Quintin Hoare. Translated by Rodney Livingstone and Gregor Benton. New York: Vintage, 1975.

———. *The First International and After.* Vol. 3 of *Political Writings,* edited by David Fernbach. Harmondsworth, Middlesex: Penguin, 1974.

———. *Grundrisse: Foundations of the Critique of Political Economy (Rough Draft).* Translated by Martin Nicolaus. Harmondsworth, Middlesex: Penguin, 1973.

———. *The Revolutions of 1848.* Vol. 1 of *Political Writings,* edited by David Fernbach. Harmondsworth, Middlesex: Penguin, 1973.

———. *Surveys from Exile.* Vol. 2 of *Political Writings,* edited by David Fernbach. Harmondsworth, Middlesex: Penguin, 1973.

Marx, Karl, and Friedrich Engels. *The German Ideology.* Pts. 1 and 3. New York: International Publishers, 1947.

———. *On Literature and Art.* Edited by Lee Baxandall and Stefan Morawski. New York: International General, 1974.

Matthews, G. M. *Shelley.* Writers and Their Work Series. Harlow: Longman, 1970.

———. "A Volcano's Voice in Shelley." *ELH* 24 (1957): 191–228.

McFarland, Thomas. *Coleridge and the Pantheist Tradition.* Oxford: Clarendon, 1969.

———. *Romanticism and the Forms of Ruin: Wordsworth, Coleridge, and Modalities of Fragmentation.* Princeton: Princeton University Press, 1981.

McGann, Jerome J. *The Romantic Ideology: A Critical Investigation.* Chicago: University of Chicago Press, 1983.

———. "The Third World of Criticism." In Levinson et al., 85–107.

McKay, Allyson M. D. "Francis Bacon: The Ideology of Utopia." Ph.D. thesis, McGill University, 1981.

McNiece, Gerald. *Shelley and the Revolutionary Idea.* Cambridge, Mass.: Harvard University Press, 1969.

McTaggart, W. J. *England in 1819: Church, State, and Poverty.* London: Keats-Shelley Memorial Society, 1970.

Mellor, Ann. *English Romantic Irony.* Cambridge, Mass.: Harvard University Press, 1980.

Mehlman, Jeffrey. *Revolution and Repetition: Marx/Hugo/Balzac.* Berkeley and Los Angeles: University of California Press, 1977.

Miller, J. Hillis. "The Critic as Host." In Bloom et al., 217–53.

———. *The Ethics of Reading: Kant, de Man, Eliot, Trollope, James, and Benjamin.* New York: Columbia University Press, 1987.

Mitchell, W.J.T., ed. *The Politics of Interpretation.* Chicago: University of Chicago Press, 1983.

Moi, Toril. *Sexual/Textual Politics.* London: Methuen, 1985.

Monod, Jacques. *Le hasard et la nécessité: Essai sur la philosophie naturelle de la biologie moderne.* Paris: Seuil, 1970.

Montrose, Louis Adrian. "'Eliza, Queene of Shepheardes,' and the Pastoral of Power." In Kinney and Collins, 34–63.

Morford, Mark P. O., and Robert J. Lenardon. *Classical Mythology.* 2d ed. New York: Longman, 1977.

Morton, Timothy. *Shelley and the Revolution in Taste: The Body and the Natural World.* Cambridge: Cambridge University Press, 1994.

Mouffe, Chantal. *The Return of the Political.* London: Verso, 1993.

Mullaney, Stephen. *The Place of the Stage: License, Play, and Power in Renaissance England.* Chicago: University of Chicago Press, 1988.

Munro, Hector. "Coleridge and Shelley." *Keats-Shelley Memorial Bulletin* 21 (1970): 35–38.

Murray, Carl. "Is the Solar System Stable?" In Hall, *Guide to Chaos,* 96–107.

Murray, E. B. "'Elective Affinity' in *The Revolt of Islam.*" *Journal of English and Germanic Philology* 69 (1968): 570–85.

Neufeldt, Leonard N. "Poetry as Subversion: The Unbinding of Shelley's Prometheus." *Anglia* 95 (1977): 60–86.

Nichols, James H. *Epicurean Political Philosophy: The De Rerum Natura of Lucretius.* Ithaca: Cornell University Press, 1972.

Nietzsche, Friedrich. *Beyond Good and Evil.* Translated by Walter Kaufmann. New York: Vintage, 1966.

———. *Daybreak: Thoughts on the Prejudices of Morality.* Translated by R. J. Hollingdale. Cambridge: Cambridge University Press, 1982.

———. *The Gay Science.* Translated by Walter Kaufmann. New York: Vintage, 1974.

———. *The Portable Nietzsche.* Edited and translated by Walter Kaufmann. Harmondsworth, Middlesex: Penguin, 1976.

———. *The Use and Abuse of History.* Translated by Adrian Collins. New York: Macmillan, 1957.

———. *The Will to Power.* Translated by Walter Kaufmann and R. J. Hollingdale. New York: Vintage Books, 1968.

Notopoulos, James. *The Platonism of Shelley: A Study of Platonism and the Poetic Mind.* New York: Octagon, 1969.

Nussbaum, Martha. *The Fragility of Goodness: Luck and Ethics in Greek Tragedy and Philosophy.* Cambridge: Cambridge University Press, 1986.

O'Neill, Michael. "'The Mind Which Feeds This Verse': Self- and Other-Awareness in Shelley's Poetry." *Durham University Journal* 85 (1993): 273–92.

Orel, Harold. "Shelley's *The Revolt of Islam:* The Last Great Poem of the English Enlightenment?" *Studies on Voltaire and the Eighteenth Century* 89 (1972): 1187–207.

Ovid. *Metamorphoses.* Translated by Mary Innes. Harmondsworth, Middlesex: Penguin, 1955.

Partner, Nancy. "Making Up Lost Time: Writing on the Writing of History." *Speculum* 61 (1986): 90–117.

Paulos, J. A. *Mathematics and Humour.* Chicago: University of Chicago Press, 1980.

Paulson, Ronald. *Representations of Revolution, 1789-1820.* New Haven: Yale University Press, 1983.

Pelletier, Robert R. "*The Revolt of Islam* and *Paradise Lost.*" *Keats-Shelley Journal* 14 (1965): 7-13.

Perkins, David. *The Quest for Permanence: The Symbolism of Wordsworth, Shelley, and Keats.* Cambridge, Mass.: Harvard University Press, 1965.

Pevsner, Nikolaus. *An Outline of European Architecture.* 7th ed. Harmondsworth, Middlesex: Penguin, 1963.

Phillips, Jane E. "Lucretian Echoes in Shelley's *Mont Blanc.*" *Classical and Modern Literature* 2 (1982): 71-93.

Plumb, J. H. *The Death of the Past.* Boston: Houghton Mifflin, 1970.

Popkin, Richard H. *The History of Scepticism from Erasmus to Spinoza.* Berkeley and Los Angeles: University of California Press, 1979.

Polan, D. "The Ruin of a Poetics: The Political Practice of *Prometheus Unbound.*" *Enclitic* 7 (1983): 35-43.

Pomian, K., ed. *La querelle du déterminisme.* Paris: Gallimard, 1990.

Poster, Mark. *Foucault, Marxism, and History: Mode of Production Versus Mode of Information.* Cambridge: Polity, 1984.

Price, Uvedale. *On the Picturesque.* Edited by T. Lauder. London: W. S. Orr & Co., 1842.

Prigogine, Ilya, and Isabelle Stengers. *La nouvelle alliance: Métamorphose de la science.* Paris: Gallimard, 1979.

———. *Order out of Chaos: Man's New Dialogue with Nature.* Toronto: Bantam, 1984.

Proust, Marcel. *A l'ombre des jeunes filles en fleurs.* Paris: Gallimard, 1954.

———. *Du côté de chez Swann.* Paris: Gallimard, 1988.

———. *Remembrance of Things Past.* Vol. 1. Translated by C. K. Scott Moncreiff. New York: Random House, 1934.

Pugin, A. W. *Apology for the Revival of Christian Architecture.* [1843.] London: Basil Blackwell, 1969.

Pulos, C. E. *The Deep Truth: A Study of Shelley's Skepticism.* Lincoln: University of Nebraska Press, 1954.

Quinn, Mary. "The Daemon of the World: Shelley's Antidote to the Skepticism of *Alastor.*" *Studies in English Literature, 1500-1900* 25 (1985): 755-74.

Quint, David. "Representation and Ideology in *The Triumph of Life.*" *Studies in English Literature, 1500-1900* 18 (1978): 639-57.

Rae, Alastair. *Quantum Physics: Illusion or Reality?* Cambridge: Cambridge University Press, Canto, 1990.

Rajan, Tilottama. *Dark Interpreter: The Discourse of Romanticism.* Ithaca: Cornell University Press, 1980.

———. "The Web of Human Things: Narrative and Identity in *Alastor.*" In Blank, *New Shelley,* 85-107.

Reibling, Barbara. "Remodeling Truth, Power, and Society: Implications of Chaos Theory, Nonequilibrium Dynamics, and Systems Science for the Study of Politics and Literature." In Easterlin and Riebling, 177-201.

Reiman, Donald. *Percy Bysshe Shelley.* New York: Twayne, 1969.

———. *Romantic Texts and Contexts.* Columbia: University of Missouri Press, 1987.

———. "Shelley as Agrarian Reactionary." *Keats-Shelley Memorial Bulletin* 30 (1979): 5-15.

———. *Shelley's "The Triumph of Life": A Critical Study.* Urbana: University of Illinois Press, 1965.

———. "Wordsworth, Shelley, and the Romantic Inheritance." *Romanticism Past and Present* 5 (1981): 1-22.

Reisner, Thomas A. "Tabula Rasa: Shelley's Metaphor of the Mind." *Ariel* 4, no. 2 (1973): 90-102.

Richardson, Alan. "The Dangers of Sympathy: Sibling Incest in English Romantic Poetry." *SEL* 25 (1985): 737-54.

Ricoeur, Paul. "Metaphor and the Main Problem of Hermeneutics." *New Literary History* 6 (1974): 95-110.

Robinson, C. E. *Shelley and Byron: The Snake and the Eagle Wreathed in Fight.* Baltimore: Johns Hopkins University Press, 1976.

Rogers, Neville. *Shelley at Work.* Rev. ed. London: Macmillan, 1967.

Rorty, Richard. *Philosophy and the Mirror of Nature.* Princeton: Princeton University Press, 1979.

Rössler, O. E. "The Future of Chaos." In Kim and Stringer, 457-66.

Royle, Edward, and James Walvin. *English Radicals and Reformers, 1760-1848.* Brighton: Harvester, 1982.

Rudé, George. *Revolutionary Europe, 1783-1815.* Glasgow: Collins, 1964.

Ruelle, David. *Chance and Chaos.* Harmondsworth, Middlesex: Penguin, 1991.

———. "Hasard et déterminisme: Le problème de la prédictibilité." In Pomian, 153-62.

Ryan, Michael. *Marxism and Deconstruction: A Critical Articulation.* Baltimore: Johns Hopkins University Press, 1982.

Ryle, Gilbert. 1971. *Collected Papers.* Vol. 2. London: Hutchinson.

———. "Thinking and Reflecting." In *Collected Papers,* 2:465-79.

———. "The Thinking of Thoughts." In *Collected Papers,* 2:480-96.

Rzepka, Charles. "*Julian and Maddalo* as Revisionary Conversation Poem." In Blank, *New Shelley,* 128-49.

Salem, Jean. *La mort n'est rien pour nous: Lucrèce et l'ethique.* Paris: Vrin, 1990.

Schama, Simon. *Citizens: A Chronicle of the French Revolution.* New York: Knopf, 1989.

Schopenhauer, Arthur. *The World as Will and Representation.* Translated by E.F.J. Payne. 2 vols. New York: Dover, 1966.

Schulze, E. J. *Shelley's Theory of Poetry: A Reappraisal.* The Hague: Mouton, 1966.

Scott, William. "Shelley's Admiration for Bacon." *PMLA* 73 (1958): 228-36.

Scrivener, Michael. *Radical Shelley: The Philosophical Anarchism and Utopian Thought of Percy Bysshe Shelley.* Princeton: Princeton University Press, 1982.

Searle, John. "Reiterating the Differences: A Reply to Derrida." In *Glyph,* 1:198-208. Baltimore: Johns Hopkins University Press, 1977.

Segal, Charles. *Lucretius on Death and Anxiety: Poetry and Philosophy in* De Rerum Natura. Princeton: Princeton University Press, 1990.

Serres, Michel. *La naissance de la physique dans le texte de Lucrèce.* Paris: Les Éditions de Minuit, 1977.

———. *Le tiers-instruit.* Paris: Gallimard, 1991.

———. "Lucretius: Science and Religion." Translated by Laurence Schehr. In *Hermes: Literature, Science, Philosophy,* edited by Josué V. Harari and David F. Bell, 98–124. Baltimore: Johns Hopkins University Press, 1982.

Simpson, David. *Irony and Authority in Romantic Poetry.* London: Macmillan, 1979.

Spencer, T.J.B. "Lucretius and the Scientific Poem in English." In Dudley, 131–64.

Sperry, Stuart. "Necessity and the role of the Hero in Shelley's *Prometheus Unbound.*" *PMLA* 96 (1981): 242–54.

———. *Shelley's Major Verse: The Narrative and Dramatic Poetry.* Cambridge, Mass.: Harvard University Press, 1988.

———. "Towards a Definition of Romantic Irony in English Literature." In *Romantic and Modern: Revaluations of a Literary Tradition,* edited by George Bornstein, 3–28. Pittsburgh: University of Pittsburgh Press, 1977.

Spivak, G. C. *In Other Worlds: Essays in Cultural Politics.* New York: Methuen, 1987.

Stallybrass, Peter. "Marx and Heterogeneity: Thinking the Lumpenproletariat." *Representations* 31 (1990): 69–95.

Stallybrass, Peter, and Allon White. *The Politics and Poetics of Transgression.* Ithaca: Cornell University Press, 1986.

Stewart, Ian. *Does God Play Dice? The Mathematics of Chaos.* Harmondsworth, Middlesex: Penguin, 1990.

Stokoe, F. W. *German Influence in the English Romantic Period, 1788–1818.* Cambridge: Cambridge University Press, 1926.

Stovall, Floyd. *Desire and Restraint in Shelley.* Durham, N.C.: Duke University Press, 1931.

Strachey, Lytton. *Eminent Victorians.* Harmondsworth, Middlesex: Penguin, 1948.

Taylor, Charles. "Foucault on Freedom and Truth." In *Foucault: A Critical Reader,* edited by David Couzens Hoy, 69–102. Oxford: Basil Blackwell, 1986.

———. *Hegel.* Cambridge: Cambridge University Press, 1975.

———. *Hegel and Modern Society.* Cambridge: Cambridge University Press, 1979.

———. *Sources of the Self: The Making of the Modern Identity.* Cambridge, Mass.: Harvard University Press, 1989.

Tetreault, Ronald. *The Poetry of Life: Shelley and Literary Form.* Toronto: University of Toronto Press, 1987.

Thompson, E. P. *The Making of the English Working Class.* Harmondsworth, Middlesex: Penguin, 1968.

Thorslev, Peter. "Incest as Romantic Symbol." *Comparative Literature Studies* 2 (1965): 41–58.

Tocqueville, Alexis de. *L'ancien régime et la révolution.* Paris: Flammarion, 1988.

Turner, Paul. "Shelley and Lucretius." *Review of English Studies* 10 (1959): 269–82.

Turner, Victor. *Dramas, Fields, and Metaphors: Symbolic Action in Human Society.* Ithaca: Cornell University Press, 1974.

Ulmer, William A. *Shelleyan Eros: The Rhetoric of Romantic Love.* Princeton: Princeton University Press, 1990.

Varnedoe, Kirk. *A Fine Disregard: What Makes Modern Art Modern.* New York: Harry N. Abrams, 1989.

Veeser, H. A., ed. *The New Historicism.* New York: Routledge, 1989.

Vivian, Charles. "The One 'Mont Blanc.'" *Keats-Shelley Journal* 4 (1955): 55–65.

Voisine, Jacques. *Jean-Jacques Rousseau en angleterre a l'époque romantique.* Paris: n.p., 1956.

Waldrop, M. Mitchell. *Complexity: The Emerging Science at the Edge of Order and Chaos.* New York: Simon & Schuster, 1992.

Walker, Joyce. "Romantic Chaos: The Dynamic Paradigm in Novalis's *Heinrich von Ofterdingen* and Contemporary Science." *German Quarterly* 66 (1993): 43–59.

Wasserman, E. R. "The English Romantics and the Grounds of Knowledge." *Studies in Romanticism* 4 (1964): 17–34.

———. *Shelley: A Critical Reading.* Baltimore: Johns Hopkins University Press, 1971.

———. "Shelley's Last Poetics: A Reconsideration." In *From Sensibility to Romanticism: Essays Presented to F. A. Pottle,* edited by F. W. Hilles and Harold Bloom, 487–512. New York: Oxford University Press, 1965.

Webb, Timothy. *Shelley: A Voice Not Understood.* Manchester: Manchester University Press, 1977.

———. "The Unascended Heaven: Negatives in *Prometheus Unbound.*" *Keats-Shelley Journal* 18 (1979): 78–101.

———. *The Violet in the Crucible: Shelley and Translation.* Oxford: Clarendon, 1976.

White, Eric Charles. "Negentropy, Noise, and Emancipatory Thought." In Hayles, *Chaos and Order,* 263–77.

White, Hayden. "The Politics of Historical Interpretation: Discipline and De-Sublimation." In Mitchell, 119–44.

———. "The Value of Narrativity in the Representation of Reality." *Critical Inquiry* 7 (1980): 5–27.

White, N. I. *Shelley.* 2 vols. London: Secker & Warburg, 1947.

———. *The Unextinguished Hearth: Shelley and His Contemporary Critics.* Durham, N.C.: Duke University Press, 1938.

Wilkie, Brian. *Romantic Poets and the Epic Tradition.* Madison: University of Wisconsin Press, 1965.

Williams, Raymond. *Culture and Society, 1780–1950.* Harmondsworth, Middlesex: Penguin, 1963.

———. *Marxism and Literature.* Oxford: Oxford University Press, 1977.

Wilson, A. M. *Diderot.* New York: Oxford University Press, 1972.

Wilson, Edward O. *The Diversity of Life.* Harmondsworth, Middlesex: Penguin, 1992.

Wilson, Milton. *Shelley's Later Poetry: A Study of His Prophetic Imagination.* New York: Columbia University Press, 1959.

Winspear, A. D. *Lucretius and Scientific Thought.* Montreal: Harvest House, 1963.

Wittgenstein, Ludwig. *Philosophical Investigations.* Oxford: Basil Blackwell, 1963.

Wood, Andelys. "Shelley's Ironic Vision: *The Witch of Atlas.*" *Keats-Shelley Journal* 29 (1980): 67–82.

Woodman, Ross Greig. *The Apocalyptic Vision in the Poetry of Shelley.* Toronto: University of Toronto Press, 1964.

Woodring, Carl. *Politics in English Romantic Poetry.* Cambridge, Mass.: Harvard University Press, 1970.

Wright, J. *Shelley's Myth of Metaphor.* Athens: University of Georgia Press, 1970.

Young, A. *Shelley and Nonviolence.* The Hague: Mouton, 1975.

Index

Havel, Václav, 437 n. 24
Hawking, Stephen, 360
Hayles, N. Katherine, 249 n. 2, 250
Hazlitt, William, 125, n. 35
Hegel, G. W. F., and Hegelianism. *See also*
  Absolute Knowing; free conformity to
  law; revolution: post-Kantian resis-
  tance to, and Hegel; Shelley, Percy
  Bysshe: and Hegel's "two thoughts";
  Sittlichkeit; world-historical individual
Absolute Knowing, 62, 66, 98, 134, 197,
  287
Bacchanalian revel, 215–16, 222
Begriff (Notion), internal teleology, 65,
  348, 361–62, 365
and free conformity to law, 62, 65, 483
and history, 65–67, 189–90, 361–62,
  368, 477
Phenomenology, 59, 62–66, 142–44,
  215–16, 360
Philosophy of History, 64–65
Philosophy of Right, 66, 347, 362–63
and revolution, 62–63, 226–27, 344;
  "fury of destruction," 1, 63, 126, 243,
  251, 259
similarities to, in Shelley's thought, 128,
  166–67, 189–92, 197, 293, 477
and *Sittlichkeit,* 62–63, 65, 177
and situated freedom, 64–65
and state, 63–65, 347–48, 350–53, 361–
  63, 483
and theodicy, 66–67, 189–90
Unhappy Consciousness, 142–44
on war, 362–63, 365
hegemony, 14–15, 172, 176–77, 235, 290,
  295 n. 1, 299–300. *See also* ideology
Heidegger, Martin, 23, 229
Heisenberg, Werner, 273, 366, 371, 486
Heraclitus, 286
hermaphrodite, 330–31
hermeneutics. *See also* atoms, atomism:
  epistemological, hermeneutic, aesthetic; charity; *clinamen;* culture: as
  hermeneutical totality; discontinuity:
  epistemological and hermeneutic;
  error: in hermeneutic process; fragment: and hermeneutics; parts and
  whole: and historicist hermeneutics;
  representative being: of individual in
  community, and historicist hermeneutics

chaotic, 272–74, 276, 278–83, 297–98,
  308, 310, 314, 317–22, 343–44, 352,
  368–70, 372, 440–43, 446, 483–84,
  486.
historicist, of culture, 18–29, 31, 57,
  263, 343–46; criticized, 74, 115, 235,
  265, 343–45, 355, 369–70, 424
idealist, 66, 92, 101–3, 179, 259, 320,
  343, 348, 423, 451–52
and identity, 232
and interminability, 310–14
textual, 136, 199–200, 293–94, 428,
  440–42, 446
Herschel, William, 244, 472, 474–75
Hesiod, 250
Hirsch, Bernard, 381 n. 25
history and historicism. *See also* context;
  entropy: and history/society; error:
  proliferation of in nonlinear interaction, in history; flux: history as;
  Hegel: and history; identity: grounded
  in history/tradition; Lucretius: and history of civilization; narrative: and history; New Historicism; organicism:
  antiorganicism, Shelley's of state/his-
  tory; organicism: of state/history; therapeutic philosophy: and history;
  turbulence: in history, politics; turbulence: *solution tourbillonaire;* turn to
  language/history; world-historical individual
disjunctive, non-narrativizable, 140, 169,
  218, 222, 230–31, 270, 282, 365–70,
  374, 378, 438, 440; and chaos, 231–
  32, 257, 262–87 passim, 301, 303–4,
  306–8, 319, 344–45, 367–70, 374,
  378, 395–98, 442, 472, 476–77, 480–
  82, 486; and poststructuralism, 3, 16–
  17, 74–75, 77, 273; and ruin, 424–25,
  424 n. 15, 442–43, 466–67, 472,
  476–77, 479–82
and literature, 1, 3, 7–28, 31, 55, 65,
  73–74, 85, 92, 101, 160, 181, 283–85,
  294, 320, 340, 347
providential, 61, 66–67, 85, 101–3, 126,
  139, 189, 192, 216, 265–66, 346–47,
  359–60, 378, 382, 413–14, 417–19,
  423, 450
therapeutic view of, 31, 33, 48, 57, 60–
  67, 70, 85, 98–99, 101, 125–26, 165,
  168–69, 189, 222, 226–27, 241, 259,

Plato, Platonism, Neoplatonism, 80–83,
85–86, 106, 129, 289–92, 294, 296–
304, 315, 319, 327–28, 337 n. 19,
340–41, 348–51, 354, 382, 394–95,
403, 430 n. 19, 464, 470, 478 n. 47.
See also leaky vessels; mimesis; organicism: of state/history, Plato's; parts
and whole: and therapeutic view of
state, in Plato; real above; therapeutic
philosophy: and Plato
Gorgias, 379, 394
myth of Er, 348–49
Republic, 289–92, 294, 296–99, 301,
327–28, 348–50
play
and chaotic creativity, 252, 258–59, 268,
271, 306, 319, 321, 374, 390; overcome by internal teleology, 358
poetry as, 70–71; and Shelley, 123, 333,
337–40
of signifier, meaning, 134–38
Polignac, Cardinal, 416–17, 417 n. 10
post-Kantian idealism, 55–107 passim, 108,
132–34, 139–40, 142–44, 152, 156,
166–67, 178–79, 217, 226, 238, 291,
347, 360, 362, 448. *See also* Absolute:
and post-Kantian idealism; Absolute
Knowing; free conformity to law; history: providential; history: therapeutic
view of; individual post-Kantians by
name; organicism; post-Kantian idealist; parts and whole: and historical
hermeneutics, post-Kantian; organicism: and narrative, post-Kantian
view; representative being; revolution:
post-Kantian resistance to; Romantic
Irony; Romanticism; *Sittlichkeit;* situated freedom; spirit of the age; sub-
ject/object; therapeutic philosophy:
and post-Kantians; world-historical individual
and religion, 61–62, 66–68, 70, 72–73,
78, 83, 97–98, 102–5, 179, 189–90
and response to Enlightenment dilemma,
54–55, 62–65, 68–70, 77, 82, 86, 96,
98, 101
and role of aesthetic object, 54–55, 61–
62, 70–73, 77, 85–86, 90–92, 102,
121, 139–40, 179, 238–39, 347, 448
and Romanticism, 1, 69–73, 85, 93–99,
103–13, 140, 152

Shelley's relationship to, 1, 49–50, 55,
67, 80–126 passim, 133–34, 139,
142–44, 152, 167, 449, 477, 482
poststructuralism, 3, 16–17, 67, 71, 73–
78, 129–30, 136–38, 140, 196–97,
200–201, 279, 310, 445. *See also*
Shelley criticism, "decentering"; theory, literary
Pound, Ezra, 342
power, corruption by, 172–81, 184, 194–
97, 297, 332
pragmatism, 16, 20–25, 28, 32 n. 3
prejudice. *See* tradition
Price, Uvedale, 422
Prigogine, Ilya, 249 n. 2, 254, 256–58,
262, 272–73, 286, 344, 366, 371–74,
394, 402, 404, 473, 486. *See also*
Stengers, Isabelle
proliferation of meaning, 11, 199–200,
267, 281–82, 314, 317. *See also* author function
Prometheus, 323, 454. *See also* Shelley,
Percy Bysshe: WORKS, *Prometheus Unbound*
promiscuity, textual, 9–13, 16–17, 21–24,
26, 74, 77, 82, 95, 208, 284, 293, 307,
314, 329. *See also* author function;
context: of production/consumption;
proliferation of meaning
Proust, Marcel, 277
Pugin, A. W. N., 269 n. 34
Pulos, C. E., 2, 35, 41 n. 13, 129

quantum physics, 254, 272–74, 319, 345,
364, 366, 371–72, 377, 398, 402
Quint, David, 200, 202, 210 n. 29, 295 n.
1, 400

Radcliffe, Ann, 239–41, 282–83, 447–48.
See also Gothic
Rae, Alistair, 273
Rajan, Tilottama, 446
real above, 348, 354–57, 359–60, 363
reason. *See also* Enlightenment
criticized, 42–43, 53–54; by Shelley,
215–16, 390–92, 391 n. 26, 399–400,
434
cunning of, 167, 169
and Enlightenment, 52, 84–85, 88, 422,
456, 458; and nineties radicals, 38–44,
52, 418